Library of
Davidson College

ECONOMIC POLICY AND PLANNING IN THIRD WORLD DEVELOPMENT

International Development Resource Books
Pradip K. Ghosh, editor

Industrialization and Development: A Third World Perspective
Urban Development in the Third World
Technology Policy and Development: A Third World Perspective
Energy Policy and Third World Development
Population, Environment and Resources,
and Third World Development
Health, Food, and Nutrition in Third World Development
Economic Policy and Planning in Third World Development
Development Policy and Planning: A Third World Perspective
New International Economic Order: A Third World Perspective
Foreign Aid and Third World Development
Multi-national Corporations and Third World Development
Economic Integration and Third World Development
Third World Development: A Basic Needs Approach
Appropriate Technology in Third World Development
Development Co-operation and Third World Development
International Trade and Third World Development
Disarmament and Development: A Global Perspective
Developing South Asia: A Modernization Perspective
Developing Latin America: A Modernization Perspective
Developing Africa: A Modernization Perspective

ECONOMIC POLICY AND PLANNING IN THIRD WORLD DEVELOPMENT

Pradip K. Ghosh, *Editor*

Foreword by Gamani Corea, Secretary-General of UNCTAD

Prepared under the auspices of the Center for International Development, University of Maryland, College Park, and the World Academy of Development and Cooperation, Washington, D.C.

International Development Resource Books, Number 7

Greenwood Press
Westport, Connecticut • London, England

Library of Congress Cataloging in Publication Data

Main entry under title:

Economic policy and planning in Third World development.

   (International development resource books, ISSN 0738-1425; no. 7)
   Bibliography: p.
   Includes index.
   1. Developing countries—Economic policy—Addresses, essays, lectures. 2. Economic development—Addresses, essays, lectures. I. Ghosh, Pradip K., 1947-
II. Series.
HC59.7.E312 1984   338.9'009172'4   83-26493
ISBN 0-313-24143-0 (lib. bdg.)

Copyright © 1984 by Pradip K. Ghosh

All rights reserved. No portion of this book may be reproduced, by any process or technique, without the express written consent of the publisher.

Library of Congress Catalog Card Number: 83-26493
ISBN: 0-313-24143-0
ISSN: 0738-1425

First published in 1984

Greenwood Press
A division of Congressional Information Service, Inc.
88 Post Road West, Westport, Connecticut 06881

Printed in the United States of America

10 9 8 7 6 5 4 3 2 1

Copyright Acknowledgments

Reprinted with the permission of the Population Council from "The urban prospect: Reexamining the basic assumptions," by Lester R. Brown, *Population and Development Review* 2, no. 2 (June 1976): 267-277.

Reprinted with the permission of the Population Council from "Food for the future: A perspective," by D. Gale Johnson, *Population and Development Review* 2, no. 1 (March 1976): 1-19.

Reprinted with the permission of the Population Council from "Population, development, and planning in Brazil," by Thomas W. Merrick, *Population and Development Review* 2, no. 2 (June 1976): 181-199.

Reprinted with the permission of the Population Council from "Observations on population policy and population program in Bangladesh," by Paul Demeny, *Population and Development Review* 1, no. 2 (December 1975): 307-321.

Reprinted with the permission of the Population Council from "Population policy: The role of national governments," by Paul Demeny, *Population and Development Review* 1, no. 1 (September 1975): 147-161.

Reprinted with the permission of the Population Council from "Asia's cities: Problems and options," by Kingsley Davis, *Population and Development Review* 1, no. 1 (September 1975): 71-86.

Articles from *Impact of Science on Society,* Vol. XXIX, no. 3, © Unesco 1979. Reproduced by permission of Unesco.

Articles from *Impact of Science on Society,* Vol. XXIII, no. 4, © Unesco 1973. Reproduced by permission of Unesco.

Articles from *Impact of Science on Society,* Vol. XXV, no. 1, © Unesco 1975. Reproduced by permission of Unesco.

Articles from *Impact of Science on Society,* Vol. XX, no. 3, © Unesco 1972. Reproduced by permission of Unesco.

Articles from *Impact of Science on Society,* Vol. XXIII, no. 2, © Unesco 1973. Reproduced by permission of Unesco.

Articles from *Impact of Science on Society,* Vol. XXV, no. 3, © Unesco 1975. Reproduced by permission of Unesco.

Articles from *Impact of Science on Society,* Vol. XXIV, no. 2, © Unesco 1974. Reproduced by permission of Unesco.

Articles from *Scientists, the Arms Race and Disarmament,* © Unesco 1982. Reproduced by permission of Unesco.

Articles from *The Use of Socio-Economic Indicators in Development Planning,* © Unesco 1976. Reproduced by permission of Unesco.

Articles from *Methods for Development Planning: Scenarios, Models and Micro-Studies,* © Unesco 1981. Reproduced by permission of Unesco.

Article from *Socio-Economic Indicators for Planning: Methodological Aspects and Selected Examples,* © Unesco 1981. Reproduced by permission of Unesco.

TO

W. ARTHUR LEWIS

IN GRATEFUL RECOGNITION OF HIS HIS LEADERSHIP ROLE
IN DEVELOPMENT RESEARCH

DEVELOPMENT CAN NOT BE CONSIDERED AS A SERIES OF DISCONNECTED SECTORAL ACTIVITIES OR PURELY TECHNOLOGICAL CHOICES. IT IMPLIES GLOBAL COHERENCE AND THE POLITICAL WILL TO BRING ABOUT SOCIAL CHANGE. IT OFTEN OCCURS THROUGH INSTITUTIONAL CHANGE : IT ASSUMES A CERTAIN DEGREE OF ARTICULATION AND ORGANIZATION ON THE PART OF THE AGENTS OF SOCIAL CHANGE.

Paul-Marc Henry

WHAT IMPROVES THE CIRCUMSTANCES OF THE GREATER PART CAN NEVER BE REGARDED AS AN INCONVENIENCE TO THE WHOLE. NO SOCIETY CAN SURELY BE FLOURISHING AND HAPPY, OF WHICH THE FAR GREATER PART OF THE MEMBERS ARE POOR AND MISERABLE.

Adam Smith,

The Wealth of Nations

Contents

The Third World	xix
Abbreviations	xxiii
Foreword	xxv
Preface	xxvii

PART I CURRENT ISSUES, TRENDS, ANALYTICAL METHODS, STRATEGIES AND POLICIES, COUNTRY STUDIES

Introduction	3
The Meaning of Development Dudley Seers	7
Economic Trends and Prospects of Developing Countries Organization for Economic Cooperation and Development	17
Economic Growth and Major Streams of Production: Some Basic Problems in Hard-core Developing Countries Centre for Development Planning, Projections and Policies of the Department of Economic and Social Affairs of the United Nations Secretariat	38
Development Trends Since 1960 and Their Implications for a New International Development Strategy Centre for Development Planning, Projections and Policies of the Department of International Economic and Social Affairs of the United Nations Secretariat	79

Contents

Some Economic Concepts and Policy Issues in Developing Countries U. Tun Wai	154
Inflation and Growth: A Reconsideration of the Evidence from the LDCs Constantine Glezakos	163
Income Differentials and the Dynamics of Development Jacques Lecaillon and Dimitrios Germidis	176
The Supply of International Liquidity to Developing Countries Klaus Boeck	195
Growth, Distribution and Motivation in LDCs Wolfgang Arnold	204
The Debt Problem of Developing Countries Gamani Corea	216
Employment Strategies and Poverty Reduction Policies of Developing Countries Centre for Development Planning, Projections and Policies of the United Nations Secretariat	244
The Fiscal Policy Aspect of Development Strategy Dirk J. Wolfson	302
Planned Mobilization of Financial Resources for Development Centre for Development Planning, Projections and Policies of the Department of Economic and Social Affairs of the United Nations Secretariat	314
External Finance for Development: Recent Experience and Its Implications for Policies Centre for Development Planning, Projections and Policies of the Department of Economic and Social Affairs of the United Nations Secretariat	341
The Production Structure and the Dynamics of Development Gerard Fichet and Norberto Gonzalez	362
Third World Countries: Problems of Economic Development and Ways of Solving Them Mai Volkov	408

PART II STATISTICAL INFORMATION AND SOURCES

    I. Bibliography of Information Sources   415

    II. Statistical Tables and Figures   431

PART III RESOURCE BIBLIOGRAPHY

    I. Books   483

    II. Selected Periodical Articles   611

    III. Specialized Publications (Reports, Documents, and Directories)   659

    IV. Bibliographic Subject Index   668

PART IV DIRECTORY OF INFORMATION SOURCES

    I. United Nations Information Sources   675

    II. Bibliography of Bibliographies   685

    III. Directory of Periodicals   690

    IV. Research Institutions   694

Appendix   706

Index   709

LIST OF TABLES

PART I

ECONOMIC TRENDS AND PROSPECTS OF DEVELOPING COUNTRIES

Table 1.	Some basic facts on the world economy	19
Table 2.	Growth of production and production sectors by groups of countries	20
Table 3.	Growth of per capita food production in developing countries, 1971-1976	21
Table 4.	Growth of gross domestic investment (GDI) and GDP by groups of countries	24
Table 5.	Growth of production, exports and imports by groups of countries	25
Table 6.	Volume indices of imports by groups of countries	27
Table 7.	Current account balances by groups of countries	29
Table 8.	External debt and debt service of developing countries by groups of countries	30
Table 9.	Financing of current balance deficits of non-oil LDCs 1973, 1976-1978	34

ECONOMIC GROWTH AND MAJOR STREAMS OF PRODUCTION: SOME BASIC PROBLEMS IN HARD-CORE DEVELOPING COUNTRIES

Table 1.	Level and growth of gross domestic product and population	40
Table 2.	Expansion of gross domestic product and its principal components at constant factor cost	42
Table 3.	Increases in levels of gross investment, gross national saving and external resources	44
Table 4.	Increase in level of consumption	45
Table 5.	Net international flow of official donations and long-term official and private capital, 1971-1973, annual averages	47
Table 6.	Percentage annual rate of increase in total agricultural production, 1961-1965 to 1971-1973	49
Table 7.	Percentage annual rate of increase in <u>per capita</u> agricultural production, 1961-1965 to 1971-1973	51
Table 8.	Percentage annual rate of increase in area harvested and yield per unit of area harvested, 1961-1965 to 1971-1973	51
Table 9.	Land use and irrigation	54
Table 10.	Consumption of fertilizers	59
Table 11.	Expansion of production, apparent consumption and net imports of cereals, 1961-1965 to 1971-1973	60
Table 12.	Expansion of production, apparent consumption and net imports of raw cotton, 1961-1965 to 1971-1973	60
Table 13.	Expansion of production, apparent consumption and net exports of raw cotton, 1961-1965 to 1971-1973	62
Table 14.	Percentage share of agricultural goods in total imports, early 1960s and early 1970s	63

Table 15. Percentage share of agricultural goods in
total exports, early 1960s and early 1970s 65
Table 16. Expansion of gross output of manufacturing
industries 65
Table 17. Percentage shares of principal industrial branches
in the gross output of manufacturing industries
in 1970 66
Table 18. Expansion in output of selected manufactures . . . 67
Table 19. Production and installed generating capacity
of electric energy 70
Table 20. Percentage share of manufactured goods in total
imports, early 1960s to early 1970s 73
Table 21. Percentage share of manufactured goods in total
exports, early 1960s and early 1970s 74

DEVELOPMENT TRENDS SINCE 1960 AND THEIR IMPLICATIONS FOR A NEW
INTERNATIONAL DEVELOPMENT STRATEGY

Table 1. Population and growth of real output, by group
of countries, 1961-1975 80
Table 2. Population and growth of gross domestic product,
by income groups of developing countries,
1961-1975 83
Table 3. Population and growth of gross domestic product,
by developing region, 1961-1975 84
Table 4. Average annual rate of increase in total and
per capita real gross domestic income, by income
group of developing countries, 1961-1975 86
Table 5. Average annual rate of increase in total and
per capita real gross domestic income, by
developing region, 1961-1975 88
Table 6. Average annual rate of increase in _per capita_
private consumption at constant prices, by income
group of developing countries, 1961-1975 89
Table 7. Average annual rate of increase in per capita
private consumption at constant prices, by
developing region, 1961-1975 90
Table 8. Distribution and increase in population of
developing countries, 1961-1975 92
Table 9. Distribution and increase in urban and rural
population of developing countries, 1961-1975 . . . 95
Table 10. Distribution and increase in labour force of
developing countries, 1961-1975 98
Table 11. Distribution and increase in major components
of the labour force of developing countries,
1961-1975 99
Table 12. Indicators of health facilities in developing
countries, 1960 and 1970 102
Table 13. Indicators of nutrition in developing countries,
1960 and 1970 103
Table 14. Indicators of education in developing countries,
1960 and 1970 104
Table 15. Change in agricultural production, by income
group of developing countries, 1966-1975 106

xiv List of Tables and Figures

Table 16. Change in agricultural production, by developing regions, 1966-1975 109
Table 17. Expansion of production and apparent consumption of cereals, by income group of developing countries, 1961-1965 to 1971-1975 111
Table 18. Expansion of production and apparent consumption of cereals, by developing region, 1961-1965 to 1971-1975 112
Table 19. Change in industrial production, by income group of developing countries, 1966-1975 116
Table 20. Change in industrial production, by developing region, 1966-1975 118
Table 21. Average annual rate of increase in quantum of international trade, by income group of developing countries, 1961-1975 122
Table 22. Average annual rate of increase in quantum of international trade, by developing region, 1961-1975 124
Table 23. Change in composition of exports of developing countries, 1960-1961 to 1974-1975 125
Table 24. Investment in relation to gross domestic product, by income group of developing countries, 1960-1975 129
Table 25. Investment in relation to gross domestic product, by developing region, 1960-1975 130
Table 26. Average annual rate of increase in gross domestic product at constant prices per economically active person in developing countries, 1961-1975 . 132
Table 27. Gross national saving in relation to gross domestic product and to total supply of saving, by income group of developing countries, 1960-1975 135
Table 28. Gross national saving in relation to gross domestic product and to total supply of saving, by developing region, 1960-1975 136
Table 29. External resources in relation to gross domestic product and to total supply of saving, by income group of developing countries, 1960-1975 138
Table 30. External resources in relation to gross domestic product and to total supply of saving, by developing region, 1960-1975 139
Table 31. Net receipts of bilateral official development assistance from developed market economies and of resources at concessional terms from multilateral agencies, by income group of developing countries, 1970 and 1975 141
Table 32. Net receipts of bilateral official development assistance from developed market economies and of resources at concessional terms from multilateral agencies, by developing region, 1970 and 1975 142

List of Tables and Figures xv

INFLATION AND GROWTH: A RECONSIDERATION OF THE EVIDENCE FROM
THE LDCs

Table 1. Summary results of the income growth, inflation
and price instability regressions 170

EMPLOYMENT STRATEGIES AND POVERTY REDUCTION POLICIES OF
DEVELOPING COUNTRIES

Table 1. Estimates of income distribution in developing
countries 279
Table 2. Targets for gross product and employment in
selected countries of Latin America and the
Caribbean 282

PLANNED MOBILIZATION OF FINANCIAL RESOURCES FOR DEVELOPMENT

Table 1. Planned average annual changes in percentage
shares of gross national saving, external
resources and total supply of saving in gross
domestic product from base year to final year
of plan 315
Table 2. Configuration of countries according to planned
shares of gross national saving and external
resources in gross domestic product in final
year of plan 318
Table 3. Configuration of countries according to planned
annual rate of growth of gross domestic product
from base year to final year of plan and
planned share of external resources in gross
domestic product in final year of plan 320
Table 4. Gross national saving and external resources
as percentage of total investment (or total
supply of saving) in base year and final year
of plan 323
Table 5. Planned marginal rate of gross national saving
and planned annual rate of increase in consumption
from base year to final year of plan 326
Table 6. Planned expansion of public and private saving
from base year to final year of plan 329
Table 7. Planned distribution of gross national saving
in base year and final year of plan 333
Table 8. Planned expansion of current expenditure and
current revenue of general government from base
year to final year of plan 336
Table 9. Planned expansion of direct and indirect taxes
from base year to final year of plan 337
Table 10. Planned sectoral allocation and origin of total
supply of saving during plan period 337

THE PRODUCTION STRUCTURE AND THE DYNAMICS OF DEVELOPMENT

Table 1. Structure of foreign trade 367
Table 2. Structure of industrial production 368

xvi List of Tables and Figures

Table 3. Imports and exports of some strategic sectors . . . 369
Table 4. Comparison of some variables, 1972 386
Table 5. Latin America: percentage structure of imports
          of industrial goods 387
Table 6. OECD countries and Latin America: degree of
          coverage of extra-regional imports by exports to
          the rest of the world 392
Table 7. Latin America: coefficients of imported supply in
          relation to total demand in the mid-1970s 393
Table 8. Latin America: proportion of demand supplied
          externally and annual growth rates of the
          industrial sectors covered by the regional
          programme of industrial and trade co-operation . . 394
Table 9. Latin America: imports of goods and non-financial
          services in the mid-1980s 397
Table 10. Latin America: coefficients of imported supply
          of total demand 400

PART II

STATISTICAL INFORMATION AND SOURCES

Table 1. Social indicators by income group of countries . . 432
Table 2. Social indicators by geographic areas
          (developing countries) 435
Table 3. Comparative social indicators for developing
          countries (by geographic area and country) 437
Table 4. Selected economic development indicators:
          population and production (average annual real
          growth rates) 441
Table 5. Selected economic development indicators:
          expenditure (average annual growth rates) 453
Table 6. Economic structure indicator: expenditure
          (percentage of GDP at current market prices) . . . 455
Table 7. Economic structure indicators: product (percentage
          of GDP at current factor cost) 457
Table 8. Foreign trade structure: export composition
          (percentage of total merchandise exports) 459
Table 9. Foreign trade structure: import composition
          (percentage of total merchandise imports) 461
Table 10. Capital flows 463
Table 11. Selected economic indicators - I 465
Table 12. Selected economic indicators - II 467
Table 13. Growth of population, GNP and GNP per person,
          1960-90 469
Table 14. Capital flows and debt of the developing
          countries and oil exporters, 1975-90 470
Table 15. Investment and savings ratios, developing
          countries, 1976 and 1990 471
Table 16. Net disbursements of medium and long-term capital
          to developing countries, by type of capital and
          country income group, 1970-85 472
Table 17. Developing countries: structure of production,
          1975 and 1990 473

Table 18. Growth of merchandise exports, by product category and country group, 1960-77 and 1977-90 474
Table 19. Shares of regions in world exports of goods 475
Table 20. Regional structure of exports of developing regions 476
Table 21. Shares of regions in world imports 477
Table 22. Import dependence of developing regions 478
Table 23. Regional structure of imports of developing regions 479
Table 24. Trade in manufactures among developing countries, 1976 480

LIST OF FIGURES

Figure 1. Structure of industrial production, 1963 and 1972 . 365
Figure 2. OECD countries: Coefficient of imports with respect to size of domestic demand in some industrial sectors, in various years 372
Figure 3. OECD countries: Pattern of exports as a proportion of imports in relation to domestic demand in the chemical industry, 1971 373
Figure 4. Trade balances of the OECD countries with Latin America in some industrial sectors, 1969-1974 ... 375
Figure 5. OECD countries and Latin America: Coefficients of imported supply of transport equipment in relation to the domestic demand of the same industrial sector 376
Figure 6. Latin America: Comparative structure of exports, imports, gross value of production and domestic demand in the mid-1970s and mid-1980s, by industrial origin 389
Figure 7. OECD countries: Coefficient of imported supply in relation to demand for non-electrical machinery, 1963, 1966, 1967 and 1969 390
Figure 8. Latin America: Import coefficients with respect to domestic demand in selected sectors of industry and their relative position with respect to the reference curve of the OECD countries 401

The Third World

Afghanistan
  Republic of Afghanistan
Algeria
  Democratic and Popular
  Republic of Algeria
Angola
  People's Republic of Angola
Argentina
  Argentine Republic
Bahamas
  Commonwealth of the Bahamas
Bahrain
  State of Bahrain
Bangladesh
  People's Republic of
  Bangladesh
Barbados
  People's Republic of
  Barbados
Benin
  People's Republic of Benin
Bhutan
  People's Republic of Bhutan
Bolivia
  Republic of Bolivia
Botswana
  Republic of Botswana
Brazil
  Federative Republic of Brazil
Burma
  Socialist Republic of the
  Union of Burma
Burundi
  Republic of Burundi

Cambodia
  Democratic Kampuchea

Cameroon
  United Republic of Cameroon
Cape Verde
  Republic of Cape Verde
Central African Empire
Chad
  Republic of Chad
Chile
  Republic of Chile
Colombia
  Republic of Colombia
Comoro Islands
  Republic of the Comoros
Congo
  People's Republic of the
  Congo
Costa Rica
  Republic of Costa Rica
Cuba
  Republic of Cuba
Dominican Republic
Ecuador
  Republic of Ecuador
Egypt
  Arab Republic of Egypt
El Salvador
  Republic of El Salvador
Equatorial Guinea
  Republic of Equatorial
  Guinea
Ethiopia
Fiji
  Dominion of Fiji
Gabon
  Gabonese Republic
Gambia
  Republic of the Gambia

Ghana
  Republic of Ghana
Grenada
  State of Grenada
Guatemala
  Republic of Guatemala
Guinea
  Republic of Guinea
Guinea-Bissau
  Republic of Guinea-Bissau
Guyana
  Cooperative Republic of Guyana
Haiti
  Republic of Haiti
Honduras
  Republic of Honduras
India
  Republic of India
Indonesia
  Republic of Indonesia
Iran
  Imperial Government of Iran
Iraq
  Republic of Iraq
Ivory Coast
  Republic of Ivory Coast
Jamaica
Jordan
  Hashemite Kingdom of Jordan
Kenya
  Republic of Kenya
Kuwait
  State of Kuwait
Laos
  Lao People's Democratic Republic
Lebanon
  Republic of Lebanon
Lesotho
  Kingdom of Lesotho
Liberia
  Republic of Liberia
Libya
  People's Socialist Libyan Arab Republic
Madagascar
  Democratic Republic of Madagascar
Malawi
  Republic of Malawi
Malaysia
Maldives
  Republic of Maldives
Mali
  Republic of Mali
Mauritania
  Islamic Republic of Mauritania
Mauritius
Mexico
  United Mexican States
Mongolia
  Mongolian People's Republic
Morocco
  Kingdom of Morocco
Mozambique
  People's Republic of Mozambique
Nepal
  Kingdom of Nepal
Nicaragua
  Republic of Nicaragua
Niger
  Republic of Niger
Nigeria
  Federal Republic of Nigeria
Oman
  Sultanate of Oman
Pakistan
  Islamic Republic of Pakistan
Panama
  Republic of Panama
Papua New Guinea
Paraguay
  Republic of Paraguay
Peru
  Republic of Peru
Philippines
  Republic of the Philippines
Qatar
  State of Qatar

Adopted from THE THIRD WORLD: PREMISES OF U.S. POLICY by W. Scott Thompson, Institute for Contemporary Studies, San Francisco, 1978.

Rhodesia
Ruanda
  Republic of Ruanda
Samoa
Sao Tome and Principe
  Democratic Republic of
  Sao Tome and Principe
Saudi Arabia
  Kingdom of Saudi Arabia
Senegal
  Republic of Senegal
Seychelles
Sierra Leone
  Republic of Sierra Leone
Singapore
  Republic of Singapore
Somalia
  Somali Democratic Republic
Sri Lanka
  Republic of Sri Lanka
Sudan
  Democratic Republic of
  the Sudan
Surinam
Swaziland
  Kingdom of Swaziland
Syria
  Syrian Arab Republic
Tanzania
  United Republic of Tanzania

Thailand
  Kingdom of Thailand
Togo
  Republic of Togo
Trinidad and Tobago
Tunisia
  Republic of Tunisia
Uganda
  Republic of Uganda
United Arab Emirates
Upper Volta
  Republic of Upper Volta
Uruguay
  Oriental Republic of Uruguay
Venezuela
  Republic of Venezuela
Vietnam
  Socialist Republic of Vietnam
Western Sahara
Yemen
  People's Democratic Republic
  of Yemen
Yemen
  Yemen Arab Republic
Zaire
  Republic of Zaire
Zambia
  Republic of Zambia

Countries which have social and economic characteristics in common with the Third World but, because of political affiliations or regimes, are not associated with Third World organizations:

China
  People's Republic of China
Cyprus
  Republic of Cyprus
Israel
  State of Israel
Kazakhstan
Kirghizia
Korea
  Democratic People's Republic
  of Korea
Romania
  Socialist Republic of Romania

South Africa
  Republic of South Africa
South West Africa
  Namibia
Tadzhikistan
Turkmenistan
Uzbekistan
Yugoslavia
  Socialist Federal Republic
  of Yugoslavia

Abbreviations

ADC	Andean Development Corporation
AsDB	Asian Development Bank
ASEAN	Association of South-East Asian Nations
CARIFTA	Caribbean Free Trade Association
DAC	Development Assistance Committee (of OECD)
ECA	Economic Commission for Africa
ECE	Economic Commission for Europe
ECLA	Economic Commission for Latin America
ECOWAS	Economic Commission of West African States
EDF	European Development Fund
EEC	European Economic Community
EFTA	European Free Trade Association
ESCAP	Economic and Social Commission for Asia and the Pacific
FAO	Food and Agriculture Organization of the United Nations
GATT	General Agreement on Tariffs and Trade
GDP	gross domestic product
GNP	gross national product
IBRD	International Bank for Reconstruction and Development (World Bank)
IDA	International Development Association
IDB	Inter-American Development Bank
IFC	International Finance Corporation
IIEP	International Institute for Educational Planning
ILO	International Labour Office
IMF	International Monetary Fund
LAFTA	Latin American Free Trade Association
ODA	official development assistance
OECD	Organisation for Economic Co-operation and Development
OPEC	Organization of Petroleum Exporting Countries
UNDP	United Nations Development Programme
UNEP	United Nations Environment Programme
UNESCO	United Nations Educational, Scientific and Cultural Organization
UNHCR	Office of the United Nations High Commissioner for Refugees
UNITAR	United Nations Institute for Training and Research
UNICEF	United Nations Children's Fund
UNIDO	United Nations Industrial Development Organization
WFP	World Food Programme
WHO	World Health Organization

Foreword

I am pleased to know of the International Development Resources Book project. The 20 resource books which are published under this project, covering the whole spectrum of issues in the fields of development economics and international co-operation for development, and containing not only current reading materials but also up-to-date statistical data and bibliographical notes, will, I am sure, prove to be extremely useful to a wide public.

I would like to commend the author for having undertaken this very ambitious and serious project and, by so doing, rendered a most valuable service. I am confident that it will have a great success.

Gamani Corea

Secretary-General
United Nations Conference on Trade and Development

Preface

Stimulus for the publication of an international resource book series was developed in 1980, while teaching and researching various topics related to third world development. Since that time, I have built up a long list of related resource materials on different subjects, usually considered to be very important for researchers, educators, and public policy decision makers involved with developing country problems. This series of resource books makes an attempt for the first time to give the reader a comprehensive look at the current issues, methods, strategies and policies, statistical information and comprehensive resource bibliographies, and a directory of various information sources on the topic.

This topic is very important because within the framework of the current international economic order, developing an effective economic policy and planning: a third world perspective policy is envisaged as a dynamic instrument of growth essential to the rapid economic and social development of the developing countries, in particular of the least developed countries of Asia, Africa and Latin America.

Much of this work was completed during my residency as a visiting scholar in the Center for Advanced Study of International Development at Michigan State University. Suzanne Wilson, Mary Ann Kozak, Kathy White and Susan Costello, students at the University, provided much needed assistance with the project. I am thankful to the M.S.U. Sociology department for providing necessary support services and Dr. James T. Sabin, Vice President, editorial of Greenwood Press who encouraged me in pursuing the work and finally agreeing to publish in book form.

I would also like to gratefully acknowledge the encouragement given to me by Dr. Denton Morrison to pursue this project and Dr. Mark Van de Vall who has been an inspiration to me since my graduate school days.

Finally, preparation of this book would not have been completed without the contributions from Dudley Seers, U. Tun Wai, Constantine Clezakos, Jacques Lecaillon, Dimitrios Germidis,

Klaus Boeck, Wolfgang Arnold, Gamani Corea, Dirk J. Wolfson, Gerard Fichet, Norberto Gonzalez, Mai Volkov and many experts of the OECD and the Center for Development Planning, Projections and Policies of the Department of Economic and Social Affairs of the U.N. Secretariat. I am also gratefully indebted to Journal of Economic Literature, U.N. Documents and World Bank Publications for the much needed annotations, and a very special thanks to Tom and Jackie Minkel fot their assistance in the preparation of this book in camera ready form.

PART I
CURRENT ISSUES, TRENDS, ANALYTICAL METHODS, STRATEGIES AND POLICIES, COUNTRY STUDIES

Introduction

This resource book has two multifaceted purposes. Firstly, to document and analyze the current trends in the development of an effective economic policy and planning of the third world countries--and to evaluate the progress made by them during the past decade in attaining long term objectives of a sustained economic growth and improvement in the quality of living future populations.

We are all very much familiar with the problems of Third World countries, usually described by Latin America (excluding Cuba) the whole of Africa, Asia (excluding its socialist countries, Japan and Israel) and Oceania (excluding Australia and New Zealand). They are plagued by poverty, very high rates of population growth, low growth rates of gross domestic product, low rates of industrialization, extremely high dependence on agriculture, rate of unemployment, and uneven income distribution. Although the expression "Third World countries" no longer has a clear meaning, majority of the international development experts would consider the poor developing countries to belong in the third world irrespective of their affiliation as aligned or non-aligned characteristic.[1]

Secondly, major purpose of this volume is to provide the researchers with the much needed knowledge about the different sources of information and available data related to the objectives and goals of economic policy and planning programs in the third world countries. Economic policy and planning programs in the developing countries have raised many complex issues. While these issues are largely dependent on national policies and priorities, their solution is of international concern.

The pace and pattern of economic policy and planning programs have varied widely among the developing countries partly because of differences in objectives, strategies and policies those countries have pursued. The issues affecting strategies and policies differ considerably at the present time from those that were important a decade ago and policy design is thus now more complex and difficult than before.

World opinion has shifted dramatically in recent years, placing emphasis on greater equity and social progress as the essential objective of international development. While the focus is on people, the impulse for greater equality of opportunity also is applied to nations. It is increasingly accepted that situations of too sharp inequalities provide neither a sound basis for progress within nations or for the maintenance of stable international relations among nations. It is recognized as well that the developing countries must be the masters of their own destiny and share fully in the collective decisions affecting the world economy. Consequently, the marked and growing disparities of income and way of life between most people in the industrial countries and those in the developing world are widely regarded as evidence of a biased and improperly functioning global system. Others explain the great income disparities as resulting from different resource endowments, and the historical and technological developments affecting their use. Disputes on the origin of poverty and wealth are certain to continue, but the search today is for development strategies which will achieve decent standards of life for all people by the end of this century.

Although a number of developing countries have sustained high levels of economic growth during the last twenty years, and there has been much social and economic progress in the Third World, little progress has been made by the poorest people and countries. Hardly anywhere have impressive rates of economic growth been matched by growth in employment or by an improvement in the relative distribution of income. Large numbers of people have shockingly low levels of income. Rates of job creation have lagged well behind the expansion of labour forces throughout most of the developing world. People who lack reliable means of livelihood are unable to assure the basic needs of adequate food, clothing and shelter. Often safe water, decent sanitation, and simple health and education facilities for their children are not available. The growing disparities of life have left ever larger numbers of people entrapped in extreme poverty, potential victims of incipient disaster.

Planning for economic and social progress has made considerable headway in the developing countries during the past two decades. Since the early years of the 1950s, country after country has adopted development planning as a rational and pragmatic instrument for the expansion and modernization of the economy and for bringing about far-reaching social changes. The record of the past two decades shows a wide array of improvements. By historical standards, the economies of developing countries have, on the average, expanded at significant rates; their industrial and other modern activities have shown a measure of dynamism; and their social amenities have gained in a variety of ways.

Yet, despite all such improvements, there is a great deal of dissatisfaction with the results of the planning process. In some quarters, the dissatisfaction has even reached the point where the value of planning as an instrument of development has been questioned. Doubts and misgivings have emerged, partly because the curve of expectations itself has risen sharply over the years and partly because some social blights have assumed a grave intensity. By far the most nagging problem today is the widespread unemployment and attendant poverty prevailing in developing countries. It is the seriousness of this problem which has called for a searching look at the planning process, not to demolish it but to ensure that the contours of national development are in harmony with the emerging needs of the society.

This book focuses attention on some of the major economic problems faced by the third world countries and the policy issues posed by those problems. It's aim is to highlight some generalizations that serve as pointers to needed economic policies. The limited extent to which statistical information is cited in this book is solely for illustrative purposes.

This volume examines the experience of a substantial number of the third world countries in implementing development plans during approximately the 1970's and draws some general conclusions for policy action during the years ahead.

Attention has been focused on some of the major problems faced by hard core developing countries and policy issues posed by those problems. However, the development needs of hard-core developing countries are very large and call for much greater interest and attention from world community than has been the case for. A systematic attack on the acute problems of countries facing extreme poverty and underdevelopment should therefore now be at the center of the policies designed to usher in a new international economic order.

It is hoped that this resource book will be of use not only to those directly involved in the formulation and implementation of development policies but also will help to acquaint a wide reading audience with the thrusts planned by developing countries for accelerated progress. In addition, the intercountry comparative analysis may be of use to planners and policy makers in developing countries, especially from the viewpoint of harmonizing national plans in order to strengthen economic co-operation with respect to economic planning among interested countries.

The plan of the reading materials in Part I of the book and the selection of the seventeen pieces represents a specific orientation, or bias. They present current international issues and trends affecting economic policy and planning in third world development, analytical methods, strategies and policies for development and selected third world country studies.

Part II includes statistical information and a descriptive bibliography of information sources related to economic planning and development in the third world countries.

Part III is a select bibliography of books, documents and periodical articles published since 1970, relevant to economic policy and planning in the developing countries. Annotations for the different titles have been compiled from The Journal of Economic Literature, International Social Sciences Index, U.N. Documents Index, World Bank Publications, Finance and Development, Book Publisher's promotion brochures and the IMF-IBRD Joint Library Publications.

6   Introduction

Part IV consists of a directory of information sources. This section is in four parts, directory of United Nations information sources, listing of bibliographic sources, titles of selected periodicals published around the world and a directory of institutions involved in research relevant to development problems in the third world countries.

---

[1]Rodwin Lloyd, "Regional Planning Perspectives in Third World Countries," in TRAINING FOR REGIONAL DEVELOPMENT PLANNING: PERSPECTIVES FOR THE THIRD DEVELOPMENT DECADE, ed. by, Om Prakash Mathur, UNCRD, 1981.
Thompson, W. Scott, THE THIRD WORLD: PREMISES OF U.S. POLICY Institute for Contemporary Studies, San Francisco, 1978.

The Meaning of Development

DUDLEY SEERS

The challenges of any period depend on the tasks that face those living in it. I believe we have misconceived the nature of the main challenge of the second half of the twentieth century. This has been seen as achieving an increase in the national incomes of the "developing countries, formalized in the target of 5% growth rates set for the first development decade.

Why do we concentrate on the national income in this way? It is of course convenient. Politicians find a single comprehensive measure useful, especially one that is at least a year out-of-date. Economists are provided with a variable which can be quantified and movements which can be analyzed into changes in sectoral output, factor shares or categories of expenditure, making model-building feasible. While it is very slipshod for us to confuse development with economic development and economic development with economic growth, it is nevertheless understandable. We can after all fall back on the supposition that increases in national income, if they are faster than the population growth, sooner or later lead to the solution of social and political problems.

But the experience of the past decade makes this belief look rather naive. Social problems and political upheavals have emerged in countries at all stages of development. Moreover, we can see that these afflict countries with rapidly rising per capita incomes as well as those with stagnant economies. In fact, it looks as if economic growth may not merely fail to solve social and political difficulties; certain types of growth can actually cause them.

Now that the complexity of development problems is becoming increasingly obvious, this continued addiction to the use of a single aggregative yardstick in the face of the evidence takes on a rather different appearance. It begins to look like a preference for avoiding the real problems of development.

From **INTERNATIONAL DEVELOPMENT REVIEW**, 1977-2, (2-7), reprinted by permission of the publisher.

The starting point in discussing the challenges we now face is to brush aside the web of fantasy we have woven around "development" and decide more precisely what we mean by it. "Development" is evitably a normative term and we must ask ourselves what are the necessary conditions for a universally acceptable aim -- the realization of the potential of human personality.

If we ask what is an <u>absolute</u> necessity for this, one answer is obvious -- enough food. Below certain levels of nutrition, a man lacks not merely bodily energy and good health but even interest in much besides food. He cannot rise significantly above an animal existence. Recent studies show that undernourishment of children leads to permanent impairment of both their physical and their mental capacities.

Since to be able to buy food is a matter of income, the criterion can be expressed in terms of income levels. This enables it to take account also of certain other minimum requirements. People will never spend all their money and energy on food, however poor they are. To be enough to feed a man, his income has also to cover basic needs of clothing, footwear and shelter, but the utility of money clearly declines sharply as these needs are satisfied.

Another basic necessity, in the sense of something without which personality cannot develop, is a job. This does not just mean employment; it can include studying; working on a family farm or keeping house. But to play none of these accepted roles -- i.e., to be chronically unemployed, dependent on another person's productive capacity, even for food -- is incompatible with self-respect, especially for somebody who has been spending years at school, perhaps at university, preparing for an active role.

It is true of course that both poverty and unemployment are associated in various ways with per capita income. If per capita incomes are falling, absolute poverty can hardly be reduced much, nor can unemployment (except in the very short run and exceptional circumstances). But certainly increases in per capita income are far from enough, as the experience of petroleum economics shows, to achieve either of these objectives. In fact, a rise in per capita income, as we very well know, can be accompanied by, can even cause, growing unemployment.[1]

The direct link between per capita income and the numbers living in poverty is income distribution. It is a truism that poverty will be eliminated much more rapidly if any given rate of economic growth is accompanied by a decline in concentration of incomes. Equality should however be considered an objective in its own right, the third element in development. Inequalities to be found now in the world, especially (but not only) outside the industrial countries, are objectionable by any religious or ethical standards. The social barriers and inhibitions of an unequal society distort the personalities of those with high incomes no less than of those who are poor. Trivial differences of accent, language, dress, customs, etc., acquire an absurd importance and contempt is engendered for those who lack social graces, especially country dwellers. Perhaps even more important, since race is usually highly correlated with income, economic inequality lies at the heart of racial tensions.

The questions to ask about a country's development are therefore: What has been happening to poverty? What has been happening to unemployment? What has been happening to inequality? If all three of these have declined from high levels, then beyond doubt this has been a period of development for the country concerned. If one or two of these central problems have been growing worse, especially if all three have, it would be strange to call the result "development," even if per capita income doubled.[2]

I. PROBLEMS OF MEASUREMENT

The challenges for the remainder of this century arise out of the analysis above. The first is how to find measures of development to replace the national income, or, more precisely, to enable the national income to be given its true, somewhat limited, significance, as a measure of development potential. (A big increase in the national income at least makes it easier in the future to achieve a reduction in poverty, if appropriate policies are adopted.)

There are two points to make here. The first is that the national income figures published for most "developing" countries have very little meaning. This is partly because of lack of data, especially on farm output, but also because, when income distributions are so unequal, prices have very little meaning as weights in "real" income comparisons.

Secondly, the lack of data on poverty, unemployment and inequality reflects the priorities of statistical offices rather than the difficulties of data collection.

The conceptual problems of these measures do not seem to be more formidable than those of the national income. We have just grown accustomed to ignoring the latter. But there are also practical problems. All the measures require information about supplementary incomes, age-and-sex composition of receiving units, etc., additional to that obtained from statistics which are prepared as a by-product of administration, at least in countries where only a small proportion of income receivers pay direct taxes.[3] It is also hard to measure even overt unemployment where unemployment registration does not exist or covers only part of the labor force. But again we must not be diverted by such technical problems from attempting the reassessment which really matters.[4]

II. INTERNAL CONSISTENCY OF DEVELOPMENT PROCESS

The second set of challenges to the social scientists, politicians and administrators in the decades ahead is to find paths of development which enable progress to be made on all these criteria. Since development is far from being achieved at present, the need is not, as is generally imagined, to accelerate economic growth -- which could even be dangerous -- but to change the nature of the development process.

A major question is whether the criteria are mutually consistent. The answer is that in many respects development on one of the criteria implies, or helps bring about, or is even a necessary condition for, development on one or more of the others.

To reduce unemployment is to remove one of the main causes of poverty and inequality. Moreover, a reduction in inequality will of course reduce poverty, ceteris paribus.

These propositions beg many questions, however. The reduction of unemployment means in part finding techniques which are labor-intensive, with the least damage to the expansion of production. This is of course a discussion to which many have contributed, notably A. K. Sen.

There is a well-known, indeed classical, argument that inequality is necessary to generate savings and incentives and thus to promote economic growth -- which, as we have seen, can be taken as an indicator of some types of development potential. I find the argument that the need for savings justifies inequality unconvincing in the Third World today. Savings propensities are after all very low precisely in countries with highly unequal distributions; the industrial countries with less concentration of income have, by contrast, much higher savings propensities. Savings are of course also affected by the absolute level of incomes, but the explanation must also lie in the high consumption levels of the rich, designed to maintain the standards so important in an unequal society.

Moreover, the rich in most countries tend to have extremely high propensities, not merely to spend, but to spend on goods and services with a high foreign exchange content, and, for countries suffering from an acute foreign exchange bottleneck, this is a major obstacle to development. It is true that import demand can be held in check (as in India) by administrative controls, but this leads to the elaboration of a bureaucratic apparatus which is expensive, especially in terms of valuable organizing ability, and which in some countries becomes riddled with corruption. In any case, in a highly unequal society, personal savings often flow abroad or go into luxury housing and other investment projects of low or zero priority for development.

The argument that only inequality can provide the incentives that are necessary is also obviously of limited validity in a country where there are barriers of race or class to advancement. Still, we cannot dismiss it out of hand. The needs for private entrepreneurial talent vary according to the circumstances of different economies, but there are very few where this need is small. Countries relying on growing exports of manufacturers, as many are, depend heavily on the emergence of businessmen with drive to penetrate foreign markets. All countries depend in some degree on the appearance of progressive farmers. Will these emerge without financial rewards on a scale that will make nonsense of an egalitarian policy? Are rising profits of companies, especially foreign companies, an inevitable feature of growth in many countries? Or are we exaggerating the importance of financial incentives? Can other, non-financial rewards partially take their place? Can social incentives be developed to a point where people will take on such tasks with little or no individual reward (as the governments of China and Cuba are trying to prove)? This is one of the great issues to be decided, and the 1970's will throw a good deal of light on the answer.

The compatibility of equality and rising output and employment has recently become doubtful for an additional set of reasons. Can the people who are professionally necessary be kept in the country if they can earn only a small fraction of what they could earn elsewhere? Yet what are the costs in terms of human welfare and even efficiency if they are prevented from leaving?

On the other hand, there are equally serious reasons for questioning the compatibility of <u>inequality</u> and economic growth. Can a structure of local industry be created to correspond to the structure of demand that arises in a highly inequitable society (leaving aside the question of whether it <u>should</u> be created)? Will production rise rapidly if the proportion of the labor force too badly nourished for full manual and mental work is only sinking slowly? Can the government obtain the cooperation of the population in wage restraint, and in many other ways that are necessary for development, if there is visible evidence of great wealth which is being transmitted from generation to generation, so that the wage earner sees his children and his children's children doomed indefinitely by subordinate positions? Can it mobilize the energies of the total population and break down social customs which obstruct development, especially in rural areas?

I do not pretend to know the answers to this complex of questions, which point to a set of "internal contradictions" in the development process far more severe than those to which Marx drew attention. What is more, the economic and political objectives are linked closely together. An economic system with large numbers of under-nourished and unemployed at the bottom end of a long social ladder, especially if they are racially distinguishable, can never provide a firm basis for political rights or for civic order. Those with high incomes from profits or salaries are not merely slow to tackle the great social problems of poverty and unemployment; they will inevitably try to find ways of maintaining privilege, resorting (as dozens of historical examples show) to political violence rather than give it up. Conversely, those without jobs or adequate incomes will sooner or later try to obtain them through a regime which would not allow organized opposition. Judging from present trends in the climate of opinion, especially among the young, it is very doubtful whether inequalities on anything like the present scale could co-exist with political liberties in the 1970's and 1980's. Yet it is hard to envisage how inequality can be reduced setting in motion, from one direction or another, forces that reduce political liberty.

There are administrative limits to the main weapon against inequality, direct taxation, apart altogether from any conflict with incentives. Inequality cannot really be reduced so long as property ownership is heavily concentrated. So conversion of incomes from large holdings of property into life pensions (as in Cuba) or bond interest (as in Chile) or their reduction through death duties (as in Britain) are likely to be more effective than taxation, though they may be beyond the bounds of the politically feasible in many countries.

But a great deal can be done even without attacking property ownership. Practically every decision taken by government officials has implications for the degree of equality -- to lend to big farmers or small, to set prices of public corporations at levels that tax or subsidize rich consumers, to build roads for private motor cars or for goods vehicles, to put the best equipment in rural or urban schools. It would not be a bad thing to put up in every civil service office a sign: "Will it reduce inequality?" Secondly, if the administrative and political organization is motivated and trained to report tax evasion, corruption, etc., all sorts of egalitarian policies, including capital taxation, become more feasible. (Where such a spirit is weak, one can hardly expect rapid development in the sense I have used the word here.)

Lastly, a reduction in inequality is very hard, if not impossible, so long as a country is dependent on a major power and shows the influence of its consumption tastes and salary levels. So is a reduction in unemployment, because one of the marks of dependence is reliance on the technology of the countries which play a dominant role in the national life, and this may well be inappropriate to local problems. On the other hand, a country that leaves its social problems unsolved is unlikely to be strong enough to achieve or maintain genuine independence; it may not even survive as a political unit.

III. ENDS AND MEANS

When political liberty is considered as an end, its importance, though high, is secondary so long as a substantial fraction of the people are undernourished and unemployed. But it appears in quite a different light as a <u>means</u>. Societies lacking open opposition have shown themselves extremely inflexible in meeting the challenge of changing circumstances, whether one considers the continuation by Germany of a war for months after it was already lost, or the stubbornness of Communist regimes in clinging to unsuccessful agricultural policies. Moreover, as Soviet experience shows, there is no guarantee that political liberties will reappear as economic problems are eased.

Higher educational levels are ends in themselves, but

education is also a means. Economists have, somewhat belatedly, come to see it as a source of development; but they treat it narrowly as a factor in the growth of national income, relating stocks of manpower with certain qualifications (e.g. university degrees) to national income levels.

But if development is not just or even mainly an increase in the national income, education takes on an entirely different aspect. We need to go a long way beyond the Harbison approach, valuable though this has been. What are important are not the "man years" at school but the methods of selection and the content of education. Inequality can be reduced (and also economic efficiency increased) if secondary and higher education are made genuinely available to those with the lowest incomes (belonging to minority races), which means of course that special methods of selection must be found. Secondly, by easing shortages of high-level manpower, education can reduce the need for high salaries for those with scarce professional skills. In that case, however, the whole structure of education needs reconsideration; education will hardly fulfil this function if it produces on the one hand a few distinguished academic scholars who, as in Britain, think of themselves as superior to the rest of the population and on the other mass of people with the wrong qualifications.

The third function of education, and this applies also to adult education and the content of radio and TV programs, is to prepare professional classes conscious of the realities of development, both the internal realities and the realities of the world scene, with such an understanding of their historical origins that they see what needs to be done and voluntarily accept the sacrifices implied. Many of the obstacles to policies which would reduce poverty and unemployment have their origin in attitudes to manual work, especially in the countryside, to imported consumer goods, to foreign technologies, etc. Since each generation is in some degree a copy of the preceding one, through parental influences, such attitudes can hardly be changed except by a conscious educational policy, broadly defined.

Finally, one policy area which looks different if one discards the aggregative approach is population. Conventionally, population growth is seen simply as a subtraction from the increase in the national income; the closer the growth rates of population and income, the slower the rise in per capita income. This line of argument is fundamentally somewhat suspect because it assumes that population and income are independent of each other. But the real case for an active population policy is simply that, so long as the labor force is growing fast, it is almost impossible to relieve unemployment and poverty, since a plentiful supply of labor keeps the wages of the unskilled, apart perhaps from a privileged modern sector, near levels of barest subsistence. Moreover, the growing pressure of population on the budget makes it very difficult to expand educational and other social services. An additional argument, on the above criteria, is that this growing pressure increases the need for foreign aid and thus postpones the attainment of genuine independence.

IV. INTERNATIONAL POLICY

It is misleading to talk about "development" when we consider the world scene, on the criteria suggested above. One cannot really say that there has been development for the world as a whole, when the benefits of technical progress have accrued to minorities which were already relatively rich, whether we are speaking of rich minorities within nations or the minority of nations which are rich. To me, this word is particularly misleading for the period since the war, especially the "development decade" when the growth of economic inequality and unemployment must have actually accelerated. (I am alarmed at the phrase, a "second development decade." Another "development decade" like the 1960's, with unemployment rates and inequality rising by further large steps, would be politically and economically disastrous, whatever the pace of economic growth!)

Certainly in some respects, as I have said, a basis has been laid in many countries for possible development in the future. But there has not been any basic improvement in international institutions. It is true that there are now opportunities for poor countries at least to talk to the rich, but one cannot speak of international order; the international institutions lack the power to impose solutions. There is not much to show for the tremendous efforts which went into the New Delhi UNCTAD. Virtually no safeguards have been set up against a world recession -- the creation of SDR's is by no means adequate in itself. Nor has much been done to open the markets of industrial countries to imports of manufactures, the only real possibility of export expansion for the Third World as a whole.

There is no fiscal system for the world. This may perhaps be foreshadowed by 1% aid targets, but these targets are in fact ignored and aid programs remain at very low levels. As Gunnar Myrdal warned us many years ago, the establishment of the national welfare state has turned the attention of the public in the rich countries inwards, making them less interested in the welfare of the world as a whole. The aid that does exist often plays an important economic role, but, like immigration and trade policies, it is very largely motivated by the self-interest of donors, sometimes by very short-term commercial and political interest. This often in effect leads them to support, or even help install, governments which oppose the redistribution of income and in other ways block development.

Many countries have in fact slipped further under the influence of one or another of the big powers. This itself hinders development. Independence is not merely one of the aims of development; it is also one of the means. It is a force for mobilizing popular support and the force is blunted if a government is obviously far from independent.

Yet clearly there is a basic inconsistency. Can a world system be created which will accommodate nationalism while providing a truly international and much more equitable economic and political order? And can this be done just by cerebration and logical clarity, or does it require the poorer countries of the world to organize themselves, perhaps by continent, to use what cards they possess to bring it about? How can nationalism be reconciled on the other hand with the strong tribal and regional forces which are emerging? What form of decentralization do these imply?

Such are the challenges we now face. The role of the practitioner, the politician or the civil servant is the extremely difficult one of finding a politically and administratively feasible path of development in a grossly unequal world. They can be helped by the theorist if he refrains from trying to adapt uncritically models and measures designed in and for industrial countries, where priorities are very different, but helps instead to develop policies, national and international, to mitigate the great social problems of the Third World.

By so doing, indeed, he may incidentally provide the social scientists in the rich countries with food for thought. After all, poverty and unemployment are not so starkly obvious in the North Atlantic area, compared to the conditions before the last war (and this helps explain the reduced interest of their social scientists in these problems until quite recently). Although economic inequality diminished too up to about 1950, it now seems to be growing again and to be accompanied by increasingly severe inequality between races in multi-racial societies. But above all, the aim must be to change international attitudes so that it becomes impossible for the political leaders and social scientists of Europe and North America to continue overlooking, and aggravating, often inadvertently, the obscene inequalities that disfigure the world.

NOTES

[1] Thus in Trinidad the growth in per capita income averaged more than 5% a year during the whole period 1953 to 1968, while overt unemployment showed a steady increase to more than 10% of the labor force.

[2] Of course, the fulfilment of human potential requires much that cannot be specified in purely economic terms. I cannot spell out all the other requirements, but it would be very unbalanced if I did not mention them at all. They include adequate educational levels, freedom of speech, and citizenship of a nation that is truly independent, both economically and politically, in the sense that the views of other governments do not largely predetermine its own government's decisions.

[3] Technical problems of measuring distribution are discussed in an unpublished paper, "On the possibility of measuring personal distribution of income," by Professor Dich of Aarhaus.

[4] I cannot explore here the measurement of the educational and political elements in development. In as far as the former is covered by the formal educational system, a technique for showing the changing profile over time has been developed by Richard Jolly. (See A. R. Jolly, "Planning Education for African Development," East African Publishing House, Nairobi, 1969.) Measurement of the extent to which the political aims have been achieved is of course much more difficult; possible clues include the number of prisoners held for political or quasi-political reasons; the social and racial composition of parliaments, business boards, senior public administrative grasdes, etc., and also of those enjoying secondary and university education; the incidence of petty theft; rates of suicide and alcoholism.

Clues on the degree of national independence include the extent to which the country votes in the same way as a great power at the United Naitons, the existence of foreign military bases and overflying rights, the ratio of aid from the largest donor to total foreign exchange receipts, etc. Indirect indicators are the proportion of assets, especially subsoil assets, owned by foreigners, the extent to which one trading partner dominates the partner of trade, and the proportion of the supply of capital (or intermediate goods) which is imported.

Economic Trends and Prospects of Developing Countries

ORGANIZATION FOR ECONOMIC COOPERATION AND DEVELOPMENT

I. INTRODUCTION

The serious economic and financial difficulties—some temporary, others more permanent—experienced by many developing countries in recent years called for special efforts of international co-operation to meet immediate problems. From about mid-1975 the world economy has slowly, and uncertainly, regained some stability although both inflation and unemployment remain at unacceptably high levels. The return to comparative stability provides an opportunity to take stock of the longer-term performance and prospects of the developing countries.

Over the past decade, some significant new financial and industrial powers have emerged at a time when the developing world as a whole was registering quite rapid rates of economic advance. With large current account surpluses since 1973, most OPEC countries have dramatically increased their external financial strength and as a group OPEC has accumulated one quarter of the world's official reserve assets. Over a longer period other developing countries, including notably Brazil, Korea (Rep.) Mexico, Taiwan and several European developing countries have grown rapidly, modernising their economies in various ways and creating efficient export sectors. Despite this aggregate economic advance, serious problems of poverty and structural imbalance remain in these countries. The lesson to be learnt from this experience is that economic progress does not necessarily equal social progress. Indeed some forms of economic progress make little or no contribution to social advance. This is particularly found in countries which have pursued rapid economic growth policies

From **DEVELOPMENT CO-OPERATION**, 1977, (37-49), reprinted by permission of the publisher, OECD, Paris.

without regard to employment or general welfare objectives. Social progress has many dimensions, some of which—such as calorie intake, literacy rates and life expectancy—tend to rise with average income; but information on other dimensions such as employment, income distribution and access to basic services often reveals a much less satisfactory trend, casting doubt on the effectiveness of unconstrained growth maximisation as a means of achieving social progress.

In the remaining countries, where the majority of the people in the Third World live, economic and social progress has been much slower and the problems of under-development and poverty remain acute. The traditional prescription would be for these countries to implement policies which raise investment rates and improve its efficiency (thereby raising aggregate growth rates): the former involves a whole panoply of measures to mobilise more domestic savings and to induce more investment; the latter involves difficult policy choices between manufacturing and agriculture, export promotion and import substitution, and between alternative technologies, where much depends on the resources, circumstances and objectives of individual countries. However, the traditional prescription has failed almost everywhere to improve the lot of the poor majority. If the aim of development is to promote the satisfaction of basic human needs as well as income growth there is a need for policies and instruments which combine these twin objectives. It is not enough simply to raise aggregate income.

The principal concern in the following section is to illustrate various dimensions of the developing countries' economic performance over the longer term, keeping in mind that achievement is due to a combination of domestic and external factors[1] and that aggregate data hide internal inequalities of all kinds. The selection of economic aggregates is largely dictated by what is available rather than what would be ideal. The chapter finishes with a discussion of prospects, picking out some of the key economic variables in the short and medium term.

II. ECONOMIC TRENDS

a) Output

By historical standards, the world's output has expanded at an unprecedented rate since the end of the Second World War. From 1950 to 1965, the OECD area experienced the fastest rates of growth; subsequently output growth in the developing world exceeded that in the industrialised world, with the most rapid advances registered by some middle-income developing countries, including both oil-rich and resource-poor countries. In per capita terms only the oil-producing and middle-income groups have reduced the relative gap which separates them from the average for

TABLE 1. SOME BASIC FACTS ON THE WORLD ECONOMY[a]

	Low income countries[b]	Middle-income countries		Industrialised countries[e]
		Lower middle-income[c]	Higher middle-income[d]	
1. Population (million, 1976)	1,210	300	612	685
2. GNP ($ billion, 1976)	193	117	841	4,184
3. Average GNP *per capita* ($, 1976)	160	390	1,370	6,110
4. GNP *per capita* (annual average percentage real increase, 1965-1974)	1.4	3.4	4.9	4.0
5. Merchandise exports ($ billion, 1976)	21	27	223	633
6. Life expectancy at birth	46	53	61	72

a. The data in the table include oil-producing countries (Algeria, Bahrain, Ecuador, Gabon, Indonesia, Iran, Iraq, Kuwait, Libyan Arab Republic, Nigeria, Oman, Qatar, Saudi Arabia, United Arab Emirates, Venezuela) but xclude Mainland China (population 820 million, GNP/cap $350 in 1975), and other centrally-planned-economy countries (population 380 million, GNP/cap $2,650 in 1975).

b. 39 countries with an average per capita income in 1975 below $265, the threshold income presently used by the World Bank to identify poorer countries. Most of these countries are in Southern Asia and Africa.

c. 42 countries with an average per capita income in 1975 between $265 and $520. Above a level of $520, a country would not, as a general rule, have access to IDA financing.

d. All other developing countries on the DAC list. Includes countries like Iran, Korea Rep., Brazil, Colombia, Peru, Malaysia, Mexico, Taiwan and Algeria (in descending order) which have recorded particularly dynamic growth, with recent annual average increases in their real GNP per capita of 7 per cent or higher, and also the following main high-income countries: Saudi Arabia, Libya, Venezuela, United Arab Emirates, Oman, Bahrain (oil exporters), Singapore, Bahamas, Israel and Bermuda (in descending order).

e. All OECD Members except Mediterranean countries in the DAC list of developing countries. Also includes a few non-OECD developed countries.

Sources: Derived from World Bank, UN and IMF sources. GNP data, shown in 1976 US dollars, are taken from, or calculated on the method used in the World Bank Atlas.

TABLE 2. GROWTH OF PRODUCTION AND PRODUCTION SECTORS BY GROUPS OF COUNTRIES

AVERAGE ANNUAL REAL GROWTH RATES, 1965-1973

Per cent.

Country group[a]	GDP	Agriculture	Manufacturing
Industrialised	4.6	1.9	4.7
Developing	6.0	3.0	7.3
of which:			
Low-income	3.3	3.2	3.7
Middle-income: lower	5.7	3.0	8.3
Middle-income: higher	6.6	2.9	8.7
Oil-producing	8.1	3.0	8.4

a. *Source and definition*: World Bank, *World Tables, 1976.*

2. Unless otherwise stated, the data in this section are drawn from World Bank publications. See in particular, the *World Tables (1976)*.

TABLE 3. GROWTH OF PER CAPITA FOOD PRODUCTION IN DEVELOPING COUNTRIES, 1971-1976

	1971	1972	1975	1976	Annual increase (per cent)	
					1961-70	1970-76
	(Index 1961-1965 = 100)					
Developing regions	101	99	103	104	0.4	0.1
Latin America	103	101	102	107	0.7	0.1
Far East	103	97	106	105	0.2	0.2
Near East	103	108	109	109	0.5	0.9
Africa	99	95	93	94	—	1.2

Source: FAO.

industrialised countries. Trends in the components of GDP^2 indicate that output growth was generally accompanied by growing shares of manufacturing, investment and exports.

Geographically, the best performances among developing countries with respect to growth of per capita GDP were achieved in Southern Europe (5 per cent for annum) and the Middle East (5.9 per cent per annum); and the weakest performances were evident in Africa (2.5 per cent per annum) and South Asia (1.2 per cent per annum). Among the major non-oil developing countries particularly good performances were registered by the Republic of Korea (8.9 per cent per annum), Greece (7.5 per cent per annum), Taiwan (7.3 per cent per annum) and Portugal (6.8 per cent per annum) Countries which fared less well included Egypt (0.8 per cent per annum), Uruguay (0.2 per cent per annum), South Vietnam (-0.2 per cent per annum), Bangladesh (-0.3 per cent per annum), and Cambodia (-5.2 per cent per annum). Most of the Sahelian countries also registered very low growth rates in per capita terms.

From a sectoral viewpoint, growth in GDP was generally accompanied by an increasing share of manufacturing. Table 2 shows that the middle-income and oil-producing countries' manufacturing sectors grew on average by more than 8 per cent per year. Of the seven non-oil countries with GDP growth rates over 6 per cent per annum for which sectoral detail is available, five had manufacturing growth rates in excess of 10 per cent per annum.

Agricultural output generally kept pace with population growth in this period. For developing countries as a whole, it grew at 3.0 per cent per annum, with the best performance occuring in East Asia (3.6 per cent per annum) and the weakest in Africa (2.4 per cent per annum). However, in a number of instances, the growth of agricultural output was well below average population growth: in Syria it was less than half the population growth rate and in the Sahel counties growth rates of agricultural output were nearly all negative.

From 1970 to 1976 food production kept pace with population growth by a slight margin (+0.1 per cent), although the situation fluctuated widely from year to year and from region to region. After several years of bad harvest at the beginning of the decade, combined with a decrease in world food production in 1974, two successive years of bumper harvest, 1975 and 1976, have eased the food situation and have averted famine. These two years of good harvest, during which the annual growth rate averaged 4 per cent, boosted the annual average increase during the Second Development Decade to 2.7 per cent, a rate still far behind the 4 per cent target and slightly lower than the rate achieved during the previous decade (2.9 per cent).

Although the situation has recently improved, major problems remain. 1975/76 food production restored per capita levels to about the 1968/71 average, itself far from adequate for many people. In some developing countries, the recent replenishment of cereal stocks may have partly reflected the inability of the poorest consumers to purchase adequate quantities for their nutritional needs. Food production failed to match population growth in no less than 50 developing countries in 1970-1976, and declined noticeably in Africa (see Table 3). In the countries most seriously affected by the economic crisis (largely synonymous with the low-income group) food production levels remained far below the average during the 1970s and in some of them (especially in Burundi, Ethiopia, Honduras, Mozambique, Rwanda, the Sahelian countries and Sri Lanka) per capita cereal production was much below the 1969/71 levels.

Growth in GDP can be expected to be related to similar growth of investment, either simultaneously or in preceding periods. Available data suggests a growing differentiation among groups of countries in investment as a share of GDP. In higher middle-income countries investment has steadily grown as a share of GDP over the past 20 years (from 18 per cent in 1955 to about 22 per cent in 1973). In the case of the lower middle-income group the share increased by some 5 percentage points. Among low-income countries, however, the investment share has risen no more than a percentage point over the past 20 years. As a result, the investment performance gap between the top and bottom groups widened from 3.7 percentage points in 1955 to 6.3 percentage points in 1973.

In general, investment grew at a faster rate than total GDP, suggesting either longer gestation periods or declining investment efficiency, but the pattern varied considerably among income groups. In higher middle-income developing countries, investment accelerated in the period 1965-1973; in lower middle-income countries, it tended to decelerate. In low-income countries, the annual rate of growth of investment fell from 7.3 per cent in 1960-1965 to 3.7 per cent in 1965-73.

Simply in terms of output and its main components over a relatively short period there is evidence of growing divergence. That is not to say, however, that the potential for fast economic growth will remain with higher middle-income countries or, conversely, that low-income countries will continue to grow relatively slowly.

b) External Trade

Before the oil crisis, the share of non-oil developing countries in world trade tended to decline in both nominal and real terms in the context of very rapidly rising total trade. Comparison between the three income groups underscores the particularly weak performance (both in exports and imports) of the low-income countries. In the years since the oil crisis the non-oil developing group has tended to increase as shares in both world exports and world imports against a background of erratic movements, and a slower underlying growth, in world trade.

Table 4. GROWTH OF GROSS DOMESTIC INVESTMENT (GDI) AND GDP BY GROUPS OF COUNTRIES

Country group	Growth 1965-1973 Per cent per annum		Per cent GDI as share of GDP		
	GDP	GDI	1965	1970	1973
Industrialised	4.6	5.4	20.6	22.7	23.4
Developing	6.0	7.3	16.8	19.6	20.3
of which:					
Low-income	3.3	3.7	14.2	15.3	15.6
Middle-income: lower	5.7	7.1	14.2	20.2	19.6
Middle-income: higher	6.6	8.3	18.3	21.0	21.6
Oil-producing	8.1	9.7	17.8	20.0	21.1

TABLE 5. GROWTH OF PRODUCTION, EXPORTS AND IMPORTS
BY GROUPS OF COUNTRIES

Per cent.

Country group	GDP	Average annual real growth rates, 1965-1973	
		Exports	Imports
Industrialised	4.6	9.2	9.3
Developing	6.0	8.0	8.3
of which:			
Low-income	3.3	3.7	2.0
Middle-income: lower	5.7	7.2	7.6
Middle-income: higher	6.6	7.6	9.6
Oil-producing	8.1	10.8	10.9

i) Exports

Between 1965 and 1973, world exports trebled in value terms and doubled in real terms. The exports of developing countries grew by somewhat more than this--primarily because of the inclusion of the oil-exporting countries. Among non-oil developing countries, the higher middle-income group maintained their share in world trade over this period. The export share of lower middle-income countries fell marginally, from 3.0 per cent in 1965 to 2.6 per cent in 1973. The share of the low-income group dropped from 2.7 per cent in 1965 to 1.5 per cent in 1973.

Looking more closely at export sectors of individual countries it appears that a high share, and rapid growth, of manufactures contributed to good performance. Examples of non-oil developing countries with particularly rapid growth of exports (more than 15 per cent per annum) include Israel, Korea (Rep.), Lebanon, Malta, Portugal, Spain, and Taiwan, where manufactures account for more than 50 per cent of exports, and Brazil, Costa Rica, Greece, and Singapore where they account for between 20 and 50 per cent. In some of these cases, manufactured exports have grown at annual rates of 25 per cent or more. The share of these countries, and indeed all non-oil developing countries, in world export markets for manufactures is still relatively small, although growing. However, in some product markets, including not only traditional items such as textiles and footwear but also advanced items such as steel and ships and electrical machinery, these middle-income developing countries have obtained a significant share.

Twenty-one non-oil developing countries had growth rates of exports below 5 per cent, of whom nine had negative growth. Many of these countries were involved in wars (Indo-China, Guinea-Bissau) or subject to political unrest or natural disasters (Chad and Upper Volta). Geographic isolation and landlockedness also place the exporting country at some disadvantage. The main economic reason, however, was the possession of an undiversified export sector based on agricultural products or unprocessed raw materials of the type available in many of the low-income, slow-growing countries.

ii) Imports

The growth of domestic output depends in part on sufficient growth of imports. A key role is played by imports of capital goods, particularly in those countries which have a low domestic capacity to produce such goods. How did these countries fare with respect to import volume over the last 15 years?

Long-term trend growth prior to the oil crisis and the recession averaged some 6-7 per cent, usually with only small departures from trend. The trends in import volume summarised in

TABLE 6. VOLUME INDICES OF IMPORTS BY GROUPS OF COUNTRIES

(1970 = 100).

Country group	1960	1965	1974	1975
Industrialised	42	63	130	121
Developing	64	76	137	151
of which:				
Low income	88	108	96	105
Middle-income: lower	63	83	114	123
Middle-income: higher	62	70	133	130
Oil-producing	67	75	181	248

Source: UNCTAD, *Handbook of International Trade and Development Statistics*, 1976.

Table 6 show, not surprisingly, a dramatic increase for oil-producing countries since 1973. Apart from minor divergencies in the trends for industrialised and middle-income countries since 1970, the main points to note include the relatively rapid growth of industrialised countries' imports in the 1960s and the slow growth and fluctuations of low-income countries' imports.

The financing facilities provided to the non-oil developing countries in 1973-75 enables them to maintain and slightly enlarge their share of world imports (by value), reversing the trend of the preceding fifteen years. However, this occurred against a background of very rapid inflation, relative price shifts and changes in composition due to poor harvest, making it difficult to assess trends in import volumes. On balance, the record appears favourable, with the exception of only one year (1975) when the non-oil developing countries probably experienced a modest decline in import volumes. Once again, there were marked differences between sub-groups. Low-income countries were forced to pare down imports in 1974, but were less affected than middle-income countries by the recession.

iii) Current Account Balances

The fairly steady growth in imports (by value) during 1973-1975 combined with a slower underlying growth of exports and an adverse shift in barter terms of trade inevitably led to increases in current account deficits. Without such increases, levels of consumption and investment would have suffered; with them, the cost to future output (in the form of debt service) began to rise--see sub-section iv.

Table 7 provides data on current account balances of groups of developing countries both before and after the oil crisis. Exclusion of the oil-producing countries has a pronounced effect in 1973 and subsequent years. Taking the average for these four years prior to the oil crisis, the higher middle-income group accounted for just over half of the deficit on average, the lower middle-income group for less than one-fifth and the low income group for nearly one-third. While the share of the low-income group has declined over the whole period, that of the higher middle-income group has increased.

In 1974, the combined current account deficit of the non-oil developing countries rose to some $38 billion, more than three times the 1973 level, largely as a result of the oil price increase. In 1975 it widened further as a consequence of the recession, but narrowed somewhat in 1976. As a share of GNP, this deficit now runs at a level of 4-5 per cent, compared with 2-3 per cent prior to the oil crisis.

TABLE 7. CURRENT ACCOUNT BALANCES BY GROUPS OF COUNTRIES

$ billion.

Country group	1960[a]	1965[a]	1970[a]	1973[a]	1974[b]	1975[b]
Industrialised	+6.1	+9.5	+13.7	+16.8	−26.0	+4.0
Developing	−4.5	−5.2	−12.7	−7.9	+27.3	−22.7
of which:						
Low-income	−1.5	−2.9	−2.6	−2.8	−5.2	−6.7
Middle-income: lower	−0.9	−0.9	−2.9	−1.6	−3.0	−7.5
Middle-income: higher	−2.3	−1.2	−6.7	−8.0	−29.8	−40.7
Oil-producing	+0.3	−0.2	−0.5	+4.6	+65.3	+32.2
Total non-oil LDCs	−4.8	−5.0	−12.2	−12.5	−38.0	−54.9

a. World Bank: *World Tables (1976)*.
b. OECD.

TABLE 8. EXTERNAL DEBT AND DEBT SERVICE OF DEVELOPING COUNTRIES BY GROUPS OF COUNTRIES

$ billion.

Country group	1967	1973	1974	1975	1976 (prov.)
Developing countries:					
Debt	48.4	112.4	137.2	172.9	206.8
Debt service	6.2	15.9	19.8	26.0	32.0
of which:					
Low-income:					
Debt	10.7	21.1	23.7	27.7	31.4
Debt service	0.8	1.4	1.7	2.1	2.3
Middle-income:					
Debt	30.9	68.9	89.1	116.4	140.8
Debt service	5.0	11.5	14.1	18.7	23.3
Oil-producing:					
Debt	6.8	22.4	24.4	28.8	34.6
Debt service	0.4	3.0	4.0	5.2	6.4
Non-oil LDCs:					
Debt	41.6	90.0	112.0	144.1	172.2
Debt service	5.8	12.9	15.8	20.8	25.6

Note: For more details see section E of the Statistical Annex.

iv) External Debt

The past decade has witnessed both a dramatic increase and significant changes in the structure of developing countries' external debt. During 1973-76 most categories of debt increased strongly, in particular debt arising from private bank financing, loans from OPEC countries, export credits and loans from international organisations. In 1977 there were large debt increases for the last two categories only. The general trend in debt and debt service is summarised in Table 8. The figures relate to total disbursed debt at year-end and to annual debt service.

It should be remembered that the rise in the nominal value of developing countries' indebtedness looks much less dramatic if seen in the light of inflation which has eroded the real value of their debt and debt service (as it has, of course, also eroded the real value of their external reserves which have risen rapidly in nominal terms). It must be kept in mind, however, that it is difficult to measure precisely the complex effect of inflation on the debt burden, taking into account such factors as the terms of trade.

Table 8 shows that (a) the more-than-fourfold increase in debt and debt service between 1967 and 1976 was mainly incurred by middle-income non-oil developing countries; (b) the sharpest increases were registered by OPEC countries; and, most important, (c) the share of low-income non-oil developing countries in total debt and total debt service has fallen steadily since 1967.

The increase in debt of non-oil developing countries was particularly marked during 1974-75 (some 26 per cent per annum). In 1977 it is expected to return to the 1960-1973 trend rate of about 15 per cent per annum. As regards debt service, the return to the pre-oil-crisis trend (also around 15 per cent increase per annum) may take somewhat longer, partly because of the time-lags resulting from grace periods.

The low and declining share of low-income countries in total debt (15 per cent in 1976) and particularly in total debt service (7 per cent) largely reflects the fact that these countries receive the bulk of their external financing in the form of grants or very soft loans, which generate little or no debt service, and to a lesser extent in semi-concessional loans such as export credits. Some of these poorer countries could have had access to international capital markets but so far have preferred not to resort to this more costly form of financing.

The debt of most middle-income countries is on much "harder" terms. In particular the largest part of international bank financing to developing countries remained concentrated throughout the period with middle-income and, since 1973, with oil-exporting countries, which have access to these resources and can afford market terms thanks essentially to their more dynamic export performance.

The indebtedness of OPEC countries as a group also increased as some of these countries (e.g. Indonesia and Algeria) still have massive recourse to export credits and capital markets to help finance their industrialisation.

III. ECONOMIC PROSPECTS OF NON-OIL DEVELOPING COUNTRIES

a) Short-Term Prospects

A number of key variables point to a relatively favourable outlook for the short-term although actual developments will, of course, be importantly affected by the future course of the world economic conjuncture. Per capita income growth saw an acceleration in 1976 from the very slow rates of advance registered in 1975. In large part this was due to good harvest, particularly in Asia.

	1975 %	1976 %
Industrialised countries	-2.1	4.2
Non-oil developing countries	0.8	3.2
of which:		
Low income	1.0	2.5
Middle-income: lower	1.2	3.7
Middle-income: higher	0.8	3.5

The cyclical upturn in the OECD area, which started around the middle of 1975, has also had a favourable, but unevenly distributed, effect on non-oil developing countries' export earnings. For the group as a whole, export earnings rose by some 20 per cent in 1976 and are expected to increase by a further 20-25 per cent in 1977. However, the rapidity with which the export earnings of some of the higher middle-income countries increased in 1976 and 1977 (notably Hong Kong, Korea (Rep.) and Taiwan) contrasts with the slow rate registered by the majority of low-income African countries.

From a balance-of-payments point of view, non-oil developing countries as a group were in a relatively comfortable position in 1976. Their current account deficit (excluding official transfers) narrowed substantially from about $55 billion in 1975 to a still large, but more sustainable, $44 billion in 1976. Despite this improvement, their aggregate borrowing on international capital markets was not reduced and gross international reserves rose by about $12 billion. The volume of non-oil developing countries' exports in 1976 grew rapidly in response to buoyant demand for primary products in the OECD area, and manufactured goods exports by the South-East Asian countries continued to gain shares in OECD markets. This development was paralleled by a firming of these countries' export prices. Imports of non-oil developing countries picked up much more slowly, partly a lagged response to the large--and possibly unanticipated--increase in export revenues, but partly also as a result of deliberate measures in some countries to curtail import growth for balance-of-payments reasons. By mid-1977, with the exception of certain South-East Asian countries, there were still few signs of any general rebound in these countries' imports.

The non-oil developing countries' export earnings prospects in 1978 are particularly difficult to assess in view of the uncertainty which currently surrounds the progress of the OECD countries out of the recession. This is a vitally important factor since some 70 per cent of their exports go to the OECD area. According to the latest OECD forecasts at the time of writing (October) economic expansion in the OECD area in 1978 may decline to below 4 per cent (year-on-year change). A major question arising from the forecasts is whether, on present policies, the expansion will be self-sustaining in many OECD countries as the prospects of weak trends in productive investment, more than two years after the recovery started, may cast some doubt on this in virtually all OECD countries other than the United States.

The expansion of OECD import volumes from non-oil developing countries slowed from over 20 per cent in 1976 to an estimated 2-4 per cent at annual rate in the first half of 1977 as stockbuilding ended in most OECD countries. With weak demand for commodities likely to persist, the OECD area's import volumes from non-oil developing countries may grow only moderately in 1978.

Prospects for non-oil commodity prices are highly uncertain because relatively small changes in underlying supply or demand conditions have been increasingly amplified by speculative activity. Assuming that further supply difficulties are avoided and there is no speculative stock-piling, prices of commodities are likely to ease somewhat in 1978 compared with the average for 1977, reflecting the relatively limited buoyancy of forecast demand. At the same time, and given the same outlook for demand, export prices of manufactures (which now account for about 32 per cent or non-oil developing countries' exports) may increase by some 6 and 1/2 -7 per cent in 1978, i.e. about the forecast rate of domestic inflation in the OECD area. The result of these tentative forecasts is a rather small (5-10 per cent) increase in non-oil developing countries' export earnings in 1978.

On the financing side, much still depends on the attitude of private lenders. Euro-currency lending which, contrary to general expectation, rose markedly in 1976, fell back somewhat in 1977. The difficulties some countries have experienced in increasing this form of indebtedness, coupled with a reduced need by some large market borrowers and the beginnings of substantial service payments on past borrowings, may lead to a further decline in 1978, unless an overadjustment of imports (to improved current balance positions) occurs. Structural, or autonomous, financial flows are expected to increase moderately in both 1977 and 1978, with ODA and other official financing leading the way. The build-up of reserves continued during the first half of 1977 but at a decelerating rate. This element, and use of IMF credit, are particularly sensitive to import adjustment, including both food import requirements (depending largely on harvest performance) and changes in import

TABLE 9. FINANCING OF CURRENT BALANCE DEFICITS OF NON-OIL LDCs[a] 1973, 1976-1978

	$ billion			
	1973	1976	1977 forecast	1978 projection
Exports f.o.b.	80.3	133.3	159.0	*169.0*
Imports f.o.b.	96.3	172.9	199.0	*224.0*
Trade balance	-16.0	-39.6	-40.0	*-55.0*
Services + private transfers	+3.0	-4.5	-5.4	*-4.0*
Current balance deficit	-13.0	-44.0	-45.4	*-59.0*
	Financing items			
1. Official transfers	6.2	10.4	11.0	*11.6*
a) DAC	4.2	6.1	(6.8)	
b) Multilateral agencies	0.9	1.9	2.1	
c) OPEC	0.9	2.1	1.8	
d) Centrally-planned-economies	0.2	0.3	0.3	
2. Long-term official + private capital net	15.0	26.7	25.9	*27.9*
ODA (loans)	4.0	7.5	7.9	
a) DAC	2.2	2.7	3.0	
b) Multilateral agencies	0.8	1.7	2.0	
c) OPEC	0.3	2.4	2.2	
d) Centrally-planned-economies	0.7	0.7	0.7	
OOF (loans)	3.4	5.2	5.5	*5.6*
a) DAC	1.8	1.7	1.8	
b) Multilateral agencies	1.3	-2.1	2.3	
c) OPEC	0.2	1.2	1.2	
d) Centrally-planned-economies	0.1	0.1	0.2	
Private (DAC)	7.5	14.0	12.5	*14.0*
a) Direct investment	3.9	4.5	4.5	
b) Portfolio investment	3.1	5.6	4.5	
c) Export credits	0.6	3.8	3.5	
3. Other	6.3	21.6	13.5	*15.5*
a) IMF oil facility	0.1	0.6		
b) Use of other IMF credit	0.3	3.0	(4.5)	
c) Euro-currency borrowing, net	5.9	18.0	9.0	
4. Change in reserve position	+10.9	+12.0	+5.0	*-4.0*
5. Short-term capital + errors and omissions	-3.5	-2.7	—	—
6. Total (1 + 2 + 3)	27.5	58.7	50.4	*55.0*
7. Total (1 + 2 + 3 - 4)	16.6	46.7	45.4	*59.0*

a. Including Israel, Greece, Malta, Portugal, Spain, Turkey and Yugoslavia.

Source: OECD, DAC.

Note: These figures are recorded on a balance-of-payments reporting basis. "Transfers" and "long-term capital" exclude grants for military purposes, debt relief and reinvested earnings. The figures are therefore not directly comparable with resource flow figures elsewhere in the report.

policies.

So far as food imports are concerned, the situation is moderately encouraging, although harvest failures in some countries may still occur, requiring concerted international action. The non-oil developing countries' gross cereal imports, which had increased sharply and continuously since the beginning of the decade, declined in 1975 and 1976. World food security has improved through the build-up of cereal stocks, mostly in the major food-exporting countries, but also in developing countries such as India and the Philippines. World stocks reached a peak level of 162 million tons in 1976/77 (crop year), representing about 18 per cent of world food consumption, a level judged adequate for security. At the same time, cereal prices have tended to stabilize at levels lower than at the time of the oil crisis. The time would seem to be ripe for establishing an international world food security system. Prospects for 1977, without being as promising as 1976, are good (especially for coarse grains) except in regions such as North Africa and parts of the Near East. Following good harvests, the MSAs' cereal import requirements were expected to decline from 19 million tons in 1975/76 to 15 million tons in 1976/77.

Given these broad considerations, the way would seem to be open for some increase in import volume growth in 1977 and 1978, perhaps back to long-term trends (6-7 per cent) as an average for the two years. There will be significant differences in rates (and timing) between countries and regions depending on the precise evolution of (and expectations concerning) export earnings and external financing. A general slackening of import regimes, in response to improved external financial positions in 1976 and the first half of 1977, would be welcomed by OECD exporters but might lead to an overadjustment of imports, requiring use of reserves and/or greater resort to IMF credit (recently boosted by the $10 billion Witteveen facility). Clearly, policy with regard to imports should continue to err on the side of caution in most countries because, as noted earlier, the size of current account deficits has risen somewhat (in relation to GNP) and their cost has generally increased. Also, many countries are still some way from full adjustment to the oil price increases. Table 9 summarises the main developments in the aggregate current account deficit and its financing, and includes a forecast for 1977 and a tentative projection for 1978.

b) Medium-Term Prospects

Prospects in the medium-term are more difficult to judge in view of the greater range of possibilities for key variables such as the growth of output and world trade, flows of capital and relative prices. How one views the medium-term future depends largely on judgements about the relative importance of determining factors.

The recently-published OECD report "Towards Full Employment and Price Stability"[3]—the McCracken Report—chooses as its critical determining factor continued economic growth in the OECD area, with an expansion of demand somewhat greater than the growth of potential supply. More specifically, the report states that a period of sustained increases in real incomes and employment is a reasonable prospect, with growth rates for real GNP averaging around 5 and 1/2 per cent a year for the OECD area as a whole over the five years from 1975 to 1980 so long as the rate of inflation can be brought down to low levels. This recalls the output projection contained in the OECD "Growth Scenario to 1980"[4] Under this scenario, world trade would grow by some 8 to 8.5 per cent per annum. The authors of the McCracken Report also believe that the terms of trade are likely to shift in favour of countries—many developing, some developed—with large resources of certain raw materials and land.

If these conditions are satisfied and if, as the McCracken Report strongly urges, the international targets for official development assistance are achieved (along with larger non-concessional capital flows and measures to enhance the purchasing power of developing countries) the medium-term growth prospects of the non-oil developing countries would look rather good, despite the heavy costs of financing the recent large current account deficits and of adjusting to higher oil prices. In particular, the possible terms of trade improvement coupled with a shift in official development assistance towards low-income countries would do much to improve these countries' trade and growth prospects.

There is however, the possibility that one or more of these conditions will not be met. This was explicitly recognised in the OECD growth scenario preamble (July 1976) which stated that the projections "should in no way be interpreted as representing either national or OECD Secretariat estimates of most likely developments over the coming four years". Since the publication of this scenario, OECD output has grown more slowly than the 5 and 1/2 per cent average. Indeed for the 5 and 1/2 per cent average to be achieved, OECD output would have to grow by just over 6 per cent on average in the years 1978-1980 in order to make up lost ground and this may be too fast a rate for reasonable price stability. As the McCracken report points out, "a major question (is) whether sufficient productive investment will be forthcoming to provide the additional capacity and jobs needed to support the return to full employment.

The possibility of not achieving 5 and 1/2 per cent growth cannot be discounted. Quite apart from the direct effect which lower growth rates would have on non-oil developing countries' exports (and possibly terms of trade), slower growth would also delay achievement of full employment in the OECD area. If the hoped-for decline in OECD unemployment were to be delayed by this in the coming years, the pressure to strengthen protection, already noted in the IMF's 28th Annual Report on Exchange Restrictions and in the 1977 GATT Annual Report, might not abate. This might in turn further damage the non-oil developing countries' export prospects, in particular those of the more dynamic middle-income countries.

These considerations underline the increased degree of economic/financial interdependence between industrial and developing countries. Future prospects of developing countries will depend heavily on the ability of industrial countries to resume economic growth in conditions of stability and to cope with the difficult structural problems they are facing, including the problem of absorbing rapidly rising imports from developing countries. Developing countries have, in recent years, shown considerable economic resilience and impressive skills in maintaining growth momentum in the face of difficult external conditions. Overall propsects for further economic advance remain, on balance, good. But the real challenge is to enable the poorer countries, and the poor majority more generally, to participate more equitably in the overall advance. This will require adjustments both in international economic co-operation and in national policies—a recurrent theme in Chapters I and V of this report.

NOTES

[1] Performance Compendium—Consolidated Results of Analytical Work on Economic and Social Performance of Developing Countries, OECD, 1973. This report noted that economic progress was difficult to define and even more difficult to measure because of the lack of suitable indicators. It also suggested that a distinction be drawn between efforts due to endogenous factors and policies, and achievements, which may also be due to exogenous factors and policies.

[2] Unless otherwise stated, the data in this section are drawn from World Bank publications. See in particular, the World Tables (1976).

[3] OECD, June 1977.

[4] OECD Economic Outlook, July 1976.

Economic Growth and Major Streams of Production: Some Basic Problems in Hard-core Developing Countries

CENTRE FOR DEVELOPMENT PLANNING, PROJECTIONS AND POLICIES OF THE DEPARTMENT OF ECONOMIC AND SOCIAL AFFAIRS OF THE UNITED NATIONS SECRETARIAT

For over a quarter of a century now, the question of an assault on underdevelopment has loomed large in policy discussions held at a wide variety of public forums. As country after country, first in Asia and then in Africa and the Caribbean, gained independence from colonial rule after the end of the Second World War, their Governments sought and have continued to spearhead national economic and social progress through assertive intervention in development matters. Deliberations in world forums, too, have accorded a great deal of attention to forging measures that could help to speed up the progress of developing countries. Undoubtedly, as a result, much success has been achieved, and several developing countries are now well on the road to self-sustained progress.

It is also true, however, that many developing countries have been left far behind on the road to progress. Despite all the efforts made at the national and international levels, extreme poverty, widespread unemployment and underemployment, and undiversified economic structures remain their distinguishing features. These problems of underdevelopment are found in their most stubborn and pronounced form in South Asia and in several African countries, most among the latter being characterized in the United Nations as the least developed among the developing countries.

The present paper focuses attention on some of the major problems faced by such hard-core developing countries and the policy issues posed by those problems. While the experience of a number of African and Asian countries has been drawn upon in this connexion, the paper does not purport to be a systematic empirical inquiry. Rather, its aim is to highlight some generalizations that serve as pointers to needed policies. The limited extent to which

From **JOURNAL OF DEVELOPMENT PLANNING**, No. 10, 1976, (131-165), reprinted by permission of the publisher.

statistical information is cited in the text is solely for illustrative purposes.[1]

I. MAIN CONTOURS OF DEVELOPMENT

Poverty and Sluggish Change

Hard-core developing countries, as just noted, are characterized by extreme poverty and pervasive symptoms of marked underdevelopment. Their per capita annual income is very low, commonly around $100. Some of these countries do have a per capita annual income $40 or $50 above $100, while some others have an income substantially smaller than $100 (see table 1). Such differences, however, are more apparent than real. The underlying coverage of the available estimates of gross domestic product or national income varies a great deal among countries. The components of gross domestic product relating to the subsistence sector of the economy--farms and hamlets whose produce hardly enters the market stream--and to handicraft industries, which are often not integrated into the market sector, are usually underestimated. The degree of underestimation, moreover, varies from country to country. Intercountry comparisons, since they must be made in a common unit of account, are also affected to a varying degree by the distortions introduced by the failure of the rate of exchange to reflect with adequate accuracy the relative purchasing power over domestic goods and services between countries. Such considerations provide a reminder that the economic distance between, say, a country with a per capita income of $50 and another with a per capita income of $150 is not as great as might appear from an uncritical use of nominal estimates.[2] There is no doubt, however, that such countries do have a common denominator, namely, extreme poverty and its attendant ills of malnutrition, disease, illiteracy and slum dwelling.

Adding to the gravity of the problems faced by hard-core developing countries is the high rate of population expansion. Typically, their population has been increasing at the annual rate of 2.5 per cent. In some of them, in fact, the annual increase of population amounts to 3 per cent or more. In such a situation, unless the total gross domestic product in constant prices expands at a substantially higher rate--say, at the annual rate of 5.5 or 6 per cent--which makes it possible to raise per capita income annually by around 3 per cent, a significant impact on extreme poverty can hardly be expected. An improvement of this magnitude has generally been conspicuous by its absence in hard-core developing countries during the past decade or so. Since the early 1960s, their total gross domestic product has in general increased at a very modest pace, with adverse consequences for per capita income. Several hard-core developing countries have, in fact,

TABLE 1. LEVEL AND GROWTH OF GROSS DOMESTIC PRODUCT AND POPULATION

Country[a]	Annual average, 1970-1972[b]					Percentage annual rate of increase, 1960-1962 to 1970-1972[b]		
	Gross domestic product at current market prices		Population			Gross domestic product at constant prices		Population
	Per capita (dollars)	Total (millions of dollars)	Total (millions)	Density (number per square kilometre)		Per capita	Total	
Mali	53	273	5.2	4		−1.7	0.4	2.2
Afghanistan	57	983	17.4	27		0.1	2.3	2.2
Upper Volta	67	368	5.5	20		0.7	2.9	2.1
Ethiopia	74	1,904	25.5	21		2.0	4.5	2.4
Chad	75	281	3.7	3		−2.4	−0.3	2.1
Bangladesh	90	6,292	70.2	489		−0.9	2.0	2.9
Somalia	92	264	2.9	4		−0.3	2.0	2.3
Niger	94	387	4.1	3		0.8	4.0	3.2
India	99	55,826	562.3	168		1.0	3.5	2.3
Benin	101	279	2.8	25		0.5	3.1	2.5
United Republic of Tanzania	102	1,395	13.6	14		2.5	5.1	2.6
Sudan	124	2,005	16.2	6		−1.2	1.7	2.9
Central African Republic[c]	138	227	1.6	3		0.3	2.3	2.0
Uganda	140	1,415	10.1	43		2.5	5.2	2.7
Pakistan	150	9,599	64.0	77		3.1	6.3	3.1
Sri Lanka	171	2,186	12.8	195		2.9	5.4	2.4

SOURCE: Centre for Development Planning, Projections and Policies of the Department of Economic and Social Affairs of the United Nations Secretariat, based on data from Statistical Office of the Department, *Yearbook of National Accounts Statistics* (various issues); from the Population Division of the Department; and from other national and international sources.

[a] Countries are listed in ascending order of their *per capita* annual gross domestic product at market prices in 1970-1972.

[b] Gross domestic product data for Bangladesh, Benin, India, Pakistan and the Sudan refer, as relevant, to financial years 1960/61-1962/63 and 1970/71-1972/73.

[c] Pending a new population census, data on population and consequently the subsistence component of gross domestic product are subject to a wide margin of error. The actual *per capita* gross domestic product may be lower, while the total gross domestic product may be somewhat higher than shown here.

suffered a decline in their per capita income. Several others have recorded only a meagre annual increase in their per capita income--1 per cent or less. Some examples of a significant annual increase in per capita income, such as Pakistan (3 per cent) and the United Republic of Tanzania (2.5 per cent), can be cited, but they are few and far between.

While extreme poverty is a common denominator of hard-core developing countries, they also display a number of strikingly different traits. For example, some of these countries have large economies, whether judged in terms of their population or the total volume of their annual output of goods and services. In this respect, India stands out as a country whose population is almost equal to the combined population of all other countries with a per capita annual income of less than $200. Inevitably, therefore, it is in India that the largest concentration of poor people is to be found. Though numerically much smaller than in India, the second largest concentration of the poor dwells in Bangladesh. The problems of poverty in Bangladesh are compounded by the high density of its population: there are more than two and a half times as many people per square kilometre in Bangladesh than in India, and this differential is widening because of the higher rate of population increase in Bangladesh. By contrast, most of the African countries with markedly underdeveloped economies are sparsely populated. On the other hand, the very small size of their economies is often a serious impediment to rapid economic growth and diversification. There are also wide differences among hard-core developing countries with respect to the availability of national resources, the typology of terrain and the vulnerability of their economies to external economic forces.

The generally modest pace of increase in total gross domestic product in hard-core developing countries has been shaped to a large extent by the performance of agriculture, which bulks large in the economy of virtually all of them. Agriculture commonly contributes two fifths to one half of total gross domestic product in these countries (see table 2). Thus, unless agricultural production expands at a vigorous pace, the over-all expansion of the economy is prone to be retarded. Such countries as Pakistan and the United Republic of Tanzania whose economies grew since the early or the middle 1960s at an annual rate of 5 per cent or more are the ones whose agricultural and related activities (value added in agriculture, hunting, forestry and fishing) increased annually by more than 3 per cent.

During the same period, manufacturing activity did generally expand faster than agricultural and related activities in hard-core developing countries, though scarcely at a spectacular rate. The United Republic of Tanzania is probably the only such country that achieved an annual increase of about 10 per cent in value added in manufacturing. It also needs to be remembered that manufacturing activity accounts for no more than one tenth of gross domestic product in most hard-core developing countries. Therefore, even where the industrial thrust did inject some dynamism, as in the United Republic of Tanzania, its contribution to lifting the over-all pace of economic expansion, though very significant, was relatively small.

TABLE 2. EXPANSION OF GROSS DOMESTIC PRODUCT AND ITS PRINCIPAL COMPONENTS AT CONSTANT FACTOR COST[a]

Country[b]	Percentage annual rate of increase, early 1960s to early 1970s			Principal components as percentage share of gross domestic product in early 1970s [c]	
	Gross domestic product	Agriculture	Manufacturing	Agriculture	Manufacturing
Mali	...	...	...	d	9
Afghanistan	...	...	...	d	e
Upper Volta	...	...	...	d	9
Ethiopia	4.0	2.1	8.0	52	9
Chad	...	...	...	d	e
Bangladesh	...	...	...	52	9
Somalia	...	...	...	d	e
Niger	...	...	...	d	e
India	3.4	1.6	4.8	40	17
Benin	...	...	...	39	9
United Republic of Tanzania	5.5	3.3	9.8	39	10
Sudan	...	...	...	35	10
Central African Republic	...	...	...	d	11[f]
Uganda	4.1	3.3	5.9	50	8
Pakistan	5.0	3.1	6.6	33	14
Sri Lanka	4.2	2.3	7.1	36	10

SOURCE: See table 1.

[a] The time period is as follows: Sri Lanka, 1960-1961 to 1970-1971; Uganda, 1963-1964 to 1971-1972; United Republic of Tanzania, 1964-1965 to 1971-1972; Ethiopia, 1959/60-1960/61 to 1970/71-1971/72; India and Pakistan, 1960/61-1961/62 to 1971/72-1972/73; Afghanistan, Central African Republic, Chad, Mali and Upper Volta, 1970-1971; Bangladesh, 1969/70 and 1972/73; Benin 1971/72; Sudan, 1969/70-1970/71; Somalia, 1970; Niger 1969.

[b] Countries are listed in ascending order of their *per capita* annual gross domestic product in 1970-1972.

[c] Data are at current market prices for Bangladesh, Benin, the Central African Republic, Chad, Mali, the Sudan and the Upper Volta.

[d] Close to 50 per cent.

[e] Less than 10 per cent.

[f] Includes some activities other than manufacturing; the share of manufacturing alone may therefore be below 10 per cent.

Comparing the early 1970s with the early 1960s, there does appear to have been some structural transformation in the economies of hard-core developing countries. The share of manufacturing activity in total gross domestic product has increased somewhat, and correspondingly the share of agricultural and related activities has decreased somewhat. But the rate of structural transformation has been slow. In India and to a smaller extent in Pakistan, the size of the industrial base is now significant. By and large, however, the force of the characteristics noted in the preceding paragraph remains undiminished in hard-core developing countries.

Allocation of Resources for Development

To bring about a sustained expansion or diversification of the economy, developing countries need to raise their levels of capital formation or investment. If there is underutilized productive capacity in an economy, output can be expanded without adding to the stock of existing capital. Indeed, examples of underutilized capacity, are readily available in the historical record of developing countries and there can be no dispute that prompt steps should be taken to rectify such a situation wherever it prevails. Underutilization of capacity, however, is a problem relevant in the context of discussions pertaining to a comparatively short span of time--for example, a year or two. Over a longer time span, such as a decade, it is the increase in the productive capacity itself that is the most relevant element for economic expansion.

Thus, a major clue to the rather sluggish pace of economic expansion in hard-core developing countries since the early 1960s is provided by their investment record of their endeavour to expand productive capacity. Hard-core developing countries have sought to raise the ratio of their gross investment to gross domestic product, but the success has been limited (see table 3). The United Republic of Tanzania once again serves as a rare example of a hard-core developing country which has managed to raise its investment ratio annually by more than 1 percentage point in recent years, from 12 per cent in the early 1960s to 23 per cent in the early 1970s. Mali and the Upper Volta managed to raise their investment ratio at a more moderate pace--by about half a percentage point per annum. But generally in hard-core developing countries the investment ratio rose rather slowly or not at all. In a number of countries, in fact, the investment ratio in the early 1970s was smaller than that in the early 1960s, though in some cases--notably Bangladesh and Pakistan--this feature is explained, in large part if not wholly, by the extraordinary turn of political events. The available information does suggest, therefore, that a major factor responsible for the slow economic growth of hard-core developing countries has been the inadequate expansion of investment for enlarging productive capacity.

In turn, the ability to expand investment has hinged on the

TABLE 3. INCREASES IN LEVELS OF GROSS INVESTMENT, GROSS NATIONAL SAVING AND EXTERNAL RESOURCES[a]
(*Percentage of gross domestic product*)

Country [b]	Average annual increase in level, 1960-1962 to 1970-1972			Level, 1970-1972		
	Gross investment	Gross national saving	External resources	Gross investment	Gross national saving	External resources
Mali	0.5	(0.9)	(−0.4)	16.6	(12.1)	(4.5)
Afghanistan	−0.2	(−0.1)	(−0.1)	5.6	(4.2)	(1.4)
Upper Volta	0.6	0.1	0.5	15.7	4.3	11.3
Ethiopia	−0.1	−0.1	—	12.1	10.0	2.2
Chad	0.2	(0.2)	—	13.3	(4.5)	(8.8)
Bangladesh[c]	−0.2	−0.4	0.2	8.0	5.3	2.8
Somalia	0.4	0.5	−0.1	15.3	7.0	8.3
Niger	−0.2	−1.1	0.9	9.0	6.9	2.1
India	—	0.2	−0.2	16.6	15.3	1.3
Benin	0.1	0.2	−0.1	18.2	11.0	7.2
United Republic of Tanzania	1.1	0.4	0.7	23.3	17.5	5.9
Sudan	−0.2	(−0.1)	(−0.1)	13.1	(11.5)	(1.6)
Central African Republic	0.1	(0.4)	(−0.3)	18.4	(13.6)	(4.7)
Uganda	0.3	—	0.3	13.7	12.9	0.8
Pakistan	−0.4	0.2	−0.6	14.8	13.7	1.1
Sri Lanka	0.3	0.3	—	18.4	15.8	2.6

SOURCE: See table 1.

[a] Gross national saving is defined as gross domestic product minus net factor income payments minus consumption. Because of lack of data on factor income payments, the ratios shown for some countries refer to gross domestic saving, defined as gross domestic product minus consumption; such ratios are shown in parentheses ( ) and may overstate the extent of internal savings. It should be noted also that country practices differ in respect of factor income, which further affects the intercountry comparability of the figures shown.

External resources are defined as gross investment minus gross national saving. Estimates have been derived from data in current prices.

[b] Countries are listed in ascending order of their *per capita* annual gross domestic product in 1970-1972.

[c] Data are distorted because of the serious economic dislocations affecting especially 1970 and 1971. The extent of the dislocations may be gauged from data for 1967-1969, which show average shares of gross investment, gross national saving and external resources in gross domestic product of, respectively, 12.6 per cent, 9.6 per cent and 3.0 per cent. Thus, whereas investment and national saving fell as a share of gross domestic product between 1960-1962 and 1970-1972, they had shown an upward trend up to the end of the 1960s.

TABLE 4. INCREASE IN LEVEL OF CONSUMPTION[a]
(Percentage of gross domestic product)

Country[b]	Average annual increase in level, 1960-1962 to 1970-1972			Level, 1970-1972		
	Total	Private	Public	Total	Private	Public
Mali	−0.9	−1.1	0.2	87.9	70.6	17.3
Afghanistan	0.1	−0.3	0.5	95.8	89.0	6.8
Upper Volta	−0.3	−0.3	—	96.0	79.6	16.4
Ethiopia	—	−0.2	0.2	89.3	79.4	9.9
Chad	−0.2	−0.8	0.6	95.5	75.6	19.9
Bangladesh	0.4	−0.4	0.8	95.3	80.7	14.6
Somalia	−0.5	−0.9	0.4	93.0	74.0	19.0
Niger	0.8	1.0	−0.2	98.0	84.9	13.1
India	−0.2	−0.5	0.3	85.9	73.1	10.8
Benin	−0.2	0.1	−0.3	88.2	71.9	16.3
United Republic of Tanzania	−0.4	−0.7	0.3	82.1	69.5	12.6
Sudan	0.1	−1.1	1.2	87.5	62.4	25.1
Central African Republic	−0.4	−0.3	−0.1	86.4	68.5	17.9
Uganda	—	−0.4	0.4	85.7	72.6	13.1
Pakistan	−0.2	−0.1	−0.1	86.6	75.2	11.4
Sri Lanka	−0.4	−0.3	−0.1	83.2	69.6	13.6

SOURCE: See table 1.

[a] Estimates have been derived from data in current prices.
[b] Countries are listed in ascending order of their *per capita* annual gross domestic product in 1970-1972.

availability of requisite flows of national and international financial resources. In the International Development Strategy for the Second United Nations Development Decade, the General Assembly of the United Nations has urged developing countries to raise the ratio of their national saving to gross product annually by half a percentage point.[3] In general, hard-core developing countries do not seem to have achieved an increase of this magnitude since the early 1960s. In a majority of countries, the saving ratio has increased but at a sluggish pace. In some countries, the saving ratio has actually declined in recent years.

An adequate increase in the saving ratio is undoubtedly one of the hardest tasks to accomplish in countries where the average income and the average standard of living are very low. The withholding of a part of production from immediate consumption for the purpose of enlarging benefits in the future is difficult but essential. Only by means of adequate self-discipline in this regard can an economy surge forward from stagnation to expansion. This does not, of course, imply a decrease in the absolute level of consumption. What it means is that consumption should rise but at a rate sufficiently slower than gross domestic product so that the consequently declining ratio of consumption to gross product makes it possible to achieve the required increase in the saving ratio--for example, as suggested in the International Development Strategy, by half a percentage point per annum. The available evidence indicates that the ratio of private consumption to gross product has declined significantly in developing countries but the ratio of public consumption to gross product has, more often than not, been on the increase. Thus, generally, the ratio of total consumption to gross product either has been declining rather slowly or has, in fact, risen (see table 4).

A part of what is conventionally called public consumption is really not consumption in the normal sense of the term. Current expenditures of Governments on educational and health services are intrinsically nearer to capital expenditures than are the more general categories of their current expenditures. A society trying to break the shackles of poverty may often have little choice in this regard. On the other hand, there is a great deal of scope for economizing by restraints on a wide variety of current expenditures of Governments, such as those incurred on armed forces and general administration. Through such restraint and through mobilization of additional revenue, Governments of hard-core developing countries need to expand public saving and thereby make a contribution to the raising of the ratio of gross national saving to gross product. The fiscal policies of Governments also need to be so designed as to evoke an adequate expansion of private saving.

Broadly speaking, the attainment of a ratio of gross national saving to gross product of about 15 per cent represents a critical test of a company's ability to be within sight of self-sustained economic and social progress. A few low-income countries--notably India, Sri Lanka and the United Republic of Tanzania--appear to have crossed this threshold. Indeed, if a systematic effort is made, these countries have a much longer road to traverse in this respect. But however formidable, the task has to be fulfilled.

For the financing of capital formation in hard-core developing

TABLE 5. NET INTERNATIONAL FLOW OF OFFICIAL DONATIONS AND LONG-TERM OFFICIAL AND PRIVATE CAPITAL, 1971-1973, ANNUAL AVERAGES[a]

Country[b]	Net flow (millions of SDR)				Total net flow per head of population (SDR)
	Total	Official donations	Long-term official capital	Long-term private capital	
Mali	33.2	25.5	6.6	1.2	6.3
Upper Volta	32.0	32.1	−1.8	1.7	5.7
Ethiopia	55.9	12.2	24.6	19.1	2.2
Chad	25.5	25.5	−0.4	0.4	6.7
Bangladesh	308.3	211.2	97.1	—	4.2
Somalia	26.7	11.2	13.4	2.1	9.1
Niger	34.2	27.4	6.0	0.8	8.3
India	581.5	72.0	521.5	−12.0	1.0
Benin	28.8	19.5	6.0	3.3	10.0
United Republic of Tanzania	130.3	4.0	114.3	12.0	9.3
Sudan	12.6	2.0	11.7	−1.1	0.8
Central African Republic	19.1	17.7	−1.5	2.9	11.4
Uganda	10.6	1.4	33.3	−24.1	1.0
Pakistan	237.0	38.5	166.0	32.5	3.5
Sri Lanka	60.2	14.5	45.4	0.3	4.6

SOURCE: Centre for Development Planning, Projections and Policies of the Department of Economic and Social Affairs of the United Nations Secretariat, based on financial data from International Monetary Fund, *Balance of Payments Yearbook* (Washington, D.C.), vol. 26, and on gross product and population data from national and international sources.

[a] Data refer to 1971 for the Niger; to 1971-1972 for Benin, India, Uganda and the Upper Volta; to 1972-1973 for Pakistan; and to 1973 for Bangladesh.
No sign indicates net inflow; minus sign indicates net outflow.

[b] Countries are listed in ascending order of their *per capita* annual gross domestic product in 1970-1972.

countries, a role of critical importance has been played by the flow of resources from abroad. This is especially true of countries in Africa, as is attested by the fact that the external resource received by a number of them in the early 1970s (for example, Benin, Chad, Somalia, the United Republic of Tanzania and the Upper Volta) amounted to as much as 6-11 per cent of their gross domestic product. In some of these countries (Chad, Somalia and the Upper Volta), by far the larger part of capital formation was financed by external resources than by national saving. The external resources received by the United Republic of Tanzania since the early 1960s have reflected a markedly upward trend and have served as a major force responsible for the strikingly large increase achieved by that country in the level of capital formation in recent years. At the other end are such countries as India, the Sudan and Uganda, where external resources have played a rather small role in the financing of capital formation: in the early 1970s, the external resources received by these countries amounted to only about 1 per cent of their gross domestic product. As per head of population, in the early 1970s, the net annual flow of official donations and long-term official and private capital received from abroad by India, the Sudan and Uganda amounted to just about the equivalent of one special drawing right (SDR) of the International Monetary Fund (or a little more than one United States dollar); whereas in Benin, Chad, Somalia, the United Republic of Tanzania and the Upper Volta, the net annual flow was in the range of SDR 6-SDR 10 (see table 5).

These examples indicate that there has been a wide divergence in the relative magnitudes of external resources received by various hard-core developing countries. It is also known, as is shown in two companion papers,[4] that the low-income developing countries in general--a group that would include all hard-core developing countries and some others--received, in relation to their population, a far smaller amount of external finance than did the higher-income and the middle-income developing countries. If a meaningful attack is to be made on extreme poverty and pronounced underdevelopment through concerted national and international measures, the world community will need to direct a rapidly growing proportion of concessional economic assistance to low-income developing countries, and within this group to countries which constitute the hard core of underdevelopment.

The resources mustered by hard-core developing countries need to be devoted to enlarging the productive capacity of the economy in a harmonious way so as to ensure that the streams of goods and services produced are in consonance with the national development objectives. Particularly important are the tasks relating to the expansion and diversification of the two principal sectors of production, agriculture and industry, the former because it constitutes the mainstay of the economy in hard-core developing countries and the latter because it serves as the engine of modernization. It is, then, to aspects of agricultural and industrial progress that the next two sections of the present paper are devoted.

TABLE 6. PERCENTAGE ANNUAL RATE OF INCREASE IN TOTAL AGRICULTURAL PRODUCTION, 1961-1965 TO 1971-1973 [a]

Country [b]	All agriculture		Food	
	FAO estimate	USDA estimate	FAO estimate	USDA estimate
Mali	−0.6	−0.5	−0.9	−1.9
Afghanistan	2.0	...	1.9	...
Upper Volta	1.0	−1.4	0.6	−1.9
Ethiopia	2.6	1.9	2.5	1.9
Chad	−2.1	...	−2.5	...
Bangladesh	1.0	1.1	1.3	1.2
Somalia	2.1	...	2.1	...
Niger	−1.4	−2.3	−1.4	−2.5
India	2.2	2.5	2.2	2.5
Benin	2.8	1.5	2.0	1.4
United Republic of Tanzania	2.9	2.1	3.3	2.4
Sudan	5.0	3.1	5.0	3.6
Central African Republic	1.7	...	1.5	...
Uganda	2.3	2.0	2.4	1.7
Pakistan	4.7	5.3	4.4	5.2
Sri Lanka	1.7	2.1	1.7	2.5

SOURCE: Centre for Development Planning, Projections and Policies of the Department of Economic and Social Affairs of the United Nations Secretariat, based on data from Food and Agriculture Organization of the United Nations, *Production Yearbook, 1973* (Rome, 1974), vol. 27, and United States of America, Department of State, Agency for International Development, *A.I.D. Economic Data Book* (Washington, D.C.), April 1975 for South Asia and June 1975 for Africa.

[a] Data refer to estimates of gross value of output published by the Food and Agriculture Organization of the United Nations (FAO) and the United States Department of Agriculture (USDA).

[b] Countries are listed in ascending order of their *per capita* annual gross domestic product in 1970-1972.

II. AGRICULTURAL EXPANSION

As noted in the preceding section, agriculture (including not only farming but also the related activities of hunting, fishing and forestry) generally contributes two fifths to one half of the total output of goods and services in hard-core developing countries. Some two thirds to four fifths of the population in most of these countries derives its livelihood from agriculture. This pivotal sector provides both the crucial food-stuffs for the work force engaged in the other sectors of the economy and the raw materials that keep the wheels of industry moving. Agriculture typically also makes a large contribution to the exports of hard-core developing countries and thereby to their capacity to import machinery and other essential goods from abroad. Clearly, therefore, hard-core developing countries cannot spring forward and maintain the momentum towards economic and social progress if their agriculture fails to show sufficient dynamism.

Trends in Production

It is indeed the lagging output of agriculture that explains in large part the slow economic and social progress of hard-core developing countries. Countries in the Sahel zone of Africa, where a severe drought resulted in a sharp downturn in agricultural output during the early 1970s, have been the worst affected in this respect. The record since the early 1960s shows that the gross value of agricultural output in such countries as India and Uganda has been increasing but at a rather modest annual rate of 2-2.5 per cent. Pakistan and the Sudan serve as the two examples among the hard-core developing countries about which it can be said with some confidence that agricultural production has been expanding at a significantly high annual rate: at about 5 per cent in Pakistan and probably at a somewhat smaller rate in the Sudan. What is true for agricultural output as a whole is also generally valid for food production (see table 6).[5]

In several hard-core developing countries, although agricultural output or food production has been increasing, the increase has proved to be too small even to be able to keep pace with the growth of population. Given the fact that the output contracted sharply in the Sahel countries, the available evidence leaves little doubt that agricultural output on a __per capita__ basis has suffered serious setbacks (see table 7). The widespread decline in __per capita__ production of agriculture, and more so of food, is a particularly disturbing feature of the contemporary world economic scene. It has made the lives of millions of people agonizingly grave. Programmes of economic expansion and social improvement in hard-core developing countries will have little meaning without a reversal in this trend. And the reversal of the

TABLE 7.   PERCENTAGE ANNUAL RATE OF INCREASE IN *per capita* AGRICULTURAL PRODUCTION, 1961-1965 TO 1971-1973 [a]

| | All agriculture | | Food | |
Country [b]	FAO estimate	USDA estimate	FAO estimate	USDA estimate
Mali	−2.7	−2.8	−3.2	−4.0
Afghanistan	−0.4	...	−0.5	...
Upper Volta	−1.1	−3.4	−1.4	−3.9
Ethiopia	0.5	−0.3	0.4	−0.3
Chad	−4.4	...	−4.7	...
Bangladesh	−2.3	−1.5	−2.2	−1.3
Somalia	−0.1	...	−0.1	...
Niger	−4.2	−5.0	−4.2	−5.2
India	—	0.3	—	0.3
Benin	0.2	−1.0	−0.5	−1.0
United Republic of Tanzania	0.3	−0.4	0.7	−0.2
Sudan	1.9	0.2	1.9	—
Central African Republic	−0.5	...	−0.7	...
Uganda	−0.4	−0.5	−0.2	−0.9
Pakistan	1.6	2.3	1.4	2.2
Sri Lanka	−0.8	—	−0.8	0.3

SOURCE AND FOOT-NOTES: See table 6.

TABLE 8.   PERCENTAGE ANNUAL RATE OF INCREASE IN AREA HARVESTED AND YIELD PER UNIT OF AREA HARVESTED, 1961-1965 TO 1971-1973

| | Cereals | | Cotton | |
Country [a]	Area harvested	Yield	Area harvested	Yield
Mali	0.8	−2.4	7.3	3.8
Afghanistan	−0.1	1.4	−6.8	7.7
Upper Volta	−0.3	−0.9	8.6	12.5
Ethiopia	1.1	1.0	13.3	7.8
Chad	−3.1	−4.7	−0.5	1.5
Bangladesh	0.8	−0.1	−3.7	−2.5
Somalia	0.5	0.8	−14.1	17.8
Niger	−0.4	−1.0	6.4	0.5
India	0.6	2.1	−0.5	2.3
Benin	−2.2	0.7	7.3	22.0
United Republic of Tanzania	3.0	1.0	2.4	1.3
Sudan	4.4	−1.1	1.4	3.3
Central African Republic	0.9	2.7	0.5	5.7
Uganda	1.8	1.8	3.1	−0.6
Pakistan	1.3	4.2	3.3	3.4
Sri Lanka	2.5	1.1	14.2	2.6

SOURCE: Centre for Development Planning, Projections and Policies of the Department of Economic and Social Affairs of the United Nations Secretariat, based on Food and Agriculture Organization of the United Nations, *Production Yearbook* (Rome), various issues.

[a] Countries are listed in ascending order of their *per capita* annual gross domestic product in 1970-1972.

trend calls for a serious and sustained effort to invigorate and modernize the agricultural sector.

Sometimes a charge has been made that the disquieting performance of agriculture has resulted from the relative neglect of this critical sector on the part of Governments. It has been said in this context that Governments of developing countries have a propensity to favour industry to the detriment of agriculture. Data on the distribution of investment among different sectors of the economy in hard-core developing countries are deficient, but such information as is available does not bear out this charge. The investment targets specified in national development plans and the data on actual outlays, wherever available, indicate that agriculture (including irrigation) has commonly accounted for one quarter to one third of total investment in hard-core developing countries. Such an allocation is by no means small. Often, in fact, a larger proportion of total investment has been allocated to agriculture than to manufacturing activity. Within the component of public investment--generally a rising component of total investment in hard-core developing countries--the share of agriculture has usually been large. This is because irrigation and certain other crucial agricultural services can be rendered only by public authorities. It is not the relative allocation of total investment to agriculture but rather the over-all shortage of resources for investment that appears to have been a major impediment to agricultural progress. Since the early 1960s, as mentioned earlier, the level of investment has risen quite slowly in most hard-core developing countries.

It is true that poor weather contributed a great deal to the dismal performance of agriculture in many developing countries during the early 1970s. There are, however, also a number of other factors of a longer-term nature that have exerted a strong influence, and some comments on these are pertinent.

Some Farming Problems

Hard-core developing countries have sought to bring additional area under cultivation as a means of increasing agricultural production, but the results have varied a great deal. The Sudan is a particularly notable example of a country where the area under cultivation of cereals has increased annually by 4.4 per cent since the early 1960s. In the United Republic of Tanzania and Sri Lanka, the comparable increase amounted to 3 per cent and 2.5 per cent, respectively. A modest increase, in the range of 1-2 per cent, was also recorded in Ethiopia, Pakistan and Uganda. But in a majority of hard-core developing countries, either the increase was small or there was even a decline (see table 8). In some countries, the increase in area under cultivation appears to have been at the expense of other crops. For example, in Bangladesh, India and Somalia, the increase in the acreage devoted to cereal production was accompanied by a decline in the area under cultivation of cotton; in India, there was also a decline in the acreage devoted to jute cultivation.

These countries where there appears to have been a shift from fibre cultivation to cereal production, however, represent a minority. Most hard-core developing countries have sought to enlarge the acreage devoted to commercial crops, especially cotton. Indeed, since the early 1960s, the annual rate of increase in the area under cotton cultivation has been striking in a number of such countries: 14 per cent in Sri Lanka, 13 per cent in Ethiopia, 6-9 per cent in Benin, Mali, the Niger and the Upper Volta and 3 per cent in Pakistan and Uganda.

Given the urgent need to expand agricultural production, it is logical that the potential for bringing additional land under cultivation should be fully tapped. In densely populated developing countries, however, the scope for enlarging land under cultivation is severely limited. Even in many of the sparsely populated countries with pronounced problems of underdevelopment, the scope is not as large as it may seem at first sight. By means of desert, rocky terrain and the intrinsic quality of soil, nature itself has put a constraint on the availability of arable land in many cases. Further, the land that can be brought under cultivation often requires a great deal of preparation and capital investment before it can be sown. In all such cases, the availability of resources and competing objectives pose a problem. While every possible effort has to be made to extend cultivation, it also has to be remembered that much more needs to be done to enhance the efficiency of land already under cultivation.

Unfortunately, average yield of cereals per unit of tilled land has increased but little in most hard-core developing countries. Since the early 1960s, cereal yield has increased annually by 4.2 per cent in Pakistan, 2.7 per cent in the Central African Republic and 2.1 per cent in India. But these are the only examples of a sizable or moderate increase in average yield that can be cited from the recent experience of hard-core developing countries. In many hard-core developing countries, cereal yield has recorded minimal increases, or has even fallen. The increases in cereal production that these countries did register came mainly or exclusively from extension of land under cultivation. In contrast, average yield of cotton has increased at a substantial rate in a number of countries--for example, in Benin, Somalia and the Upper Volta.

The past trend of inadequate increase in the average yield of cereals accompanied by a small increase in land under cereal cultivation cannot continue into the future without serious consequences for competing crops and uses. It is important that impediments to increases in average yields of all major crops be addressed with urgency. A sustained increase in agricultural yields can be achieved only through the application of a range of complementary inputs. Particularly important among the inputs are irrigation and better water management, fertilizer, improved seeds, pesticides and improved storage.

The lack of adequate water supply and control is the single biggest obstacle to the raising of agricultural yields. Irrigation is a necessity not merely in the "green revolution" technology

TABLE 9. LAND USE AND IRRIGATION

Country [a]	Land use		Irrigation	
	Year	Arable land (thousand hectares)	Year	Area (thousand hectares)
Mali	1970	11,600	1971	66
Afghanistan	1968	7,844	1968	813
Upper Volta	1970	5,315	1970	0.4
Ethiopia	1970	13,250	1961	...
Chad	1972	7,000		...
Bangladesh	1968	9,069	1969	1,058
Somalia	1960	957	1970	162
Niger	1972	15,000	1972	5
India	1971	161,340	1971	31,290
Benin	1963	1,546		...
United Republic of Tanzania	1970	15,192	1968	40 [b]
Sudan	1968	7,100	1967	711
Central African Republic	1968	5,840		...
Uganda	1967	3,772	1967	4
Pakistan	1969	19,235	1971	12,974
Sri Lanka	1971	895	1970	465 [c]

SOURCE: Food and Agriculture Organization of the United Nations, *Production Yearbook, 1973* (Rome), vol. 27.

[a] Countries are listed in ascending order of their *per capita* annual gross domestic product in 1970-1972.

[b] Tanganyika only.

[c] Irrigated rice only.

based on high-yielding seeds, which require a controlled and adequate water supply. With traditional seeds and farming practices, too, water control is needed to reduce the uncertainty ever present in agriculture and the vulnerability to the amount and timing of precipitation in the crop-growing season. Pakistan and Sri Lanka are the two prominent examples of low-income countries where a substantial proportion of arable land--two thirds in the former and one half in the latter--is purposely provided with water, including flooding by river water, for crop production or pasture improvement. But in most hard-core developing countries the proportion is small (see table 9).

The proportion of arable land under irrigation is, in fact, abysmally small in some of the African countries, especially those in the Sahelian zone, a 200-mile wide fringe on the south of the Sahara Desert, where extreme crop failures were experienced for a number of years recently. There seems to be some debate whether the droughts that caused the crop failures constitute a haphazard or cyclical phenomenon, but there is no doubt that a future recurrence would be greatly reduced in its impact with the implementation of a comprehensive water management programme in the region. In the absence of such a programme, which, as in other regions, would require an exploitation of both surface and underground water potential, population increase in the Sahel region has been accompanied by an expansion of the extensive margin of agriculture northward into areas of increasingly uncertain rainfall. This has, in turn, reduced areas used for grazing by nomadic populations engaged in the raising of livestock, an important product of the region. It was in this context, therefore, that the devastation caused by the drought in the early 1970s assumed the proportions it did. Water management in the Sahel region would set the stage for a more intensive higher-yield cultivation and reduce the pressure on grazing lands, although any programme of river settlement would succeed only with control of river blindness and other diseases endemic to the region. Other necessary schemes include range management to prevent overgrazing by livestock, together with an integration of cultivation and livestock rearing so as to provide fodder for the animals during the three-month dry season of the year. Obstacles to the successful implementation of these schemes include political problems stemming from the fact that major river basins in the region cut across national boundaries. A beginning has been made, however, with plans for two dams on the Senegal River.

Next to a controlled and predictable water supply, the increased use of fertilizer is a critical element in the package of inputs needed for improved crop yields. While beyond a point the continued application of chemical fertilizer is likely to be counter-productive, that stage is probably still remote in countries with markedly underdeveloped economies. Use of chemical fertilizer has indeed increased dramatically in most hard-core developing countries since the early 1960s (see table 10). The increased use has been stimulated in some countries by Government subsidies--for example, in Bangladesh. In the United Republic of Tanzania, the ujamaa villages--a particular form of co-operative village organization promoted in that country--have been the recipients of fully subsidized fertilizer, the Government bearing the entire cost,. These subsidy schemes have strained the financial resources of the countries concerned, especially in recent years with the sharp hike in the price of fertilizer, amounting to as much as a three-or fourfold increase over the 1970/71 level. The problems posed by the upward spiralling of the price of fertilizer have been recognized, and international assistance to cope with them has been given through the United Nations Emergency Operation and the International Fertilizer Supply Scheme. The need for both short-term help and long-term sources of supply within developing countries has also been recognized. But much still remains to be done at both international and national levels.

While the rate of increase in the use of chemical fertilizer is impressive, the intensity of use is still very low in most hard-core developing countries. In some cases, the published data on use of chemical fertilizer perhaps overstate the actual or effective application. There are, for example, known instances of organizational impediments that delayed deliveries to cultivators beyond the point during the crop cycle up to which the fertilizer would have been useful.

Chemical fertilizer is, of course, not the only possible source of soil nutrient. There is a large potential source in organic fertilizer. This possibility needs to be fully exploited for eliminating what is a key obstacle to higher agricultural yields in hard-core developing countries.

Since the early 1960s, high-yielding varieties of wheat, rice and maize have been introduced in several hard-core developing countries and, as already noted, a few of the countries have achieved significant increased in the average yields of these three crops. However, the general record is not as good as it might have been. As also mentioned earlier, the high-yielding seeds need heavy complementary doses of water and fertilizer for a full exploitation of their potential. In addition, the new varieties which have usually been obtained from abroad have proved susceptible to local plant diseases and pests. In this context, there is an important need to cross-breed high-yielding varieties obtained from abroad with local varieties in order to develop hardy strains adapted to local conditions. Also in some cases, there appear to have been short-comings in the administrative apparatus for the distribution of improved seeds to cultivators. Recognition of this problem has led to the creation in a number of countries--for example, in Bangladesh and the Sudan--of Government departments or units specifically for the expansion and improvement of seed-distribution schemes.

High-yielding varieties have also been developed for millets and sorghum, but these varieties do not seem to have been introduced on anywhere near the same scale as for wheat, rice and maize. This suggests that there is a great deal of scope for increasing yields in Africa where millet and sorghum are the predominant cereals grown. The introduction of improved seeds with respect to these two cereals appears to have encountered the same factors that have prevented greater success with respect to wheat and rice, namely, inadequate availability of complementary inputs and hybrid strains of seeds that are better suited to local conditions.

Benefits resulting from increases in output of food grains are often sharply reduced by the encroachment of pests and animals on food supplies. Adequate availability of pesticides and storage facilities is, therefore, also a critical element of agricultural development policy. While a number of important steps have been taken in this regard, the deficiencies are still very great in hard-core developing countries.

The physical inputs that have been mentioned so far require a complement of intangible inputs by way of agricultural extension services and credit, so that farmers can have both the knowledge and the financial wherewithal to realize the potential for crop yields. The ratio of extension workers to farms in need of extension services is very low in hard-core developing countries. The usual problem here, to start with, is the small size of the available pool of the educated people from whom extension workers might be recruited and, then, the unsuitability of the existing educational systems to the practical needs of agriculture. Intermediate education designed to provide practical training is woefully deficient in hard-core developing countries. In its stead, there exist systems of higher education that have a pronounced tendency to make the students not merely unfit but also unwilling to serve in rural areas. In many countries, a thorough overhaul of educational systems is needed to ensure that the knowledge imparted to students is in tune with the development requirements of the nation. Future policies might also include the use of telecommunications that help to maximize the impact on farm practices in particular and rural life in general of the suitably trained corps of extension workers. There have been moves in some countries, most recently in Benin, India and Sri Lanka, to restructure the agricultural extension service so as to make it a more attractive career option.

With regard to agricultural credit, the problem is especially acute for the small farmer who is usually considered too risky a borrower by non-institutional lenders, who are still the only or main recourse for the farmer in most hard-core developing countries. Typically, such moneylenders impose onerous terms on borrowers. Institutional sources of credit backed by the Government have existed in a number of hard-core developing countries for many years, but the coverage of farm activity by such institutions is thin. Innovative measures are required not only to expand the coverage but also to attune lending procedures to the special circumstances of agricultural activity.

The need for a sustained adequate increase in food-grain production has loomed large in the foregoing discussion because of the crucial importance of this component of agricultural activity in underdeveloped economies. Attention also has to be given, however, to the protein supplements, especially pulses.[6] The production of pulses is conditioned by many of the same factors that affect cereal production. High-yielding varieties of pulses have not been widely developed or used, and the limitations of water and fertilizer available are the same as for cereals. Thus, it needs to be stressed that the raising of yields in food production in general has to be a pivotal element of the strategy designed to transform agriculture from a sluggish activity into a thriving force in hard-core developing countries.

Production, Consumption and International Trade

Inevitably, recent developments in agricultural production in hard-core developing countries have strongly influenced the patterns of not only their consumption or use of agricultural commodities but also their international trade. On balance, it is the trend in food production that has exercised the dominating influence.

In the face of inadquate expansion or even outright decline in the output of cereals, most hard-core developing countries have had to enlarge their imports of food grains in recent years. Indeed, an annual rate of increase of 10 per cent or more in net imports of cereals from the early 1960s to the early 1970s has been a common occurrence in these countries. The annual rate of increase in net imports during this period was particularly large in the drought-affected countries of the Sahel region of Africa--for instance, 27 per cent in Mali, 18 per cent in the Upper Volta and 15 per cent in Chad (see table 11). But in a number of countries the large increases in imports were insufficient to offset the shortfalls in production, with the result that their total apparent consumption (that is production plus net imports) of cereals actually declined. In the face of a rapidly expanding population, the decline in _per capita_ apparent consumption of cereals was very large in some countries. Several hard-core developing countries did manage to increase their consumption of cereals at a modest rate, but at the cost of enlarging their dependence on imports. India and Pakistan are two notable examples of a diminished dependence on imports: from the early 1960s to the early 1970s, the share of net imports in apparent consumption declined from 6 to 2 per cent in India and from 9 to 3 per cent in Pakistan. The share also declined in Sri Lanka, but even so net imports accounted for about two fifths of total apparent consumption of cereals in that country during the early 1970s. In most hard-core developing countries, however, the share of imports in the apparent consumption of cereals has increased.

As a result of these developments, the supply of food grains in hard-core developing countries has generally remained tight. A 4 to 5 per cent annual increase in the supply is needed to cope with the annual expansion of population (typically, 2.5 per cent) and the annual growth of demand resulting from the increase in incomes. The latter factor--that is, the income effect--tends to be of considerable significance because, at low levels of income, the demand for food rises rapidly as income increases. If hard-core developing countries wish to reduce their dependence on imports, production of food grains will have to expand at a still higher rate--that is, annually by 5 per cent or more. The lagging

TABLE 10. CONSUMPTION OF FERTILIZERS

Country [a]	Index, 1971/72-1972/73, annual average (annual average, 1961/62-1965/66 = 1)			Annual average, 1971/72-1972/73 (thousand metric tons)		
	Nitrogenous fertilizer	Phosphate fertilizer	Potash fertilizer	Nitrogenous fertilizer	Phosphate fertilizer	Potash fertilizer
Mali	23	29	...	3.3	5.4	...
Afghanistan	250	55	...	10.5	5.5	0.3
Upper Volta	...	6	...	0.5	0.5	...
Ethiopia	15	7	...	5.8	6.6	1.9
Chad	8	15	...	1.2	0.8	0.4
Bangladesh	3	9	7	83.2	60.3	10.8
Somalia	3	...	...	2.3	0.4	1.0
Niger	4	5	...	0.2	0.1	0.1
India	4	5	6	1,769.0	574.5	317.5
Benin	31	13	5	2.3	1.2	1.9
United Republic of Tanzania [b]	5	6	3	9.7	5.3	3.2
Sudan	2	—	...	49.5	0.2	...
Central African Republic	6	6	2	1.5	0.6	0.2
Uganda [b]	3	2	2	4.2	2.3	1.4
Pakistan	7	46	...	374.7	43.8	1.0
Sri Lanka [b]	1	7	1	50.5	9.7	32.7

SOURCE: See table 8.

[a] Countries are listed in ascending order of their *per capita* annual gross domestic product in 1970-1972.

[b] Data refer to 1971-1972. The base period for calculating indexes is 1961-1965.

TABLE 11. EXPANSION OF PRODUCTION, APPARENT CONSUMPTION[a] AND NET IMPORTS OF CEREALS, 1961-1965 TO 1971-1973

Country [b]	Percentage annual rate of increase			Net imports as percentage of apparent consumption	
	Production	Apparent consumption	New imports	1961-1965	1971-1973
Mali	−1.5	−0.7	27.1	1	8
Afghanistan	1.4	1.9	16.6	2	6
Upper Volta	−1.1	0.5	17.9	1	6
Ethiopia	2.3	2.3	13.0	—	—
Chad	−6.8	−6.6	14.9	—	3
Bangladesh	0.8	1.5	10.7	5	11
Somalia	1.5	4.2	8.1	35	49
Niger	−1.3	−0.9	[c]	−4	—
India	2.8	2.4	−9.1	6	2
Benin	−1.5	−1.0	8.6	3	8
United Republic of Tanzania	4.1	3.9	1.9	8	6
Sudan	3.3	3.8	18.6	2	6
Central African Republic	3.7	4.4	11.5	7	12
Uganda	3.7	3.8	9.5	2	4
Pakistan	5.6	4.9	−6.4	9	3
Sri Lanka	3.7	2.5	0.9	45	39

SOURCE: Centre for Development Planning, Projections and Policies of the Department of Economic and Social Affairs of the United Nations Secretariat, based on data from Food and Agriculture Organization of the United Nations, *Production Yearbook* and *Trade Yearbook*, various issues.

[a] Apparent consumption equals production plus imports minus exports.

[b] Countries are listed in ascending order of their *per capita* annual gross domestic product in 1970-1972.

[c] Net exports declined at the average annual rate of 23.4 per cent.

TABLE 12. EXPANSION OF PRODUCTION, APPARENT CONSUMPTION[a] AND NET IMPORTS OF RAW COTTON, 1961-1965 TO 1971-1973

Country [b]	Percentage annual rate of increase			Net imports as percentage of apparent consumption	
	Production	Apparent consumption	Net imports	1961-1965	1971-1973
Ethiopia	22.5	9.4	−20.2	65	4
Bangladesh	−6.2	...	...	...	96
India	1.9	1.6	−2.1	8	6
Sri Lanka	12.4	−1.6	−9.3	82	39

SOURCE AND FOOT-NOTES: See table 11.

supplies in relation to needs have sparked sharp increases in prices of food grains. And since food grains constitute a large proportion of household budgets in low-income countries, the food prices have affected the whole economy, resulting in widespread inflation.

Despite the increases recorded in recent years, net imports generally constitute a relatively small proportion of total consumption of cereals in hard-core developing countries. Somalia, where net imports contributed nearly half of consumption of cereals in the early 1970s, is one notable exception (apart from Sri Lanka, the exception mentioned earlier). Given the potential for substantially increasing average yields of cereals, with appropriate efforts most of these countries should be able to meet their consumption requirements of food grains through domestic production. The achievement of food security is vital not only for its own sake, but also to ease inflationary pressure and strain on the balance of payments and, above all, to inject momentum into agricultural activity in general so that employment opportunities are enlarged and the economy as a whole moves forward.

The foregoing considerations are also relevant with regard to the production, consumption and trade of agricultural raw materials. Raw cotton provides an outstanding example in this respect. Such countries as Ethiopia, India and Sri Lanka which are net importers of raw cotton have been able, through increased domestic production, to reduce their dependence on imported supplies of this important raw material (see table 12). Many hard-core countries, however, are net exporters of raw cotton, and several of them have achieved substantial increases in the production and exports of this item in recent years (see table 13). Nevertheless, a great deal of scope with regard to the production of not only cotton but also a number of other raw materials remains to be tapped, both to serve as a base for the expansion of domestic industries and to enlarge foreign exchange earnings. The need for striking a harmonious balance between food production and raw material production will, of course, have to be kept in the forefront in designing and implementing policies for agricultural development.

A criticism used to be voiced not too long ago that developing countries had kept the prices of their agricultural goods, especially food grains, deliberately low in favour of the urban elite, while letting the prices of their industrial goods increase at a faster rate. This feature, it was said, acted as a disincentive for the farmer and was a major cause of slow agricultural progress. Agricultural prices were probably kept low in several countries during the 1950s and the early 1960s, but since then the picture appears to have changed. Although the available data are meagre, there is evidence that agricultural prices have risen substantially since the mid 1960s. Such a conclusion emerges from the information relating to both the domestic sales and the exports of agricultural goods. The signals that domestic and world markets have offered by means of their price behaviour since 1972 strongly point to the need for expansion of output of crucial agricultural goods.

As already emphasized, with the growth of population and

TABLE 13. EXPANSION OF PRODUCTION, APPARENT CONSUMPTION[a] AND NET EXPORTS OF RAW COTTON, 1961-1965 TO 1971-1973

Country[b]	Percentage annual rate of increase			Net exports as percentage of production	
	Production	Apparent consumption	Net exports	1961-1965	1961-1973
Mali	12.6	5.9	14.5	72	84
Afghanistan	0.7	0.9	0.6	60	60
Upper Volta	20.8	15.4	24.6	50	67
Chad	1.6	[c]	0.5	102	93
Somalia	−1.2	3.9	−49.0	36	—
Niger	3.1	−28.5	10.6	52	98
Benin	34.4	34.2	34.4	79	80
United Republic of Tanzania	4.8	10.7	3.9	90	83
Sudan	4.8	−2.0	6.8	90	106
Central African Republic	6.3	15.8	5.9	97	93
Uganda	1.0	−2.4	1.6	84	88
Pakistan	6.8	...	...	...	31

SOURCE: See table 11.

[a] See table 11, foot-note *a*.
[b] See table 11, foot-note *b*.
[c] Apparent consumption was negative in base period.

TABLE 14. PERCENTAGE SHARE OF AGRICULTURAL GOODS IN TOTAL IMPORTS, EARLY 1960s AND EARLY 1970s [a]

Country [b]	All agricultural goods		Food-stuffs	
	Early 1960s	Early 1970s	Early 1960s	Early 1970s
Mali	22	33	19	28
Upper Volta	25	26	19	21
Ethiopia	10	10	6	7
Chad	19	21	16	19
Somalia	33	33	30	28
Niger	27	15	23	13
India	25	19	15	10
Benin	23	20	23	17
United Republic of Tanzania	11[c]	8	11[c]	7
Sudan	19	24	17	22
Central African Republic	15	17	14	16
Uganda	6	7	5	5
Pakistan [d]	21	18	17	14
Sri Lanka	41	48	39	46

SOURCE: Centre for Development Planning, Projections and Policies of the Department of Economic and Social Affairs of the United Nations Secretariat, based on data from Statistical Office of the Department, *Yearbook of International Trade Statistics* (various issues).

[a] Data for the early 1960s refer to 1961-1962 except for the following countries: Ethiopia and the Sudan, 1962-1963; Pakistan, 1963-1964. Those for the early 1970s refer to 1971-1972 except for Benin, the Central African Republic, Chad, Mali, the Niger, Pakistan and Sri Lanka, where they pertain to 1970-1971.

All agricultural goods refer to sections 0 (food and live animals), 1 (beverages and tobacco) and 2 except 27 and 28 (crude materials, inedible, except fuels, fertilizers, minerals, metalliferous ores and metal scrap) of the Standard International Trade Classification (SITC). Food-stuffs refer to sections 0 and 1 of SITC. Both product groups—that is, all agricultural goods and food-stuffs—include some processed items.

In some cases, the shares of product groups in total trade have been calculated on the basis of incomplete data. Thus, for Uganda and the United Republic of Tanzania the data exclude local produce and locally manufactured goods traded between member States of the East African Community; for the Central African Republic data exclude trade with Chad (1961-1962), the Congo, Gabon and (for 1970-1971) the United Republic of Cameroon; for Benin and Mali, the Niger and the Upper Volta (especially in 1961-1967), trade, particularly with neighbouring States, may be considerably understated, and as a consequence, the share of food, beverages and raw materials may be underestimated in relation to the share of manufactures.

[b] Countries are listed in ascending order of their *per capita* annual gross domestic product in 1970-1972.

[c] Tanganyika only. In Zanzibar, the share of all agricultural goods in total imports amounted to 46 per cent and the share of food-stuffs to 39 per cent.

[d] Including transactions of the former Eastern Wing of Pakistan which is now Bangladesh.

average income, demand for agricultural goods is bound to expand substantially in hard-core developing countries. Although net imports of food generally constitute a small proportion of apparent consumption, such imports do often form a significant part of the total import bill. Indeed, the imports of agricultural goods by hard-core developing countries consist largely of food-stuffs (see table 14). There is thus a significant scope for releasing scarce foreign exchange by replacing agricultural imports by domestic production. For earnings of foreign exchange, hard-core developing countries generally depend very heavily on exports of agricultural goods. Except in such countries as India and Pakistan, where industrialization has made some headway, and in mineral economies (the Central African Republic, for instance, has developed a flourishing export trade in diamonds in recent years), agricultural goods constitute the bulk of the exports of hard-core developing countries (see table 15). Given their large foreign-exchange requirements, in order to import machinery and other essential development goods, these countries need to make every possible effort to increase exports of agricultural goods wherever scope exists. All these features reinforce the argument that a vigorous agricultural expansion is an essential ingredient of economic growth and welfare in countries with markedly underdeveloped economies.

III. INDUSTRIAL PROGRESS

Along with agriculture, attention also has to be given to manufacturing activity, which serves as the engine of expansion, diversification and modernization of the economy. Because of lack of adequate information, it is not possible to pinpoint figures from the composition of actual investment in recent years, but the development plans of a number of hard-core developing countries suggest that usually one fourth to one fifth of total investment is allocated to the manufacturing sector. Further, an even greater proportion of total investment is usually devoted to expanding such basic facilities as power, transport and communication which have a profound bearing on the process of industrialization. A great deal of industrial activity in these countries is now undertaken in the public sector of the economy, often because it is not profitable for private enterprise to undertake the production of certain crucial goods. However, as in the case of agriculture, the problem currently lies not in the relative allocation of investment among various functional sectors of the economy but in finding additional resources for raising the level of investment in general.

TABLE 15. PERCENTAGE SHARE OF AGRICULTURAL GOODS IN TOTAL EXPORTS, EARLY 1960s AND EARLY 1970s [a]

Country [b]	All agricultural goods		Food-stuffs	
	Early 1960s	Early 1970s	Early 1960s	Early 1970s
Mali	56	84	40	45
Afghanistan	85	72	27	32
Upper Volta	84	92	74	51
Ethiopia	98	96	69	71
Chad	95	94	14	25
Somalia	93	97	82	88
Niger	90	78	28	27
India	46	35	36	29
Benin	80	65	21	33
United Republic of Tanzania	86 [c]	78	30 [c]	48
Sudan	99	94	9	8
Central African Republic	81	59	31	26
Uganda	91	92	53	69
Pakistan [d]	70	41	11	11
Sri Lanka	92	91	70	67

SOURCE: See table 14.

[a] See table 14, foot-note a.

[b] See table 14, foot-note b.

[c] Tanganyika only. In Zanzibar, the share of all agricultural goods in total exports amounted to 89 per cent and the share of food-stuffs to 72 per cent.

[d] See table 14, foot-note d.

TABLE 16. EXPANSION OF GROSS OUTPUT OF MANUFACTURING INDUSTRIES [a]

Country [b]	Percentage annual rate of increase, 1960-1961 (annual average) to 1970			Percentage distribution of manufacturing output in 1970		
	Total	Mainly light manufacturing	Mainly heavy manufacturing	Total	Mainly light manufacturing	Mainly heavy manufacturing
India	5.6	3.3	8.8	100	50	50
United Republic of Tanzania	11.6	10.3	15.9	100	72	28
Uganda [c]	7.5	7.7	6.3	100	79	21
Pakistan [d]	9.5	8.9	10.9	100	67	33
Sri Lanka [c]	8.4	6.1	12.7	100	60	40

SOURCE: Centre for Development Planning, Projections and Policies of the Department of Economic and Social Affairs of the United Nations Secretariat, "Industrialization and development: progress and problems in developing countries" in *Journal of Development Planning*, No. 8 (United Nations publications, Sales No. E.75.II.A.1).

[a] For coverage of light and heavy manufacturing industries, see table 17.

[b] Countries are listed in ascending order of their *per capita* annual gross domestic product in 1970-1972.

[c] End period data refer to 1969.

[d] Including data for Bangladesh. Annual rate of increase calculated from data for 1961-1962.

TABLE 17. PERCENTAGE SHARES OF PRINCIPAL INDUSTRIAL BRANCHES IN THE GROSS OUTPUT OF MANUFACTURING INDUSTRIES IN 1970

Industrial branch	Country[a]				
	India	United Republic of Tanzania	Uganda[b]	Pakistan[c]	Sri Lanka[b]
Mainly light manufacturing industries					
Food, beverages and tobacco products	27	41	50	32	38
Textiles, wearing apparel and leather products	19	21	24	32	16
Wood and wood products, including furniture	1	7	3	—	1
Paper and paper products, printing and publishing	4	3	2	3	4
Mainly heavy manufacturing industries					
Chemicals and chemical, petroleum, coal, rubber and plastic products	16	9	3	17	17
Non-metallic mineral products, except products of petroleum and coal	3	3	3	3	3
Basic metals	10	1	9	3	2
Fabricated metal products, machinery and equipment	21	15	6	10	18
Total manufacturing output	100	100	100	100	100

SOURCE: See table 16.

[a] Countries are listed horizontally in ascending order of their *per capita* annual gross domestic product in 1970-1972.

[b] 1969.

[c] Including data for Bangladesh.

TABLE 18. EXPANSION IN OUTPUT OF SELECTED MANUFACTURES
(*Percentage annual rate of increase, 1962-1963 to 1971-1972*)

Country[a]	Refined sugar	Beer	Cigarettes	Cotton woven fabrics	Fertilizer [b]	Cement
Afghanistan	...	...	...	6.4	...	5.7
Upper Volta	...	7.6	...	...	...	...
Ethiopia[c]	...	12.4	14.8	15.1	...	16.5
Bangladesh[d]	3.5	...	22.5	−3.5	6.1	−4.2
Somalia[e]	13.5	...	...	...	...	...
India	3.7	11.7	5.2	0.3	19.2	6.2
United Republic of Tanzania	...	24.0	13.7	43.5[f]	...	25.0[g]
Sudan	29.5	−0.3[h]	10.2	5.3[i]	...	5.8
Central African Republic	...	1.5	...	5.3	...	...
Uganda	...	24.5	6.1	5.0	21.0	14.3
Pakistan	10.3	8.2	8.9	1.8	25.5	8.2
Sri Lanka	...	5.5	8.8	20.5	...	19.0

SOURCE: Centre for Development Planning, Projections and Policies of the Department of Economic and Social Affairs of the United Nations Secretariat, based on data from Statistical Office of the Department, *The Growth of World Industry* (various issues).

[a] Countries are listed in ascending order of their *per capita* annual gross domestic product in 1970-1972.

[b] Nitrogenous, phosphatic (including superphosphates), potassic and multi-nutrient fertilizers.

[c] 1965 to 1971.
[d] 1962-1963 to 1970-1971.
[e] 1964-1965 to 1970-1971.
[f] 1966-1967 to 1972-1973.
[g] 1966 to 1972.
[h] 1965-1966 to 1970-1971.
[i] 1964 to 1971.
[j] 1965-1966 to 1972-1973.

Patterns of Manufacturing Output

Information on the pace of expansion and composition of manufacturing output in recent years is available for only a few hard-core developing countries. None the less, some conclusions of a general validity can be drawn from even such limited information. Generally, manufacturing activity appears to have expanded at a faster rate than the economy as a whole. However, during the decade since the early 1960s, the annual rate of expansion of manufacturing activity was large or moderately large in very few of the hard-core developing countries. The rate was high in the United Republic of Tanzania (10 per cent) and moderately high in Ethiopia, Pakistan and Sri Lanka (7-8 per cent). In India, which has a longer record of industrialization than other hard-core developing countries, manufacturing activity expanded at less than 5 per cent per annum. Moreover, except in India and Pakistan, the share of manufacturing in total output of goods and services remains small in hard-core developing countries--usually less than 10 per cent.[7]

Within the manufacturing sector. The output of relatively heavy manufacturing industries has generally tended to grow faster than that of relatively light manufacturing industries (see table 16). The relatively heavy industries produce a wide variety of producer goods: cement, coal-based products, chemicals, tools and equipment, to name only a few. Such producer goods are required to strengthen the linkages within the manufacturing sector itself as well as to expand production in other sectors of the economy.

Notwithstanding the faster pace of expansion of producer goods industries, the relatively light manufacturing industries--which generate mainly consumer goods--predominate in the industrial structure of hard-core developing countries. A rare exception in this respect is India, where light and heavy manufacturing industries contributed to the total output in virtually equal proportions (about 50 per cent each) at the outset of the 1970s. In Uganda and the United Republic of Tanzania, in contrast, the share of relatively light manufacturing industries in total manufacturing output at the beginning of the 1970s was 79 and 72 per cent, respectively. These two examples from Africa are fairly representative of the prevailing structure of manufacturing production in hard-core developing countries.

The predominance of relatively light manufacturing industries in the industrial structure of hard-core developing countries is readily understandable. These are mostly industries that produce processed food-stuffs, beverages, tobacco products, textiles, wearing apparel and leather goods (see tables 17 and 18). Such industries require, per unit of output, comparatively light doses of capital and skills. Since these factors of production tend to be comparatively scarce in underdeveloped economies, it is only to be expected that light manufacturing activities will be proportionately more important at earlier stages of development. With the passage of time, as the historical experience of countries which are no longer at an early stage of industrial development has shown, the share of light manufacturing activities in total manufacturing output is likely to diminish.

Since the demand for producer goods is prone to expand rapidly, hard-core developing countries need to devote a great deal of attention to expanding the production of these critical manufactures wherever the potential exists. The drive to expand cement output is discernible in virtually all hard-core developing countries. Some of these countries are also pushing ahead with the manufacture of chemical fertilizer; India, Pakistan and, to a smaller extent, Bangladesh now manufacture a sizable amount of this crucial input for agriculture. A push ahead is also being made with the output of metals and metal products in some low-income countries, including not only India and Pakistan but also the United Republic of Tanzania. These developments provide a broad indication of progress, but they are also a reminder that the problem of achieving adequate expansion of the output of producer goods so as to strengthen forward and backward linkages within the economy will need to be kept constantly at the forefront of policy decisions.

Production Problems

Impediments to the expansion and diversification of manufacturing activity in hard-core developing countries are many. For example, often a serious problem is posed by an inadequate base of raw materials. Inadequate expansion of electricity and other basic facilities frequently obstructs rapid growth of industries. Shortages of skills also impede industrial expansion. As stressed earlier, barring a small number of exceptions, hard-core developing countries have not been able to raise their level of capital formation at a significant pace in recent years, and this has seriously affected their ability to expand the industrial sector and the rest of the economy.

The relatively light manufacturing industries, which predominate in the industrial structure of hard-core developing countries, are based largely on agricultural raw materials. It is therefore often the inadequate increase in agricultural output that has hindered industrial progress in recent years. Numerous examples are available of the deleterious effects of shortfalls in the supply of agricultural materials on the manufacture of such items as sugar, cooking oil and textiles. Sometimes the downturn in agricultural output, by diminishing the purchasing power of agriculturists, has resulted in an unintended build-up of unsold goods; the case of cotton textiles in India is a noteworthy example in this respect. Efforts to impart vigour to agricultural activity should therefore also lead to an improved rhythm of industrial expansion.

To cope with their growing needs, both for industrialization and for consumer use, hard-core developing countries have been expanding the generation of electricity. And the annual rate of

TABLE 19. PRODUCTION AND INSTALLED GENERATING CAPACITY OF ELECTRIC ENERGY [a]

Country [b]	Percentage annual rate of increase, 1961-1962 to 1971-1972 [c]		Annual average, 1971-1972 [d]	
	Production	Installed capacity	Production (kilowatt hours per capita)	Installed capacity (kilowatts per 1000 persons)
Mali.	10.8	7.2	9.3	4.4
Afghanistan.	11.8	15.3	24.5	14.2
Upper Volta	11.5	12.8	6.3	2.6
Ethiopia	14.1	7.4	15.6	6.6
Chad	16.4	20.7	13.1	9.0
Bangladesh	9.5	14.3	14.9	7.7
Somalia	...	...	11.4 [e]	2.1 [f]
Niger	15.6	10.4	11.1	3.6
India.	10.8	38.4	120.2	30.6
Benin	13.4	16.7	15.2	3.6
United Republic of Tanzania [g]	9.3	9.4	32.5	9.2
Sudan	10.7	8.3	19.9	7.2
Central African Republic . .	16.0	8.4	28.5	9.9
Uganda	6.2	1.9	78.9	17.0
Pakistan	14.3	16.0	112.9	28.6
Sri Lanka.	9.8	9.2	73.2	21.7

SOURCE: Centre for Development Planning, Projections and Policies of the Department of Economic and Social Affairs, based on data from Statistical Office of the Department, *Statistical Yearbook* (various issues).

[a] Countries are listed in ascending order of their *per capita* annual gross domestic product in 1970-1972.

[b] For Benin, Chad, Ethiopia, Mali, Pakistan, Somalia, Uganda and the United Republic of Tanzania, production and installed capacity in enterprises generating primarily for public use.

[c] Ethiopia, 1961-1962 to 1970-1971; Bangladesh and Pakistan, 1963-1964 to 1971-1972.

[d] Ethiopia, 1970-1971.

[e] Production in Mogadiscio, Merca, Giohar and Hergeisa only.

[f] Installed capacity in Mogadiscio only.

[g] Excluding Zanzibar.

increase in both the installed capacity and production of electricity since the early 1960s has generally been quite significant (see table 19). Yet, the output of electricity remains very small in these countries. Moreover, there are wide differences in this respect even among hard-core developing countries themselves: for instance, in the early 1970s, the annual per capita production of electricity in the Upper Volta was merely 6 kilowatt hours, compared with 120 kilowatt hours in India (which in turn was tiny in comparison with the output in industrialized countries). The demand for electricity greatly exceeds supply, and power failures caused by overstrained machinery are a frequent occurrence in hard-core developing countries. Their dependence on imported supplies of petroleum is very heavy, and the already difficult situation in this respect has been made precarious by the sharp increase in the price of petroleum since 1973. The need for economical sources of energy remains very great.

Transportation problems also loom large in hard-core developing countries. In countries of South Asia, the railway system is fairly extensive, but is overstrained. Industrial production often suffers because of inordinate delays in moving both the essential inputs and the products of factories. In low-income countries of Africa, railways play a much less important role. Some of those countries, in fact, do not have railways. Roads serve as the main arteries of transportation; but deficiencies, especially in respect of feeder roads that connect villages with the main routes that link urban centres, are serious. Much has been done to extend the transportation network, but much more remains to be done.

Next to an adequate physical infrastructure, an endowment of mineral raw materials is vitally important for a viable manufacturing sector. Mineral deposits serve as important nuclei of manufacturing activity; in fact, a major deposit of a mineral resource can give rise to a network of physical infrastructure that would not otherwise have been brought into existence. As the requirements of producer goods increase, so do the needs for mineral raw materials. Geological explorations are being undertaken in hard-core developing countries, but limitations of finance and skills often impose a severe constraint.

There are known to be sizable deposits of coal in India and the United Republic of Tanzania and of natural gas in Afghanistan and Pakistan. The known reserves of petroleum in hard-core developing countries appear to be small; but such estimates, whether in relation to petroleum or other minerals, do not include an allowance for what may be discovered through the exploration now under way. For instance, no estimates are as yet available with regard to off-shore discoveries in Benin, India and the United Republic of Tanzania. Even so, the pattern of endowment appears to be sparse and meagre in these countries, and their dependence on imported supplies of energy seems unlikely to diminish significantly in the foreseeable future.

Among metallic ores, there are sizable reserves of iron ore and bauxite in India and of copper in Uganda. Tin ore exists in small quantities in the Niger, Uganda and the United Republic of Tanzania. Among other minerals, the pattern of raw material availability for the manufacture of chemical fertilizer is very sparse indeed. India and Uganda have some phosphate rock. Potash seems to be virtually non-existent in low-income countries of Africa and Asia. The Central African Republic and the United Republic of Tanzania have diamond mines; for these two countries, export trade in diamonds, by enhancing their ability to import needed minerals, could serve as a partial substitute for lack of a wider mineral-resource base.

In the years ahead, systematic explorations may lead to important new discoveries of mineral deposits in hard-core developing countries. There is indeed a strong case for mounting geological explorations. In the absence of sizable discoveries, however, most of these countries will have to import a variety of mineral raw materials for establishing or expanding domestic industries. This consideration once again emphasizes the need to expand agricultural production for which a potential exists so that, through both import substitution and export promotion of relevant agricultural commodities, additional foreign exchange is made available for the wherewithal of industrialization.

Deficiencies of the existing educational systems mentioned earlier in the context of agricultural problems are also pertinent with regard to the industrial progress of hard-core developing countries. Particularly urgent is the need to enlarge the base for middle-level technicians--for example, mechanics and foremen. It is true that industrialization itself helps to enlarge the available pool of skills by imparting on-the-job training and experience, but this process by itself cannot yield the required results. A requisite base and orientation for technical education of various types and levels has to be created by means of active measures designed to modify the current educational systems.

Markets for Manufactures

The question of markets for the goods manufactured in hard-core developing countries also poses important policy issues. The issues embrace aspects of both the domestic market and the external market for products of industries.

Manufactured goods bulk large in the imports of hard-core developing countries. This feature is an indication not only of the low level of industrialization in these countries but also of the fact that a ready domestic market exists which, in respect of many (though usually not all) types of goods, can be catered to through the establishment and expansion of domestic industries. The domestic market, moreover, is expanding, in part because of the growing population and in part because of the rising (though not at a spectacular rate) average income which is usually accompanied by a more rapidly increasing demand for manufactured goods. It is against this framework that hard-core developing countries have been striving to promote a wide variety of import-substituting industries.

TABLE 20. PERCENTAGE SHARE OF MANUFACTURED GOODS IN TOTAL IMPORTS, EARLY 1960s TO EARLY 1970s [a]

| | All manufactured goods | | Basic manufactures | | | |
| | | | Total | | Textiles | |
Country [b]	Early 1960s	Early 1970s	Early 1960s	Early 1970s	Early 1960s	Early 1970s
Mali	72	55	31	19	21	6
Upper Volta	70	62	30	24	15	8
Ethiopia	80	80	30	23	17	6
Chad	66	59	27	19	11	7
Somalia	60	58	28	25	15	8
Niger	65	73	32	33	21	21
India	64	65	19	24	1	—
Benin	67	75	32	37	11	24
United Republic of Tanzania	76 [b]	81	37 [c]	28	14 [c]	4
Sudan	73	68	32	32	17	19
Central African Republic	77	79	29	24	15	10
Uganda	76	90	33	28	19	7
Pakistan [d]	69	68	24	19	2	1
Sri Lanka	50	48	24	21	10	8

SOURCE: See table 14.

[a] All manufactured goods refer to sections 5 (chemicals), 6 (basic manufactures), 7 (machines and transport equipment) and 8 (miscellaneous manufactured goods) of SITC. Basic manufactures refer to SITC section 6 and textiles to SITC division 65.
For differences in time period and coverage of trade data, see table 14, foot-note a.

[b] Countries are listed in ascending order of their *per capita* annual gross domestic product in 1970-1972.

[c] Tanganyika only. In Zanzibar, the share of all manufactured goods in total imports amounted to 44 per cent and the share of basic manufactures to 9 per cent.

[d] Including transactions of the former Eastern Wing of Pakistan which is now Bangladesh.

TABLE 21. PERCENTAGE SHARE OF MANUFACTURED GOODS IN TOTAL EXPORTS, EARLY 1960s AND EARLY 1970s[a]

Country [b]	All manufactured goods		Basic manufactures			
			Total		Textiles	
	Early 1960s	Early 1970s	Early 1960s	Early 1970s	Early 1960s	Early 1970s
Mali	2	9	2	7	1	6
Afghanistan	14	14	14	9	14	9
Upper Volta	9	7	4	5	3	2
Ethiopia	—	1	—	1	—	—
Chad	1	2	—	1	—	—
Somalia	5	2	—	—	—	—
Niger	2	3	1	1	—	1
India	44	55	40	42	35	26
Benin	4	8	1	5	—	4
United Republic of Tanzania	13[c]	11	12[c]	10	—	2
Sudan	—	1	—	—	—	—
Central African Republic	1	41[d]	—	39[d]	—	1
Uganda	9	7	9	7	—	—
Pakistan[e]	29	57	25	49	22	43
Sri Lanka	1	2	—	1	—	—

SOURCE: See table 14.

[a] See table 20, foot-note a.

[b] See table 20, foot-note b.

[c] Tanganyika only. In Zanzibar, the share of all manufactured goods in total exports amounted to 1 per cent, virtually the whole of it being accounted for by "basic manufactures" (SITC section 6).

[d] This high figure is very largely accounted for by diamonds.

[e] See table 20, foot-note d.

The impact of their drive towards import substitution, especially in African countries, has been most strikingly evident in consumer-goods industries. The share of "basic manufactures"--the category of the Standard International Trade Classification that includes textiles, leather products, rubber articles, paper products, along with cement, glass and metals--in total imports has declined significantly in several hard-core developing countries in the early 1970s, compared with the early 1960s. Frequently, it is the decline in the share of imports of textiles that is responsible in large part for this trend (see table 20). The domestic availability of raw cotton has been the major contributory factor for the growth of cotton textile industry in these countries. In fact, the domestic availability of agricultural raw materials, in general has been the key element of the success of import-substitution efforts.

The import-substitution drive, however, has varied greatly among hard-core developing countries in recent years. For instance, India appears to have largely exhausted the scope for import substitution with regard to manufactured consumer goods. Pakistan, too, seems to have nearly reached this stage of industrial development. These two countries now increasingly need to enlarge the domestic base for industries manufacturing producer goods, especially machinery, tools and equipment. Given their relative scarcity of foreign exchange, without an adequate expansion of domestic output of capital goods their ability to raise the level of capital formation for accelerated economic growth will be circumscribed. In hard-core developing countries of Africa, by contrast, there is probably still considerable room for economical import substitution regarding manufactured consumer goods. But these countries also have to turn to the manufacture of a variety of producer goods, such as cement, chemicals and certain metal products.

Among hard-core developing countries, India and Pakistan are the only major exporters of manufactured goods, in the sense that more than half of their exports consist of manufactures. In most other hard-core developing countries the share of manufactures in total exports is less than one tenth (see table 21). Pakistan's exports of manufactured goods consist largely of textiles. India's exports of manufactured goods are comparatively more diversified but textiles still are the most important item.

In their endeavour to expand exports of manufactured and semi-manufactured goods, those hard-core developing countries which have already developed an export capacity inevitably face the critical question of adequate access to the markets of economically advanced countries. The generalized scheme of preferences for the imports of manufactures and semi-manufactures from developing countries has gained wide acceptance among developing countries. But there are often many loop-holes and escape clauses in the practices adopted which impede the effectiveness of the scheme. This is especially true with regard to such manufactures as cotton textiles and shoes which frequently encounter quantitative import ceilings in a number of developed countries. These are precisely the sort of labour-intensive goods for whose production poorer countries have a distinct comparative advantage. Such examples suggest that much still remains to be done in developed countries to ease the entry of goods manufactured by developing countries, especially those goods whose production can be a particularly effective means of making an attack on extreme poverty and unemployment.

The more advanced developing countries can also do a great deal to encourage imports of manufactures from the poorer developing countries. Thanks to the new economic power gained by several developing countries in recent years, the scope for such trade has greatly enlarged. The full potential of the scope, however, can be tapped only if a systematic effort is made to do so.

While the domestic market for many manufactured consumer goods is generally sufficient in hard-core developing countries to permit an economical scale of production, this is often not true with regard to manufactured producer goods. A number of consumer manufactures—bicycles and electric fans, for example—are akin to producer goods in this respect. The constraints imposed by the small size of the domestic market are great in many hard-core developing countries of Africa. To overcome such constraints and reap economies of scale, it is vital for these countries to undertake appropriate schemes for economic co-operation and development. Indeed, through mutually beneficial arrangements for production and trade, it should be possible to steer industrialization on to an efficient path of progress. A number of economic co-operation and integration schemes do exist in Africa. However, as yet, they fall short of what has been achieved in certain other parts of the developing world, notably in Latin America.

IV. NEEDED POLICY THRUST

The problems that hard-core developing countries face are numerous and complex. Clearly, there are no simple solutions to the intense and stubborn poverty that is the most distinguishing and unfortunate characteristic of these countries. Extreme poverty and underdevelopment can be alleviated, and ultimately eradicated, only if a development strategy that dovetails requisite national and international measures into a coherent whole is pursued with fervour over a sustained period of time.

The central theme of the discussion in the preceding sections is that, because agriculture is by far the dominant sector of the economy in hard-core developing countries, it is axiomatic that their economy cannot surge forward unless there is rapid agricultural progress. The expansion and modernization of agriculture is vital not only for accelerated economic growth but also for easing inflationary pressures and strains on the balance of payments, for enlarging employment opportunities, for improving nutrition and for enhancing incomes where poverty displays its worse scars.

The pre-eminence of agriculture does not imply that industry can be neglected. Indeed, industry has to expand at a more rapid rate than agriculture. For only in this way can the required diversification of the economy and the modernization of all its sectors be achieved. Manufacturing and other industrial activities, especially power generation and transportation, need to be closely integrated with agriculture through a combination of policies that converge harmoniously on the most acute problems facing a society. The policies inevitably entail the whole range of measures designated to mobilize human, physical and financial resources.

How a country goes about organizing its pattern of production and the means to achieve its basic national objectives rests essentially on its own discipline and dedication. There are no innate laws of economics which provide ready-made answers. Much can, of course, be gleaned from the experience of economies that have successfully completed the transition from poverty to plenty. But when national histories, social cultures and economic endowments vary as widely as they do, rigid imitation of some other country's development path can hardly be the right solution. In the end, it is for the country itself to translate its aspirations into reality in consonance with its own genius.

It is also, however, a distinguishing feature of the contemporary world scene that the international community has accepted an obligation to help speed up the economic and social progress of developing countries. Neither the problems nor the needs of developing countries are identical. The neediest among developing countries are those which suffer from extreme poverty and underdevelopment. A systematic attack on the acute problems of these hard-core developing countries should therefore now be at the centre of the policies designed to usher in a new international economic order.

NOTES

[1] The tables included in the present paper contain data on relevant variables for 16 developing countries, 11 in Africa and five in Asia, which appear to be prominent examples of hard-core developing countries--that is, where problems of poverty and under-development are acute. These countries were selected solely for the purpose of drawing, on the basis of their development experience since the early 1960s, the generalizations set forth in the paper. The selection was also influenced by whether at least a modicum of information was available that could help to provide a valid quantitative picture of the unfolding developments in recent years. For some of the variables, data are not available for all of the 16 countries.

[2] For a discussion of relevant methodological and empirical problems, see Irving B. Kravis, Zoltan Kenessey, Alan Heston and Robert Sommers, A System of International Comparisons of Gross Product and Purchasing Power (Baltimore, the Johns Hopkins University Press, 1975).

[3] General Assembly resolution 2626 (XXV) of 24 October 1974, para. 17(a).

[4] See "Foreign aid and development needs" and "External finance for development: recent experience and its implications for policies" in the present issue of the Journal of Development Planning.

[5] It should be stressed that the output data just cited refer to gross value of agricultural production, whereas in the preceding section the corresponding data referred to value added in agricultural production. The time periods underlying the two sets of data also differ in a number of cases.

[6] Also important is the production of beverage crops (coffee, tea and cocoa), especially for export. But since beverage crops are major sources of foreign exchange for a number of hard-core developing countries, the Governments concerned have usually paid greater attention to the problems of beverage crop production in their agricultural policies. Beverage crops, moreover, are grown to a substantial extent on plantations, which are more akin to a modern industry than to the small-scale farming that is a common characteristic of hard-core developing countries.

Animal husbandry, too, is an important component of agricultural activity, but it also has a number of special facets. In order to keep the discussion brief, questions relating to animal husbandry are not discussed in the present paper.

[7] The data cited in this paragraph refer to value added in manufacturing. Comments in the next few paragraphs regarding the composition of manufacturing output are based on gross value of production.

Development Trends Since 1960 and Their Implications for a New International Development Strategy

CENTRE FOR DEVELOPMENT PLANNING, PROJECTIONS AND POLICIES OF THE DEPARTMENT OF INTERNATIONAL ECONOMIC AND SOCIAL AFFAIRS OF THE UNITED NATIONS SECRETARIAT

The concept of the United Nations Development Decade is intended to serve as a focus for concerting national and international action to speed up the economic and social progress of developing countries. Thus, in 1961, designating the 10-year period 1961-1970 as the [First] United Nations Development Decade, the General Assembly called upon the Member States and their peoples to "intensify their efforts to mobilize and to sustain support for the measures required on the part of both developed and developing countries to accelerate progress towards self-sustaining growth of the economy of the individual nations and their social advancement so as to attain in each under-developed country a substantial increase in the rate of growth, with each country setting its own target, taking as the objective a minimum annual rate of growth of aggregate national income of 5 per cent at the end of the Decade."[1] Nine years later, proclaiming the 10-year period 1971-1980 as the Second United Nations Development Decade, the Assembly suggested that "the average annual rate of growth in the gross product of the developing countries as a whole during the ... Decade should be at least 6 per cent". Furthermore, it specified that "This target and those derived from it are a broad indication of the scope of convergent efforts to be made during the Decade at the national and international levels; it should be the responsibility of each developing country to set its own target for growth in the light of its own circumstances."[2]

Well in advance of the terminating point of the Second United Nations Development Decade (31 December 1980), the General Assembly has initiated preparation of a new international development strategy, and for this purpose has enlisted support from organizations of the United Nations system and from the Committee for Development Planning.[3] As affirmed by the Economic and Social

From **JOURNAL OF DEVELOPMENT PLANNING**, No. 13, 1978, (173-192), reprinted by permission of the publisher.

TABLE 1. POPULATION AND GROWTH OF REAL OUTPUT, BY GROUP OF COUNTRIES, 1961-1975

Country group[a]	Population (1970)		Average annual rate of increase[b] in gross domestic product at constant prices (percentage)					
			Total			Per capita		
	Millions	Percentage share[c]	1961-1965	1966-1970	1971-1975	1961-1965	1966-1970	1971-1975
Developing countries	1 638	60.1	5.1	5.8	5.9	2.5	3.1	3.2
Developed market economies	739	27.1	5.2	4.5	2.8	3.9	3.4	1.8
Centrally planned economies[d]	348	12.8	6.1	7.4	6.3	4.8	6.4	5.5

Sources: Centre for Development Planning, Projections and Policies of the United Nations Secretariat, based on data from *Yearbook of National Accounts Statistics* (United Nations publication; various issues) and from other international and national sources.

[a] *Developing countries:* Afghanistan, Algeria, Angola, Argentina, Barbados, Bangladesh, Benin, Bolivia, Botswana, Brazil, Burma, Burundi, Cape Verde, Central African Empire, Chad, Chile, Colombia, Comoros, Congo, Costa Rica, Dominican Republic, Ecuador, Egypt, El Salvador, Equatorial Guinea, Ethiopia, Fiji, Gabon, Gambia, Ghana, Guinea, Guinea-Bissau, Guatemala, Guyana, Haiti, Hong Kong, Honduras, India, Indonesia, Iran, Iraq, Israel, Ivory Coast, Jamaica, Jordan, Kenya, Kuwait, Lesotho, Liberia, Libyan Arab Jamahiriya, Madagascar, Malawi, Mali, Malaysia, Mauritania, Mauritius, Mexico, Morocco, Mozambique, Namibia, Nepal, Nicaragua, Niger, Nigeria, Pakistan, Panama, Paraguay, Peru, Philippines, Republic of Korea, Réunion, Rwanda, Saudi Arabia, Senegal, Sierra Leone, Singapore, Somalia, Southern Rhodesia, Sri Lanka, Sudan, Surinam, Swaziland, Syrian Arab Republic, Thailand, Togo, Trinidad and Tobago, Tunisia, Uganda, United Republic of Cameroon, United Republic of Tanzania, Upper Volta, Uruguay, Venezuela, Zaire, Zambia.

Developed market economies: Australia, Austria, Belgium, Canada, Cyprus, Denmark, Finland, France, Germany, Federal Republic of, Greece, Iceland, Ireland, Italy, Japan, Luxembourg, Malta, Netherlands, Norway, New Zealand, Portugal, Puerto Rico, South Africa, Spain, Sweden, Switzerland, Turkey, United States of America, United Kingdom.

Centrally planned economies: Bulgaria, Czechoslovakia, German Democratic Republic, Hungary, Poland, Romania, Union of Soviet Socialist Republics.

[b] Annual compound rate calculated from the data for the year immediately preceding the time period indicated.

[c] Percentage of the combined population of the countries listed in foot-note *a* above.

[d] Data for output refer to net material product, which differs conceptually from, and is therefore not exactly comparable to, gross domestic product.

Council, "the new international development strategy should be
directed towards the objective of the establishment of the New
International Economic Order and within this framework should
encompass results achieved at major United Nations meetings and
conferences held during the Second United Nations Development
Decade on world economic and social problems".[4] The General
Assembly intends to adopt "the new international development
strategy for the 1980s" at a special session in 1980.[5]

It is only to be expected that the new international
development strategy will take into account the results of the
comparable strategies for the decades of the 1960s and 1970s. The
present paper therefore provides a broad assessment of the major
development trends since 1960 and, from this assessment, draws some
general implications for a new international development strategy.
The discussion is focused on a limited number of variables, namely,
those for which a reasonable amount of quantitative information is
available to permit valid intercountry comparisons. In order to
keep the presentation relatively compact, the emphasis in the paper
is on development issues, and the relevant conclusions are put
forward more as broad descriptions of the emerging patterns than as
systematic enumerations of the statistical results. The
statistical tables contained in the paper do, however, provide more
detail than might be apparent from a perusal of the text alone.

I. WIDENING DISPARITIES

In the 15-year period stretching from 1960 to the midpoint of
the Second United Nations Development Decade, the developing
countries sustained an average annual rate of increase in their
gross domestic product at constant prices of over 5.5 per cent.
From a rate of increase of 5.1 per cent a year over the first half
of the 1960s, the pace quickened to 5.8 per cent in the latter half
of that decade, and thus the record of economic growth in the 1960s
turned out to be better than had been anticipated in the General
Assembly's decision to designate it as the First United Nations
Development Decade. In the first half of the next decade, the
annual rate of economic growth was close to 6 per cent (see table
1). While not actually reaching the 6 per cent figure stipulated
for the 1970s as a whole in the International Development Strategy
for the Second United Nations Development Decade, the pace of
expansion achieved over the 15-year period as a whole was
by historical standards a remarkable one. It not only represented
substantial improvement over the rate of expansion achieved in
decades prior to 1960 by developing countries but it also compared
favourably with what had been achieved over a comparable time span
by the economically more advanced countries when they were
themselves in an earlier phase of development. The pace of
expansion compared favourably, too, with the rate of growth
registered by the developed market economies over the same 15 years
since 1960, and especially over the five years since 1970; but it

lagged behind the rate of growth of material production in the centrally planned economies of Europe.

Per capita gross production in developing countries increased by 2.5 per cent annually in the first half of the 1960s, and at above 3 per cent annually over the subsequent 10 years. In absolute figures, it increased from $169 in 1960 to $222 in 1970 and then to $260 in 1975, all expressed in the prices and rates of exchange prevailing in 1970.[6]

These figures, while showing the magnitude of the upward movement, provide in the very same instant a vivid illustration of the low absolute level of per capita gross domestic product still prevailing in the developing countries, especially when set against the level prevailing in the developed countries, as shown below (again expressed in 1970 dollars):

	1960	1965	1970	1975
Developing countries	169	190	222	260
Developed market economies	1,988	2,403	2,946	3,123

The ratio of about 12 to 1 between the average per capita product in the two groups of countries has remained nearly constant over the period, increasing slightly between 1960 and 1970, thus signifying a widening gulf between the two groups of countries, and then narrowing somewhat between 1970 and 1975;[7] but this small narrowing in recent years has to be seen against the fact that the developed market economies experienced a severe recession in 1974 and 1975. The absolute gap, as can be readily judged, widened in each of the five-year periods in question. Simply because it is very large, the absolute gap can be expected to widen in the foreseeable future. The danger is that, without requisite efforts, even the "modest beginning towards narrowing the gap" in relative terms as visualized in the International Development Strategy for the Second United Nations Development Decade[8] may turn out, in retrospect, to have been an elusive goal.

It should also be noted in this context that, given the nature of the conventional method (involving the use of official rates of exchange between currencies) by which the estimates of gross product of different countries are converted into a common measure (usually, the United States dollar) for purposes of intercountry comparisons or aggregation, the existing ratio of roughly 12 to 1 revealed by the figures is only a crude measure of the economic distance between the average incomes of developed and developing countries. Alternative methods of comparing gross domestic products across countries--based, for instance, on the purchasing power parities of currencies--suggest that the real distance is probably less.[9] Even so, the most typical style of life for the mass of people living in the developing countries is that of extreme poverty, and much remains to be done to raise their standards of living to a tolerable minimum.

Out of the total population of developing countries of around 1.6 billion at the outset of the present decade, roughly 1.2 billion lived in countries with a per capita gross domestic product in 1970 below the nominal $222 average for all developing countries, and a slightly smaller number (accounting for 70 per

TABLE 2. POPULATION AND GROWTH OF GROSS DOMESTIC PRODUCT, BY INCOME GROUPS OF DEVELOPING COUNTRIES, 1961-1975

Country group[a]	Population (1970)		Average annual rate of increase[b] in gross domestic product at constant prices (percentage)						
			Total				Per capita		
	Millions	Percentage share[c]	1961-1965	1966-1970	1971-1975		1961-1965	1966-1970	1971-1975
I. Countries with *per capita* gross domestic product in 1970 of less than $200	1 151	70.2	4.0	4.5	3.6		1.5	2.0	1.1
Petroleum-exporting countries	175	10.7	3.2	5.6	7.1		0.6	2.9	4.3
Other countries	976	59.5	4.2	4.4	3.0		1.6	1.8	0.5
II. Countries with *per capita* gross domestic product in 1970 of $200 or more but less than $400	222	13.5	5.2	5.7	6.0		2.5	2.9	3.2
Petroleum-exporting countries	30	1.8	3.6	6.2	7.5		0.9	2.6	4.1
Other countries	192	11.7	5.6	5.7	5.8		2.8	2.9	3.0
III. Countries with *per capita* gross domestic product in 1970 of $400 or more	266	16.2	5.9	6.7	7.5		3.0	3.9	4.6
Petroleum-exporting countries	51	3.1	8.1	8.6	11.1		5.1	5.5	7.9
Other countries	215	13.1	5.5	6.3	6.5		2.6	3.5	3.7
TOTAL	1 638	100.0	5.1	5.8	5.9		2.5	3.1	3.2
Petroleum-exporting countries	255	15.6	5.7	7.3	9.5		3.0	4.4	6.5
Other countries	1 383	84.4	5.0	5.5	5.2		2.4	2.8	2.5

Sources: See table 1.

[a] *Group I: petroleum-exporting countries*—Indonesia, Nigeria; *other countries*—Afghanistan, Bangladesh, Benin, Botswana, Burma, Burundi, Cape Verde, Central African Empire, Chad, Comoros, Ethiopia, Gambia, Guinea, Guinea-Bissau, Haiti, India, Kenya, Lesotho, Madagascar, Malawi, Mali, Mauritania, Nepal, Niger, Pakistan, Philippines, Rwanda, Sierra Leone, Somalia, Sri Lanka, Sudan, Thailand, Togo, Uganda, United Republic of Cameroon, United Republic of Tanzania, Upper Volta, Zaire.

Group II: petroleum-exporting countries—Algeria, Ecuador, Iraq; *other countries*—Angola, Bolivia, Colombia, Congo, Dominican Republic, Egypt, El Salvador, Equatorial Guinea, Ghana, Guatemala, Guyana, Honduras, Ivory Coast, Jordan, Liberia, Malaysia, Mauritius, Morocco, Mozambique, Nicaragua, Paraguay, Republic of Korea, Senegal, Southern Rhodesia, Swaziland, Syrian Arab Republic, Tunisia.

Group III: petroleum-exporting countries—Gabon, Iran, Kuwait, Libyan Arab Jamahiriya, Saudi Arabia, Trinidad and Tobago, Venezuela; *other countries*—Argentina, Barbados, Brazil, Chile, Costa Rica, Fiji, Hong Kong, Israel, Jamaica, Mexico, Namibia, Panama, Peru, Réunion, Singapore, Surinam, Uruguay, Zambia.

[b] Annual compound rate calculated from the data for the year immediately preceding the time period indicated.

[c] Percentage of the combined population of countries in groups I-III.

TABLE 3. POPULATION AND GROWTH OF GROSS DOMESTIC PRODUCT, BY DEVELOPING REGION, 1961-1975

Developing region[a]	Population (1970)		Average annual rate of increase[b] in gross domestic product at constant prices (percentage)						
			Total			Per capita			
	Millions	Percentage share[c]	1961-1965	1966-1970	1971-1975	1961-1965	1966-1970	1971-1975	
Africa	330	20.2	4.6	5.4	4.1	2.0	2.7	1.4	
Lower-income countries[d]	214	13.1	3.6	4.9	4.6	1.1	2.3	1.8	
	(159)	(9.7)	(3.0)	(4.3)	(3.4)	(0.4)	(1.7)	(0.8)	
Other countries	116	7.1	5.5	5.8	3.7	3.0	3.0	1.0	
Asia	1 039	63.4	5.1	5.7	6.3	2.4	3.0	3.6	
Lower-income countries[d]	933	56.9	4.2	4.5	3.4	1.6	1.8	0.9	
	(813)	(49.7)	(4.4)	(4.4)	(2.9)	(1.9)	(1.9)	(0.4)	
Other countries	106	6.5	7.6	8.7	11.5	4.6	5.8	8.6	
Latin America and the Caribbean	270	16.4	5.3	6.0	6.4	2.4	3.1	3.5	

Sources: See table 1.

[a] For a list of countries included in each group, see foot-note *a* to table 2.

[b] See foot-note *b* to table 2.

[c] Percentage of the combined population of countries in the three regions, as listed in foot-note *a* to table 2.

[d] Countries with a *per capita* gross domestic product in 1970 of less than $200; for a list of such countries included here, see foot-note *a* to table 2. Data in parentheses refer to lower-income countries excluding petroleum exporters.

cent of the total population) in countries with a per capita product of less than $200. Strikingly, it was precisely this group of the poorest countries in which the rate of increase in gross domestic product lagged, both in the 1960s and in the first half of the 1970s. Moreover, while the rate of increase accelerated over the three quinquennia for both the middle-income group (that is, the group comprising countries with per capita gross domestic product in 1970 of $200 or more but less than $400) and the higher-income group (that is, the group comprising countries with per capita product in 1970 of $400 or more, in some cases much more), the rate of increase for the lower-income group slowed down in the first half of the 1970s, to an annual rate of only 3.6 per cent as against the corresponding rates of 6 per cent and 7.5 per cent, respectively, for the other two groups (see table 2). The lower-income developing countries other than those that are net exporters of petroleum--mainly agrarian countries whose agricultural production expanded slowly in this period--recorded an annual rate of increase in gross domestic product of no more than 3 per cent. While the annual rate of increase in the first half of the 1970s averaged 5.9 per cent for developing countries as a whole, the corresponding figure for the petroleum exporters among them was 9.5 per cent.[10]

The disparate rates of increase in total gross domestic product are also reflected in the disparate rates of increase in per capita product. For the lower-income countries the rate of increase in per capita product came to below 2 per cent a year in the 1960s and not much more than 1 per cent a year in the first half of the 1970s (only 0.5 per cent a year if the petroleum-exporting countries in this group, Indonesia and Nigeria, are excluded). This compares with annual rates of increase for the middle- and higher-income groups of developing countries of about 2.7 per cent and 3.5 per cent, respectively, in the 1960s and 3.2 per cent and 4.6 per cent, respectively, in the first five years of the 1970s.

The record of lower-income countries showed no marked regional difference between Africa and Asia when the entire 15-year period is considered, but there were differences in the respective rhythms of growth within the period (see table 3). All but one of the countries with an annual per capita gross product of less than $200 are in fact situated in two large areas stretching across southern Asia and middle Africa. In these two "depressed regions of the world", as the Committee for Development Planning has put it, the problem of mass poverty and underdevelopment "is so extreme in terms of the human suffering it entails that it becomes a problem involving the conscience of the whole world".[11]

The effect of contrasting performance of different groups of developing countries may be summarized by the following figures of average per capita gross domestic product (expressed in 1970 dollars):

TABLE 4. AVERAGE ANNUAL RATE OF INCREASE IN TOTAL AND *PER CAPITA* REAL GROSS DOMESTIC INCOME,[a] BY INCOME GROUP OF DEVELOPING COUNTRIES, 1961-1975
(*Percentage*)

Country group[b]	Total			Per capita		
	1961-1965	1966-1970	1971-1975	1961-1965	1966-1970	1971-1975
I. Countries with *per capita* gross domestic product in 1970 of less than $200	3.9	4.5	4.5	1.4	1.9	1.9
Petroleum-exporting countries	2.6	5.6	13.8	0.1	3.0	10.9
Other countries	4.1	4.4	2.7	1.6	1.8	0.2
II. Countries with *per capita* gross domestic product in 1970 of $200 or more but less than $400	4.9	5.9	8.0	2.2	3.0	5.1
Petroleum-exporting countries	3.3	6.3	17.8	0.7	2.7	14.0
Other countries	5.2	5.8	5.7	2.5	3.0	3.0
III. Countries with *per capita* gross domestic product in 1970 of $400 or more	5.7	6.7	12.8	2.8	3.9	9.8
Petroleum-exporting countries	6.3	7.9	30.2	3.3	4.8	26.4
Other countries	5.5	6.4	6.3	2.6	3.6	3.5
TOTAL	4.9	5.8	9.4	2.3	3.1	6.5
Petroleum-exporting countries	4.6	7.0	24.6	1.9	4.1	21.2
Other countries	4.9	5.6	5.0	2.3	2.9	2.3

Sources: See table 1.

[a] Gross domestic product at constant (1970) prices, adjusted for changes in the terms of trade. See also foot-note *b* to table 2.

[b] For the list of countries included in each group, see foot-note *a* to table 2.

	1960	1965	1970	1975
Lower-income developing countries:				
Petroleum exporters	82	85	98	121
Others	93	100	110	112
Middle-income developing countries:				
Petroleum exporters	278	291	331	404
Others	207	237	274	318
Higher-income developing countries:				
Petroleum exporters	408	522	681	994
Others	487	554	658	789

Within the group of higher-income developing countries, there are a number whose per capita gross product is well above the average for the group; indeed, some of those countries--thanks to their resource endowments--have a per capita output higher than that of any of the developed countries.

The figures just cited, striking as they are, provide only a partial picture of the income disparities among developing countries. As a result of sharp changes in international prices, particularly in the first half of the 1970s, important divergences occurred in the rates of growth of real gross domestic product--that is, the quantum of goods and services produced--and real gross domestic income--that is, the gross domestic product adjusted for changes in the terms of trade. These divergences affected most particularly the relative positions of the petroleum exporters as against other developing countries. For the period as a whole, while the latter's rates of increase were virtually the same for both real product and real income, for the former the increase in real income was considerably faster (see table 4). The figures of per capita real domestic income for the different groups of developing countries, which are shown below (expressed in relation to 1970 dollars), indicate the relative gain made by petroleum exporters, especially those in the middle-income and higher-income groups of developing countries.

	1960	1965	1970	1975
Lower-income developing countries:				
Petroleum exporters	84	85	98	165
Others	93	100	110	110
Middle-income developing countries:				
Petroleum exporters	281	290	331	638
Others	209	236	274	316
Higher-income developing countries:				
Petroleum exporters	458	538	681	2,192
Others	484	551	658	783

TABLE 5. AVERAGE ANNUAL RATE OF INCREASE IN TOTAL AND *PER CAPITA* REAL GROSS DOMESTIC INCOME,[a] BY DEVELOPING REGION, 1961-1975

(Percentage)

Developing region[b]	Total			Per capita		
	1961-1965	1966-1970	1971-1975	1961-1965	1966-1970	1971-1975
Africa	4.4	5.6	7.8	1.9	2.9	5.0
Lower-income countries[c]	3.4	5.0	6.8	0.9	2.4	4.0
	(2.9)	(4.5)	(2.6)	(0.3)	(1.9)	(—)
Other countries	5.2	6.1	8.5	2.7	3.3	5.6
Asia	4.8	5.7	12.2	2.1	3.0	9.4
Lower-income countries[c]	4.0	4.5	3.9	1.5	1.9	1.4
	(4.3)	(4.4)	(2.7)	(1.8)	(1.8)	(0.2)
Other countries	7.0	8.5	24.3	4.0	5.6	21.0
Latin America and the Caribbean	5.1	6.0	7.2	2.2	3.1	4.3

Sources: See table 1.

[a,b] See corresponding foot-notes to table 4.

[c] For definition of lower-income countries, see foot-note *d* to table 3. Data in parentheses refer to lower-income countries excluding petroleum exporters.

TABLE 6. AVERAGE ANNUAL RATE OF INCREASE[a] IN *PER CAPITA* PRIVATE CONSUMPTION AT CONSTANT PRICES, BY INCOME GROUP OF DEVELOPING COUNTRIES, 1961-1975
(*Percentage*)

Country group[b]	1961-1965	1966-1970	1971-1975
I. Countries with *per capita* gross domestic product in 1970 of less than $200	0.5	1.3	1.4
Petroleum-exporting countries	-0.1	1.8	5.3
Other countries	0.6	1.2	0.7
II. Countries with *per capita* gross domestic product in 1970 of $200 or more but less than $400	1.8	2.4	3.2
Petroleum-exporting countries	0.5	1.0	7.1
Other countries	2.1	2.6	2.5
III. Countries with *per capita* gross domestic product in 1970 of $400 or more	2.4	3.7	4.4
Petroleum-exporting countries	1.8	4.8	10.6
Other countries	2.5	3.5	3.3
TOTAL	1.6	2.6	3.2
Petroleum-exporting countries	0.9	3.1	8.3
Other countries	1.8	2.5	2.2

Sources: See table 1.
[a] See foot-note *b* to table 2.
[b] For a list of countries included in each group, see foot-note *a* to table 2.

TABLE 7. AVERAGE ANNUAL RATE OF INCREASE[a] IN *PER CAPITA* PRIVATE CONSUMPTION AT CONSTANT PRICES, BY DEVELOPING REGION, 1961-1975

(*Percentage*)

Developing region[b]	1961-1965	1966-1970	1971-1975
Africa	0.8	1.6	2.2
Lower-income countries[c]	0.1	1.3	2.3
	(0.3)	(0.7)	(0.8)
Other countries	1.6	2.0	2.1
Asia	1.1	2.1	6.0
Lower-income countries[c]	0.6	1.3	1.2
	(0.7)	(1.4)	(0.7)
Other countries	2.8	4.8	8.5
Latin America and the Caribbean	2.2	3.2	3.2

Sources: See table 1.

[a] See foot-note *b* to table 2.

[b] For a list of countries included in each group, see foot-note *a* to table 2.

[c] For definition of lower-income countries, see foot-note *d* to table 3. Data in parentheses refer to lower-income countries excluding petroleum exporters.

The effect of terms-of-trade changes on the various developing regions also differed considerably, in large part due to the particular regional configuration of petroleum exporters. By comparison with the other regions, Asia experienced a very high rate of increase in real income during the first half of the 1970s. But this pattern was dominated by the experience of West Asian countries (mainly petroleum exporters); in the lower-income Asian countries, which are situated in the southern half of the continent, real income increased slowly in the first half of the 1970s--by less than 1.5 per cent yearly on a per capita basis. Even the averages for the lower-income countries are strongly influenced by the petroleum exporters among them. If petroleum exporters are excluded, the lower-income countries of both Africa and Asia recorded a nil or nominal annual increase in per capita income in the first half of the 1970s (see the figures in parentheses in table 5).

Differences in the rates of growth of per capita real gross domestic product and income were responsible also for differences among countries in rates of increase in private consumption, the most immediate indicator of current changes in the level of material well-being (see tables 6 and 7). Particularly high rates of increase in consumption were recorded during the first half of the 1970s by petroleum exporters. At the same time, it may be noted that for the various groups of countries, whether for petroleum exporters or others, or for lower-, medium- or higher-income developing countries, per capita consumption rose less quickly than per capita real income, thus leaving a greater margin for financing investment and meeting the factor payments on past investments financed with external resources. Only in the poorest group--excluding petroleum exporters--did the per capita increase in consumption, meagre as it was, move ahead of the increase in income during the first half of the 1970s. This implied an increasing relative dependence on external resources for financing of capital formation.

II. RISING POPULATION AND URBANIZATION

The preceding discussion has indicated that the annual increase in per capita gross domestic product in developing countries since 1960, though remarkable by historical standards, has by no means been spectacular or sufficient to meet the requirements of most of those countries. In the developing countries other than those that are net exporters of petroleum, the annual increase in the 15 years since 1960 amounted to less than 3 per cent, and in the lower-income countries among them it averaged less than 1.5 per cent (see table 2). Part of the explanation for the modest or small annual increase in average output or income lies in the rapid expansion of population that has been taking place in much of the developing world.

The population of developing countries as a whole has

TABLE 8. DISTRIBUTION AND INCREASE IN POPULATION OF DEVELOPING COUNTRIES, 1961-1975

Country group[a] or region	Number (1970)		Average annual rate of increase[b] (percentage)		
	Millions	Percentage distribution[c]	1961-1965	1966-1970	1971-1975
By income group of developing countries					
I. Countries with *per capita* gross domestic product in 1970 of less than $200	1 145	69.3	2.51	2.55	2.56
II. Countries with *per capita* gross domestic product in 1970 of $200 or more but less than $400	239	14.5	2.68	2.73	2.68
III. Countries with *per capita* gross domestic product in 1970 of more than $400	268	16.2	2.81	2.73	2.77
TOTAL	1 652	100.0	2.58	2.61	2.61
By developing region					
Africa	327	19.8	2.50	2.60	2.67
Low-income countries[d]	212	12.8	2.52	2.56	2.67
Other countries	115	6.9	2.45	2.69	2.67
Asia	1 055	63.9	2.55	2.56	2.55
Low-income countries[d]	928	56.2	2.51	2.55	2.55
Other countries	127	7.7	2.83	2.62	2.59
Latin America and the Caribbean	270	16.3	2.82	2.79	2.79

Source: Centre for Development Planning, Projections and Policies of the Department of Economic and Social Affairs of the United Nations Secretariat, based on data from the Population Division of the Department.

[a] *Group I*: Afghanistan, Bangladesh, Benin, Burma, Burundi, Central African Empire, Chad, Democratic Kampuchea, Ethiopia, Gambia, Guinea, Haiti, India, Indonesia, Kenya, Lesotho, Madagascar, Malawi, Mali, Mauritania, Niger, Nigeria, Pakistan, Philippines, Rwanda, Sierra Leone, Somalia, Sri Lanka, Sudan, Thailand, Togo, Uganda, United Republic of Cameroon, United Republic of Tanzania, Upper Volta, Zaire.

Group II: Algeria, Angola, Bolivia, Colombia, Congo, Dominican Republic, Ecuador, Egypt, El Salvador, Ghana, Guatemala, Guyana, Honduras, Iraq, Ivory Coast, Jordan, Liberia, Malaysia, Mauritius, Morocco, Mozambique, Nicaragua, Paraguay, Republic of Korea, Republic of Viet-Nam (now part of Viet Nam), Senegal, Southern Rhodesia, Swaziland, Syrian Arab Republic, Tunisia.

Group III: Argentina, Barbados, Brazil, Chile, Costa Rica, Fiji,

TABLE 8. *(continued)*

Gabon, Hong Kong, Iran, Israel, Jamaica, Kuwait, Lebanon, Libyan Arab Jamahiriya, Mexico, Panama, Peru, Saudi Arabia, Singapore, Surinam, Trinidad and Tobago, Uruguay, Venezuela, Zambia.

[b] Annual compound rate calculated from the data for the year immediately preceding the year indicated.

[c] Percentage of the combined population of groups I-III.

[d] Countries with *per capita* gross domestic product in 1970 of less than $200. For names of such countries, see foot-note *a* above.

been increasing yearly at about 2.6 per cent since 1960. The annual rate of increase has tended to be somewhat smaller in the lower-income developing countries, and somewhat higher in the middle-income and higher-income developing countries (see table 8). For developing countries as a whole, the rate of increase was slightly higher in the first half of the 1970s than in the corresponding period of the preceding decade.

In Asia, the densely populated region which has more than three fifths of the people of all developing countries, the rate of increase of population has been somewhat below the over-all average for developing countries. It has been somewhat above the average of Africa, which accounts for about a fifth of the population of the developing world. Population growth in Africa, moreover, has tended to accelerate; the annual rate of expansion rose from 2.5 per cent during the first half of the 1960s to nearly 2.7 per cent during the first half of the 1970s. In Latin America and the Caribbean, the annual rate during the first half of the 1970s was almost 2.8 per cent, only fractionally smaller than what it was a decade earlier.[12]

An important assumption of the International Development Strategy adopted in 1970 was that the average annual increase in the population of the developing countries as a whole during the period 1971-1980 would be 2.5 per cent.[13] It is evident from the preceding two paragraphs that this assumption has not been borne out by the trends recorded so far in the 1970s. Some developing countries have registered a significant slackening in the pace of their population growth, but some have also experienced a significant acceleration. For the developing countries as a whole, a slowing down of population increase is yet to come.

The clue to the continued surge in the population of developing countries is to be found in the trends in rates of death and birth. By virtue of a variety of health and sanitation measures, developing countries have continued to achieve substantial declines in death-rates. Between the first half of the 1960s and the first half of the 1970s, the number of deaths per 1,000 persons is estimated too have declined from 23.1 to 19.8 in Africa, from 20.2 to 16.7 in Asia, and from 11.2 to 9.2 in Latin America and the Caribbean. On the average, the crude death-rate in Latin American and the Caribbean is now about as low as that in developed countries. Between the same two time periods, the number of births per 1,000 persons appears to have declined from 47.7 to 46.3 in Africa, from 44.8 to 41.9 in Asia, and 39.5 to 36.9 in Latin American and the Caribbean. The crude birth-rate in each of these three developing regions is still more than twice as large as the corresponding average for developed countries.[14] Evidently, the death-rates in developing regions of the world are close to reaching a low magnitude beyond which a further decline may not be possible, but their birthrates have a long way to decline in order to equal the low average for developed countries.

Thanks to continuing improvement of health, life expectancy has been increasing significantly in developing countries. Between the first half of the 1960s and the first half of the 1970s, average life expectancy increased from 40.8 to 45 years in Africa, from 44.6 to 48.5 years in Asia, and from 57.7 to 61.4 years in

TABLE 9. DISTRIBUTION AND INCREASE IN URBAN AND RURAL POPULATION OF DEVELOPING COUNTRIES, 1961-1975

Country group[a] and population group	Number (1970) Millions	Percentage distribution[c]	Average annual rate of increase[b] (percentage)		
			1961-1965	1966-1970	1971-1975
By income group of developing countries					
I. Countries with *per capita* gross domestic product in 1970 of less than $200					
Urban population	207	18.1	3.89	4.25	4.39
Rural population	937	81.9	2.25	2.20	2.14
II. Countries with *per capita* gross domestic product in 1970 of $200 or more but less than $400[d]					
Urban population	88	37.0	4.99	5.14	4.68
Rural population	150	63.0	1.60	1.44	1.44
III. Countries with *per capita* gross domestic product in 1970 of more than $400					
Urban population	154	57.4	4.58	4.35	4.01
Rural population	114	42.6	1.00	0.77	0.99
TOTAL					
Urban population	449	27.2	4.33	4.46	4.23
Rural population	1 202	72.8	2.04	1.96	1.95
By developing region					
Africa					
Urban population	66	20.2	4.94	5.25	5.16
Rural population	261	79.8	2.02	2.03	2.01
Asia[d]					
Urban population	230	21.8	4.06	4.30	4.25
Rural population	824	78.1	2.18	2.10	2.06

TABLE 9. *(continued)*

Country group[a] and population group	Number (1970)		Average annual rate of increase[b] (percentage)		
	Millions	Percentage distribution[c]	1961-1965	1966-1970	1971-1975
Latin America and the Caribbean					
Urban population	153	56.8	4.50	4.37	4.06
Rural population	117	43.2	1.13	0.90	1.02

Source: See table 8.
[a-b] See corresponding foot-notes to table 8.
[c] Percentage of the population of the country group indicated.
[d] The sum of urban and rural population for this group falls somewhat short of the corresponding total shown in table 8 owing to incomplete information for the Republic of Korea.

Latin America and the Caribbean.[14] Although these regional averages inevitably conceal intercountry differences, they do provide a strong indication of continuing divergences in the records of various parts of the developing world. There is ample evidence that life expectancy is still quite low in many countries of the two "depressed regions" of the world, namely, middle Africa and southern Asia.

The demographic trends experienced by developing countries in recent years indicate that, until birth-rates in these countries decline significantly, their population will continue to increase at a high rate. Indeed, the current development plans of many of these countries have been based on the assumption that population expansion during the second half of the 1970s will be rapid.[15] A continuing high rate of increase in population would have far-reaching implications for material production, for services that have a bearing on the quality of life and for mobilization and allocation of resources to satisfy the burgeoning requirements. The wide variety of strains and imbalances that might emerge in the economies of these countries would pose serious challenges to policy makers.

The rapid increase in population has magnified the demand for jobs and has accentuated the search for a better life in the cities. Thus, urban population has been increasing at a much faster rate than rural population in developing countries. During the first half of the 1970s, for example, urban population expanded more than twice as fast as rural population in the lower income developing countries, more than three times as fast in the middle-income developing countries and more than four times as fast in the higher-income developing countries (see table 9).

This contrasting pattern is also reflected in the regional averages. In the developing regions of Asia and Africa, urban population expanded during the first half of the 1970s by two and two-and-a-half times as fast, respectively, as rural population, while in Latin Americaand the Caribbean, it expanded four times as fast. At the outset of the 1970s, about 57 per cent of the people in Latin America and the Caribbean were living in urban areas, while the corresponding proportion in the developing regions of Asia and Africa amounted to 22 per cent and 20 per cent, respectively. The trends experienced in recent years suggest that by 1980 the proportion will have risen significantly in all developing regions, but the contrast among the regions in this regard will still be sharp.

Rapid urbanization has created a variety of strains and social costs. These have been notably evident in the growth of slums and shanty towns, in the pressing demand for schools and hospitals, in the overloading of transportation facilities.

In the wake of a rapid increase in population, the average annual increase in labour force of developing countries as a whole accelerated from 1.9 per cent during the first half of the 1960s to 2.2 per cent during the first half of the 1970s. The annual rate of increase during the first half of the 1970s amounted to about 2.1 per cent in the lower-income developing countries and to about 2.6 per cent and 2.7 per cent in the middle-income and the higher-income developing countries, respectively. In geographical

TABLE 10. DISTRIBUTION AND INCREASE IN LABOUR FORCE OF DEVELOPING COUNTRIES, 1961-1975

Country group[a]	Number (1970)		Average annual rate of increase[b] (percentage)		
	Millions	Percentage distribution[c]	1961-1965	1966-1970	1971-1975
By income group of developing countries					
I. Countries with *per capita* gross domestic product in 1970 of less than $200	460	74.0	1.77	2.02	2.07
II. Countries with *per capita* gross domestic product in 1970 of $200 or more but less than $400	78	12.5	2.03	2.39	2.55
III. Countries with *per capita* gross domestic product in 1970 of more than $400	84	13.5	2.35	2.49	2.71
TOTAL	622	100.0	1.88	2.13	2.21
By developing region					
Africa	129	20.7	2.00	2.16	2.17
Low-income countries[d]	92	14.8	2.04	2.21	2.11
Other countries	36	5.9	1.91	2.05	2.31
Asia	408	65.6	1.75	2.05	2.11
Low-income countries[d]	366	58.8	1.70	1.98	2.06
Other countries	42	6.8	2.19	2.59	2.57
Latin America and the Caribbean	85	13.7	2.29	2.48	2.77

Source: See table 8.

[a-d] See corresponding foot-notes to table 8.

TABLE 11. DISTRIBUTION AND INCREASE IN MAJOR COMPONENTS OF THE LABOUR FORCE OF DEVELOPING COUNTRIES, 1961-1975

Country group[a] and activity	Number (1970)		Average annual rate of increase[b] (percentage)		
	Millions	Percentage distribution[c]	1961-1965	1966-1970	1971-1975
By income group of developing countries					
I. Countries with *per capita* gross domestic product in 1970 of less than $200					
Agriculture	310	67	0.90	1.12	1.01
Industry	64	14	4.22	4.15	4.61
Services	86	19	3.88	3.95	3.75
II. Countries with *per capita* gross domestic product in 1970 of $200 or more but less than $400					
Agriculture	46	59	1.00	1.29	1.19
Industry	11	15	4.24	4.21	4.70
Services	20	26	3.77	4.07	4.23
III. Countries with *per capita* gross domestic product in 1970 of more than $400					
Agriculture	33	40	0.90	0.98	0.92
Industry	20	24	3.68	3.74	3.98
Services	31	36	3.39	3.50	3.62
TOTAL					
Agriculture	389	63	0.91	1.12	1.02
Industry	96	15	4.10	4.07	4.49
Services	137	22	3.75	3.87	3.79
By developing region					
Africa					
Agriculture	95	74	1.34	1.52	1.38
Industry	13	10	4.49	4.13	4.65
Services	21	16	4.10	4.12	4.00
Asia					
Agriculture	258	63	0.75	1.00	0.88

TABLE 11. (continued)

Country group[a] and activity	Number (1970)		Average annual rate of increase[b] (percentage)		
	Millions	Percentage distribution[c]	1961-1965	1966-1970	1971-1975
Industry	64	16	4.16	4.13	4.57
Services	86	21	3.80	3.91	3.78
Latin America and the Caribbean					
Agriculture	36	42	0.97	1.01	1.13
Industry	19	23	3.68	3.83	4.12
Services	30	35	3.39	3.53	3.71

[a-b] See corresponding foot-notes to table 8.   [c] See foot-note c to table 9.

Source: See table 8.

terms, the annual rate during this period was 2.1 per cent in Asia, nearly 2.2 per cent in Africa and about 2.8 per cent in Latin America and the Caribbean (see table 10). The current indications are that the rate is likely to accelerate generally in developing countries. The projections made by the International Labour Organisation put the average annual rate of increase in labour force of developing countries as a whole during the 1980s at 2.5 per cent.

Experience has shown that productivity--that is, output per workers--tends to increase generally by 3 to 4 per cent per annum. This suggests that a 6 per cent yearly growth of gross domestic product in the coming decade may not be sufficient to absorb the new entrants into the labour force and at the same time make a significant impact on the backlog of unemployment in developing countries. By the same token, a 6 per cent annual rate of economic growth may not be sufficient to accelerate the increase in their per capita income or the rise in their average standard of living.

Because urban population has been expanding much faster than rural population, the labour force seeking entry into industrial and service activities has also been expanding much faster than its counterpart in rural activities (see table 11). Clearly, therefore, industrial and service activities will need to acquire a dynamic thrust if the social ailments currently prevailing in developing countries are to be alleviated. The development plans and policies for the 1980s will need to be fully cognizant of the emerging needs in this regard.

III. SEARCH FOR A BETTER QUALITY OF LIFE

Rapid increases in population, rising incomes and heightened expectations have all reinforced the search for a better quality of life in developing countries. The search can be seen in the endeavours of these countries to expand and improve housing, health facilities and systems of education and training.

On housing conditions in developing countries, unfortunately, the available quantitative information is far too meagre to permit a meaningful assessment of trends since 1960. All that can be said, on the basis of a few case studies and general observations, is that housing conditions remain very deficient in most developing countries. Indeed, in the lower-income countries among them, the situation continues to be grave. In the rural areas of developing countries, the typical abode of people has not changed much from what it was decades ago. Rapid urbanization, on the other hand, has often led to glaring contrasts: while large income disparities within countries have stimulated the rise of luxury housing for a minority of the people, the housing situation for a majority of them has not improved significantly or has even worsened.

Some improvement has been recorded in the supply of piped water to occupied dwellings and in the development of

TABLE 12. INDICATORS OF HEALTH FACILITIES IN DEVELOPING COUNTRIES, 1960 AND 1970

Country group[a]	Population per physician		Population per nurse		Population per hospital bed	
	1960	1970	1960	1970	1960	1970
I. *Lower-income developing countries*						
Those with *per capita* gross national product in 1970 of $100 or less	26 754	21 821	8 064	8 243	2 161	1 883
Those with *per capita* gross national product in 1970 of $101-$200	9 413	8 879	4 284	2 980	1 328	1 228
II. *Middle-income developing countries:* those with *per capita* gross national product in 1970 of $201-$375	3 950	3 437	3 480	1 794	607	500
III. *Higher-income developing countries:* those with *per capita* gross national product in 1970 of $376-$1,000[b]	2 093	1 729	1 790	1 508	425	406

Source: World Bank, *World Tables, 1976* (Baltimore, Johns Hopkins University Press, 1976), pp. 518-521.

[a] Data in each case refer to adjusted group average, which is defined as the population-weighted geometric mean derived for each indicator from a group of countries for which data relating to both 1960 and 1970 are available (but excluding the largest countries and extreme indicator values). For further details, see the World Bank publication mentioned above.

[b] Including some that are not conventionally listed as developing countries in United Nations reports.

TABLE 13. INDICATORS OF NUTRITION IN DEVELOPING COUNTRIES, 1960 AND 1970

Country group[a]	Per capita calorie supply (percentage of requirements)		Per capita protein supply (grams per day)	
	1960	1970	1960	1970
I. *Lower-income developing countries*				
Those with per capita gross national product in 1970 of $100 or less	88.4	89.7	54.0	56.5
Those with per capita gross national product in 1970 of $101-$200	92.8	98.1	55.2	57.7
II. *Middle-income developing countries:* those with per capita gross national product in 1970 of $201-$375	88.9	98.8	52.9	59.3
III. *Higher-income developing countries:* those with per capita gross national product in 1970 of $376-$1,000[b]	100.8	103.2	65.7	68.2

Source: See table 12.

[a,b] See corresponding foot-notes to table 12.

TABLE 14. INDICATORS OF EDUCATION IN DEVELOPING COUNTRIES, 1960 AND 1970

Country group[a]	Adjusted school-enrolment ratio				Vocational enrolment as percentage of secondary enrolment[d]	
	Primary[b]		Secondary[c]			
	1960	1970	1960	1970	1960	1970
I. *Lower-income developing countries*						
Those with *per capita* gross national product in 1970 of $100 or less	24.1	38.0	2.8	6.9	8.4	6.9
Those with *per capita* gross national product in 1970 of $101-$200	40.2	48.2	5.7	8.8	7.7	4.3
II. *Middle-income developing countries:* those with *per capita* gross national product in 1970 of $201-$375	72.1	85.8	12.8	23.3	17.0	12.7
III. *Higher-income developing countries:* those with *per capita* gross national product in 1970 of $376-$1,000[e]	78.8	94.4	17.0	33.7	15.7	14.5

Source: See table 12.

[a] See foot-note *a* to table 12.

[b] Enrolment of all ages in primary schools as percentage of primary-school age, adjusted to take into account differences in national systems of education.

[c] Enrolment of all ages in secondary schools as percentage of secondary-school age, adjusted to take into account differences in national systems of education.

[d] Vocational enrolment as percentage of total secondary education (general, vocational and teacher training).

[e] See foot-note *b* to table 12.

sewage-disposal systems. But such improvement has been confined largely to urban areas. And even so, the intercountry differences remain sharp.

The available information on aspects of health, though by no means complete, is detailed enough to demonstrate that significant progress has been made. For example, as already mentioned, death-rates have been declining and average life expectancy has been increasing in developing countries. Through concerted national and international efforts--the most notable among the latter being the eradication programme launched in 1967 by the World Health Organization--smallpox has been virtually eliminated. Similarly, the incidence of malaria was greatly diminished during the 1960s, but a recrudescence of this disease is reported to have taken place in certain areas in recent years.

Improvements in health have been made possible in part by expansion of health facilities. The numbers of physicians, nurses and hospital beds have generally been increasing faster than population in developing countries. As a result, the ratio of population to each of these instruments of better health has usually been falling (see table 12). The ratio, however, varies a great deal among countries. It is very high in the lower-income developing countries, and progressively lower in higher-income groups of countries.[16] The disparities among individual countries are, of course, far greater than those indicated by group averages. The current development plans of countries envisage significant further expansion of health facilities in relation to population, but even so it appears that large disparities will continue to prevail in the foreseeable future.

Similar conclusions emerge from nutrition indicators. For example, <u>per capita</u> calorie supply and <u>per capita</u> protein supply have increased significantly in developing countries in recent years; but the average supply varies among countries, being significantly lower in the lower-income countries (see table 13). However, the differences among developing countries in regard to calorie supply and protein supply are not great; and, through suitable policies, including measures to promote the use of nutritive but inexpensive food-stuffs available in developing countries, it should be possible to raise levels of nutrition and diminish intercountry differences.

Progress is also being made with regard to education. Ratios of student enrolment to population of relevant age groups have generally been increasing at primary, secondary and tertiary levels of education in developing countries. Again, however, intercountry differences continue to be sharp. For example, higher-income developing countries in general are close to reaching full enrolment at the primary level, but most lower-income developing countries have a long way to go to reach that level (see table 14). Similarly, considerable differences prevail among countries in respect of enrolment at higher levels of education.

Developing countries have adopted a variety of measures to expand and strengthen their systems of education. The measures have involved revision of curricula in order to make education development oriented, to reduce urban/rural and male/female disparities and to alleviate wastage caused by dropping out of

TABLE 15. CHANGE IN AGRICULTURAL PRODUCTION, BY INCOME GROUP OF DEVELOPING COUNTRIES, 1966-1975[a]

Country group[b]	Average annual rate of increase at constant market prices[c] (percentage)				Ratio of agricultural production to gross domestic product (percentage)		
	Agricultural production[d]		Gross domestic product		Average annual change in ratio		
	1966-1970	1971-1975	1966-1970	1971-1975	1966-1970	1971-1975	Ratio, 1975
I. Countries with *per capita* gross domestic product in 1970 of less than $200	2.4	1.4	4.0	3.9	−0.7	−1.0	38.6
II. Countries with *per capita* gross domestic product in 1970 of $200 or more but less than $400	2.8	3.4	6.2	6.8	−0.9	−0.8	22.5
III. Countries with *per capita* gross domestic product in 1970 of $400 or more	2.9	4.9	6.7	7.7	−0.5	−0.3	10.8
TOTAL	2.6	2.6	5.7	6.3	−0.8	−0.8	20.9

Sources: See table 1.

[a] Agricultural production refers to value added in agriculture (including animal husbandry), hunting, forestry and fishing.
Estimates are based on country data which are in some cases available only in terms of fiscal years beginning or ending in the calendar years shown here. For some countries data for 1975 are preliminary and subject to revision.

[b] Group I: *Africa*—Burundi, Cape Verde, Central African Empire, Chad, Comoros, Ethiopia, Gambia, Guinea, Guinea-Bissau, Kenya, Madagascar, Mauritania, Niger, Nigeria, Somalia, Togo, Uganda, Upper Volta, United Republic of Cameroon, United Republic of Tanzania; *Asia*—Burma, India, Indonesia, Pakistan, Philippines, Sri Lanka, Thailand. Group II: *Africa*—Algeria, Angola, Congo, Ghana, Morocco, Mozambique, Senegal, Swaziland, Tunisia; *Asia*—Iraq, Republic of Korea, Syrian Arab Republic; *Latin America and Caribbean*—Bolivia, Colombia, Dominican Republic, El Salvador, Ecuador, Honduras, Nicaragua, Paraguay. Group III: *Africa*—Libyan Arab Jamahiriya, Namibia, Réunion, Zambia; *Asia*—Iran, Saudi Arabia, Singapore; *Latin America and Caribbean*—Argentina, Brazil, Chile, Jamaica, Mexico, Panama, Peru, Trinidad and Tobago, Uruguay, Venezuela.

[c] Annual compound rate calculated from the data for the year immediately preceding the time period indicated.

TABLE 15. *(continued)*

^d For the following countries the data refer to original estimates of value added at current prices to which a gross domestic product deflator has been applied: Angola, Burundi, Central African Empire, Chad, Congo, Guinea, Madagascar, Mozambique, Niger, Senegal.

For the following countries values at constant market prices have been estimated from data on (gross) domestic product at factor cost: Algeria, Bhutan, Brazil, Burundi, Cape Verde, Central African Empire, Chad, Congo, Comoros, Ethiopia, Gambia, Ghana, Guinea, Guinea-Bissau, Honduras, India, Indonesia, Iran, Iraq, Lesotho, Libyan Arab Jamahiriya, Madagascar, Mauritania, Morocco, Mozambique, Namibia, Niger, Nigeria, Pakistan, Panama, Réunion, Senegal, Singapore, Somalia, Sri Lanka, Swaziland, Togo, Tunisia, Trinidad and Tobago, Uganda, United Republic of Cameroon, United Republic of Tanzania, Upper Volta, Uruguay.

^e Derived from data showing the sum of value added in the different sectors of economic activity. Rates of increase shown here may diverge somewhat from those shown in tables 1-3; the latter are derived from data on expenditure on the gross domestic product. The country coverage is smaller in the case of data on the sectoral origin of economic activity, and for some countries the data are incomplete, preliminary or cover a slightly different time period.

students from enrolment or by their repetition of grades. Such problems, however, continue to persist in varying degree.

An important area of concern for developing countries is vocational education. The ratio of vocational enrolment to secondary enrolment has generally tended to decline in these countries (see table 14), while the demand for trained persons to fill middle-level technical jobs has been mounting rapidly. The shortages of mechanics, foremen and other similar personnel are widespread in developing countries, even in some of those that have adequate numbers of higher-level professional persons, such as engineers and scientists. Improvement in education and training is an important fruit of economic growth, but education and training must also help to achieve and sustain economic growth by an efficient and rational use of the available productive capacity. This duality continues to be a major challenge to planners and policy makers in developing countries.

IV. LAGGING AGRICULTURAL PRODUCTION

Because agriculture bulks large and plays a pervasive role in the economies of most developing countries, the course of agricultural activity has usually had a profound influence on the expansion and diversification of those economies. In developing countries as a group, value added in agriculture, fishing, hunting and forestry (hereafter, for brevity, referred to as agricultural production) increased annually on the average by 2.6 per cent during both the second half of the 1960s and the first half of the 1970s, an annual rate well below the target of 4 per cent specified in the International Development Strategy (see table 15).[17] Since population also expanded yearly by 2.6 per cent, agricultural production per inhabitant recorded no increase at all for developing countries as a group. The stagnation or decline in per capita agricultural production experienced by many developing countries has had a deleterious effect not only on the course of production in general but also on the course of employment and income distribution.

Agricultural production has lagged especially badly in the lower-income developing countries, increasing yearly by no more than 1.4 per cent during the first half of the 1970s as against 2.4 per cent during the preceding quinquennium. This implies that there was a substantial decline in per capita output. Since these lower-income countries are predominantly agrarian, the lag in agricultural production has naturally circumscribed the possibilities of their over-all economic expansion. Slow growth of this major activity has been directly responsible for the slow pace of over-all economic growth. Lack of dynamism in agriculture has also restricted the availability of investment and foreign exchange resources for other sectors of the economy and, through the various links of the agricultural sector with the rest of the economy on both the demand and supply side, has affected adversely the entire

TABLE 16. CHANGE IN AGRICULTURAL PRODUCTION, BY DEVELOPING REGIONS, 1966-1975[a]

Developing region[b]	Average annual rate of increase at constant market prices[c] (percentage)				Ratio of agricultural production to gross domestic product (percentage)		
	Agricultural production[d]		Gross domestic product[e]		Average annual change in ratio		
	1966-1970	1971-1975	1966-1970	1971-1975	1966-1970	1971-1975	Ratio, 1975
Africa	2.4	1.9	6.7	3.7	−1.5	−0.5	29.5
Lower-income countries[f]	2.8	1.5	5.4	4.8	−1.2	−1.4	39.2
Other countries	1.8	2.7	7.7	2.8	−1.4	—	21.1
Asia	2.6	2.5	5.0	6.9	−0.9	−1.4	29.8
Lower-income countries[f]	2.3	1.4	3.7	3.6	−0.6	−0.9	38.4
Other countries[g]	4.0	8.7	9.4	14.7	−1.1	−0.9	14.7
Latin America and the Caribbean	2.9	3.4	6.0	6.4	−0.4	−0.4	11.8

Sources: See table 1.

[a-e] See corresponding foot-notes to table 15.

[f] Countries with a *per capita* gross domestic product in 1970 of less than $200; for the list of lower-income countries included in each developing region, see foot-note *b* to table 15.

[g] Figures based on limited sample; see foot-note *b* to table 15.

process of diversification and transition from an agrarian to an industrial society. The share of agriculture in total gross domestic product has of course been falling in the lower-income developing countries no less fast than in most other developing countries, thus giving the superficial impression that the process of diversification was maintaining momentum throughout the developing world. But in the lower-income developing countries these figures imply not a dynamic diversification but rather a precarious balance in which a slow rate of increase in gross domestic product has gone hand in hand with an even slower rate of increase or, during the first half of the 1970s, with even a decline in per capita terms in agricultural production.

The low rate of increase in agricultural production affected the lower-income countries in both Africa and Asia (see table 16). The rate of increase in production recorded during the second half of the 1960s was just sufficient to exceed the rate of increase in population in Africa and not quite sufficient in Asia. In both regions the rate of increase in production of lower-income countries slowed dramatically during the first half of the 1970s, to a rate well below the rate of population increase. Part of that decline in both regions resulted from highly adverse climatic conditions: the prolonged drought across the middle of Africa which affected the Sudano-Sahelian countries and East Africa, and the three successive weather-induced poor harvests in South Asia during 1972/73-1974-75. But, bearing in mind that the period 1966-1975 also witnessed what has come to be known as the Green Revolution, the slow progress during this 10-year period in a sector accounting for around two fifths of the total output of the lower-income developing countries is highly disturbing. In Africa, the slow agricultural progress has only partly been redeemed, as the rates of increase in gross domestic product show, by the relative buoyancy of industry--a buoyancy that was possible only because of the embryonic state of the manufacturing sector in lower-income African countries, and the relatively significant impact of new mining activity.

The more rapid rates of agricultural growth in the period as a whole were registered by the middle-and higher-income developing countries, particularly those in Asia and in Latin America and the Caribbean. Over the whole period since 1965, the middle- and higher-income developing countries of Asia taken together and, in the first half of the 1970s, the higher-income developing countries taken as a whole, were the only groups to reach the 4 per cent annual increase suggested in the International Development Strategy for agricultural output in developing countries as a whole.

Progress among countries within the middle- and higher-income groups was by no means uniform--far less indeed than among the lower-income countries. But, in general, the countries in which agricultural production increased fastest tended to be those in which the agricultural sector was relatively small in terms of its contribution to both over-all output and employment. By and large, these were the countries with either better diversified economies and a relatively more highly productive agriculture--including many smaller countries that had developed their economies with the help of imported food--or those with the ability to channel resources

TABLE 17. EXPANSION OF PRODUCTION AND APPARENT CONSUMPTION[a] OF CEREALS, BY INCOME GROUP OF DEVELOPING COUNTRIES, 1961-1965 TO 1971-1975
(*Percentage*)

Country group[b]	Average annual rate of increase				Ratio of net imports to apparent consumption	
	Total		Per capita		Average annual rate of change	Ratio, 1971-1975
	Production	Apparent consumption	Production	Apparent consumption		
I. Countries with *per capita* gross domestic product in 1970 of less than $200	2.6	2.7	0.1	0.2	—	3.3
II. Countries with *per capita* gross domestic product in 1970 of $200 or more but less than $400	2.4	3.6	−0.3	0.9	1.0	23.5
III. Countries with *per capita* gross domestic product in 1970 of $400 or more	3.5	4.3	0.7	1.5	0.8[c]	5.1
TOTAL	2.8	3.1	0.2	0.5	0.3	6.5

Sources: Centre for Development Planning, Projections and Policies of the United Nations Secretariat, based on population data from the Population Division of the Department of International Economic and Social Affairs of the United Nations Secretariat and cereals data from Food and Agriculture Organization of the United Nations, *Production Yearbook* and *Trade Yearbook* (Rome), various issues.

[a] Apparent consumption refers to production plus imports minus exports.

[b] Group I: *Africa*—Benin, Botswana, Burundi, Cape Verde, Central African Empire, Chad, Comoros, Ethiopia, Gambia, Guinea, Kenya, Lesotho, Madagascar, Malawi, Mali, Mauritania, Niger, Nigeria, Rwanda, Sierra Leone, Somalia, Sudan, Togo, Uganda, United Republic of Cameroon, United Republic of Tanzania, Zaire; *Asia*—Afghanistan, Bangladesh, Bhutan, Burma, India, Indonesia, Lao People's Democratic Republic, Nepal, Pakistan, Philippines, Sri Lanka, Thailand, Yemen; *Latin America and the Caribbean*—Haiti. Group II: *Africa*—Algeria, Angola, Congo, Egypt, Ghana, Ivory Coast, Liberia, Mauritius, Morocco, Mozambique, Namibia, Senegal, Southern Rhodesia, Swaziland, Tunisia; *Asia*—Iraq, Jordan, Malaysia, Republic of Korea, Syrian Arab Republic; *Latin America and the Caribbean*—Bolivia, Colombia, Dominican Republic, El Salvador, Ecuador, Guatemala, Guyana, Honduras, Nicaragua, Paraguay. Group III: *Africa*—Gabon, Libyan Arab Jamahiriya, Namibia, Réunion, Zambia; *Asia*—Fiji, Hong Kong, Iran, Israel, Kuwait, Lebanon, Saudi Arabia, Singapore; *Latin America and the Caribbean*—Argentina, Barbados, Brazil, Chile, Costa Rica, Jamaica, Mexico, Panama, Peru, Surinam, Trinidad and Tobago, Uruguay, Venezuela.

[c] Change from net exports equivalent to 2.6 per cent of apparent consumption in 1961-1965, to net imports equivalent to 5.1 per cent of apparent consumption in 1971-1975.

TABLE 18. EXPANSION OF PRODUCTION AND APPARENT CONSUMPTION[a] OF CEREALS, BY DEVELOPING REGION, 1961-1965 TO 1971-1975

(Percentage)

Developing region[b]	Average annual rate of increase				Ratio of net imports to apparent consumption	
	Total		Per capita		Average annual rate of change	Ratio, 1971-1975
	Production	Apparent consumption	Production	Apparent consumption		
Africa	1.8	2.6	−0.8	—	0.7	14.3
Lower-income countries[c]	1.5	1.9	−1.1	−0.7	0.4	5.8
Other countries	2.3	3.4	−0.3	0.8	0.9	24.6
Asia	2.8	3.0	0.2	0.4	0.2	6.7
Lower-income countries[c]	2.9	2.8	0.4	0.3	—	2.9
Other countries	2.5	4.4	−0.2	1.7	1.3	32.0
Latin America and the Caribbean	3.5	4.1	0.7	1.3	0.6[d]	−0.7[e]

Sources: See table 17.

[a,b] See corresponding foot-notes to table 17.
[c] See foot-note b to table 16.
[d] Decline in net exports.
[e] Ratio of net exports to apparent consumption.

into agriculture that had been generated elsewhere in the economy, such as by mineral exports. On the other hand, the middle-and higher-income developing countries in which the rural sector was still substantial, particularly the traditional sector engaged in stape-food production for domestic consumption, were among those with the slower rates of agricultural growth. While many of these latter countries still managed to register rates of over-all economic growth that were above those of the lower-income countries, the fact that agricultural production--especially food output--has lagged, appears to have extorted a price; first, in an impoverished countryside and its concomitant, an exodus to the towns, and, secondly, in a much enlarged import bill for food-stuffs.

Food production, as represented by what happened to cereal output between the first half of the 1960s and the first half of the 1970s, managed to stay ahead of population increases, if only just, for the lower-income countries--the group for which, as noted, agriculture as a whole had lagged most conspicuously (see table 17). For the middle-income developing countries, however, cereal production lagged behind the rate of increase in population, even though agriculture as a whole did considerably better than that for the lower-income developing countries. The per capita decline in cereal output appears to have been the typical experience of the middle-income countries in Africa and Asia, but not in Latin America and the Caribbean. In the higher-income developing countries, cereal output generally managed to stay comfortably ahead of population increase. Nevertheless, in the higher-income group, as in the other two groups--or, indeed, also in each of the three regional groups--the rate of increase in cereal production lagged behind demand, as may be gleaned from trends in net imports and apparent consumption (see tables 17 and 18). In the lower-income groups where the consumption and production of food staples follow each other fairly closely and import dependence in normal times is minimal, there was still some net increase in imports over the decade that sustained increases in consumption at rates above those allowed by increased internal production. In Asia, this was largely due to the need to maintain a minimum level of consumption in periods of poor harvests (often weather induced). In Africa, it was partly a result of the inability of production to keep pace with changes in consumer preferences, in favour of cereals and away from other staples (such as starchy roots) or substitution among cereals, and partly due to the need to provide for minimum consumption in periods of crop failure in the wake of natural calamities, such as the droughts in the Sudano-Sahelian region and elsewhere. In the middle-income group, which includes many countries that have long relied on substantial imports of food-staples to meet a part of their wage-goods needs, the combination of a relatively rapid increase in gross domestic product and lagging cereal output resulted in a rapid increase in imports and a large increase in their over-all dependence on imported foodstuffs; during 1971-1975 cereal imports accounted for 23.5 per cent of apparent consumption in this group, as against an average for all developing countries of 6.5 per cent (see table 17). In the higher-income countries, where both cereal production and cereal consumption increased faster than in each of the other two groups, consumption still outpaced production; as a consequence, net exports of cereals amounting to 2.6 per cent of apparent consumption during 1961-1965 were converted to net imports amounting to 5.1 per cent of apparent consumption during 1971-1975.

The figures for some of the key aggragates in agriculture in developing countries, then, cannot be considered as telling anything other than a sombre story. What they suggest for the future seems no less sombre. And yet, it would be misleading, in attempting to assess the present situation and what it bodes for the future, to dwell only on the trends in the main aggragates of output. Over the years there has been progress in many individual areas, at both the national and international level, which has been altering the setting for agriculture in developing countries.

There are indications that agriculture is now being accorded enhanced attention. The treatment of agriculture in the current development plans provides an illustration of this change.[18] Of course, when earlier development plans were formulated, agriculture was probably not accorded the low priority that a review of past performance tends to suggest. At the level of general intentions, continuity rather than change is in evidence, but what appears to give the latest treatment of agriculture the significance that previous attestations of its high priority lacked is the attention now being placed on food production. More and more, countries are adopting a battery of measures to increase food output.

Promotional policies include more public or publicly induced investment, effort to increase the supply of land suitable for cultivation, more extensive irrigation, provision of agricultural inputs and farmer services, enhanced and better focused training, improvement in the functioning of markets, and better rural infrastructure. Such policies have been prompted not simply by the need to step up food production but also by the need to find more direct and effective ways of fighting mass poverty or narrowing personal and regional income disparities within countries.

It appears that the new agricultural orientation stands a better chance of bearing fruit now than if it had occurred, say, a decade earlier. In terms of the resources that can be mobilized for agricultural development, both nationally and internationally, the opportunities have improved over the recent past. This is borne out at the national level by the investment allocations contemplated in plans for the latter half of the 1970s, and the much greater readiness of international financing institutions to provide large sums for agricultural and rural development (including investments through the newest United Nations specialized agency, the International Fund for Agricultural Development, which became operational in 1977).

Reinforcing the effect of increased availability of financial resources is the impact that can be expected from basic research and accumulated practical experience in overcoming some of the major obstacles to both improved food cultivation and improved animal rearing. Most relevant here is that cluster of international agricultural institutions carrying out strategically directed, methodical, coordinated research that is supported by a network of facilities to test, monitor, modify, apply and promote the use of strains and methods developed to increase output and yields.[19] The pioneering work that led to the Green Revolution has been extended in the past few years to cover many more staples besides rice, wheat and maize--the world's three most important crops--and to examine the potential of crops in a wide variety of settings representative of agriculture in different climatic areas of the developing world. A priority effort is research on reducing economic as well as agronomic risk by developing strains and varieties that are more robust or require much reduced inputs of chemical fertilizer, or grow on less carefully measured applications of water; much of this research by its very nature is thus concerned with the needs of small farmers. In addition, the quest continues to raise the level and quality of protein in a wide variety of crops.

What gives these efforts in research special significance--and special strength--is the international and interinstitutional co-operation that has been achieved for the purpose of pursuing specific solutions that are capable of early and wide application. The emergence of a similar spirit of co-operation on an ever increasing range of problems that individual countries cannot hope to tackle on their own is another reason for distinguishing the current climate in agriculture from that of the recent past. Such efforts include programmes to combat desertification, as in the Sudano-Sahelian region (supported by the recently formed Club des amis du Sahel of aid donors), and more generally, to prevent ecological catastrophes; or to reclaim land for agriculture through control or eradication of specific diseases (human and animal), or to develop jointly river basins and border areas.

Sight cannot be lost, either, of the consequence for rural development in general, and agricultural development in particular, of changing policies and changing approaches in other, but related, fields. In health, for example, the repercussions of a greater emphasis on rural, preventive and public health-oriented medicine could be far-reaching by way of increased productivity resulting from greater physical well-being and alertness and, as a result of the greater economic security so made possible, from greater receptivity to new techniques and new crops. Changes in education, in the form of a greater rural and technical orientation, greater reliance on informal work-oriented methods, greater enrolment of girls in rural schools and so on, are similarly going to leave their mark on agriculture. Improved training for the extension services and public-sector management and middle-level technical personnel, too, could be important; it is now estimated, for example, that half of all water available through irrigation schemes is wasted largely because of poor system upkeep and management, or lack of user supervision. Then there is the critical question of farmer or land organization for improving agriculture; this is closely related to a wide range of local political, social and other developments. It embraces questions of land ownership and control (for example, individual <u>versus</u> communal ownership or control); types of farmer co-operation for production, marketing or acquisition of inputs; forms of organizing and providing agricultural services at different levels of government, and so on. A considerable body of experience of how different

TABLE 19. CHANGE IN INDUSTRIAL PRODUCTION, BY INCOME GROUP OF DEVELOPING COUNTRIES, 1966-1975[a]

Country group[b]	Average annual rate of increase at constant market prices[c] (percentage)		Ratio to gross domestic product (percentage)		
			Average annual change in ratio		
	1966-1970	1971-1975	1966-1970	1971-1975	Ratio, 1975
I. Countries with *per capita* gross domestic product in 1970 of less than $200					
All industry	6.7	5.3	0.5	0.3	23.6
Manufacturing	5.0	4.7	0.1	0.1	12.7
II. Countries with *per capita* gross domestic product in 1970 of $200 or more but less than $400					
All industry	6.5	9.4	0.1	0.7	31.0
Manufacturing	10.1	10.5	0.5	0.5	16.7
III. Countries with *per capita* gross domestic product in 1970 of $400 or more					
All industry	8.5	7.3	0.6	−0.1	37.7
Manufacturing	7.8	8.1	0.2	0.1	23.1
TOTAL					
All industry	7.8	7.1	0.6	0.2	32.4
Manufacturing	7.4	7.7	0.3	0.2	19.0

Sources: See table 1.

[a] Based on value-added data. All industry comprises manufacturing, mining and quarrying, electricity, gas and water, construction. For other details, see foot-note *a* to table 15.

[b,c] See corresponding foot-notes to table 15.

forms of organization perform in given circumstances has now been amassed. How all such problems will be faced and resolved, often entailing difficult policy decisions, will help to set the pace of agricultural expansion. At the same time this will help to determine such other issues as the relation between agricultural output, productivity and incomes, the level and distribution of employment, and the intersectoral, interregional and interpersonal distribution of income.

V. DRIVE FOR ACCELERATED INDUSTRIALIZATION

Industrialization, especially the creation of a thriving manufacturing sector, has long been regarded as the quintessence of development and modernization. While agriculture has currently reclaimed a greater share of attention, the appeal and importance of industrialization appear greater than ever for developing countries. At the same time, views and plans for industry are being formed in a climate that has been conditioned by several decades during which substantial industrial progress has been made, intermingled with some disappointments and set-backs. Important lessons have been learnt from past experience, one of them being that sectoral balance and adequate linkages between industry and other activities are no less crucial to the success of the industrial drive itself than they are to over-all national development.

As is only to be expected, value added in all industrial activities or in manufacturing alone (hereafter, for brevity, referred to as industrial or manufacturing production) has generally increased faster than total gross domestic product. In developing countries as a group, industrial production expanded annually by 7.8 per cent during the second half of the 1960s and by 7.1 per cent during the first half of the 1970s. The manufacturing component of this production increased yearly during these two time periods by 7.4 per cent and 7.7 per cent, respectively. The annual increase in manufacturing production recorded during the first half of the 1970s was thus somewhat smaller than the average annual increase of 8 per cent specified for the 1970s as a whole in the International Development Strategy. The share of manufacturing in gross domestic product rose significantly and by 1975 equalled 19 per cent for developing countries as a group (see table 19).

The average rate of increase in industrial production in the lower-income developing countries was substantially smaller than that in the middle-and higher-income developing countries during the decade 1966-1975, with annual rates of 6.7 per cent during the second half of the 1960s and only 5.3 per cent during the first half of the 1970s in the lower-income group, against average annual rates for the other two groups of 6.5 per cent and 8.5 per cent during the earlier period, and 9.4 per cent and 7.3 per cent during the more recent half decade. For manufacturing activity alone the disparities among the three groups of developing countries were

TABLE 20. CHANGE IN INDUSTRIAL PRODUCTION, BY DEVELOPING REGION, 1966-1975[a]

Developing region[b]	Average annual rate of increase at constant market prices[c] (percentage)		Ratio to gross domestic product (percentage)		
			Average annual change in ratio		
	1966-1970	1971-1975	1966-1970	1971-1975	Ratio, 1975
Africa					
All industry	11.7	2.3	1.2	−0.4	26.9
Manufacturing	8.3	4.1	0.1	—	5.3
Lower-income countries:[d]					
All industry	13.0	5.6	1.3	0.2	23.6
Manufacturing	8.0	4.8	1.0	—	3.9
Other countries:					
All industry	11.0	0.4	0.9	−0.8	29.8
Manufacturing	8.5	3.7	—	0.1	6.5
Asia					
All industry	8.1	9.1	0.7	0.6	30.3
Manufacturing	7.2	9.2	0.3	0.3	16.0
Lower-income countries:[d]					
All industry	5.6	5.2	0.4	0.3	23.5
Manufacturing	4.8	4.7	0.1	0.1	14.6
Other countries:					
All industry	12.6	14.1	1.1	−0.2	40.1
Manufacturing	15.5	18.4	0.7	0.6	18.5
Latin America and the Caribbean					
All industry	6.9	6.9	0.3	0.2	36.0
Manufacturing	7.4	7.1	0.3	0.1	24.7
TOTAL					
All industry	7.8	7.1	0.6	0.2	32.4
Manufacturing	7.4	7.7	0.3	0.2	19.0

Sources: See table 1.
[a] See foot-note *a* to table 19.
[b,c] See corresponding foot-notes to table 15.
[d] See foot-note *f* to table 16.

greater still. For instance, during the first half of the 1970s, the lower-income developing countries recorded an annual increase in manufacturing production of only 4.7 per cent, compared to the annual rates of 10.5 per cent and 8.1 per cent experienced by the middle-income and higher-income developing countries. The contrast during this period was even more striking within Asia, with manufacturing activity expanding annually by 4.7 per cent in the lower-income Asian countries as against 18.4 per cent in the other developing countries of that continent (see table 20). Generally, for the three groups of developing countries, the pattern of expansion of both industry as a whole and of its manufacturing component was similar to the pattern of expansion of both agricultural production and total gross domestic product.

Within each of these three groups, as would be expected, there has been a considerable diversity of experience. Not all countries that saw a relatively rapid expansion of manufacturing, for instance, also experienced rapid rates of increase in agricultural or over-all production, nor did all lower-income countries necessarily record slow rates of increase in production of both agriculture and industry. However, the combination of a lagging agriculture and a buoyant industrial or manufacturing sector has been confined generally to countries in which petroleum or mineral extraction has been the leading sector, or in which industry simply has been a minor element in the total economy.

As a result of disparate rates of increase in production, the distance in terms of industrial advance among developing countries has lengthened appreciably in recent years. In 1975, for instance, the share of manufacturing in total gross domestic product amounted to nearly 13 per cent in the lower-income countries, to about 17 per cent in the middle-income countries and to over 23 per cent in the higher-income developing countries. Viewed in geographical terms, it is evident that the African countries are far behind other developing countries in this regard. The share of manufacturing in total gross domestic product amounted in 1975 to only a little more than 5 per cent in developing countries of Africa, compared to 16 per cent in developing Asian countries and nearly 25 per cent in Latin America and the Caribbean.

An important aspect of the manufacturing story, which has involved most developing countries irrespective of their level of income or actual rate of expansion of total manufacturing activity, has been the changing composition of output in favour of heavy industries--in other words, in favour of such manufactures as chemicals and chemical products or fabricated metals, machinery and equipment as against food products, or textiles, wearing apparel and footwear. At the same time, the preponderance of mainly light manufacturing activity is still in evidence, although an increasing number of countries, especially the economically larger countries--including some lower-income countries--have become both relatively and absolutely important producers of heavy industrial goods. The plans for the second half of the 1970s suggest that the trend towards heavy industry is generally expected to continue.[20] This would seem to be in line with the emerging patterns of demand in developing countries which are expected to be influenced to an important degree by the increasing claim of investment on gross domestic product.

In earlier periods of industrialization in developing countries, much of the impetus has come from import-substitution, focusing principally but not exclusively (as in some larger countries) on substituting domestically produced goods for imported light manufactures. In the 1960s, the contribution of import substitution to the expansion of manufacturing production was not as significant as it had been earlier. Most of its impact came in lower-income countries which are typically also at a lower stage of industrialization. Over-all import substitution was important in only rare instances to the growth of light industries, but it had an important influence in the area of heavy industry. Here, the potential for import substitution, particularly in the more sophisticated goods, remains large.

For smaller economies the limitations of their narrow internal markets have continued to curtail their potential in this regard. In order to break out of the limitaions so imposed, countries have traditionally attempted to seek import-substitution opportunities within the wider markets offered by economic-integration arrangements with neighbouring countries, as for instance, through formal subregionl market integration schemes, or (a more recent variant), joint ventures and enterprises across countries to meet their needs in the products of heavy industry. Such schemes have been gaining momentum at the very time that their importance in the context of an industrial drive that stresses the role of heavy industry is coming to the fore.

In the context of subregional integration schemes, import substitution and exports of industrial goods are intricately bound up; sometimes indeed the transactions are the same ones but viewed from two different sides by the respective trade partners. The emphasis place on integration schemes during the 1960s, and with renewed vigour again more recently, has been part of an important new trend towards seeking a greater dynamic for industry by way of promoting expansion of production for the export market. As a result of a number of key policy changes in a spectrum of developing countries, reinforced by the general buoyancy of world trade in manufactures in the 1960s and early 1970s, exports--destined to developed countries and also to other developing countries--have made an important contribution to the expansion of manufacturing at a time when the over-all impetus of import substitution in many sectors had begun to wane. A number of developing countries have emerged as forceful international competitors in manufacturing, some relying on labour-intensive light or assembly industries, but others increasingly on capital goods, many of a technical complexity. In the latter regard, the changes that have occurred in the aftermath of the increases in petroleum prices since 1973 have been instrumental in enhancing co-operation among developing countries, often across regions, on specific industrial ventures, with the technology used in many cases coming from developing country sources.[21]

Against the background of the growing importance of manufacturing activity in total economic activity in developing countries, a considerable impact has come from the sharp changes that have occurred in the first half of the 1970s in the supply and price of certain minerals, and especially petroleum. The positive developments for the petroleum-exporting countries, and in a more limited sense, for some mineral-exporting countries, and the negative effect of a sharply increased import bill for net importers among developing countries, need hardly be elaborated upon except to say that one consequence has been to alter relative costs of manufacturing activity as a whole, and of particular branches of manufacturing, as between different developing countries. Those countries that have stimulated economic growth largely on the basis of manufactured exports and that are dependent on imports of energy and raw materials are now facing the twin problems of higher production costs and the threat--even reality--of rising barriers against their products in developed countries. On the other side, new industrial opportunities now exist for countries with plentiful energy supplies or certain minerals whose long-term price prospects are likely to be favourable to the producers because of, among other things, possible scarcities in the future. For the developing countries as a group the scope for fruitful co-operation has been widened as the need for such co-operation has become more urgent; clearly, too, such co-operation is gaining momentum.[22]

While the contribution of industry to the economy of developing countries has been important already in terms of the quantity and range of goods produced for the home market and for exchange on international markets, the importance of industry far transcends these aspects. Its importance has to be seen in terms also of its dynamic, modernizing potential, its tonic effect on other sectors and on technological capacity and skills, as well as on social change and on incomes and employment. A variety of considerations therefore attest to the need for accelerated industrial progress of developing countries during the 1980s.

VI. EMERGING PATTERNS OF INTERNATIONAL TRADE

The patterns revealed by the trends in production, income and consumption have their counterparts in the trends in international trade of developing countries. The familiar theme that the lower-income developing countries have lagged behind the other developing countries emerges with equally striking clarity in the record of both exports and imports.

For developing countries as a whole, the annual rate of expansion of quantum of exports of goods and non-factor services accelerated from 6.3 per cent in the first half of the 1960s to 6.7 per cent in the second half of that decade and then slowed down to 4.8 per cent in the first half of the 1970s. The expansion recorded by developing countries during the first half of the 1970s has thus fallen substantially short of the target of somewhat more than 7 per cent indicated for the decade as a whole in the International Development Strategy. In the 1960s, the petroleum-exporting developing countries registered a rate of increase in the

TABLE 21. AVERAGE ANNUAL RATE OF INCREASE IN QUANTUM OF INTERNATIONAL TRADE, BY INCOME GROUP OF DEVELOPING COUNTRIES, 1961-1975[a]

(*Percentage*)

Country group[b]	Exports of goods and non-factor services			Imports of goods and non-factor services		
	1961-1965	1966-1970	1971-1975	1961-1965	1966-1970	1971-1975
I. Countries with *per capita* gross domestic product in 1970 of less than $200	4.7	4.8	4.0	3.9	4.5	7.3
Petroleum-exporting countries	6.0	8.3	7.7	1.4	9.2	21.9
Other countries	4.4	4.0	3.0	4.4	3.6	2.6
II. Countries with *per capita* gross domestic product in 1970 of $200 or more but less than $400	4.7	6.0	6.3	2.3	8.2	10.6
Petroleum-exporting countries	4.6	5.8	3.8	−4.4	9.2	25.3
Other countries	4.8	6.0	6.8	3.8	8.1	6.7
III. Countries with *per capita* gross domestic product in 1970 of $400 or more	7.9	7.8	4.4	4.5	9.8	15.1
Petroleum-exporting countries	12.2	9.3	2.5	7.6	8.6	28.1
Other countries	5.8	6.9	5.5	3.4	10.2	8.7
TOTAL	6.3	6.7	4.8	3.8	7.9	12.2
Petroleum-exporting countries	9.8	8.6	3.5	3.5	8.8	26.3
Other countries	5.1	5.9	5.3	3.8	7.7	6.7

Sources: See table 1.

[a] See foot-note *b* to table 2.

[b] See foot-note *a* to table 2.

quantum of exports that was well above the corresponding figure for other developing countries. In the first half of the 1970s, the pattern was reversed: the quantum of exports expanded yearly on the average by only 3.5 per cent for the petroleum-exporting countries and by 5.3 per cent for other developing countries (see table 21).

Of course, for the petroleum-exporting countries, the quantum figures for the first half of the 1970s are deceptive; part of the slow-down is accounted for by voluntary reduction of production and exports by some countries, while the increase in price made it possible for export value to increase by an annual average of roughly 45 per cent (as against the corresponding increases in export value for the next petroleum-importing countries of 20 per cent). The combination of trends in the quantum and unit price of exports and unit price of imports resulted in an annual rate of increase in the purchasing power of exports over the first half of the 1970s of 24.6 per cent for petroleum exporters and only 2.3 per cent for other developing countries.[23]

Among these other developing countries, the experience of the lower-income group of countries has been markedly different from that of the middle-income and higher-income groups of developing countries. During the 1960s, in a period of buoyant world trade, the quantum of exports of this lower-income group increased by only just over 4 per cent a year, as against a rate of around 6 per cent for the other two groups taken together. In the first half of the 1970s, the rate of increase for the lower-income group slowed to an annual rate of only 3 per cent, whereas the middle-income and high-income groups recorded annual increases of 6.8 per cent and 5.5 per cent, respectively. Among the two subregions that account for almost all countries with a per capita gross domestic product of less than $200, lower-income Africa experienced an annual expansion of exports in real terms of only 2 per cent during the first half of the 1970s; the corresponding figure for lower-income Asia was 3.6 per cent.

During the first half of the 1970s, the sharp annual increase in the purchasing power of exports of the petroleum-exporting countries (24.6 per cent) enabled these members of the developing world to expand the quantum of their imports of goods and non-factor services at an average yearly rate of 26.3 per cent (see table 21). In contrast, the import figure for other developing countries (6.7 per cent annual increase) exceeded several times the increase in the purchasing power of their exports (2.3 per cent). Moreover, among these other developing countries, the implied increase in the ratio of imports not financed by export earnings affected most notably the groups of middle-income and higher-income countries. The rate of increase in import quantum of the lower-income group (2.6 per cent) was not much greater than the rate of increase in the purchasing power of its exports.

For the lower-income countries other than the net exporters of petroleum, the rate of increase in import quantum has tended to trail that in export quantum since 1965 (see table 21). But this was wholly as a result of the trend experienced by the Asian countries among them. The import quantum of those Asian countries rose annually at a very sluggish rate, 1.7 per cent during

TABLE 22. AVERAGE ANNUAL RATE OF INCREASE IN QUANTUM OF INTERNATIONAL TRADE, BY DEVELOPING REGION, 1961-1975[a]

(Percentage)

Developing region[b]	Exports of goods and non-factor services			Imports of goods and non-factor services		
	1961-1965	1966-1970	1971-1975	1961-1965	1966-1970	1971-1975
Africa	5.7	6.9	-0.2	3.1	7.2	9.7
Lower-income countries[c]	4.2	6.6	3.7	5.3	7.3	8.5
	(2.5)	(6.0)	(2.0)	(6.1)	(7.6)	(3.5)
Other countries	6.6	7.0	-2.4	2.0	7.2	10.4
Asia	7.1	8.4	7.9	5.2	8.4	15.5
Lower-income countries[c]	5.1	3.7	4.3	3.3	3.0	6.6
	(5.7)	(3.0)	(3.6)	(3.8)	(1.7)	(2.0)
Other countries	8.4	10.8	0.1	6.9	12.3	19.4
Latin America and the Caribbean	5.9	4.4	3.8	2.5	7.8	9.1

Sources: See table 1.

[a] Data in parentheses refer to lower-income countries excluding petroleum exporters. For other details, see foot-note b to table 2.
[b] See foot-note a to table 2.
[c] See foot-note d to table 3.

TABLE 23. CHANGE IN COMPOSITION OF EXPORTS OF DEVELOPING COUNTRIES, 1960-1961 TO 1974-1975

Item and period (SITC sections)[a]	All merchandise trade (0-9)	Mineral fuels and related materials (3)	Non-fuel trade (0-9 except 3)	Food, beverages, tobacco (0-1)	Raw materials (excluding fuels) (2+4)	Manufactured goods (5-8)
Average annual rate of increase in value (percentage)						
All exports:						
1960-1961 to 1969-1970	7.2	8.8	6.6	4.6	3.4	12.8
1969-1970 to 1974-1975	33.1	50.2	20.0	18.1	16.4	24.9
Exports to other developing countries:						
1960-1961 to 1969-1970	6.0	4.1	7.0	3.4	4.5	11.3
1969-1970 to 1974-1975	35.5	50.9	25.9	25.0	18.9	29.3
Percentage share of trade represented by the commodity group indicated						
All exports:						
1960-1961	100.0	28.6	71.4	30.1	26.4	14.9
1969-1970	100.0	32.4	67.6	23.9	18.9	23.4
1974-1975	100.0	59.6	40.4	13.3	9.8	17.0
Exports to other developing countries:						
1960-1961	100.0	37.7	62.3	24.6	16.4	19.7
1969-1970	100.0	32.0	68.0	20.4	15.5	30.3
1974-1975	100.0	54.3	45.7	13.5	8.0	23.6

Source: Centre for Development Planning, Projections and Policies of the United Nations Secretariat, based on *Yearbook of International Trade Statistics*, and *Monthly Bulletin of Statistics* (United Nations publications), various issues.

[a] Standard International Trade Classification, revised.

1966-1970 and 2 per cent during the following quinquennium (see table 22); in so far as this meant inadequate expansion of imports of capital goods, the ability to raise the level of gross capital formation was seriously constrained. For the corresponding group of African countries, import quantum expanded substantially faster than export quantum. For the higher-income countries (excluding petroleum exporters), import quantum has moved ahead of export quantum since 1965. This pattern also prevailed for the corresponding middle-income countries in the second half of the 1960s; but in the first half of the 1970s, their import quantum moved roughly in line with export quantum.

Given that the starting point was one of negative balance between export and import outlays, the excess of imports over exports of goods and services was possible only because of a large increase in capital flows, much of it by private international banks. At the same time, the relatively slow increase in concessional official development assistance on which the lower-income countries largely rely is reflected in their failure to increase imports at a rate much above the very slow rate of increase in the purchasing power of their exports. (Aspects of financial flows received by developing countries are examined in a subsequent section of the present paper.)

The different experience of the petroleum-exporting developing countries from the rest, and also among the other country groups identified earlier, serves to focus attention on the fact that export performance generally is linked to the particular range of commodities on which different groups of countries tend to depend, and on the particular fortunes of these various commodities in world markets. One of the strong currents running through the 1960s and the first half of the 1970s has been the changing composition of the exports of developing countries. Thus, exports of mineral fuels (including petroleum) from developing countries to the rest of the world were more buoyant than their non-fuel merchandise exports as a group (see table 23). Similarly, among non-fuel commodity groups, exports of manufactures increased most rapidly while exports of food, beverages and tobacco, and of raw materials lagged behind. A similar pattern may be observed in the mutual trade of developing countries, except that in this case the value of mineral fuel trade increased more slowly than the value of other merchandise trade in the 1960s.

As a result of the different rates of increase in the export value of different commodity groups, the composition of the exports of developing countries has changed in the following way since 1960. Mineral fuel exports, from representing only just under 29 per cent of the value of all exports in 1960-1961, jumped to almost 60 per cent by 1974-1975. The share of raw materials other than fuels, on the other hand, diminished by almost two thirds, from over 26 per cent to under 10 per cent of all exports, while the relative importance of manufactures rose from nearly 15 per cent to 17 per cent, or, from about 21 per cent to over 42 per cent of the value of exports other than mineral fuels.

In respect of the changing composition of exports in mutual trade among developing countries, the rise in the share of mineral fuels, while sharp, has not been as pronounced as the rise in its share of exports to all countries. In the same way, raw materials other than fuels fell in relative importance, but again not as sharply as in trade with all countries. On the other hand, the share of manufactures rose more; by 1974-1975 manufactures accounted for more than half of all intra-developing trade in non-fuel merchandise. Considered from the point of view of the relative importance of mutual trade among developing countries for different commodity groups, then, such trade has increased in importance, on the export side, for all major commodity groups barring mineral fuels; on the import side, on the other hand, developing countries as source of supply of each other's need have become relatively less significant in raw materials other than fuels, and in the food, beverages and tobacco group, but more significant in mineral fuels and in manufactures.

Over all, the geographical distribution of the exports of developing countries was virtually identical in 1960-1961 and 1974-1975: 73 per cent of their exports went to the developed market economies and 4-5 per cent to the centrally planned economies, and the remainder (about 22 per cent) constituted mutual trade among developing countries. In the intervening period, the share of mutual trade declines slightly in relation to the shares of exports to the developed market economies and the centrally planned economies, but the decline of the 1960s was reversed in the first half of the 1970s. On the side of imports, the share of mutual trade of developing countries rose from about 21 per cent to almost 26 per cent during this period, and the share of imports from the developed market economies in the total imports of developing countries declined from 74 per cent to 68 per cent.[24]

The growing importance of mutual trade, especially in manufactures, has been paralleled by enhanced co-operation among developing countries. A number of countries have already profited considerably in terms of increased sales of exports--and the stimulus to manufacturing that has been given--by their participation in subregional integration schemes. Over a dozen such schemes have come into being since 1960, affecting each of the developing regions.[25] Their over-all impact on trade cannot really be fully judged as yet. The period in question has been dominated by forces (such as buoyancy of trade in a period of unprecedented world economic expansion, a strong current towards world trade liberalization and the upheavals of the late 1960s and the first half of the 1970s) that have tended to overwhelm the efforts at subregional co-operation among developing countries. But there is no doubt that such co-operation is itself an emerging force with the potential of being a major trade influence, especially when seen in the context of the new, wider efforts at interregional co-operation in trade among developing countries, the substantial financial resources that some capital-surplus developing countries can now deploy and the rapid growth of joint production ventures, many with important trade implications.

While enhanced co-operation through a variety of schemes, and the effects of a long and gradual effort at establishing physical as well as institutional links among developing countries in the post-colonial era have had their roles to play in increased trade, their ability to step up exports has been determined to a very important extent by the success of domestic efforts to increase production. While demand for exports plays a leading role, and the spotlight has tended to be on it, the past decade has demonstrated forcefully the importance of supply; it is exactly because of efforts made on that side that many countries were in a position to respond to the generally buoyant demand conditions--and enlarged access to markets of developed countries--in the 1960s and early 1970s, for manufactures, and later also for a very wide range of other commodities. This cycle was again repeated in the post-1973 buoyant demand conditions prevailing in petroleum-exporting countries, to which some other developing countries managed to respond vigorously. Conversely, countries that could not step up supply were severely handicapped, and this affected particularly a considerable number of the lower-income countries. In addition, specific supply problems helped to cause temporary world shortages of specific commodities, and contributed to wild price swings which, while giving windfall gains to producers, also had a disrupting influence on both producers and consumers. At the same time, world demand has not been uniformly buoyant for all products; this adversely affected countries highly dependent on commodities with weak markets, among which were many of the lower-income countries.

At this juncture, the prospects for trade are possibly more unclear than they are for any other major factor influencing the economic advancement of developing countries. At the same time, in this uncertain period, since trade most intimately and directly concerns all countries, both developed and developing, much of the interested concern will inevitably focus on trade issues, such as how to escape protectionism and improve market access for developing countries; how to stabilize commodity markets and provide for fair remuneration to commodity producers, in the wider context of questions relating to the prices of energy and food, and of manufactures imported by developing countries; or how to take advantage of the positive contributions that can be made by transnational corporations, while ensuring adequate safeguards and controls over them. Even so, while the broad nature of the main longer-run issues is clear, given the background of current payments imbalances, currency instability and acute debt problems, expectations on what progress can be made on specific trade questions are likely to change rapidly.

VII. RAISING LEVELS OF CAPITAL FORMATION

In order to expand the diversify their economies, developing countries have been making efforts to raise their levels of investment. For these countries as a group, in terms of constant prices, the share of gross investment in gross domestic product rose from 17.1 per cent in 1960 to 19.2 per cent in 1970. At that point the difference in the shares for petroleum-exporting countries and other developing countries was not large, with shares

TABLE 24. INVESTMENT IN RELATION TO GROSS DOMESTIC PRODUCT, BY INCOME GROUP OF DEVELOPING COUNTRIES, 1960-1975

Country group[a]	Share of gross investment in gross domestic product at constant prices (percentage)				Implicit incremental capital/output ratio[b]		
	1960	1965	1970	1975	1961-1965	1966-1970	1971-1975
I. Countries with *per capita* gross domestic product in 1970 of less than $200	13.6	15.6	17.0	17.3	3.6	3.6	4.5
Petroleum-exporting countries	8.7	11.8	14.5	21.6	3.2	2.0	2.4
Other countries	14.4	16.2	17.4	16.5	3.7	3.9	5.4
II. Countries with *per capita* gross domestic product in 1970 of $200 or more but less than $400	17.5	16.5	20.0	25.2	3.2	3.1	3.4
Petroleum-exporting countries	26.4	16.4	24.9	46.9	6.1	2.9	4.2
Other countries	15.6	16.5	19.1	20.6	2.8	3.1	3.3
III. Countries with *per capita* gross domestic product in 1970 of $400 or more	19.9	19.7	20.6	26.3	3.3	2.9	3.1
Petroleum-exporting countries	22.5	22.8	20.9	37.3	2.6	2.7	2.2
Other countries	19.4	19.0	20.5	23.0	3.5	3.0	3.5
TOTAL	17.1	17.7	19.2	23.4	3.4	3.1	3.5
Petroleum-exporting countries	18.5	18.4	19.8	34.8	3.2	2.6	2.5
Other countries	16.8	17.5	19.1	20.5	3.4	3.5	3.8

Sources: See table 1.

[a] *Group I: petroleum-exporting countries*—Indonesia, Nigeria; *other countries*—Afghanistan, Bangladesh, Benin, Botswana, Burma, Central African Empire, Ethiopia, Gambia, Guinea, Haiti, India, Kenya, Madagascar, Malawi, Mali, Namibia, Nepal, Niger, Pakistan, Philippines, Sierra Leone, Sri Lanka, Sudan, Thailand, Togo, Uganda, United Republic of Cameroon, United Republic of Tanzania, Upper Volta, Zaire.

Group II: petroleum-exporting countries—Algeria, Ecuador, Iraq; *other countries*—Bolivia, Colombia, Congo, Dominican Republic, Egypt, El Salvador, Ghana, Guatemala, Guyana, Honduras, Ivory Coast, Jordan, Liberia, Malaysia, Mauritius, Morocco, Nicaragua, Paraguay, Republic of Korea, Southern Rhodesia, Senegal, Syrian Arab Republic, Swaziland, Tunisia.

Group III: petroleum-exporting countries—Gabon, Iran, Kuwait, Libyan Arab Jamahiriya, Saudi Arabia, Trinidad and Tobago, Venezuela; *other countries*—Argentina, Barbados, Brazil, Chile, Costa Rica, Fiji, Hong Kong, Israel, Jamaica, Mexico, Panama, Peru, Singapore, Suriname, Uruguay, Zambia.

[b] Implicit incremental capital/output ratio equals gross investment as percentage of gross domestic product for period indicated (but with a one-year lag) divided by the annual rate of growth of gross domestic product in the period.

TABLE 25. INVESTMENT IN RELATION TO GROSS DOMESTIC PRODUCT, BY DEVELOPING REGION, 1960-1975

Developing region[a]	Share of gross investment in gross domestic product at constant prices (percentage)				Implicit incremental capital/output ratio[b]		
	1960	1965	1970	1975	1961-1965	1966-1970	1971-1975
Africa	17.0	17.2	18.3	26.1	3.5	3.1	4.9
Lower-income countries[c]	11.3	14.5	16.4	20.0	3.4	2.9	3.7
	(11.8)	(13.8)	(16.8)	(19.1)	(4.1)	(3.4)	(5.2)
Other countries	22.0	19.5	19.8	31.0	3.5	3.3	6.0
Asia	14.7	16.6	18.5	23.0	3.1	3.1	3.0
Lower-income countries[c]	14.2	15.9	17.2	16.7	3.6	3.7	4.8
	(14.9)	(16.7)	(17.6)	(16.0)	(3.6)	(4.0)	(5.4)
Other countries	16.4	18.4	21.2	32.3	2.3	2.3	2.0
Latin America and the Caribbean	19.4	18.9	20.3	22.9	3.6	3.2	3.5

Sources: See table 1.

[a,b] See corresponding foot-notes to table 24.

[c] For definition of lower-income countries, see foot-note d to table 3. Data in parentheses refer to lower-income countries excluding petroleum exporters.

of 19.8 per cent for the former and 19.1 per cent for the latter. Thereafter, the share for petroleum-exporting countries rose sharply to equal 34.8 per cent in 1975, whereas for other developing countries it rose only to 20.5 per cent (see table 24).

Although the difference in the experience of the petroleum exporters from that of the other developing countries is the eye-catching contrast during the first half of the 1970s, divergent trends in the three groups of developing countries at different levels of per capita income were both marked and significant, especially in terms of their implications for the coming decade. The higher-income group among the non-petroleum exporters, which had experienced the slowest increase in the share of investment in gross domestic product during the 1960s--although starting from a relatively high initial share--recorded by far the fastest increase in the corresponding share during the first half of the 1970s, from 20.5 per cent to 23 per cent. The trends in the other two income groups were different in that rapid increases during the 1960s were followed by a much slackened pace of increase during the 1970s. For the lower-income group of non-petroleum-exporting countries, in fact, the share of investment in gross domestic product declined between 1970 and 1975, from 17.4 per cent to 16.5 per cent. The decline really took place in the lower-income non-petroleum-exporting countries of Asia: from 17.6 per cent in 1970 to 16 per cent in 1975. This outcome, as already mentioned, was shaped in part by the inadequate increase in their imports of capital goods. The corresponding group of African countries, whose total imports and imports of capital goods expanded at a significant rate, managed to sustain a significant increase in the level of gross investment. Even so, their level of investment remained well below the corresponding level for the middle-income and higher-income developing countries.

One aspect of the link between investment and expansion of gross domestic product is thus clearly illustrated by the divergent experience of the various groups of developing countries since 1960. By and large, countries that could allocate a high share of their resources to investment had rapid economic growth, and those that could not had moderate or slow growth. The implications of this for the future are self-evident.

At the same time, the relation between investment and increases in output, as may be observed from trends in the incremental capital/output ratio, has differed over time and among different groups of countries (see tables 24 and 25). The relation over time has differed for such familiar reasons as cyclical movements in capacity utilization, weather-induced fluctuations in farm output, bunching of investments (as in petroleum extraction) or concentration in different plan periods on projects with short or long gestation periods. While such factors have also been responsible for some of the differences in the relation between investment and increases in output among countries at different income levels, there appears to have been, in addition, a tendency for the lower-income countries--which had the lower rates of investment and output growth--to require larger increments of capital for each unit of additional output.

A part of the explanation for this tendency is to be found in

TABLE 26. AVERAGE ANNUAL RATE OF INCREASE IN GROSS DOMESTIC PRODUCT AT CONSTANT PRICES PER ECONOMICALLY ACTIVE PERSON IN DEVELOPING COUNTRIES, 1961-1975[a]

Country group or developing region[b]	1961-1965	1966-1970	1971-1975
	By income group of developing countries		
I. Countries with *per capita* gross domestic product in 1970 of less than $200	2.2	2.4	1.5
II. Countries with *per capita* gross domestic product in 1970 of $200 or more but less than $400	3.1	3.2	3.4
III. Countries with *per capita* gross domestic product in 1970 of $400 or more	3.5	4.1	4.7
TOTAL	3.2	3.6	3.6
	By developing region		
Africa	2.5	3.2	1.9
Lower-income countries[c]	1.5	2.6	2.4
Other countries	3.5	3.7	1.4
Asia	3.3	3.6	4.1
Lower-income countries[c]	2.5	2.5	1.3
Other countries	5.3	6.0	8.7
Latin America and the Caribbean	2.9	3.4	3.5

Sources: See tables 1 and 9.
[a] See foot-note *b* to table 2.
[b] See foot-note *a* to table 2.
[c] See foot-note *d* to table 3.

the different rates of increase in agricultural production. In addition, a variety of other, often conflicting, factors have had some bearing on it. For instance, certain types of capital formation have gone hand in hand with certain economic structures. Countries at lower levels of income and an inadequate endowment of basic facilities--such as power, roads and railways, or housing and urban infrastructure--have required large investments with little immediate impact on the economy's productive capacity; on the other side, however, some relatively advanced economies have required complex, sophisticated and expensive investments for advancing to the next level of development in particular sectors.

It must also be stressed that investment, though crucial over anything but the short run, is not the sole factor that generates production. Land has been important, especially in countries that have been able to bring additional acreage under cultivation without expensive preparation. And everywhere, labour supply has been vital, not only in terms of numbers but also in terms of quality. Moreover, an important part has been played by the efficiency with which capital has been employed through such means as the appropriateness of the investment choices made, the maintenance of the existing capital stock, and effective management of productive activities.

Some indication of the effect of policies to increase efficiency of production can be obtained by relating the increase in gross domestic product with the increase in labour force. Since 1960, generally, production per worker has increased faster in the higher-income developing countries than in the middle-income developing countries, and faster in the middle-income countries than in the lower-income countries (see table 26). Between 1970 and 1975, the lower-income developing countries experienced not only a nominal increase in the share of investment in gross domestic product (from 17 per cent to 17.3 per cent) but also a small annual increase in output per worker (1.5 per cent).

To an important extent, increased output per worker has been influenced by new investment and its efficiency. At the same time, the relationship has also worked the other way around, in that capital productivity has been partially determined by the skill and efficiency of the labour force. In a number of countries, more widespread and better education and training, as well as better health and nutrition, have helped to raise worker skills and efficiency, and hence their performance and ability collectively to handle and manage even more complex and sophisticated undertakings. With a continuing move away from subsistence or traditional agriculture, and greater range and depth in secondary and tertiary activities, the resulting practical experience and technical competence, as well as the generally higher work standards brought about by the better living standards that come with higher incomes, will undoubtedly continue to have a major bearing on trends in the productivity of both labour and capital.

Capital, of course, is not a homogeneous item. Not only does its composition differ from country to country and change over time but so also do the underlying technology, the organization of production, the factor proportions, and the input mix of a unit of capital. While the choice of allocation among different sectors will remain a major preoccupation, increasingly the challenge will also become one of meeting the often competing demands for investment, on the one side, in technologically advanced and often capital-intensive activities that will carry countries on to more ambitious forms of industrial endeavour but which may increase employment only in the longer run, and, on the other side, in activities, with a more direct and immediate impact on employment. None the less, increasing investment in the aggregate has to remain an important aim. In so far as investment has to come from the private sector, there has to be sufficient opportunity for investors to make a return and, in many cases also, active inducement by government. The development plans drawn up for the latter half of the 1970s indicate that the public sector itself is intended to spearhead the investment effort in an increasing number of countries. The plans also indicate that, in general, developing countries envisage a significant rise in the level of capital formation in the coming years.

VIII. MATCHING FINANCE FOR CAPITAL FORMATION

To raise their levels of capital formation, developing countries have deployed a wide variety of measures to secure matching levels of finance. They have, as is only to be expected, given a good deal of attention to tapping their own financial potential. Many countries, in fact, have reiterated in their successive development plans their aim to enhance self-reliance for accelerated economic and social progress. However, in order to supplement their domestic saving as well as to overcome the shortages of foreign exchange, many countries have also sought financial resources from abroad in the form of official grants and loans and/or loans from external private institutions. Indeed, for a large number of developing countries, the extraordinary events that impinged heavily on international economic relations during the first half of the 1970s strongly reinforced the need for, as well as the relative dependence on, external financial resources.

For developing countries as a whole, the ratio of gross national saving to gross domestic product measured in current prices rose from 15.2 per cent in 1960 to 16.9 per cent in 1970, or on the average yearly by 0.34 percentage point during the 1960s. Between 1970 and 1975, the average yearly rise in the saving ratio was sharp--1 percentage point--and the ratio in 1975 almost equalled 22 per cent. The International Development Strategy, it may be recalled, called for an average annual increase of 0.5 percentage point in the saving ratio of the developing countries as a group during the 1970s as a whole.[26] At first glance, then, the annual increase of 1 percentage point recorded in the saving ratio might suggest that developing countries generally were exceptionally successful in mobilizing domestic financial

TABLE 27. GROSS NATIONAL SAVING IN RELATION TO GROSS DOMESTIC PRODUCT AND TO TOTAL SUPPLY OF SAVING, BY INCOME GROUP OF DEVELOPING COUNTRIES, 1960-1975[a]

(Percentage)

Country group[b]	Share of gross national saving in gross domestic product				Share of gross national saving in total supply of saving (including factor income)			
	1960	1965	1970	1975	1960	1965	1970	1975
I. Countries with *per capita* gross domestic product in 1970 of less than $200	10.9	13.2	14.5	14.8	76.2	83.0	85.3	80.4
Petroleum-exporting countries	2.2	9.4	11.3	21.8	24.4	79.7	77.9	102.3
Other countries	12.1	13.6	15.0	12.6	80.7	82.9	86.2	72.0
II. Countries with *per capita* gross domestic product in 1970 of $200 or more but less than $400	15.0	13.2	15.2	18.8	86.2	80.5	76.0	70.1
Petroleum-exporting countries	24.8	14.4	21.9	31.9	91.9	88.3	88.0	82.0
Other countries	13.0	12.9	13.8	14.9	83.9	78.7	72.3	64.5
III. Countries with *per capita* gross domestic product in 1970 of $400 or more	19.1	20.6	19.2	26.4	92.7	100.5	93.2	114.3
Petroleum-exporting countries	24.0	25.5	24.8	44.8	126.3	123.8	118.7	198.2
Other countries	17.9	19.4	17.9	17.5	85.2	95.1	87.3	74.8
TOTAL	15.2	16.5	16.9	21.9	86.4	91.7	88.0	97.8
Petroleum-exporting countries	17.8	19.1	20.6	37.7	101.7	109.8	103.0	153.9
Other countries	14.7	16.0	16.2	15.5	83.5	88.4	84.8	71.8

Sources: See table 1.

[a] Total supply of saving equals gross capital formation. Gross national savings equals total supply of saving minus the excess of imports over exports of goods and services (including factor income). Data are at current prices.

[b] See foot-note *a* to table 24.

TABLE 28. GROSS NATIONAL SAVING IN RELATION TO GROSS DOMESTIC PRODUCT AND TO TOTAL SUPPLY OF SAVING, BY DEVELOPING REGION, 1960-1975[a]

(Percentage)

Developing region[b]	Share of gross national saving in gross domestic product				Share of gross national saving in total supply of saving			
	1960	1965	1970	1975	1960	1965	1970	1975
Africa	14.0	13.6	18.3	20.1	82.8	83.4	96.3	75.3
Lower-income countries[c]	8.6	10.7	13.5	16.7	78.2	77.0	82.3	80.7
	(10.2)	(9.2)	(13.4)	(7.9)	(92.5)	(76.1)	(79.5)	(41.3)
Other countries	20.3	16.8	23.2	23.3	85.7	88.9	106.4	71.7
Asia	12.0	14.4	15.1	24.9	78.9	85.2	82.5	120.3
Lower-income countries[c]	11.4	13.7	14.7	14.2	76.0	83.5	85.5	80.2
	(12.4)	(14.3)	(15.3)	(13.6)	(79.3)	(83.6)	(87.1)	(79.2)
Other countries	13.7	16.8	15.8	34.9	85.6	89.6	78.2	148.5
Latin America and the Caribbean	19.0	19.5	18.3	19.3	93.1	99.0	90.1	85.0

Sources: See table 1.
[a] See foot-note a to table 27.
[b] See foot-note a to table 24.
[c] For definition of lower-income countries, see foot-note d to table 3. Data in parentheses refer to lower-income countries excluding petroleum exporters.

resources during the first half of the Second Development Decade. Such a conclusion, however, would be spurious.

The key fact to note is that the trend in the saving ratio of developing countries as a whole has been overwhelmingly dominated by the experience of the petroleum exporters (see table 27). The ratio of gross national saving to gross domestic product of petroleum-exporting countries rose at an average of only 0.28 percentage point during the 1960s, from 17.8 per cent in 1960 to 20.6 per cent in 1970. But by 1975 it had risen dramatically to 37.7 per cent. The other developing countries also made a gain, though a very modest one, during the 1960s; their saving ratio rose from 14.7 per cent in 1960 to 16.2 per cent in 1970, or on the average yearly by 0.15 percentage point during the 1960s. But thereafter, in marked contrast to petroleum-exporting countries, the saving ratio of the other developing countries declined to 15.5 per cent in 1975. Among these latter countries, the most adversely affected were the lower-income developing countries, whose saving ratio declined form 15 per cent in 1970 to 12.6 per cent in 1975 (table 27). Such a decline took place in the lower-income countries of both Africa and Asia--indeed, very steeply in Africa, from 13.4 per cent to 7.9 per cent (see table 28). These figures provide another telling testimony of the severe constraints facing the countries situated in the two depressed regions of the world that suffer from acute problems of mass poverty and unemployment.

Among the countries other than petroleum exporters, although the saving ratio suffered a serious setback in the first half of the 1970s, the share of gross investment in gross domestic product (as noted in the preceding section) fortunately did increase significantly during this period. The increase in their level of capital formation for expansion of productive capacity was made possible by means of increased relative dependence on external resources. This can be readily seen from the fact that, for this group of developing countries, the share of gross national saving in total supply of saving (which, by definition, equals gross capital formation) declined from 85 per cent in 1970 to 72 per cent in 1975, the decline implying that the share of external resources in total supply of saving correspondingly increased (table 27). Among the lower-income countries of Africa in this group, the share of gross national saving in total supply of saving became as low as 41 per cent in 1975 (table 28).

Recent trends in gross national saving have been greatly influenced by the role played in many developing countries by export incomes in generating financial resources for higher levels of investment. The saving ratio rose during the first half of the 1970s not only in petroleum-exporting countries, which gained new economic power from the sharp increase in petroleum price, but also in some other developing countries that experienced a buoyant export trade. Another factor that played an important part in determining the magnitude of the saving ratio was the course of agricultural activity. Lagging agricultural production, especially in the lower-income countries of Africa and Asia, depressed rural incomes and also (because of shortages of food-stuffs) sparked an upward spiralling of prices in urban areas which benefited mainly traders and other middlemen at the cost of the rest of the society.

TABLE 29. EXTERNAL RESOURCES IN RELATION TO GROSS DOMESTIC PRODUCT AND TO TOTAL SUPPLY OF SAVING, BY INCOME GROUP OF DEVELOPING COUNTRIES, 1960-1975[a]

(Percentage)

Country group[b]	Share of external resources in gross domestic product				Share of external resources in total supply of saving			
	1960	1965	1970	1975	1960	1965	1970	1975
I. Countries with *per capita* gross domestic product in 1970 of less than $200	3.4	2.7	2.5	3.6	23.8	17.0	14.7	19.6
Petroleum-exporting countries	6.8	2.4	3.2	-0.5	75.6	20.3	22.1	-2.3
Other countries	2.9	2.8	2.4	4.9	19.3	17.1	13.8	28.0
II. Countries with *per capita* gross domestic product in 1970 of $200 or more but less than $400	2.4	3.2	4.8	8.0	13.8	19.5	24.0	29.9
Petroleum-exporting countries	2.2	1.9	3.0	7.0	8.1	11.7	12.0	18.0
Other countries	2.5	3.5	5.3	8.2	16.1	21.3	27.7	35.5
III. Countries with *per capita* gross domestic product in 1970 of $400 or more	1.5	-0.1	1.4	-3.3	7.3	-0.5	6.8	-14.3
Petroleum-exporting countries	-5.0	-4.9	-3.9	-22.2	-26.3	-23.8	-18.7	-98.2
Other countries	3.1	1.0	2.6	5.9	14.8	4.9	12.7	25.2
TOTAL	2.4	1.5	2.3	0.5	13.6	8.3	12.0	2.2
Petroleum-exporting countries	-0.3	-1.7	-0.8	-13.2	-1.7	-9.8	-3.0	-53.9
Other countries	2.9	2.1	2.9	6.1	16.5	11.6	15.2	28.2

Sources: See table 1.

[a] External resources equal excess of imports over exports of goods and services (including factor income). Minus sign indicates net outflow of resources. For other details, see foot-note *a* to table 27.

[b] See foot-note *a* to table 24.

TABLE 30. EXTERNAL RESOURCES IN RELATION TO GROSS DOMESTIC PRODUCT AND TO TOTAL SUPPLY OF SAVING, BY DEVELOPING REGION, 1960-1975[a]

(Percentage)

Developing region[b]	Share of external resources in gross domestic product				Share of external resources in total supply of saving			
	1960	1965	1970	1975	1960	1965	1970	1975
Africa	2.9	2.7	0.7	6.6	17.2	16.6	3.7	24.7
Lower-income countries[c]	2.4	3.2	2.9	4.0	21.8	23.0	17.7	19.3
	(0.8)	(2.9)	(3.4)	(11.3)	(7.5)	(23.9)	(20.5)	(58.7)
Other countries	3.4	2.1	−1.4	9.2	14.3	11.1	−6.4	28.3
Asia	3.2	2.5	3.2	−4.2	21.1	14.8	17.5	−20.3
Lower-income countries[c]	3.6	2.7	2.5	3.5	24.0	16.5	14.5	19.8
	(3.2)	(2.8)	(2.3)	(3.6)	(20.7)	(16.4)	(12.9)	(20.8)
Other countries	2.3	1.9	4.4	−11.4	14.4	10.4	21.8	−48.5
Latin America and the Caribbean	1.4	0.2	2.0	3.4	6.7	1.0	9.9	15.0

Sources: See table 1.
[a] See foot-note a to table 29.
[b] See foot-note a to table 24.
[c] For definition of lower-income countries, see foot-note d to table 3. Data in parentheses refer to lower-income countries excluding petroleum exporters.

Consequently, the saving ratio suffered a setback in the mid 1970s.

Fiscal and financial policies of Governments are of course important for mobilizing domestic financial resources and for steering the resources into productive uses in line with national priorities. Developing countries have continued to make efforts to widen their tax base as one means of expanding public saving and, through monetary and other promotional measures, to stimulate private saving. Pursued with vigour, these efforts should lead to a significant increase in the availability of financial resources during the coming years. But much will also depend on the zeal with which institutional and organizational measures are applied to expand production. For, while resources are needed to increase production, the growth of production itself contributes to the availability of resources. In many developing countries, the need for institutional and organizational measures is nowhere so urgent as it is in agricultural activity.

The economic power gained by the petroleum-exporting countries has made them large suppliers of capital to the rest of the world. The net outflow of financial resources from these countries in 1975 amounted to more than 13 per cent of their gross domestic product, compared to less than 1 per cent in 1970 and less than 2 per cent in 1960.

The net inflow of financial resources received by other developing countries as a proportion of their gross domestic product, which had risen comparatively slowly from 2.1 per cent in 1960 to 2.9 per cent in 1970, rose sharply to 6.1 per cent in 1975. The proportion averaged a little less than 5 per cent for the lower-income countries, over 8 per cent for the middle-income countries and somewhat less than 6 per cent for the higher-income countries (see table 29). Whereas the proportion doubled between 1970 and 1975 for the lower-income countries as a group, it more than trebled for the corresponding subgroup of African countries--rising from 3.4 per cent in 1970 to 11.3 per cent in 1975 (see table 30).

At the outset of the 1970s, external resources financed 15 per cent of gross investment in developing countries other than the petroleum exporters. In 1975, the proportion had risen to 28 per cent; for the lower-income countries in this group, the corresponding figures was 28 per cent, whereas for the middle-income and higher-income countries, it was about 36 per cent and 25 per cent, respectively (table 29). Within the group of the lower-income countries, the contrast between the African countries and the Asian countries was very sharp: external resources financed almost three fifths of gross investment in the African countries, compared to just over one fifth in the Asian countries. For this group of African countries, the relative dependence on external resources has increased phenomenally since 1960; but for the comparable group of Asian countries, the relative dependence on external resources in 1975, though higher than in 1970, was virtually of the same order as in 1960 (table 30).

The sharply increased dependence of these developing countries on external financial resources in 1975 resulted from the cumulative impact of a number of adverse factors encountered since 1972. First, there was the escalation in prices of food-grains

TABLE 31. NET RECEIPTS OF BILATERAL OFFICIAL DEVELOPMENT ASSISTANCE[a] FROM DEVELOPED MARKET ECONOMIES AND OF RESOURCES AT CONCESSIONAL TERMS FROM MULTILATERAL AGENCIES, BY INCOME GROUP OF DEVELOPING COUNTRIES, 1970 AND 1975

Country group[b]	Net receipts as percentage of gross domestic product		Net receipts per inhabitant in dollars	
	1970	1975	1970	1975
I. Countries with *per capita* gross domestic product in 1970 of less than $200	2.25	2.60	2.40	4.64
Petroleum-exporting countries	3.30	1.43	3.24	4.00
Other countries	2.08	2.98	2.24	4.75
II. Countries with *per capita* gross domestic product in 1970 of $200 or more but less than $400	2.21	1.70	5.74	8.84
Petroleum-exporting countries	1.53	0.75	5.06	6.69
Other countries	2.35	2.00	5.84	9.18
III. Countries with *per capita* gross domestic product in 1970 of $400 or more	0.39	0.40	2.29	4.93
Petroleum-exporting countries	0.24	0.09	1.18	1.38
Other countries	0.41	0.49	2.56	5.78
TOTAL	1.38	1.32	2.83	5.26
Petroleum-exporting countries	1.51	0.63	3.04	3.79
Other countries	1.35	1.54	2.79	5.53

Sources: Centre for Development Planning, Projections and Policies of the United Nations Secretariat, based on data from Organisation for Economic Co-operation and Development, *Development Co-operation, 1976 Review* (Paris, 1976), and from sources indicated in table 1.

[a] Publicly financed capital on concessional terms of at least a 25 per cent grant element.

[b] *Group I: petroleum-exporting countries*—Indonesia, Nigeria; *other countries*—Afghanistan, Bangladesh, Benin, Botswana, Burma, Burundi, Cape Verde, Central African Empire, Chad, Comoros, Ethiopia, Gambia, Guinea, Guinea-Bissau, Haiti, India, Kenya, Lesotho, Madagascar, Malawi, Mali, Mauritania, Nepal, Niger, Pakistan, Philippines, Rwanda, Sierra Leone, Somalia, Sri Lanka, Sudan, Thailand, Togo, Uganda, United Republic of Cameroon, United Republic of Tanzania, Upper Volta, Zaire.

Group II: petroleum-exporting countries—Algeria, Ecuador, Iraq; *other countries*—Angola, Bolivia, Colombia, Congo, Dominican Republic, Egypt, El Salvador, Equatorial Guinea, Ghana, Guatemala, Guyana, Honduras, Ivory Coast, Jordan, Liberia, Malaysia, Mauritius, Morocco, Mozambique, Nicaragua, Paraguay, Republic of Korea, Senegal, Southern Rhodesia, Swaziland, Syrian Arab Republic, Tunisia.

Group III: petroleum-exporting countries—Gabon, Iran, Kuwait, Libyan Arab Jamahiriya, Saudi Arabia, Trinidad and Tobago, Venezuela; *other countries*—Argentina, Barbados, Brazil, Chile, Costa Rica, Fiji, Hong Kong, Israel, Jamaica, Mexico, Panama, Peru, Réunion, Singapore, Surinam, Uruguay, Zambia.

TABLE 32. NET RECEIPTS OF BILATERAL OFFICIAL DEVELOPMENT ASSISTANCE FROM DEVELOPED MARKET ECONOMIES AND OF RESOURCES AT CONCESSIONAL TERMS FROM MULTILATERAL AGENCIES, BY DEVELOPING REGION, 1970 AND 1975[a]

Developing region[b]	Net receipts as percentage of gross domestic product		Net receipts per inhabitant (dollars)	
	1970	1975	1970	1975
Africa	3.14	3.21	4.61	9.67
Lower-income countries[c]	3.35	3.43	3.75	8.22
	(4.40)	(5.86)	(4.40)	(10.43)
Other countries	2.94	2.97	6.22	12.35
Asia	1.86	1.76	2.34	4.22
Lower-income countries[c]	1.97	2.30	2.09	3.78
	(1.66)	(2.30)	(1.83)	(3.60)
Other countries	1.50	0.90	4.52	8.07
Latin America and the Caribbean	0.44	0.34	2.56	3.85

Sources: See table 31.
[a] See foot-note a to table 31.
[b] See foot-note b to table 31.
[c] For definition of lower-income countries, see foot-note d to table 3. Data in parentheses refer to lower-income countries excluding petroleum exporters.

(following widespread crop failures in 1971 and 1972), petroleum (after the actions initiated by the Organization of Petroleum Exporting Countries in October 1973), fertilizer and capital goods (in the wake of increases in prices of other key commodities); and this was followed by a pronounced recession in economic activity in industrial countries. To cover the very large deficit that emerged in their balance of payments on current account, these developing countries turned to both official and private sources of external finance. The relative importance of these two sources of external finance, however, differed widely among countries.

Among the developing countries excluding petroleum exporters, the relative importance of concessional assistance from official sources has been much greater in recent years for the lower-income countries than for the corresponding middle-income and higher-income groups. For example, the net receipts of official development assistance of the lower-income group from the developed market economies and of resources at concessional terms from multilateral agencies in 1975 amounted to about 3 per cent of the gross domestic product of recipient countries (up from 2.1 per cent in 1970), whereas the corresponding figures for the middle-income and higher-income countries were 2 per cent (down from nearly 2.4 per cent in 1970) and 0.5 per cent (up from 0.4 per cent in 1970), respectively (see table 31). Within the group of lower-income countries, the African countries were the increasingly larger recipients, in that their net receipts of concessional assistance from the same sources, as a proportion of gross domestic product, increased from 4.4 per cent in 1970 to 5.9 per cent in 1975. During the same period, the net receipts of Asian countries increased from 1.7 per cent to 2.3 per cent, but remained proportionally much smaller than the net receipts of African countries (see table 32).[27]

Similar information on net receipts of official development assistance from the centrally planned economies is not available. But the amounts involved are known to have been much smaller than the net receipts of financial aid from the developed market economies. The aid provided by petroleum-exporting countries to other developing countries since 1974 as a proportion of the gross national product of the aid givers has been well above the target specified in the International Development Strategy for aid from developed countries. It has gone largely to countries with which the aid givers have close ethnic, cultural and religious ties.[28] On the whole, because financial assistance received by developing countries from the developed market economies and multilateral agencies has constituted probably more than four fifths of the total concessional assistance received by developing countries, such assistance serves as a close approximation of the past trends in over-all official aid.

It will have been apparent from the foregoing comments that a shift is beginning to be perceptible in the flow of concessional finance from the developed market economies and multilateral agencies towards lower-income developing countries. Even so, the disparities in receipts of aid have remained marked, and the receipts have fallen well short of needs.

The point about aid disparities and needs comes out sharply

from the data on per capita receipts of financial assistance. Among the developing countries other than petroleum exporters, the per capita net amount of official assistance received by the lower-income countries from the developed market economies and multilateral agencies registered an encouraging increase from $2.25 in 1970 to $4.75 in 1975, but even so the amount received in the latter year remained substantially smaller than the corresponding figures of $9.18 and $5.78 for the middle-income and higher-income countries, respectively (table 31).[29] Within the lower-income group, it was the subgroup of Asian countries that continued to have the most unfavourable experience in this respect: its per capita receipts in 1975 amounted to only $3.60, compared to $10.43 for the corresponding subgroup of African countries (table 32). Ideally, there should be an inverse relation between per capita receipts of aid and per capita income of receiving countries, the underlying premise being that relatively larger flows of assistance should be provided to poorer countries. Recent trends in the flow of international assistance to developing countries indicate that the ideal relation is not yet in sight.

Had the flow of official development assistance from the economically advanced countries equalled the target indicated for it in the International Development Strategy, a significant impact on the problem of mass poverty in developing countries might have already become discernible. During 1971-1975, the net flow of official development assistance from the developed market economies averaged 0.33 per cent of their gross national product.[30] The average was not even half as large as the target of 0.7 per cent set in the Strategy. The corresponding ratio for disbursements of assistance from the developed countries with centrally planned economies is not available, but some estimates suggest that it is much smaller than the figure of 0.33 per cent for the developed countries with market economies.[31] In 1976, drawing attention to the problem of human suffering in the depressed regions of middle Africa and southern Asia, the Committee for Development Planning emphasized the need for action "on a new and dramatic scale" to alleviate acute poverty.[32] Action on such a scale requires, among other things, a large increase in the flow of concessional aid to the needy countries. These of course are encouraging signs; but in the fact of persisting stagnation (in relative terms) in over-all official development assistance, it is hard to envisage that concessional assistance to the needy countries "on a new and dramatic scale" is in the offing. The need for it, however, continues to loom large. Indeed, without a marked expansion of such assistance, a new international strategy can hardly offer the promise of a significant and reasonably quick improvement in standard of life for a large majority of people in developing countries.

The sharp deterioration in balance of payments on current account around the mid 1970s compelled many developing countries to seek loans from international private capital markets. As in the past, however, international private capital has been attracted mainly to higher-income and middle-income developing countries, which possess a buoyant export trade and/or a relatively large domestic market for manufactured products. This conclusion is borne out by the available information on publicized Euro-currency credit. For example, in 1975, the publicized amount of Euro-currency loans extended to developing countries was $10.7 billion, of which the sum of $3.2 billion was accounted for by loans to petroleum-exporting countries. Of the balance of $7.5 billion, $5.9 billion (78 per cent) went to higher-income developing countries, $1.4 billion (18 per cent) to middle-income countries and only $0.3 billion (4 per cent) to lower-income countries. Even more striking is the fact that the Euro-currency credits obtained in 1975 by just two higher-income developing countries, Brazil and Mexico, amounted to as much as $4.3 billion or 57 per cent of the sum of all such credits to developing countries other than the petroleum exporters.[33] The credit extended by the International Monetary Fund, particularly through its Oil Facility, eased to an extent the severe constraint faced by deficit countries, but many countries also had to run down substantially their international monetary reserves to finance external deficits.

The increased relative dependence on external finance in recent years has compounded the external debt problems of developing countries which had already become serious by the end of the 1960s. Information on total external indebtedness of developing countries is lacking. However, some pertinent conclusions can be drawn from data on external public debt. For illustrative purposes, information on external public debt of developing countries other than petroleum exporters as a percentage of their gross domestic product is shown below for 1970 and 1975.[34]

	1970	1975
Lower-income countries	20	24
Middle-income countries	27	34
Higher-income countries	13	16
Total	18	21

This information indicates that the relative level of external public debt has become very high for middle-income countries and fairly high for lower-income countries. Within the group of lower-income countries, external public debt as a percentage of gross domestic product in 1975 averaged 36 per cent for African countries and 21 per cent for Asian countries. By contrast, in the same year, the average for countries of Latin America and the Caribbean (all but one of which belong to the middle-income and higher-income groups of developing countries) was 15 per cent. In many developing countries, a substantial proportion of export earnings is currently absorbed by the service payments they have to make on external debt.

Thus, there is an urgent need not only for a substantially enlarged flow of concessional assistance, particularly to lower-income countries which face stubborn poverty and underdevelopment but also for measures to alleviate the debt problem meaningfully. Alleviation of the burden of past debt, however, is merely one aspect of a critical problem. Measures are also required to prevent the emergence of unmanageable debt burdens in the future, by providing assistance to the needy countries wholly or mainly as grants.

IX. POINTERS FOR THE 1980'S

Economic and social development is a complex process that requires vigorous efforts on a wide front over a long span of time. In such a context, the current International Development Strategy is merely one link in a chain of action programmes devised by the world community to accelerate the progress of developing countries and to diminish economic and social disparities among nations. It is only logical to expect therefore that the issues highlighted in the current Strategy, many of which have been touched upon in the foregoing review of development trends since 1960, will figure in a new international development strategy that the General Assembly intends to adopt for the 1980s. However, in the light of experience, there are bound to be some new development issues or at least changes in emphasis among the current ones that will require new measures and shifts in current policies. This aspect is foreshadowed in the current Strategy in the statement that the policy measures already agreed upon by the world community "should be viewed in a dynamic context, involving continuing review to ensure their effective implementation and adaptation in the light of new developments, . . . and to seek new areas of agreement and the widening of the existing ones".[35]

The analysis contained in the preceding sections indicates that the need for rapid economic growth remains urgent in developing countries. Only through expansion, diversification and modernization of their economies will it be possible for these countries to provide their people with increasing opportunities for a better life. As a group, developing countries recorded an annual increase in total output or income of 5.5 per cent in the 1960s and not far short of 6 per cent in the first half of the 1970s. Taking into account both needs and possibilities, it can be legitimately argued that the annual rate of economic growth of developing countries in the 1980s should be higher than 6 per cent. It is relevant to note in this context that recent national development plans suggest that these countries are seeking on the average an annual rate of more than 7 per cent during the second half of the 1970s.[36]

An average for all developing countries, however, tends to be highly deceptive, as is vividly demonstrated by the record of recent development trends. While the average annual rate of economic growth for developing countries as a whole in the first half of the 1970s was almost equal to the target specified in the International Development Strategy for this decade (6 per cent), the average for the lower-income developing countries (those with a per capita annual gross domestic product of less than $200 at the outset of the 1970s) that are not exporters of petroleum was only 3 per cent or just about half as large as the average for all developing countries. Per capita output increased yearly by only

0.5 per cent, and per capita income adjusted for terms of trade changed by only 0.2 per cent, in those lower-income countries in which about 60 per cent of the people of the developing world live. It is not that those countries did not seek rapid economic growth; rather, it is the stranglehold of diverse constraints that obstructed the attainment of their development targets.[37] Thus, despite the efforts made to relieve human suffering, immense poverty continues to be the unfortunate trait of these countries, all but one of which are situated in middle Africa and southern Asia. Such facts suggest that special development strategies need to be formulated for the countries that have acute problems of poverty.

A problem encountered by most developing countries, irrespective of their average income or level of development, has been the rapid increase of population. On the average, the population of developing countries has been growing annually since the mid 1960s by over 2.6 per cent, or at a rate higher than the average of 2.5 per cent assumed for the 1970s in the International Development Strategy. Of course, a country's capacity to cope with rising population is influenced by such factors as its current level of development and current density of population. Notwithstanding differences among developing countries in regard to such factors, rapid growth of population has imposed heavy social costs in most of them. Rapid urbanization has been especially costly, because of the heavy demand it has generated for the social infrastructure of housing, systems of piped-water supply and sewage disposal, transportation and other urban amenities. Rapid growth of population has also strained educational and health facilities and has aggravated the unemployment problem. The population issue cannot therefore be set aside from discussions on requirements of accelerated economic and social progress.

The need for expansion and improvement of educational and health facilities will continue to be strong in the years ahead. A number of significant achievements have been made in respect of these facilities, but shortages and short-comings remain pressing. It appears particularly urgent to enhance sharply the capacity of people to tackle a wide variety of development tasks. Vocational education and training, designed to expand much needed occupational skills, deserve a far greater attention than has been accorded them in the past.

A slackened pace of population growth, even if achieved fairly soon, will contribute significantly to alleviation of the unemployment problem only in the long run, since those who will be seeking employment in the 1980s are already born. Although the available quantitative information is meagre, there is little doubt that the unemployment problem has continued to be serious in much of the developing world. The problem calls for a bold and imaginative attack through commensurate expansion and modification of the activities that yield useful goods and services.

For much of the developing world, nowhere is the need for a dynamic expansion of production greater than in agricultural activity. The lagging output of agriculture has severely impeded the economic and social progress of many developing countries, especially those at the lower end of the income scale. These countries need a rapid agricultural expansion to provide food security, generate adequate supplies of agricultural raw materials for industries, absorb people without work into gainful employment, improve distribution of income, stem rapid urbanization, contain inflationary pressures, increase exports--indeed, to invigorate the whole economy. Fortunately, policy discussions at both national and international levels have recently been giving considerably attention to the requirements of agricultural development, and the receptivity to new ideas on this subject appears to be growing. The international community can play a valuable role in invigorating the agricultural activity of developing countries, <u>inter alia,</u> by helping to build irrigation systems so as to make agriculture immune from the vicissitudes of weather and by helping to develop seeds suitable for cultivation in dry areas. Much of the agricultural success, however, will depend on national efforts, which will often entail difficult policy decisions.

Relatively, the performance of industry in developing countries during recent years has been encouraging. But again, over-all group averages do not convey the full picture. The available evidence clearly shows that industrial production in the lower-income developing countries has been increasing at a tardy pace compared to the pace in the rest of the developing world. Signs are also unmistakable that, had agricultural production not languished, the recent industrial record of developing countries would have been more encouraging. Rapid industrialization will surely remain a basic objective of these countries. But their planners and policy makers will also need to give renewed attention to the promotion of a pattern of industrial output that is in consonance with the country's development requirements. The policy thrust needs to be in favour of the manufacture of those goods that create greater employment opportunities and improve the living standards of lower-income people or that help to increase earnings of foreign exchange and strengthen the base for further industrial expansion.

The trading pattern of developing countries has experienced some changes in recent years. Recent changes have stemmed from a number of factors, prominent among them being the major shifts in prices of internationally traded goods, the recession in economic activity of many industrial countries in the middle years of the 1970s and the rise in protectionist forces that have impeded access to their markets for a variety of goods manufactured or processed by developing countries. The latter two developments are danger signals for the export trade of developing countries. To be meaningful, a new international development strategy will have to pave the way for an upward trend in the export earnings and the capacity to import of developing countries, especially those whose needs are urgent. A series of interrelated measures are required for this purpose which, by and large, have been under negotiation in international forums for some time. The outcome of those negotiations appears clouded at present, but their success is vital for a new international development strategy.

In part, the recent changes in the trading pattern of developing countries have also resulted from their efforts to strengthen economic co-operation among themselves. Indeed, their growing co-operation holds forth a new promise. Not only has their mutual trade gained significantly in recent years but their collaborative activities to expand industrial and agricultural production as well as physical and financial infrastructure have acquired some momentum. Although some of the earlier economic integration schemes of developing countries have suffered setbacks, a number of newer ones have displayed vitality. To an important extent, the new momentum of the mid 1970s was prompted by world economic events. But the more important point is that many countries did rise to the challenge of those events. A crucial need now is not to let joint efforts slacken. Whether through formal integration schemes or through ad hoc arrangements, developing countries need to push for greatly strengthened economic co-operation among themselves.

The efforts of developing countries to enhance their individual and collective self-reliance are but a logical element of their development thrust. In this context, they will certainly need to tap fully their financial resources and to use those scarce resources efficiently for expansion of productive activity. The fiscal, financial and institutional policies required to help achieve these objectives have undergone substantial changes in many developing countries, but experience also shows that much still remains to be done.

Even with dynamic national policies, which should yield an expanding flow of their own financial resources, many developing countries will require a greatly enlarged flow of finance from abroad. The countries most in need of concessional assistance from abroad are those that face crushing poverty. Will the years ahead witness the attainment of the aid target that has so far proved elusive--the target for the net flow of official development assistance from the economically advanced countries? Will such assistance increasingly go to the neediest countries? Will there be adequate monitoring and control of international flows of private finance and technology to developing countries in a framework acceptable to both borrowers and lenders? Will the burden of external indebtedness that many developing countries currently bear be removed or substantially alleviated? These are not new questions; they have been at the forefront of international discussions on development matters for a long time. But without adequate responses to them, there can hardly be a new international development strategy.

New and old issues are prone to intermingle in a new international development strategy. The ultimate test of both the viability and the success of the new strategy will be the vigour with which the policy measures prescribed in it are applied both by the developing countries themselves and by the rest of the world community in a spirit of global solidarity. If the required vigour is displayed and sustained through the 1980s, the world will have made an important stride towards the establishment of a new international economic order.

NOTES

[1] General Assembly resolution 1710 (XVI), adopted on 19 December 1961, para. 1.

[2] General Assembly resolution 2626 (XXV), adopted on 24 October 1970, para. 13.

[3] General Assembly resolution 31/182, adopted on 21 December 1976, para. 1.

[4] Economic and Social Council resolution 2125 (LXIII), adopted on 4 August 1977. sect. III, para. 2, The Declaration and the Programme of Action on the Establishment of a New International Economic Order are contained in General Assembly resolutions 3201 (S-VI) and 3202 (S-VI), which were adopted on 1 May 1974.

[5] General Assembly resolution 32/174, adopted on 19 December 1977, para. 2.

[6] The data are expressed in United States dollars.

[7] No direct comparisons are available between the level of output in developing countries and that of the centrally planned economies of Eastern Europe and the Union of Soviet Socialist Republics; however, the trend in per capita output of the latter, as measured by their rate of increase in per capita net material product implies that the relative distance between these two groups has increased somewhat.

[8] General Assembly resolution 2626 (XXV), para. 14.

[9] See, for example, Irving B. Kravis and others, A System of International Comparisons of Gross Product and Purchasing Power (Baltimore, Johns Hopkins University Press, 1975).

[10] Hereafter the shorter term "petroleum exporters" will be used for convenience.

[11] See International Finance, Depressed Regions and Needed Progress (United Nations publication, Sales No. E.76.II.A.8), p. 26. Only one country of Latin America and the Caribbean, Haiti, had a per capita gross domestic product in 1970 of less than $200.

[12] Because of differences in country coverage, the data in table 8 and the two related tables containing information on expansion of rural and urban population and labour force that follow differ somewhat from those set out in the tables contained in the preceding section. The tables in that section deal with countries for which information on gross domestic product is available for the period 1960-1975. The tables in the present section focus on countries for which comparable data on population and its major components (urban and rural population or population by occupational groups) are available.

[13] General Assembly resolution 2626 (XXV), para. 15.

[14] Estimates of the Population Division of the Department of International Economic and Social Affairs of the United Nations Secretariat. Because of lack of data, the country coverage underlying these estimates differs somewhat from that specified in foot-note a to table 8. This difference, however, does not affect the conclusions emerging from the estimates.

[15] See "Planning for development: goals and policies of developing countries for the second half of the 1970s", study prepared by the Centre for Development Planning, Projections and Policies, Journal of Development Planning, No. 11 (United Nations publication, Sales No. E.77.II.A.14), chap. I.

[16] The averages shown in table 12 and the following two tables are taken from a recent publication of the World Bank. The system of country classification used in that publication differs from that underlying all but these three tables contained in the present paper. The differences, however, do not affect the broad generalizations relating to lower-income, middle-income and higher-income developing countries--that is, the three country groups around which much of the analysis set out in the present paper is built.

[17] In order to base such conclusions on information for a reasonably large number of countries, the data in table 15 refer only to 1966-1970 and 1971-1975. The relevant comparisons with information for 1961-1965 are possible only for a much smaller number of countries than that underlying table 15 (and the related table that follows). Even so, owing to lack of information on components of gross domestic product by origin for several developing countries, the number of countries covered in table 15 is smaller than of those that form the basis of the corresponding tables in the section entitled "Widening disparities" (tables 1-7). This explains in large part why the rates of economic growth shown in table 15 differ somewhat from those indicated in earlier tables.

[18] See "Planning for development: goals and policies . . .", chaps. I and II.

[19] See Consultative Group on International Agricultural Research, International Research in Agriculture (New York, 1974).

[20] Detailed information on industrial progress during the 1960s and on industrial plans for the 1970s is given in two papers and a study prepared by the Centre for Development Planning, Projections and Policies. See "Industrialization and development: progress and problems in developing countries", and "Planning for industrial progress: goals and policies of developing countries for the 1970s", Journal of Development Planning, No.8 (United Nations publication, Sales No. E.75.II.A.1), and "Planning for development: goals and policies . . . .".

[21] See "Salient features of economic co-operation among developing

countries" in the present issue of the Journal of Development Planning.

[22] Ibid.

[23] Supplement to World Economic Survey, 1975 (United Nations publication, Sales No. E.77.II.C.2), table III.1.

[24] See "Salient features of economic co-operation among developing countries" in the present issue of Journal of Development Planning.

[25] Ibid.

[26] General Assembly resolution 2626 (XXV), para. 17.

[27] The conclusion that the relative importance of concessional assistance from official sources in recent years has been much greater for the lower-income petroleum-importing countries emerges even more forcefully from a comparison of the data on net receipts as a percentage of gross domestic product shown in tables 31 and 32 with the data on external resources as a percentage of gross domestic product shown in tables 29 and 30. Of course, the country coverage underlying the two pairs of tables differs owing to short-comings of the available information. However, the coverages of each of the two pairs is sufficiently large to permit drawing of valid generalizations for broad groups of developing countries.

[28] See "Salient features of economic co-operation among developing countries" in the present issue of Journal of Development Planning, tables 11-13.

[29] The data in tables 31 and 32 refer only to those countries for which comparable information on gross domestic product was available. If the aid data for the countries that are not covered in those tables are included, the disparities in per capita receipts of concessional assistance from the developed market economies and multilateral agencies appear to be greater than those suggested by the figures mentioned in the text above. The more inclusive coverage yields the following averages for per capita net receipts of petroleum-importing developing countries in 1975: lower-income countries, $4.79; middle-income countries, $10.85; higher-income countries, $7.73. The more inclusive coverage refers to the countries listed in foot-note b to table 31 and the countries listed below:

Group I: Bhutan, Democratic Kampuchea, Democratic Yemen, Lao People's Democratic Republic, Macao, Maldives, Solomon Islands, Timor, Samoa and Yeman.
Group II: Gilbert Island, Pacific Islands (Trust Territory), Papua New Guinea, Republic of Viet Nam (now part of Viet Nam), Sao Tome and Principe, Tonga Tuvalu and West Indies not identified elsewhere.

Group III: Bahamas, Belize, Bermuda, Cuba, Djibouti, French Guiana, French Polynesia, Guadeloupe, Lebanon, Martinique, New Caledonia and New Hebrides.

[30] *Economic and Social Progress in the Second Development Decade* (United Nations publication, Sales No. E.77.II.A.11), p.111.

[31] See, for instance, Organisation for Economic Co-operation and Development, *Development Co-operation, 1976 Review* (Paris, 1976), p. 59.

[32] *International Finance, Depressed Regions and Needed Progress* (United Nations publication, Sales No. E.76.II.A.8).

[33] Estimates of group averages were made by the Centre for Development Planning, Projections and Policies of the United Nations Secretariat, on the basis of country data from World Bank, *Borrowings in International Capital Markets* (Washington, D.C., December 1976), No. EC-181/763.

[34] Estimates of group averages were made by the Centre for Development Planning, Projections and Policies of the United Nations Secretariat, from country data on external debt given in World Bank, World Debt Tables, vol. II (Washington, D.C.), 2 September 1977, No. EC-167/77 and from country data on gross domestic product given in sources mentioned in table 1. The country coverage is as follows: lower-income countries--Afghanistan, Bangladesh, Benin, Botswana, Burma, Burundi, Central African Empire, Chad, Ethiopia, Gambia, India, Indonesia, Kenya, Lesotho, Madagascar, Malaw, Mali, Mauritania, Niger, Pakistan, Philippines, Rwanda, Sierra Leone, Somalia, Sri Lanka, Sudan, Thailand, Togo, Uganda, United Republic of Cameroon, United Republic of Tanzania, Upper Volta and Zaire; middle-income countries--Bolivia, Colombia, Congo, Dominican Republic, Ecuador, Egypt, El Salvador, Ghana, Guatemala, Guyana, Honduras, Ivory Coast, Jordan, Liberia, Malaysia, Mauritius, Morocco, Nicaragua, Paraguay, Republic of Korea, Senegal, Swaziland, Syrian Arab Republic and Tunisia; higher-income countries--Argentina, Brazil, Chile, Costa Rica, Fiji, Jamaica, Mexico, Peru, Singapore, Uruguay and Zambia.

[35] General Assembly resolution 2626 (XXV), para. 20.

[36] See "Planning for development: goals and policies . . ."

[37] Recent experience of developing countries in implementing their national plans is dealt with in some detail in another paper. See "Implementation of development plans: the experience of developing countries in the first half of the 1970s", paper prepared by the Centre for Development Planning, Projections and Policies, *Journal of Development Planning*, No. 12 (United Nations publication, Sales No. E.78.II.A.1).

Some Economic Concepts and Policy Issues in Developing Countries

U. TUN WAI

> This articles examines some of the economic concepts and issues confronting economic policymakers in developing countries. While many of these concepts and issues are common to developed countries, considerable differences arise mainly from the way they are manifested in the context of economic problems.

How do the economics of developing countries compare with those of developed countries? The answer depends largely on the definition of economics.

If economics is the study of economies, then each country's economic problem is unique and no generalization can be made. But if one defines economics as a field of study which attempts to derive universal principles regarding the allocation of scarce resources toward competing ends, then one would have to conclude that these principles of economics are applicable universally. Nevertheless, one could still discuss the relevance of a given set of principles to a particular situation.

The confrontation of a given theory with economic reality helps to determine its relevance. It also enables economists to improve a theory and make it more applicable to developing countries. From this point of view, there is scope for discussing economic concepts and issues which may be different from those in developed countries. Two further points will help to clarify the relationship between concepts and policy issues and between theories and economic realities.

The first point concerns the relevance of macroeconomic models for developing countries. Most macroeconomic models, built with developed countries in mind, are designed to approximate reality. Therefore, there is bound to be a gap (G) between the model (M) and

From **FINANCE AND DEVELOPMENT**, June 1980, reprinted by permission of the publisher.

reality (R). The relevance of the model becomes greater when G approaches zero or when the difference is one of degree and not of kind. The gap will be large if the assumptions of the model are not realistic. Since economic reality is different for developing and developed countries, one should not be surprised if the gap between the model and reality is greater for developing countries than for developed countries. Even for developed countries, when policy issues are under consideration one needs complicated models. R.G.D. Allen in the preface to his book, <u>Macro-Economic Theory: A Mathematical Treatment</u> (1968), states: "The models considered here, despite their formidable appearance at times, are many stages removed from policy applications. They attempt to explain how things work in precise terms. But just because of their precision, they are not easily used in any consideration of how the working of the economic system should be viewed in practice, when the strategic variables change from one situation to another. Moreover, in order to obtain precision, the models are drastically simplified to keep down the number of variables and parameters."

The second point may be made through an analogy with medicine. Even though human beings have the same anatomy and physiology, tropical medicine is studies as a separate field of specialization. For similar reasons, development economics is studied separately in many universities throughout the world. Thus one would expect to find economic problems in developing countries very different from those in developed countries. This analogy also helps to explain why certain parameters and the strength of some variables may be different in the two types of countries.

The techniques of economic analysis that are universally useful include <u>ceteris paribus</u> (other things being equal), marginal analysis, and trade-offs. <u>Ceteris paribus</u> enables the economist to break up a complicated problems into its components and into manageable units. Marginal analysis helps to show the policymaker the additional effort needed to solve an economic problem. Trade-offs between conflicting objectives and between alternative policy instruments highlight the nature of economics. Bearing these points in mind, we examine below some of the important economic concepts and issues facing policymakers in developing countries, without relating them to specific theories or to particular economic situations. There are other important problems which are not dealt with in this article, for example, the need to develop domestic financial markets and bring about social and other institutional changes to obtain a high rate of economic growth.

I. CONCEPTS AND ISSUES AT THE NATIONAL LEVEL

Per Capita Income

The one measure used widely by economists and policymakers to indicate material progress is per capita income (national income divided by total population). When this measure is deflated by prices to give real per capita income over time in a given country, one cannot quarrel with this indicator. But when it is used to make international comparisons, there are many pitfalls because the exchange rate does not measure the purchasing power of currencies for goods and services that are not internationally traded. Then, again, consumption patterns and needs between countries may be so different for climatic, social, and institutional reasons that per capita income may be a poor measure of economic welfare -- not to mention the social costs of pollution, overcrowding of cities, and other factors which are not taken into account in computing national income.

Despite these shortcomings in evaluation material progress, policymakers in developing countries can place great weight on development plans to increase total output and to reduce the so-called gap between standards of living in developing and developed countries. The first objective is desirable if it is regarded only as a first approximation of what a country really wants and if other equally desirable social objectives, such as more equal distribution of income, are not disregarded. The second objective is desirable, politically speaking, but it will be very difficult to reduce the gap since the standards of living in developed countries are rising rapidly.

Unemployment

Two views can be taken of the unemployment problem in developing countries. One is to regard the problem in the same way as in developed countries -- that is, to be very concerned with it either in the form of open unemployment or of disguised unemployment. Consequently, considerable impetus must be given in development plans to increasing employment. The other view would be to point to the evils of unemployment but to put less pressure on the government to solve this problem on the grounds that the family is still an economic unit in developing countries and provides private social security. Both view are valid -- the former for urban areas; the relevance of the two views depends in part on whether the country is generally overpopulated (as, for example, India and Bangladesh) or on whether it is not overpopulated (as many African and Southeast Asian countries).

The availability of unemployed labor is both a challenge and a possibility for more rapid growth in developing countries, says W. Arthur Lewis ("Economic Developed with Unlimited Supplies of Labour," The Manchester School, May 1954). However, Ragnar Nurkse (Problems of Capital Formation in Underdeveloped Countries and Patterns of Trade and Development, 1967) believes that there are a number of problems to be overcome before excess workers in rural areas can be put to work on new investment projects in urban areas, including the cost of transporting food from farms to projects and the need to give tools to workers on these new investment projects. In short, any sizable reduction in unemployment depends on additional free resources to finance investment for infrastructure and to train unemployed workers.

Besides the question of supply of labor, there is the problem of factor proportions in developing countries, which has an important bearing on the choice of projects and the relative use of labor and capital. Since developing countries have to import capital equipment it may be desirable to choose more labor intensive projects to save foreign exchange and give employment to nationals. Furthermore, since these innovations are based on relative prices of labor and capital in developed countries, the latest machinery is not necessarily the best choice for developing countries. Hence, there should be more research and development expenditures for capital saving innovations specially suited to their needs. If the innovations can be both capital and labor saving, as for example improved higher yielding seeds suited to the local climate, then the needs of developing countries would be well served.

Sometimes the unemployment problem in developing countries is said to originate from structural factors which are nonexistent in developed countries. A number of explanations have been given for the existence of structural unemployment in developing countries, many of which are related to structural disequilibrium at the factor (input) level. For example, market imperfections, technological restraints, and overpopulation have been stressed by R.S. Eckaus, (The Factor Proportions Problem in Underdeveloped Areas," in <u>American Economic Review,</u> September 1955). The policy implications of this analysis for developing countries is that one needs to improve the institutional framework and adapt existing technology to developing countries.

Nonmonetized Sector

A nonmonetized sector exists in developing countries because a certain part of output produced by the villagers is purely for home consumption. It can also exist when goods are bartered rather than bought with money. The size of the nonmonetized sector is believed to be important in a large number of developing countries, even though it has never been measured accurately. Such a sector also exists in developed countries -- for example, when wives provide services in the home without direct monetary gain -- but it is generally believed to be less important than in developing countries.

Should the authorities take this sector into account in planning? Should they take steps to monetize the sector gradually or merely ignore it? Most economists would say that it cannot be ignored and that if developing countries are to grow rapidly one must integrate such a sector into the rest of the economy, not only o motivate villagers to produce more and be more responsive to the objectives of the plan but also to enable the government to tax more heavily. Further, growth can be more rapid if there is specialization and division of labor. What better way is there to do this than to make the villager more specialized, selling his product to the market and buying practically all his needs from the market?

If the objective is growth per se and not stability of income, this view is valid. The production of goods for home consumption provides the villager with his own built-in stabilizer except when there are widespread droughts or floods. Therefore, perhaps, what is needed is not to reduce the size of the nonmonetized sector absolutely, but only relatively, by increasing the monetized sector. This can be done only if the villager will either work longer hours or use more capital to produce goods for the market without diminishing production for home consumption.

II. CONCEPTS AND ISSUES AT THE INTERNATIONAL LEVEL

Terms of Trade

In the international field, terms of trade is perhaps the most widely used concept by policymakers, partly because it is relatively easy to understand and partly because it is convenient to explain difficulties in a country's balance or payments. The technicalities of terms of trade are the same for both developed and developing countries. But owing to the greater sensitivity of prices of raw materials over the business cycle of developed countries, the greater dependence on fewer export commodities by developing countries, and the importance of international trade to growth, this subject has been associated more with the problems of developing countries than those of developed countries.

By the terms of trade is meant the ratio of export prices to import prices over time with a fixed base year. Terms of trade are said to improve when export prices rise more rapidly (or fall less rapidly) than import prices or when export prices rise while import prices fall. When this occurs a country is able to obtain a larger volume of imports for a given quantum of exports. There is a deterioration in the terms of trade when the reverse happens.

There are a number of technical questions before terms of trade can be used as a basis for policymaking. First, the terms of trade should be measured in foreign currency prices; they can also be measured in local currency prices provided the conversion factors are the same for both exports and imports. Complications arise when there is a marked shift over a period in the commodity mix of exports and imports. Then there is the question of the choice of the base year. If the chosen year is one when export prices are relatively high, then the terms of trade will appear to be unfavorable in the subsequent period. If export prices are low in the base year, then the terms of trade will appear unrealistically favorable. While policymakers may have special reasons for choosing one year over another, one could partly avoid the base year problem by fitting trend lines to export prices and import prices and then compare the two trends. Even here, there is the question of what overall period one should consider. How far back should one go to make such a comparison?

The policy objective of not wishing to allow a country's terms of trade to deteriorate is commendable but the means to achieve this objective are neither simple nor clear cut. Judging from innumerable speeches at international conferences, policymakers in developing countries rely a great deal on urging their more developed trading parties to maintain the demand for raw material exports from their countries, while taking appropriate steps to prevent the prices of industrial products from rising. Such exhortations have some propaganda value from fluctuating or deteriorating according to changes in market conditions.

More recently, the oil producing countries have succeeded in improving their terms of trade through restricting output and raising the export price of oil. Their success has resulted partly from the solidarity shown by the OPEC (Organization of Petroleum Exporting Countries) countries and partly by the inelastic demand for oil, at least in the short run. While other developing countries would like to take similar measures to improve their terms of trade, cartels for other commodities are not likely to have the same success as OPEC because there are close substitutes for other raw materials.

International Inflation

In the 1950s and early 1960s it used to be thought that mainly developing countries suffered from chronic inflation. During the past ten years, inflation has become a world-wide phenomenon, and there are many developed countries, such as Italy, Japan, the United Kingdom, and the United States, where the inflation level is now measured in double digits (that is, above 9 per cent a year), and exceeds that of many developing countries. This phenomenon is all the more remarkable when we consider that most industrial countries experienced a long period of about two decades of relative price stability and growth. The recent period of inflation is different from some of the earlier ones because price increases are accompanied by declining output and rising unemployment, and hence the term "stagflation."

While it is not our main concern to analyze the causes of this change in the world situation, all periods of inflations have excess demand situations with some cost-push elements; some of the basic reasons might be

--a slowing down of the rate of technical advance in industrial countries which formerly helped to raise labor productivity to

match the demand for higher money wages,
- --pre-empting by governments in developed countries of bigger shares of the gross national product for government consumption and national defends, financed to a large extent by central bank credit,
- --the rapid expansion of output in industrial countries leading to a world-wide boom in prices of primary products which, in turn, through the foreign trade multiplier, increased imports of industrial products by the developing countries,
- --the breakdown of the built-in safeguards among industrial countries; in the past there was considerable slack in the capacity to produce output in other countries whenever one country was in a boom period. (In other words, the timing of business cycles was not coincidental in the early postwar period, but in the last decade business cycles have become more synchronized.),
- --the breakdown of the Bretton Woods system and the temporary abandonment of the fixed exchange rate system.

The interrelationships between inflation and exchange flexibility were discussed by H. Johannes Witteveen, the Managing Director of the Fund, in the March issue of <u>Finance and Development</u>. Although dealing mainly with developed countries, his views are also relevant to some developing countries.

A major policy issue before planners in developing countries is how to take policy measures to reduce the impact of world-wide inflation, or alternatively how to learn to live with a changed world situation. First, before a developing country can take offsetting measures, it should ensure that domestic pressures are not adding to domestic or world-wide inflation. Otherwise it will be pointless to take measures to fight international inflation while letting domestic inflation go unchecked. Second, it must have the financial strength to resist the effect of world-wide inflation which many developing countries do not possess. The ability to counteract imported inflation is lower in developing countries than in industrial countries.

In brief, the policymaker has to decide how to insulate the domestic economy from the effects of inflation abroad. If the prices of exports rise at least as fast as import prices and foreign exchange reserves are adequate or rising, then an appreciation of the exchange rate would tend to keep domestic prices in local currency unchanged. Since all export prices and all import prices do not move in step, some adjustment problems may have to be faced, such as a slowing down of the growth rate (especially if prices of imported capital goods rise faster than imported consumer goods), or a loss of foreign exchange reserves, or a combination of both.

It is not possible for any economy to insulate itself completely. Therefore, domestic incomes policy, especially the determination of wage rates in different sectors, that is, export versus home market, changing the relative size of government and private sector, and the relative shares of fixed income versus business profits, and so on, will have to be reviewed and adapted.

Floating Exchange Rates

The Bretton Woods system of fixed exchange rates based on an international dollar-gold exchange standard received a considerable setback in August 1971 when the United States suspended the convertibility of the dollar into gold, and the de jure or de facto floating of more and more key currencies since that date. Therefore, in recent years most developing countries have had to make a choice from among complete floating, pegging, or maintaining the value of their currencies in relation to one key currency while allowing the value in relation to other key currencies vary. This has been in marked contrast to the situation under the Bretton Woods system when a developing country could be assured that linking the value of its currency to one key currency automatically maintained its relation with respect to other key currencies as well.

For some countries in the French franc area (mainly in Africa) and the dollar currency area (mainly in Latin America), the choice has been made with little hesitation because of important trading and financial relations with the dominant key currency country. But even for them, there have been adjustment problems not only for some transactions in the balance of payments, such as travel and minor exports, but also for long range policies aimed at diversifying international trade. For other developing countries in Africa (for example, the Malagasy Republic, Nigeria, and Zambia) and in Asia (for example, Sri Lanka and India) which had become integrated with many currency areas and where trade and financial relationships were not dominated by any one country, neither the choice nor the adjustment problems have been easy. In the three East African countries of Kenya, Tanzania, and Uganda, which belong to a common customs area and share certain intergovernmental services, such as transport, the choice has been further complicated by differences of opinion as to what key currency their currencies should be pegged to.

It is for these reasons that in the recent discussions on international monetary reform, the developing countries generally have been very strongly in favor of restoring the par value system as it operated before August 1971. In the envisaged new system the exchange rate mechanism will remain based on stable but adjustable values, but there is provision for countries to adopt floating rates in particular situations, subject to Fund authorization, surveillance, and review. ("Outline of Reform, June 14, 1974" in International Monetary Reform Documents of the Committee of Twenty). Meanwhile, the Executive Board of the Fund on June 13, 1974 adopted a decision on guidelines for countries with floating exchange rates. The Fund Executive Board decision is too recent to fully assess how it will operate. The important policy question, however, is what key currency a developing country should be linked to. This in part depends on whether the key currency itself is floating or fixed in relation to other key currencies.

This policy question can be decided in part by comparing the net benefits to be gained from linking to alternative key currencies. Although noneconomic considerations will play a role, the following economic considerations should be taken into account: the prospects of the provision of a stable and expanding market for the exports of the developing countries by the key currency country; the aspects of foreign capital, both private and official, flowing in to finance temporary balance of payments deficits and to provide additional resources for financial economic development; the relative official strength of the key currency in connection to other currencies, especially whether it is more inflation-prone than that of other industrial countries. This point is particularly important in view of the present phenomenon of world-wide inflation, and the efforts of most developed countries to resist the importation of inflation.

One could add to the list of considerations by including the amount owed to the various key currency countries, the stock of foreign investment in the developing countries, and so on. All these points can be included in the category of relative financial strength of the developing country and the key currency country. It is natural for a country to wish its currency to be linked to the strongest currency, but if its currency is likely to lag greatly behind, then the developed country will suffer from an undervalued currency. On the other hand if its currency is linked to too weak a currency, then it is apt to find that foreign assets in terms of other key currencies will rapidly diminish in value. Therefore, a policymaker can choose the key currency only slightly stronger, and actively speaking, in the balance of payments field. It may also be possible to link with a very strong key currency and not follow suit, either in whole or part, whenever the key currency is reissued. Similarly, a country could link to a less strong key currency and not follow suit, either in whole or in part, when the key currency is devalued. But the alternative approaches will not, of course, provide the advantage of at least a bilateral "par value-fixed exchange rate" in a floating world.

Specialization Needed

The developing countries' preoccupation with growth, as well as the structural differences between them and the developed countries, will justify the specialization in techniques of economic analysis. This can be achieved by exerting care in applying the basic principles of economics and models to developing countries, because, in a one-world economy, the interests of developed countries may not always coincide with the interests of developed countries, at least in the short run.

Inflation and Growth: A Reconsideration of the Evidence from the LDCs

CONSTANTINE GLEZAKOS

Although inflation has been among the most extensively discussed topics by both academic economists and practitioners, the problems arising from inflation are still very much with us. Especially for most of the post-World War II period, both the rate of inflation and the controversy over its effects have been, and remain, relatively greater in less developed countries (LDCs) than in developed countries (DCs).

Controversy rages over the causes of inflation and its effects. In the present study I deal only with the latter issue, concentrating on the alleged relationship between the rate of inflation and economic growth. Specifically, the purpose of the present study is to investigate the extent to which the heretofore neglected "pattern of inflation" might contribute to clarifying the relationship between inflation and growth.[1] Simply stated, the contention of this study is that economic growth is affected more by the pattern of price changes than by the rate of inflation per se. Furthermore, it is argued that, unless the way in which inflation proceeds is properly taken into account, no significant relationship between inflation and economic growth can be revealed, especially by cross-country studies.

I. REVIEW OF THE LITERATURE

Few, if any, of the authors who have dealt with the relation between inflation and economic growth have succeeded in supporting their arguments with adequate empirical evidence. Moreover, to the extent that statistical analysis has been undertaken, the methods utilized have been rudimentary and the results inconclusive. This has prompted several economists to consider the attempt to identify the direction and significance of the relationship between inflation and growth as a hopeless cause. Mikesell, for example, contends that "the economic indicators do not in themselves provide satisfactory explanation of either the causes or the consequences of inflation," while Harberger asserts that "it is abundantly clear from the available evidence that there is no close relation between the rate of inflation and the rate of economic growth."[1]

The use of international cross-section data has facilitated the investigation of the relationship between inflation and growth by several authors, yet even such studies have not enjoyed great success.[2]

The pattern of inflation has been mentioned occasionally as a relevant factor in theoretical or descriptive studies in inflation and growth. It nevertheless has been neglected in most empirical studies on the monetarist-structuralist controversy. For example, at the 1963 Rio de Janeiro Conference on Inflation and Growth, Massad stated that "it may be more important to consider the changes in the rate of inflation rather than the average rate over a period, particularly when emphasis is placed on the elements of uncertainty introduced by inflation."[3] Johnson similarly asserted that inflation might impede growth in LDCs as a result of the fact that it "does not proceed at a steady and well anticipated rate, but proceeds erratically with large politically determined variations in the rate of price increase."[4]

In recent years the pattern of inflation concept has received appreciably greater attention in both theoretical and empirical studies but mainly in distinguishing between anticipated and actual inflation in the context of estimating short-run tradeoffs between inflation and unemployment.[5] Unfortunately, however, the same concept has been ignored in empirical studies of the relationship between inflation and long- or medium-term economic growth.

II. THE PATTERN OF INFLATION AND ECONOMIC GROWTH

Those who consider that the nature of changes in the rate of inflation has an influence on the overall rate of economic growth generally believe that it affects growth by affecting the accuracy with which economic units formulate their expectations regarding future prices, and hence the appropriateness of their behavior. It can be argued on an a priori basis that if a relatively steady rate of inflation persists in a country, some of its alleged detrimental effects[6] would more likely be ameliorated as the rate of inflation is more or less accurately anticipated.[7] Even accurately anticipated inflation rates can cause some waste of economic resources to the extent that people try to hedge against inflation by substituting inventories of real goods and foreign exchange reserves for idle cash balances.[8] Indeed, such behavior might be relatively more common in LDCs where financial markets are extremely underdeveloped.

However, even in such cases the losses in allocative efficiency as a result of anticipated inflation might not be extensive due to the limited degree of monetization in the LDCS. On the other hand, the economic costs of unanticipated inflation may be considerably greater. If the rate of inflation cannot be predicted, the possibility of successful hedging against inflation by both businessmen and wage earners is reduced, and the economic risks and social disruption associated with widely fluctuating inflation rates is significantly increased. Furthermore, the increased risk from future uncertainty would especially discourage long-term private investments, and thus impair economic growth.

Finally, it can be argued that, if inflation rates could be anticipated correctly, saving and lending activities might not be curtailed severely since nominal interest rates can be arranged so as to avoid the undesirable transfer of assets from creditors to debtors. This in turn can conceivably improve the existing bad situation of "fragmented capital markets,"[9] which so typically characterize LDCs and, possibly, increase their investment efficiency.[10] The present study attempts to test the conflicting claims regarding the effects of the pattern of price changes on economic growth. More specifically, the goal of the present study is the verification or refutation of the a priori contention that price change instability or inflation rate unpredictability is more deleterious to the economic growth of the LDCs than the rate of inflation per se.

III. THE MEASUREMENT OF PRICE INSTABILITY

In order to test the alleged effects of price instability, one needs a measure of such instability. From the discussion of the previous section it should be clear that price instability is conceived here as the degree of discrepancy between observed and anticipated prices.[11]

Therefore, although the variance or standard deviation of a price index time series might seem to be the obvious measures of price fluctuations over the relevant time period, it is evident from the preceding analysis that they do not qualify as measures of price instability in the context of the present study. This is because the variance of a price index time series measures deviations from the average price of the time period under consideration and not from expected prices. To put it differently, even if prices in a certain country were rising at a steady and thus accurately predictable rate, the variance of the country's price index series would be different than zero and hence indicate price instability in a case where price instability, according to my definition of the term, does not exist.[12]

It is evident, therefore, that an appropriate measure of price instability requires the development of a procedure for the estimation of expected prices.

Price Expectations Model

The definition and estimation of expected prices has become an increasingly popular topic in recent years and a considerable number of published studies, especially on money demand, have covered it extensively. Therefore, my discussion of price expectations is very concise. Its main objective is to explain basically the rationale and the procedure developed for the empirical estimation of expected prices.

Price expectations are attitudes and judgments regarding future prices and, as such, they have two dimensions: uncertainty and time. Since I am dealing with annual data, I have set the time horizon equal to one year. Thus, my main effort is to select or develop an expectations model which will represent, in a simple but rational fashion, the way in which price expectations are supposedly formed in the minds of individual decision units in an economy. Needless to say, such a model has to be simple enough so that it can be used for all countries in the sample.

On an a priori basis, two kinds of factors shape future price expectations in the minds of the decision-making agents. The first is <u>inertia</u> around a "normal" price level and the second is the <u>dynamic</u> force of a recent change in the price level. This general conceptual framework, in which price expectations might be perceived, can be expressed in several mathematical forms. On the one hand, there are various ways in which the normal price level can be determined and, on the other, there are different forms in which past "trends" or "projections of recent changes" might be taken into account.

Inasmuch as my study is in the exploratory stage, I did not delve deeply into the experimentation regarding alternative price expectations models. My intent is not the determination of an optimum price expectations model as such, but rather the investigation of the effects of price instability on economic growth, as long as price instability has been measured on the basis of a reasonable price expectations model. This was done by selecting two expectations models that, on the one hand, could be considered as representing, at least in general terms, how long-run expectations are formed and, on the other, allow for variation in such behavior among countries.

The two basic price expectations models that I have utilized in this study are the "adaptive expectations" model[13] for price levels and annual price changes:

$$P_t^e = P_{t-1}^e + \beta(P_{t-1} - P_{t-1}^e) \qquad (1)$$

$$\dot{p}_t^e = \dot{p}_{t-1}^e + \beta(\dot{p}_{t-1} - \dot{p}_{t-1}^e) \qquad (2)$$

and an "extrapolative" model for price levels:

$$P_t^e = P_{t-1} + \lambda(P_{t-1} - P_{t-2}) + \lambda^2(P_{t-2} - P_{t-3}) \qquad (3)$$

where: P_t^e denotes the price level expected to prevail at year t and formed during the year preceding it, and P_t denotes the actual price level at year t. Also, $\dot{p}_t^e$ and $\dot{p}_t$ denote the expected and actual annual price changes respectively, i.e., $\dot{p} = \frac{\Delta P_t}{P_t}(100)$.

The adaptive expectations model can be easily reduced to a distributed lag model of past prices. Indeed, through successive substitutions, equations 1 and 2 can be reduced respectively to:[14]

$$P_t^e = \beta P_{t-1} + \beta(1-\beta)P_{t-2} + \beta(1-\beta)^2 P_{t-3} + \cdots \qquad (4)$$

and

$$\dot{p}_t^e = \beta \dot{p}_{t-1} + \beta(1-\beta)\dot{p}_{t-2} + \beta(1-\beta)^2 \dot{p}_{t-3} + \cdots \qquad (5)$$

Similarly, equation 3 can be rearranged as a truncated distributed lag model:

$$P_t^e = (1+\lambda)P_{t-1} - \lambda(1-\lambda)P_{t-2} - \lambda^2 P_{t-3} \qquad (6)$$

Estimation of the Adjustment Coefficients

In equations 4 through 6 expected prices (or price changes) have been expressed as weighted sums of past observed prices (or price changes). For the empirical estimation of expected prices, therefore, it is necessary to obtain estimates of the weights, which are actually functions of the respective adjustment coefficients and β, λ. Since the dependent variable, P_t^e or $\dot{p}_t^e$, of these equations is not an observed one, some of the standard estimation methods, especially the ordinary least squares (OLS) methods, cannot be used to obtain sample values of their parameters.[15] This is why I opted for an alternative estimation procedure, a maximum likelihood type method, that is not only computationally simple, but also avoids the statistical problems associated with the estimation of distributed lag models.

Briefly, the procedure used for the estimation of expected prices consists of the following steps:

1. The lagged terms of equations 4 and 5 were restricted to three, which incidentally coincide with those of equation 6. It might be mentioned here that limiting the distributed lag model to three terms should not be considered as a problem regarding the accuracy of the estimated expected prices. Actually, there is evidence from empirical studies that expected prices are influenced only by the most recent price changes rather than the more remote ones.[16] One probable objection that might be raised against the restriction of the number of terms in a distributed lag model is that its weights would not add up to one.[17] However, this might not be a deficiency

with any significant consequence since, as Sargent has pointed out regarding prices, for expectations to be optimal forecasts, they should be formed as a weighted average of past inflation with weights summing to less than unity.[18]

2. The partial adjustment coefficients β and λ were estimated by minimizing the average losses from forecasting errors in the quadratic loss function $Q = \Sigma [P_t - P_t^e]^2$. This estimation procedure was dictated by the need to apply a choice criterion consistent with economic rationality. Indeed, if an economic agent were to choose a relevant criterion to accurately forecast future prices in the face of uncertainty, it would be reasonable to expect that the economic agent would select one that minimizes his expected losses from forecast errors. Computationally, the values of β and λ were obtained by searching the parameter space 0 to 1 in intervals of .1, and finding the value that minimizes the quadratic loss function $Q = \Sigma [P_t - P_t^e]^2$,[19] where P is given by each of the reduced form models 4 through 6. Such an estimation procedure has an advantage over iterative methods because it provides a global minimum for Q.[20]

Price Instability Index

Having completed the estimation procedure for the expected prices with the described alternative price expectations models, the last remaining task in determining price instability was the selection of an appropriate price instability measure. To complete this task, it was decided to use a price instability index defined as the "average of the absolute deviations between observed and expected prices expressed as percent of the expected prices."[21] In other words, our price instability index is:

$$I_i = \frac{1}{n} \Sigma \frac{|P_t - P_t^e|}{P_t^e}(100) \qquad (7)$$

Since three different price expectations models were used, three alternative price instability indexes were obtained denoted by I_1, I_2 and I_3 with the subscripts corresponding to the respective models.

Data

The choice of the price index representing the actual price movements in a country might be considered as one of the most critical points of every empirical study dealing with inflation. Conceptually, the GNP (or GDP) deflator is regarded as the most representative measure of the general price level of a country.

However, deflators have not been used frequently in cross-sectional inflation studies. This might be attributed to two factors: unavailability and unreliability.

Although the consumer or cost-of-living price index is a selective index not designed to measure the movement in the overall price level, it has nevertheless been widely used in inflation studies. This is primarily the result of its availability and, secondly, its reliability.

In the present study the consumer price index was employed for the estimation of both the inflation rates and the price instability indexes.[22] The data cover the period 1953 to 1968 inclusive. Given that the price expectations models involve lagged values, however, the estimation of expected prices for 1953 and subsequent years required the use of prices for some years prior to 1953.

Fitted growth rates were estimated for both inflation and income growth.[23] In other words, logarithmic trends were estimated for the consumer price index and the real per capita GDP time series for each country of this sample.[24] The estimated price and income growth rates for the individual countries in the sample, as well as the three price instability indexes, are presented in table A of the Statistical Appendix. Finally, the LDCs that are included in the sample were chosen simply on the basis of availability of data, especially on real income, for the period under consideration.[25]

IV. TEST RESULTS

Regression analysis was used to test the hypothesis that price instability is more detrimental to economic growth than inflation. More specifically, nonlinear regressions were employed because it might be reasonable to assume that the relationship between income growth and inflation or price instability is not a proportional one.

Indeed, one should not expect that the doubling of a country's inflation rate or price instability would result in a proportional decrease (or increase) of the country's income growth rate.

The two general regression models tested in this study are:

$$\ln \dot{g} = a + b \ln \dot{p} + c \ln I_i + u \qquad (8)$$

and

$$\dot{g} = a + b \ln \dot{p} + c \ln I_i + u \qquad (9)$$

Where $\dot{g}$ denotes the real per capita income growth rate, $\dot{p}$ the inflation rate, and I_i the price instability index corresponding to model i.

The results of the regressions estimated with the OLS method

TABLE 1

SUMMARY RESULTS OF THE INCOME GROWTH, INFLATION
AND PRICE INSTABILITY REGRESSIONS

EQUATION	DEPENDENT VARIABLE	INTERCEPT	COEFFICIENTS OF EXPLANATORY VARIABLES				$\bar{R}^2$	F-RATIO/d.f.
			$\ln \dot{p}$	$\ln I_1$	$\ln I_2$	$\ln I_3$		
1.1	$\ln \dot{g}$	4.630 (1515.74)	−0.0019 (1.035)				0.0274	1.071/(1,38)
1.2	$\ln \dot{g}$	4.636 (1182.26)		−0.0061* (2.302)			0.1224	5.298*/(1,38)
1.3	$\ln \dot{g}$	4.638 (1268.79)			−0.0089** (3.143)		0.2063	9.876**/(1,38)
1.4	$\ln \dot{g}$	4.637 (1180.33)				−0.0072* (2.559)	0.1470	6.548*/(1,38)
1.5	$\ln \dot{g}$	4.639 (1119.60)	0.0058 (1.757)	−0.0136** (2.725)			0.1900	4.338*/(2,37)
1.6	$\ln \dot{g}$	4.638 (1275.72)	0.0027 (1.222)		−0.0119** (3.189)		0.2371	5.748**/(2,37)
1.7	$\ln \dot{g}$	4.638 (1160.54)	0.0035 (1.339)			−0.0116* (2.690)	0.1864	4.240*/(2,37)
1.8	$\dot{g}$	102.570 (326.47)	−0.1918 (1.019)				0.0266	1.039/(1,38)
1.9	$\dot{g}$	103.129 (255.71)		−0.6249* (2.293)			0.1215	5.256*/(1,38)
1.10	$\dot{g}$	103.339 (275.13)			−0.9136** (3.150)		0.2070	9.221**/(1,38)
1.11	$\dot{g}$	103.224 (255.53)				−0.7373* (2.554)	0.1465	6.523*/(1,38)
1.12	$\dot{g}$	103.422 (242.89)	0.5985 (1.775)	−1.4066** (2.736)			0.1905	4.352*/(2,37)
1.13	$\dot{g}$	103.358 (276.93)	0.2794 (1.251)		−1.2266** (3.125)		0.2392	5.816**/(2,37)
1.14	$\dot{g}$	103.354 (251.68)	0.3683 (1.360)			−1.1990** (2.703)	0.1872	4.260*/(2,37)

SOURCE: Table A of the Statistical Appendix.

NOTE: R^2 denotes the coefficient of determination, and the figures in parentheses below the regression coefficients are the t-values of the coefficients. * and ** indicate significant at 5 and 1 percent respectively.

are presented in table 1. The first 7 regression equations correspond to model 8 and its variants, while the regression equations 8 through 14 correspond to model 9.

The following observations are among those that may be noted from the inspection of the results presented in table 1:

1. The negative effects of inflation on growth are insignificant as is indicated by equations 1.1 and 1.8.
2. Price instability, regardless of the price expectations model used for its estimation, has significant negative effects on income growth. Furthermore, as can be seen from equations 1.3 and 1.10, the price instability index estimated with the use of the partial adjustment model of price changes, model 2, shows the best fit in terms of explained variation in g.
3. The multiple regressions do not show significantly better fit than the simple regressions. This is mainly due to multicollinearity. Indeed the correlation coefficients between inflation rates and price instability indexes exceed 0.7. This is also the reason why the inflation coefficient, although still insignificant, turns out to be positive in the multiple regressions.
4. From the determination coefficients it can be seen that price instability explains from about 12 to 21 percent of the observed variation in income growth rates in the countries of my sample. This range is probably well within reasonable expectations since, admittedly, a host of factors, other than price instability, determine the income growth in each country.

V. CONCLUSIONS

On the basis of the empirical evidence adduced by this study one might contend that for the average LDC price instability (or price change unpredictability) is more detrimental to economic growth than inflation.

However, some restraint is required as far as the generalization of the findings is concerned due to the fact that statistical testing conducted here is based on cross-country data. It should be recognized that each country has its own economic, social, and institutional characteristics. Furthermore, economic growth is the result of the combination of a wide variety of contributing factors. Nevertheless, one might be justified in deriving an important policy implication from the results of the present study. Since steady inflation does not seem to seriously impair economic growth in the LDCs, their governments should not be constantly preoccupied with attempts to stop inflation entirely. In view of these findings, it is reasonable to suggest that a more sensible policy for these governments would be to direct their efforts primarily toward the stabilization of inflation rates rather than the complete elimination of inflation. Only after this is accomplished, and provided that the reduction in inflation rates would not require severe recessionary measures, should a government proceed to gradually lessen or eliminate inflation.

At this point one should resist the temptation of making any further or more specific policy recommendations, since it does not seem plausible that there is a single price stabilization policy prescription suitable for all LDCs. Inasmuch as inflation rate instability might be caused either by economic factors external to each country, or by natural phenomena such as the weather, or by erratic domestic economic policies, obviously the appropriate stabilization policy for each case would be different. The only general recommendation that can be safely given to the governments of the LDCs, especially in those countries suffering from chronic inflation, is that their economic policies should be exercised in a manner that does not constantly frustrate expectations.

NOTES

[1] Raymond F. Mikesell, Inflation in Latin America," in Latin America: Problems in Economic Development, ed. Charles Nisbet (New York: Free Press, 1969), p. 150. Arnold C. Harberger, "Some Notes on Inflation," in Inflation in Latin America, ed. Werner Baer and Isaac Kerstenetzky (Homewood, IL: R. D. Irwin, 1964), p. 320. Dudley Seers also states that "it is meaningless to set up a hypothesis that inflation helps or hinders growth." A Theory of Inflation and Growth in Under-Developed Economies Based on the Experience of Latin America," Oxford Economic Papers 14 (June 1962): 191.

[2] See Graeme S. Dorrance, "Inflation and Growth: The Statistical Evidence," IMF Staff Papers 13 (March 1966): 82-102; A. P. Thirlwall and C. A. Barton, "Inflation and Growth: The International Evidence," Banca Nazionale del Lavoro-Quarterly Review 28 (September 1971): 263-75.

[3] Carlos Massad, "Comment," in Baer and Kerstenetzky, Inflation, p. 106.

[4] Harry G. Johnson, "Is Inflation the Inevitable Price of Rapid Development or a Retarding Factor in Economic Growth?" Malayan Economic Review 11 (April 1966): 27.

[5] See, for example, Robert J. Gordon, "Steady Anticipated Inflation: Mirage or Oasis?" Brookings Papers on Economic Activity (1971), pp. 449-510; and Edmund S. Phelps, Inflation Policy and Unemployment Theory (New York: Norton, 1972).

[6] The beneficial and detrimental effects of inflation in the LDCs

have been adequately discussed by several authors so that their enumeration here would be merely superfluous. See, for instance, the concise discussions by Gerald H. Anderson and Thomas D. Curtis, "Inflation and Economic Development: A Review of Theory and Empiricism," Quarterly Review of Economics and Business 18 (1968): 7-20; Werner Baer, "The Inflation Controversy in Latin America: A Survey," Latin America Research Review 2 (Spring 1967): 3-25; and Thirlwall and Barton, "Inflation and Growth," pp. 264-65.

[7] See Milton Friedman, "Monetary Policy in Developing Countries," in Nations and Households in Economic Growth, ed. Paul A. David and Melvin W. Reder (New York: Academic Press, 1974), pp. 275-76. To be sure, the degree to which steady price increases would remain harmless would depend, as Emile Despres put it, "Upon expectations being (a) highly uniform . . . among economic entities, (b) precise, i.e., out to be the realized path." "Inflation and Development: Brazil," in International Economic Reform: Collected Papers of Emile Despres, ed. Gerald M. Meier (New York: Oxford University Press, 1973), p. 186.

[8] Benjamin Higgins, for instance, claims that "any rate of steady price increase -- even a modest increase 1/2 percent per month -- will become a built-in factor in expectations of investors, and lead to the misallocation of new investment to land, buildings, speculation in inventories, short-run trading operations, and away from long-run productive enterprises." Economic Development: Problems, Principles, and Policies, rev. ed., (New York: Norton, 1968), p. 491. It has also been claimed that predictable inflation rates impair economic growth because they deprive an economy of the positive redistributive effects of "surprise" inflation. See Arthur Buttler and Philip Della Valle, "'Surprise' Inflation, Economic Growth and Employment," International Labour Review 104 (December 1971): 489-504. However, as Rosemary Thorp points out, "in a prolonged inflation in Latin America the redistributive effects are negligible, as far as this can be determined from the available data on labor's share in GNP." "Inflation and the Financing of Economic Development", in Financing Development in Latin America, ed. Keith B. Griffin (London: St. Martin's Press, 1971), p. 199.

[9] See Ronald I. McKinnon, Money and Capital in Economic Development (Washington, DC: Brookings Institution, 1973), esp. chap. 2.

[10] Such increase in efficiency could come about from the fact that under steady inflation rates it would be more advantageous to small businessmen and farmers to accumulate funds for relatively sizeable or worthwhile investments. On the contrary, under unpredictable inflation conditions, they have to invest their small annual savings into minor or marginal improvements in the old technology in order to prevent the value of their savings from being seriously reduced by inflation. For more details on capital market "indivisibilities" in LDCs, see McKinnon, Money and Capital.

[11] Since, as Gordon points out, "most of the evils commonly associated with inflation occur only when the actual inflation rate deviates from that which is expected," if one intends to identify the effects of price unpredictability on economic growth, one should define and measure price instability accordingly, "Steady Anticipated Inflation," p. 499.

[12] Other measures of price instability utilized in similar studies suffer from the same type of weaknesses. For different measures of price instability see Gordon, "Steady Anticipated Inflation," and Buttler and Della Valle, "'Surprise' Inflation."

[13] For a succinct exposition of various expectations models, see Jan Kmenta, Elements of Econometrics (New York: Macmillan, 1971), pp. 473-87; and John F. Muth, "Rational Expectations and the Theory of Price Movements," Econometrica 29 (July 1961): 315-35.

[14] The adaptive expectations model is sometimes presented as:

$$P_t^e - P_{t-1}^e = (1 - \delta)(P_{t-1} - P_{t-1}^e)$$

which is reduced to the following distributed lag model:

$$P_t^e = (1-\delta)P_{t-1} + \delta(1-\delta)P_{t-2} + \delta^2(1-\delta)P_{t-3} + \ldots$$

The above model is computationally identical with (4) when one sets $\beta = 1 - \delta$.

[15] Furthermore, fitting a Box-Jenkins autoregressive moving average model to obtain future price predictions based on past prices, considering the price series as a stochastic process, was not possible due to the limited size of the sample.

[16] Toshihisa Toyoda, for example, in his "Price Expectations and the Short-Run and Long-Run Phillips Curves in Japan, 1956-1968," Review of Economics and Statistics 54 (1972): 271, states that he found "some evidence that current price expectations are formed exclusively on the basis of the most recent history of actual price movement.

[17] The implicit assumption behind such requirement is that if inflation persists, sooner or later people will come to fully anticipate inflation.

[18] Thomas J. Sargent, "A Note on the Accelerationist Controversy," Journal of Money, Credit and Banking 3 (August 1971): 721-25.

[19] Actually, for the adaptive expectations model, I searched the parameter space from -0.9 to 0.9 in order to examine the possibility that the adjustment coefficient could be greater than 1. This could happen if in the form the adaptive expectations model is given in n. 15 above, is negative.

[20] It might be mentioned in passing that the estimation method

utilized here gives unique values for the adjustment coefficients and in addition their values are independent of the reference base of the time series used. Furthermore, my method for estimating expected prices has two other advantages. First, it does not impose any restrictions on the weights of the lagged terms, and second, it avoids the computational problems associated with the estimation of distributed lags.

[21] It can be easily shown that this price instability index would be zero for a country whose prices rise at a steady rate during the period under consideration, regardless of the size of the annual rate of inflation.

[22] As far as estimation of price expectations and instability indexes is concerned, the consumer price index might also be a more appropriate price index to use, since it is the index that most economic units are familiar with and thus the one that they take into consideration in their future plans.

[23] The fitted growth rate, say for prices, is $P_t = a(1 + \dot{p})^t$, where P_t is the consumer price index for year t, and $\dot{p}$ is the "fitted" annual inflation rate. Growth rates estimated with this approach have two basic advantages. They do not depend heavily upon the values of the first and last years of the series, and they are also less sensitive than average growth rates to extreme values.

[24] The use of the real per capita income for the estimation of income growth rates seems more appropriate on two accounts: it provides a better measure than total income for a country's living standard and its improvement over time, and it is free from the effects of the population growth.

[25] The classification of countries as less developed ones is based on the list made by the Commission on International Development. See Lester B. Pearson, Partners in Development: Report of the Commission on International Development (New York: Praeger, 1969), pp. 358-59.

Income Differentials and the Dynamics of Development

JACQUES LECAILLON[2]
DIMITRIOS GERMIDIS[3]

In a market economy the function of unequal income distribution may be viewed in different ways.

Seen as a price system, the structure of remuneration helps to determine the allocation of productive resources. The theory here is that income disparities induce labour to move from one sector or branch of activity to another as economic considerations dictate, and disappear when the necessary shifts have taken place and equilibrium has been restored. The question arises, however, whether this conception remains wholly valid when the effectiveness of market mechanisms is inhibited by structural or behavioural factors.

It is often thought that development manifests itself through a decline in the rural population caused by migration towards the towns (i.e. "urbanisation"). In fact, several phenomena overlap here. In the first place, demographic growth may be such that the population increases in both rural and urban areas. Moreover, the modern sector is not the exclusive preserve of the towns, and population movements can be of several kinds. In addition to analysing the phenomenon of rural-urban migration and the part played by income differentials in instigating it, therefore, full account needs to be taken of changes in the employment structure of the receiving areas.

Seen as the cause of disparity in the standard of living of different social classes, income distribution is one of the factors determining the volume of savings available for investment and hence the potential for economic growth. From, this point of view a less egalitarian distribution may be necessary to boost savings inasmuch as only the wealthier classes are in a position to save and invest. It may, however, be asked whether the use of income in developing countries is similar to that in industrialized ones. In other words, is there a close correlation between the distribution of income and the use to which it is put? These problems need to be carefully investigated.

In the pages that follow we shall be attempting such an investigation chiefly on the basis of information from a number of countries in French-speaking Black Africa, particularly the United Republic of Cameroon, the Ivory Coast, Madagascar and Senegal.

I. RURAL-URBAN MIGRATION AND INCOME DIFFERENTIALS

Contrary to what happened at the same stage of development in Europe, North America and, more recently, in Japan, the rapid growth of certain urban agriculture making it possible--thanks to improved strains, techniques and productivity--to produce the surplus needed for urban growth.[4] Nor is the origin of urbanisation in Africa to be sought in the growth of industry around the larger population centres. In fact the latter, which grew up partly as a consequence of colonialism, were originally more or less enclaves in the service of foreign economies.

Since independence, the process of urbanisation has speeded up considerably. There are various reasons for this, the most important of which are probably the widening gap between nominal urban and rural incomes, and the emergence of new employment possibilities with the beginnings of industrialisation in certain centres. The attraction of the towns has also been strengthened by the Africanisation of civil services and of many other jobs, especially in the tertiary sector. This is a case where prospects of higher remuneration and the desire for social status have coincided.

Nevertheless, urbanisation rates[5] generally remain low. Thus the average for West Africa as a whole is only 14 per cent, even though Senegal with 29 per cent and the Ivory Coast with 21 per cent are well above this. In the future, however, it seems that these rates may rise to more alarming levels, as rural-urban migration has recently begun to accelerate. If this occurs two sets of problems will arise, relating on the one hand to social integration (the need to absorb the newcomers harmoniously without upsetting the urban balance) and on the other to over-all economic efficiency (the need to ensure optimum utilisation of the country's production factors).

It follows that economic policy should give high priority to the problem of socio-demographic equilibrium, and hence to income equilibrium. Population shifts may be useful in the process of development, but they must be adapted to a country's capacity for change--and that of its towns. In practice a move to the city often entails exchanging a situation of underemployment (hidden unemployment) for one of open and total unemployment. Moreover, urbanisation creates new needs, notably as regards the provision of infrastructure and food supplies, and these can only be satisfied gradually. Urban development is expensive and usually quite slow.

As for suburban market-gardening zones, they do not build up fast enough into the necessary green belts and their output generally remains inadequate, even when the effective demand is limited.

While better income opportunities and new employment prospects attract country-dwellers to the towns, it is also possible to distinguish other factors which have the same effect by inducing them to break away from rural society. These serve to swell--in some cases considerably--the migratory flows set in motion by the pull factors and sometimes even provoke such flows themselves, a sort of flight to the cities such as that which led to the growth of the notorious favelas or shanty-towns in Brazil. Whereas the pull factors are both social and economic, the push factors are often predominantly, though not exclusively, social. They include the desire for independence or social standing, the rejection of a certain way of life, and so on.

To measure the relative influence of these different factors by reference to the level of development attained would call for continuous series of migration statistics for each country concerned. Unfortunately the existing data are very fragmentary and only cover certain regions at certain times. Since the statistical basis is so imperfect, the following remarks, value judgments and general conclusions can obviously be of only limited value. This is not to say, however, that they are totally unfounded.

The distinction between pull and push factors is a convenient way of grouping the motives of migration, even if some of them do not always fall exclusively within one of these two categories.

The Pull Factors

Seen from the rural point of view, these are exogenous factors creating a suction effect towards the city. Without making any claim to exhaustiveness, we shall consider mainly the prospect of securing employment and the hope of attaining higher incomes.

Employment

There can be no doubt that the desire to find a better job--or any job at all--is a fundamental motive in decisions to migrate. The existence (and sometimes only the presumed existence) of job vacancies in urban centres is a powerful magnet to available labour, but the prospects of success differ according to region. Expansion of the public and semi-public sector tends to follow, or sometimes even to precede, the concentration of private sector activities in certain areas. The population follows in its turn. The extent of this concentration is illustrated by the fact that in the Ivory Coast, for example, the southern <u>department</u> provides over 88 per cent of all wage employment.[6]

Unfortunately, the growth of the urban population tends to outstrip that of employment. In the Ivory Coast, Cameroon and Senegal the rural exodus exceeds the capacity of the secondary and tertiary sectors to absorb the unskilled or semi-skilled jobseekers, so that the large towns are filling up with unemployed and underemployed immigrants. The situation threatens to take a dramatic turn as the economy becomes increasingly monetised[7] and it gets more and more difficult to maintain any degree of self-sufficiency in the bigger centres of population. This phenomenon is more marked in the Ivory Coast than in the other countries mentioned.

<u>Incomes</u>

The hope of finding employment is not the only pull factor. Separately or in combination with the employment incentive, income disparities also influence the scale of migratory flows, with inter-regional differences apparently playing a larger part than occupational ones. Inter-regional differences in incomes—and particularly in cash incomes—are always attractive in a good year and go a long way to explain the migratory movements taking place within the rural sector, for incomes can vary widely from one agricultural area to another.[8]

If we take household incomes rather than incomes per head, however, there is less difference between urban and rural areas, especially when there are grown-up children able to do their share of agricultural work. As a logical consequence, and also because they have more drive and fewer ties, it is mainly the young who migrate. It has been estimated that in the Ivory Coast, between 1965 and 1970, half of all rural-urban migrants were aged 15 to 29, and that within this bracket those under 25 formed an overwhelming majority.[9] The same phenomenon has been observed in Cameroon, where half of those migrating to the capital city of Yaounde between 1960 and 1965 were between the ages of 15 and 24, and 90 per cent between 15 and 44.[10]

The Push Factors

Not all the newcomers, however, are merely drawn in by the magnet of the towns. In many cases the decision to break away from the home environment is due to a variety of reasons and to endogenous forces acting centrifugally. The fact that young people are so much in the majority in these migratory flows is not without significance. Apart from their greater vitality, the oppressive weight of traditional authority, the lack of opportunity for social or occupational advancement and the comparative poverty of the rural environment combine with the pull factors to incite them to leave.

The Weight of Authority

The desire to escape the ties of family, clan or tribe is often an important motivation to leave, inasmuch as the discipline of established authority can scarcely be evaded in any other way.[11]

From an economic point of view, family authority is exercised through a system of ownership that discriminates against the young. The land generally belongs to the older members of the family, who are loath to loosen their grip until they reach a very advanced age. Thus it is difficult to own or manage a farm or plot of land before reaching middle age, and the young usually have no say in the family's affairs. The fact that they naturally do the hardest physical work does not make this state of affairs any easier to bear.

Undeniably, this rigid structure of authority seriously impedes the modernisation of agriculture. It retards the adoption of new methods and techniques which could lead to better products and higher output. Dissatisfaction and the desire to migrate are most marked among the educated young, who are not only the ones most likely to find urban employment but also those to whom family or social constraints seem least justifiable and least tolerable.

Environmental Shortcomings

Compared with the bright lights and distractions of the city, the countryside appears to have little to offer. Those who migrate on these grounds are therefore influenced by push and pull factors acting simultaneously. They seek to get away from primitive surroundings where there is no electricity, no running water, little possibility of study, few medical services and so on. Moreover, as subsistence farming is still very widespread, young people generally have no cash income of their own even when their standard of living is otherwise acceptable, so that their independence is reduced accordingly. The imagined delights of city life appear all the more attractive in comparison, even if they may not be within everybody's reach or can be enjoyed only at the cost of some new servitude such as prostitution.

Social Monotony

The rigidity of rural family and social structures tends to drown the individual in the mass, so that his or her personality has little chance to assert itself. The prospects of advancement and of being able to change one's status or role in life seem problematical and remote, whereas moving to the city offers some hope of improving one's social position more rapidly. Occasional brief visits to urban centres have generally nurtured this belief, which--even though it often proves illusory--is an important inducement for all that.

Thus, the fascination of the big city is reinforced by the desire for social standing. Employment in the public service, which combines the advantages of good income, prestige and job security, is much sought after for this purpose.[12]

* * *

The new factor in all this is the growing feeling of impatience. People are becoming more and more clearly aware of the differences between individuals, social and occupational groups, regions and ways of life. The desire to live in the present, the increasing rejection of passivity and the determination to possess or even to become "something new" are shortening reaction times and hastening the process of change. Moreover, this impatience is infectious and is therefore intensified by all the modern information media, while the pull and push factors combine to extend and amplify their effects.

Of course, income differentials play their part here. With the growing monetisation of the economy these disparities, increasingly seen and measured in monetary terms, gain in importance. Actual or nominal purchasing power becomes the yardstick. The point to be noted here is that the differentials work in the same direction as the psycho-sociological pull and push factors: they increase the net advantage of migration in the eyes of persons tempted by the urban adventure and thus perpetuate the disequilibrium between town and country. Consequently, migrations from one sector to another cannot be analysed as though they were simply transfers of production factors in a more or less perfect market. If this were the case, income disparities would duly exercise a regulatory function, adjusting labour demand and supply in the various sectors of the economy, whereas in fact there exists a permanent tendency to excess supply in the secondary and tertiary sectors and to rising urban unemployment. The numbers of would-be workers flooding in from the countryside exceed the amount of employment, especially wage-earning employment, available in modern sector enterprises and would probably still do so even if the superiority of urban over rural incomes were eliminated.

II. INCOME DIFFERENTIALS AND EMPLOYMENT STRUCTURE IN NON-AGRICULTURAL SECTORS

As noted above, the exodus of an appreciable fraction of the rural population is partly motivated by income differentials between town and country. This migration creates a permanent excess labour supply in the cities owing to the limited opportunities for wage-earning employment there. This being so, the problem of the relationship between income differentials and the employment structure in non-agricultural activities has two sides to it: that of the distribution of labour between wage-earning and non-wage-earning employment on the one hand, and that of the structure of wage-earning employment on the other.

The distribution of non-agricultural labour between wage-earning and non-wage-earning employment

When there exists a chronic imbalance on the labour market, the stimulation of artisanal activity, especially in urban centres, can obviously help to provide employment for workers who will, for the most part, not be wage earners.[13]

In a good many industrialised countries self-employment was until quite recently a sign of social status, and the increase in the number of self-employed workers outside agriculture helped to absorb the labour leaving the land. Only when the concentration of enterprises in the secondary and tertiary sectors reaches a very advanced stage does the self-employed category begin to decline in favour of wage-earning employment, and it still remains a constant source of new ideas and individual initiative. It is thus widely agreed that a policy of developing artisanal activity and small-scale industry helps to improve economic and social conditions generally in African countries.[14]

The role of small enterprises[15]

As regards employment, the existence of small enterprises provides a sort of stepping-stone or relay by absorbing migrant labour which the modern sector is unable to use.

These small enterprises create employment in so far as their establishment and expansion presuppose the investment of personal savings which would not spontaneously find their way to the modern sector. In countries where the capital market is insufficiently organised and where the investment of money is not a widespread practice, personal savings are generally hoarded. Their investment in artisanal activities therefore represents a net increase in the volume of employment and a contribution to national output even if the productivity of such enterprises is lower than that of modern sector ones.

Independent entrepreneurs also play a part in the distribution of income. In low-productivity units the attraction of self-employment does not in any way endanger the recruitment of labour by modern enterprises, but by enabling families to obtain at least some supplementary income these small enterprises help to reduce inequalities in standards of living and thus, in rural areas, to stem the tide of urban migration.

Finally, small-scale enterprises make a useful contribution to training, particularly of apprentices and family workers, which can only upgrade the labour supply in general. Moreover, competition in this sector is so keen that the branches in which self-employed workers predominate constitute a reserve of entrepreneurs that should clearly enhance the growth potential of the economy.

In the countries considered in the present article these independent small enterprises, which form the backbone of what is often called the informal sector, perform their relay function to the full. In the Ivory Coast they have absorbed the bulk of the growing labour force over the past few years and seem likely to go on doing so.[16] It is the same story in Madagascar[17] and Cameroon, where the informal sector supplies many young people with a temporary solution while they look around for regular wage-earning jobs--which are, however, becoming harder and harder to find. The existence of this sector has no doubt prevented a serious employment crisis from occurring before now.[18]

Income Differentials as a Regulator

The informal sector's relay function highlights the regulatory role of income differentials. If surplus labour is attracted towards this sector, it is because of the shortage of wage-earning employment in the modern private sector and the public sector. In other words, since average incomes in the informal sector are generally below the statutory minimum wage, the direction of labour flows depends on the availability of jobs rather than on rates of remuneration.

Data gathered during a number of surveys[19] show that the urban informal sector contains extremes of poverty and relative affluence, ranging from the penniless newly arrived migrant to the employee with a wage equal or even above the statutory minimum. The sector therefore provides incomes at a level mainly between those of agricultural workers and those of employees in the urban modern or public sectors who receive at least the official minimum wage.

Thus any attempt to introduce a minimum wage in the informal sector is generally regarded as the best way of destroying it.[20] If migration is to help close the gap between rural and urban incomes, it is best to let the latter find their own level as a function of supply and demand rather than impose minima which are unrealistically high in relation to the productivity of many informal sector activities.

The observer may therefore question the value of a minimum wage policy in an economy where labour is constantly in excess supply and where earnings below the legal minimum must be tolerated in order to preserve "traditional" jobs.[21] Is the build-up of surplus labour in the cities not likely to force down the lower levels of urban wages, leading to regular breaches of the legislation? And will not the fixing of a minimum favour wage earners at the expense of the self-employed and thereby discourage individual initiative?

These questions, which need further consideration, call the entire wage structure into question.

Wage disparities and the structure of wage-earning employment

Disparities between the primary, secondary and tertiary sectors

Intersectoral differentials often reflect the rural-urban dichotomy mentioned above. In many of the French-speaking African countries there are in fact two minimum wage systems: the salaire minimum interprofessionnel garanti (SMIG) for industrial workers, and the salaire minimum agricole garanti (SMAG) for agricultural ones. Public employees who get the SMIG may also receive fringe benefits such as housing allowances.

Taking all this into account, the monthly incomes per head of certain categories of employee in the Ivory Coast around 1970 have been estimated[22] as follows:

	CFA francs
Agricultural workers (average)	5,600
SMIG manual workers, Grade 1	10,100
SMIG white-collar workers, Grade 1	13,000
Public employees (minimum)	14,000

Thus manual and white-collar private employees earn approximately twice as much as agricultural workers, and public employees two and a half times as much.

Although the skill levels and types of work involved are scarcely comparable, such differentials seem difficult to justify. We shall not revert to the question of rural-urban migration, but is is hard to understand why such a gap should be maintained between the SMIG and the SMAG when there is already a natural tendency for the population to drift into the cities--to such an extent, indeed, that there is sometimes a risk of labour shortage in agriculture.

The gap between the private and public sectors is no easier to justify. Contrary to what generally happens in the industrialised countries and many developing ones, where government officials earn appreciably less than their counterparts in the private sector (but are compensated by the prestige and security attaching to public employment), in French-speaking Africa the wages and salaries of civil servants and other public employees are often the highest of all and prove a great draw. Only for the top jobs does the private sector pay better than the public.

The state of affairs is partly due to historical factors. Feeling themselves in some way responsible for the economic and social development of their countries, civil servants no doubt considered that the importance of this role entitled them to large salaries, and certain attitudes inherited from colonial times lent support to this idea. There is an error of perspective here, however. The tertiary sector, whether public or private, depends for its existence on the wealth created by productive activities. In Africa, where the power of colonial administration appeared detached from its productive base in the metropolitan country, this elementary fact of life may have too often been overlooked.[23] Here again, it is the practical effect which should be the criterion. In view of the attractiveness of careers in the public service to increasing numbers of young people with various levels of educational qualification, it seems impossible to justify the maintenance of pay differentials that tend to accentuate the imbalance between supply and demand.

Industrial and regional differentials

The average level of remuneration differs from one industry and from one area to another.[24] In the former case the disparity can no doubt be attributed partly to differences in the skill and nationality profile of the workforce on the one hand[25] and in location on the other. Even when these factors have been discounted, however, disparities persist albeit in attenuated form; they seem to be linked to the type of activity carried on and the size of firm. It follows that narrowing them depends mainly on the modification of economic structures, which is a long-term task.

Regional disparities are less admissible. The only factor that might justify them is differences in the cost of living, but the measurement of regional cost-of-living trends is fraught with all kinds of difficulty. The important thing is that wage earners inhabiting the remoter parts of a country should not be forgotten in any attempt to achieve fairer distribution of the fruits of growth.

Differentials according to nationality

The existence of differentials according to nationality, and especially as between Africans and non-African "expatriates", understandably excites a good deal of attention in all the countries in question. In many cases these expatriates are useful and even indispensable, and in order to attract them some financial inducement is required, whence the differential. In the circumstances it would seem that interim measures are called for. In order not to upset the economic balance of the employment market one could in such cases distinguish the salary, which could be kept in line with that paid to Africans, and the expatriation allowance. This may look like a subterfuge for maintaining the disparities, but it would equally well serve as a means of gradually reducing them as the need for overseas personnel becomes less urgent.

In any event, one thing is certain: an employment policy (within the broader framework of a strategy for economic and social development) can only be coherent if it covers all groups of wage earner. It must also be borne in mind that excessive disparities will not be tolerated much longer and that those remaining will have to be justifiable by reference to skill levels, working conditions or other imperatives.

III. SAVINGS, INCOME DISPARITIES AND DEVELOPMENT PATHS

If we analyse the very long process of economic growth leading from underdevelopment to industrialisation, we find that between the two extremes there lies a transitional phase during which the concentration of income increases. This phenomenon is probably inevitable: when a column of vehicles accelerates, the distance between them naturally tends to increase. A certain minimum of inequality in the distribution of income is thus ineluctable, but it is not something that can be rigorously determined. It follows that government measures to reduce disparities will not necessarily impede the growth of production or the rate of increase of output per head. This observation can be verified in particular with respect to the relation between income distribution and utilisation. Various kinds of distribution can therefore be compatible with development.

The relation between distribution and utilisation of income

It is widely believed that, other things being equal, the effect of a move towards more egalitarian income distribution is to reduce total savings and stimulate consumption, thereby hampering the accumulation of capital which is so vital during the take-off phase of the economy. However, studies carried out in various parts of the world[26] have shown that such changes in distribution do not automatically entail any reduction in savings and that their effects on consumption are probably negligible apart from an increased demand for foodstuffs. Such an increase will nevertheless be unlikely to stimulate growth, and the most probable hypothesis is that there will be a slight fall in the growth rate, representing the reasonable price that has to be paid for greater equity.

Application of this analysis to African countries would call for additional research going beyond the scope of the present article. What can be stated, however, is that neither the volume of savings nor the structure of consumption is necessarily related to income by a sufficiently straightforward link for a change in distribution to have automatic and predictable consequences.

The situation in the traditional sector

In the traditional sector, which contains the great majority of the population, the various ways of accumulating capital (hoarding or investing) and the forms the process takes (individual or collective) depend largely on the social system in force and thus on ethnic factors. The differing economic status of individuals only comes into play as a secondary factor within a particular ethnic group. In certain regions there even exist more or less hidden sources of income, ranging from religious donations to usury and fraudulent business operations, which provide the recipients with a surplus to consumption that can be assimilated to potential savings. The scale and destination of such savings undoubtedly depend on the social system. Their mobilisation for productive ends presupposes an evolution in customs and a reform of financial structures going well beyond a mere redistribution of individual incomes. This means that the impact of redistributional measures on the volume of savings and the choice of investment depends essentially on the nature of the measures themselves; it is not irrevocably fixed in advance.

Similarly, it is a mistake to assume that variations in income are always the main determining factor in variations in consumption, as is normally the case in industrialised economies. In particular, it has been found that the determining factor in food consumption can be the rigidity or flexibility of supply, which in turn depends on the effectiveness of marketing networks. In Senegal, for example, the income elasticity of food consumption varies from one village to another according to its trading relations with the outside world.[27] Thus changes in the distribution of income do not in themselves suffice to bring about major changes in its utilisation.

. . . and in the modern sector

If we look at the situation in the modern sector, we arrive at much the same conclusions. This is so, in the first place, because in an open economy a proportion of the higher incomes accrues to foreign firms and personnel, while the volume of foreign investment is determined by considerations that as a rule are quite unconnected with the inequality of income distribution in the country. The sums saved by expatriate staff from their high salaries are often sent home, so that any fluctuations in their amount have only a very minor effect on investment and economic activity in the host country.

To take one example, it has been estimated that in the Ivory Coast only some 6 to 8 per cent of disposable household income is saved, which is only half the rate observed in developed countries. But if we include the sums exported by expatriate personnel (salary transfers and money spent abroad during leave), we obtain a rate of saving similar to that prevailing in developed countries. In absolute terms the transfers of funds abroad actually exceed local savings, amounting in 1973 to 40,000 million CFA francs compared with 25,000 million.[28]

The amount saved by nationals in the modern sector, on the other hand, is no doubt influenced by the level of their incomes. A more unequal distribution could therefore increase the propensity to save. However, the effect of emulation, whereby those in receipt of high incomes tend to model their life style on that of Europeans, should not be overlooked; experience shows that large increases in incomes lead to corresponding increases in imports. Besides, household savings are channelled chiefly into high-yielding real estate investment or simply kept in liquid form: "In view of the low level of their medium- and long-term investments, it can be said that the contribution of households to financing economic development is minute."[29] This being so, a more even income distribution would not necessarily produce any major contraction of national savings and its effect on investment would doubtless be fairly limited.

It should be added that savings and investment rates depend less on the spontaneous behaviour of economic agents than on a complex of political factors including taxation, monetary policy, financial structures and foreign economic relations.[30] It may be postulated that, within certain limits, the pace of economic growth is more or less independent of income distribution. A smaller degree of inequality is compatible with continued economic development, particularly since increases in the standard of living of the poorest classes of the population should make it possible to improve productivity. There is no scientifically determined relation between economic development and the inequality of income distribution.

Development paths and income inequalities

It is clear from what has been said above that there can be different development models corresponding to different patterns of income distribution.

The role of dualism

The diversity of such models will depend chiefly on the degree of dualism between the traditional and modern sectors and on the distribution of <u>human</u> as much as material resources[31], inasmuch as structural changes in wages and thus the general distribution of income are determined by the distinction between skilled and unskilled employment and differences in levels of education.

As long as the economy remains underdeveloped, the distribution of income in the non-agricultural sector is always very unequal because so few people possess any capital or education. However, the degree of income concentration within this sector is of negligible weight because of the predominance of the agricultural sector at this stage. The over-all degree of income inequality therefore depends essentially on the dispersion of agricultural incomes and thus, in the last resort, on the structure of agriculture.

When an economy enters its take-off stage the growth of the modern sector, capitalistic in nature and mainly consisting of secondary and tertiary activities, automatically produces a concentration of incomes that have hitherto been rather dispersed. The modern sector's productivity (and capital/labour ratio) being far higher that the traditional sector's, it can create a large proportion of the domestic product despite employing only a small minority of the labour force. In addition, as the remuneration of unskilled labour is kept low by the abundance of supply from the traditional sector, the income accruing to material and human capital (the latter in the form of high salaries for the highly educated) accounts for a big percentage of the income of the modern sector. In other words, the degree of income concentration reflects the allocation of the fruits of growth to the minority controlling production factors that are in short supply. This phenomenon may be more or less pronounced, but it is likely to persist as long as the relative scarcities of the factors involved remain unchanged.

This is where the degree of dualism between the modern and traditional sectors is so important. The productivity gap between them is wider or narrower according to the extent to which the traditional sector attracts investment capital and its products are in demand by the modern sector.[32] A moderate degree of dualism presupposes a progressive injection of capital/labour ratio: the farmers enlarge their holdings and improve their equipment and cultivation techniques, the craftsmen modernise their workshops. If on the other hand the modern sector exports most of its production, imports most of its inputs and in general has few dealings with the traditional sector, and if, in addition, public and private investment is channelled exclusively into the modern sector, then the small entrepreneurs in the traditional sector will be starved of capital and their standard of living will stagnate. In this case, despite the effort to accumulate capital and the increase in output per head, the concentration of income will be considerable.

Investment in education, which determines the diffusion of human capital, may also heighten income concentration if reserved to the wealthier classes, or, on the contrary, may reduce it if extended to all gifted children whatever their social origin. Even if the return on material capital remains constant, the structure of wages and of the wage-earning population may greatly alter the distribution of income and its evolution: the difference between the earnings of unskilled workers and those of supervisory and technical personnel enables the latter to save and to invest in the education of their children. Thus it is in no way surprising that a high rate of enrolment in secondary and university education is usually associated with a lower concentration of income.[33]

The interdependence of policy options

The fact that the pattern of income distribution can evolve in various ways means that policy-makers enjoy a certain latitude of decision. However, the initial choices are generally interdependent and, once made, set off processes that acquire a momentum of their own.

A highly concentrated and unequal distribution of income, for example, tends to consolidate the position of groups endowed with material or human capital. These prefer to invest in the modern sector, thus helping to keep per capita incomes in the traditional sector at a very low level. In this way the modern sector maintains a reservoir of cheap labour, accentuating the concentration of income still further. The high earnings in the modern sector lead to consumer spending on goods that are not produced in the traditional sector but are generally imported. Such spending creates little employment apart from some local demand for domestic service, and the maintenance of a high rate of underemployment is a further source of inequality.

Conversely, a more even income distribution leads to a less dualistic economy. Higher agricultural incomes can encourage investment in the traditional sector, just as credit facilities for small entrepreneurs and artisans and the generalisation of education help to raise the level of material and human resources there. The result is higher per capita incomes in the traditional sector which, even if they rise more slowly than national output per head, encourage the development of a national market for consumer goods. The expansion of such a market creates jobs, since the manufacture of local mass-consumption goods relies on more labour-intensive techniques than those used to produce the goods sought by the wealthier classes.

A more even income distribution also tends to limit imports, leaving more funds available for the purchase of capital goods and semi-finished products needed for further job creation. In turn, a reduction in unemployment and a rise in the lowest incomes, which should lead to higher productivity, militate against an unequal distribution.

* * *

The early stages of economic development and the transition from underdevelopment to self-sustaining growth entail structural upheavals which cannot fail to affect the pattern of income distribution. It seems nevertheless that the tendency towards greater inequality can be restrained without endangering economic growth provided that income distribution objectives are incorporated into development plans and reconciled with other national goals.

The priorities involved cannot be decided on the basis of economic analysis alone. In Africa as elsewhere the rate of development, the scale and distribution of the sacrifices it calls for and the degree of inequality that can be tolerated all depend on the will of the people and the wisdom of their rulers. In the last resort, technical considerations must yield to the decisions of the politicians.

NOTES

[1] The present article is based on a more general study of income inequalities among wage earners and self-employed workers in a number of African countries (J. Lecaillon and D. Germidis: Inegalites de revenue et developpement economique (Paris, Presses universitaires de France, forthcoming)). The underlying research was carried out within the framework of the ILO's World Employment Programme under the guidance of Felix Paukert, whom the authors would like to thank for his help and encouragement.

[2] Professor of Economics at the University of Paris I.

[3] OECD. Professor at the Institut de'etude du developpement economique et social (IEDES), University of Paris I.

[4] See Colin Rosser: Urbanization in Tropical Africa: a demographic introduction, An International Urbanization Survey report to the Ford Foundation (New York, Ford Foundation, 1973), p. 49.

[5] The percentage of total population living in agglomerations.

[6] Ministere de l'Enseignement technique et de la Formation professionnelle, Office national de formation professionnelle (ONFP), and ministere du Plan, Direction des etudes de developpement (DED): Le secteur prive et parapublic en Cote-d'Ivoire, 1971: Resultats de l'enquete main-d'euvre 1971, Part 4 (Abidjan, 1972), p. 32.

[7] See G. Tixier: Etude comparee des politiques economiques du Cameroun et de la Cote-d'Ivoire (Paris, Librairie generale de droit et de jurisprudence, 1973), p. 161.

[8] For furtther details on this point see Lecaillon and Germidis, op. cit.

[9] Ministere du Plan, DED: Ressources humaines et perspectives d'emploi--Cote-d'Ivoire, 1968-1975, etude realisee par A. Achio (Abidjan, 1969), pp. 304 ff. For similar data on Madagascar see Centre national de la recherche scientifique, France: La croissance urbaine en Afrique noire et a Madagascar (Paris, 1972), Vol I, pp. 261 ff.

[10] Societe d'etudes pour le developpement economique et social, France: Enquete sur le niveau de vie a Yaounde, 1964-65, Note de synthese (Paris, 1965).

[11] See H. Joshi, H. Lubell and J. Mouly: Abidjan: urban development and employment in the Ivory Coast (Geneva, ILO, 1976), pp. 32-33.

[12] See International Bank for Reconstruction and Development (IBRD): Ivory Coast: special report on employment (Washington, 1974; Report No. 279a-IVC), Vol. II.

[13] See ILO: *Rapport au gouvernement de la Republique malagasy sur les problemes de l'emploi* (Geneva, doc. OIT/TAP/Malagasy/R.6, 1972), p. 156.

[14] See ILO: *Rapport au gouvernement de la Republique federale du Cameroun sur le developpement de l'artisanat et des petites industries* (Geneva, doc. OIT/OTA/Cameroun/R.2, 1972); and idem: *Rapport au gouvernement de la Republique federale du Cameroun sur l'organisation, la planification et le developpement de l'artisanat et de la petite industrie* (Geneva, doc. OIT/TAP/Cameroun/R.10, 1968).

[15] See Joshi, Lubell and Mouly, op. cit., Ch. 3.

[16] IBRD: *Ivory Coast: special report on employment*, op. cit., Vol. II, p. 97.

[17] ILO: *Rapport au gouvernement de la Republique malagasy sur les problemes de l'emploi*, op. cit.

[18] Ministere de l'Education nationale, Cameroon: *Enquete sur le devenir des eleves de l'enseignement technique* (Yaounde, 1973).

[19] See IBRD: *Ivory Coast: special report on employment*, op. cit., Vol. II, pp. 31-32.

[20] Ibid., p. 102.

[21] This question is examined in S. Watanabe: "Minimum wages in developing countries: myth and reality", in *International Labour Review*, May-June 1976, pp. 345-358.

[22] IBRD: *Ivory coast: special report on employment*, op. cit., Vol. II, pp. 27-28.

[23] Cf. Secretariat d'Etat aux Affaires etrangeres, charge de la cooperation, France: *Cote d'Ivoire 1972-73, Dossier d'information* (Paris, 1973), p. 43.

[24] For further details see Lecaillon and Germidis, op. cit.

[25] Composition by age and sex is certainly also significant in this respect, but detailed analysis has not been possible owing to lack of data.

[26] See for example W. R. Cline: "The potential effect of income redistribution on economic growth in four Latin American countries", in *Development Digest* (Washington), Oct. 1971, pp. 9-23; R. Prebisch: "Income distribution in Latin America: structural requirements for development", ibid., pp. 38-50; F. Paukert, J. Skolka and J. Maton: *Redistribution of income, patterns of consumption and employment*, World Employment Programme research working paper (Geneva, ILO, 1974); and ILO: *Towards full employment: a programme for Colombia* (Geneva,

1970), p. 149.

[27] See Institut de science economique appliquee, France: Besoins nutritionnels et politique economique, Senegal (Paris, 1965).

[28] Ministere du Plan, Ivory coast: Travaux preparatoires au Plan 1976-1980: prix, revenus, consommation, epargne (Abidjan, 1975), p. 104.

[29] Ibid., p. 106.

[30] J. Mouly and E. Costa: Employment policies in developing countries: a comparative analysis (London, George Allen and Unwin on behalf of the ILO, 1974), p. 27.

[31] On this point see C. Morrisson: La repartition des revenue dans les pays du tiers monde (Paris, Cujas, 1968), p. 323.

[32] See Morrisson, op. cit., p. 329.

[33] I. Adelman and C. T. Morris: "An anatomy of income distribution patterns in developing nations", in Development Digest, Oct. 1971, p. 36.

The Supply of International Liquidity to Developing Countries

KLAUS BOECK

The gravamen of the comments by the developing countries on the problem of the supply of international liquidity is that since 1970 they have been at a great disadvantage as far as the distribution of the newly created international liquidity is concerned. At the annual IMF meeting in Manila in early October 1976 they therefore put forth a demand for a fresh allocation of SDRs.[1] The question that has to be asked in this connection is whether the developing countries are justified in their criticism concerning the supply of liquidity and whether another SDR allocation is needed in order to solve their liquidity problems if any exist.

A discussion of problems of the supply and distribution of international liquidity calls, even more definitely than many other economic subjects, for an incontrovertible delimination of the object of investigation, for the number of liquidity concepts in vogue is too large.[2]

I. THE MONETARY RESERVE CONCEPT

The developing countries appear to base their line of argument on the currency reserve concept, for in their critique of the supply of international liquidity they are referring explicitly to the regression of international reserves relative to world imports.[3] The monetary reserves -- also known as unconditional liquidity -- consist of the gold, foreign currencies and SDRs held by the monetary authorities plus their drawing rights on the

From **INTERECONOMICS**, No. 5/6, 1977, (129-133), reprinted by permission of the publisher.

so-called gold tranche with the International Monetary Fund (IMF).

A comparison of the changes in the monetary reserves of the developing countries with those of the total world reserves does not bear out the assertion that there has been a permanent deterioration in the position of the developing countries. After a distinct decline in 1971 compared with 1970 the developing countries' share of the total monetary reserves showed between 1971 and 1973 an equally distinct increase which in turn was followed by a substantial downturn due to the oil crisis up to the end of 1975. In the first half of 1976 however the developing countries' reserves rose again much faster than the total reserves, so that by August 1976 they were back to 15.3 p.c. of all reserves -- a figure surpassed only once before in the seventies, namely by that for 1973.

The actual changes in the monetary reserves and their distribution thus do not show the developing countries to have been at a disadvantage. It is questionable however whether these figures can be quoted at all as sufficient evidence for the equitableness or adequacy of the supply of international liquidity.

II. VALUE CHANGES

The movements of the monetary reserves as recorded by the IMF indicate either value or volume changes in the reserve-stocks. As the reserves are valued in SDR, value changes cannot occur in the SDR accounts or the reserves with the IMF. The value of the gold holdings of monetary authorities could not change either as long as the gold-SDR ratio was prescribed by the official gold price.[4] The impending second amendment to the IMF's Articles of Agreement however will abolish the official gold price[5] and thus open the possibility in principle of gold holdings changing in value.

Value changes in the reserves held in foreign currencies on the other hand have long been common occurrences. This reserve component is regularly revalued whenever the rate of the reserve currency in question to the SDR changes. About four-fifths of all foreign currency reserves in 1975 were held in dollars, according to IMF estimates. As the dollar was revalued by 4.6 p.c. against the SDR in that year, the total monetary reserves increased by about SDR 4.2 bn in consequence of this parity change.[6]

If all monetary authorities held identical reserve portfolios, value changes in the monetary reserves would be neutral in their effect on the reserve distribution. In actual fact however gold and foreign currencies carry widely differing weights in the reserve portfolios of the industrialized and developing countries. At the end of the first half of 1976 gold accounted for 6 p.c. of all monetary reserves of developing countries but for as much as 27 p.c. of those of the industrialized countries. If the gold holdings are revalued, as is to be expected in view of the present world market price for gold if for no other reasons, the reserve position of the developing countries will therefore clearly worsen.

The Supply of International Liquidity   197

At the same time 89 p.c. of the monetary reserves of the developing countries were held in the form of foreign currencies -- a much higher percentage than the corresponding 58 p.c. of the industrialized states. As a result the developing countries benefited from the mentioned revaluation of the US dollar much more than the industrialized states. The opposite of course happens in the case of a dollar devaluation as was seen in 1973 and 1974.

As the gold value changes have not yet shown up in the books and the value changes in foreign currency reserves apparently did not follow a uniform trend, they do not allow any definite statements about advantages or disadvantages for the developing countries in regard to the supply of international liquidity in the past.

III. RESERVE-STOCK CHANGES

Quantitative change, i.e. movements in the monetary reserve-stocks, are the outcome of balance of payments disequilibria or IMF decisions on the allocation of extra SDR. So far such allocations have been made only in the triannual period from 1970 to 1972. They are thus playing no part in the current supply of liquidity and may be disregarded for the following observations.

As regards the role of balance of payments surpluses and deficits for the supply of liquidity, a distinction must be made between those in reserve currency countries and those in non-reserve currency countries. The surpluses and deficits of the former affect both the total amount of the world monetary reserves and their distribution. States with a balance of payments surplus vis-a-vis the reserve currency country for instance will accumulate additional foreign currency reserves equal to the deficit of the reserve currency country. Their reserve position vis-a-vis all other participants in this reserve system will improve coincidentally.

Balance of payments disequilibria between non-reserve currency countries on the other hand affect only the distribution but not the total amount of the world°s monetary reserves. This however holds good only if deficits are financed from their own reserve-stocks and not by foreign loans.

Foreign currency loans from another monetary authority, the Euro-markets or the IMF on the other hand increase the total world monetary reserve-stock. They also alter the distribution of the reserves in favour of the states with a balance of payments surplus vis-a-vis the borrower. If the borrower's balance of payments before acceptance of the loan was in equilibrium, his own monetary reserves will increase by the amount of the additional indebtedness incurred.

The distribution effects of the creation of additional foreign currency reserves are the only relevant factor as regards the question whether a country or group of countries is put at a disadvantage in respect of the supply of liquidity. These effects can only be calculated from the total of the bilateral balances of payments of all the participants in the reserve system and not from the statistics of monetary reserve changes which are published by the IMF, for the IMF figures aggregate the distribution effects of the creation of additional reserves with those of drawings on existing reserves.

There are no adequate statistical data available yet for the necessary analysis of the bilateral balances of payments however, and quantitative statements about the distribution of the additional foreign currency reserves created in recent years cannot therefore be made, at least not at present. But even if the required information on the distribution of new foreign currency reserves could be culled from currently available statistics, it could not either prove or disprove the developing countries' thesis of a handicap in regard to the supply of international liquidity.

IV. FUNCTIONAL LIQUIDITY CONCEPT

The distribution of the newly created monetary reserves may for instance conceivably shift over a certain period in favour of the industrialized states because they needed larger reserves during this time than the developing countries and therefore made correspondingly greater efforts to increase their reserves. The existence of a disadvantage can therefore be proved only if the access to new reserves is made relatively more difficult for developing countries while the reserve requirements of both groups of countries, industrialized and developing, are assumed to be changing at the same rate. This line of argument rests no longer on the largely formal interpretation of the concept of reserve liquidity. International liquidity is now understood in a functional sense[7] as the ability to obtain international means of payment.

Possibilities for at least a nominal increase in the supply of liquidity are inherent in the mere possession of monetary reserves -- in the case of gold reserves through higher prices and in regard to foreign currency accounts through the earning of interest. With a reserve increase in this form neither group of countries is discriminated against if the rise of the gold price matches the interest earned on foreign currency accounts. But if the gold price rises more strongly than the interest earned on foreign currency accounts, the industrialized countries will profit more. Conversely, the developing countries will be the ones to profit more if the gold price rises less than the interest income from foreign currency accounts. It is certainly not possible to predict which of these conjunctures will predominate in future, but disregarding the non-recurrent adjustment effects of the freeing of the official gold price, it is quite feasible that the interest earnings on foreign currency accounts and the increase of the gold price will be kept more or less in balance by a yield-oriented investment policy of the monetary authorities.

The Supply of International Liquidity   199

The industrialized states will of course derive especially large profits from the adjustment of the price of monetary gold to the world market price following the parting with the official gold price. Since however monetary gold, unlike the reserves held in foreign currencies, did not earn interest, the gold price adjustment is to be interpreted as compensation for interest forgone rather than as an advantage or disadvantage bestowed on a particular group of countries.

As well as by a higher gold price and interest income from foreign currency accounts, the supply of liquidity can be improved by intervention of monetary authorities in the foreign exchange markets or by the raising of loans in foreign currencies. Exchange market intervention for the purpose of increasing the foreign currency reserves offers little prospect of success unless there is relatively flexible exchange rate management and the country's own currency can be expected to be alternatively subject to upward and downward tendencies. Most developing countries meet neither of these conditions.

The IMF Interim Committee legalized the floating of exchange rates at its meeting in Jamaica in January 1976 and thereby put the monetary authorities in a position to pursue a flexible exchange rate policy. Most developing countries however have made no use of this possibility. They continue to keep their currencies.[8] This linkage is often maintained exclusively by foreign exchange controls. Exchange controls make it possible to raise the monetary reserve, e.g. by tightening the foreign currency allocations to importers, i.e. by curtailing imports and/or undervaluing the national currency so as to promote exports, but the developing countries are for both these measures less favourably placed than the industrialized states.

V. DISADVANTAGES TO THE DEVELOPING COUNTRIES

Undervaluation of its currency is unlikely to provide a significantly larger foreign currency income for a developing country. Obviously it will not increase the foreign currency income if the exporters do not pass on the benefit from the lower exchange rate in their prices. If they do reduce their prices in foreign currencies on the other hand, the foreign currency income will increase only in consequence of a more than proportionate rise of demand and supply. The price elasticity of demand cannot be expected to be high for the kind of goods which developing countries supply except perhaps for semi-manufactures and finished products. Extra capacity would be needed to cope with a more than proportionate rise in the foreign demand for these. In this sector however the developing countries are even worse off for spare capacity and the resources for capacity extensions than in the raw materials sector.

With floating exchange rates industrialized countries achieve an undervaluation of their currency if the latter is exposed to revaluation pressure which is neutralized by corresponding intervention. In this case price concessions by the exporters of the industrialized country are much more likely to result in an increase of the foreign currency income because their supply flexibility will probably enable them to make an adequate response to a more than proportionate rise of the demand from abroad.

An increase of the monetary reserves may however, as mentioned, follow from curtailment of imports as well as from additional exports. Recourse to import restrictions on the part of developing countries can however in certain circumstances interfere with the realization of their development aims or result in an immediate noticeable worsening of goods supplies.

The imports of an industrialized state with a depreciation-prone currency are also apt to be affected if the authorities do not intervene at all or only on a relatively moderate scale in order to preserve their reserves, but the advanced state of development and high level of supplies in industrialized countries mitigate the impact of such import reductions.

The advantage accruing to industrialized states from their more advanced development, which is reflected by the diversity and flexibility of their exports, explains in great measure why their currencies can be expected to show alternative upward and downward tendencies. In the developing countries this cannot be expected, at least not in like measure. Developing countries have more reason to expect permanent downward pressure; hence a more flexible exchange rate policy would probably do nothing for their liquidity.

Finally, developing countries are also at a disadvantage compared with the industrialized states in the raising of balance of payments loans. They are rarely in a position to tap such bilateral lines of credit with other monetary authorities as the USA in particular has opened to the central banks of the other industrialized states. Besides, most developing countries have no or only very limited access to the international credit and capital markets.[9] An approach to the IMF is thus the only possible remedy left to them.

VI. COMPENSATION THROUGH IMF LOANS

Until the outbreak of the oil crisis approximately, IMF loans were obtainable in the framework of the so-called credit tranches, the compensatory financing facility and the buffer stock financing facility. While resort to the credit tranches is open to industrialized and developing countries alike, the compensatory and buffer stock facilities are primarily intended to cover the requirements of the developing countries. Drawings on these credit lines are in any case subject to quite definite conditions.

The general prerequisite for them is an acute balance of payments need. Drawings on the credit tranches involve, besides, economic policy impositions designed to help to restore the balance of payments. The compensatory financing facility on the other hand is available for the bridging of short-term shortfalls in export earnings due to external causes outside the control of the deficitary country. Loans from the buffer stock facility are provided for payments arising from membership of international commodity agreements.

This traditional arsenal of IMF credit instruments is intended as stop-gap aid against cyclical or seasonal balance of payments deficits. As means of disposing of the balance of payments problems thrown up by the oil crisis they have proved largely inadequate. It has also been realized that, especially in developing countries, balance of payments deficits may be the result of mistakes in the structural and growth policy which take much more time to correct than for instance adjustments to compensate for cyclical oversteer.

The IMF responded to these additional demands by offering new lines of credit. In June 1974 the oil facility was created; it could only be used for balance of payments deficits caused by the increased cost of imported oil.[10] In August 1975 the IMF supplemented it by an Interest Subsidy account for the purpose of lowering the interest burden of drawings from the oil facility -- by about 5 p.c. -- on the most severely affected developing countries (the MSAC).[11] The oil facility was at first provided for one year only as its main purpose was to avoid the material overreactions to which, it was feared, the oil price explosion would give rise, but it was later extended until the spring of 1976. The Interest Subsidy account has been opened for a correspondingly limited period only; it will be closed on the last interest date.

No closing date has been set for the extended IMF facility which was created in September 1974 or for the Trust Fund set up in May 1976. Both these measures were taken with the particular balance of payments problems of the developing countries in mind. The extended facility allows drawings for much longer periods and appreciably larger sums than are common with other credit lines. The Trust Fund provides balance of payments loans on concessional terms for developing countries in special need. The grant of credit is however in both cases conditional upon initiation of an IMF-approved programme to restore the balance of payments.

Besides providing new credit facilities, the IMF at the beginning of 1976 raised the credit limit for the compensatory financing facility and the buffer stock financing facility. These measures together resulted in a considerably larger expansion of drawing rights for developing countries than for the industrialized states. At the end of the IMF year of 1973/74 the drawing rights of the developing countries amounted to SDR 12.7 bn and were thus markedly smaller than the credit facilities of SDR 18.1 bn available to the industrialized states. Two years later a total of SDR 24.2 bn was at the disposal of the developing countries compared with an amount of SDR 28.0 bn for the industrialized states.[12] When the IMF members have given their assent to the sixth general review of quotas, the ratio will change further in favour of the developing countries: the countries in this group will be able to dispose of SDR 28.7 bn and the industrialized states only of SDR 21.7 bn.

This review of the IMF's recent credit measures warrants the conclusion that the IMF has shown adequate flexibility, especially in respect of the particular concerns of the developing countries. It has proved its flexibility by its ability to create new instruments to cope with new situations typical of developing countries, but also by the substantial additions to the total volume of finance -- about SDR 12 bn in no more than two years. The credit policy of the IMF may thus be considered to have provided an adequate equivalent for the handicap from which the developing countries are undeniably suffering in regard to the supply of international liquidity from other sources.

VII. NO NEW SDR ALLOCATION

In view of the available financing facilities and their impending increase by another SDR 4.5 bn there is no manifest need for an immediate new SDR allocation, especially bearing in mind that SDR drawings differ from IMF loans only in one respect, namely in that their use is not contingent on any economic stipulations whatsoever and may in certain circumstances be allowed for longer periods. The individual developing country may consider the resulting greater scope of action an advantage but it only creates a possibility of deferring necessary adjustment measures. For the viability of the world monetary system it is if anything a drawback. The economic impositions by the IMF on the other hand are aimed at perfecting the adjustment process. It follows that, from the point of view of monetary policy, an enlargement of liquidity subject to "conditionality" within the IMF framework is clearly preferable to any new SDR allocation.

NOTES

[1] Cf. Press Communique of the Ministers of the Group of 24, issued following their meeting in Manila on Oct. 2, 1976, in: IMF Survey, Vol. 5 (1976), No. 20, p. 313.

[2] Cf. John Williamson, International Liquidity, in: The Economic Journal, Vol. 83 (1973), No. 331, p. 686ff.

[3] Cf. Press Communique, ibid., p. 313.

[4] 35 SDR = one ounce of pure gold.

[5] Cf. International Monetary Fund, Proposed Second Amendment to the Articles of Agreement of the International Monetary Fund, Washington, D.C., 1976, p. 40.

[6] Cf. International Monetary Fund, Annual Report 1976, p. 34f.

[7] Cf. John Williamson, ibid., p. 687.

[8] On the reasons for this measure cf. Barbara Erhardt, Floating Exchange Rates and their Problems for the Developing Countries, in: Intereconomics, 12th year (1977), No. 1/2, p. 29f.

[9] Cf. Jacob A. Frenkel, The Demand for International Reserves by Developed and Less-Developed Countries, in: Economica, February 1974, p. 21.

[10] Cf. IMF, Annual Report 1975, p. 53.

[11] Cf. IMF, Annual Report 1976, p. 58f.

[12] These figures are based on the assumption that the extended facility is used exclusively by developing countries. Moreover, the drawing rights against the gold tranche were not taken into account because they are counted as official monetary reserves.

Growth, Distribution and Motivation in LDCs

WOLFGANG ARNOLD

In 1955 Kuznets[1] propounded the thesis that the income distribution in countries with a very low average per-capita income was at first relatively egalitarian, that in the course of economic growth a differentiation process was then initiated which resulted in inordinately gross income disparities, and that it was only from a certain state of development onwards that a levelling process took place. At that time Kuznets was not yet able to provide adequate empirical evidence in support of his thesis. In the meantime however a number of empirical studies have been presented, especially by Kravis[2] (1960), Oshima[3] (1962), Kuznets[4] (1963), Adelman-Morris[5] (1973) and Paukert[6] (1973), which seem to confirm the existence of a connection as stated by Kuznets.

If Kuznets' thesis is interpreted as an immutable historic law of development, this would imply that one has to presume the existence in the case of the developing countries of an actual insoluble conflict between the objectives of accelerating economic growth and a relatively egalitarian distribution of incomes.[7] The consequence of this for development policy would be that the developing countries would have to forgo economic growth for the sake of a relatively egalitarian distribution or to abandon the distribution objective in the interest of the growth objective.

I. TWO OBJECTIONS

If Kuznets' thesis and its historical interpretation is subjected to a critical analysis, there are two objections above

From **INTERECONOMICS**, Nov.-Dec. 1979, (298-303), reprinted by permission of the publisher.

all which can be formulated: Most of the mentioned empirical studies which seem to bear out Kuznets' thesis rest on cross-section analyses; they thus assume implicitly that the development in every country follows the same course in regard to the level of growth and the distribution structure. There are however a number of developing countries, such as Taiwan, Sri Lanka, Costa Rica, Tanzania and Colombia for instance, in which the income distribution has -- at least temporarily -- improved with progressing growth.[8] Moreover, there is no reason why a certain uniformity of the development of economic and social indicators observed in the past should necessarily be assumed to apply likewise to the future.

Kuznets' assertion that the disparity of incomes increases in the first phase of the growth process for instance can be explained in the case of the present developing countries by pointing out that in the practice of development policy attention focused hitherto almost entirely on the achievement of the growth objective which was largely in line with the development concepts of the industrialized Western nations, and that the social discrepancies were caused or aggravated by this specific policy. Conceivably special measures of distribution policy could create in the developing countries conditions which impinge on events in the sphere of economic growth and income distribution in such a way that the differences between incomes are flattened or at least further differentiation is countered and these same measures do not impair growth but possibly even advance it.

II. OPPORTUNITIES FOR REDISTRIBUTION OF INCOMES

Starting from this position, one has to ask what can be done to realize the distribution objective. Besides, the effects of certain measures of distribution policy on economic growth have to be assessed.

There are fundamentally two ways of changing the income distribution:

1. The political authorities can tackle the determinants of income distribution in the production process: they can thus try to influence the decisive factors for primary distribution so as to achieve the desired equalization;

2. The state has the possibility of effecting a redistribution through taxes and transfer payments in the framework of its revenue and expenditure policy and of thus correcting the income distribution retrospectively.

The discussion on distribution policy concentrated for a long time almost entirely on the second of these alternatives. Its redistributive effectiveness must however be doubted, especially since Fohl's criticism of progressive taxation. Fohl's criticism is essentially that the intended redistribution is in great measure thwarted by tax shifting processes and the efficiency of such fiscal devices is therefore low.[9]

A sceptical view of revenue and expenditure measures is especially justified in view of the specific situation in the developing countries. The scope for taxation and transfer income payments is narrowly limited in these countries, and their market structure would presumably make it even more difficult to prevent tax shifting processes than in the industrialized countries.

In view of these arguments against retrospective action on distribution it seems advisable to examine the determinants of primary distribution for a solution of the problem. It is best to focus on theories which offer an immediate explanation for the personal income distribution because they alone are socially relevant.[10]

III. THE ABILITY THESIS

What was probably the first attempt at an explanation of the personal income distribution was undertaken by Galton.[11] Taking Quetelet's observation that the distribution of certain physical characteristics among human beings is in line with a Gaussian normal distribution as his starting point, Galton claimed that the human abilities are also normally scattered around a mean and that there exists a linear dependence between the distribution of abilities and that of incomes. Hence the income distribution was also normal. Later empirical investigations, starting with Pareto's well-known studies on personal distribution, indicated however that the distribution curve postulated by Galton did not match the facts. In reality incomes are not positioned symmetrically around a mean but they are scattered asymmetrically, showing a marked positive skewness. Galton's thesis that the income distribution is determined by the distribution of abilities was nevertheless the point of departure for many of the explanations attempted later.

The dominant hypothesis aside from the ability thesis is the explanation by stochastic processes offered in particular by Champernowne,[12] Gibrat,[13] Friedman,[14], Rutherford[15] and Mandelbrot[16] in their studies which are based on the Paretian or the normal logarithmic distribution. A fault common to all these stochastic attempts at an explanation is their lack of empirical content. Empirically established deviations from the supposed distribution can always be explained <u>ad hoc</u> by the claim that the -- incomputable -- chance is a co-determinant of distribution. Besides, these theories offer no criteria for distributive measures because chance is by definition not susceptible to the exertion of influence.

The ability thesis was developed further mainly by Rhodes[17], Roy,[18] Lydall,[19] Chiswick and Becker,[20] and Tinbergen.[21] Rhodes and Roy do not however define the concept of ability in such a way that their statement could be refuted in principle. Lydall's theory suffers from the crucial shortcoming that his explanation relates only to part of the distribution curve and his approach can therefore only solve part of the problem. Tinbergen's demand-supply theory and the human capital theory to be ascribed mainly to Becker and Chiswick seem to be more suitable for explanatory purposes. Both these theories employ concepts of ability which are operationable.

IV. THE HUMAN CAPITAL THEORY

The human capital theory rests on the perspective of a connection between the distribution of investments in education and the distribution of earned incomes. The instrumental paradigma is the conventional theory of capital including Joel Dean's capital model in particular. The profit maximization assumption in Dean's model is replaced by an income maximization assumption. Individuals will accordingly invest in education up to the level at which the economic benefit or income reaches it maximum. It is assumed furthermore that every individual similar to the entrepreneur, is faced with a specific conjuncture of supply and demand in the capital market for educational investments, with the result that the individual supply and demand conditions for education capital determine the size of a person's investment in education.

As in accordance with the specific definition of the demand curve the rates of return from investment in education are known and the income from work depends by virtue of the so-called earnings equation upon the size of the investment and the rates of return, it is possible to determine the size of the investment and income simultaneously with the help of the model. The distribution of earned incomes as well as the distribution of the investments in education are on these premises determined by the supply and demand conditions facing the individuals in the market for education capital.

The crucial shortcoming of this theory for the solution of the problem is the fact that the premises in regard to the course of the individuals' supply and demand curves are not precise enough to allow the deduction from the theory of a specific connection between the distribution of investments in education and the distribution of earned incomes. Given the assumed premises a falling (or rising) inequality of investments can go hand in hand with an increasing, declining or constant inequality of earned incomes.[22]

In support of this position one will in fact have to rely more on econometric investigations carried out in connection with the human capital theory.[23] It was thought that the existence of a close positive connection between a person's educational level and the size of his earned income could be proved with the aid of these studies. A narrowing of the differences in education was therefore thought to lead of necessity to a reduction of the income differences. Other studies show however that the lengthening of the average time spent on education which normally attends the lessening of differences in education involves increased income differences.[24]

Reder[25] offers for this phenomenon the explanation that the lessening of differences in education aimed at equalizing incomes led to a simultaneous relative scarcity of innate abilities and for this reason gave considerable income advantages to the more gifted. Another criticism which may be made is that almost all empirical and econometric studies relate to developed countries and therefore fail to take into account the fact that in the developing countries persons with an academic education often fail to find employment while there is frequently a high surplus demand for personnel whose training period was much shorter; the latter therefore earn high incomes.

V. THE DEMAND-SUPPLY THEORY

Tinbergen's demand-supply approach, in contrast to the human capital theory, follows up the perspective that the distribution of earned incomes does not depend solely on factors of labour supply, i.e. the distribution of investments on education, but is at the same time also determined by the structure of the demand for labour. Tinbergen predicates that the labour market is not a uniform market in which services can be treated as homogeneous or in their entirety mutually exchangeable but consists of a large number of separate compartments. The criterion for distinctions between the individual compartments is the intensity or degree of the supply or demand for certain attributes or qualities.

The employers as a body specify a frequency distribution of the required abilities: they present a demand for certain amounts of labour in the various compartments of the labour market. On the supply side of the labour market on the other hand there are a large number of individuals with certain abilities; all these together show a certain frequency distribution of available qualities. If the frequency distributions of the required and available qualities coincide, production can, according to Tinbergen, be organized in such a way that every individual occupies an occupational position commensurate with his abilities.

It must be assumed however that the two distributions differ in reality so that a permanent element of tension with the well-known phenomena of excess supply or demand is a characteristic feature of the labour market and its sub-markets. In order to bring about a migration of labour and thus a harmonization of the two frequency distributions the employers must offer income incentives, i.e. they must pay higher wages in the labour market compartments in which the demand for labour exceeds the supply. Differences between earned incomes thus result in the model from ex ante imbalances in the various sub-markets. The wider the frequency distributions of available and required qualities diverge, the greater will be the degree of inequality between earned incomes. If they coincide, the result will be an egalitarian distribution of earned incomes.

VI. "AMOUNT OF SCHOOLING"

For a long time Tinbergen's theory was largely ignored. The main reason for this was that the concept of quality was at first left undefined. In later econometric studies Tinbergen, following up suppositions of the human capital theory, made use of education as measured by the "amount of schooling" as a quality indicator.[26] The degree of inequality of the earned incomes depends in this case upon the degree of divergence of the educational distribution on offer from that in demand. The political authorities interested in flattening the income distribution must accordingly use production and education measures to bring the two distributions into harmony.

The econometric tests of this theory by Tinbergen[27] may be regarded as perfectly satisfactory under statistical aspects. Tinbergen has arrived at relatively high determination coefficients. The question is however to what extent econometric investigations can be used at all in support of hypotheses and theories, i.e. whether a successful statistical or econometric test can be regarded as providing empirical confirmation for the theory.

The main objection to taking this position is that confutative instances are obscured, or interpreted as "normal abnormalities" and consequently accepted, because of the inference theory at the basis of econometrics. Besides, econometric tests, including those mentioned here, are usually arranged in such a manner as to provide confirmation, "verification" of preconceived opinions and not their refutation. In concrete terms, the tests are not carried out against a background of alternative and competing theories but the econometric structural equation presupposes certain theoretical dependences including for instance the dependence of the income distribution on the demand and supply distribution in the present case. Insofar as this is true one can hardly describe Tinbergen's hypothesis as an empirically confirmed theory.

Moreover, as in the case of the tests applied to the human capital theory, the empirical studies are open to the objection that they all relate to developed countries and do not take the specific conditions of developing countries into account. It is somewhat difficult to imagine that the labour market in the developing countries is as "perfect" as Tinbergen's theory presupposes. One need only think of the lack of labour mobility and the greatly reduced market transparence compared with the industrialized countries. Besides, the confinement of the investigations to school education neglects the component of vocational training which is certainly of great importance for incomes, a serious shortcoming in the developing countries where typically the school system is inadequate and instruction outside the schools, and especially on-the-job training, is of crucial importance for the development of the ability potential of the individual.

VII. THE ACHIEVEMENT MOTIVATION THESIS

Both the human capital theory and the demand-supply theory have a close connection with thoughts which have their origin in the theory of growth. This is especially striking in the case of the human capital theory which derived directly from the at first one-sidedly growth-oriented education economics. This aspect suggests a reference to considerations developed by McClelland[28] in the framework of the achievement motivation thesis.

McClelland presented the hypothesis, going back to Weber[29] and Tawney,[30] that periods of economic ascent and descent in history are always preceded by epoch-making psychological changes in achievement motivation: the high achievement motivation of a society is the decisive cause of economic growth. Crucial is according to this view that persons with a high achievement motive possess the typical attributes of successful entrepreneurs and managers and that successful entrepreneurial activities bring about economic growth. McClelland was able to support his growth hypothesis by empirical tests. An increase of achievement motivation was seen to be followed by an increase of economic growth.

The translation of the achievement motivation thesis -- similar to that applied to the human capital theory by its adherents -- to the area of income distribution leads to the hypothesis that a decline (increase) of the inequality of achievement motivation intensity results in a decline (increase) of the inequality of income distribution. This hypothesis is based on the supposition that persons of high achievement motivation act in an entrepreneurial spirit (in the widest sense), that they are, for instance, interested in doing something better, take an activist forward-looking view of future prospects or tend to assess their occupational and economic opportunities with cautious optimism and will therefore achieve high incomes whereas persons of a lower achievement motivation, who do not possess these qualities or possess them only to a smaller degree, will receive lower incomes.

The distribution hypothesis evolved on the basis of the achievement motivation theory seems to be superior to the human capital theory and also to Tinbergen's theory, chiefly because the concept of achievement motivation allows the component of on-the-job training which is probably highly relevant to incomes, to be taken into account.[31] This is so because it may be assumed in view of the specific behaviour syndrome of highly motivated persons that people with a strong urge for achievement will make greater use of opportunities for advanced vocational training and for this reason have better promotion and income opportunities. Success at school and duration of school education have also been shown by empirical studies to depend decisively on the degree of achievement motivation.[32]

That this is a fruitful hypothesis is illustrated by the fact that training courses for adults to increase their achievement motivation in the Indian region of Andhra Pradesh led to noticeable economic gains, i.e. improved incomes, for those who attended them.[33] The hypothesis can, moreover, be extended with the aid of the Atkinson model[34] which assigns to the opportunity structure a crucial role in motivation effectuation and thus conforms to Tinbergen's thesis of the additional influence of labour demand factors on distribution. To do so may be advisable in view of the specific situation in the developing countries. Other motives such as the desire for power and affiliation which have also been found to act as income determinants can be included in the analysis.

VIII. GROWTH ASPECTS

No matter whether the human capital theory, the demand-supply theory or the thesis of achievement motivation offer a better explanation of the income distribution and are thus more suitable for application to distribution policy, our reflections show that measures based on these theories will not -- at least not immediately -- result in an impairment of growth. The close connection of these theories with the theory of growth and other considerations of relevance to a growth policy suggest on the contrary that such measures, insofar as their <u>direct</u> effects are concerned, have a positive influence on economic growth.

Possible <u>indirect</u> effects ensuing from the changed distribution must however also be taken into consideration. Economists under the influence of the classical and Keynesian schools maintain that an egalitarian or relatively egalitarian income distribution is detrimental to growth in the developing countries. The majority of the people in the developing countries subsist, so they say, on a level close to the physical minimum, so that their incomes enter fully into consumption. The number of people capable of saving part of their income was relatively small. If their incomes were in the course of a levelling process reduced to a point near the general average, most of them would cease to be savers while the average income would rise by so small a margin that this savings shortfall could not be compensated for. A more egalitarian income distribution resulted therefore in a smaller savings rate, and the investment ratio would decline at the same time. A sufficient capital accumulation was however of crucial importance for the achievement of an adequate growth rate of the national product. Besides, a more egalitarian income distribution inevitably leading to increased consumer demand would result in larger consumer goods imports as the level of production in the developing countries is so low. This would be at the expense of the urgently needed imports of capital goods.

As against this line of argument it has however to be pointed out that the upper class in the developing countries often use the bulk of their income for purposes of consumption and not for investment. Schumpeter already remarked that the assumption that an inegalitarian income distribution automatically increases the investment propensity was an uncritical idealization and generalization of what had been observed in a particular historical situation. The consumer demand of the wealthy people is, it must also be noted, largely concentrated on goods of a higher standard which have to be imported. Consequently a levelling of incomes will probably merely change the composition of the consumer goods imports but not necessarily impose an extra burden on the balance of payments. A more egalitarian income distribution makes for uniformity of consumption structures, with the possible result of increased demand for mass consumption goods imparting impulses to production and bringing economies of scale into play.

Although it seems hardly possible and is not intended here to give a final answer, our reflections lead to the view that there is no convincing case for a development policy with a one-sided growth orientation. Cross-section analyses of the kind mentioned at the beginning do not warrant the abandonment of distribution objectives and measures in the developing countries. There seems to exist the possibility of achieving advances in growth and distribution at the same time and thus to approach more closely to the fundamental aim of development policy: to raise the standard of living of the whole population.

NOTES

[1] S. Kuznets: Economic Growth and Income Inequality, in: The American Economic Review, Vol. XLV, 1955, p. 1-28.

[2] I. B. Kravis: International Differences in the Distribution of Income, in: The Review of Economics and Statistics, Vol. XLII, Supplement: August 1960, p. 408-416.

[3] H. T. Oshima: The International Comparison of Size Distribution of Family Incomes with Special Reference to Asia, in: The Review of Economics and Statistics, Vol. XLIV, 1962, p. 439-445.

[4] S. Kuznets: Quantitative Aspects of the Economic Growth of Nations: Distribution of Income by Size, in: Economic Development and Cultural Change, Vol. XI, 1963, p. 1-80.

[5] I. Adelman, C. T. Morris: Economic Growth and Social Equity in Developing Countries, Stanford 1973.

[6] F. Paukert: Income Distribution at Different Levels of Development: A Survey of Evidence, in: International Labour

Review, Vol. 108, 1973, p. 97-125.

[7] This position is taken by I. Adelman for instance. She says with reference to her own empirical studies: "These results imply that, for a lengthy portion of the process of economic development, there is a conflict between the growth of overall national income and an increase in the welfare of the poor. Equally important, there is an analogous conflict with respect to policy instruments for systematic intervention." I. Adelman: Development Economics -- A Reassessment of Goals, in: The American Economic Review, Vol. 65, 1975, p. 303.

[8] Cf. H. Chenery: Introduction, in: Redistribution with Growth, Oxford 1974, p. XV. Cf., e. g., also A. Berry: Changing Income Distribution under Development: Columbia, in: The Review of Income and Wealth, Series 20, 1974, p. 289-316.

[9] C. Fohl: Kritik der progressiven Einkommensbesteuerung (Critique of progressive income taxation), in: Finanzarchiv, N. F., Vol. 14, 1953/43, p. 88-109; cf. also by the same author: Das Steuerparadoxon (The tax paradox), in: Finanzarchiv, N. F., Vol. 17, 1956/57, p. 1-37.

[10] There seems little point in dealing with the theories of functional distribution, more especially because of the blatant income differences within the group of wage and profit recipients in the developing countries and the high degree of cross-sectional distribution. Other kinds of distribution, such as the regional or sectoral distribution, are also only an inadequate approximation to the personal distribution.

[11] F. Galton: Hereditary Genius, London 1869.

[12] D. G. Champernowne: A Model of Income Distribution, in: Economic Journal, Vol. 63, 1952, p. 318-351; cf. also by the same author: The Distribution of Income between Persons, London 1973.

[13] R. Gibrat: Les inegalites economiques (The economic inequalities), Paris 1931.

[14] M. Friedman: Choice, Chance and the Distribution of Income, in: The Journal of Political Economy, Vol. 61, 1953, p. 277-290.

[15] R. S. G. Rutherford: Income Distribution, A New Model, in: Econometrica, Vol. 23, 1955, p. 277-294.

[16] B. Mandelbrot: The Pareto-Levy Law and the Distribution of Income, in: International Economic Reivew, Vol. 1, 1960, p. 79-106.

[17] E. C. Rhodes: The Pareto Distribution of Income, in: Economica, Vol. XI, 1944, p. 1-11.

[18] A. D. Roy: The Distribution of Earnings and Individual Output,

in: Economic Journal, Vol. LX, 1950, p. 489-505.

[19] H. F. Lydall: The Distribution of Employment Incomes, in: Econometrica, Vol. 27, 1959, p. 110-115: and by the same author: The Structure of Earning, ibid., p. 127ff.

[20] G. S. Becker, B. R. Chiswick: The Economics of Education, Education and the Distribution of Earnings, in: The American Economic Review, Papers and Proceedings, Vol. LVI, 1966, p. 358-369; G. S. Becker: Human Capital and the Personal Distribution of Income: An Analytical Approach, Ann Arbor 1967.

[21] J. Tinbergen: On the Theory of Income Distribution, in: Weltwirtschaftliches Archiv, Vol. 77, 1956, p. 155-175; by the same author: A Positive and a Normative Theory of Income Distribution, in: The Review of Income and Wealth, Series 16, 1970, p. 221-234; by the same author: Income Distribution, Analysis and Policies, Amsterdam-Oxford, 1975.

[22] On this and other shortcomings of the human capital theory cf. W. Arnold: Personelle Einkommensverteilung in Entwicklungslandern. Eine entwicklungspolitisch orientierte Analyse personeller Verteilungstheorien (Personal income distribution in developing countries. A development policy-oriented analysis of personal distribution theories). Tubingen-Basle 1979.

[23] Cf., amongst others, G. S. Becker, B. R. Chiswick: op. cit., p. 365ff: J. Mincer: The Distribution of Labor Income, in: The Journal of Economic Literature, Vol. VIII, 1970, p. 1ff; by the same author: Schooling, Experience, and Earnings, New York 1974, p. 43ff.

[24] Cf., e. g., B. R. Chiswick: Earnings Inequality and Economic Development, in: Quarterly Journal of Economics, Vol. 85, 1971, p. 21-39; B. R. Chiswick, J. Mincer: Time-Series Changes in Personal Income Inequality in the United States from 1939, with Projections to 1985, in: Journal of Political Economy, Vol. 80, 1972.

[25] M. W. Reder: A Partial Survey of the Theory of Income Size Distribution, in: L. Soltow (ed.): Six Papers on the Size Distribution of Wealth and Income, New York-London 1969, p. 226.

[26] Cf. J. Tinbergen: Can Income Inequality be Reduced Further?, in: H. J. Niedereichholz (ed): Festschrift fur Walter Georg Waffenschmidt, Meisenheim am Glan 1972, p. 165 ff; by the same author: The Impact of Education on Income Distribution, in: The Review of Income and Wealth, Series 18, 1972, p. 255-265. In more recent studies Tinbergen has extended the range of quality indicators. Cf. by the same author: Income Distribution: Second Thoughts, in: The Economist 125, No. 3, 1977, p. 315-339.

[27] Cf. J. Tinbergen: Can Income Inequality be Reduced Further?, op. cit.; by the same author: The Impact of Education on Income

Distribution, op. cit.

[28] D. C. McClelland: The Achieving Society, Princeton (N.J.), 1961.

[29] M. Weber: Die protestantische Ethik und der Geist des Kapitalismus (The protestant ethics and the spirit of capitalism), reprint from Max Weber: Gesammelte Aufsatze zur, Religionssoziologie I, Tubingen 1934.

[30] R. H. Tawney: Religion and the Rise of Capitalism, London 1926.

[31] Cf. also the attempts by the adherents of the human capital theory to deal with this income component by using age group statistics. Cf. espec. J. Mincer: Schooling, Experience, and Earnings, op. cit.

[32] Cf., e. g., D. C. McClelland: Erziehung zur Tuchtigkeit (Education for efficiency), in: W. Edelstein, D. Hopf (eds.): Bedingungen des Bildungsprozesses, Stuttgart 1973, p. 40-59.

[33] Cf. D. C. McClelland, D. G. Winter: Motivating Economic Achievement, New York-London 1969.

[34] Cf. J. W. Atkinson: Motivational determinants of risk-taking behavior, in: Psychological Review, Vol. 64, 1957, p. 359-372.

The Debt Problem of Developing Countries

GAMANI COREA

I. BACKGROUND

The debt problem of developing countries is a matter of growing concern to the international community. After more than two decades of borrowing, developing countries find themselves encumbered with an increasing burden of debt service payments. Their ability to meet these payments at all, or to meet them without seriously disrupting their economies is now a matter of some urgency. The studies now being undertaken by the World Bank and other bodies will help to determine the precise magnitude of the problem--both globally and in respect of individual countries. But the evidence already at hand is sufficient to underline the need for a serious appraisal of the debt problem and for new approaches that might serve to alleviate it.

The fact that the servicing of debt obligations has proved to be a problem at all suggests that something is amiss. Apart from official aid and short-term financing, most of the credits made available to developing countries were linked to commercial transactions relating to sales of goods and equipment.[1] These credits were presumable extended in good faith and with confidence in the ability of the recipient to honour the terms agreed upon. Repayment of the credits was often formally guaranteed by the recipient Government. This was considered to be sufficient security in itself; it freed commercial suppliers offering credits from the need to make a strict appraisal of the viability of the projects financed. They presumed that irrespective of the merits of the project, the recipient country would so order its affairs that its borrowing operations would always remain well within the

From **JOURNAL OF DEVELOPMENT PLANNING**, No. 9, 1976, (53-78), reprinted by permission of the publisher.

The Debt Problem of Developing Countries 217

limits of its capacity to repay.

In the light of these considerations any failure to meet contractual debt service obligations, apart from being a breach of faith, must appear to be the result of mismanagement, if not irresponsibility, on the part of the borrowing country. It might seem that such a situation need not have arisen had those countries been judicious in selecting the projects of the uses to which the credits were applied. Accordingly, any request for relief from debt service difficulties must be treated with the utmost reserve. Concessions in the way of debt relief could only encourage laxity in financial management, discriminate against prudent borrowers, and encourage requests for similar treatment by other debtors. Relief should be provided only in the most exceptional situation--where no other alternative is available. Moreover, relief, where provided, might even be used to exact a price from the debtor--in such a way that any relief provided by reduction in payments in the short term is gained at the cost of enhanced payments later. A relief operation which is a traumatic experience to debtors is a warning to all.

As long as debt service problems were an isolated phenomenon affecting only a handful of debtor countries there was little inducement to reconsider the validity of the view that these problems basically reflect failures in management and should be treated accordingly. The very fact that they are beginning to engulf an increasing number of developing countries and that there are real fears--suggested by statistical projections--that debt crises may cease to be exceptional occurrences, indicates the need for a reappraisal of the whole question. Should debt problems, in other words, continue to be regarded as a manifestation of management problems and be treated in that light? Or are there wider and more complex issues involved which require new approaches both in diagnosing the problem and in formulating remedies? There is evidence already of a changed approach in the way certain debt situations have recently been handled. Cases in point are the Indian and Indonesian debt rearrangements, which reflect a somewhat broader approach. But there is, as yet, little evidence that this approach signifies the acceptance of new techniques or principles of general applicability. On the contrary, it is the exceptional character of these arrangements that are currently being stressed.[2] The need for a fuller acceptance of the issues involved in the debt question still remains.

The first question that needs examination is the relationship between debt service problems and the management issue. Obviously irresponsibility and lack of discipline can lead countries to seek external credits for implementing ill-conceived projects which contribute little or nothing towards strengthening the economy. In the process, liabilities are incurred which bear no relationship to the country's capacity to discharge them. It is idle to pretend that these occurrences are exceptional. Even when planning authorities in developing countries are strong, which is by no means the universal rule, there are many occasions when pressures to initiate projects of doubtful soundness or lesser priority are not successfully resisted. The planners' strongest practical argument--the non-availability of resources--is weakened when ministries point to offers of external credits as a means of financing favoured projects. Commercial suppliers of machinery and equipment seldom have an overriding concern about the viability of the projects undertaken. The feasibility reports with which they buttress their proposals are not always objective or independent. The supplier has, in fact, no stake in the success of the project. His return is assured by the government guarantee irrespective of whether or not the project is a success. Furthermore, corruption and venality are sometimes part of the salesman's armoury and have played a significant role in the debt history of some countries.

Nevertheless, although mismanagement and laxity have been aspects of the debt problem, it would be erroneous to conclude that they have been the main element. It is possible and important to distinguish between situations where debt repayment is handicapped because of a misuse of resources through, for example, poor project selection and those where a debt service problem remains even though the resources have been put to good use. In the past, when currency convertibility was the rule in developing countries--largely by virtue of their adherence to a 100 per cent exchange standard--there was no problem of debt service capacity in terms of the balance of payments. The relevant issue was namely whether the domestic revenues generated directly or indirectly, by the projects financed out of credits would suffice to bear the amortization and interest charges involved. It is perhaps true to say that it was in this context that the conventional rules and criteria for loan financing evolved and that the issue of debt service came to be looked upon as a question of the internal viability of a project--transfer payments in foreign currencies being taken for granted. Today the situation is different. Developing countries, having adopted more flexible currency systems in the interests of growth and stability, often face serious balance-of-payments problems. The internal viability of a project in the conventional sense will not guarantee that adequate foreign exchange resources have been generated to meet the service charges on the external loans which may have financed the projects.

It may appear, at first sight, that this transfer problem might be overcome if the earning or saving of foreign exchange was introduced into the criteria for project selection. But this approach is not wholly satisfactory either. On the one hand, most commercial credits carry a relatively short amortization period--averaging, in the past, about five years, although there has been a trend towards longer maturity dates in the most recent period. The range of projects that could successfully meet, whether directly or indirectly, amortization and service charges in so short a period must indeed be extremely limited. On the other hand, even where projects are self-financing in the sense of generating adequate foreign exchange resources to meet service charges, there is no assurance that debt service would not be burdensome to the recipient country. A country facing acute payments problems for other reasons might find it difficult to meet its debt obligations even though the projects undertaken with the use of foreign credits have made a positive contribution to the over-all external resource position.[3]

The fact of the matter is that there can be no easy rule of

thumb prescription to determine the appropriate use of external credits. The best that a country can do is to gear its external borrowing to as good an assessment as possible of its future debt service capacity--taking into account all relevant factors, such as export prospects, existing debt service obligations, expectations about future concessional aid and the impact which all these will have on the levels of future imports. This will help it to establish a rough limit to the further increases that it might incur by way of payment obligations. But even this is not an infallible means of avoiding debt service difficulties. The imponderables are many even if the time horizon involved is the five-year period common to medium-or longer-term commercial credits.

It is, of course, true that despite its limitations, an approach on the basis mentioned above would greatly assist the developing countries in the problem of debt management. But even this leaves out another aspect of the debt problem, an aspect which perhaps overshadows all the other causal factors. It is true that developing countries could have minimized or even avoided debt service difficulties altogether by rigorously confining their borrowing operations to the narrow limits of what they knew, with certainty, to be their minimum capacity to repay. But this would still leave unresolved the problem of how such countries are to secure the additional external resources needed to support their economic and social development. The Governments of these countries face increasing internal pressure to cope with such problems as unemployment and low incomes. The dilemma which confronts them has been expressed in a report of the Organisation for Economic Co-operation and Development (OECD) as follows:

> "To what extent are recipients justified (or should donors acquiesce) in undertaking borrowing for needed investment in development at terms that seem likely to be too hard to sustain because the amounts thought to be required are not forthcoming at sufficiently concessional terms, or should they rather slow down the pace of their development?"[4]

Policy makers in developing countries might rightly be asked to eschew goals which are unrealistic and ambitious. But they cannot be expected to be so meticulous about the need to avoid taking future risks if the cost is to be stagnation and disruption today.

The extent to which an inadequacy of external resources on concessional terms has played a part in the accumulation of commercial credits in individual countries can only be established by case studies. But there can surely be little doubt that the insufficiency of capital flow on appropriate terms in the past has been a significant factor, possibly the major factor, behind the growing debt problems of developing countries taken as a whole. If this were not the case, there would be but little validity in the universal acceptance today of the need for a substantial improvement in the terms of future lending to developing countries. This is a tacit recognition of the fact that the problem of growth and of debt service could not be overcome by improvements in management alone. It is, moreover, likely that management itself is improved when countries are in receipt of significant amounts of official aid. This is particularly true where there is a measure of aid co-ordination through aid consortia or even consultative groups and where attention is focused on management efficiency and over-all performance. In these situations improvements take place in the whole area of project formulation and selection and this is reflected not only in the projects submitted to official aid agencies and lending institutions but also in those financed out of suppliers' credits.

The foregoing discussion emphasizes the difficulty of prescribing rules for the sound management of external debt in circumstances where developing countries are unable, due to the inadequacy of external resources, to meet even the most modest of development objectives. In these situations they will be driven, in the words of the OECD report, "[to] accept expensive aid to get done things the country urgently needs in the hope that exports will do better than expected so that one can pay the new debts, or in the confidence that creditors have no choice but to refinance rather than have debts repudiated".[5] But what of future situations in which the external resource situation might be improved by increases in export earnings or, especially, by increases in the flow of official aid on concessional terms so that countries are not driven to the excessive use of credits on hard terms? Would there still be scope for commercial credits and what rules of management can be suggested to govern their use in a manner that would avoid debt problems in the future?

In the type of situation now envisaged the yardsticks described earlier for regulating borrowing operations could be applied more readily. A country, having assessed its future payments situation in the light of its export prospects, it expectations about new concessional aid, its debt service obligations on past debt, and future aid, could estimate the extent to which it could prudently incur further obligations by way of additional borrowing on commercial terms. This would clearly be possible in cases where the investments, directly or indirectly, generate repayment capacity in foreign exchange through additional export earnings or import savings. It would also be possible in situations where this condition may not prevail, but where debt repayments, although resulting in a future slowing-down of imports and possibly of growth, only does so to an extent which the country considers to be wholly tolerable. In such a case the country is exercising a preference for greater expansion now to what might otherwise be possible in the future. But it would remain satisfied that the payments burden it incurs is still consistent with tolerable development goals. It would not need to seek relief from payments obligations on the grounds that these result in the disruption or dislocation of the economy.

What this means is that a country could supplement concessional aid with commercial credits to the extent that the additional service payments to not impair its export capacity beyond the limits deemed tolerable. This implies, in effect, that the country is able to incur average terms of debt service somewhat harder than those embodied in the official aid it receives. The alternatives in this situation are to reach the appropriate average by a mix of aid and commercial credits or--if its total external capital flows are to be provided through concessional aid--to increase the quantum of the latter on harder terms.

The foregoing discussion has examined the possible causes of debt problems in developing countries. The core of the problem is that, in the context of the world trading system that has prevailed up to now, developing countries have been unable to secure the external resources needed for development out of their own export earnings. They have been obliged to supplement their earnings through inflows of capital from abroad. They had, moreover, to obtain this capital from the sources and on the terms available to them. When access to capital inflows on concessional terms was limited, they had to supplement these flows by credits on harder terms. Commercial credits provided by developed countries as instruments to help promote sales of equipment and other items were a means of obtaining supplementary capital resources. Other than official aid and private investment, they were often the only source available. Most developing countries had lost the access they sometimes had in colonial times to international capital markets.

It is not argued, of course, that commercial credits are the sole cause of debt problems. Many developing countries have experienced debt difficulties arising from excessive short-term borrowings from foreign banks and other sources of short-term funds. But here the terms have been even harder--high interest rates and short maturity periods. But short-term borrowing and commercial credits apart, there is also the possibility that official credits themselves could also result in debt problems if the concessional element is too small. Had all capital inflows into developing countries in the past been in the form of official aid on the terms that have governed such aid up to now, the debt problem in the period ahead would undoubtedly have been less. But individual countries receiving such credits might still experience difficulties if their prospective external resources position remains unfavourable in the light of their future import needs. It should be remembered that non-commercial credits from international financial institutions such as the World Bank and the regional development banks bear market rates of interest. It is very likely that debt service difficulties will still have been widespread had all capital inflows into developing countries in the past been governed by the terms of these credits.

II. CRITERIA FOR INDENTIFYING DEBT PROBLEMS

A rising volume of debt service payments may not in itself be a cause of any difficulty if the total external resources available to a country are in some sense adequate to enable these payments to be made. The conventional debt service ratio is of value in that it relates service payments to the major source from which these payments have to be made--a country's export earnings. But a high debt service ratio need present no problem to countries whose total external resources--whether through exports or capital flows--are rising sufficiently rapidly. What is important is an understanding of the over-all situation of the country and the several factors that are relevant to an assessment of this situation. Various numerical indicators may be devised which provide prima facie evidence of debt service difficulties. But these can hardly take account of all the pertinent factors and cannot, therefore, serve as infallible guides in identifying debt problems.

An issue that needs clarification is the precise sense in which debt service payments can be regarded as posing a problem for an individual country. It would seem that a distinction could be made between situations where varying interpretations of a debt service problem are possible. The first of these is the most immediate and obvious: a situation in which a country finds that its total commitments for external payments on account of imports or debt exceed the resources currently available to it. This is a situation in which a country is in danger of default not only on its debt service obligations but also on other kinds of contractual payments including payments for imports on which orders have already been placed. Countries which have depleted their external reserves and exhausted the possibilities for further short-term borrowing constantly face the nightmarish prospect of a crisis of this type if, for example, there were to be an unexpected shortfall in export earnings. In such an event a country would probably choose to default on debt service payments rather than on normal payments for imports. This is, of course, a situation that can only occur in the very short term because it is one in which there is no flexibility whatsoever to reduce imports since these have already been committed. Whether any effective relief could be provided through debt relief or refinancing along will depend on the relative scale of the debt service burden. But in any attempt to forecast early debt service problems, special attention would need to be given to the situation in countries with low international reserves and volatile export earnings.

A second case, in many ways similar to the first, is of a less immediate nature. This occurs where imports may not have been actually committed but where it could be foreseen that a crisis would arise in which there was the prospect of default in debt service payments. This could happen where the external resources likely to be available to the country would not suffice to finance debt service payments without causing a drastic and disruptive reduction in imports beyond the minimum amounts needed for the maintenance of normal economic activity. The impending situation is one of crisis in the sense that a country would clearly be unable to meet its debt obligations and remedial measures of one kind or another would be unavoidable. In the past, crises of this kind have generally not been forecast in time and remedial action has been forthcoming only when the crisis has taken place and defaults had already occurred or were imminent. It can be one of the purposes of an early warning system to predict occurrences of this kind so that measures might be taken in advance to avoid an actual breakdown in debt service payments and a total dislocation in foreign exchange management. It will be necessary for purposes of forecasting to determine, for each country, the minimum level of imports below which economic activity will be sharply dislocated. If a country's external resources do not permit the minimum quantum of imports without impeding debt service payments, an acute crisis, carrying with it the possibility of default, would be imminent.

But such a concept of debt service difficulties is restrictive although, unfortunately, the one most commonly involved in past approaches to the debt problem. The notion of capacity to pay is here interpreted in its most literal sense and a debt problem is recognized as such only when the very limits of this capacity have been reached. In the absence of detailed country studies, it is not possible to determine the number of countries that may face this extreme situation in the period ahead. But the number may not be altogether negligible, in the context of existing debt service commitments, if countries are able to obtain their future needs of capital only on relatively hard terms and if export earnings were to fare particularly poorly.

Besides this extreme and restrictive concept, however, there is another and somewhat broader one which looks upon the debt problem not merely in terms of the critical point at which service payments themselves are jeopardized but also in terms of its impact on the country's economic and social goals. Debt service payments can pose problems for a country not only in the extreme situation in which its capacity to honour its obligations is in doubt but also where these payments so reduce the external resources available to it that its ability to meet its minimum economic and social objectives is impaired. A country which is paying its debts but which in consequence is suffering a negative rate of economic growth has a problem of debt service in a very fundamental sense. It is this aspect of the problem that needs most of all to be taken into account in any new approach to the debt issue. It is important to identify not only the extreme crisis cases as described above but also the far more numerous cases where debt service problems are gravely impeding the performance of countries in respect of economic growth and other objectives. It is, in other words, this criterion of minimum economic and social goals that needs somehow to be developed into an effective guide for identifying debt service difficulties.

The relationship between the debt problem and wider economic objectives might perhaps be further clarified. Of fundamental importance to developing countries in the pursuit of these goals is the capacity to import. The extent to which individual countries depend on imports for the supply of essential consumer goods, of production inputs, and of machinery and equipment for further development will doubtless vary. But as long as imports are indispensable for these purposes, their availability in adequate amount is of critical importance to the life and growth of the economy. The external resources accruing to a country are made up of its export earnings on goods and services and the inflow of new capital. But the total of these resources do not constitute import capacity. Debt service payments need to be deducted from this total before the amounts available for imports can be determined.

For any developing country, differing objectives in respect of economic growth will have varying implications in regard to the amount of imports needed. Conversely, variations in the amount of imports possible will have implications for growth objectives. Of critical importance in determining the extent to which debt service obligations have a bearing on growth objectives is the relationship between debt service obligations and import capacity. In arriving at a judgement on whether or not a country is facing, or will face, a debt service problem, it is necessary to project the course of import capacity and the extent to which such capacity is affected by debt service payments. If projections of import capacity—based on projections of future earnings, new capital flows, and service payments, both on debts already incurred and on new capital flows—show a rapidly rising trend for any country, that country is less likely to be concerned with service problems than if the projections indicated a static or falling trend. The trend of import capacity is a more significant indicator of problems than the trend of the conventional debt service ratio. Of course, the debt service problem will be regarded as important only if service payments significantly reduce import capacity. The ratio of debt service payments to total external outlays is for this reason important. But a high ratio of debt service payments is unlikely by itself to prove excessively burdensome if import capacity is rising rapidly.

Looked at in this way, a country could be said to be experiencing or facing debt service problems in situations where two conditions prevail: first, where its prospective import capacity falls short of what is needed for the attainment of its minimum economic and social objectives, and secondly, where debt service payments are likely to absorb a significant share of its total external outlays. The second condition has to be interpreted differently in varying circumstances and particularly as between the short and the long run. Debt service payments, being contractual obligations, are normally regarded by developing countries as having prior claim on their external resources. In a short-run crisis of the kind described earlier, where a country finds it difficult to meet its committed external outlays, any payments abroad including debt service payments, will constitute a problem. This would be so whether the ratio of service payments to total external outlays is large or small. In the longer run, the ratio assumes greater significance. A country may find that its prospective import capacity falls hopelessly short of requirements for its minimum objectives. But there is little sense in saying that such a country has a debt service problem if service payments are small and make only a minor difference to import capacity.

The more difficult problem of interpretation, however, centres around the concept of minimum economic and social objectives against which the adequacy of import capacity must be tested. Here there is room for a host of varying definitions. As usual, the extremes are more easy to describe. There is first the extremely restrictive concept of the minimum imports needs to avoid a breakdown or crisis situation. Every country would have some notion of the "rock bottom" level of imports it needs for essential consumption purposes and for sustaining normal levels of economic activity. The concept of minimum consumption needs is, of course, difficult, but countries which have been grappling with payments problems are likely to have already eliminated imports of non-essential consumer items and to have identified their minimum requirements for imported food-stuffs, textiles etc. needed to avoid or minimize political and social tensions. Usually, per capita consumption levels of essential food-stuffs will need to be maintained and import requirements could be estimated after taking account of the contribution of local production to the total supply. In regard to other items, developing countries, in the course of preparing and administering foreign exchange budgets, are aware of minimum requirements to maintain normal levels of activity in the various sectors of the economy--requirements, for example, of fertilizer, industrial raw materials, spares and construction materials. These requirements are determined on the basis of what is needed for the utilization of productive capacity already existing or in process of being established. It is seldom a static amount since some increases in imports would be needed--over the medium term at least--to satisfy the needs of current investments that would mature in the near future. This concept of minimum needs would, on the other hand, rule out further new investments and the import requirements that would flow out of these investments. A concept of this kind--a maintenance needs concept--implies no growth in the economy in so far as this is dependent on additional imports. For this reason it will usually imply a sustained decline in per capita income. It is, as indicated, the most restrictive of concepts possible and cannot figure as an economic and social objective, however minimal.

A somewhat wider interpretation of a minimum goal would be one in which over-all economic growth suffices at least to sustain per capita incomes. Debt services burdens could then be related to the import capacity needed to attain this objective. But this again is, from any point of view, an obviously restrictive interpretation. The mere maintenance in developing countries of per capita incomes at present levels is clearly not part of the economic and social objectives of these countries, or of the donors who are their "partners in development". It cannot be argued that the problems of countries with heavy debt service payments might be ignored as long as they are "holding their heads above water" by barely matching economic growth with increase in population. The fact is that, in this situation, heavy debt service payments stand in the way of a better growth performance by these countries; a better performance sorely needed on any reckoning. The employment situation alone, to take one example, is likely to deteriorate severely if over-all economic growth is no more than 2.5 or 3.0 per cent per annum.

These restrictive interpretations are of some value in that they serve as a rough guide in assessing the extent to which different countries are affected by the debt service problem. They are among the indicators that may be used to establish priorities between countries for the purpose of applying remedial solutions. But from the viewpoint of the debt problem of developing countries as a whole and of individual countries, a wider interpretation of minimum economic and social goals is needed. On what considerations should such an interpretation be based?

A straightforward approach that suggests itself is one based on the norms and targets of development that have been adopted by the international community--for example, the 6 per cent average annual rate of economic growth set for the Second United Nations Development Decade. But an approach on these lines is, in turn, unsatisfactory, not because these targets are in any sense ambitious from the viewpoint of needs, but because they are too mechanistic to be applied universally irrespective of the circumstances of individual countries. It is too simple and undiscriminating an approach to measure the severity of a country's problems by the extent to which it has succeeded in attaining the 6 per cent target. The situation needs to be assessed more comprehensively in terms of factors of particular relevance to each country. Although growth models might sometimes suggest that growth rates could be smoothly adjusted to varying resource availabilities, it is seldom that countries have such a continuum of possible growth objectives to choose from. The responses of the economy may be such that changes in the quantum of resources available would result in discontinuous changes in growth and performance. A given increase in the flow of resources available might make possible a more than proportionate increase in over-all growth. Similarly, a contraction in resources might so dampen or thwart growth impulses that a substantial deceleration in growth might take place. These and a host of other considerations need to be taken into account in determining the economic and social goals appropriate for an individual country. The considerations that are of relevance in determining whether debt service payments pose problems for a country are essentially those pertinent to the assessment of aid needs. It is essentially the flow of resources that is affected by debt service payments and by aid, and in both cases over-all development perspectives need to be taken into account.

What all this implies is that while the debt problem has to be viewed in a wider context than the limited one of extreme crisis situations, there are no precise yardsticks or criteria that could serve as a ready reckoner for the purpose. Apart from the difficulties of establishing quantitative measures of appropriate or even minimum economic and social objectives, there is the complex question of how these objectives might be related to the efforts which a country is itself making. Clearly, any assessment of external resource needs must assume that the country itself is allocating and utilizing resources in the most appropriate and efficient manner practicable. Purely quantitative indices or yardsticks that seek to measure debt service difficulties can hardly take these issues into consideration in a satisfactory way. They can only be assessed against the background of a full evaluation of the situation in a country. Qualitative elements and judgements must inevitably play a part in such an evaluation.

These issues are of relevance to efforts to devise an early warning system for identifying debt service problems. It is clearly desirable that emerging difficulties be detected in advance. It is also important that early warnings should point not merely to those crisis situations where defaults are likely but also to those where debt service payments will constitute a barrier to the attainment of even minimum development goals. For both these purposes it is, of course, necessary to have accurate projections, on a country-by-country basis, of future service payments on existing and new debt. It is also useful to relate these magnitudes to other indices of resource availability. From this point of view, concepts such as the debt service ratio, and particularly those which adjust this concept to take account of the maturity pattern of debts (for example, the indicators devised by OECD and other institutions and countries[6]) are of value. But, as already mentioned, the concept of import capacity is also important as an indicator in assessing debt service problems. It would be desirable to have projections of this capacity in respect of individual countries. A country with a prospective decline in import capacity is likely to be in a far more serious position than countries whose per capita import capacity is likely to rise or even to remain constant.[7] But whatever their merits, these indicators only serve to override prima facie evidence that debt service problems may arise. Only a detailed case-by-case study can establish the true nature of such a problem and its likely impact on a country's objectives.

III. REMEDIAL APPROACHES

Previous sections discussed the origins and nature of the debt problem. The present section is concerned primarily with the question of what might be done about these problems. The present-day approach to debt problems is essentially an ad hoc one. Action to provide relief to countries suffering from these problems is generally taken in crisis situations when defaults have taken place or are imminent and creditors are left with no alternative to debt relief. If there is any principle which may be said to guide debt relief operations it is that the relief afforded should be the minimum needed to ensure the early resumption of service payments and that the cost to creditors by way of any postponement of amortization and interest payments should be matched by additional interest charged at commercial rates. This is the so-called moratorium interest levied on the postponed amortization and contractual interest receipts that would otherwise have accrued to creditors. Debt relief provided in this way is equivalent to a loan at commercial interest rates of an amount equal to the contractual service payments due and bearing a maturity period equal to the duration of the moratorium on these payments.

It is now being increasingly recognized that this approach to debt problems is totally inadequate. The short-comings are many. In the first place, by delaying until action is virtually forced by events themselves, unnecessary disruption and damage is caused to the economy of the debtor country which cannot but impair its capacity to recover and to shoulder future debt service payments. More timely relief might have better served the interests of creditors and debtors alike. But it is not only the timing which is wrong; the quantum of relief provided is also inadquate. The "commercial approach" to debt rearrangements involving the levy of moratorium interest, and the very short duration of the relief provided does not, save in a few cases, serve to overcome the problems and difficulties of the debtor. It might suffice in instances where the problem is purely temporary, brought on, for example, by a shortfall in export receipts likely not only to be short-lived but also to be compensated by a vigorous upswing in future receipts. But when the payments problems of the debtor country are of a more chronic and deep-seated character, the "short leash" approach can only compound its difficulties and undermine its efforts to find a lasting and viable solution.

It is not surprising that many countries that have had debt relief arrangements in the past have found it necessary to seek repeated reschedulings. Thus, during the period 1957-1970, Argentina had its debts rescheduled on four occasions, Brazil twice, and Ghana, Indonesia and Turkey three times each. Indeed, of the eight countries which had their debts rescheduled under multilateral arrangements in the 19670s, only Chile and India had merely one rescheduling arrangement during that decade.[8] In the case of Ghana, total external debt obligations increased by 39 per cent after the rescheduling arrangement of 1968. This was due to the levy of moratorium interest at 6.5 per cent.[9] It is evident from these citations that past approaches to debt problems have been inadequate and have not succeeded in finding durable solutions. As long as the countries affected are few in number it is possible to view debt problems as isolated occurrences where the solutions adopted, even if proved inadequate, are of limited relevance in the international setting. If debt problems are, as current projections suggest, to become more pervasive in the future, the question of appropriate remedial measures assumes a new significance. Inadequate or unsatisfactory approaches to the debt problem could clearly impair the attainment, on a global scale, of objectives in the field of development and economic management.

There are two aspects to the question of a new look at the debt problem. One is the need for a more flexible approach to remedial solutions. The other is the need for a wider and more liberal interpretation of debt problems themselves. The latter issue was discussed in the preceding sections in which it was argued that debt problems exist even outside the extreme crisis situations recognized in the past and that remedial measures need to be applied to countries facing debt problems as defined in this wider sense. The extension of liberal solutions to countries in crisis situations only will not be altogether equitable. A new approach must clearly combine both a more flexible definition of debt problems and more appropriate solutions. The present section is concerned with the question of solutions. Assuming, in other words, that it has been established that a given country is facing a debt problem, how best could this problem be overcome? The identification of a debt problem should not be understood to imply that the need for debt rescheduling has been automatically established. There are other ways of relieving the burden of debt service payments and these should form part of the solution.

In what ways could the debt problem be dealt with and what are their comparative merits? The fundamental issue is that the debt problem is an aspect of the inadequacy of external resources in relation to a country's minimum economic and social goals. It follows that any method of augmenting the resources available to a country is a means of affording relief to its debt service burden. It is a means, in other words, of enhancing the country's import capacity. Since the prospects for increasing its external resources through aid and the inflow of new capital that might normally be expected have already been taken into account in projecting import capacity, the remaining ways by which the latter could be increased are additional flows of capital and a reduction in the external resources that would otherwise be devoted to debt service payments. Thus, additional flows of new capital beyond the amount initially expected and debt relief arrangements are both sources of relief for the debt burden.

Each of these items might usefully be considered in turn. Take first the question of additional capital flows. As already indicated, an estimate of future capital flows must play an important part in the forecasting of debt problems. If estimates of future capital flows and their terms are based on the maximum possible under any circumstances, and a debt service problem still remains, then obviously only debt rescheduling is available as a remedy. But if estimates of future flows are based on more limited assumptions such as, for example, the continuance of present gross flows on current terms, it would be pertinent to consider the extent to which an improvement in future flows and in terms might contribute towards an easing of the debt problem. The amount of additional resources which new capital flows provide is determined both by the quantum of these flows and by the terms on which they are made available. The terms, that is, the interest and amortization schedule, determine the reverse flow of resources brought about by new lending. The contribution of new capital flows to the total resource availability of recipient countries during a given period is thus measured by the difference between the gross flows and the reverse service payments during that period. The harder the terms on which new capital is provided the smaller is this contribution.

It follows that the future debt problem of developing countries is intimately bound up with the question of the quantum and the terms of future new lending. Whatever the merits of the argument for treating debt and aid as separate issues, the fact remains that aid and other types of capital flow contribute to the external resources which developing countries obtain and out of which debt service payments are made. To the extent that ways and means are being sought for reducing debt service difficulties, attention needs, therefore, to be paid to the possible role of new capital flows. Could the debt service problems which developing countries may encounter in the period ahead be avoided or significantly ameliorated by improvements affecting the flow of new capital alone? If the answer is in the affirmative, it would follow that debt rescheduling as a remedial instrument could be avoided or utilized only in extreme cases. Since creditors have shown a marked disinclination to agree to rearrangements of obligations on past debts, the answer is of more than limited interest in the context of the debt service problem. The Development Assistance Committee of OECD has recently recommended new norms intended to govern the terms of future official assistance. It lays much emphasis on the part which an improvement in the terms of new lending can play in avoiding future debt service crises. Whether these improvements will also contribute significantly to the amelioration of the problems caused by existing debt service burdens can only be answered by quantitative studies based on varying assumptions concerning the quantum and terms of future capital flows.

There are, however, a number of considerations that are relevant to this issue. The first is that if debt service problems, in the wide sense, are to be overcome largely by new capital flows, the quantum of new capital will need to be considerable indeed. The developing countries as a whole need a net transfer of resources in order to pursue their economic and social objectives. Even a zero net transfer of resources--that is, a new gross flow of capital of an amount equal to service payments on existing and new debt and on dividend remittances on private foreign investments--will require substantial gross capital flows whose quantum will depend on the terms of these new flows. A net transfer of resources equal to that obtaining at present would involve a much larger gross flow. The implications for gross capital flows if the targets specified in the International Development Strategy with regard to financial resource transfers to developing countries--namely, a net flow equal to 1 per cent of the gross national product of economically advanced countries, with at least 70 per cent of that flow being in the form of official development assistance--are to be realized at current levels of interest rates would appear to be far-reaching.

A relevant issue concerns the practicability of obtaining parliamentary or political support in donor countries for gross lending on a substantially increased scale. Present trends leave little ground for optimism. But there are other issues as well. For example, if the solution to the debt problem is to be a by-product of additional aid or of new lending provided outside the context of the debt problem, the question arises of the distribution among donors of the implied debt relief assistance. One of the questions that already arises today is the extent to which concessional aid provided by some donors for enhancing the tempo of development is used rather to service debt obligations to other donors or creditors whose past terms have been harder.[10] The use of new aid or new lending to meet debt service problems would not pose a problem of this sort if a single donor or creditor was concerned with both aspects of the question. But the problem does become a difficult one where the donors and creditors are numerous. This issue has, perhaps, already played some part in helping all concerned to view the need for debt relief in the wider context of aid needs and development goals. It will assume supreme importance in a situation where new capital flows are assumed, <u>inter alia,</u> to look after the whole debt problem. This situation differs, of course, from one in which new lending is directly linked to a debt relief operation; where refinancing, for example, is made available to countries for the specific purpose of meeting debt service payments. This is debt relief in the direct sense and needs to be considered in the category of direct relief measures as a solution to the debt problem. Here the question of burden sharing among creditors could more easily be linked to their past lending activities.

Another aspect of the use of new capital flows to ease debt problems concerns the question of the distribution of new resources among recipients. Even in conditions where the total quantum of new capital flows to developing countries would provide an adequate net transfer of resources to these countries taken as a whole, this action will not by itself ensure that a similar result will prevail in respect of each developing country. Attainment of this end may require that countries with large debt service obligations receive greater gross inflows of capital than others. All this raises complex problems of resource distribution among recipients. Clearly, if the total resources made available by donors is a fixed quantity, there is no way making more resources available to debtor countries without making less resources available to others. This would place the heavy borrowers of the past in a better position vis-a-vis other, possibly more prudent, borrowers. The same kind of problem will, of course, arise in attempts to provide aid to countries which have, for example, neglected exports in the past. These issues cannot be resolved by abstract formulae. The most that can be said is that the equity problem would be better dealt with if debt issues were to be considered jointly with aid issues on a country-by-country basis in the context of each country's over-all prospects and performance. This should provide a better result than any automatic debt relief formula. The problem of distribution will not arise, of course, if the quantum of external resources available to developing countries is not a fixed amount. Other solutions to the debt problem—such as debt rescheduling—may in certain circumstances overcome the difficulties caused by a fixed total of resources.

There is yet another facet to the relationship between new capital flows and the debt problem. The foregoing discussion assumed that no technical problems would arise in using new capital flows for debt service payments. Debt service payments must usually be paid in free exchange, that is, convertible currencies. Capital flows, on the other hand, do not always provide additional free exchange resources. They are usually provided for specified purposes and are also tied to purchases from the donor country. These limitations pose special problems regarding the use of capital flows to service debt payments. Take, for example, the linking of capital flows to specified purposes. Financing could be provided either for projects or for the purchase of imported supplies in support of a programme. This is the familiar distinction between project and programme aid. Finance provided for projects will facilitate debt service payments only if the recipient country would, in the absence of external financing, have initiated the project out of its own free exchange resources. By obtaining external financing for such a project, free exchange resources that would otherwise have been committed to it are released for other uses including debt service payments. It is true that developing countries would normally import machinery and capital out of their own free exchange resources for new investments and that if these investments could be successfully presented as projects for external financing, a release of free exchange could take place. But, in practice, the scope for this is likely to be restricted. Countries facing payments problems are likely to have already explored and utilized these possibilities. If imports of machinery and equipment, paid for out of free exchange resources, still figure in their import schedules, it is probably because these cannot easily be "dressed up" for presentation as projects. In this situation these countries can only obtain additional project financing through the presentation of new projects which, however important in themselves, do not serve the purpose of releasing free exchange resources.

In the case of programme aid there is somewhat greater flexibility. Programme aid is used for the importation of commodities which form part of an accepted programme of imports. These commodities could be raw materials, inputs of various kinds, spares and equipment and even consumer goods. The extent to which programme aid releases free exchange resources for other purposes depends on whether or not programme aid is used to finance additional imports or imports which would otherwise be obtained out of free exchange resources. It is only in the latter case that a release of resources could take place. However, in view of the wider range of commodities that could be imported under programme aid, it is undoubtedly easier to utilize such aid to release free exchange for other purposes. Hence, to the extent that new capital flows are looked upon as a means of easing debt problems, it is programme aid rather than project aid that is of greater importance.

The practice of tying capital flows to purchases from the donor introduces yet another limitation. The problems raised by tying aid have been widely discussed. But here again it is important to note that to the recipient, tied programme aid is often a more effective and flexible means of relieving payments problems than tied project aid. Administrators of foreign exchange budgets in developing countries face formidable management problems in endeavouring to fit offers of programme aid from a number of donors into a programme of priority imports. Normal trade practices and trading patterns are invariably disturbed in the process.[11] But to the extent that the administrators succeed, programme aid, even when tied, gives the recipient country greater scope for using aid resources to free foreign exchange resources for other essential purposes than does project aid.

It will be apparent, in the light of this discussion, that not only the quantum but also the type of new capital flows is of vital importance in the context of debt problems. A question of some significance is whether the increased emphasis now being placed on multilateral as against bilateral aid will affect the relationship between aid and debt problems in the future. Today, a fair proportion of total official aid flows from major donors, such as the United States of America, is in the form of programmed aid. Finance provided by multilateral lending agencies, such as the World Bank and the regional development banks, is on the other hand intended primarily for projects. It follows that any substitution of multilateral for bilateral finance can mean a shift from programme to project lending. This could, if uncorrected, weaken the link between new capital flows and debt problems. The solution would, of course, be for multilateral lending institutions to adopt greater flexibility in their lending practices. In the past programme aid financing has been undertaken on a limited scale by institutions such as the World Bank. It would be desirable to expand this kind of lending in the future. Another method of providing free exchange resources to developing countries is to finance the local costs of projects in foreign exchange. But this will make foreign exchange available to relieve other pressures only to the extent that the additional local expenditure on new projects does not generate additional import demands. Also, it is not an expeditious way of providing new resources.

There is, finally, a consideration of the greatest importance in connexion with the role of new capital in easing debt problems. To the extent that new capital takes the form of loans rather than grants and that these loans help service rather than pay off past debt, the total indebtedness of the recipient increases cumulatively. Depending on the terms, this practice extends the period during which the recipient has to depend on new capital flows. It will need to borrow even after it reaches the point at which it ceases to require a net transfer of resources abroad. Other things being equal, the period of dependence on external aid and capital flows is less the greater the share of grants in the total.[12]

IV. DEBT RELIEF OPERATIONS

The preceding discussion considered new capital flows as a means of providing resources to countries with heavy debt service obligations. The present section deals with the alternative method of making resources available by a reduction in the debt service burden itself through debt rescheduling, or by the provision of finance for the specific purpose of meeting those obligations, that is, by refinancing. Refinancing is, of course, the same as providing new capital flows. But it is best discussed under debt relief arrangements since refinancing provisions, unlike aid flows in general, are made within the context of direct debt relief operations and are directly aimed at the debt problem.

As mentioned above, creditors have been averse to encouraging debt relief operations except as an exceptional and unavoidable event.[13] Whether the need for such operations will continue to be minimal will depend on the extent to which debt service problems will engulf developing countries, bearing in mind the need for a more flexible interpretation of debt problems. It will also depend, as shown earlier, on the course of future capital flows. If, as is possible, future capital flows prove to be inadequate for dealing with debt problems in the wider context of developing goals, then a newer and more flexible attitude to debt relief operations will be necessary. It has been the argument of this paper that a country has a case for debt relief when debt service payments are a significant element in lowering import capacity below certain desirable levels. This assumes that the maximum possibilities in respect of export earning or import saving, as well as of aid and other capital flows, have been taken into account. It assumes, in other words, that the debt problem is viewed in the over-all context of the country's economic situation and of its minimum objectives in the economic and social fields.

It remains to consider some issues that are relevant to the granting of debt relief. One of these is based on a distinction between short-term and long-term debt and on the question of whether such debts should be treated in different ways. It has been argued that countries whose debt service difficulties are due to a bunching of debt of early maturity are in a different position to countries which face heavy debt service payments over a longer period. It is this distinction that is highlighted in some reviewed indicators of debt service ratios that have been suggested.[14] The OECD index, for example, expressed amortization and interest payment on adjusted "net debt" accumulated over 15 years as a percentage of current annual exports. Countries with heavy debt payments in the short term will have high annual debt service ratios during this period but also have a lower index for the 15-year period than countries whose debt service-payments continued at high levels over a longer period. It is argued that countries in the latter category are in a more serious position than those in the former and thus have a stronger case for debt rearrangements on a long-term basis. The short-term character of the debt is said to explain why certain countries such as Australia and New Zealand were able, in the 1930s, to avoid debt rearrangements although their annual debt service ratios reached nearly 40 per cent and also why the situation in countries such as Mexico is less critical today than their relatively high annual debt service ratios would suggest. This factor is also said to explain, at least in part, why previous debt rearrangements--mostly in Latin America where debt difficulties arose out of a bunching of early maturing debts--were of the "short leash" type, whereas more recent debt reschedulings for India and Indonesia, whose debt difficulties are of a more extended character, have been on a longer-term basis.

It has been suggested that the debt problems of countries whose debts are of a short-term character are relatively easy to manage. The "rolling" of these debts by new borrowing or, at most, by rescheduling over a relatively short period might suffice. The problem of long-term indebtedness is less tractable, on the other hand, and requires more drastic solutions. This is true in the sense that specific annual debt service obligations spread over a short period are indicative of a lower level of total indebtedness than is the case where these same outlays are extended over a longer term. But excessive short-term debt burdens could also prove severely disruptive. The "rolling" of these debts by new borrowing or refinancing would not provide a basic solution to the problem except in cases where the debt service difficulties are due to purely temporary shortfalls in external resources. In fact, such a device might only aggravate the problem on account of the high cost of borrowing. The rescheduling of these debts with the aim of reducing annual debt service payments is likely to prove a more effective solution, even if the rescheduling is over a relatively short period. Here again, the aim of the relief operation should not be limited to what is only needed to avoid a breakdown in payments. If wider goals are neglected, difficulties are likely to persist and to result in the need for repeated reschedulings.

Where the problem of heavy debt service payments persists over a longer term, there is little point at all to "short leash" relief operations. This would only provide a very temporary palliative and will gravely handicap all attempts at planning and economic management over a longer period. The credit-worthiness of the country and hence its capacity to mobilize external resources for the purpose of strengthening its economy would be jeopardized. It is clear that in this situation relief provided must take the form of reducing the debt service payments due over a number of years.

Whatever the character of the debt problem--whether short-term or long-term--the relief provided must take into account each country's needs in terms of its over-all goals. In revising contractual amortization and interest arrangements on existing debt, attention must be paid to the fact that a country would be needing new capital flows in the future and would have to bear service charges on these flows. Debt rescheduling must not pre-empt future resources that might be devoted to debt service.

In determining the terms of debt rescheduling the guiding criterion should be the average terms of borrowing most appropriate to each country in the future. If the terms of new capital flows are given, the revision of those on past debt must be such as to be consistent with the appropriate average terms. To the extent that a country's debt service problems are a reflection of inappropriate terms in the past, debt rescheduling must be an instrument for correcting the anomaly. This approach will leave scope for adapting the terms of debt relief operations to the requirements of each country. As a general rule, however, there would appear to be little justification, in the context of a wider approach, for the imposition of moratorium interest, that is, of additional interest charges on service payments that are postponed. The objective of a debt relief operation should be to reduce rather than increase a country's total outstanding debt service commitments. Moratorium interest at commercial rates has the effect of enhancing total debt--the increase, as mentioned earlier, was as much as 39 per cent in the case of Ghana. It is in fact difficult to see how debt relief can provide anything more than short-term and temporary assistance if the concept of moratorium interest is retained. This is an aspect of the commercial approach which needs to be modified.

In terms of the approach suggested, the appropriate rescheduling in certain situations might imply a reduction or write-off, in whole or in part, of past debt.[15] This would happen, for example, if it appears that a country's situation is such that the annual service payments it can make on past debt might suffice only for the payment over a widely extended period of amortization charges only. This would require a waiver of contractual interest. This arrangement may alternatively be presented as a write-off in principal, with continuing interest payments. In the recent rescheduling arrangement for Indonesia, moratorium interest was not levied on rearranged payments of principal while interest on the rescheduled debt will not be paid until the second half of the revised 30-year repayment period. Further flexibility was introduced into the agreement by providing for an option to defer part of the principal repayments due during the first eight years. According to the World Bank report, the Indonesian agreement "cannot be considered as a precedent for general application". But it is difficult to see why the objective of the new agreement should be unique to any country. In the words of the Bank, the agreement will "improve Indonesia's present external debt structure, facilitating orderly planning for her economic recovery and long-range growth".[16] These should be the standards applied in the debt relief arrangements of all developing countries.

An alternative to debt rescheduling is refinancing. Debt rescheduling requires a change in contractual arrangements for amortization and interest payments. This may give rise to technical and legal complexities which creditors wish to avoid. A refinancing credit provided for the specific purpose of paying off past debts would avoid these difficulties. It could serve much the same purpose as a rescheduling of debt in that it reduces the extent to which other external resources need to be directed to debt service payments. Once again the terms of the refinancing credits are crucial. A refinancing credit with a long maturity period and concessional interest rates which suffice to pay off old hard debt will serve to improve the recipients' external debt structure. On the other hand, borrowing at interest to pay only annual amortization and interest charges on past debt will be equivalent to the payment of moratorium interest in a debt-rescheduling operation.

An important aspect of the relative merits of rescheduling and refinancing is the impact on total capital flows. If refinancing credits are provided out of budgetary appropriations for aid, they might reduce the total aid available for developing countries. The manner in which rescheduling arrangements are financed by creditor countries may vary. It is likely that, when the debt service schedules on commercial credits guaranteed by the Government of the creditor country are rearranged, the revised payments are made to the Governments which would repay the financial agencies responsible for the internal financing. To the extent that the governmental resources needed for these adjustments do not come out of aid appropriations, debt rearrangements would not involve a corresponding reduction in aid flows.

Another problem is that of burden sharing among creditors. One of the difficulties expressed in debt renegotiations stems from the multiplicity of creditors. This has made it necessary for successful debt renegotiations to take place in a multilateral setting so as to avoid, as far as possible, unequal treatment of various creditors. Since it is, usually government or government-generated debt that is brought within the ambit of debt rearrangements, negotiations are generally between Governments.

The question of equality of treatment raises a number of issues. The conventional approach has been to share the burden of any relief provided among the creditors in proportion to the total debt owed to each creditor.[17] This approach does not, however, take account of differences in the terms of lending imposed by different creditors and weighs more heavily on the soft creditors than on the hard lenders. Other formulae which take account of differences in terms have been opposed on the grounds that a harmonization of terms after the fact is involved—generally in circumstances where creditors have not agreed on the harmonization of terms for current or future lending. In some recent negotiations a compromise formula was agreed upon. Thus, in the Indian case,

> "It was decided how much India could afford to pay per year (around 20 per cent of exports), and this was divided by total debt outstanding. This came to 6 per cent. Every creditor was then to reschedule whatever service payments were over the limit. Countries under the limit (like the U.S.) were required to make a minimum contribution to the rescheduling. It seems likely that this idea will be used more often in the future.

It would seem that the recent Indonesian rescheduling also departed from the traditional concept of burden sharing. Amortization payments on the total debt rescheduled was spread over a 30-year period, while interest payments on the rescheduled debt was postponed for a 15-year period. This suggests that the burden placed on the hard lenders is correspondingly greater.

Similar problems of burden sharing arise in connexion with refinancing arrangements. A possible formula for determining the contribution of each creditor to the total refinance fund would be to make contributions proportional to debt service receipts. But whatever the formula adopted, it is evident that effective debt relief operations would need to depart from the traditional concept of burden sharing and to make some differentiation in the distribution of the burden among creditors in accordance with the terms of their previous lending. All this merely underlines the importance of the multilateral character of relief operations.

V. POLICIES TO BE PURSUED BY DEBTOR COUNTRIES AND THE PROBLEM OF SURVEILLANCE

It has been argued in this paper that solutions to debt problems of developing countries need to take into account the wider goals of economic and social development. This would result in considerable changes in customary approaches to the debt problem. These changes will embrace the criteria used in establishing a country's case for remedial measures as well as the measures themselves. However, the corollary to the need for a wider approach is the need for institutional arrangements under

which the over-all situation of a country could be reviewed. There
has to be a measure of agreement on a country's economic and social
goals, on the import capacity needed to attain these goals, on the
efficacy of its over-all development strategy and so on. Countries
providing additional resources, whether by way of debt relief or
aid, must have reasonable assurance that these resources will be
put to good use.

These issues touch the complex problem of the appraisal and
evaluation of the performance of developing countries. Such a
review must inevitably form part of a new approach to debt
problems. An important question concerns the forum in which this
review can best take place. Past debt negotiations have taken
place under a variety of arrangements, sometimes under "clubs"
sponsored by donors or creditors (e.g., the "Paris Club" and the
"Hague Club"), sometimes under a consortium of donors sponsored by
the World Bank or the Organisation for Economic Co-operation and
Development, and sometimes under the auspices of the International
Monetary Fund (IMF). Whatever the sponsorship, however, IMF has
played a significant part in virtually all recent cases of debt
rearrangement by providing additional resources under stand-by
facilities and by securing the adherence of the recipient country
to programmes of stabilization. In this way, a measure of
surveillance over the recipients' policies has been provided for
and this has been a means of winning the confidence of creditors.

The stabilization agreements entered into with IMF are,
however, of relatively short duration. The undertakings on policy
given by a member country apply during the period of the stand-by
agreement only -- usually one year. Moreover, IMF is a source of
short-term resources for countries facing payments difficulties.
For a country facing a heavy burden of short-term debt, Fund
drawings, repayable over a three- to five-year period, are a means
of "rolling over" this debt. The magnitude of these drawings is,
however, determined by the size of a country's quota; this limits
the direct relief which the Fund can provide. It is, moreover,
likely that a country facing debt service difficulties would
already have had early access to the Fund to strengthen its general
payments situation. Nevertheless, Fund stand-by agreements are of
great importance in that they enhance a country's chances of
obtaining supplementary support from other sources, such as foreign
commercial banks. Short-term indebtedness to foreign commercial
banks is sometimes an important element in a country's total
foreign debt and can be a factor in debt service difficulties. In
the Philippines the commercial banks, following the stabilization
programme which the Government instituted in consultation with the
Fund, agreed to reschedule short-term debts over a six-year
amortization period.

It is not certain, however, that the type of policy measures
that are incorporated in stand-by agreements are sufficient or
appropriate from the point of view of a country's wider goals. The
emphasis could fall too heavily on restoring the country's capacity
to resume contractual debt obligations at the earliest opportunity,
even if this were to result in a marked slowing-down in economic
growth. Deflationary measures are sometimes taken with a view to
improving the balance of payments by depressing import outlays, or

to generating sufficient budgetary resources to service debt by curtailing government expenditures. Ceilings are also imposed on the quantum of new commercial credits that might be contracted in order to prevent the external debt situation from worsening further. The impact of these measures might well be to stifle economic growth and to aggravate problems on the social, political, and economic front. Unemployment, for example, which is usually a serious problem in developing countries, might well increase much further. These approaches might be the only options available in situations where debt problems are viewed outside the context of a country's economic and social goals. However, as the Commission on International Development (Pearson Commission) has stated, although "Some debt rearrangements in the past have stipulated that the debtor government agree to a stringent program of economic stabilization. . . [generally] these agreements have emphasized restraint on government spending and credit policies and neglected the need to mobilize domestic resources more effectively, generate new export earnings, and sustain sound development outlays. . . A case in point, is the limit on new export credits which many debt rearrangements impose on debtor governments. Such a ceiling is obviously necessary. . . [but it] is equally important to suggest how export credits are to be replaced by external resources on more suitable terms so that the growth momentum is sustained."[19] The need is for a package of policies more wide ranging and more long term in scope than those which usually fall within the ambit of stabilization programmes. These policies will take account of the relationship betwen debt problems and future capital flows, viewed against the background of development objectives.

This raises the question of the appropriate forum in which debt service difficulties might be discussed and solutions negotiated. It has been pointed out that there is today no established forum to which a country facing debt service problems could turn. Past debt negotiations have been instituted in an <u>ad hoc</u> fashion, sometimes through the initiative of a leading creditor, sometimes through a multilateral agency. Whether such a forum ought to be established and what form it should take is a question that needs to be discussed. It would probably be undesirable, in the light of the various issues discussed here, to establish specialized machinery to deal with debt problems alone.[20] Since debt issues need to be examined in the context of development goals and aid requirements, the appropriate forum would be one which considers these issues as well. It is perhaps not accidental that in those cases where debt relief arrangements have departed from the traditional mould -- for example, in the cases of India and Indonesia -- aid consortia had already been in existence. It is usually the case that Governments which are creditors of a country are also providers of aid to that country. It would be incongruous if steps taken in the one field were to ignore steps taken in the other. The establishment of aid consortia may be regarded as exceptional, but the World Bank has sponsored a number of consultative groups to strengthen aid co-ordination.[21] These might prove useful as a means of co-ordinating debt and aid questions even if actual debt relief agreements are negotiated under other arrangements.

It should be noted that where consortia or consultative groups exist a comprehensive review already takes place of a country's development goals and efforts, thus assuring donors of the efficacy of a country's policies. It would seem inevitable, if problems of aid and debt are to be effectively dealt with, that developing countries will need to have their problems discussed and their performance evaluated in a multilateral setting. Such a review becomes pertinent to a number of other purposes as well -- purposes connected for example, with the attainment of international targets set for the Second United Nations Development Decade, for the establishment of claims for support under schemes of supplementary financing etc. The question of the type of machinery most suited to these purposes has yet to be resolved. It is important for developing countries themselves have sufficient representation. Furthermore, it is essential, in the global setting, that review and evaluation encompass the policies of donor countries as well. Only in this way can the concept of development as an international problem acquire true meaning.[22]

NOTES

[1] Towards the end of the 1960s debt service payments -- that is, payments on amortization and interest -- on export credits and other private loans accounted for about 50 per cent of total debt service payments by developing countries. Their share of total debt outstanding, however, was only about 25 per cent. The difference in proportions reflected the comparatively harder terms of commercial credits. (Cf. Partners in Development; Report of the Commission on International Development (New York Praeger Publisher, 1969), p. 155.) In 1973 the ratios were about 58 per cent and 33 per cent, respectively. These estimates for 1973 were made by the UNCTAD secretariat on the basis of information provided by the International Bank for Reconstruction and Development.

[2] "In April [of 1970], an agreement was reached with Indonesia by a number of donor countries to provide major, long-term debt relief. . . Nevertheless, the agreement is unique to Indonesia and cannot be considered as a precedent for general application". World Bank, International Development Association, Annual Report, 1970 (Washington, D. C.), p. 52.

[3] It is likely that the main factor underlying the debt service difficulties of developing countries is the pressure on the balance of payments caused by the slow expansion of exports and the strong upward pressure on imports generated by the process of economic growth itself. These forces were probably stronger than

anticipated by the authorities and thereby undermined the assessment of debt service capacity made when incurring debt.

[4] Organisation for Economic Co-operation and Development, Development Assistance; 1969 Review. (Paris, 1969), p. 233.

[5] Ibid., p. 213.

[6] The OECD has devised a multiyear adjusted debt index ratio. This is the 1 to 15-year cumulative debt burden, adjusted for reserves and divided by annual exports. This helps to differentiate, in a way that the conventional debt service ratio does not, between countries whose debt service payments are likely to make a heavy drain on export earnings over a relatively long period and those whose debt service payments are of short-term duration. (Cf. Organisation for Economic Co-operation and Development, Development Assistance; 1969 Review, p. 277.) A similar purpose is served by an index which combines debt service ratio with the average maturity of all loans. (Cf. Charles R. Frank, Jr., Debt and Terms of Aid (Washington, D.C., Overseas Development Council, 1970), p. 34).

[7] In assessing the adequacy of import capacity in terms of the requirements for economic growth, allowance must be made for the replacement of imports by domestic substitutes.

[8] Cf. Charles R. Frank, Jr., op. cit., p. 26.

[9] Since 1970 there have been further reschedulings of the external debts of Chile, Ghana and India.

[10] "For one thing, there is the awkward 'bail out' problem. Many donors, providing the softest kinds of assistance, very much wish to avoid situations in which their soft aid flows can be viewed as providing the resources to repay financing by other donors at harder terms. A minimum way of avoiding this problem may be for all donors at hard terms, to remain at least 'neutral' during the period (which may last for many years) when a net transfer of resources is required by the particular developing country. That is, donors would agree as a minimum to offset any payments due them with new financing flows. Of course, mere 'neutrality' would not contribute to the needed net transfer of resources, but it would at least avoid the awkward 'bail out' problem." Organisation for Economic Co-operation and Development, Development Assistance; 1969 Review, p. 234.

[11] The cost of imports is also invariably increased, although it is possible that the extra prices paid by recipients for goods finances out of tied aid is lower for programme aid than for project aid. This is because programme aid is used for the purchase of general supplies that are usually available "over the counter" and whose prices are widely known, and because the scope is somewhat larger for competitive bidding by a number of suppliers within a donor country. These factors are less likely

to prevail where highly specialized equipment is sold under tied project aid.

[12] ". . . the economic cost to donors of further concessions at the soft end of the spectrum is rather small, as the present value of interest payments of 2% 30 years hence is negligible. . . probably the time is not far away when a concerted effort has to be made to put development assistance not merely on a soft, but on a grant basis". Goran Ohlin, Aid and Indebtedness (Paris, Organisation for Economic Co-operation and Development, 1966), pp. 38-39.

[13] "Donors have been extremely reluctant to provide such relief, and do so only when no other alternative is available. Relief is difficult, at best, with unfortunate side effects, leading often to a breakdown in the orderly flow of assistance and the disruption of development progress". Organisation for Economic Co-operation and Development, Development Assistance; 1969 Review, p. 235.

[14] Cf., for example, Organisation for Economic Co-operation and Development, Development Assistance; 1969 Review, p. 277, et seq., and Charles R. Frank, Jr., op. cit., pp. 34-35.

[15] "The Bank Staff proposal for the Indian renegotiation noted that debt cancellation would be by far the best technique in terms of quality and suggested that the minimum terms which would meet the purpose of the exercise would be a 10-year interest-free postponement of service payments." International Bank for Reconstruction and Development, Multilateral Debt Renegotiations, 1956-65, (Washington, D.C., 1969), p. 18.

[16] World Bank, International Development Association, Annual Report, 1970, p. 52.

[17] "The Anglo-Saxon legal tradition of bankruptcy and debt settlement generally does not distinguish among different types of creditors in assessing the 'cause' of the whole problem. Each creditor is expected to absorb a burden relative to the portion of total debt owed him". Charles R. Frank, Jr., op. cit., p. 28.

[18] Ibid., pp. 28-29.

[19] Cf. Partners in Development, p. 157.

[20] The opposition of creditor countries is based on different premises. "Creditor countries have repeatedly insisted that debt rearrangement must be regarded as an exceptional course of action and that no permanent machinery should be established to deal with renegotiation requests since the existence of such machinery could have the undesirable effect of stimulating demands for consolidation of external debts". International Bank for Reconstruction and Development, Multilateral Debt Renegotiations, 1956-1968, p. 3.

[21] Aid consortia provide a multilateral framework within which individual donors make pledges of specific aid commitments. Consultative groups provide an occasion for reviewing a country's aid needs but are not forums where pledges are made. The World Bank at present sponsors two consortia, one aid group, and 11 consultative groups. It also participates in aid co-ordination groups, sponsored by other agencies. <u>Cf.</u> World Bank, International Development Association, <u>Annual Report</u>, <u>1970</u>, p. 30.

[22] For recent developments on the question of appropriate forum, see <u>Debt Problems of Developing Countries</u> . . . (United Nations publication, Sales No. E.75.II.D.14), p. 9.

Employment Strategies and Poverty Reduction Policies of Developing Countries

CENTRE FOR DEVELOPMENT PLANNING,
PROJECTIONS AND POLICIES OF THE
UNITED NATIONS SECRETARIAT

Planning for economic and social progress has made considerable headway in the developing countries during the past two decades. Since the early years of the 1950's country after country has adopted development planning as a rational and pragmatic instrument for the expansion and modernization of the economy and for bringing about far-reaching social changes. The record of the past two decades shows a wide array of improvements. By historical standards, the economies of developing countries have, on the average, expanded at significant rates; their industrial and other modern activities have shown a measure of dynamism; and their social amenities have gained in a variety of ways.

Yet, despite all such improvements, there is a great deal of dissatisfaction with the results of the planning process. In some quarters, the dissatisfaction has even reached the point where the value of planning as an instrument of development has been questioned. Doubts and misgivings have emerged, partly because the curve of expectations itself has risen sharply over the years and partly because some social blights have assumed a grave intensity. By far the most nagging problem today is the widespread unemployment and attendant poverty prevailing in developing countries. It is the seriousness of this problem which has called for a searching look at the planning process, not to demolish it but to ensure that the contours of national development are in harmony with the emerging needs of the society.

The present paper offers a general view of the main problems and policy issues relating to unemployment and poverty in the developing countries in the light of experience in development planning. In order to provide a compact picture, detailed information has been deliberately eschewed, and the discussion

From **JOURNAL OF DEVELOPMENT PLANNING**, No. 5, 1972, (3-48), reprinted by permission of the publisher.

consists mainly of a set of generalizations. While these generalizations inevitably conceal intercountry differences, their underlying reasoning would appear to be widely valid. Concrete illustrations of the problems encountered in a number of individual countries and of the policies devised to cope with them are contained in the annex to the paper.

I. UNEMPLOYMENT AND POVERTY

It is difficult to say how much unemployment there really is in developing countries. The compilation of statistics on this subject has not been a vigorous activity in these countries. The estimates yielded by the decennial censuses of the population have usually left much to be desired and the sample surveys have not, thus far, received as much attention as they deserve. Small wonder, then, that development plans which commonly provide a wealth of detail on such variables as output and trade are often reticent with regard to employment. It is true that the measurement of unemployment and inadequate employment is not an easy task; and in the developing countries, with their age-old traditions and social institutions, especially in the rural areas, the task is formidable. But if policy-making is to have a rational basis, it is imperative that earnest efforts should be made to fill the gaps in knowledge.

In this spirit, recently, Governments have evinced a new interest in the question of unemployment data, and in their contemporary development plans have begun to cast a keener eye on both the conceptual problems and the policy issues. The estimates adduced in the annex to the present paper show a progressive accentuation of unemployment in many developing countries. In several of these countries, 8-12 per cent of the labour force is reported to be currently unemployed. The creators of successive generations of development plans in some countries, in assessing the achievements of their predecessors, have candidly stated that in each plan period the new employment opportunities have failed to absorb the new entrants to the labour force and that, consequently, the backlog of unemployment has continued to mount. The estimates generally refer to what is called visible or open unemployment. It is well known that in developing countries a great many people are only partially employed; in other words, they would be willing to undertake additional work if such work were available. Usually they eke out an existence through activities whose productivity is low. A number of development plans provide estimates of low-productivity employment--sometimes called disguised unemployment or underemployment--in terms of open unemployment, and the figures of total unemployment which then emerge appear staggering.

Adding to the gravity of the problem is the continuing migration of people in search of jobs and better remuneration from the rural to the urban areas. The more rapid absorption of the labour force in urban activities is surely an essential ingredient of the development process; but the trek of the people to urban centres has almost invariably far surpassed what could be handled in the prevailing circumstances. Too often the glitter of the cities has proved to be a mirage and a chimera; and the migrants have found themselves merely swelling the ranks of the unemployed, accentuating the spread of slums all around and enhancing the misery of poverty. The social institutions of most developing countries are such that poverty is more bearable in the rural setting than in the urban environment. In villages, it is possible at least for a person to lend a helping hand in the family field or occasionally to put in some labour for remuneration in wage or kind; but in cities the unemployed are left to contend with too many forces beyond their control.

Indeed, the overriding problem of poverty, both rural and urban, has figured prominently in some recent development plans. Development experts are now increasingly emphasizing that unemployment and underemployment are only one element, albeit a dominating one, of the grinding poverty which afflicts large masses of people in many developing countries. These people have inadequate work opportunities, earn low incomes, suffer from malnutrition and live in miserable hovels, while a very small segment of society enjoys startling affluence. The limited data that are available show a highly uneven distribution of income and wealth. If social justice is to have any meaning, it is beginning to be stressed, the problems of unemployment and of the maldistribution of income and wealth need to be tackled as an integral part of the attack on mass poverty.

One low-income group, comprising young people, has been particularly hard hit by the lack of adequate job opportunities. The degree of unemployment is generally much greater among persons of 15 to 25 years of age, and this is a major cause of social unrest in the developing world. In many developing countries, the growing unemployment among the educated has further complicated the situation. Education should certainly be an important development goal, but the goal should be consonant with the ability to absorb the educated in needed occupations. Unfortunately, it is a common experience in developing countries that so-called educated unemployment has been growing, while at the same time shortages of persons with comparatively simple skills--mechanics and foremen, for instance--have frequently impeded the pace of production. Despite the growing sophistication of development plans, educational and manpower planning remains a weak component of the planning process in developing countries.

When some developing countries launched their initial development plans in the 1950's, there was hardly any realization that the prime force contributing to the upsurge of the supply of labour would be far stronger than had been envisaged by the planners. In the initial arithmetic of planning, the prospective rate of growth of population in the years immediately ahead was typically assumed to be not much more than what it had been during the 1940's. In the event, the rate of population growth turned out to be much higher. During the 1960's, in the aggregate, the population of developing countries is estimated to have expanded at the average annual rate of growth of 2.6 per cent. Thanks to the expansion of medical facilities and the progress in medical science--in themselves welcome fruits of development--the death-rates tumbled rapidly; but as the birth-rates did not show a parallel decline, there inevitably appeared a sharp upsurge in the growth of population. The population of working age appears to have increased at an average annual rate of about 2.4 per cent during the 1960's. While it is not possible to pinpoint the rate of increase in the actual number of job seekers, it would seem that the labour force (employed and unemployed) expanded at a rate not far short of the growth rate of the working-age population. The new educational facilities, by keeping potential workers in classrooms, probably stemmed the growth of the labour force to a certain extent; but the increasing participation of women in paid work, equally probably, added to its growth.

Had the growth of labour force been accompanied by a vigorous expansion in the demand for labour, the imbalance epitomized by the unemployment and underemployment prevailing in the developing countries today would not have arisen. The aggregate production of goods and services, as measured by the concept of the gross domestic product, rose on the average by about 5 per cent during the period 1960-1969 in the developing countries, and this increase undoubtedly provided new employment opportunities. It is, however, inherent in the process of change that, because of technological and other improvements, economic growth takes place simultaneously with an increase in the productivity of labour. The precise magnitude of the increase in labour productivity during the past decade is not known, but a figure of around 3 per cent per annum--a number of countries have recorded higher figures--would not appear unreasonable. This would suggest that the demand for labour rose by less than the increase in the supply of labour. To take care of both the new entrants to the labour force and at least to make a small reduction in the backlog of unemployment, the developing countries as a group would have required an annual rate of growth of gross domestic product during the past decade of significantly more than 5 per cent. Even then many developing countries with growth rates below the average for the group would still have accumulated a growing backlog of unemployment.

II. EMPLOYMENT OBJECTIVES AND RELATED GOALS

The fact that unemployment has loomed large in developing countries does not imply that planners and policy-makers have ignored the question of employment creation. Employment objectives have been put forward in one form or another in all development plans. In fact, some of the earliest plans of developing countries even emphasized the need for attaining, to use their own words, full employment or full utilization of manpower resources. The earlier optimism was, however softened when the magnitude of the underlying problem was more clearly perceived. Realizing that full employment could not be achieved in a few years, the subsequent plans started using such phrases as fuller employment, large or substantial expansion in employment opportunities, fuller utilization of human resources, and greater equality of opportunities through gainful employment and other means. The more recent plans reflect a sharper concern about the prevailing unemployment and underemployment, but there is no illusion that the problem can be easily solved.

Although the expansion of employment opportunities has been universally accepted as a key objective of development planning, the delineation of employment goals in operationally meaningful terms has in general left much to be desired. A frequent plea has been that the absence of relevant data makes the task well-nigh impossible. But even when some information is available, planning efforts have often not gone beyond the estimation of the prospective increase in the labour force and the linking of it in a general way to the projected expansion of total output and the level of capital formation. Many a development plan stops short at the statement that the planned rate of economic growth will (or is expected to) absorb in gainful employment the new entrants to the labour force and perhaps make a reduction in the existing unemployment and underemployment. In a number of countries, the practice of estimating requirements of labour in individual industries has been followed, but these industries cover only a small component of the work force; in agriculture, the mainstay of the economy in most developing countries, and in service activities, which together provide far greater employment than does industry, very little is said in the plans by way of quantitative estimation of additional employment. The conclusion therefore seems inescapable that the planning of employment is still rather rudimentary in developing countries. The employment targets that are set are generally too broad and too simplistic. Although on the whole the targets have been modest, there has commonly been failure to achieve even these.

In the face of mounting unemployment, some observers have wondered whether the planners and policy-makers in developing countries have not sacrificed the objective of greater employment on the altar of a higher rate of economic growth. While it is true that employment opportunities have not expanded as fast as they should, evidence does not show that the pursuit of unbridled economic growth has been the cause. In the aggregate, the annual rate of economic growth of developing countries in the 1960's was modest, not spectacular. In a number of countries where the unemployment problem is especially acute, the rate of economic growth was significantly smaller than the average for the developing world. Given the dimensions of poverty, there would, in fact, seem to be a case in favour of a higher rate of economic growth than that achieved during the past decade. It cannot be forgotten that the growth rate in question is merely a summary statement of the tempo of production of goods and services. It is through expanding production that developing countries have to seek new employment opportunities and to find the means for improving the levels of living.

At the same time, however, logic demands that the

pattern of production should be so designed as to facilitate the task of making a concerted attack on unemployment and low incomes. The methods of production should be such as to bring about a significant increase in employment; the output of goods and services should be geared to the needs of the masses; and the additional saving made possible by the expansion of output should be directed to productive investment. These need not be conflicting aims. While the policy measures adopted by the developing countries need to be continually scrutinized within the framework of these aims, it could hardly be concluded that the over-all pace of production should be reduced.

With a growing recognition of the problems of mass poverty, planners are now beginning to devote attention to the plight of the people on the lowest rung of the income ladder. It is felt that a desired increase in per capita income or consumption in a country would not automatically ensure a significant improvement for the poorest among the poor; planning must therefore entail special efforts in favour of such people. In the latest development plan of India, for example, the goal of attaining a national minimum of consumption by the poor figures prominently among the egalitarian aims. The broader objective of reductions in income disparities among different groups of people is, of course, emphasized in many development plans, as is attested by the information contained in the annex to this paper. It is pointed out that a better distribution of income is of major importance for the creation of additional jobs. The resulting shift in the pattern of demand in favour of the goods consumed by the lower income groups—goods which have a larger component of labour and a smaller component of capital (the scarce factor of production) than many of the luxury articles catering to the rich—should help to stimulate employment.

The possible negative effect of better income distribution on the rate of saving has, however, vexed planners a great deal. Some of the earlier development plans were explicit in stating that in the initial stages of development, maldistribution of income had to be tolerated because the upper income groups had a higher propensity to save and that if egalitarian norms were pushed too quickly the saving ratio of the country would be adversely affected, thereby slowing down the expansion of both output and employment. In more recent years, however, there has been a reassessment of such reasoning. With the expanding role of public saving in the development process, arguments based on the assumption that the private sector was the sole determinant of a country's saving have become suspect. There is also the feeling that analogies drawn from the historical experience of industrial countries are not valid in this respect in the case of developing countries. There are many avenues for inducing, with appropriate incentives, an average family in a typical developing country to enlarge its saving for productive investment; saving for housing or for education is cited as a common example. The limited amount of empirical work done on the subject is suggestive, but it needs to be carried further to obtain more definitive answers.

The ideas that are now being expressed on the subject of social justice do not suggest that egalitarian goals should be achieved in a country by making everybody poor. The basic premise is that there are many more complementarities in the development process than had been previously considered possible. It is now up to the planners and policy-makers to seize the opportunities for such complementarities and to forge ahead with programmes which aim at achieving a well-rounded progress.

III. MAJOR POLICY ISSUES

The task of making an attack on unemployment and poverty has thrown up a wide range of policy issues. It cannot be said that clear-cut solutions to the prevailing problems have been found; but in the patterns of development of the past two decades, there are a number of important lessons for the design and implementation of a forceful development policy during the 1970's.

Industrialization and Employment

As is only to be expected, industrialization is a major goal of the developing countries. Almost every development plan stresses the importance of industrialization as the source of dynamism and as the engine of modernization. Industrial development is sought in order to initiate technological advances in the economy, to raise productivity of labour, to expand output in all sectors and to lay the basis of a continuing momentum of economic growth. Where foreign exchange earnings from traditional exports have tended to stagnate, the search for new outlets through manufactured and semi-manufactured exports has also been stressed. In some of the earlier development plans in particular it was argued that the scope for absorbing the increase in the labour force in traditional activities was small, and therefore the bulk of the new employment opportunities had to be found in industry.

There is no doubt that the developing countries have made significant progress in their drive towards industrialization. Their industrial output (mining, manufacturing, electricity, gas and water) expanded annually on the average by 7 per cent during the period 1960-1969, and at least some of these countries have also made notable advances in their endeavour to promote manufactured exports. However, industrial employment, although steadily expanding, has not had a significant effect on the prevailing unemployment and poverty. The comparable data, compiled by the Statistical Office of the United Nations for the period 1960-1969, show that while the industrial output of developing countries rose at the annual average rate of 7.3 per cent,[1] the industrial employment increased by only 3.2 per cent; whereas the components of mining and manufacturing output expanded annually by 8.4 and 6.6 per cent respectively, the corresponding increases in employment in these two components were only 0.1 and 3.5 per cent. Clearly, under the impact of technological improvements, the labour content of a unit of industrial output has been steadily diminishing, the impact in mining being dramatic. By itself a 3.2 per cent annual increase in industrial employment is not unimpressive; it is, after all, greater than the annual rate of growth of population or of the labour force. However, this has to be seen against the fact that industry accounts for a relatively small part of total activity in developing countries. On the whole, industry provides less than a quarter of their total output of goods and services, and its share in total employment must therefore be even smaller. Thus, it is apparent that the expansion of industrial employment has absorbed only a small part of the increase in the labour force of the developing countries. By far the larger number of the new job seekers have had to look for employment in other activities; and in the absence of a coherent employment policy, many of them have merely added to the pool of the unemployed and to the growth of slums and shanty towns in urban areas.

The increase in the capital-intensity of the industrial output is a well-established element of the development process, and to a certain extent therefore the recent experience of the developing countries is no exception. A good deal of evidence is, however, appearing which suggests that the allocation of resources in most developing countries has been unduly biased in favour of capital, a scarce factor of production. Tariff policies, exchange rates and fiscal policies (tax exemptions and accelerated depreciation allowances being the most common among them) have frequently been such as to make the market price of machinery and equipment much lower than its true scarcity value or what the economists call its social opportunity cost. Often, the interest rates charged on industrial loans have been quite low. Policies of aid-giving countries, too, have commonly favoured the establishment and expansion of capital-intensive projects in developing countries. Several observers have also commented that the growth of profits in the industrial sector has worsened the distribution of income in many instances. The anti-monopoly measures adopted or contemplated by a number of developing countries are pointers to the growing awareness of this feature.

Given the scarcity of capital, it is astonishing how often examples of underutilization of industrial capacity are encountered in the developing countries. The policy bias in favour of capital has, in many cases, encouraged the installation of an unnecessarily large capacity. In some countries, the tendency for the prices to increase sharply has, by stimulating the desire to protect against future increases in prices and against drastic changes in foreign exchange rates and by making the real cost of loan finance still lower, contributed to further encouragement in this direction. Such factors as shortages of imported machine parts and declines in the supply of raw materials resulting from poor crops have also been important causes of underutilization of capacity. But the persisting nature of the problem suggests that industrial policy needs to be sharply geared to ensuring maximum utilization of the existing industrial capacity and concomitant absorption of additional workers in gainful activity.

The question of the full utilization of the existing industrial capacity has another facet which warrants close attention. Capacity is often understood to mean that there is only one shift of workers operating the industry concerned each day. In the circumstances prevailing in the developing countries--namely, scarcity of capital and abundance of labour--there is indeed a great need to operate factories on a multiple-shift basis. Additional employment opportunities can be created in this manner with utmost economy in the use of machinery and equipment. Development plans have generally been reticent on the subject of multiple-shift operations. It is true that such operations call for stronger organization and greater management skills--elements which are also scarce in the developing world. But if these basic characteristics are not inculcated into society, the value of planning itself is greatly diminished.

When embarking on new programmes of industrial development, calling for additional capacity, planners should obviously look into their likely effects on the creation of employment. However, merely because unemployment is very great and capital very scarce, it cannot be concluded that developing countries must always opt for a labour-intensive type of industrialization. In choosing both a suitable pattern of industrial production and appropriate methods of production, development planners have encountered a number of complexities which have a bearing on this issue.

So far as the design of industrial production for exports is concerned, developing countries usually have little choice to exercise. Many of the labour-intensive products, such as textiles and shoes, that several of these countries can produce efficiently for export, are also those that encounter resistance from the developed countries through the imposition of trade barriers. Some notable successes have no doubt been achieved by the developing countries in expanding their manufactured exports, but by and large the size of industrial activity for export purposes remains small in the developing countries as a group. Developing countries should undoubtedly seek new outlets for their industrial goods, and the economically advanced nations should strengthen their co-operation for this purpose; but if the developing countries are to emerge as successful competitors in international markets, the choice of industrial products and of methods of production will have to take into account the criterion of efficiency, which may not always be compatible with the criterion of labour-intensity.

The scarcity of foreign exchange has also played a pivotal part in shaping the pattern of industrial production for domestic use. Apart from expanding the consumer goods industries which are traditionally known to the labour-intensive, many developing countries have also fostered an array of producer goods industries which are relatively greater users of capital. The typical argument has been that, in the absence of a vigorous expansion of export earnings, the growing requirements of producer goods cannot continue to be satisfied through imports. It has also been cogently argued that a shift in the pattern of production from consumer to investment goods is in itself a means of increased saving. In so far as the availability of resources and the requirements imposed by the links prevailing among industries have warranted the promotion of intermediate and capital goods industries, it would be illogical to contend that such industries should not be encouraged if they do not fulfill the criterion of labour-intensity.

Although this reasoning has a great deal of validity, it should not lead to the opposite conclusion that there is no room for labour-intensive industrial products. The possibilities of such industries are far from fully exploited. Especially in the light of the growing emphasis on the need for a better distribution of income, there would appear to be a case for restraints on the consumption of luxuries in order to release resources for increasing the supply of the necessities of life and concurrently to create additional employment. A concerted policy to favour basic textiles as against refrigerators or washing machines is an example that seems to be relevant for many developing countries.

With regard to the methods or techniques of producing the selected range of industrial goods, the developing countries have had to contend with the fact of heavy dependence on imported technology. The available techniques of production, developed to suit the needs of the industrialized nations, are usually of an advanced type. The few attempts that have been made by developing countries to make use of the older processes of production--techniques of an earlier vintage--or of the second-hand machines that might favour a greater utilization of labour have not in general been salutary. Certain machines or machine parts that conform with the older industrial processes are often no longer in supply, and the second-hand machines have not in general proved efficient. The need for developing appropriate technologies which encourage employment and are also efficient is frequently stressed in discussions on development problems, but the development of such technologies is itself an arduous process. In the short run at least, the range of available technologies has turned out to be rather narrow.

The modifications which some Governments have recently introduced in their policies suggest, however, that the possibilities of more labour-intensive industrial production are receiving greater attention. Although the evidence is not enough to permit it to be said that a new general trend can be discerned in the developing countries, the information assembled in the annex reveals a number of remarkable examples of a critical scrutiny by Governments of their own past policies in this respect. These Governments have taken initial steps to curb the preference of industrialists for capital-intensive methods by raising the market price of capital through, for instance, modifications in tariffs or exchange rates.

The need for curbing undue increases in wages and for training workers, so as to promote greater utilization of labour has also been emphasized in a number of recent development plans. This issue naturally poses a dilemma for Governments. It is sometimes argued that substantial increases in wages are needed as a means of bringing about better distribution of income. Increasingly, however, it is becoming apparent that the urgent need is to achieve substantially greater employment at reasonable wages rather than limited employment at substantially improved wages. Rapidly expanding opportunities for productive work are, in fact, an essential complement to other measures designed to bring about a better distribution of income and wealth.

As a step towards exploring the possibilities of more labour-intensive industrial production, the need is stressed in some countries for integrating large-scale industries--through subcontracting and other means--with smaller units which may be more conducive to the expansion of employment. It is maintained that, even if the industrial product is not of a labour-intensive type, its packaging and distribution for sale should follow labour-intensive methods. That such possibilities should be fully exploited remains self-evident.

Absorption of Labour Into Rural Activities

In the long run industrialization will unquestionably bring about a fundamental transformation of the economy in developing countries. However, as the industrial sector in a large majority of these countries is at present small, the process of transformation will require a very long period of time. For many years to come, stretching over a number of successive development plans, the new openings for industrial employment in most developing countries will continue to be relatively small. Conversely, given the predominance of agriculture in a large majority of the developing countries, there is no escape from the conclusion that the greater part of the increment to the labour force will have to be absorbed somehow in rural activities. There will, in other words, have to be a much better balance between agriculture and industry than was evident in many of the earlier exercises in development planning.

It is not merely the mammoth problem of unemployment which calls for a proper emphasis on agricultural development. The experience of the past two decades is replete with examples of other types of acute pressure emanating from the relative neglect of agriculture. The inadequate expansion of agricultural output has in many instances resulted in food shortages, malnutrition, inflation and deficits in the balance of payments; and in the aggregate, the slow expansion of agriculture has impeded the over-all growth of the economy. For the developing countries as a whole, it might be noted, agricultural production (the contribution of agriculture to the total gross domestic product) rose by only 2.8 per cent per annum during the period 1960-1969.

Fortunately, there appears to be a shift now in the thinking on this subject in the developing countries. The more recent development plans have placed a sharper accent on the role of agriculture in the development strategy. There is a growing recognition of the fact that if the agricultural sector does not make sufficient progress, the drive to improve the level of living will be frustrated. As a result, agricultural policies have undergone significant modifications during the past few years in several developing countries, and the impact of these modifications has been striking. This can be shown in a broad manner by decomposing the figure mentioned in the preceding paragraph into two parts: between 1960 and 1965 agricultural by only 1.9 per cent, but the corresponding average during the period 1965-1969 was 4 per cent. An important contributory factor to the improvement has been the technological advance embodied in the new hybrid varieties of seeds which have brought about a substantial increase in yields per acre in several developing countries.

Experience in a number of countries has also led to the finding that, contrary to some prevailing notions, output per acre is usually higher on small holdings than on large farms. Because of the pressure of population on land, small farms typically have more workers per acre and a more diligent way of cultivation. While the output per worker on small holdings is lower than on large farms, output per acre is usually higher. Small-scale cultivation can therefore not only lead to a significant improvement in production but can also contribute to greater employment and better distribution of income. For making agriculture a viable entity, thereby contributing to the solution of the problem of poverty, this finding is of particular importance. It provides strong support for the argument that land reforms need to be undertaken with vigour.

The significant increase in agricultural production in the developing countries during the past few years that has resulted from the use of new varieties of seeds and improved agricultural practices--increasingly characterized as "the green revolution"--has raised some questions about its implications for employment. Thus far, on the whole, the experience has been favourable. Preparation of the fields and water management to suit the requirements of new seeds have called for an increase in the input of labour. The harvesting, winnowing and marketing of larger crops, too, have given rise to additional demand for labour. The improvement in agricultural incomes, in turn, has given impetus to new activities. It is true that in some instances shortages of labour have occasionally appeared--at the time of sowing and harvesting--which have induced some farmers to go in for mechanization.

Undue mechanization of agriculture certainly needs to be curbed. However, it cannot be categorically asserted that all mechanization should be avoided. In a number of cases, greater use of capital equipment may be essential. In many developing countries where the pressure of population is great, land is a scarce factor of production, and the use of the types of capital equipment which help to diminish the constraint of that scarcity would be quite rational. Investment in irrigation facilities and the mechanization of a number of other agricultural operations are therefore rightly considered necessary in certain circumstances, especially for promoting multiple cropping of the available land. By and large, however, both conceptual reasoning and the limited experience accumulated to date suggest that the increasing prosperity of the agricultural sector should in fact help to make a substantial contribution to the problems of unemployment and poverty in the developing countries.

Development plans normally recognize the importance of such ancillary rural activities as poultry farming, fisheries, animal husbandry and dairying. Experience does not show, however, that the scope for these valuable means of livelihood has been fully utilized. The record of the past two decades reveals several striking cases where noteworthy achievements have been made as measured by the production of eggs, poultry, fish, meat, wool, milk and other dairy products. Measures have also been adopted to provide technical and financial assistance to small farmers and producers of the items just mentioned through co-operative societies or government agencies, but a large potential still remains to be tapped. In particular, the contribution that many ancillary activities in the rural sector can make towards the reduction of unemployment and underemployment need to be fully worked out.

The role that village industries can play in advancing the cause of rural progress has also received a good deal of attention both in the general literature on development problems and in the development plans of many countries. Although the earlier contentions that the cottage or craft industries in villages are necessarily of a capital-saving variety have not always proved true, these industries are important for utilizing surplus labour. If the scale of the investment required for establishing a rural industry is such that it is within the means of artisans, this activity can be useful for promoting self-employment in various parts of a country. It seems logical to think, as has been stated in some of the development plans, that a simultaneous development of labour-intensive rural and other small-scale industries along with a number of sophisticated and capital-intensive industries may be a perfectly rational approach. This does not mean, however, that the question of the efficiency of these industries can be ignored; measures will be required to bring about an improvement in their productivity.

As the institutional and social patterns of the rural sector differ widely among the developing countries, precise solutions will naturally need to be devised in the light of specific circumstances. Institutional changes in the rural areas are also among the most difficult to achieve. The task requires not only experimentation and ingenuity but also perseverance. The renewed interest in the problems of rural development needs to be pursued with vigour. Without a prospering rural sector, comprising both field cultivation and a string of productive ancillary activities, it will not be possible to make a meaningful attack on unemployment and poverty.

Role of Construction Activity

The search for employment opportunities has also led to a revival of interest in the role that construction activity can play in this regard, particularly in the rural sector. Public construction works projects were undertaken in the past in a number of developing countries for providing employment, but in general they made little impact; at best they proved palliatives rather than cures. The resources made available for this purpose were usually small; the administrative machinery set up was commonly weak; and the enthusiastic participation of the local people was rarely forthcoming.

However, in the face of appalling poverty and unemployment, some Governments have recently sought to give construction works programmes a new impetus. A number of recent development plans provide substantial outlays for this purpose, especially to meet the needs of backward areas within the country. The new endeavours have in part been aided by the improving scale of food production; the old fear that construction activity may set into motion inflationary pressures appears to have greatly diminished as a result of the resiliency shown by the agricultural sector in recent years.

In the circumstances prevailing in most developing countries, construction activity can be an especially useful means of absorbing labour in productive work. Indeed, much of this activity can be of a labour-intensive type and therefore can avoid the dilemma encountered by policy-makers in the context of industrialization. In the rural areas, public construction works can be particularly helpful by drawing the unemployed and the off-season workers into such tasks as the improvement of land use, the building of drainage and irrigation channels and the expansion and improvement of roads from the villages to the marketing centres. In the urban areas, the clearance of slums, the building of low-income housing and the expansion of schools and hospitals can help to ameliorate both unemployment and the maldistribution of income. One lesson which emerges forcefully from past experience is that such programmes should not be undertaken in a piecemeal manner; their design and implementation should be fully integrated into development planning.

The new endeavours, if they are to succeed, will also require a much greater decentralization of planning and of administration than was the case in the past. In the matters relating to both public construction activity and rural development, there is a need for strengthening planning at the local level so that the design and execution of relevant programmes can not only gain from local initiative but also take fully into account factors of a peculiarly local character. Planning at the local level has generally been quite weak in most developing countries. This is one aspect where a thorough overhaul of planning procedures is required.

Some Longer Term Issues

The experience of the past two decades has also brought to the fore some policy issues of of a longer term nature which have a bearing on problems of unemployment and poverty. These issues relate to the emergence of imbalances in the demand and supply of various types of skills and to what is sometimes characterized as "the population explosion".

Manpower Planning

As mentioned earlier, it is a common experience of many developing countries that widespread unemployment prevails among the educated, while at the same time there are acute shortages of middle-level skills. Again and again the record shows that manpower planning has not generally been undertaken in a systematic way in the developing countries. Manpower budgets, indicating the pattern of planned development of specific skills and vocations against the framework of expanding requirements, are not commonly found in the development plans; most plans only contain general statements on this subject. To prevent future exacerbation of the problems, the balance-sheet of requirements and availabilities of basic vocations will need to be worked out carefully.

In this connexion, educational policy calls for a close scrutiny. The expanding facilities which Governments are providing to impart basic education at the primary level are of unquestioned importance. Such education helps to expand opportunities for a better life and to strengthen the participation of the public in the development process. It is, however, the outpouring of persons with no more than a general education from the secondary and higher institutions who have acquired no technical skills that has given rise to the existence of educated unemployment in several countries. From time to time, proposals have been mooted in some countries for employing such persons for a year or two in a social service scheme; but the schemes have really not been promoted in a sufficiently vigorous and organized manner. The basic idea, on the other hand, does hold forth some promise. The plight of those recently out of the educational institutions, often looking in vain for ordinary desk jobs, warrants urgent attention. A properly organized scheme that requires such persons to spend, against the payment of a stipend, a specific period working, especially in rural areas, as primary school teachers, medical assistants and disseminators of information on a range of productive tasks could help to alleviate the unemployment problem, to narrow the gulf separating the rural areas from the urban centres, and to orient the public towards development.

For longer term solutions, however, it is necessary to look in other directions. Vocational institutions imparting skills that are in short supply need to be encouraged, while the tendency observed in several countries to expand facilities for general education at the secondary and higher levels in an unplanned way needs to be curbed. Stiffer entrance examinations for a general and liberal arts education could be one solution; this could be coupled with an increase in tuition fees, which are at present quite low almost everywhere in the developing world, and an offer simultaneously of a larger number of scholarships to those who are in genuine need of financial aid for education. Other solutions could no doubt be fashioned, depending upon the prevailing circumstances. First and foremost, however, Governments need to define clearly the types of employment they deem necessary and then seek to develop education and training for that purpose.

Population Policy

From a still longer term viewpoint, a population policy is particularly relevant for the problems of unemployment and poverty. The needs of those who are already born will have to be met in one way or another, and therefore these persons have already shaped the circumstances for many years to come. But future births, and consequently the future labour force, can be influenced by a consciously designed population policy.

In this context, a number of developing countries have formulated a longer term perspective and specific targets relating to the growth of population. Some success has been achieved in lowering the rate of growth of population in recent years, but much remains to be done. It is necessary to have a sustained development policy designed to bring about both an acceleration in the rate of expansion of work opportunities and a retardation in the rate of increase in the labour force through measures to reduce the rate of population growth.

IV. INTERRELATIONS OF DEVELOPMENT TASKS

The unemployment problem in the developing countries--the predominant cause of poverty--has rightly commanded a great deal of attention. However, as the foregoing discussion has emphasized, the solutions to the problem are not simple. The have to be sought within the framework of the complex development process in its entirety. The accelerated rates of economic growth which the developing countries are seeking should yield increasing means for a concerted drive against unemployment and poverty. However economic growth is a necessary but not a sufficient condition. Steps have to be taken concurrently to ensure harmony between different objectives.

There is a far greater compatibility and complementarity between various development goals and objectives than has been commonly assumed. The links between the goals of economic growth, employment and the improved distribution of income are beginning to appear in sharper focus. To forge and strengthen those links, however, some of the conventional notions have to be dispelled.

The pattern of production has to be designed to meet the needs of the poor who constitute the majority, not those of the affluent minority; the rural sector has to be modernized and expanded; labour-intensive technologies need to be applied wherever appropriate; the possibilities of public construction works need to be fully exploited; educational bias against vocational and technical training has to be removed; population planning has to be viewed as an integral part of the development perspective. Only by weaving together these various strands will it be possible to make a meaningful attack on unemployment and poverty.

ANNEX

V. PROBLEMS AND POLICIES OF MAJOR DEVELOPING REGIONS

The three sections that follow contain concrete illustrations of the problems of unemployment and poverty encountered in South-East Asia, in Latin America and the Caribbean, and in Africa, and of the policies devised to cope with them. The account in each section is based on the experience in development planning of a few countries. Although the account is therefore not exhaustive, it does offer some idea of the evolution of thinking and policy-making with regard to development problems in individual developing regions.

A. South-East Asia

Some three fifths of the inhabitants of the developing market economies of the world live in South-East Asia,[1] and their total number is growing annually at a rate about 2.6 per cent. The region contains some of the most crowded habitations in the world. The per capita annual gross domestic product of the region was estimated to be only $110 in 1965. Large numbers of people live in immense poverty in South-East Asia. Some of the countries of the region have had nearly two decades of experience in development planning--they were in fact pioneers in the developing world in launching development plans--but their problems of unemployment and poverty still remain massive.

Characteristics of the Prevailing Problems

Although all commentators agree that there is a great deal of unemployment and underemployment in South-East Asia, the precise magnitude of the problem is not known. India and Pakistan, for example, maintain statistics on registered applicants for work; but as unemployment registration offices are usually found only in the larger towns and as, even there, the coverage is generally inadequate, the data do not provide a correct picture for the nation as a whole. The sample surveys undertaken in a number of countries, however, offer some meaningful estimates. About the end of the 1960s, the proportion of the labour force unemployed was over 12 per cent in Ceylon, 8 per cent in West Malaysia and 7.3 per cent in the Philippines. In India, the number of the unemployed was estimated to be 5.3 million in 1956 and 9 million in 1961. The Planning Commission of India which used to provide estimates of the backlog of unemployment at the beginning of each plan period has recently abandoned this practice on the ground that the conceptual and statistical difficulties are too great to yield meaningful estimates.

It is generally accepted in the official circles of several countries in the region that the unemployment problem has been seriously aggravated over the years. The earlier development plans of India, for instance, even stated at the beginning of each plan period that the number of new employment opportunities would fall short of the number of new entrants to the labour force and that the backlog of unemployment would therefore continue to rise; indeed, this appears to have happened all through the past two decades. In West Malaysia, according to the second Malaysian plan, the worsening in the unemployment situation is indicated by the fact that the proportion of the labour force unemployed rose from 6.5 per cent in 1965 to 8 per cent in 1970. In the Republic of Korea, by contrast, the level of unemployment has shown a progressive decline.

Underemployment is even more difficult to quantify. Some attempts at estimation have nevertheless been made in the region. In India, according to the third five-year plan, the underemployed, in the sense of those who have some work but are willing to take up additional work, were believed to be of the order of 15-18 million in 1961. In Pakistan, the fourth five-year plan of the country states that of the 17.7 per cent of the labour force estimated to be wholly and partially unemployed in 1969/70, the bulk would fall into the category of underemployment. In the Philippines, 21.7 per cent of the labour force was reported to be seeking additional work in 1968/69; but the four-year development plan for the years 1971/72-1974/75 also strikes a note of caution by saying that 55.7 per cent of those seeking additional work were already working at least 40 hours or more per week. Such examples do show, however, that there is a significant amount of underemployment in South-East Asia.

In general, the problem of unemployment is more acute in the urban areas and among younger persons. In the Philippines, for instance, 9.1 per cent of the labour force in urban areas was estimated to be unemployed in 1968/69, as against 6.5 per cent in the rural areas. Similarly, a sample survey in West Malaysia indicated that in 1967/68 the unemployment rate of the urban work force was 9 per cent, compared to an unemployment rate of 5.4 per cent in rural labour force. The preponderant majority of the unemployed are usually new entrants to the labour force who had never been employed before. In Malaysia, it was estimated in 1962 that 16 per cent of the persons in the age group 15-19 years were unemployed, compared to 10 per cent in the age group 20-24 years and to 3 per cent among those of 25 years of age or more. In the Philippines, the latest development plan reports that three fifths of the unemployed are below 25 years of age.

Another factor which has particularly affected younger persons is unemployment among the educated. A recent survey undertaken in Ceylon shows that among the unemployed in 1969/70, 76 per cent had proceeded beyond the primary level of education and 29 per cent had completed more than 10 years of schooling. Ceylon probably represents the extreme case in Asia; but the available evidence does indicate that the problem is also acute in a number of other countries of the region, notably India, Pakistan and the Philippines. In India, for example, 6-7 per cent of the labour force with 10 or more years of schooling was "conservatively estimated" to be unemployed in 1967.[2] Apart from the waste entailed in the provision of higher education without the assurance of prompt employment, this characteristic has been a major cause of social and political unrest.

Unemployment and underemployment have exacerbated the poverty in the region. The unemployed, those who share work and income because of insufficient opportunity for full-time productive employment, those engaged in activities using primitive and low-efficiency techniques of production and those with low earnings fall within the category of mass poverty in a number of Asian countries. The plight of the poor and the search for means to relieve their misery have demonstrated that the problems of income distribution and employment are closely interrelated. Reliable information on the distribution of income and wealth is scarce, but a number of studies have provided useful pointers. In India, the country's fourth five-year plan reports that, in 1967/68, the lowest decile of households shared 3.2 per cent of the private consumption of the country as a whole, while the richest decile absorbed 23.9 per cent of the total. A study published recently contends that, in 1960/61, 40 per cent of the rural population and 50 per cent of the urban population of India lived below the poverty line, that is, below a minimum level per capita consumer expenditure which, under the prevailing circumstances, could secure a diet adequate at least in terms of calories.[3] According to the Pakistan third five-year plan, 40 per cent of the households in East Pakistan and 24 per cent of those in West Pakistan received an income of less than 100 Pakistan rupees ($21) per month in the mid 1960s. In Ceylon, the latest development plan points out that, in 1969/70, 40 per cent of the households received an income of less than 200 Ceylonese rupees ($34) per month and 80 per cent less than 400 Ceylonese rupees ($68) per month. An earlier study indicted that, in 1962/63, the richest 10 per cent of the households in Ceylon received 29 per cent of all income.[4]

The inequalities in income have their root in the prevailing pattern of the ownership of means of production. For example, in rural India in 1953/54, the lowest quintile in the income scale owned 0.87 per cent of the total land and the highest quintile 37.24 per cent.[5] As for the ownership of industrial and finance capital, a striking example is provided by Pakistan where it was reported that, while there were over 3,000 individual firms in 1959, only seven individuals, families or foreign corporations controlled one quarter of all private industrial assets and one fifth of all industrial assets; 24 units controlled nearly half of all private industrial assets; further, 15 families owned about three quarters of all the shares in banks and insurance companies.[6]

The search for work and for improved conditions of life has commonly prompted many to migrate to the urban centres. In India, for instance, net migration from the rural areas made up one third of the increment to the urban population. In Ceylon, Malaysia and Pakistan, the urban population grew during the 1960s at a rate of around 5 per cent *per annum*, and a part of the upsurge was due to the migration from villages. This pattern has greatly aggravated the problems of housing, sanitation, transport and community services. Slums have mushroomed in many cities. Poverty and overcrowding have also provided fertile ground for the growth of crime. The problems of urban squalor cannot, however, be allowed to mask the fact that large numbers of the poor are still in the villages of South-East Asia.

Some Causal Factors

Owing to a variety of demographic, social and economic changes, the number of persons seeking employment has increased rapidly in South-East Asia. The principal demographic factor is the rapid fall in death rates after the Second World War while birth rates have shown little change. Malaria, which used to be the scourge of the region, has been virtually wiped out. There is now a greater control over other diseases also. Infant mortality rates have fallen, and the life expectancy has risen. These factors have inevitably had a powerful impact on the supply of labour.

Social changes include a rise in literacy and an exposure to a world where substantially high levels of living are the order of the day. To the young who had been in school for 10 years or more, salaried employment became a normal expectation. In some ways their education and the social milieu as a whole provided food to nurture high expectations. With the spread of education and other transformations in society, the numbers of women seeking salaried work have increased.

The breakdown of traditional modes of production has also added to the increase in the number of persons seeking employment.

This has resulted from the introduction of new technology or perhaps both new technologies and new products. Cases in point are the substitution of large and modern oil expellers for village oil presses, the use of trucks and lorries in place of animal-drawn carts for transport, and the production of asbestos sheets as substitutes for clay roof tiles.

While the labour force has been growing rapidly, the opportunities for work have not generally expanded at a sufficiently fast pace. The Republic of Korea, whose economy expanded at the average annual rate of 9 per cent during the period 1960-1969, is an exceptional case. Under the momentum of vigorous economic growth, the proportion of its labour force unemployed, though still significant (4.6 per cent in 1970), has steadily been diminishing. In marked contrast, the economies of India and Indonesia expanded at the annual rates of 3.1 and 2.2 per cent, respectively; and their problems of unemployment and poverty almost certainly worsened. Malaysia, Pakistan and the Philippines recorded moderately high annual rates of economic growth—5 to 6 per cent—but their problems of unemployment and income distribution, too, have remained acute. It is probable therefore that in a number of cases the patterns of economic growth in the past have not been in harmony with employment and related goals.

Formulation of Goals

The Governments of some of the countries in South-East Asia have stressed the problems of unemployment and poverty from the very inception of their experiments in planning. The draft outline of the first five-year plan of India, published in 1951, in fact emphasized the need for creating conditions for full employment. The full text of the plan, published a year later, expressed the same idea more cautiously by saying that the accent in the initial years of development had to be on the mobilization of idle man-power with as little increase in money incomes as possible, rather than on full employment. The ten-year plan of Ceylon, published in 1959, made the creation of employment its central strategy, and envisaged that there would be relatively full utilization of manpower resources by the end of the plan period. The first five-year plan of India also noted that the urge to economic and social change stemmed from the fact of poverty and of inequalities in income, wealth and opportunity.

The results of the initial experiments in planning did not, however, prove reassuring. The ten-year plan of Ceylon was not implemented at all. In India, a review of the progress during the first 10 years of planned development presented the conclusion that "the phenomena of unemployment, underemployment and, in consequence, low productivity per unit of labour and deficiencies in the administration of tax legislation in large measure accounted for the concentration of income".[7] The experience of a number of other countries in the region—notably, Malaysia, Pakistan and the

Philippines—with regard to the impact of their earlier efforts in planning on unemployment and income distribution has been broadly similar to that epitomized in the remark just cited.

In the face of a worsening situation, the recent development plans of several countries of South-East Asia exhibit an enhanced awareness of both the gravity and the urgency of the problem. The earlier development plans of Pakistan, for instance, did not show particular concern about the scarcity of employment opportunities; the creation of new jobs was considered a by-product of economic growth and not a matter calling for the establishment of specific targets. In the fourth five-year plan, on the other hand, the employment objective is prominent; between 1969/70 and 1974/75, the labour force is projected to increase annually by 2.9 per cent, but employment is envisaged as expanding annually by about 4 per cent and thereby making some reductions in the numbers of unemployed. In the Philippines, the calculations underlying the latest development plan envisage an annual increase of 4.4 per cent in employment during the period 1970/71-1974/75 as against a 3.5 per cent increase in the labour force; consequently, the unemployment rate (the ratio of the unemployed to the labour force), which is believed to have risen from 7.3 per cent in 1968/69 to 8.5 per cent in 1970/71, is expected to decline to 5.2 per cent in 1974/75. It is in fact argued that these calculations were based on historical parameters which reflected an undue capital bias and, with appropriate measures that it is intended to take to relieve the capital bias, the actual employment should surpass the estimates emerging from these calculations. In the Republic of Korea, where already significant achievements have been made in expanding employment, the target is to increase employment from 1970 to 1976 at the annual rate of 2.9 per cent, or slightly faster than the rate of growth of the labour force, and to reduce the unemployment rate from 4.6 cent in 1970 to 4 per cent in 1976. In Ceylon's new plan, it is proposed to reduce the number of unemployed from 550,000 in 1970 to 225,000 in 1976; this requires the creation of employment opportunities for 850,000 in the five-year span from 1972 to 1976, or an increase of about 20 per cent. In Malaysia, the target is to create new jobs by more than 3 per cent a year during the period 1971-1975 and thereby hold the unemployment rate at 7.3 per cent. The fourth five-year plan of India also emphasizes the goal of employment creation on an increasing scale during the period 1969/70-1974/75 in both urban and rural sectors; but unlike the two preceding plans of the country which had delineated specific employment creation on an increasing scale during the period 1969/70-1974/75 in both urban and rural sectors; but unlike the two preceding plans of the country which had delineated specific employment targets—9.6 million new jobs during the period 1956/57-1960/61 and 14 million during the period 1961/62-1965/66—the latest plan, in contrast, offers no quantitative targets. While in operational terms, in most Asian countries, the formulation of employment goals still suffers from serious deficiencies, the enhanced awareness of the employment problem augurs well for the 1970s.

The recent plans of South-East Asia also show a keener appreciation of the links between the problems of unemployment and income disparities. Pakistan's plans provide the most striking example of the recent shift in thinking. Unlike its predecessors, the fourth five-year plan of Pakistan places a considerable stress on the inequitable nature of the country's growth pattern in the past which, it is pointed out, gave rise to an acute impression that the development process had discriminated against poorer regions and income groups; the plan calls for a fundamental change in this respect. Both Ceylon and Malaysia, in their latest plans, emphasize the need for redressing the problems of the neglected groups in society. In India, the need for improving the distribution of income is an important objective of the fourth five-year plan, as it was of the previous plans, a call is made for more radical policies of income distribution, and the need for attaining a national minimum consumption standard by the poor is suggested.

It should be noted at the same time that there has been a consistent awareness in the countries of the region that the living standards of the lower groups cannot be raised by merely redistributing the existing wealth or income. The prior need for economic growth is explicitly recognized in their plans and other policy declarations. In general, little faith is put in fiscal measures for reducing income disparities, since, it is frequently stated surpluses from the higher incomes of the richer people are needed for investment to lay the basis for greater consumption in the future. Thus, as a recent statement from India puts it, the social and economic objectives have to be reached "through more rapid growth of the economy, greater diffusion of enterprise and of the ownership of the means of production, increasing productivity of the weaker units and widening opportunities of productive work and employment to the common man and particularly the less privileged sections of society".[8] In a similar vein, it is argued in Malaysia that "efforts to eradicate poverty, including the creation of greater employment opportunities, and to restructure the society . . . can best be undertaken in the context of an expanding economy", and therefore the country "must plan for a high rate of economic growth".[9]

Search for Solutions

The search for solutions to the grave problems of unemployment and poverty in South-East Asia has, thus, called for a reappraisal of the development process. Both the dimension and the pattern of economic growth have been subjected to a new scrutiny. New avenues of policy have also been explored with the aim of remedying the situation.

Economic Growth and Capital Accumulation

In Ceylon, India and Indonesia, the inadequate rate of economic growth in the 1960s has been a major obstacle. In the latest plan of India, for instance, it is emphasized that the tempo of economic activity in recent years has been insufficient to provide productive employment to all, to extend the base of social services and to bring about significant improvement in the living standards of the people. While, as mentioned earlier, the economies of Malaysia, Pakistan and the Philippines have recorded a moderately good rate of growth, their problem of unemployment has remained acute. Although in some instances the inability to raise the level of capital formation has been a limiting factor, the experience in the region has led many analysts to wonder whether capital has been used efficiently.

It is clearly inefficient to install productive equipment and not use it to full capacity; this way both potential output and employment out of a given stock of capital are held back. Yet there have been such cases in a number of Asian countries. The latest plan of India, for example, has identified steel, textile machinery, machine tools, commercial vehicles and fertilizers as the major industries where production has remained substantially below installed capacities in recent years, either because of low levels of demand following two years of poor crops or because of low efficiency. In Ceylon, investments made during the 1960s in several consumer-goods and producer-goods industries are reported to have resulted in the installation of capacities which remained "grossly underutilized."[10] Evidence of substantially underutilized capacity is also to be found in Pakistan and the Philippines.

That the productive potential of agriculture has not been fully utilized also remains true. In India, according to the fourth five-year plan, only 15 per cent of the net sown area was cultivated more than once a year in the mid 1960s. In Ceylon, less than half of the irrigated land is reported to be double cropped. On the other hand, it has to be recognized that the problems of multiple cropping are, in a way, different from those of the utilization of industrial capacity. For multiple cropping, it is often necessary to undertake substantial new investment, especially in irrigation and fertilizers. However, the need for better management for expanding output and employment out of the existing capacity is common to both agriculture and industry. The recent plans in South-East Asia reflect a new awareness of the relevant issues, and this aspect is touched upon in the following paragraphs dealing with the major sectors of production.

Agricultural Development

Agricultural development in South-East Asia during recent

years has given rise to a new mood of optimism. Even in Ceylon, India and Indonesia, where agricultural production was growing slowly in the early part of the 1960s, the agricultural output has begun to increase at an impressive rate. Productivity per acre has risen in virtually every country of the region. For example, in India, according to the latest plan, output per acre increased annually by 1.4 per cent during approximately the first half of the 1950s, by 1.8 per cent during the second half of that decade, and by 2.7 per cent in the last half of the 1960s. In several countries of the region, the whole series of innovations in improved seed, chemical fertilizers, weedkillers, pesticides, irrigation and farm management has made a larger agricultural output possible.

Initial evidence indicates that farm incomes and employment have risen in the South-East Asian countries where the use of the new varieties of seeds has had a strong impact. Because of the need for greater sophistication in water management, soil preparation and other farming practices, the new seed varieties are reported to have required considerably higher labour inputs than the indigenous varieties. In some areas--notably in the Punjab in India--even some localized shortages of agricultural labour have appeared at certain times of the year; but such shortages also reflect the reluctance of labour to move from one region of the country to another. The new developments in agriculture have nevertheless raised the question of appropriate technology. In the earlier plans of South-East Asia, discussions on the choice of technology were by and large confined to manufacturing; but in recent years the field of discussion has been widened to include agriculture as well. There is a new consciousness that, to quote from a current plan, "since absorption of the labour force outside agriculture is limited by the rate and nature of investment, most of the additional labour force which cannot be productively absorbed by non-agricultural sectors will have to remain on the land", therefore, to avoid a worsening of the unemployment problem, steps should be taken to prevent the undue mechanization of farming.[11]

Particularly in countries where the possibilities of bringing new land under cultivation are negligible or have been exhausted, there is a limited for greater use of capital equipment in order to raise output per acre. In India, for example, the programmes of intensive agricultural development and of the use of high-yield seed varieties have aimed at the adoption of a series of farming practices involving regulated irrigation, fertilizers and improved agricultural implements, including tractors and power tillers. Between 1960/61 and 1968/69 the number of tractors in the country is reported to have increased from 31,000 to 91,000 and power tillers from zero to 20,000. It is argued that the approach to the use of power-operated machinery on farms is influenced by the need to make optimum use of inputs and to facilitate multiple cropping, especially when the interval between two crops is very short. The planners believe that "a selective process of farm mechanization will help to shift labour to more labour-intensive agricultural activities and hence seek to avoid large scale displacement of labour while adding to productivity".[12] In Pakistan, too, the approach to farm mechanization is based on the principle that "mechanization should be introduced when it is complementary to the use of labour or for specific operations which fall in the peak season of labour shortages".[13] The need for careful study of the implications of mechanization and for continuing research to evolve new varieties of seeds and techniques of cultivation appropriate to local circumstances is generally stressed in most countries of the region.

It is, at the same time, recognized that some cases of decline in agricultural employment are bound to occur because of a substantial increase in productivity or for such reasons as the shrinking demand for a particular item. In Ceylon, for instance, the increase in tea production—a major activity in the country—is not expected to create new employment opportunities during the period 1972-1976. The basic belief behind South-East Asian plans is that, on balance, agricultural development should bring a substantial improvement in all aspects of the economy.

In some countries of the region, there is also now a special concern for the small farmer. Experience has shown that improved farming practices require assured irrigation; this tilts the balance in favour of farmers who have the means to install their own wells or other means of water-supply. Such factors as the availability of credit and facilities for storage and transport, affected as they are by the ability of the lender to supply collateral and by some familiarity on his part with the language of administration, have also favoured the larger farmer. Measures have been proposed to eliminate the tendency to discriminate against low-income agriculturists. In India, for example, the current plan calls for the establishment of the Small Farmers' Development Agency for helping farmers with potentially viable small land holdings. Under this scheme, it is expected to organize the activities of small farmers, provide credit and supplies to them in time and assist them in land preparation and marketing. In a number of countries there is a renewed call for land reform measures, such as the imposition of ceilings to the size of land-holdings, to make land for cultivation available to larger numbers of people.

In South-East Asia, growing importance is also attached to expanding the production of meat, poultry and fish and to developing dairy products. An increased tempo of such activities is sought, to bring benefits in terms not only of greater rural incomes and employment but also of improved diet.

Industrialization

In the developing market economies of Asia as a group (including West Asia), during the period 1960-1969, industrial production expanded annually by 7.6 per cent and industrial employment by 3.4 per cent. These figures also reflect, broadly, the pattern of industrial expansion in the subgroup of South-East

Asia. The share of industry in total activity is, however, small in most countries of South-East Asia, and the share of manufacturing is still smaller. Except in the Republic of Korea industrial expansion has not made a significant contribution in terms of absorbing proportionately large numbers of workers into gainful employment.

Industrialization is rightly looked upon as the spearhead of the transformation of the South-East Asian economies. The results achieved are impressive in many ways. It is equally striking, however, that the planners in the region are themselves now critically examining some of the results. In Pakistan, for example, while the incentives provided to the private sector are considered to have been a major stimulant, the planners believe that "excessive protection and extra liberal concessions have also led to the establishment of many inefficient industries and neglect of productivity in general".[14] In the Philippines, to cite another remarkable example of self-criticism, "as a result of earlier policies which cheapened foreign exchange and over-priced labour, the attractiveness of capital-intensive industries somehow relegated the development of relatively labour-intensive industries to the background. A second effect has been the predilection towards a big-scale finish-product enterprise as against fairly small- and medium-scale types of activities".[15] The policies that are mentioned in these quotations as having contributed to a capital-bias in industry include, on the one hand, low rates of interest, zero or low tariffs or a favourable exchange rate applicable to imports or capital equipment, and partial or total exemption from taxation of earnings from new fixed investment, all of which directly favour outlays on capital assets; and, on the other hand, minimum wage legislation and provisions for social security which deter entrepreneurs from employing additional labour. Recent policy show concern at the distortions created by the past policies. The creation of excess capacity promoted by some of the earlier policies and the emergence of under-utilized capacity in several industries for reasons of a short-term nature, such as shortages of raw materials or difficulties in importing spare parts of machinery, have both been subjected to increasing scrutiny. Some changes in policy can be discerned already, but it is not yet clear how far these will go.

The experience of countries in South-East Asia has also reflected a widespread understanding that labour-intensive techniques are not feasible in all branches of industry. The development plans of India, for instance, have constantly argued that in some branches of industry it was essential to adopt the scale and methods of production which would yield the largest economies. Such pervasively used intermediate goods as steel and heavy chemicals are not amenable to production at low cost except on a large scale using techniques that require a great deal of capital per worker. In initiating a strategy geared to the production of capital goods in the mid 1950s in India, it was argued that labour-saving devices in particular lines were often a necessary condition for increasing employment opportunities in the system as a whole. As considerations of competitiveness and profitability have come to the fore, particularly when greater attention has been given to the expansion of manufactured and semi-manufactured goods, countries have not found it possible to allocate resources for industrialization on the simple criterion of labour-intensity.

The necessary resort to capital-intensive techniques in certain areas does not preclude the possibility of the use of labour-intensive techniques elsewhere. The need for exploring the possibilities in this respect is emphasized in many policy statements issued in recent years in the region. The development of indigenous technologies, industrial designs and engineering skills is also receiving greater attention in some countries.

The industrial activity which is considered particularly promising for the utilization of labour in South-East Asia is cottage and small-scale manufacturing. Ceylon's new plan, for example, states that industrialization during the 1960s failed to take adequate account of the resource situation of the country, and the emphasis placed on the expansion of capital-intensive industries led to the relative neglect of the small-scale sector. In India, the development of cottage and small-scale industries has been a major component of industrial policy. Under the first five-year plan, programmes of village industries were undertaken as an integral part of rural development and small industries were viewed as a vehicle for promoting self-employment among educated persons. Village industries were protected from competition, subsidized with cesses on large-scale textile factories and oil pressing enterprises and provided with assured markets in some government organizations. However, beginning with the second five-year plan, the need for greater efforts to increase the efficiency of traditional techniques has been consistently emphasized. In a number of countries of the region, small-scale industries using efficient technology are becoming more important as a means of dispersing manufacturing activity beyond metropolitan areas and diffusing the ownership of industrial assets among a wider public. There is also a growing emphasis on the need for shaping a pattern of industrialization which has a greater impact on the development of the rural sector than in the past, and for this purpose programmes for developing agro-based industries have been drawn up.

The problems raised by the concentration of industrial incomes and wealth, resulting from the pattern of industrialization in the post-war years, have also been subjected to a searching inquiry in some countries of South-East Asia. The insulation from competition provided through high tariffs on imports ensured extraordinarily high profits in many instances and these contributed to the growth of economic power and to a deterioration in the already uneven distribution of wealth and income. The striking example of a limited number of families owning a large proportion of the industrial and financial assets in Pakistan has been mentioned earlier. As an official statement from Pakistan describes it, "concentration of industrial power in a few family groups is leading to pre-emption of new sanctions and bank credit by industrial families, resulting in a denial of fair opportunities to the late comers".[16] It is believed that, distributive justice apart, economic growth itself is likely to suffer through lack of adequate competition . A number of measures to broaden the ownership of industry and the allocation of loanable funds have therefore been proposed. In India, the nationalization of leading commercial banks followed upon the recommendation made in the fourth five-year plan that steps be taken to prevent an undue proportion of the available financial resources from being directed to large industrial houses.

The pattern of industrialization that resulted in industrial output comprising, to a significant extent, such items as motor-cars, refrigerators and air conditioners, which satisfy the demands of the affluent rather than meeting the needs of the masses, has also come in for criticism in some countries of the region. It is considered that such a pattern has not only aggravated the problems of maldistribution of income but has also resulted in forgone opportunities for the creation of greater employment through the production of labour-intensive articles of mass consumption. Examples of this type raise larger questions of development policy. Although a new line of discussion has opened up, it cannot be said that the issue has been settled.

Public Construction Works

Several countries in South-East Asia have looked to public construction works as an important labour-intensive activity which could provide substantial employment opportunities and help to harness abundant human resources to developmental tasks. A revealing example is provided by the third five-year plan of India which envisaged that rural works programmes would employ 100,000 persons in 1961/62 and that the volume of such employment would progressively increase to 2.5 million in 1965/66. The results achieved were, however, meager. The actual outlay on the programme was hampered by uncertainties, administrative delays and a shortage of experienced staff; and the new employment opportunities created were insignificant.[17] Other examples from the region also lead to the conclusion that the rural works programmes in the past have been poorly formulated and indifferently implemented. Commonly, the programmes have been too widely distributed geographically to be effective; projects have not been properly identified and formulated; and the local organizations that could initiate the projects and carry them further have been weak.

A revival of interest has, however, taken place in the possible usefulness of public construction works in several Asian countries. In India, the current plan envisages that the rural works programmes to be undertaken in 40 chronically drought-prone districts, for which an outlay of 1,000 million Indian rupees ($133.3 million) is allocated for the period 1969/70-1973/74, will prove useful in providing unemployment relief. Similarly, in Pakistan, under the current plan, a large works programme in rural and urban areas is contemplated for the period 1970/71-1974/75 as a means of relieving the problem of unemployment. These recent plans also emphasize the need for involving local civic bodies in programmes relating to public construction works, for streamlining administrative procedures so as to avoid bureaucratic delays and for carefully identifying useful outlets for construction activity.

Educational and Manpower Planning

Most countries in South-East Asia have had a particularly difficult task in providing employment for the educated. In India, the problem of the educated unemployed has been recognized ever since the inception of development planning in 1951; yet the problem has continued to grow over the years. It has also become acute in such countries as Ceylon, Pakistan and the Philippines. Often the enrolment of students at the second and third levels of education has risen faster than the enrolment at the first level. In Pakistan, for instance, the fourth five-year plan reports that enrolment at the second and third level increased in the 1960s at an annual rate of 10.2 and 11.2 per cent, respectively, whereas enrolment at the first level grew at the annual rate of only 7.5 per cent. Further, a common experience in the region has been the concentration of students in such fields as liberal arts, humanities, social studies, commerce and law. It is in these fields that the unemployment of the educated has been particularly high. In some instances, however, unemployment has also appeared in technical fields.

In recent years, a number of remedial measures have been pursued in the countries of the region. The short-term measures have included financial assistance for the unemployed to establish themselves in self-employment, provision of information regarding employment opportunities and efforts to dissuade students from the lure of white-collar employment. The longer term policies have included reforms in educational curricula in order to orient them towards technical and scientific subjects and the expansion of training in skills for which there is a growing demand.

Many serious problems, however, still remain to be solved. The importance of achieving full enrolment of the relevant age group in primary education is recognized in South-East Asia both as a basic right and as a means of providing the people with opportunities for a better life; but the actual enrolment ratios are usually well below the target. Similarly, in recent policy statements, while concern has been expressed over the rapid expansion of higher education of a general nature. the framework of a longer term policy has yet to be firmly established. The recent statement from Pakistan that "the existing organizational arrangements continue to be very inadequate to deal with the tasks and functions of manpower planning in an effective manner" because of such factors as the "wide dispersal of efforts and energies", "inconsistency and unreliability [of] vital data", and "shortage of professional staff" familiar with the techniques of manpower planning[18] provides a valid description of the situation prevailing in several other countries of South-East Asia. Some of the recent development plans in the region, on the other hand, do now put an added emphasis on the need for relating education at the higher level to the pattern of jobs and estimates of demand in the economy for educated manpower.

Population policy

Most countries of South-East Asia are looking even further ahead: through population control they are seeking to curb the problems created by the rapid growth of the labour force and the rising proportion of dependants in an average household. The Republic of Korea and Singapore have achieved significant reductions in birth-rates and the over-all rate of growth of population. Among the large countries of the region, India and Pakistan have had population control programmes for many years. The importance attached to family planning in India can be gauged from the fact that the allocation for this purpose has risen from 6.5 million Indian rupees under the first plan (1951/52-1955/56) to 3,150 million Indian rupees under the fourth plan (1969/70-1974/75); the latter plan aims at reducing the birth-rate from 39 to 25 per thousand inhabitants in 10-12 years. In Pakistan, the family planning programme began on a large scale in 1965; the allocation for this purpose has now been raised from 356 million Pakistan rupees under the third plan (1965/66-1969/70)--compared to an initial allocation of 274 million Pakistan rupees--to 695 million Pakistan rupees under the fourth plan (1970/71-1974/75); it is envisaged that the birth-rate will decline from 45 to 40 per thousand inhabitants. The new plans of Ceylon, Malaysia and the Philippines also indicate greater emphasis on family planning than in the past.

The provisional results of the census taken in India in 1971 suggest that the rate of population growth during the 1960s was smaller than had been assumed. Results of the other population censuses taken in the region recently, when available, might also reveal significant changes and pointers for the longer term erspective of population and labour force.

B. Latin America and the Caribbean

As a region, Latin America and the Caribbean has reached a substantially higher stage of material advancement than has South-East Asia or Africa. The per capita gross domestic product of Latin America and the Caribbean is three to four times as large as that of South-East Asia or Africa. The average density of population in this region is about one seventh the density of population in South-East Asia. Yet, many countries in Latin America and the Caribbean are faced with acute problems of unemployment. Compared with that in South-East Asia, development planning in Latin America and the Caribbean has been undertaken more recently; the first generation of plans was formulated, roughly speaking, between the late 1950s and the mid 1960s. However, major policy issues have been articulated in the region over a much longer period, and a sizable literature has grown up on unemployment and related problems.

General considerations

In the economic literature of Latin America and the Caribbean, the term most commonly used to characterize the nature of the employment problems is "structural unemployment". Although this concept has not been clearly defined, it is usually viewed as the result of the differentiated impact of the development process on the determinants of supply and demand for labour in the past decades. In recent years, attention has been given not only to the main factors which are traditionally considered in studying the supply and demand for labour but also to the prevailing pattern of income distribution from the viewpoint of both its effects on the production structure and consequently on employment opportunities and its implications for social tensions.

Supply of labour

Owing to a considerable drop in mortality rates, the rate of growth of the population in Latin America and the Caribbean accelerated from a level near 2 per cent during the 1930s and reached a peak during the 1960s at a level near 3 per cent. The lagged effect of this process has meant that after a while, the rate of increase in the economically active population--and consequently in the labour force--finally caught up and by the end of the 1960s was also near 3 per cent. Among other things, the attraction of the cities and better communications and transport have led to rapid urbanization. During the 1960s, compared to the annual increase of 2.9 per cent in total population, the annual increase in urban population is estimated to have been 4.4 per cent, and in the rural population 1.2 per cent. Because of the rapid growth of the urban population and because most migrants from rural to urban areas are 15 to 35 years of age, the supply of labour in the cities has risen at a considerably higher rate than the total labour force. That the labour force of the region has now become predominantly urban can be seen from the fact that the share of agriculture in the total labour force declined from 50 per cent in 1950 to 43 per cent in 1965. It is also pertinent to mention that, during the period 1950-1965, while the total labour force in Latin America increased at the annual rate of 2.6 per cent, the components of the labour force employed in agriculture and industry (mining, manufacturing and construction) expanded at the annual rates of 1.5 and 2.8 per cent, respectively; whereas the total of those employed in service activities and those who were wholly unemployed increased at the annual rate of 3.8 per cent.[19]

The inability to absorb the whole of the growth of the labour force in productive activities has resulted in considerable unemployment and underemployment--both open and disguised--in many countries of the region. For example, according to some recent development plans, open unemployment as a percentage of the labour force amounted to 10.3 per cent in Trinidad and Tobago in 1967, to 8.7 per cent in Colomiba in 1970 and to 5.4 per cent in Chile in 1970. In Colombia, according to a team organized by the International Labour Office, disguised unemployment (persons without work and who would probably seek it if the unemployment figures were much lower) among the urban working force of males amounted to 10 per cent in 1967 and underemployment (persons who were occupied but had monthly incomes of less than 200 pesos) equalled 6 per cent among the urban males in the same year.[20]

The problem of unemployment has also been aggravated by such factors as natural disasters, the instability of demand for certain products and archaic systems of education.

Apart from situations, such as soil erosion or mining exhaustion, which are not usually unexpected and therefore give people time to readjust, droughts and, in a less degree, floods and earthquakes can greatly affect the volume of employment. Droughts generally force people into the cities and permanently increase the urban supply of labour, since few return to rural areas. A typical case has been north-eastern Brazil and more recently Chile, where the drought of 1968 led to a disproportionate increase in the urban labour force.

The instability--or sudden fall--in demand for goods produced in certain degree of geographical isolation, where production is labour-intensive and where few skills are required--as is the case of many raw materials--tends to produce pockets of unemployment. The drop in demand causes massive lay-offs of unskilled workers whose regional mobility is practically nil. The cases of the coal and nitrate industries in Chile are well known in this connexion.

The educational system in Latin America has often continued to follow old ways. Physical work tends to be considered less worthy than desk work. The restricted academic approach of the curricula, where the aim is mainly to prepare the student for the next step--secondary school if he is in primary school, and university if he is in secondary school--has the effect of making the supply of labour qualitatively more rigid. In fact, relatively few of those who have formal education come back to traditional activities, and they rarely show any desire to become skilled manual workers.

Population analysts maintain that the labour force in Latin America and the Caribbean is likely to continue growing at about 3 per cent annually during the 1970s. This trend is mostly determined by the birth rates in past years. Although there is a tendency for the share of the economically active population in total population to decrease as a result of educational efforts, this tends to be offset by higher participation of women in the labour force. The drop in birth rates which many countries of the region have experienced at the end of the 1960s, by virtue of the urbanization process and family planning programmes, will not significantly diminish the growth of the labour force until the mid 1980s.

Demand for labour

During the period 1950-1965, in Latin America, the gross domestic product increased at the average annual rate of about 5 per cent, while the labour force grew by 2.6 per cent per annum. In the agricultural sector, output and productivity (output per worker) expanded at the annual rates of 3.8 and 2.2 per cent, respectively, and the corresponding increases in industrial output and productivity were 6 and 3.1 per cent.[21] Although an average annual increase of 5 per cent in the gross domestic product is not unimpressive, the increase has been inadequate to solve employment problems.

In agriculture, the lack of dynamic forces tending to encourage greater utilization of manpower has been attributed to the inadequate distribution of land and, more recently, to the insufficient growth of aggregate demand. In industry, or with regard to urban activities in general, the causes of unemployment are more numerous, as will be evident from the following paragraphs. In this connexion, it is important to bear in mind that in Latin America employers belong by and large to the private sector of the economy and their main interest--the maximization of profits--does not necessarily lead to a great increase in employment. This also reflects the fact that the private sector is not sufficiently integrated into the planning process.

Policies such as accelerated depreciation for tax purposes, low or no tariffs on imports of capital goods, a preferential exchange rate for imports of machinery and equipment, and low interest rates on loan finance have encouraged the replacement of manpower by capital goods. This process in Latin America has been reinforced by the demonstration effect (it is fashionable to have the most modern machinery), by inflation (which encourages over-expansion of capacity as a hedge against future price increases and against drastic modifications in the rate of foreign exchange) and by the fact that capital goods are generally designed to be used in countries where income is high and labour is scarce and expensive. Idle capacity is, therefore, partly a result of these policies.

Social legislation aimed at minimum wage laws, social security payments required from employers, strict regulations on lay-offs, and the growing strength of unions have also contributed to the preference of entrepreneurs for machinery rather than for workers.

The external links also condition the employment situation. Foreign investment in Latin America has usually had few multiplier effects. The leading export activities are practically not absorbing additional manpower.[22] Emigration is concentrated among highly skilled workers and professionals. Tied credits increase dependence on capital-intensive techniques.

Most Latin American countries have established institutions in charge of scientific and technological development, either in the universities or as government-sponsored agencies. But these institutions have not centred their efforts on research into new production processes that would take into account domestic availabilities of manpower. They are mainly interested in the possibilities of the technological transfers from developed countries.

Income distribution

For a long-term solution to the employment problem, the pattern of income distribution prevailing in many Latin American countries has also to be borne in mind. The pattern of income distribution affects the level of employment through its impact on the structure of consumption. Empirical evidence shows that both the import content and the direct labour content of the goods purchased by the rich and the poor tend to be different; the rich are prone to buy goods which require a proportionately larger component of foreign exchange (import input), a scarce factor of production, and a smaller component of labour, thereby compounding the problem. The prevailing pattern of income distribution may also aggravate social tensions as people in rural and urban areas become aware of the disparities among different areas and among different groups. It is only lately that the inequalities in income distribution and the problems of the marginal groups ("marginalization") in metropolitan areas where favelas have mushroomed have received serious attention by the authorities in the region. Although until now these groups have remained a minority of the urban population, their absolute numbers are considerable in some cities[23] and they are very poor.

If, as seems to be the case in parts of South-East Asia where the term has gained currency, mass poverty is understood to imply a very low per capita income, a large number of people living at bare subsistance levels and, to a certain extent, the concentration of people in certain areas, it can be said that such poverty also prevails in parts of Latin America.

Towards the end of the 1960s, according to the estimates prepared by the Economic Commission for Latin America (ECLA) using the purchasing power equivalents of Latin American countries in terms of United States dollars at 1960 prices, the per capita annual gross domestic product in Haiti amounted to only $85, in

TABLE 1. ESTIMATES OF INCOME DISTRIBUTION IN DEVELOPING COUNTRIES[a]
(Percentage shares in total national income going to population groups of different income levels)

Country and group[b]	Poorest 20 per cent	Poorest 60 per cent	Highest 20 per cent	Highest 5 per cent
Argentina	7.00	30.40	52.00	29.40
Bolivia	4.00	26.60	59.10	35.70
Brazil	3.50	22.70	61.50	38.40
Chile	5.40	27.00	52.30	22.60
Colombia	2.21	15.88	68.06	40.36
Costa Rica	6.00	25.40	60.00	35.00
El Salvador	5.50	23.60	61.40	33.00
Jamaica	2.20	19.00	61.50	31.20
Mexico	3.66	21.75	58.04	28.52
Panama	4.90	28.10	56.70	34.50
Peru	4.04	17.10	67.60	48.30
Trinidad and Tabago	3.60	18.52	57.00	26.60
Venezuela	4.40	30.00	47.10	23.20
Average of 13 Latin American and Caribbean countries	4.3	23.5	58.6	32.8
Average of 15 African countries[c]	5.6	22.1	62.6	34.8
Average of 7 Asian countries[d]	5.5	28.0	53.2	26.0

SOURCE: Irma Adelman and Cynthia Taft Morris, "An anatomy of income distribution patterns in developing nations" in United States Department of State, Agency for International Development, *Development Digest* (Washington, D.C.), vol. IX, No. 4, October 1971.

[a] Data refer to various years in the 1950s and through the 1960s.

[b] Group average refers to simple arithmetic mean.

[c] Dahomey, Gabon, Ivory Coast, Kenya, Libyan Arab Republic, Madagascar, Morocco, Nigeria, Southern Rhodesia, Senegal, Sierra Leone, Sudan, Tunisia, United Republic of Tanzania and Zambia.

[d] Burma, Ceylon, India, Iraq, Lebanon, Pakistan and Philippines.

Bolivia to $203, in the Dominican Republic to $233, in Honduras to $247 and in Paraguay to $272.[24] Further as indicated in table 1, the poorest 20 per cent of the population in 13 countries of Latin America and the Caribbean received 4.3 per cent of the total national income in the early 1960s, whereas the richest 5 per cent of the population received as much as 32.8 per cent of the national income. Assuming for illustrative purposes that the income distribution in Haiti, the Dominican Republic, Honduras and Paraguay is similar to the average just mentioned for 13 countries, it works out that 95 per cent of the total population in Haiti, around 65 per cent in the Dominican Republic, 60 per cent in Honduras, and 50 per cent in Paraguay has a per capita annual product of $60 (roughly equivalent to $50 per capita annual national income). For Bolivia, using its own income-distribution data as shown in table 1, it appears that roughly 75 per cent of the population has a per capita annual product of $60. Similarly using the data shown in table 1 and the relevant information contained in an ECLA study on income distribution,[25] the corresponding illustrative figure for Columbia is 60 per cent, for Brazil and Peru 50 per cent, and for Mexico 35 per cent.[26] In absolute terms, the number of persons belong to the group with per capita annual product of $60 towards the end of the 1960s works out as follows (in millions) Bolivia, 3.5; Brazil, 42; Colombia, 12.5; Dominican Republic, 2.5; Haiti, 4.5; Honduras, 1.5; Mexico, 17; Paraguay, 1; Peru, 6.5. Data on the concentration of these people in certain areas within the country are not available; but the north-east of Brazil, the "sierras" in Bolivia and Peru, the Oaxaca State in Mexico and the Choco region in Colombia are well-known examples of such concentration. All these indicators, however crude, point to the existence of mass poverty in many parts of Latin America.

It is not merely the absolute level of poverty that matters. Even in less constricting circumstances, if the prevailing pattern of income distribution is not acceptable to the majority of the people, conflicts may arise and jeopardize the expansion of employment opportunities. Argentina, Chile and Uruguay enjoy a per capita gross product substantially higher than the rest of Latin America. But there has been a growing realization on the part of the people that the prevailing pattern of income distribution depends more on historical elements (concentration of wealth in small groups), social-cultural factors (social status or education) and privileged access to the public sector or the financial system than on actual efforts to contribute to the national product and thus tensions in even these countries have increased. The tensions have appeared in such forms as increasing conflicts between labour and management in both the private and public sector of the economy, recurrent and more violent strikes and the take-over of farms and factories by the workers.

Recognition of the employment problem and formulation of employment targets

Development planning in Latin America in the late 1950s and early 1960s showed relatively little concern about the employment situation. Some plans did not even mention it. Only a few plans referred to it; but the problem was considered to be transitory, and the general belief was that the development process would automatically resolve it.[27] In fact, it was stated that full employment or a complete utilization of human resources would be achieved as part of this process. The reasoning was that a sufficient and sectorally balanced rate of economic growth would lead to an increase in the demand for labour at a rate compatible with the supply. In agriculture, it was thought that a proper price policy for food-stuffs, together with measures aimed at the redistribution of land and the expansion of production would ease rural unemployment and reduce the rate of urbanization. In manufacturing, it was expected to provide significant additional employment in the short run by the use of idle industrial capacity; in the long run, the increase in the level of capital formation was expected to lead to an increasing demand for labour. It was also felt that the Government, partly for stabilization reasons and partly to increase the surplus of current revenue over current expenditure to finance development activities, should refrain from creating too many jobs directly through its own activities; the common thinking was that the Government should not create employment at a rate higher than the population growth. However, in certain contexts, the importance of construction works initiated by the Government for absorbing manpower was recognized. Also recognized was the need to tackle the specially grave problems of unemployment and low incomes in the backward areas within the country.

Around the mid 1960s the approach to the employment problem began to change. Planners realized that the employment target was much more difficult to achieve than they had thought.[28] The absorption of manpower in agriculture turned out to be less than had been expected. Under the impact of technological advance, the increase in industrial output was accompanied by a much smaller expansion of industrial employment. The resulting deterioration of the employment situation in several countries of Latin Aemrica and the Caribbean aroused new anxieties. While the underlying forces remain unabated, widespread recognition has now emerged of the fact that an otherwise satisfactory rate of economic growth is not necessarily associated with an adequate increase in employment. The rapid growth of the labour force and of urbanization has brought to the fore the need for Governments to take additional and innovating measures in various sectors of the economy to tackle the problems of unemployment and underemployment. In the recent development plans of several countries of Latin America and the Caribbean greater attention has been paid to these problems than was the case in the earlier plans.[29]

In general, full employment is now viewed as a long-term

TABLE 2. TARGETS FOR GROSS PRODUCT AND EMPLOYMENT IN SELECTED COUNTRIES
OF LATIN AMERICA AND THE CARIBBEAN[a]

(Annual rate of expansion; percentage)

Country and plan	Total gross product	Per capita gross product	Total employment	Employment in agriculture	Employment in manufacturing
Brazil					
Plano Trienal de Desenvolvimento Econômico e Social, 1963-1965	7.0	3.9	...	...	...
Programa de Ação Econômica de Governo, 1964-1966	6.3	2.8	3.5	3.5	3.5[b]
Diretrizes de Governo Programa Estratégico de Desenvolvimento, 1967-1970	6.0 (minimum)	...	...	...	...
Metas e Bases para Ação de Governo, 1970-1973	9.0	6.0	3.1	...	...
Chile					
Programa Nacional de Desarrollo Económico, 1961-1970	5.5	3.0	...	...	...
Política de Desarrollo Nacional, 1967-1970	6.0	3.6	3.0	...	...
El Desarrollo Económico y Social de Chile en la Década, 1970-1980:					
Hipótesis alta	6.4	4.0	3.3	1.2	3.9
Hipótesis media	5.1	2.7	2.9	1.2	3.3
Colombia					
Plan General de Desarrollo Económico y Social, 1961-1970	5.6	2.6	3.2	1.6	4.5[b]
Plan de Desarrollo Económico y Social, 1970-1973	7.5	4.5	4.4	2.4	6.2[b]
Trinidad and Tobago[c]					
Second Five-Year Plan, 1964-1968	5.1 (5.8)	2.1 (2.8)	2.5 (2.6)	1.8 (1.8)	1.9[d] (2.6)
Third Five-Year Plan, 1969-1973	4.5 (5.8)	2.9 (4.2)	2.9 (3.0)	1.7 (1.7)	1.7[d] (2.5)

[a] Targets or projections.

[b] Non-agricultural employment. In Colombia, during the period 1970-1973, employment in manufacturing is estimated to grow by 6.8 per cent per annum (weighted average of 7.8 per cent increase in handicrafts and 5.5 per cent in the rest of manufacturing).

[c] Figures in parenthesis show the rates when petroleum and asphalt mining are excluded.

[d] Including petroleum and asphalt mining.

objective; it is believed that the objective will be reached only after the structural changes required by the economy have occurred. The recent plans have sought a firmer basis for employment projections. Though many deficiencies still remain, the improvements in the quality and quantity of data which have taken place over the years have proved to be of material help. The usual and rather mechanical approach of estimating the increase in the demand for labour as the difference between the growth of total output and the growth of productivity is still utilized; but alternative hypotheses relating to changes in productivity are now commonly used and sectoral details are worked out on an increasing scale. The evolution of targets formulated by Brazil, Chile, Colombia and Trinidad and Tobago with regard to output and employment as part of their planning exercises is depicted in table 2.

It may be noted in this connexion that the projections of employment made in several Latin American countries by the end of the 1960s show that, unless the agricultural sector is able to increase employment opportunities in the future at a higher rate than in the past, the level of urban unemployment—following the migration in search of jobs by people from rural to urban areas—will become tolerable. The latest plans have therefore been drawn up on the premise that the agricultural sector still has to be relied upon to absorb a substantial part of the increment to the labour force and that considerable increases in employment in the manufacturing sector are not to be expected.

In Brazil, the planned annual rate of economic growth of 9 per cent for the period 1969-1973 is envisaged as being accompanied by a rate of increase in employment which is virtually equal to the rate of growth of the labour force. In Chile, even if the higher of the two postulated annual rates of economic growth, 6.4 per cent, is attained, full employment will not be achieved until 1980. The 7.5 per cent annual rate of economic growth planned in Colombia for the period 1970-1973 would leave 6.4 per cent of the labour force unemployed at the end of the plan period. In Trinidad and Tobago, the fulfilment of the target for economic growth during the period 1969-1973 would leave 8 per cent of the labour force unemployed.

The results envisaged in the latest plans of these countries cannot be taken as pessimistic; nor are they to be understood to imply that the sole condition for the attainment of the employment target is the achievement of the planned rate of economic growth. For the expansion of employment opportunities on an increasing scale, the sustained and co-ordinated application of many policy measures is required; and a good deal of discussion has been taking place on the subject of policies in Latin America and the Caribbean.

Employment policies

The discussions on employment policies in recent years have covered a wide range of topics. Attention has been given to policy measures which impinge on the economy as a whole as well as to those designed for specific sectors of the economy. A growing concern about income distribution has pervaded recent policy statements. For tackling the problems of both unemployment and income disparities, increasing attention has been devoted to a spatial disaggregation of national plans through "regional" or subnational plans. Such longer term issues as manpower planning and family planning have also figured in the policy discussions. The main features of the employment and related policies adopted in Latin America and the Caribbean are described in the following paragraphs.

General policy instruments

One theme running through the policy discussions concerns the efficiency of the use of the scarce factors of production. In the recent plans, it is recognized that discriminatory policies in the past have often fostered an extensive use of capital at the expense of labour, particularly in manufacturing. Changes in policies to increase the demand for labour are recommended in many countries. However the degree of commitment of Governments to the changes is not clear; this perhaps reflects in part the difficulty entailed in clearly defining an incomes policy and in part the fear of a slump in private investment. The measures contemplated generally include an increase in the price of capital, wage guidelines and stricter regulations on foreign investment, on transfers of technology and on imports of machinery and equipment. However, to increase effectively the price of capital, action is required on several fronts: inflation has to be reduced drastically in many countries (for example, the average annual increase of consumer prices in Brazil and Chile was higher than 20 per cent during the 1960s), exchange rates and preferential tariffs have to be adjusted, interest rates in the banking system have to be raised and Governments have to increase the cost of development loans. As it is generally thought that these measures will result in an adverse reaction of the part of private investment, a long time is taken to put them into effect; and some of them may not be implemented at all. At the same time, the gradual increase in social security benefits--the financing of which in Latin American countries usually has the effect of a tax on labour use--tends to decrease rather than increase the relative price of capital.

Wage guidelines have become more important in plan documents over a period of time. However, they are still rather loose, and in many cases they contradict income-distribution targets. The usual recommendation--as stated, for instance, in the plans of Brazil and Colombia--is that wages should not increase faster than productivity; in practice, this tends to stabilize the present functional distribution of income. The main reasons for this limit are employment considerations and price stability. In Trinidad and Tobago it is felt that money wages as a whole should grow somewhat more slowly than productivity in the whole economy. Apart from the high rate of open unemployment in Trinidad and Tobago--10.3 per cent of the labour force in 1967--the underlying reasons for these measures are said to be the following:

> "First, attempts by trade unions in the less productive sectors to bring wages of their members up to the level obtaining in the petroleum and other highly capital-intensive sectors may cause these less productive sectors to go out of business or to mechanize more rapidly than they would otherwise do. Second, when wage-rates and salaries rise in the public sector--a very large employer of labour--this reduces the capacity of this sector to provide employment. Third, labour itself may be influenced by the relatively high wages obtaining in the highly capital-intensive sector and in the public sector and set a relatively high floor to the return it expects. This not only reduces the chances of the coming into being of new labour-intensive industries but may also mean that persons prefer to remain unemployed rather than accept what they consider to be too low wages."[30]

In the case of foreign investment, the purchase of foreign technology and imports of capital goods, Latin American countries are imposing new regulations. The governmental agencies charged with the final decision in these matters are giving increasing weight to employment considerations. Lately, the idea of developing indigenous technology is being accepted, and in fact increased public funds are being committed for this purpose.

Among the general policy measures, the theme of income distribution is also gaining emphasis. For instance, as stated in the Colombian plan:

> "The main cause of increasing unemployment in the country is the inequality in the different areas of life, coupled with a low saving rate. There is inequality of opportunities, a considerable concentration of income and wealth, great disparities in the development of the different regions of the country and between the urban and rural sectors."[31]

A similar viewpoint is also put forward in the Chilean plan for 1970-1980. The redistributive policies advocated in several countries include increased government expenditure on education, housing and health; income-tax reforms and greater control over the evasion of taxation by high-income groups; progressive taxes on wealth (for example, real estate taxes); discriminatory taxes on luxury goods; increased expenditure on agricultural infrastructure accompanied either by the distribution of unutilized land or the redistribution of existing farms among the peasants; and, lately, increasing participation of workers in profits and specific management functions in both public and private enterprises.

Agriculture

In the agricultural sector, increased employment is expected as a result of higher output, agrarian reform and changes in the pattern of production. For example, according to the latest plans, the target for annual increase in agricultural output amounts to 7 per cent in Brazil, 5.5 per cent in Colombia, 5 per cent in Trinidad and Tobago and 4.7 per cent in Chile. By relating these output targets to the targets for agricultural employment indicated in table 2, it can be seen that in Colombia, for each 1 per cent planned increase in agricultural output, the planned increase in agricultural employment works out to be 0.43 per cent; and the corresponding figures for Trinidad and Tobago and Chile are 0.34 and 0.26 per cent, respectively. These co-efficients for agricultural employment appear to be broadly compatible with the corresponding co-efficient of 0.39 per cent estimated for Latin America as a whole during the period 1950-1965[32] by the Latin American Institute for Economic and Social Planning.

With regard to agrarian reform, it is recognized in the latest plans that the effect on the absorption of labour during the 1960s was less favourable than had been expected. In such countries as Brazil and Columbia which have substantial amounts of unused land, a partial solution to the employment problem has been evident; but the costs of new settlements have usually turned out to be much higher than the original estimates. Programmes of land distribution--for example, in Chile where 2.9 million hectares came under agrarian reform during the period 1965-1969--did contribute to a fuller utilization of the working hours of the new owners, but did not have a significant effect on the number of workers employed. The implementation of hughe infrastructure projects, particularly irrigation, was not as successful as predicted.[33] Such findings have led to a review of both aims and policies. Public funds for agrarian reforms have been increased, and expectations with regard to results have become rather cautious.

In seeking a new pattern of agricultural production, the planners in Latin America have reflected the belief--based on a number of studies on land capability, new agricultural techniques, expansion of foreign trade and the development of agro-industries--that a change towards more labour-intensive activities in agriculture would be highly beneficial from the viewpoint of both the employment and the total income of the rural sector. The plans are increasingly providing a more detailed account of the desired expansion and diversification of agricultural output, especially food-stuffs.[34] Credit and price policies, research, extension and advisory services, infrastructure and marketing facilities are being modified to achieve the new pattern of agricultural production.

Manufacturing

Substantial increases in manufacturing output are envisaged under the current plans of Latin America and the Caribbean. The planned rate of expansion of manufacturing output is 10 per cent in Brazil, 9.3 per cent in Colombia, 7.2 per cent in Chile, 6 per cent in Trinidad and Tobago. With the help of the data shown in table 2, it can be seen that in Colombia, for each 1 per cent planned increase in manufacturing output, the planned increase in manufacturing employment equals 0.73 per cent; and the corresponding co-efficients for Chile and Trinidad and Tobago are 0.54 and 0.42 per cent, respectively. For Latin America as a whole, according to the Latin American Institute for Economic and Social Planning, the corresponding co-efficient during the period 1950-1965 was 0.47 per cent.

The expectations of a relatively high co-efficient of manufacturing employment during the 1970s are based on the assumptions of a dynamic handicrafts activity--a 10 per cent planned annual increase in the output of handicrafts in Colombia, for instance--and changes in the pattern of production. In the past, however, it has not been easy to increase employment at a fast rate in handicrafts. During the period 1950-1965, employment in handicrafts increased annually by only 1.8 per cent in Colombia, 1.7 per cent in Brazil and 0.6 per cent in Chile; in Brazil, the annual average dropped to 1 per cent during the period 1962-1968.[35] The plan for the period 1964-1968 of Trinidad and Tobago put a high reliance on employment increases in handicrafts and traditional manufacturing. However, the review of actual experience, contained in the subsequent plan, revealed that although the production target for total manufacturing had been achieved, the employment effects of institutional, fiscal and financial instruments deployed for such activity had proved to be disappointing.

In modern manufacturing activity bearing in mind that employment prospects are rather gloomy, the need for greater selectivity in the activities to be promoted is emphasized in recent plans. It is pointed out that the production process of the new industry or industries should be labour-intensive and, moreover, that there should be backward and forward linkages among industries.

The adequate choice of labour-intensive industries has also been linked to income redistribution.[36] A successful policy to redistribute income towards lower income groups should increase the demand for the goods produced by such industries. It has been realized that labour-intensive techniques are not necessarily confined to traditional industry. The production of many tools, machines and electronic devices is also labour-intensive. For capital-intensive goods whose production within the country is warranted for a variety of reasons, two approaches are suggested in some recent plans.[37] One is to choose the least capital-intensive technique available, as long as it is economical. The other is to develop an indigenous technology which takes into account the human resources of the country.

Internal backward and forward linkages are one of the main features of the industrialization process of Brazil in recent years. The industrial strategy of Brazil's plan for 1967-1970 stressed the importance of the creation of the dynamic nuclei that reciprocally stimulate industries, each providing a market for the other. By the end of the 1960s most Latin American countries stressed this approach, promoting integrated industries and particularly those activities which utilized available raw materials in all possible forms. Agro-industries became a focal point, since these combined practically all the desired features: forward and backward linkages, labour-intensity, feasibility of location in rural areas to control the urbanization process, compatibility with national goals (redistribution of income and improved diet) and good possibilities of successful autonomous research to improve technology.

Construction activities and spatial development

The possibility of creating additional employment opportunities through construction activities is emphasized in several recent plans. The planned rates of annual growth of construction are in general quite high--10 per cent in Chile (hipotesis alta), 9 per cent in Colombia, 8 per cent in Brazil and 7 per cent in Trinidad and Tobago. These rates are closely related to the planned level and distribution of public investment, and their achievement depends mainly on the ability of Governments to increase the budget surplus and on the improvement of the financial market for housing projects. Usually, measures to deal with both aspects are being implemented in Latin America, and the plans call for reinforcement of the measures.

As mentioned earlier, problems of spatial development--that is, the development of various areas within a country--are also receiving greater attention. To cope with localized unemployment and income disparity among different parts of the country, the need for special measures has been stressed. Two main sets of instruments have been used in this connexion, namely, the allocation of public expenditure for the benefit of backward areas and extra incentives for private investment in these areas.[38] Lately, development of tourism has been suggested as an activity that can provide a considerable amount of additional employment and at the same time offer a partial solution for depressed areas.[39] A more adequate territorial distribution of the population has also been suggested. In addition to the policies directly related to agriculture and manufacturing, certain new policies are being tried in an attempt to control the urbanization process; these include the dissemination of education and training facilities, the improvement of the flow of information about employment opportunities in different parts of the country, and lately, family planning.

Manpower planning

Earlier plans in Latin America had taken notice of the shortages of certain skills, and had pointed out the need for studies on human resources and manpower planning. But it is only rather recently that aspects of manpower planning have started receiving serious attention.

In order to modify during the 1970s the level and distribution of labour supply, several new measures relating to education and training and the improvement of employment services are being considered by most countries of Latin America and the Caribbean. The measures suggested include the expansion of educational services, a greater emphasis on scientific and technical education, the provision of facilities for acquiring industrial skills, the promotion of intermediate careers, the improvement of information to increase the mobility of workers, adult training, greater retention in secondary education as a means to prevent exaggerated growth of the labour supply, and an intensification of studies and research on human resources. A greater concern about welfare and social security policies has also developed; but at the same time the need to proceed gradually in the case of such welfare programmes is stressed, because it is feared that increased costs of labour might intensify the use of capital.

Family planning

As part of the discussion on human resources, family planning and population policies have also attracted attention from the authorities in Latin America and the Caribbean. The spectrum of goals and policies is very broad. At one end, in Brazil, the emphasis is on the geographical distribution of population within the country in order to exploit its potentialities.[40] At the other end, in Trinidad and Tobago, "in keeping with Government's policy to raise effectively the standard of living of the entire population, it has been found necessary to reduce considerably [the] rapid rate of population growth; the Cabinet has accorded the highest priority to a National Family Planning Programme".[41] The aim of this programme is to halve the birth-rate in 10 years. Most other countries in the region appear to follow a policy somewhere in between these two poles.

The censuses taken in Latin America in 1970 suggest a significantly smaller increase in population than do the projected estimates. Unfortunately, however, no definitive studies have been made to evaluate the impact of the family planning programmes in the region. In any event, as stated earlier, the effect of the family planning programmes launched since the mid 1960s is not expected to be discernible with regard to the supply of labour before the 1980s.

C. Africa

Much of Africa is at an early state of development. Its slow per capita gross domestic product makes the region akin to South-East Asia; but by virtue of its low density of population, Africa resembles Latin America. Most African countries have gained political independence comparatively recently, and therefore the region's experience in development planning is also rather recent. In their endeavours to transform their societies, Governments in Africa have had to cope with numerous problems. Prominent among these, especially in the past few years, has been the problem of unemployment and underemployment.

Main features of the employment problem

As is true in many developing countries, data on unemployment and underemployment in Africa are meagre. The broad dimensions of the problem can nevertheless be seen from the estimates available for some countries. In Egypt, the proportion of the labour force unemployed is estimated to have increased from 6.2 per cent in 1961 to 11.5 per cent in 1968. This corresponds to an average annual increase of 13 per cent during the period 1961-1968. About 1.5 million persons were reported to be unemployed in 1965. In Ghana, around 11 per cent of the labour force was estimated to be unemployed towards the end of the 1960s; the corresponding rates of unemployment among the wage and urban labour force were about 25 and 30 per cent, respectively. In absolute terms, some 350,000 persons were reported to be actively seeking wage employment. In Morocco, the census of 1960 showed that 21 per cent of urban males of active age were unemployed, with rates ranging up to about 25 per cent for many age subgroups in such cities as Casablanca, Kenitra and Tangier. It is also reported that the nation-wide unemployment rate among urban males probably rose to around 25 per cent by 1965. Altogether about 600,000 persons--9 per cent of the working-age population--were estimated to be unemployed in Morocco in 1965. In Nigeria, 7.8 per cent of the labour force was estimated to be unemployed in 1970.

Data on underemployment in Africa are even more scanty, but there is little doubt that substantial underemployment prevails in both rural and urban areas. In absolute numbers, underemployment in 1965 was estimated to be 2.25 million in Morocco, 1.2 million in the Sudan and 1 million each in Algeria and Egypt; but the true significance of such estimates is not clear, as they are based on heterogeneous criteria and data.[42]

Under the impact of the spurt in the growth of total population, the annual rate of increase in the population of working age in Africa rose from 2.2 per cent in the 1950s to 2.4 per cent in the 1960s. In fact, during the 1960s, the corresponding rate was close to 3 per cent in Ghana, Kenya, Morocco and the Sudan, and in the urban areas, the rate of increase was substantially greater, reaching as much as 6 per cent in some cases. These figures attest to the fact that the labour force in Africa has been growing at rapid rates.

As in the case of the rest of the developing world, the expanding supply of labour in Africa has failed to be accompanied by a vigorously expanding demand for labour. The pace of economic growth in Africa during the 1960s was slower than in the rest of the developing world. The development of transportation and power--basic facilities where were very inadequate in many African countries in the 1950s--has commonly necessitated large outlays of a capital-intensive nature. Modern industrial activities have also often followed a capital-intensive pattern; this has been particularly marked in mining. The share of manufacturing in total output is smaller in Africa than in South-East Asia or Latin America. It is apparent therefore that the absorption of the labour force in industrial activities has generally been more limited in Africa than in other developing regions. At the same time, agricultural growth during the past decade has been modest. All in all the process of economic growth has not yielded sufficient employment opportunities.

With the rise in productivity in non-agricultural activities following the application of modern technology, as is only to be expected, wage rates have risen. Particularly striking, however, are the widening wage differentials in Africa. For example, in Kenya, the development plan for 1970-1974 reports that, in 1967, the average wage income in non-agricultural activities was four and a half times greater than in farming (mainly scale farming) and seven times greater than in other rural occupations; these differentials were estimated to be greater than a decade ago. In many African countries, wages in the non-agricultural or manufacturing sector have been rising annually by 7 or 8 per cent during the 1960s; and, although precise information about the agricultural sector is lacking, the general impression appears to be that the difference between urban and rural wages has increased. This has tended to attract more workers into urban areas. Other factors have also contributed to the flow of workers to the cities. For instance, according to a survey of rural-urban migration conducted by the University of Ghana in 1963, important among these factors have been the lack of road and communication facilities, of water-supplies, of health facilities, of entertainment and of work suitable for the educated in the rural areas. In actual practice, the migration from rural areas in general merely accentuated urban unemployment.

The high wage rates have induced employers to look for capital-intensive and labour-saving techniques. Statutory minimum wages have been considered necessary in a number of African countries in order to avoid the exploitation of labour, but when strong pressure by trade unions has pushed the wage rates well above the minimum level, the implications for the creation of additional employment have tended to become serious.

Employment objectives

In the early 1960s, the development plans of Africa did not reflect much concern about the employment problem. Often the lack of adequate information about the prevailing conditions and the prospective expansion of the labour force and employment made it difficult to provide a meaningful analysis of the problem. An additional factor was the shortage of educated and skilled persons. Frequently, therefore, Governments considered it necessary to concentrate on the removal of this major impediment to development.[43]

In those African countries which have experienced substantial open unemployment, mainly in the urban areas, the problem was recognized more sharply. Even in their earlier development plans, certain employment targets were specified. In the Sudan, for example, it was stated that, during the 1960s, employment would be created to absorb the expected annual increase of 2.8 per cent in the labour force.[44] In Egypt, employment was expected to increase during the 1960s at the average annual rate of 4.1 per cent, accelerating from 3.2 per cent per annum during the first half of the 1960s to 5 per cent per annum during the second half.[45] Generally, however, the targets were not achieved. For example, as stated earlier, in Egypt the proportion of the labour force unemployed increased substantially during the 1960s.

Although the more recent development plans of Africa emphasize the growing urgency of the problem, the formulation of employment objectives still commonly encounters the old difficulties. Because of limitations of data, quantitative targets are usually set only for non-agricultural employment or for wage-earning employment; and the question of self-employment, especially in farming, is discussed in a qualitative way.

While emphasizing the importance of governmental measures for the expansion of employment opportunities, it is recognized that an adequate pace of economic expansion will remain crucial. As argued in Kenya, "the full solution in terms of the complete elimination of unproductive underemployment, can only be found in a long-term sustained high rate of economic growth, generating employment opportunities at a significantly higher rate than the annual rate of increase of the working population".[46]

In some countries, notably Kenya and the United Republic of Tanzania, the objective of employment creation is also linked with the need for enabling low incomes to grow at a faster rate than the average. The present inequalities of income between a small number of highly remunerated individuals on the one hand and the great mass of the people on the other are considered onerous. Particularly in the context of the strategy of rural development, to which considerable attention has been given in some of the recent plans, the shift in the distribution of income in favour of rural areas and activities is considered to be an important means of promoting self-employment.

Approaches to the employment problem

Utilization of existing production capacity

One way to raise the level of employment immediately would be to utilize the existing production capacity more fully. There are several reasons for the underutilization of capacity in many African countries. For instance, the departure of colonial armies and officials led to a sudden reduction in demand for a number of food products, such as white bread, pasta, biscuits and wine, particularly in northern Africa. Moreover, the shortages of technicians and managers aggravated the underutilization of capacity in the existing food-processing installations. Further, in the countries with large deficits in their balance of payments, the shortages of imported materials have proved to be an important contributory factor. To cope with these difficulties, it has become necessary to find new outlets for the products of the under-utilized industries. Where feasible, foreign skilled labour has been used to meet the immediate needs, but ultimately it is essential to develop vocational skills within the country. To avoid shortages of imports, the need for careful foreign exchange budgeting and for export promotion has become acute. The solutions are not easy, but they constitute an important task to which the planners are increasingly turning.

Wage and price policies

In a number of African countries, the need is recognized to provide an appropriate set of incentives and disincentives to establish a balance between the supply and demand for labour, in both rural and urban areas. In Ghana, for example, the Government reorganized the former Incomes Commission, which lacked both the control over prices and the legal backing to enforce its decisions, into the Prices and Incomes Board, with the aim of bringing the review of prices of essential commodities under its control; this is to be backed by legislation requiring all bodies concerned with the determination and regulation of wages and salaries to work within the framework of a national incomes policy.[47] The incomes policy in Kenya is meant to attain the general objectives of increasing production and employment with the two additional objectives of obtaining a fair distribution of national income and of holding down costs and prices to avoid balance-of-payments problems, which ultimately also affect employment. It is stated that the policy will seek to ensure that a large proportion of the gain in productivity is used to create employment opportunities rather than to increase wages.[48] In 1970, the Government, private employers and trade unions signed a one-year agreement under which private and government employment would be increased by 10 per cent, while the unions would make no new wage demands.

Industrialization

Apart from high wage rates in the modern sectors, such elements as generous tax concessions, low interest rates and liberal imports of machinery and equipment have provided an inducement for enterprises to adopt labour-saving methods of production. Some of the recent plans and policy statements in Africa show an awareness of the problem. In Ghana, for instance, the Government has announced its intention "in order to encourage the utilization of [the] factor endowments in proportions that reflect their scarcity value . . . to give preference to labour-intensive rather than capital-intensive methods wherever such choices are technically feasible and economically reasonable".[49] Compared to that in South-East Asia or Latin America, however, the discussion on policies in this particular context has been rather limited in Africa.

Recent African plans also give attention to the question of enlarging the range of industrialization which, in most countries of the region, is at present narrow. Industries producing light consumer goods have made progress, but they have also brought in their wake substantial increases in the importation of raw materials, intermediate goods and capital equipment. In order to increase employment and incomes as well as in consideration of the balance of payments, a number of countries are aiming at enlarging the domestic production of intermediate and simpler capital goods.[50]

Rural development

The importance of rural development, has been particularly emphasized in a number of the current plans in Africa. In Ghana, for instance, the Government has pointedly drawn attention to "the great imbalance in the distribution of incomes as well as employment opportunities between rural and urban communities"—a problem which has been "exacerbated by policies pursued earlier and which failed to provide suitable programmes, social infrastructure and amenities for improving the lot of rural communities". The special emphasis now laid by the Government on rural development rests on the premise that "since 60 per cent of the active labour force of the nation reside in the rural areas, a development strategy which takes no cognisance of this runs the risk of being irrelevant."[51] Similarly, in Kenya, "the Government believes that it is only through an accelerated development of the rural areas that balanced economic development can be achieved, that the necessary growth of employment opportunities can be generated and that the people as a whole can participate in the development process".[52]

The measures formulated as part of the rural development strategy in most African countries are quite similar, as can be seen from the following examples. In Ghana, the aim is to improve the economic rewards for farming and other rural activities through the availability of credit on favourable terms, the provision of extension services, the improvement of transportation, the construction of feeder roads and the expansion of marketing facilities. Further, in order to make farm careers more attractive as viable, alternatives to urban jobs and as part of the drive to improve rural living conditions, the provision of good drinking water, health facilities and electricity is considered important. In Kenya, the creation of job opportunities in the rural areas—both wage jobs and self-employment—is sought through the provision of credit, training and managerial advice. The provision of rural water-supplies, the improvement of rural housing and transport and the strengthening of administration at the local level are also stressed. In Egypt, to reduce seasonal unemployment and to expand total labour use, the rural development policy calls for the intensification and diversification of production, better water use, the introduction of new crops, the development of animal husbandry, a greater supply of agricultural requisites and the enlargement of production units to make them economically viable. In Morocco, in addition to expansion in farming, reductions in unemployment and underemployment have been sought through reafforestation, fruit growing and the improvement and extension of irrigation.

In a number of African countries—for example, in Kenya and the United Republic of Tanzania—the creation of additional employment opportunities has been sought through land settlement schemes. The opening up of new land has, however, commonly proved to be a highly mechanized and costly process.

An important element of the rural development strategy in many

African countries is the expansion of handicraft production, which is usually undertaken as part of the agricultural activity. Governments have aimed at expanding the output of handicrafts, thereby raising rural employment and incomes, by providing financial assistance and facilities for research, training and marketing.

Manpower training

As mentioned earlier, many African countries gained political independence comparatively recently, and a critical limiting factor to their economic and social progress has been the inadequacy of the number of highly trained and educated persons. In order to implement their development plans, these countries needed to increase the numbers of such persons as rapidly as possible, while often retaining substantial numbers of foreigners or "expatriates". Over the years there has been a substantial increase in national skills. While compared to those of other developing regions shortages of trained manpower are still great, some imbalance between the types of work available and the skills and preferences of job-seekers has appeared in certain instances. In Ghana, for example, a school-leaver possessing a general elementary education is not well placed for seeking employment in the labour market since the vacancies are mainly for trained craftsmen, technicians and those seeking middle-level occupations. In Egypt, which has a longer history of education expansion, the problem of unemployment among the educated, while there are shortages of middle-level technicians, bears a close resemblance to that encountered in India. In such circumstances, the need for expansion of vocational and technical institutions, for a better balance between different levels of education and for reforms in the content of education has been acute. Since 1966, a number of modifications have been introduced in Egypt to achieve these objectives. In most African countries, however, the problems of educational and manpower planning are only now beginning to receive serious attention.

Population policy

Some attention has also been paid to the longer term growth of population and of the labour force and its implications for employment opportunities. Several African countries have announced the desirability of family planning to reduce the birth-rate; but on the whole, thus far, this has had little effect. Often the implementation of family planning policies has not been vigorous. The pilot centres for promoting family planning in a number of instances have been confined to urban areas. There have also been instances of popular resistance, especially in the rural areas. In general, a firm base for a long-term population policy in Africa has yet to be laid.

Meanwhile, some African countries have promoted emigration as a means of alleviating unemployment. For example, the number of persons emigrating from Morocco to Europe and the Libyan Arab Republic increased approximately from 9,000 in 1968 to 24,000 in 1969 and 33,000 in 1970. Such a policy cannot, however, be more than a partial short-term solution; nor can it be appropriate for every country.

NOTES

[1] This rate is based on index numbers of production. The previously cited figure of 7 per cent is derived from the data on national accounts.

ANNEX

[1] The expression "South-East Asia" has been used in this paper as a convenient abbreviation to denote the group of the developing market economies in southern, south-eastern and eastern Asia, that is, the Asian countries stretching from Pakistan to the Republic of Korea.

[2] M. Blaug, R. P. G. Layard and M. Woodhall, Causes of Graduate Unemployment in India (London, 1969).

[3] V. M. Dandekar and N. Rath, "Poverty in India", Economic and Political Weekly (Bombay), 2 and 9 January 1971.

[4] Central Bank of Ceylon, Survey of Ceylon's Consumer Finances, 1963, part II (Colombo), p. 55.

[5] India, Planning Commission, Report of the Committee on Distribution of Income and the Levels of Living (New Delhi, 1964), p. 82.

[6] G. F. Papanek, Pakistan's Development: Social Goals and Private Incentives (Cambridge, Massachusetts, 1967), pp. 67-68.

[7] India, Planning Commission, Report of the Committee on Distribution of Income and Levels of Living (New Delhi, 1964-1969), p. 28.

[8] India, Planning Commission, Fourth Five-Year Plan (New Delhi, 1970), p. 19.

[9] Malaysia, Second Malaysia Plan (Kuala Lumpur, 1971), pp. 5-6.

[10] Ceylon, Ministry of Planning and Employment, The Five-Year Plan (Colombo, 1971), p. 59.

[11] Pakistan, Planning Commission, The Fourth Five-Year Plan (Islambad, 1970), p. 103.

[12] India, Fourth Five-Year Plan, p. 135.

[13] Pakistan, The Fourth Five-Year Plan, p. 106.

[14] Ibid., p. 7.

[15] Philippines, Four-Year Development Plan FY 1972-75 (Manila, 1971), p. 130.

[16] Pakistan, The Fourth Five-Year Plan, p. 15.

[17] India, Planning Commission, Plan Evaluation Organisation, Report on Evaluation of Rural Manpower Project (New Delhi, 1967), quoted in R. Gupta, "Rural works programme--where it has gone astray", Economic and Political Weekly (Bombay), 15 May 1971.

[18] Pakistan, The Fourth Five-Year Plan, p. 110.

[19] Latin American Institute of Economic and Social Planning, Transformacion y Desarrollo (Santiago, Chile, 1970). In Latin America and the Caribbean, according to the data compiled by the Statistical office of the United Nations, industrial employment increased during the period 1960-1969 at the annual rate of 2.5 per cent.

[20] International Labour Office, Towards Full Employment (Geneva, 1970), p. 21.

[21] Latin American Institute for Economic and Social Planning, Transformacion y Desarrollo. For the period 1960-1969, the data compiled by the Statistical Office of the United Nations for Latin America and the Caribbean show the annual rates of growth of output to be as follows: gross domestic product, 5 per cent; agricultural output, 3 per cent; industrial output, 6 per cent.

[22] In Chile, La Gran Mineria del Cobre has not increased employment in the past decade, and even the doubling of production capacity which occurred by the end of the 1960s did not require any significant additional manpower. Petroleum and asphalt mining in Trinidad and Tobago have decreased employment by about 20 per cent in the past decade, although output has increased considerably. In Brazil and Colombia, because of the demand situation and increases in productivity, activities related to

coffee production have failed to increase employment.

[23] About 900,000 in Rio de Janeiro in the early 1960s. See Instituto Brasileiro de Administracao Municipal, Revista de Administracao Municipal (Rio de Janeiro), No. 100, May–June 1970.

[24] Economic Survey of Latin America, 1968 (United Nations publication, Sales No. E.70.II.G.I), p. 9.

[25] Ibid., table 9.

[26] The estimates of per capita product of these countries, as explained above, are as follows: Brazil, $379; Colombia, $367; Mexico, $677; Peru, $450.

[27] For example, see Brazil, Presidencia da Republica, Plano Trienal de Desenvolvimento Economico e Social, 1963-1965 (Rio de Janeiro, 1963); Chile, Ministerio de Economia, Corporacion de Fomento de la Produccion, Programa Nacional de Desarrollo Economico, 1961-1970 (Santiago de Chile, 1961); Colombia, Consejo National de Politica Economica y Planeacion, Plan General de Desarrollo Economico y Social, 1961-1970 (Bogota, 1962); Trinidad and Tobago, Five-Year Development Programme, 1958-1962 (Government Printing Office).

[28] As it is expressed in one plan, "it is usually much easier to achieve the economic objectives than the employment objective" [Trinidad and Tobago, Second Five-Year Plan, 1964-1968 (Port-of-Spain, 1965), p. 143].

[29] For example, see Brazil, Presidencia da Republica, Metas e Bases para a Acao de Governo (Brasilia, September 1970), part I, chap. III: "Objectivos, estrategia, grandes prioridades"; Chile, Oficina de Planificacion Nacional, El Desarrollo Economico y Social de Chile en la Decada 1970-1980, cap. III, "Los recursos humanos y la politica social": Colombia, Departamento Nacional de Planeacion, Plan de Desarrollo Economico y Social, 1970-1973, cap. III, "Politica de empleo"; Trinidad and Tobago, Third Five-Year Plan, 1969-1973 (Port-of-Spain, Government Printery, 1970), part II, "Human resources and manpower planning".

[30] Trinidad and Tobago, Third Five-Year Plan, 1969-1973, p. 50.

[31] Colombia, Plan de Desarrollo Economico y Social, 1970-1973, p. 12 (unofficial translation). For a more detailed analysis, see International Labour Office, Towards Full Employment (Geneva, 1970).

[32] In the long run, however, the agricultural employment co-efficient is likely to decrease. In Argentina, in fact, the absolute level of employment decreased during the period 1950-1965, although agricultural production increased significantly. See Latin American Institute for

Economic and Social Planning, *Transformacion y Desarrollo* (Santiago, Chile, 1970).

[33] See, for example, Colombia, *Plan de Desarrollo Economico y Social 1970-1973*, chap VIII, "Sector agropecuario, reforma agraria".

[34] See, for example, Chile, *El Desarrollo Economico y Social de Chile en la Decada 1970-1980*, chap. II-B, "La politica de desarrollo del sector agropecuario"; and Trinidad and Tobago, *Third Five-Year Plan, 1969-1973*, "Sectoral programmes, agriculture".

[35] Latin American Institute for Economic and Social Planning, *Transformacion y Desarrollo*, and Brazil, *Metas e Bases para Acao de Governo*.

[36] See, for example, Chile, *El Desarrollo Economico y Social de Chile en la Decada 1970-1980* and Colombia, *Plan de Desarrollo Economico y Social, 1970-1973*.

[37] See, for example, Brazil, *Metas e Bases para a Acao de Governo*.

[38] See, for example, Chile, *El Desarrollo Economico y Social de Chile en la Decada 1970-1980* and Brazil, *Plano Trienal de Desenvolvimento Economico e Social, 1963-1965*.

[39] See Chile, *El Desarrollo Economico y Social de Chile en la Decade 1970-1980*, chap. V, "Regionalizacion del desarrollo", part B, "Modificaciones y cambios tecnologicos en transporte y comunicaciones y turismo"; Colombia, *Plan de Desarrollo Economico y Social, 1970-1973*, chap. VIII-3, "Turismo"; Trinidad and Tobago, *Third Five-Year Plan, 1969-1973*, "Sectoral programmes--tourism".

[40] Brazil, *Metas e Bases para a Acao de Governo*.

[41] Trinidad and Tobago, *Third Five-Year Plan, 1969-1973*, p. 306.

[42] See *Economic Survey of Africa*, vol. II. North African Sub-region (United Nations publication, Sales No. E.67.II.K.20), p. 129.

[43] For example, see Ethiopia, Planning Board Office, *Second Five-Year Development Plan 1963-1967* (Addis Ababa, 1962), chap. 4, para. 37.

[44] Sudan, *The Ten-Year Plan of Economic and Social Development (1961/62-1970/71)*, p. 55.

[45] United Arab Republic (now Egypt) National Planning Committee, *General Frame of the Five-Year Plan for Economic and Social Development (July 1960-June 1965)* (Cairo, Government Printing Office, 1960), p. 13.

[46] Kenya, Development Plan for the Period 1970-1974 (Nairobi, Government Printing Office, 1969), p. 106.

[47] Ghana, One-Year Development Plan, July 1970 to June 1971, pp. 145-147.

[48] Kenya, Development Plan, 1970-1974, pp. 130-140.

[49] Ghana, One Year Development Plan, p. 147.

[50] For example, see Nigeria, Second National Development Plan, 1970-1974 (Lagos, 1970), chap. 16, and Kenya, Development Plan, 1970-1974, chap. 10.

[51] Ghana, One-Year Development Plan, p. 182.

[52] Kenya, Development Plan, 1970-1974, p. 2.

The Fiscal Policy Aspect of Development Strategy

DIRK J. WOLFSON

Now that we have gained some experience in international development, policymakers and economists in both developing and capital-exporting countries are getting increasingly interested in taking stock of where the development effort is getting us. In other words, we are becoming performance-conscious.

Fiscal policy can be very helpful in improving performance. Over the years, there has been a growing discomfort with the way the "invisible hand" was handling things with respect to resource allocation, income distribution, and economic stabilisation, particularly in relatively underdeveloped areas. In these areas, indeed, the harmonisation of economic activity by means of the market mechanism leaves so much to be desired that they have been described as areas where, left to themselves, the determinants of economic development fail to harmonise effectively over a long period.[1]

Fiscal policy is the branch of economic policy best suited to deal with market failures. Its task is threefold: the improvement of the allocation of economic resources, the distribution of income, and the stabilisation of the economy. Its main instruments are taxation, financial management and government spending. This article offers a short introduction to the use of these instruments.

I. TAXATION

Before discussing tax policy generally, it should be noted

From **INTERNATIONAL DEVELOPMENT REVIEW**, 3/1973, (7-34), reprinted by permission of the publisher.

that government revenues also consist of various non-tax receipts, of which fees for services rendered are generally the most important. Although the <u>quid pro quo</u> involved and the generally voluntary nature of the transaction distinguish these from taxation and limit the extent to which resource transfers of this kind can be imposed, consistency requires that utility rates, harbour dues and the like be set in concert with a government's overall objectives in terms of taxation. Fiscal policy, therefore, should encompass <u>all</u> receipts of the public sector, regardless of whether they are labelled tax revenues or public service receipts, or whether they are chanelled through the central budget or not.

The fact that some of the services provided by a government yield readily identifiable user benefits (e.g., power, or safe anchorage in a port) which warrant a charge per unit of usage in lieu of financing out of general government revenues does not mean that these services are not part of the government revenue base. Some of these services are necessarily run at a deficit (e.g., hospitals, telecommunications) to be subsidized out of general revenues. By the same token, there is no <u>a priori</u> reason why other services should not be run at a surplus, introducing an element of taxation in the rate structure, if the demand for these services is strong enough and if the users can afford to pay. Even when these services are provided by agencies with budgetary autonomy and surpluses are kept under earmark for internal use and not paid over to the central budget, these surpluses are part of a government's "earning power" which is one and indivisible.

The Tax Effort

In the course of the development process, the level of government spending is, in real terms, determined by the sum of a country's tax effort, its ability to attract private domestic savings, and its success in contracting foreign loans and international aid. The tax effort, however, generally is the crucial factor. In the face of an insatiable need for public services, the capacity to generate public savings (the surplus of public revenues over recurrent expenditures) is often the major constraint. As raising the level of public savings tends to reduce private savings and private capital formation, a careful analysis of the tax base is called for in redistributing resources from the private to the public sector, if overall growth is to be maximised.

Considerable extra leeway may be granted, however, if a country has rich natural resources. Extractive industries attract large flows of foreign capital, the returns on which can be taxed without affecting domestic private savings. The taxing of non-resident income is shifted abroad, both for the individual and in the aggregate, as this segment of a country's tax effort is made at the cost of foreign rather than domestic private savings and capital formation.

Obviously, this way of transferring resources internationally by taxing non-resident income might endanger the investment climate and kill the goose with the golden eggs, if pushed to the extent that the overall tax burden becomes prohibitive. Any investment or business transaction that transcends the frontiers of a particular country gives rise to at least two potential tax claims -- that of the investor's country of domicile and that of the country in which the investment is made or the business transaction takes effect. Double taxation, however, is automatically avoided if the investor's country of domicile grants, as a matter of statutory law, a credit against taxes paid by its residents to foreign governments, as some of the major capital-exporting countries do, and insofar as the foreign liability does not exceed what would have been payable at home. With capital exporters that do not grant unilateral statutory relief, bilateral arrangements may be worked out, such as treaties whereby both parties agree to tax at source and forego the taxation of foreign source income of their residents. Capital-importing countries generally stand to gain from such treaties.[2]

The bulk of the tax effort, however, will have to be made at home. Therefore, tough political choices will have to be made and hardnosed judgements applied to fend off pressures for undue privileges and unjustified tax exemptions.

So much for the level of taxation, but any country's tax effort has three dimensions: level, structure and administration. The structure is really the centerpiece, as it determines the ease with which any given level can be achieved and the efficiency with which taxes will be administered. It also holds the key to allocating, redistributing and stabilising functions of tax policy.

Taxation and the Allocation of Resources

As to allocation, a consistent tax policy which covers all public receipts can do much more than just provide the resources with which a government can play its spending role in the economy. It can also directly influence the utilisation of resources in the economy at large by providing guidance to the entrepreneurial decisions made by individuals.

In the field of consumption, we have grown accustomed to the distinction between merit goods, which should be offered below cost (education), and demerit goods, which are taxed at discouraging rates (cigarettes). In the field of production, however, the steering potential of taxation is often insufficiently recognized. A properly structured stumpage fee, for example, can encourage the expolitation of hitherto unmarketable timber species by setting a low rate for these, while controlling the depletion of the more profitable species through higher rates. Likewise, harbour dues and utility rates should primarily be looked at with a view to securing the efficient use of these facilities, since, once the initial public investment is made, it is more important to make the best possible use of it than to attempt to cover just the current and capital outlays.

For example, in some cases, charges that do not cover the total cost may help an under-utilised port to generate traffic. On the other hand, a busy port could seriously consider charging more than its full cost so as to discourage marginal cargoes that sooner or later would necessitate expensive expansion. As long as cargoes pay their full cost on the basis of a properly structured rate, they are not marginal to the economy as a whole and should not be discouraged per se. But they may well become marginal to an individual port that is close to its full capacity. In this case, the rate structure may be used to divert traffic to other ports in order to achieve a better utilisation of a nation's -- or even a region's -- total port capacity.

Sectoral targets may be achieved through the earmarking of revenues for specific expenditures. In a way, this is done by creating autonomous agencies and setting aside port revenues for port development, utility revenues for utility development, etc. It could also be done through user taxes -- by setting aside gasoline and motor vehicle taxes in a road fund, for example. In these cases, there is still a direct link between the purpose of the tax and the interest of the individual taxpayer who foots the bill. But certain taxes could be earmarked regardless of such a link in order to dramatise a national commitment. In many countries, certain specified tax proceeds, such as royalties due from extractive industries, are set aside for development purposes. It is, of course, easier to do this with new sources of revenue than through diversion of existing sources from the general revenues.

The disadvantage of earmarking is that it tends to blur the basic concept of unity of a government's resources. Therefore, the political advantages of dramatising a commitment should be carefully weighed against the loss of allocative flexibility in the financial system. There is a danger of financial compartmentalisation, which in turn may lead to rigidities that prejudice allocative decisions and may reduce the efficiency of a government's intervention in the economy. This danger may be neutralised by a sophisticated management of financial resources, as elaborated upon below.

Taxation and the Redistribution of Income

As a tool of income redistribution, tax policy can be used in more than one way. In the first place it can be used within a nation, by such well-known measures as progressive taxation on income and wealth and high import or internal taxes on luxury items.

What is not always realised, however, is that such measures can also contribute to a more equitable income distribution internationally -- that is, between rich and poor countries. Particularly in a small country with an important extractive industry, a large share of the relatively well-to-do people may be expatriates, who often are in a position to shift the tax burden imposed on them to their foreign government or company by means of cost-of-living allowances. Here again, tax policy has to play the whole field. Thus port profits may be largely at the expense of foreign shareholders in mining companies -- often the major users -- or, when imports of luxury consumer goods are involved, at the expense of the well-to-do. Insofar as high port dues threatened to raise the domestic price of mass consumption items like rice, compensation could be found in lower import duties for such items. Likewise, income redistribution calls for fairly high power rates for large private consumers: "Make those who can afford air conditioners pay for bringing light bulbs to the poor."

A more direct way of redistributing income between rich and poor nations is through withholding taxes on income derived by non-resident foreigners, which has already been touched upon above. In this connection, it is gratifying to note that many developing countries have managed to conclude treaties for the avoidance of double taxation with capital-exporting countries so as to integrate foreign investments more fully into their tax base without hurting their investment climate.

Good utilisation of the potential of taxation to redistribute income internationally is of prime importance for developing countries, as it makes them less dependent on the initiatives which the rich countries of the world take.

A final word on intersectoral distribution, which marks the border line between distribution and allocation. Jacking up luxury taxes and earmarking the proceeds for the development of agriculture tends to redistribute income from the urban to the rural population. It also helps to slow down urbanisation and urban unemployment. In short, it kills a distributive and an allocative bird with one stone.

Taxation and Stability

In the larger industrial countries, fluctuations of income and employment originate mainly at home, which facilitates stabilisation efforts on the part of the government, as the roots of instability are within its own jurisdiction. In primary producing countries, however, the major destabilising impulses are fluctuations in commodity prices on the world market and the uneven flow of foreign investment capital. Such disturbances, emanating from abroad and beyond the control of the national authorities, make stabilisation policy more difficult, although not necessarily futile.[3]

One way of dampening the impact of export price fluctuations on the domestic economy is to have a sliding scale of export duties, going up as prices go up, and down as prices fall. This way, part of the burden of adjustment is shifted from the private sector to the government. A safer and more comprehensive procedure is to entrust the marketing of primary exports to a government marketing board. An active policy of price intervention by means of a marketing board has administrative advantages over the use of fluctuating export taxes; it also provides a better opportunity to shield the economy as a whole from price fluctuations by separating marketing board reserves from ordinary budget resources.

Generally, however, the marketing board approach is only realistic for the export of farm products. The marketing of plantation products (rubber, palm oil, and the like) and minerals is often firmly in the hands of large corporations and concessionaires. With respect to concessions, stabilisation might best be effected by requiring a large royalty component in their tax liability. Thus the burden of adjustment would be borne mainly by the shareholders who may not feel the need to adjust their spending patterns accordingly and who are -- more often than not -- non-residents anyway.

Tax Administration

Whatever a government's intentions in terms of growth, allocation, distribution or stabilisation, a major constraint bedevilling a developing country's tax effort is the shaky state of its tax administration. Therefore, considerations of both equity and efficiency require that, as long as checks and balances are insufficiently developed to avoid widespread tax evasion, care should be taken in the selection of the tax base to ensure that tax liabilities can be determined and enforced simply and irrefutably. During the early stages of development in particular, this introduces a certain bias towards export duties over direct taxes, and towards fees for services rendered over indirect taxes. I hesitate to bring up the subject of harbour dues once more, but it does explain my preference for taxing at a point where most goods have to pass.

II. FINANCIAL MANAGEMENT AND DEBT MANAGEMENT

Financial management encompasses everything that happens with the funds derived from public revenues from the moment they are collected until the moment they are spent or, sometimes, overspent. In other words, it includes debt management. Hence, the central issue of financial management is how to match the flow of expenditure, as planned in the annual budget appropriations, with the flow of public revenues. Since the two flows will never exactly tally, there are problems of how to provide temporary resources to secure a proper functioning of government during the lean months of the year and, alternatively, of what to do with the money during those periods that the liquid assets of a government are in excess of its current liabilities.

Financial management always seems to end up as the Cinderella of fiscal policy. With tax policy and government spending continuously in the limelight, the management of financial resources escapes the public eye and therefore is often conveniently ignored. Yet it is as important as tax and expenditure policies in achieving government objectives in the field of allocation, redistributive justice and stabilisation.

Debt and the Transfer of Resources

The connoisseur of matters monetary will have noticed that in the previous two paragraphs I have committed the misdemeanour of speaking of debt management, financial management and resource management as if they were one and the same thing. As a matter of fact, in a developing country they are more closely interlinked than is generally recognized. In those countries, the classical assumption that the creation of debt vis-a-vis private (nonbank) parties implies the transfer of real resources to the public sector more or less applies, for the simple reason that developed capital markets are virtually absent. Anyone who buys government debt parts with his money indeed and acquires an asset that, generally, is hard to sell without incurring substantial losses. Until redemption, therefore, government debt placed among the population and taxation have a similar impact on private spending.

Although the voluntary response to offerings of domestic public debt is generally limited in developing countries, it may be worthwhile to explore domestic borrowing capacity carefully. Owners of wealth who would not dream of paying taxes may well be prepared to offer their resources if they keep title to them and earn interest. And a carefully stage-managed borrowing program which succeeds in coaxing property owners to sell off their holdings of precious metals, or to start exploiting rather than just accumulating herds of cattle, means that the debt created by the government finds its counterpart in real terms. It is a simple truth that, in its early stages, development is more often hurt by conspicuous saving than by conspicuous consumption.

The attraction of such borrowing operations is that they broaden the fiscal base without increasing the tax burden. Thus negative production incentives and a decline in private savings can be avoided or at least postponed. Insofar as the amounts borrowed are put to a more productive use than they would have been in the private sector, there is a net welfare gain.

Let me reiterate that experience so far with domestic voluntary lending in most developing countries has not been encouraging. A considerable amount of sophistication and confidence in the security of property and in the value of money are essential conditions for government debt to attract private savings in competition with the accumulation of more traditional forms of wealth. What justifies my emphasis in this article on what might seem an academic point is that the dormant potential for domestic government borrowing is often insufficiently realized.[4] In recognizing this potential, governments may find additional encouragement to work towards meeting the conditions precedent to its success.

In many developing countries, however, the debt is largely foreign. Contracting foreign debt has an attraction over contracting domestic debt in that the resources are not bidden away from alternative domestic uses. Therefore, a foreign loan never affects domestic private capital formation.

Burdens, Real and Imaginary

Servicing the existing domestic debt brings about a redistribution of tax income to the holders of the debt. In real terms, therefore, it should not pose a burden on the economy as a whole, whether we like the redistributive implications of interest payments within the economy or not. When a country is spending a substantial part of its budget on debt service, however, the burden of the debt may become very real indeed, claiming an inordinate amount of the economy's taxable capacity. Insofar as it is politically impossible to raise taxes along with an increasing debt burden, other public current and capital expenditures drop below the optimal pattern, or else inflationary pressures merge.[5] Servicing foreign loans always burdens the domestic economy. Resources are not merely redistributed among residents, but transferred abroad. This highlights the need for a sophisticated policy of debt management, aimed at evening out capital flows that might throw the economy off balance.

Management, Efficiency and Control

In the absence of developed financial markets, the potential for an active policy of stabilisation through debt management is obviously small. A first prerequisite, however, is to consider, administer and control the public liquid assets in their entirety and not on the basis of where in the public sector they happen to accrue. Once the principle is recognized that non-tax public service revenues of autonomous agencies such as utility companies, port authorities, postal services, etc., conceptually are similar to those of other agencies of government that are administered under the central budget, it no longer makes sense to undermine the consistency of financial policy by scattering the financial resources of the public sector. Such financial fragmentation creates states within the state, making an inefficient maze out of what should be a clearly conceived and efficient financial structure. Moreover, bringing the management of marketing board resources within the purview of the treasury may often create the only genuine possibility for debt management.

On the other hand, the improvement in performance which is envisaged by the decentralisation of decision-making in autonomous agencies should not be infringed upon. In short, what is needed is to find ways of pooling the financial resources of the public sector, without infringing on the financial autonomy of the self-budgeting agencies.

The satisfaction of these two seemingly conflicting desiderata is probably best guaranteed in countries following French financial traditions. There, financial systems have evolved that are based on an almost complete centralisation of the financial transactions of the public sector through the treasury (not in the treasury). These treasuries pool all, or practically all, cash balances of the public sector in one balance at the central bank, but internally maintain a double bookkeeping system with separate accounts for the central government, for special funds (such as trusts funds), and for the liquid assets of autonomous public agencies. This centralisation of resources enables the treasury to function as a banker for the public sector as a whole, meeting the day-to-day credit requirements of individual public entities from its central pool, which, within certain limits, may be backed up with facilities from the central bank.

As long as a government continues to balance its budget and the autonomous public agencies are, by and large, run on a "pay as you go" basis, such pooling of resources should virtually obviate the need for overdraft facilities and substantially reduce the interest burden on the public sector. It would put an end to the absurd situation of some segments of the public sector paying high interest on overdrafts, whilst others are sitting on surplus cash generating far lower interest income only because the various agencies of government fail to see that the government's resources are one and indivisible, even if they are administered separately.

From a policy viewpoint, however, the potential interest savings constitute only part of the case for pooling the liquid resources of the public sector. It also rests on the benefits in terms of accountability, control and management of a country's resources. Rather than going through periodic exercises that "any government money that is anywhere must be somewhere" and then setting out on a treasure hunt to find it, it is much more sensible to have an accounting system that provides a comprehensive daily record of all the public sector's current assets and liabilities. This is more than a convenience; it is a prerequisite for efficient financial and monetary management. A government that wants to pursue a responsible overall fiscal policy to attain its objectives in allocation, redistributive justice and stabilisation needs an overall view of the financial state of the economy.

As briefly noted above in reference to marketing boards, the main potential of financial resource management is in stabilising the economy by ensuring that the show can go on if the financial situation gets tight and by putting on the brakes if the economy gets overheated. Great care should be taken, however, to ensure that such efforts are made in close concert with the monetary policy pursued by the central bank.[6]

III. GOVERNMENT SPENDING: THE ALLOCATIVE FUNCTION OF THE BUDGET

Public expenditures represent the main thrust of a government's intervention to improve the performance of the economy. Therefore, once the budget has been carefully prepared (in terms of both size and structure) to reflect the best policy-making government can do, it is important that the appropriations are actually spent and that the implementation of the budget is not frustrated. Underspending a good budget is a doubtful achievement. It can only mean that government activities were at a lower level than intended, or that certain areas, which were important enough to get the initial appropriations, lagged behind.

The tragedy is that the casualties always tend to be in the development effort. Development expenditures in general have longer lead periods than current expenditures, since their implementation is not routine. Dedication to economic development is not everywhere strongly ingrained, and some politicians may be tempted when they see that development appropriations remain unspent, yet current expenditures on such nice things as participation in conferences abroad seem to be handicapped for lack of money. Under such circumstances, pressures for budgetary transfers emerge. The things that slip into the budget this way are often expenditures that were rejected as of lesser priority at the time of preparation of the original budget (foreign travel, official cars, etc.), and, adding insult to injury, they tend to be disproportionately expensive in terms of foreign exchange.

It is important, therefore, that the development-oriented elements in the body politic stick to their guns and make sure that unspent development balances and their foreign exchange counterpart are safeguarded, if need be by carrying them over to the next year, or by setting development resources aside in a development fund, whence a separate development budget is administered. Again, the role of such a fund is to dramatize a commitment and, like all earmarked funds, this is done at the cost of budgetary flexibility. Moreover, it should be recognized that the availability of some real domestic resources -- such as qualified manpower -- cannot be "carried over"; once a man-year is gone, it is gone. But other resources, most notably foreign exchange, can be.

This is not to say that the amount of development spending for any year should be primarily determined by the expenditure arrears of the past regardless of the level of economic activity presently prevailing, nor that the wisdom of past appropriations should be taken for granted and considered immune to review. The point is, rather, that the development effort as expressed by the share of the national product set aside in the original budget estimate should not be allowed to dwindle away as a result of institutional factors. A country that budgets $10 million in development expenditures out of a total of $100 million fools itself by "saving" $5 million in unspent development appropriations, if the "saving" is applied to additional non-development expenditures in supplementary budgets in the course of the year. That way, development targets erode and the allocative function of the budget is jeopardised, as the increased level of recurrent spending mortgages the future capacity to invest.

The Budget as a Stabiliser

Clearly, the above argument rests on the assumptions that the budget indeed reflects the considered priorities of the government, that the underlying plans are sound, realistic and properly timed, and that expenditure controls are effective. For all the emphasis on underspending, we should not forget that overspending a budget that has been carefully matched with the overall economic situation can be just as disruptive. This matching does not mean that the budget always has to be in balance. As a matter of fact, in most countries the main stabilising function of each individual budget is to be not in balance but in surplus or deficit, depending on the state of the economy. Out of this macro-economic insight, the concept of "functional finance" developed. A policy of functional finance cannot be fully effective unless it is backed by a consistent monetary policy to reconcile the financial management of the government with the volume of credit to the private sector.

Nevertheless, the public sector remains primarily responsible for the stabilisation of the economy, both for reasons of principle (in that only the government can be expected to adjust its spending pattern on behalf of its macro-economic responsibilities) and for the more pragmatic reason that, particularly during early stages of development, the public sector comprises a very substantial part of the monetized economy. Therefore, considerations of economic stability should loom large in allocative decisions. Anything that is done to diversify the economy in a meaningful way benefits stability. Likewise, investments that reduce price swings for individual products, such as storage facilities or farm roads that widen the market, are helpful in increasing the economy's resilience. Good development programming helps too, as it tends to reduce the other -- and often overlooked -- root cause of instability: the fluctuations in the flow of foreign aid.

The Distributive Function of Public Spending

To further redistributive justice, government spending can intervene both directly and indirectly -- directly, by granting subsidies or price support (apart from considerations of economic stability and continuity of production, it may be felt that equity demands that producers should be enabled to maintain a basic income in the face of adverse price developments), and indirectly, by investing in areas, such as education, that tend to reduce inequities of opportunity.

NOTES

[1] See P. D. Hajela, "Under-developed Areas -- An Economic Perspective," The Indian Journal of Economics, July 1959.

[2] The nature and extent of the gain will have to be ascertained on a case-by-case basis in view of the many intricacies involved in this highly technical field. For a brief introduction to these problems, see Tax Treaties between Developed and Developing Countries (New York: United Nations, 1969).

[3] See Rasheed O. Khalid, "Fiscal Policy, Development Planning, and Annual Budgeting," International Monetary Fund Staff Papers, March 1969.

[4] For further reading on the difference between actual and potential economic surplus, see Raja J. Chelliah, Fiscal Policy in Underdeveloped Countries with Special Reference to India (London: George Allen & Unwin, 1960), pp. 63-67, reprinted in Richard M. Bird and Oliver Oldman, eds., Readings on Taxation in Developing Countries, Revised Edition (Baltimore: Johns Hopkins, 1967), pp. 41-44.

[5] In the professional literature, there is a lot of confusion with regard to the "burden" of the domestic debt; for an excellent survey article which puts things straight, see C. S. Shoup, "Debt Financing and Future Generations," The Economic Journal, December 1962, pp. 887-98, reprinted in J. M. Ferguson, Public Debt and Future Generations (Chapel Hill: University of North Carolina Press, 1964), pp. 204-19.

[6] On the difficulties involved and the dangers of insufficient coordination of the fiscal and monetary authorities, especially in currency areas, see Petrus J. van de Ven and Dirk J. Wolfson, "Problems of Budget Analysis and Treasury Management in French-speaking Africa," International Monetary Fund Staff Papers, March 1969, pp. 148-56.

Planned Mobilization of Financial Resources for Development

CENTRE FOR DEVELOPMENT PLANNING, PROJECTIONS AND POLICIES OF THE DEPARTMENT OF ECONOMIC AND SOCIAL AFFAIRS OF THE UNITED NATIONS SECRETARIAT

In general, as indicated in Chapter I, most developing countries have planned to raise sizably their total investment in relation to gross domestic product during the latter part of the 1970s in order to expand the production of a wide range of goods and services that are required for accelerated economic and social progress. The increase planned in the level of investment can be achieved only if it is matched by a parallel increase in the total supply of saving. A pivotal element of development planning, thus, has lain in the mobilization of the requisite financial resources.

Developing countries have given considerable attention in their current plans to the financial resources that need to be mobilized nationally. Thought has been given in this context to the contribution warranted from both the public and the private sectors of the economy. The requirements of financial resources from abroad, too, figure prominently in most current plans. However, while appropriate efforts can help, the inflow of funds from abroad is not something for the which recipient country has the sole determining voice. Bearing in mind this axiomatic constraint, developing countries have increasingly looked to their own efforts to finance the rise in the level of investment determined by them.

I. TARGETS FOR NATIONAL SAVING AND EXTERNAL RESOURCES

The shifts contemplated by developing countries in the components of the supply of saving to match the planned changes in

From **JOURNAL OF DEVELOPMENT PLANNING** No. 11, 1977, (143-168), reprinted by permission of the publisher.

Table 1 PLANNED AVERAGE ANNUAL CHANGES IN PERCENTAGE SHARES OF GROSS NATIONAL SAVING, EXTERNAL RESOURCES AND TOTAL SUPPLY OF SAVING IN GROSS DOMESTIC PRODUCT FROM BASE YEAR TO FINAL YEAR OF PLAN[a]

Country[b]	Gross national saving	External resources	Total supply of saving
Countries indicating a planned annual increase of 1 percentage point or more in percentage share of gross national saving in gross domestic product			
Jordan	3.8	−5.1	−1.3
Iran	3.7	−2.9	0.8
Sierra Leone	2.1	−1.2	0.9
Argentina	1.9	−0.9	1.0
Morocco	1.9[c]	−0.3[d]	1.6
Indonesia	1.6	−0.5	1.1
Nicaragua	1.6	−0.7	0.9
Philippines	1.4	−0.9	0.5
Bolivia	1.2	−0.2	0.9
Ecuador	1.1	−0.8	0.4
Countries indicating a planned annual increase of 0.4 percentage point or more but less than 1 percentage point in percentage share of gross national saving in gross domestic product			
Guatemala	0.8	−0.7	0.1
Chile	0.7[c]	−0.1[d]	0.6
Costa Rica	0.7	−0.4	0.3
India	0.7	−0.2	0.5
Panama	0.7	−0.1	0.5
Madagascar	0.6[c]	−0.3[d]	0.2
Mali	0.5	1.3	1.7
Uruguay	0.5[c]	0.7[d]	1.2
Barbados	0.4[c]	−0.8[d]	−0.4
Botswana	0.4	−5.3	−5.0
El Salvador	0.4	0.2	0.6
Malawi	0.4	−0.4	0.1

Table 1 (continued)

Country[b]	Gross national saving	External resources	Total supply of saving
Countries indicating a planned annual increase of less than 0.4 percentage point in percentage share of gross national saving in gross domestic product			
Dominican Republic	0.2[c]	−0.2[d]	0.1
Malaysia	0.2	0.1	0.3
Kenya	0.1	0.2	0.3
Venezuela	−0.8[c]	0.5[d]	−0.2
Nigeria	−1.2	2.5	1.3

Source: See table 1.

[a] Estimates have been derived from data in constant prices, generally the prices of the base year of plans.

For Indonesia, Panama and Venezuela, data refer to changes from first year to final year of plan. For details on time periods and differences in concept of gross domestic product, see table 1.

Total supply of saving equals gross domestic capital formation, except for Iran, where it equals gross fixed investment. External resources equal excess of imports over exports of goods and services, including factor income. Gross national saving equals total supply of saving minus external resources.

No sign indicates increase; minus sign indicates decrease. See also footnote 20.

[b] Countries are listed in descending order of their planned annual change in the percentage share of gross national saving in gross domestic product.

[c] Gross domestic saving.

[d] External resources equal excess of imports over exports of goods and services, excluding factor income.

the level of investment during the latter part of the 1970s are depicted in table 1. Since, as mentioned in earlier chapters, the underlying time periods of current development plans differ, the data in that table are shown as annual averages.

It is striking that over a third of the countries -- 10 out of 27 -- have planned to raise the percentage share of the gross national saving in gross domestic product annually by more than one percentage point. The planned yearly increase in the saving ratio as just defined amounts to nearly four percentage points in Iran and Jordan, and to about two percentage points in Argentina, Morocco and Sierra Leone. In more than two fifths of the countries -- 12 out of 27 -- the planned annual increase in the ratio is in the range of 0.4 to 0.8 percentage point, with Guatemala; Chile, Costa Rica, Indian and Panama are nearer the upper end of this range. Among the remaining five of the 27 countries, the Dominican Republic, Kenya and Malaysia have projected a small yearly increase in the ratio, whereas Nigeria and Venezuela -- two major petroleum-exporting countries that have built up a large portfolio of financial assets in recent years -- have signalled their intention to reduce their saving ratios.

The average of the annual increases planned by developing countries in their saving ratios amounts to 0.7 percentage point. While this average is substantially higher than the indicative average of 0.5 percentage point specified for the developing countries as a whole in the International Development Strategy for the Second United Nations Development Decade, it must also be seen against the fact that the developing countries as a group achieved an average annual increase of about 0.8 percentage point in their saving ratio during the first half of the Second Development Decade. Of course, much of the impressive increase recorded in the average resulted from the vigour exhibited by petroleum-exporting countries.

A vivid counterpart of the planned thrust to raise the level of national saving in relation to total output of the economy is the drive in a large majority of developing countries to diminish their relative dependence on external finances. Twenty of the 27 countries listed in table 1., or nearly three fourths of the total number, have planned either to reduce their net inflow of external resources as a proportion of gross domestic product or, in some cases, to augment relatively the net outflow of resources.[1] The dominating tendency, clearly, is to seek a reduction in the relative dependence on external resources as just defined. A particularly sharp reduction has been planned by Botswana and Jordan, followed at some distance by Sierra Leone and thereafter by Barbados, Ecuador, Nicaragua and a number of other countries. In Iran, the net inflow of external resources at the outset of the current plan is expected to give way to a net outflow of resources by the end of the plan. Argentina, Chile, Guatemala and the Philippines expect some increase by the end of their current plans in the net outflow of resources as a proportion of gross domestic product.

Of the seven countries (just over one fourth of the total number) that have indicated an opposite trend with respect to

Table 2 CONFIGURATION OF COUNTRIES ACCORDING TO PLANNED SHARES OF GROSS NATIONAL SAVING AND EXTERNAL RESOURCES IN GROSS DOMESTIC PRODUCT IN FINAL YEAR OF PLAN[a]

Planned share of external resources in gross domestic product (stated as second figure against each country)	Country and planned share of gross national saving in gross domestic product (stated as first figure against each country)[b]						Number of countries
	20 per cent or more		15 per cent or more but less than 20 per cent		Less than 15 per cent		
Nil or target indicating a net outflow of resources as percentage of gross domestic product	Iran	41.2	Chile	18.4[c] −3.4[d]			9
	Venezuela	37.3[c] −12.6	Guatemala	17.4 −4.7			
	Nigeria	35.7 −9.8					
	Argentina	30.1 −11.8					
	Malaysia	29.5 −5.1					
	Dominican Republic	26.1[c] −9.9					
	Philippines	25.7 −0.1					
		−4.4					
Less than 6 per cent	Bolivia	22.4 5.4	Morocco	18.9[c] 4.0[d]	El Salvador	13.9 3.7	9
			Sierra Leone	18.9 5.5	Madagascar	13.3[c] 1.7	
			Ecuador	18.1 4.3	Uruguay	12.7[c] 2.4	
			Indonesia	17.8 5.2			
			India	15.7 0.6			
6 per cent or more	Costa Rica	21.4 7.3	Kenya	19.6 6.2	Mali	12.7 13.0	9
			Nicaragua	16.7 9.1	Barbados	8.7[c] 11.8	
			Botswana	15.8 7.1	Malawi	8.0 10.3	
			Panama	15.2 14.9	Jordan	1.8 20.1	
Number of countries	9		11		7		27

Source: See table 1.
[a] For details on time period and differences in concept of gross domestic product, see table 1.
For definitions of gross national saving and external resources,
Minus sign indicates net outflow of resources.
[b] Countries are listed within each category in descending order of their percentage share of gross national saving in gross domestic product in final year of plan.
[c] Gross domestic saving.

external resources, only four countries -- namely, El Salvador, Kenya, Mali and Uruguay -- have postulated, in a real sense, an increase in relative dependence on external resources. In other words, these four countries expect a deterioration in their balance of payments on current account in relation to gross domestic product, which would need to be covered by an enlarged financial flow from abroad. For the remaining three countries -- Malaysia, Nigeria, and Venezuela -- the indication from table 1 of an increased relative dependence on external resources is more apparent than real; these three countries, in fact, have posited a continued net outflow of resources, albeit at a reduced level in relation to gross domestic product by the end of their current development plans.

If the targets specified for financial resources were achieved, as may be seen from table 2, in one third of the countries for which it has been possible to obtain the relevant information -- 9 out of 27 -- gross national saving in the final year of current plan would amount to more than 20 per cent of gross domestic product. By far the highest target in this respect, 41 per cent, has been set by Iran. Notwithstanding the decline in saving ratio contemplated by Venezuela and Nigeria during the time period of their current plans, these two countries would be among the highest savers in the world, with their saving ratios of 37 per cent and 36 per cent, respectively. Indeed, the fact that these two countries had a very high saving ratio at the outset of their current plans (41 per cent and 42 per cent, respectively), a good part of which was absorbed by a net outflow of external resources to the rest of the world (equal to 12 per cent of gross domestic product in Venezuela and nearly 25 per cent of gross domestic product in Nigeria), by itself helps to explain why these two countries has posited a decline in the saving ratio; their thrust now is to bring about a relative reduction in the net outflow of resources. By the final year of current plan, the ratio of gross national saving to gross domestic product is targeted to amount to about 30 per cent in Argentina and Malaysia and to about 26 per cent in the Dominican Republic and the Philippines. Two fifths of the countries -- 11 out of 27 -- project that the ratio of gross national saving to domestic product in the final year of current plan will be in the range of 15 per cent or more but less than 20 per cent, with Kenya indicating a target that is almost equal to 20 per cent.

In a broad sense, as experience has shown, the attainment of a saving ratio of 15 per cent represents a critical test of a country's ability to be within sight of self-sustained economic and social progress. Thus, if the targets indicated in current plans were achieved, about three fourths of countries -- 20 out of 27 -- would have crossed that critical threshold. In contrast, prominent among the low savers would be Barbados, Jordan and Malawi, whose targets for the saving ratio in the final year of their current plans amount to less than 9 per cent.

It is readily evident from table 2 that one third of the countries -- 9 out of 27 -- expect to have no dependence at all on a net inflow of financial resources from abroad by the final year of their current plans. All of these nine countries, in fact,

Table 3 CONFIGURATION OF COUNTRIES ACCORDING TO PLANNED ANNUAL RATE OF GROWTH OF GROSS DOMESTIC PRODUCT FROM BASE YEAR TO FINAL YEAR OF PLAN AND PLANNED SHARE OF EXTERNAL RESOURCES IN GROSS DOMESTIC PRODUCT IN FINAL YEAR OF PLAN[a]

Country group	Country and planned share of external resources in gross domestic product[b]						Number of countries
	6 per cent or more		Less than 6 per cent		Net outflow (percentage)		
Countries indicating a planned annual rate of growth of gross domestic product of 8 per cent or more	Jordan	20.1 (21.9)	Ecuador	4.3 (22.4)	Venezuela	−9.8 (27.5)	9
	Malawi	10.3 (18.3)			Malaysia	−9.9 (19.5)	
	Botswana	7.1 (22.9)			Nigeria	−11.8 (23.9)	
	Kenya	6.2 (25.7)			Iran	−12.6 (28.6)	
Countries indicating a planned annual rate of growth of gross domestic product of 6 per cent or more but less than 8 per cent	Panama	14.9 (30.1)	Indonesia	5.5 (23.0)	Dominican Republic	−0.1 (26.0)	14
	Mali	13.0 (25.7)	Sierra Leone	5.5 (24.5)	Chile	−3.4 (15.0)	
	Nicaragua	9.1 (25.8)	Bolivia	5.4 (27.7)	Philippines	−4.4 (21.3)	
	Costa Rica	7.3 (28.7)	Morocco	4.0 (22.9)	Guatemala	−4.7 (12.7)	
			El Salvador	3.7 (17.6)	Argentina	−5.1 (25.0)	
Countries indicating a planned annual rate of growth of gross domestic product of less than 6 per cent	Barbados	11.8[c] (20.5)	Uruguay	2.4 (15.1)			4
			Madagascar	1.7 (15.0)			
			India	0.6 (16.3)			
Number of countries		9		9		9	27

Source: See table 1.
[a] For details on time period and differences in concept of gross domestic product, see table 1.
For definitions of external resources and total supply of saving, Minus sign indicates net outflow of resources.
[b] Figures in parentheses refer to total supply of saving as percentage of gross domestic product.
Countries are listed within each category in descending order of their percentage share of external resources in gross domestic product.

expect a net outflow of resources. In another one third of the countries, the net inflow of external resources in the final year of plan is estimated to be positive but less than 6 per cent of gross domestic product. The target as just defined is not far short of 6 per cent in Indonesia and Sierra Leone; whereas in Ecuador, El Salvador and Morocco, it amounts to about 4 per cent. Conspicuous among this group is India whose corresponding target amounts to substantially less than 1 per cent. The remaining one third of the countries expect to be heavily dependent on external resources, in the sense that their net inflow of external finance is estimated to amount to 6 per cent or more of gross domestic product in the final year of plan. The estimated requirement of net external finances is in the range of 10-20 per cent of gross domestic product in Barbados, Jordan, Malawi, Mali and Panama.[2]

The countries that have projected a net outflow of resources by the final year of their plans are mainly those that expect to be high savers -- that is, countries indicating a target of 20 per cent or more for the ratio of gross national saving to gross domestic product. However, two of the nine countries that expect to be high savers -- namely, Bolivia and Costa Rica -- also envisage a substantial net inflow of external resources -- more than 5 per cent and more than 7 per cent, respectively, of gross domestic product in the final year of plan. At the other end of the scale, countries in which the saving ratio is expected to be low -- less than 15 per cent of gross domestic product -- are seeking a large or moderately large inflow of external resources in relation to the size of their economies.

The relation of the planned rate of expansion of the economy to the estimated requirement of the net inflow of external resources, and by inference to the planned level of gross national saving, is brought out in table 3. It is striking that a substantial number of countries that have planned a high (8 per cent or more) or a moderately high (6 per cent or more but less than 8 per cent) annual rate of growth of gross domestic product expect to receive a substantial or large stimulus to economic growth from external resources. This pattern holds for Botswana, Costa Rica, Jordan, Kenya, Malawi, Mali, Nicaragua and Panama. In contrast, Argentina, Chile, the Dominican Republic, Guatemala, Iran, Malaysia, Nigeria, the Philippines and Venezuela have planned to achieve a high nor moderately high rate of economic growth exclusively or largely by means of their own saving effort. In between these two groups of countries are Bolivia, Ecuador, El Salvador, Indonesia, Morocco and Sierra Leone, which expect to achieve a moderately high or even a high rate of economic growth not only by means of their own efforts but also a moderately large contribution from external resources.[3]

The targets set by countries for total supply of saving in the final year of their plans -- that is, the sum of gross national saving and external resources -- are shown in parentheses in table 3. These data help to explain how, for example, Iran and Jordan, although they are at the opposite ends of the spectrum in terms of the target for their own saving, have both planned a high rate of economic growth. Because Iran has postulated a net outflow of resources, whereas Jordan expects to receive a large inflow of external resources, the targets for the total supply of saving in these two countries are not markedly apart. In countries seeking a high or moderately high rate of economic growth, the target for total supply of saving -- which, by definition, equals total gross domestic capital formation -- is generally in excess of 20 per cent of their gross domestic product. Chile and Guatemala are two exceptions to this general pattern. In Chile, as indicated in chapter I, much of the increase in production is expected to come from better use of the under-utilized productive capacity; Guatemala, too, thanks to the vigorous increase expected in agricultural output and to the coming into fruition of some of the investments made prior to the current plan, anticipates that the economy will expand substantially with comparatively little capital formation. In countries seeking a comparatively low rate of economic growth, the target for the total supply of saving is also in general comparatively low -- 15 or 16 per cent of gross domestic product in India, Madagascar and Uruguay, for instance.

Notwithstanding the decline planned in the relative dependence on external resources, many countries expect that a substantial part of their total investments by the end of their current plans will still be financed by external resources. Thus, seven of the 27 countries listed in table 4 specify that more than 30 per cent of total investment is to be financed by external resources; in descending order of magnitude of the relative contribution of external resources to the financing of investment, the seven countries are Jordan, Barbados, Malawi, Mali, Panama, Nicaragua and Botswana. In another five countries -- Costa Rica, El Salvador, Indonesia, Kenya and Sierra Leone -- the corresponding proportion is in the range of 20-25 per cent. In four other countries -- Bolivia, Ecuador, Morocco and Uruguay -- 16 to 19 per cent of total investment would be financed by means of external resources.[4]

The substantial or large increase planned by most developing countries in their saving ratios does not imply that their intention is to reduce consumption levels or to put severe restraints on the expansion of consumption. Indeed, as may be seen from table 5, the annual increases planned in total and _per capita_ consumption are generally quite substantial. The underlying strategy in all countries is that while a substantial part of the increment to gross domestic product would be saved in order to expand productive capacity, a substantial part of it would also be allocated for consumption. About three fourths of the countries listed in table 5 plan to expand total consumption annually by more than 5 per cent. In about two thirds of the countries for which relevant information is available, consumption per inhabitant is slated to increase yearly by 3 per cent or more. Although it is postulated that public consumption will increase faster than private consumption in a majority of countries, the yearly increase contemplated in private consumption per inhabitant is generally quite significant.

The targets set for the expansion of consumption help to demonstrate that side by side with the endeavour to raise the level of national saving in relation to total output, developing countries are seeking to bring about a significant improvement in living standards. Nevertheless, there can be no doubt that the

Table 4 GROSS NATIONAL SAVING AND EXTERNAL RESOURCES AS PERCENTAGE OF TOTAL INVESTMENT (OR TOTAL SUPPLY OF SAVING) IN BASE YEAR AND FINAL YEAR OF PLAN[a]

Country[b]	Gross national saving		External resources	
	Base year	Final year	Base year	Final year
Countries indicating a planned annual increase of 1 percentage point or more in percentage share of gross national saving in gross domestic product				
Jordan	−60	8	160	92
Iran	93	144	7	−44
Sierra Leone	43	77	57	23
Argentina	107	120	−7	−20
Morocco	69[c]	82[c]	31	18
Indonesia	61[e]	78[e]	39	22
Nicaragua	41	65	59	35
Philippines	104	121	−4	−21
Bolivia	72	81	28	19
Ecuador	60	81	40	19
Countries indicating a planned annual increase of 0.4 percentage point or more but less than 1 percentage point in percentage share of gross national saving in gross domestic product				
Guatemala	111	137	−11	−37
Chile	125[c]	123[c]	−25	−23
Costa Rica	65	74	35	26
India	89	96	11	4
Panama	45[e]	50[e]	55	50
Madagascar	76[c]	89[c]	24	11
Mali	59	49	41	51
Uruguay	112[c]	84[c]	−12	16
Barbados	29[c]	42[c]	71	58
Botswana	25	69	75	31
El Salvador	82	79	17	21
Malawi	31	44	67	56

Table 4 (continued)

Country[b]	Gross national saving		External resources	
	Base year	Final year	Base year	Final year
Countries indicating a planned annual increase of less than 0.4 percentage point in percentage share of gross national saving in gross domestic product				
Dominican Republic	93[c]	100[c]	7	—
Malaysia	158	151	−58	−51
Kenya	79	75	21	25
Venezuela	142[c]	136[c]	−42	−36
Nigeria	242	149	−142	−49

Source: See table 1.

[a] For details on time period, see table 1.

For definitions of total supply of saving, gross national saving and external resources, see foot-note *a* to table 48.

Minus sign in first two columns indicates dissaving; in last two columns, it indicates net outflow of resources.

[b] Countries are listed in descending order of their planned annual change in the percentage share of gross national saving in gross domestic product.

[c] Gross domestic saving.

attainment of targets for saving will pose a major challenge to these countries. The target for the marginal rate of saving -- that is, the planned increment in gross national saving as a proportion of the planned increment in gross domestic product -- exceeds 30 per cent in one third of the countries listed in table 5, and in another one third of the countries, the target is in the range of 25-30 per cent. To achieve such a target, vigorous efforts will be necessary on a wide front in both the public and private sectors of the economy. The course of action planned by developing countries in this respect is examined in the next section.

II. TARGETS AND POLICIES FOR PUBLIC AND PRIVATE SAVING

Although comparable information on the increases planned in public and private saving is available for only about half of the countries listed in the preceding tables, the broad thrust of policy in developing countries seems to be fairly clear. In general, as indicated by the data assembled in table 6, both public (or government) and private saving are expected to increase at a significant marginal rate. More often than not, the planned marginal rate of increase in each of these two components of gross national saving is higher than the corresponding average rate or ratio prevailing at the outset of the plan. Thus, by directing significant proportions of the planned increment in gross domestic product into public and private saving, the general objective is to raise the average ratio of each of these two components of national saving to gross domestic product by the end of the current development plan.

The data show that in Bolivia and Nigeria the marginal rate of public saving -- the absolute increase planned in public saving from the base year to the final year of the current plan as a proportion of the corresponding absolute increase in gross domestic product -- amounts to more than 20 per cent. Although Nigeria is an exception to the general pattern in the sense that its projected average ratio of public saving to gross domestic product will have declined by the final year of the current plan, the ratio is none the less expected to be very high in that year -- 27 per cent. Bolivia expects its public-saving ratio to rise and amount to about 17 per cent by the end of its current plan. The high ratios of public saving to gross domestic product planned by these two countries reflect in large part their expectation that a vigorous export trades will make relatively large contributions to the national exchequer. In other countries, the ratio of public saving to gross domestic product by the end of the current plan is envisaged as being much smaller; the target in several cases is in the range of 4-8 per cent. But even so, compared to the situation prevailing before the start of the plan, the target of such countries generally implies a substantial rise in the ratio. This feature is particularly evident in respect of the targets set by

Table 5 PLANNED MARGINAL RATE OF GROSS NATIONAL SAVING AND PLANNED ANNUAL RATE OF INCREASE IN CONSUMPTION FROM BASE YEAR TO FINAL YEAR OF PLAN[a]

(*Percentage*)

Country[b]	Marginal rate of gross national saving	Planned annual rate of increase in consumption[c]			
		Total	Per inhabitant		
			Total	Public	Private
Countries indicating a planned annual increase of 1 percentage point or more in percentage share of gross national saving in gross domestic product					
Jordan	27.4	7.2	...	...	...
Iran	50.6	19.3	15.9	23.7	12.1
Sierra Leone	48.4	3.6	1.0	1.9	0.9
Argentina	53.1	4.8	3.2	−1.2	4.0
Morocco	41.1[d]	5.5	2.3	...	...
Indonesia	36.4	5.5	...	...	...
Nicaragua	37.6	4.3	0.9	3.5	0.6
Philippines	43.7	5.1	2.0	2.2	1.9
Bolivia	35.3	5.1	2.3	4.4	2.0
Ecuador	27.5	8.5	4.9	5.9	4.8

Table 5 (continued)

Country[b]	Marginal rate of gross national saving	Planned annual rate of increase in consumption[c]			
		Total	Per inhabitant		
			Total	Public	Private
Countries indicating a planned annual increase of 0.4 percentage point or more but less than 1 percentage point in percentage share of gross national saving in gross domestic product					
Guatemala	26.2	6.6	3.6	5.0	3.5
Chile	27.7[d]	5.7	3.7	−0.1	4.2
Costa Rica	28.9	6.2	3.3	2.5	3.5
India	25.9	5.3	3.4	4.8	3.2
Panama	23.5	5.8	2.9	3.1	2.8
Madagascar	29.9[d]	2.5	...	...	...
Mali	19.6	5.7	...	...	...
Uruguay	25.5[d]	1.9	0.7	...	...
Barbados	16.9[d]	4.2	3.7	4.2	3.5
Botswana	17.7	11.8	9.3	13.4	8.1
El Salvador	18.4	6.2	2.5	3.0	2.5
Malawi	12.1	8.0	5.3	5.8	5.0
Countries indicating a planned annual increase of less than 0.4 percentage point in percentage share of gross national saving in gross domestic product					
Dominican Republic	29.0[d]	7.1	...	...	...
Malaysia	30.9	7.8	5.0	8.7	3.6
Kenya	20.8	7.8	4.4	6.7	3.7
Venezuela	25.8[d]	7.8	4.4	3.3	4.6
Nigeria	30.0	13.6	10.8	11.9	10.6

Source: See table 1.

[a] Marginal rate of gross national saving refers to increase in gross national saving as percentage of increase in gross domestic product from base year to final year of plan. For Indonesia, Panama and Venezuela, marginal rate calculated from first year to final year of plan.

For details on time period and differences in concept of gross domestic product, see table 1.

[b] Countries are listed in descending order of their planned annual change in the percentage share of gross national saving to gross domestic product.

[c] Average annual compound rate.

[d] Marginal rate of gross domestic saving.

Costa Rica and India, for example.

Notwithstanding the general endeavour to expand public saving, most countries expect private saving to remain by far the larger source of supply for gross national saving. As may be seen from table 7, prominent in this regard are Argentina, Botswana, Costa Rica, Indonesia, Jordan, Kenya and Nicaragua. Even in India, for instance, where about two thirds of the planned investment is entrusted to the public sector of the economy, it is the private sector that is expected to provide about two thirds of the gross national saving during the plan period as a whole; and even after the decline postulated from the beginning to the end of that period, the share of the private sector in the supply of gross national saving is expected to be about 62 per cent in the final year of the current plan.

Policies to Expand Public Saving

Developing countries have proposed a variety of steps to expand public saving during the latter part of the 1970s. The measures undertaken or contemplated are directed towards increasing not only general government saving (comprising the central Government, state governments and local governments) but also saving by public enterprises and autonomous government agencies.

In order to expand government saving as one element of action a number of countries are seeking to restrain the expansion of current government expenditure. The increases posited by countries in current government expenditure in relation to their planned expansion of gross domestic product are shown in table 7. It is evident from the table that six of the 17 countries for which relevant information is available -- namely, Argentina, Bolivia, Jordan, Panama, the Philippines and Sierra Leone -- project that current government expenditure will increase more slowly than the total output of the economy. These six countries, it may be recalled, have planned to bring about a substantial to large annual increase in the percentage share of gross national saving in gross domestic product -- more than one percentage point, with the exception of Panama, where the comparable figure is 0.7 percentage point. Two of the 17 countries -- namely, Botswana and the Dominican Republic -- specify that current government expenditure will increase only slightly faster than gross domestic product; indeed, the difference in the planned rates of expansion of current government expenditure and total output is too small to be considered significant. At least half of the countries listed in table 7, current government expenditure is expected to increase significantly faster than domestic product. This does not mean, however, that these countries are not making efforts to restrain such expenditure. While pointing out the need to avoid unnecessary expenditure, many countries have emphasized that increased current expenditure is necessary for such activities as agricultural promotion, education, health and family planning. A number of

Table 6 Planned expansion of public and private saving from base year to final year of plan[a]
(Percentage)

	Marginal rate of saving[c]			Percentage share in gross domestic product in final year of plan[d]		
	Public		Private	Public saving		Private saving
Country[b]	Total	General government		Total	General government	
Countries indicating a planned annual increase of 1 percentage point or more in percentage share of gross national saving in gross domestic product						
Jordan	...	19.9	7.5	...	0.5	1.2 [e]
Iran	...	...	...	...	13.0 [f]	20.9 c, [f]
Sierra Leone	...	16.3	...	4.7 [f]	3.6 [f]	11.5 [f]
Argentina	...	12.6	24.1 [e]	...	2.5	27.6 [e]
Indonesia[g]	...	5.0	12.8 [e]	...	8.6	9.2 [e]
Nicaragua	4.4	16.6	33.1	4.0	3.7	12.7
Bolivia	27.3	...	8.0	16.7	10.0	5.7
Ecuador	9.3	...	5.0	7.8	...	10.3
Countries indicating a planned annual increase of 0.4 percentage point or more but less than 1 percentage point in percentage share of gross national saving in gross domestic product						
Costa Rica	12.5	0.9	16.4	5.5	−0.6	15.9
India	15.4	9.7	10.6	6.0	3.6	9.7
Panama	10.9	8.9	12.6	6.9	2.3	8.3
Botswana	...	...	...	...	3.6	12.2 [e]
El Salvador	10.0	8.4	8.3	4.6	3.4	9.3

Table 6 (continued)
(Percentage)

Country[b]	Marginal rate of saving[c]				Percentage share in gross domestic product in final year of plan[d]			
	Public		Private		Public saving			Private saving
	Total	General government			Total	General government		
Countries indicating a planned annual increase of less than 0.4 percentage point in percentage share of gross national saving in gross domestic product								
Kenya	...	4.3	16.5[e]		...	2.3		17.3[e]
Nigeria[g]	22.6	...	7.4		26.6	19.8		9.1

Source: See table 1.

[a] Unless otherwise stated, estimates have been derived from data in constant prices, generally prices of base year of plan.
 For Argentina, Ecuador, Indonesia and Panama, marginal rates shown in first three columns refer to expansion from first year to final year of plan. For details on time periods, see table 1.
 Public saving equals surplus in the consolidated current account of the public sector (general government, autonomous agencies, public corporations). Private saving equals the difference between gross national saving

[b] Countries are listed in descending order of their planned annual change in the percentage share of gross national saving in gross domestic product.

[c] Marginal rate refers to increase in saving as percentage of increase in gross domestic product from base year to final year of plan. For differences in concept of gross domestic product, see foot-note a to table 1.

[d] Minus sign indicates deficit.

[e] Including surplus on current account of autonomous agencies and public enterprises not transferred to the general government.

[f] Plan period as a whole.

[g] Estimates derived from data in current prices.

countries have also mentioned the constraints they face in their endeavour to restrain current government expenditure.

For example, India expects current government expenditure on social services to increase faster than gross domestic product; but at the same time, in order to restrain over-all expansion of current government expenditure, it intends to prevent an increase in food subsidies. In India, an important limiting factor to such restraint is the interest on the national debt. It is estimated that this will double during the plan period and will constitute nearly 10 per cent of current government expenditure in 1978/79. In Botswana and Nicaragua, too, the interest on the national debt is expected to increase at a fast rate -- in fact, twice as fast as the total output of the economy.

Along with efforts to restrain current government expenditure, developing countries are seeking to bring about a substantial increase in current government revenue. Current revenue is projected to increase faster than gross domestic product in 15 of the 16 countries for which relevant information is available. Indeed, in most countries the percentage increase postulated in current government revenue is substantially greater than the percentage increase planned in total output. The striking examples in this regard are offered by Barbados and El Salvador and thereafter, in descending order of magnitude of the planned elasticity of current government revenue, by Argentina, Sierra Leone, India, Malaysia, Morocco, the Philippines and Costa Rica. Among the countries listed in table 8, only Botswana has postulated that current government revenue will increase more slowly than total output, on the grounds that a number of projects that would yield, during their construction phase, substantial revenue to government byn way of customs and excise duties would have been completed by the end of the current plans.

Of particular importance is the fact that the planned elasticity of current government revenue is greater than the planned elasticity of government expenditure in 12 of the 16 countries for which such a comparison can be made. Since these elasticities have been calculated in relation to the planned increase in gross domestic product, the fact just mentioned implies not only that current government expenditure but also that the ratio of government saving to gross domestic product, as has been noted, is expected to rise and contribute to increasing the national saving ratio in a large majority of countries.

Since the bulk of current government revenue usually comes from taxation, it is to the expansion of tax revenue that Governments have given major attention in their attempts to increase public saving. Typically, tax revenue is projected as increasing substantially faster than total output. Among the countries listed in table 8, Indonesia has postulated by far the sharpest increase in this respect; but also noteworthy are the efforts anticipated by Argentina, Costa Rica, El Salvador, India, Morocco, the Philippines and Sierra Leone. If the efforts contemplated by Governments prove successful, tax revenue will exceed 15 per cent of gross domestic product in two thirds of countries -- 10 out of 15 -- by the end of their current plans, with Costa Rica, Indonesia and Morocco appearing near the top of the list, with a tax ratio well above this percentage.

In their search for expansion of tax receipts, a number of countries -- for example, Argentina, Costa Rica, Malaysia and Venezuela -- have emphasized the need to improve the machinery for tax collection. Some countries, such as India and Nepal, have also stressed the need to prevent tax evasion and other malpractices, which deprive the national exchequer of important revenues. In addition, a great deal of attention has been given to the question of modifying the tax system, not only to make it yield greater tax revenue but also to stimulate capital formation and to improve the distribution of income.

Brazil, for example, intends to modify its income-tax law with a view to making the underlying system more functional and equitable by rationalizing and simplifying its clauses, especially those affecting low-income taxpayers. To widen the tax base for people who have the capacity to pay "-- mostly those who are self-employed -- is an important concern in Bangladesh, Ecuador and India. With respect to corporate profits, Afghanistan, India, Malawi, Mali and the Philippines contemplate changes in the tax structure in order to increase revenue and to plough back dividends into new investment.

The difficulties encountered by most developing countries in taxing agricultural incomes have led them to rely on land taxes. For example, Ecuador and Uruguay intend to reassess land values in order to have a realistic basis for tax purposes. A number of countries -- notably Afghanistan, Bangladesh, India and Nepal -- intend to widen the reach of the land tax and to introduce some progressivism into its rate structure.

Many countries also envisage important changes in indirect taxes, not only to expand current government revenue but also to improve both the allocation of resources for development and the distribution of income. Morocco, for example, intends to widen the differentiation in the tax rates applied to luxury goods and mass-consumption goods. Kenya expects that excise and sales taxes will increasingly replace tariffs on imports. Major changes in tariffs on internationally traded goods are contemplated by Afghanistan, Brazil, Chile, Iran, Panama and Venezuela.

Many countries are also seeking to enlarge public saving through enhanced contributions from public enterprises and autonomous government agencies. Most efforts in this regard focus on improving the productivity of these entities and on rationalizing the prices charged for their products or services. The themes of greater efficiency, realistic prices and satisfactory rates of return by public enterprises and agencies figure prominently in the current plans of Afghanistan, Bangladesh, India, Mauritius, Panama, Peru, Sierra Leone and Uruguay.

Policies to Expand Private Saving

As indicated earlier, while a large majority of developing

Table 7 PLANNED DISTRIBUTION OF GROSS NATIONAL SAVING IN BASE YEAR AND FINAL YEAR OF PLAN[a]
(Percentage)

Country[b]	Base year[c]			Final year		
	Public saving		Private saving	Public saving		Private saving
	Total	General government		Total	General government	

Countries indicating a planned annual increase of 1 percentage point or more in percentage share of gross national saving in gross domestic product

Country	Total	General govt	Private	Total	General govt	Private
Jordan	...	[c]	...	...	30[d]	70[e]
Iran	...	...	...	...	38[f]	62[e,f]
Sierra Leone	...	...	...	29[f]	22[f]	71[f]
Argentina	...	−6	106[e]	...	8	92[e]
Indonesia	...	46	54[e]	...	48	52[e]
Nicaragua	45	37	55	24	22	76
Bolivia	72	42	28	74	45	26
Ecuador	36	...	64	43	...	57

Countries indicating a planned annual increase of 0.4 percentage point or more but less than 1 percentage point in percentage share of gross national saving in gross domestic product

Country	Total	General govt	Private	Total	General govt	Private
Costa Rica	9	−8	91	26	−3	74
India	23	12	77	38	23	62
Panama	44	1	56	45	15	55
Botswana	...	...	...	...	23	77[e]
El Salvador	21	12	79	33	24	67

Table 7 (continued)
(Percentage)

Country[b]	Base year[c]			Final year		
	Public saving		Private saving	Public saving		Private saving
	Total	General government		Total	General government	
Countries indicating a planned annual increase of less than 0.4 percentage point in percentage share of gross national saving in gross domestic product						
Kenya	...	14	86[e]	...	12	88[e]
Nigeria	77	...	23	75	55	25

Source: See table 1.

[a] For definitions of gross national saving and its components, see foot-note *a* to table 48 and foot-note *a* to table 53. Unless otherwise indicated, estimates have been derived from data in constant prices, usually prices of base year. For details on time period, see table 1.

Minus sign indicates dissaving.

[b] Countries are listed in descending order of their planned annual change in the percentage share of gross national saving in gross domestic product.

[c] First year of plan for Argentina, Ecuador, Indonesia and Panama.

[d] Dissaving by general government amounted to 45 million Jordanian dinars out of a gross national dissaving of 56 million Jordanian dinars.

[e] Including surplus on current account of autonomous agencies and public enterprises not transferred to the general government.

[f] Plan period as a whole.

[g] Estimates derived from data in current prices.

countries have sought to raise the share of public saving in gross national saving, by far the larger contribution to national saving is still expected to come in most countries from the private sector of the economy. Considerable importance, therefore, attaches to efforts designed to expand private saving.

In developing countries, especially those that have a comparatively large agricultural sector in which modern activities are relatively scarce, a significant volume of non-monetary saving takes place in the subsistence sector of the economy through such activities as land improvement, construction and additions to cattle. A number of African and Asian countries envisage that general measures to promote agriculture will help to step up such saving.

In most countries, however, the two most important groups with a potential for increased private saving are business enterprises and wage and salary earners in urban areas. As membership in these two groups increases with expanding income, private saving also usually increases. For example, the maturing of some projects and the over-all dynamics of development are expected to lead to increases in the saving of private enterprises at an annual rate of about 30 per cent in Bolivia, 12 per cent in Kenya and about 20 per cent in the Philippines during the time period of their current plan. In Argentina and Chile, the use of under-utilized productive capacity is expected to lead to increases in corporate profits and hence in private saving for new investment. Brazil, Costa Rica, Jordan, Malaysia, Mauritius and Nigeria intend to continue, with some marginal adjustments, their commercial and fiscal policies; this feature, it is contended will remove uncertainties and thereby help to promote private saving and investment.

To promote private saving, especially household saving, many countries deem it important to modify interest rates and to expand or create financial institutions that cater to different groups of potential savers. For example, Bangladesh, Kenya and Sierra Leone have stressed that a significant increase in interest rates is needed not only to encourage private saving but also to help direct individual savings into desirable uses. The Philippines and Uruguay, too, have looked to a more realistic interest rate as a way to increase personal savings. Panama intends to eliminate ceilings on the interest rates paid to savers and to strengthen savings and loan institutions as a way to widen outlets for savings by individuals and to increase competition among various types of financial institutions. In order to ensure that inflation does not act as a deterrent to private saving, Brazil intends to continue its system of periodic adjustments of savings deposits in line with price increases. Among other outlets for individual savings, for instance, Bangladesh has looked to agricultural co-operatives, and Sierra Leone and Somalia to post office savings banks.

In some developing countries, particularly those at a somewhat advanced stage of industrialization and where private enterprise plays a major role, the need to expand or strengthen capital markets has been stressed. Brazil, Malaysia, Morocco and Venezuela are prominent examples in this respect. An important objective in such countries is to enable a wider spectrum of society to hold part of their savings in the form of company shares. Venezuela,

Table 8 PLANNED EXPANSION OF CURRENT EXPENDITURE AND CURRENT REVENUE OF GENERAL GOVERNMENT FROM BASE YEAR TO FINAL YEAR OF PLAN[a]

Country[b]	Planned elasticity in relation to gross domestic product[c]			Tax revenue as percentage of gross domestic product in final year of plan
	Current expenditure	Current revenue		
		Total	Taxes	
Countries indicating a planned annual increase of 1 percentage point or more in percentage share of gross national saving in gross domestic product				
Jordan	0.61	1.43	1.14	18.6
Sierra Leone	0.95	1.74	1.79	16.7
Argentina	0.88	1.87	1.84	17.4
Morocco	1.30	1.59	1.55	20.7
Indonesia[d]	...	...	2.07	21.9
Nicaragua	1.12	1.20	1.23	13.9
Philippines	0.97	1.59	1.59	16.0
Bolivia	0.92	1.32	1.24	14.9[e]
Countries indicating a planned annual increase of 0.4 percentage point or more but less than 1 percentage point in percentage share of gross national saving in gross domestic product				
Costa Rica	1.46	1.57	1.67	23.9
India	1.27	1.69	1.71	17.6
Panama	0.80	1.36	1.44	14.3
Mali	...	...	1.01	13.9
Barbados	2.78	2.70	...	...
Botswana	1.02	0.76	...	...
El Salvador	1.56	2.25	1.62	12.6
Countries indicating a planned annual increase of less than 0.4 percentage point in percentage share of gross national saving in gross domestic product				
Dominican Republic	1.07	...	1.45	17.5
Malaysia	1.39	1.60	...	...
Kenya	1.24	1.17	1.23	16.7
Nigeria	2.12	1.20	...	...

Source: See table 1.

[a] Unless otherwise indicated, estimates derived from data in constant prices. For El Salvador, Nigeria and Panama, expansion estimated from first year of plan. For details on time period, see table 1.

[b] Countries are listed in descending order of their planned annual change in percentage share of gross national saving in gross domestic product, as indicated in table For differences in concept of gross domestic product, see foot-note *a* to table 1.

[c] Ratio of planned change in expenditure or revenue to planned change in gross domestic product.

[d] Estimates derived from data in current prices.

[e] Net current income of central Government.

Table 9 PLANNED EXPANSION OF DIRECT AND INDIRECT TAXES FROM BASE YEAR TO FINAL YEAR OF PLAN[a]

	Percentage annual rate of increase		Percentage distribution of total tax revenue			
			Direct taxes		Indirect taxes	
Country[b]	Direct taxes	Indirect taxes	Base year	Final year	Base year	Final year
Jordan	22.7	11.0	16	24	84	76
Morocco	13.6	8.6	27	31	73	69
Indonesia[c]	43.1	21.7	57	75	43	25
India	10.6	9.5	21	22	79	78
Malaysia	17.5	11.5	...	...	...	...
Kenya	8.2	9.4	36	35	64	65

Source: See table 1.

[a] Unless otherwise stated, estimates have been derived from data in constant prices, generally prices of base year.
 For Kenya, expansion calculated from first year of plan. For details on time period, see table 1.
[b] Countries are listed in descending order of their planned annual change in the percentage share of gross national saving in gross domestic product, as indicated in table 1.
[c] Estimates derived from data in current prices. The plan implies that prices will rise from the base year to the final year at an average annual rate of 8.9 per cent.

Table 10 PLANNED SECTORAL ALLOCATION AND ORIGIN OF TOTAL SUPPLY OF SAVING DURING PLAN PERIOD[a]

	Percentage allocation of total supply of saving		Percentage composition of total supply of saving			Excess of sectoral saving over sectoral investment as percentage of total supply of saving[c]	
Country[b]	Public investment	Private investment	Public saving	Private saving	External resources	Public sector	Private sector
Sierra Leone	46	54	20	47	33	−26	−7
Nicaragua	40	60	18	43	39	−22	−17
Bolivia	70	30	55	14	31	−15	−16
Ecuador	40	60	33	51	16	−7	−9
Costa Rica	30	70	16	53	31	−14	−17
India	66	34	32	63	5	−34	29
Panama	60	40	21	27	52	−39	−13
El Salvador	33	67	22	55	23	−11	−12
Nigeria[d]	67	33	114	38	−52	47	5

Source: See table 1.

[a] For definitions of total supply of saving and its components, see foot-note a to table 48 and foot-note a to table 53.
 For details on time period, see table 1.
[b] Countries are listed in descending order of their planned change in percentage share of gross national saving in gross domestic product.
[c] Minus sign indicates deficit.
[d] Estimates derived from data in current prices.

for instance, is seeking increased participation by workers in shareholding.

III. MEASURES TO CANALIZE FINANCIAL RESOURCES

Developing countries have also given attention in their plans for the latter part of the 1970s to the question of canalizing financial resources into the expansion of the productive capacity in activities that are in line with national objectives and priorities. It is, of course, recognized that in a number of activities, especially those encountered in the subsistence and traditional sectors of the economy, savings and investments are often synonymous terms. For instance, farmers who undertake land improvements and construction through their own efforts or, similarly, individuals who set up productive enterprises are saving and investing at the same time. In such cases, the problem of canalizing savings from some components of the economy into investments undertaken by others does not arise. As already mentioned, the need to promote self-financed activities by individuals and businesses has been stressed in many current plans.

However, as the economy becomes increasingly complex, the problem of canalizing financial resources assumes greater and greater importance. In many developing countries, commercial banks confine their lending operations to the provision of short-term working capital, with the result that the needs of investment capital in agriculture and industry often remain inadequately fulfilled. It is for this reason that the importance of specialized financial institutions that help to meet such needs continues to be stressed in the national plans and other policy statements of developing countries.

The general expectation in developing countries is that public saving will continue to fall short of public investment in the foreseeable future. It is evident from table 10 that this pattern is expected for the latter part of the 1970s in all but one of the nine countries for which it has been possible to obtain the relevant information. The sole exception to the general pattern reflected by this group of countries in Nigeria which, for reasons already mentioned, envisages a net outflow of financial resources to the rest of the world. It is postulated that public saving will fall considerably short of public investment in Panama and, thereafter, in descending order of the relative magnitude of shortfall, in India, Sierra Leone and Nicaragua. Private saving, too, is envisaged as falling considerably short of private investment in most of the countries listed in the table. However, in India and Nigeria, the private sector is expected to have a surplus of saving over investment. The surplus specified by India is, in fact, relatively large.

The shortfalls in total saving over total investment have to be covered by net inflows of financial resources from abroad. Anticipating such a pattern, among others, Bolivia, Jordan,

Morocco, Nicaragua and Sierra Leone have specified their requirements for external resources in considerable detail. Requirements for external financial resources have also been detailed by India, though it plans to cover a large part of its deficit in public saving over public investment through net borrowing from the private sector of the economy.

Among other countries, El Salvador has identified the internal and external sources of funds, year by year, over the time period of its current plan, for each major project in the public sector. Kenya, similarly, has specified requirements for foreign resources for the investment programmes to be implemented by various ministries. Panama and the Philippines have indicated not only the requirements for foreign loans and assistance by end-use but have also identified potential sources of such funds.

Several countries, moreover, have sought to encourage inflows of foreign private capital. For instance, Chile, Kenya, Jordan and Malaysia have outlined the broad incentives they are offering to private capital from abroad. Mauritius, Nigeria and the Philippines, apart from indicating in some detail the incentives offered by them, have given guidance on prospective areas of activity for foreign private capital.

Whether the public sector of the economy is a net borrower from the private sector or vice versa, considerable flows of certain types of finance from one sector to the other are envisaged in order to step up investment in desired activities. For instance, Bangladesh, Costa Rica, India, Kenya, Malaysia, Panama and Sierra Leone have planned to borrow substantial sums from the private sector of the economy by means of selling government securities, savings bonds or prize bonds. These countries expect that such financial instruments will be absorbed by banking institutions, provident funds, social security organizations and the general public.

For their part, Governments intend to continue providing loan capital to certain activities undertaken in the private sector of the economy. In this connexion, reference is commonly made to the industrial banks or development corporations established by governments to promote industrialization. Also mentioned are the specialized institutions set up to meet the credit needs of agriculturists.

In sum, as the analysis of targets and policies put forward in the present chapter has shown, developing countries are intensifying their drive to mobilize financial resources for development. Action is designed not only to raise the level of national saving and move towards greater self-reliance but also to improve the functioning of financial institutions. Financial planning and physical planning have been viewed as twin sides of the same critical process -- namely, the concerting of deliberate efforts to speed up economic and social progress.

NOTES

[1] It should be noted that a decrease in the net inflow of external resources and an increase in the net outflow of resources in relation to total output of the economy both imply a relative improvement in the balance of payments on current account; consequently, since in accounting terms such decreases and increases are both equivalent to a reduced relative dependence on external resources, they are indicated in the middle column of table 1, where relevant, with a minus sign. By the same token, an increase in the net inflow of resources and a decrease in the net outflow of resources in relation to total output, both of which imply a relative deterioration in the balance of payments on current account (in accounting terms, these are both equivalent to an increased relative dependence on external resources), appear in the middle column of the table, where relevant, without a sign.

[2] In Jordan, if remittances of the Jordanians working abroad were included as part of gross national saving rather than of external resources (as is done in the country's plan), gross national saving and external resources in the final year of the plan would amount to 12.8 per cent and 9.1 per cent of gross domestic product, respectively.

[3] It should be noted that the estimates of gross national saving and external resources have been derived from data in constant prices, generally the prices prevailing in the base year of plans. If prices of exports and imports change significantly over the plan period, the magnitudes of these financial flows could run out or be quite different from the estimates derived from constant prices. Five of the countries whose plans have been examined have specified estimates of their external account in both constant and current prices. For illustrative purposes, the relevant data are shown as follows:

[4] For a number of countries, external resources refer to excess of imports over exports of goods and services, excluding factor income. The relevant figures are identified in table 4 by foot-note d. In such cases, the proportion of external resources in total supply of saving tends to be underestimated.

[5] Even the sole exception to the general pattern indicated by the data in table 9 is perhaps more apparent than real. A large part of the increase in tax receipts projected by Indonesia is envisaged as coming from the mining, refining and export of petroleum. All of Indonesia's expected petroleum revenue, in the absence of detailed information, has been treated as receipts from direct taxes in the table. However, a substantial proportion of tax revenue from petroleum -- the revenue that normally takes the form of excise and export duties -- belongs, in fact, to the category of indirect taxation.

External Finance for Development: Recent Experience and Its Implications for Policies

CENTRE FOR DEVELOPMENT PLANNING, PROJECTIONS AND POLICIES OF THE DEPARTMENT OF ECONOMIC AND SOCIAL AFFAIRS OF THE UNITED NATIONS SECRETARIAT

Most developing countries are heavily dependent on inflows of financial resources from abroad as a means of speeding up their economic and social progress. While their own efforts to mobilize domestic financial resources have yielded appreciable results in recent years, the level of domestic saving in many developing countries is still comparatively low. Understandably, countries whose average incomes are low, and consequently average levels of consumption barely sufficient to meet the requirements of human existence, find it difficult to expand domestic saving rapidly. Commonly, therefore, external financial resources have been a valuable addition to the means for expanding capital formation for accelerated progress in developing countries.

The importance of external financial resources, however, goes beyond their role as a supplement to domestic saving in developing countries. Even if it were possible to expand domestic saving to match the needed level of capital formation, the foreign exchange requirements of many developing countries are so great that without inflows of external financial resources they would not be able to attain that level of capital formation or investment. As the development process gathers momentum, the requirements of machinery, heavy equipment, fertilizer, petroleum and other critical producer goods increase rapidly. Most developing countries find it necessary to meet a large proportion of such requirements through imports; but frequently their own exports have not been expanding at a rate that could enable them to pay for increased imports through their own foreign exchange earnings. Countries whose export commodities have encountered a markedly sluggish expansion of world demand have been singularly unfortunate in this respect. In addition to burgeoning requirements of imports of crucial goods, developing countries typically have to make

From **JOURNAL OF DEVELOPMENT PLANNING**, No. 10, 1976, (23-57), reprinted by permission of the publisher.

rising net payments for the shipping and insurance services of foreign countries which they utilize for their international commerce. Moreover, most developing countries have to make substantial payments abroad for the servicing of their external debts. Often unforeseen developments or emergencies have compounded the difficulties faced by many of these countries. For all these reasons, developing countries have generally encountered a large excess of imports over exports of goods and services; and to meet the payments requirements of this excess or external deficit, they have needed inflows of official and private funds from abroad.

The international flows of financial resources, as is only to be expected, figure prominently in the deliberations of intergovernmental forums concerned with development problems. Those deliberations are generally based on the information emanating from countries and international institutions that extend grants and loans to developing countries. Such information is, of course, useful and merits close attention.[1] However, one major deficiency of this type of information is that the data on the funds provided by various aid-givers, investors and lenders to a developing country cannot be added up for all sources of funds to derive a meaningful estimate of how much total external finance that country did actually receive. This is because not all aid-giving or capital-exporting countries publish data on their disbursements of funds to developing countries; for the centrally planned economies, as well as for the petroleum-exporting countries that have recently emerged as important sources of external finance, it is possible to make estimates of only their commitments of economic assistance to developing countries, with little or no indication regarding the lag between commitments and disbursements. Even for the countries that publish data on their disbursements of funds to developing countries, the available information is detailed enough to provide indications of only the official funds given to individual recipient countries. The information is not accompanied by comparable detailed indications of the flows of their private capital to individual countries.

An important additional source of information in this respect, but which avoids the snags just mentioned, is the set of balance-of-payments data compiled by developing countries. The balance-of-payments data have the advantage of providing comparable information on different types of financial flows--official <u>versus</u> private, grants <u>versus</u> loans, long-term <u>versus</u> short-term--received by a country during a certain time period from the rest of the world. There is, of course, the drawback that not all developing countries publish information on their balance of payments. However, if the purpose is not to add up the balance-of-payments data for all developing countries in order to arrive at some global estimates for the developing countries as a whole, the absence of information for some countries is not an impediment for an exercise designed to draw broad policy conclusions on the basis of information for a sufficiently large number of recipient countries. By virtue of the intrinsic advantages of the balance-of-payments data, such an exercise could serve as a useful supplement to the analyses based on the information published by capital-exporting or aid-giving countries and institutions with regard to the financial resources provided by them to developing countries.

Accordingly, the present paper contains an examination of external finance for development based on the balance-of-payments statements of 65 developing countries for which comparable information was available for a moderately long span of time in the recent past. In terms of economic variables, these 65 countries represent the overwhelming bulk of the developing world. This is true whether judged in terms of their population, production or international trade. Thus, even if the number of countries represented in this analysis falls short by about one third the total number of the developing countries that are members of the United Nations, the policy conclusions emerging from the analysis can be considered applicable to developing countries in general and should be of help in formulating and implementing new approaches to international resource transfers for the accelerated progress of the developing world.

I. AN OVER-ALL VIEW OF INTERNATIONAL FINANCIAL FLOWS

The data on major components of the balance of payments on capital account of 65 developing countries for the six-year period 1968-1973, but expressed as annual average, are shown in table 1. Since this period was characterized by realignments of rates of exchange among various currencies, the data are shown not in the currency of any particular country but in terms of the special drawing rights (SDR) of the International Monetary Fund. One SDR was originally, in 1970, denominated as the equivalent of one United States dollar; but, following the devaluation of the dollar and later the emergence of a regime of floating exchange rates, the dollar value of the SDR has been undergoing changes.[2]

One initial over-all conclusion to be drawn from table 1 is that all but six of the 65 developing countries had an excess of imports over exports of goods and services during the period 1968-1973 and therefore required inflows of external finance and/or withdrawals from their international reserves to finance the excess. In other words, the balance of payments on capital account of the six countries with a seemingly different pattern appears with a negative sign (last column of table 1), indicating that those six countries exported more goods and services than they imported and consequently recorded a net outflow of financial resources and/or additions to their international reserves. However, the data for the six countries need to be interpreted with caution. Four of the six countries, namely, Iraq, Malaysia, Venezuela and Zambia, were really not exporters of capital. Iraq, Malaysia and Venezuela made substantial additions to their international reserves. Moreover, Malaysia and Venezuela recorded a net outflow of private donations--a financial component which is of a rather different character from the rest of the balance of payments on capital account. In Zambia, the net outflow of private donations was large. Taking into account these factors, it is apparent that the initial conclusion needs to be modified. In terms of the components of the balance of payments on capital account that are of crucial relevance for the financing of development—official donations, long-term official capital and long-term private capital—those four countries were really importers of capital. It follows, then, that only two of the 65 countries, the Libyan Arab Republic and Saudi Arabia, were net exporters of capital during the six-year period reviewed here. Therefore, for the purpose of analysis, those two countries have been treated as a category apart in the present paper (group I in table 1); and the focus has been kept mainly on the 63 countries that were net importers of capital (group II).

The combined balance of payments on capital account of the 63 capital-importing developing countries exceeded SDR 9.6 billion per annum during the period 1968-1973. A little more than one seventh of that amount, SDR 1.4 billion, was accounted for by the net receipts of donations from abroad by private institutions and individuals in those countries. The largest recipient of such private donations was Israel whose extraordinarily large annual receipts—SDR 737 million—resulted from a pattern of cultural and religious ties with institutions and individuals abroad which is scarcely to be found in the case of any other recipient country. The other relatively large recipients of net annual flows of private donations were Algeria (SDR 241 million), India (SDR 177 million), the Republic of Korea (SDR 115 million), the Philippines (SDR 112 million), Morocco (SDR 97 million) and Pakistan[3] (SDR 83 million), with Democratic Yemen, Mexico, Tunisia, Jamaica and Guatemala—in that order—following at some distance (in the range of SDR 42-21 million). For such North African countries as Algeria and Morocco, the prime force in this respect came from the remittances of their migrant workers earning a livelihood, often for short spells of time, in the industrial countries of Western Europe. For such countries as India, Jamaica, Pakistan and the Philippines, the remittances came mainly from their erstwhile nationals who had more or less permanently settled abroad. In contrast, several developing countries recorded a net annual outflow of private donations. These included not only the two countries characterized in table 1 as exporters of capital, Saudi Arabia (SDR 205 million) and the Libyan Arab Republic (SDR 69 million) but also Zambia (SDR 108 million), Venezuela (SDR 84 million), Zaire (SDR 63 million), Malaysia (SDR 62 million) and the Ivory Coast (SDR 46 million). A significant part of economic activity in several of these countries depends on migrants from other countries, and some of these countries also have sizable minorities of different national origins. As a result, these countries usually experience a significant net outflow of private donations.

In many developing countries, short-term capital movements also play a part of some significance. However, short-term capital, according to the internationally accepted definition, covers loans or credits with a maturity period of up to one year.[4] In a single year, movements of this type of capital often exert a strong influence; but over a moderate span of time, such as the six-year period reviewed in table 1, the inflows and outflows of short-term loans or credits tend to cancel out. In line with this reasoning, the main conclusion emanating from the data in the penultimate column of table 1--which relate to short-term capital movements plus changes in international reserves and errors and omissions--[5] is not that net movements of short-term capital during the period 1968-1973 as a whole were significant, but that developing countries generally tended to accumulate international reserves during this period.[6]

The most pertinent over-all conclusion emerging from the data in table 1 is that it was really the combined net inflow of official donations and long-term official and private capital that was of profound importance in financing the external deficit of developing countries. For the 63 capital-importing developing countries listed in the table (group II), the total net inflow of these components amounted on the annual average to SDR 9.5 billion. This international flow, which for reasons of both conceptual significance and verbal convenience may be called the net flow of development finance, was almost equal to the combined external deficit of the 63 countries (SDR 9.6 billion). Clearly, then, in the context of discussions on development problems and policies, it is this flow that matters most. Accordingly, the remainder of the present paper deals exclusively with the net international flow of development finance.

Even a cursory glance at the first column of table 1 would reveal that there were enormous intercountry variations in the net flow of development finance received from abroad by developing countries during 1968-1973. Some countries received a very large net flow of development finance, while some received little or nothing. In absolute terms, the 12 largest recipients of the annual flow of development finance from the rest of the world were Brazil (SDR 1,026 million), Mexico (SDR 857 million), India (SDR 704 million), Israel (SDR 656 million), the Republic of Korea (SDR 569 million), Pakistan (SDR 524 million), Iran (SDR 485 million), Indonesia (SDR 390 million), Egypt (SDR 335 million), Colombia (SDR 239 million), Nigeria (SDR 237 million) and Chile (SDR 208 million). At the other end of the spectrum, the 12 smallest recipients of development finance (those with net annual receipts of less than SDR 20 million or those with little or no net inflow or even a net outflow) were--in descending order of the flow--Togo, El Salvador, the Central African Republic, the Sudan, Sierra Leone, Haiti, Democratic Yemen, Uganda, Mauritius, Western Samoa, Zambia and Guyana. Since the countries are listed in table 1 in descending order of the magnitude of their per capita annual income, it is evident even at this first glance that some of the higher-income developing countries--for instance, Brazil and Mexico--fared very well, whereas some of the low-income countries--such as Democratic Yemen and Haiti--fared very poorly in respect of the net international receipts of development finance. It needs to be remembered, however, that the economies of countries vary greatly in size, and therefore absolute amounts of external finance do not provide a correct picture; this aspect is dealt with later in the paper.

Of the combined net annual flow of development finance

received by the 63 developing countries (SDR 9.5 billion), around 60 per cent was accounted for by the funds received by Governments and official institutions (16 per cent in the form of donations and 44 per cent in the form of long-term capital) and the remaining 40 per cent by the long-term capital (comprising direct investment and loans) received by private entities. While in principle there is no reason why Governments and official institutions of developing countries should have received external grants and loans only from Governments and official institutions abroad and that, similarly, private entities should have received external finance only from private entities abroad, in practice a broad relationship of this sort (though obviously not of one-to-one type) does prevail. Therefore, for the sake of brevity, and without unduly distorting the picture, hereafter these flows are referred to simply as official donations, long-term official capital and long-term private capital.

It is evident from table 1 that the relative importance of these three components of external finance for development varied greatly among the recipient countries. Some received large flows of both official and private finance, some others received little of both components, and others obtained these flows in a variety of permutations. Of course, the word "large" or "small" has a different connotation for different countries, depending on the size of their economies.

It follows, therefore, that the data set out in table 1 are suggestive but by no means conclusive. In fact, not surprisingly, they give rise to an array of cogent questions. Were there any significant upward or downward trends discernible in the flow of external finance for development within the six-year period reviewed? Why did some countries receive very large flows of external finance and others very little? Did official finance from abroad play an offsetting role in countries which received little or no private capital from the rest of the world? Were flows of external finance, judged in relation to some meaningful economic yardsticks, distributed equitably among developing countries? What lessons emerge from recent experience for needed policies or new approaches to transfer of financial resources to developing countries? An attempt is made in the remainder of the paper to throw light on these and related questions.

II. TRENDS IN INTERNATIONAL FLOWS OF DEVELOPMENT FINANCE

As may be seen from table 2, which contains data on annual averages of international flows of development finance separately for 1968-1970 (the last three years of the First United Nations Development Decade) and 1971-1973 (the first three years of the Second United Nations Development Decade), the two capital-exporting developing countries, the Libyan Arab Republic and Saudi Arabia, expanded their net outflow of development finance dramatically: the combined net annual outflow from these two countries increased from about SDR 50 million in 1968-1970 to SDR 711 million in 1971-1973.[7] This more than fourteenfold increase was clearly a reflection of the economic power gained by these countries through the exploitation and exports of their large natural resource endowments of petroleum. There is little doubt that the data for the period after 1973 (say, for 1974-1976), when available, will tell an even more dramatic story in this respect. At least for some years of the 1970s, if not for the whole decade, other petroleum-exporting developing countries will also show large net outflows of development finance.

The net annual flow of development finance received by the 63 capital-importing developing countries increased from SDR 7.9 billion in 1968-1970 to SDR 11.3 billion in 1971-1973, or by about 43 per cent. Proportionately, the largest increase (98 per cent) was recorded by countries with a per capita income of $400-$799 and the smallest increase (4 per cent) by countries with a per capita income of less than $100. The increase amounted to 39 per cent for countries with a per capita income of more than $800 and about 24 per cent for countries with a per capita income of $200-$399 as well as for countries with a per capita income of $100-$199.

III. COMPONENTS OF DEVELOPMENT FINANCE

Among the three components of the net international inflow of development finance, for the 63 capital-importing countries as a whole, long-term private capital expanded from 1968-1970 to 1971-1973 by 65 per cent (from /SDR 2.9 billion to 4.8 billion), official donations by 36 per cent (from SDR 1.3 billion to 1.8 billion) and long-term official capital by 28 per cent (from SDR 3.7 billion to 4.7 billion). As a result of these disparate rates of increase, the share of long-term private capital in the combined net flow of development finance received by the 63 capital-importing countries rose from 37 per cent in 1968-1970 to 43 per cent in 1971-1973, and in fact became the largest of the three components (see table 3). During the same period, the shares of both the official donations and the long-term official capital received by these countries declined: the former, from 17 to 16 per cent, and the latter, from 46 to 41 per cent.

The relative importance of these three components in the net flow of development finance varied considerably among developing countries. The relative importance of long-term private capital was generally large in the higher-income developing countries. For example, in countries with a per capita income in the range of $400-$799, private capital accounted for 65 per cent of the net flow of development finance from abroad in 1971-1973, representing a significant increase from 1968-1970. The share of private capital was also substantial in countries with a per capita income of more than $800, though this is not readily apparent from the information summarized in table 3. The average for the top-income group shown in the table is heavily influenced by the large net flows of official donations and official capital received by Israel; for the countries other than Israel in that group, even after recording a substantial decline from 1968-1970, the share of long-term private capital amounted to as much as 40 per cent in 1971-1973.

Long-term official capital was relatively more important in countries with a _per capita_ income of less than $200. In 1971-1973, this component accounted for 61 per cent of the total net flow of development finance into countries with a _per capita_ income of less than $100, and for 47 per cent in countries with a _per capita_ income of $100-$199. However, the share of long-term official capital was by no means small in other developing countries; it amounted to more than one half of the total in the top-income group of developing countries (with or without Israel) and to around one third of the total in countries with a _per capita_ income of $400-$799 as well as in the middle-income group of developing countries (those with a _per capita_ income of $200-$399).

The share of official donations in the net inflow of development finance was the largest in the middle-income group (31 per cent). But just as the average in this respect for the top-income group is dominated by the experience of Israel, the average for the middle-income group is largely a reflection of the experience of Egypt and Jordan. In such cases, political developments were the main force shaping the pattern of inflow of official donations. The share of official donations in the flow received by the lowest-income group of countries did increase significantly, as did the share of long-term private capital. But, as may be seen from the absolute values shown in table 2, these shares were essentially a reflection of the experience of one country--Zaire. In most developing countries, the relative importance of official donations from abroad has tended to decline.

In the simplistic statistical sense, as already noted, the general decline in the share of official funds (both grants and loans) in the net international flow of development finance implies that there was an upsurge in the other component of this flow--that is, private capital. This decline, however, is also a reflection of the fact that, not only was there little progress towards achieving the aid target specified in the International Development Strategy for the Second United Nations Development Decade but there has actually been a retrogression with regard to official development assistance from the economically advanced countries to the developing world. It is a matter of concern that the component of development finance that is of particular importance to developing countries--namely, official donations--now plays a rather small role. As mentioned earlier, the share of official grants in the net flow of development finance received by the 63 capital-importing developing countries declined from 17 per cent in 1968-1970 to 16 per cent in 1971-1973. Of course, one redeeming feature of this recent experience is that official grants, which carry no burden of repayment and interest charges, did rise faster than official capital. But even so, as can be seen from the data in absolute values shown in table 2, the grant component remained much the smaller part of official funds.

While the faster increase in the grant component of official funds in recent years is to be welcomed, this tendency has thus far proved to be too mild to offset the trends that have been evident since the early 1960s. Unfortunately, data are not available to permit demonstration of the trends for all of the 63 countries covered in table 3. However, the data for 42 of these 63 countries summarized in table 4 are sufficiently representative to serve as a basis for generalization. From the early 1960s to the early 1970s, as can be seen from the table, the net flow of official donations received by the 42 capital-importing countries expanded by a little more than one third, whereas the net flow of long-term private capital to them more than quadrupled. Annually, in money terms, official donations expanded at the rate of a mere 3 per cent. In real terms, the annual increase was very small indeed. And the share of official donations in the total flow of development finance tumbled from 26 to 14 per cent.[8] At a time when the burden of external debt has become large for many developing countries, the diminished role of official grants from abroad (which impose no economic burden on recipients) poses a serious problem for these countries.

IV. DISTRIBUTION AMONG COUNTRIES

From the viewpoint of international development policy, the question of distribution of the net international flow of development finance among countries is of particular importance. A consciously designed distribution of this flow can be a critical means of narrowing international economic disparities and bringing about an integrated world economy. The foregoing discussion has already yielded hints that the distribution tended to be uneven or inequitable. This aspect, however, calls for a more searching analysis than what is apparent from those hints; therefore, it is to this aspect that the next few paragraphs are addressed.

As may be seen from table 5, the international flow of private capital to the developing world has, in particular, been heavily concentrated in a small number of countries. It is striking that the 11 countries with a __per capita__ annual income of $400-$799, which accounted for no more than 13 per cent of the combined population of the 63 capital-importing developing countries, received as much as 54 per cent of the net flow of long-term private capital to these 63 countries in 1971-1973. The degree of concentration in fact increased substantially, as is attested by the fact that the corresponding proportion received by these 11 countries in 1968-1970 was 40 per cent. The shares of countries with a __per capita__ income of $800 or more and those in the income range of $200-$299 did decline but, even so, remained well above their corresponding population shares. The experience of lower-income developing countries was strikingly different in this respect: countries with a __per capita__ income of $100-$199, which accounted for 32 per cent of the combined population of the 63 capital-importing countries, received only 15 per cent of the total net flow of long-term private capital. And countries with a per capita income of less than $100 and with a population share of 40 per cent received merely 3 per cent of this flow. In fact, over two thirds of the net flow of the long-term private capital received by the seven countries in the lowest-group went to only one among them--namely, Zaire; the share of the other six in this flow, thus, was less than 1 per cent.

Actually, the degree of concentration in the international flow of private capital to the developing world has tended to be much greater than what appears from the group averages shown in table 5. Of the net annual flow of long-term private capital to the 63 capital-importing developing countries in 1971-1973 (SDR 4.8 billion), Brazil alone received nearly 26 per cent and Mexico about 21 per cent. In other words, just two of the 63 countries received close to half of this flow. Among the other prominent recipients of private capital were the Republic of Korea, Nigeria and Israel--in that order, each receiving about 6 per cent of the flow; Indonesia and Singapore (each getting about 4 per cent); Jamaica (3 per cent); Ecuador, Zaire, Malaysia, Pakistan, Thailand, Colombia and Iran (each around 2 per cent). Together, these 15 countries accounted for nearly nine tenths of the flow of long-term private capital to the 63 capital-importing developing countries.

There appear to have been two major contributory factors to this high degree of concentration--one stemming from the market prospects offered to foreign investors in the capital-importing countries themselves and the other from the market prospects offered to them in the world at large via the exports from those countries. To illustrate the role of these two factors in a simple but nevertheless economically meaningful manner, the relevant information has been arranged in a synoptic form in table 6. The role of the two contributory factors is depicted separately in the two parts of the table.

In the first place, along the vertical axis in the table, the 63 capital-importing developing countries have been grouped according to whether their net annual inflow of long-term private capital in 1971-1973 was relatively large, moderate or small. The 17 countries that received a net annual flow of long-term private capital equivalent to SDR 60 million or more are characterized as recipients of large flows. Those which received a net flow in the range of SDR 10 million to 59 million--there were 21 such countries--are considered to have received a moderate amount. The remaining countries are considered as recipients of small flows, or as those which experienced a net outflow of this component of development finance. These limiting values of the net flow of long-term private capital were selected so as to derive three broad but meaningful country groupings for the purpose of generalization. Next, along the horizontal axis, on the right-hand side of the table, account has been taken of whether the economies of these countries are relatively large, medium-sized or small. For this purpose, the groupings are based on the magnitude of the total gross domestic product of each country in 1971. Countries with a total gross domestic product of $6 billion or more are considered in this illustrative exercise to be economically large, those with a total gross domestic product of $1 billion or more but less than

$6 billion as economically medium-sized, and those with a total gross domestic product of less than $1 billion as economically small. It is readily apparent that the countries cluster along the diagonal from the top right-hand corner to the point where the vertical and horizontal axes meet at the bottom of the table. A majority of the economically large countries--for instance, Brazil, Mexico, the Republic of Korea and Nigeria--received comparatively large flows of private capital. Similarly, a majority of the countries with medium-sized economies received moderate amounts of private capital; and a majority of the economically small countries--such as Haiti, Sierra Leone, the Central African Republic and Togo--received small flows.

Also shown on the right-hand side of the table, in parentheses, are the annual average rates of growth of total gross domestic product for the three-year period 1971-1973. These rates provide an indication of the expansion of the domestic market in individual developing countries during recent years. It is evident that the countries receiving large (moderate/small) flows of private capital were often those which had not only large (moderate/small) domestic markets to begin with but also domestic markets that were expanding at a fast (moderate/slow) rate. In this manner, generally, the market prospects held out for foreign investors in the capital-importing countries themselves were reinforced.

The attraction exercised by the relative buoyancy of exports--external market prospects--is depicted along the horizontal axis on the left-hand side of the table. In that part of the table, account has been taken of whether the exports of goods and services of the countries concerned were expanding at a comparatively vigorous, moderate or slow pace--that is, at an annual rate of respectively, 12 per cent or more, 6 per cent or more but less than 12 per cent, and less than 6 per cent. Once again it is readily apparent that the countries cluster along the diagonal from the top left-hand corner to the point where the vertical and horizontal axes meet at the bottom of the table. In some countries, it is the traditional commodities--most notably petroleum and metals--that enjoyed vigorous world demand. At the same time, in a number of developing countries, substantial export prospects were also opening up for manufactured and semi-manufactured goods. Not only did such export prospects attract foreign investors, but foreign private capital also contributed to expansion of exports.

For many countries, it is evident, the domestic and external market prospects reinforced each other. Some countries enjoyed vigour on both domestic and external fronts; these included, for example, Brazil, the Republic of Korea, Israel and Iran. Some other countries, in contrast, encountered unfavourable experience on both fronts; among others, these included Haiti, Sierra Leone, the Central African Republic and Togo.

Of course, some other factors were also at work. The experience of Chile and Egypt, for example, was undoubtedly influenced by political developments. The net outflow of long-term private capital from Iraq and Venezuela (to cite another illustration) was a reflection of the nationalization activities of these countries. By and large, however, it is the two major contributory factors discussed above that provide the main explanation.

It will not have escaped notice that the countries clustering near the intersection of axes at the bottom of the table, whether looked at in relation to the size of the economy (the right-hand side) or the buoyancy of exports (the left-hand side) are mostly low-income developing countries. For such countries, the international flow of private capital served neither as a large supplement to domestic saving nor as a large means of overcoming the foreign exchange constraint. In contrast, several of the higher-income developing countries had the best of both worlds in this respect: by virtue of their higher income levels, they were in a position to generate higher levels of domestic saving; and they also gained substantially from large inflows of private capital from abroad. While some policy measures may help in enlarging the flow of private capital to those countries whose recent experience has been rather negative and which are desirous of receiving such capital, it will not be logical to expect a great deal on this score. The flow of capital is an autonomous activity, which is determined by commercial considerations.

For countries which do not receive substantial flows of private capital from abroad, the flows of official funds--donations and long-term loans--are especially important. In order to judge whether the flows of official funds from abroad played a major role in filling this kind of void, the relevant information is once again depicted in an illustrative form in table 7. Countries have been grouped along the horizontal axis of the table according to whether their net inflow of long-term private capital during 1971-1973 was relatively large, moderate or small. This characterization is according to the limiting values shown for private capital in the preceding table. Along the vertical axis of table 7 is to be found the key aspect of the illustrative exercise under discussion--namely, whether the net annual inflow of official donations and long-term official loans was comparatively large, moderate or small. The flow of official funds being larger than the flow of private capital in most countries, the limiting values used to categorize countries as large, moderate or small recipients of official funds differ from those used with regard to private capital. The limiting values were so chosen as to have, for illustrative purposes, three broadly comparable groups of countries.

Ideally, given the high degree of concentration of private capital, one would wish to see an inverse relationship between the inflows of the official and private components of development finance from abroad. In other words, needy countries which receive little or no private capital should receive a large flow of official funds, and vice versa. If this were so, countries would cluster in table 7 along the diagonal from the top left-hand side to the bottom right-hand side. Unfortunately, however, this kind of relationship is elusive at present. The notable tendency that does appear in table 7 is the clustering along the diagonal from the top right-hand side to the bottom left-hand side. Put differently, several countries which received a large flow of private capital also received a large flow of official funds; these countries were Israel; Brazil, Iran, Pakistan, Indonesia, the Republic of Korea, Colombia and Zaire. Five of these eight countries belong to the higher- or middle-income groups of developing countries. At the other end were Chad, Somalia, Togo, Uruguay, the Central African Republic, the Sudan, El Salvador, Sierra Leone, Haiti, Democratic Yemen, Mauritius and Western Samoa which received small flows of both official and private funds (or even recorded an outflow of private capital); several of these are countries with low incomes, and a number of them are listed in the United Nations as the least developed among the developing countries. For some countries, of course, the flow of official funds did play a significant offsetting role. Among these were India, Egypt, Jordan, Chile and--to a smaller extent--Sri Lanka, Uganda and Burma; but such countries were clearly in a minority.[9]

One explanation of why official funds from abroad did not generally play an offsetting role lies in the fact that in a number of instances a significant part of the foreign funds obtained by Governments or official institutions in developing countries consisted of loans obtained from foreign private institutions. Strictly speaking, this part should be called private capital, and the major factors that shaped its flow are those discussed above--namely, the market prospects in individual countries and the export prospects for their products. Therefore, so far as this part is concern, the degree of concentration is not surprising. From the balance-of-payments data, it is unfortunately not possible to gauge how much of the official loan total falls into the category of official development assistance. Official donations, however, largely belong to this category. In so far as this component, too, has reflected a high degree of concentration--notably in Egypt and Jordan among the middle-income group of countries and Israel among the higher-income group--it is because political factors have been a major influence in shaping the aid policies of donor countries.

That the flows of official funds from abroad were also, in general, unevenly distributed among developing countries, although not to the same degree as foreign private capital, is clearly evident from the data shown earlier in table 5. Countries in the lowest-income group (those with a per capita income of less than $100), which account for 40 per cent of the combined population of the 63 capital-importing developing countries, received in 1971-1973 only 15 per cent of the combined net flow of official donations and only 13 per cent of the combined net flow of long-term official capital. Their share of official donations in 1971-1973 was a little larger than in 1968-1970, but their share of official capital was substantially smaller. The contrast was not so sharp for countries with a per capita income of $100-$199, but even so the distribution remained significantly disproportionate: with a population share of 32 per cent, these countries received 22 per cent of the total flow of official donations and 21 per cent of the total flow of long-term official capital--the percentage flow of official donations representing a substantial decline since 1968-1970. The largest share of official donations (44 per cent) went to the middle-income countries (those with a per capita income of $200-$399) and the largest share of official capital (29 per cent) to the next higher-income group of countries (those with a per capita income of $400-$799); these shares of official funds were substantially greater than the corresponding population shares of the countries concerned.

Because lower-income countries received disproportionately small flows of both official and private capital, the contrasts are even sharper in terms of the total flow of development finance. In 1971-1973, the lowest-income group of countries, with a population share of 40 per cent, received merely 9 per cent of this total flow; and countries with a per capita income of $100-$199, whose population share was 32 per cent, received just about 19 per cent. At the other end, countries with a per capita income of $400-$799 and a population share of 13 per cent secured as much as 35 per cent of the total flow; and those with a still higher per capita income, whose population share was only 3 per cent, obtained 14 per cent of the total flow. These data demonstrate that the world community is still far away from designing an international development policy that helps to bring about, through its pattern of international flows of development finance, a significant reduction in economic disparities among developing countries.

V. ECONOMIC CONTRIBUTION OF INTERNATIONAL FLOWS OF DEVELOPMENT FINANCE

While the economic significance of the international flow of development finance varied considerably for the recipient developing countries, there is little doubt that on the whole this flow has made an important contribution to the drive for accelerated economic and social progress. An exhaustive discussion of the economic contribution made by the international flow of development finance is beyond the scope of the present paper, but some illustrative indicators are worth examining in order to draw conclusions with regard to needed policies.

The extent to which the net international flow of development finance has supplemented the foreign exchange earned by developing countries through exports of goods and services is depicted in table 8. For the 63 capital-importing developing countries, 16 per cent of the combined receipts of foreign exchange from these two major sources was accounted for by the net flow of development finance, both in 1968-1970 and in 1971-1973. Countries with a per capita income of $400-$799 experienced a substantial increase in the relative importance of the net international flow of development finance as a source of foreign exchange: the share of this source increased from 15 per cent in 1968-1970 to 19 per cent in 1971-1973. The middle-income and lower-income countries, in contrast, experienced a decline in the relative importance of this source. Nevertheless, the share of the net flow of development finance in the combined receipts of foreign exchange was the highest in countries with a per capita income of less than $100 (21 per cent); and in countries with a per capita income of $100-$199, the share was at least above the average for developing countries as a whole. The counterpart of these tendencies is to be seen in the data presented in table 9. In countries with a per capita income of $400-$799, the proportion of imports of goods and services financed by the net flow of development finance from abroad increased from 19 per cent in 1968-1970 to 25 per cent in 1971-1973; whereas in countries with a per capita income of less than $100, the proportion declined from 26 to 23 per cent during the same time span, but nevertheless remained above the average for developing countries as a whole. The proportion remained unchanged for other income groups of countries and was well below the figure for countries with a per capita income of $400-$799.

While therefore it is correct to infer from the data in table 8 that the international flow of development finance has been an important means of enlarging imports in most developing countries--and to the extent imports of machinery and other investment goods have been favoured by these countries, the flow has been an important means of enlarging productive capacity--these data fail to indicate that the flow fell short of needs in countries where the problems of underdevelopment and poverty are pronounced, namely, the low-income developing countries. The latter conclusion emerges clearly from the indices of expansion of international trade and finance which are shown in table 10. The evidence is unmistakable that the experience of the lowest-income group of countries with regard to both major sources of foreign exchange presents essentially a story of relative stagnation. Between 1968-1970 and 1971-1973, the net flow of development finance received by these countries from abroad increased by a mere 4 per cent and their exports by only about 11 per cent. These figures stand out in striking contrast to the experience of the higher-income countries. For example, the corresponding figures for countries with a per capita income of $400-$799 were 98 per cent and 46 per cent, respectively. The imports of the lowest-income group of countries increased by barely 16 per cent or, proportionately, less than the imports of any other group--indeed, much less than the imports of higher-income developing countries. This increase is calculated in current prices. In real terms--that is, taking into account the rise in prices--there appears to have been very little increase in the imports of the lowest-income group of countries. The experience of countries with a per capita income of $100-$199 was not so bleak. Their exports at least expanded at a rate somewhat above the average for the developing world; but in respect of increases in the flow of development finance from abroad and imports, these countries were far behind the higher-income developing countries. This evidence demonstrates that the economic significance of development finance from abroad has, unfortunately, been weak in those very countries where the need for such finance is strong.

The analysis set out in the preceding section has already indicated that, in relation to population, the international flow of development finance has remained very inequitably distributed among the recipient countries. A summary view yielded by that analysis is contained in table 11, which shows data on per capita net receipts of development finance from abroad. The contrasts presented by this information are striking. If international development policy had been geared to a narrowing of economic disparities among developing countries, the lower-income developing countries would have received higher amounts of external finance per head of population than the higher-income developing countries. Actually, the pattern has been just the opposite, and marked by a very wide divergence. In 1971-1973, the per head receipts of the net annual flow of international development finance amounted to nearly SDR 30 in countries with a <u>per capita</u> income of $800 or more, to about SDR 19 in countries with a <u>per capita</u> income of $400-$799, to SDR 13 in countries with a <u>per capita</u> income of $200-$399, to SDR 4 in countries with a <u>per capita</u> income of $100-$199 and to not even SDR 2 in countries belonging to the lowest-income group. Moreover, between 1968-1970 and 1971-1973, the receipts of higher-income developing countries per head of population increased very substantially. But in the lower-income group of countries, there was no increase at all. By and large, the lower-income developing countries fared poorly in respect of all three components of development finance. Much of the inter-country divergence in per head receipts of the net international flow of development finance resulted from the movements of capital that are governed by commercial considerations. In essence, it is only official development assistance that can help to narrow or eliminate the divergence. The component of such assistance that is readily identifiable from table 11--namely, official donations--has been not only small but also not geared to achieving this objective. The conclusion is therefore inescapable that, instead of helping to achieve some narrowing, international flows of official and private finance have contributed to a widening of economic disparities among developing countries.

VI. IMPLICATIONS FOR POLICIES

For many developing countries, the need for financial resources from abroad remains acute. Low average income, paucity of domestic saving and inadequate expansion of export earnings continue to figure prominently among the problems encountered in many parts of the developing world. Since the end of the period reviewed in the present paper, some of the problems have in fact become seriously aggravated. The sharp increases in the prices of petroleum, fertilizaer, food-grains and crucial investment goods, such as machinery and heavy equipment, have imposed an alarming burden on many developing countries. Further, as a result of economic recession in developed countries with market economies, which absorb by far the largest part of the exports of developing countries,[10] there is currently a downward slide in the export trade of all but a few developing countries whose export commodities (most notably, petroleum) enjoy vigorous world demand.

Thus, the constraint imposed by the scarcity of foreign exchange has frequently become severe.

These developments on the trade front have taken place at a time when the net flow of financial resources from developed to developing countries continues to hover persistently well below the target specified in the International Development Strategy. During 1971-1973, the net flow of public and private financial resources from the developed market economies—the only group of economically advanced countries for which data on disbursements of funds are available—amounted to 0.7 per cent of their gross national product, compared to the target of 1 per cent indicated in the Strategy. This target is a key element of the International Development Strategy, and current developments in the world economy have simply reinforced its importance.

Recent experience has vividly demonstrated that the international flow of private capital to developing countries is prone to be concentrated in a few of them. Since international movements of private capital are shaped by commercial considerations, it is futile to think that the factors that serve as a magnetic attraction for foreign investors can be duplicated universally. This experience demonstrates that the target denominated in the International Development Strategy with regard to official development assistance is far more meaningful than the target relating to total resource transfers which lumps together public and private capital flows. Autonomous movements of private capital across national frontiers, however important they may be for recipient countries, can hardly be considered to be of the same genus as official grants and concessional loans to developing countries.

Although not all developing countries can realistically expect to attract large flows of private capital from abroad, certain measures can help them in this respect. A particularly helpful role as intermediaries can be played by specialized international institutions. For example, the International Finance Corporation, which is an affiliate of the International Bank for Reconstruction and Development (IBRD), is specifically charged with the task of promoting the flow of private capital to developing countries. In association with private investors, the Corporation provides equity and loan capital to private enterprises without entailing a guarantee of repayment by the Government of the country where such enterprises are located; it also helps to establish joint ventures. An enlargement of the role played by the Corporation could be one possible means of help. Another valuable source of help could be the establishment of similar mechanisms within or as affiliates of the regional and subregional development banks. By virtue of their specialization of activities in a particular geographical area, the regional and subregional development banks are in an especially good position to be able to assess the local requirements and problems.

Those developing countries which wish to obtain private capital from abroad also need to be aware and provide a clear indication of their obligations to foreign investors. Ambiguity and uncertainty are particularly detrimental in this regard. Here again, international organizations can play a useful part by helping, on request, to streamline rules and regulations governing foreign private investment, by supplying information about access to international capital markets, and even by helping to resolve disputes.

For many developing countries, however, the importance of official financial flows from abroad will remain supreme. Particularly important in this regard is the role of grants which, unlike loans, impose no burden of amortization and interest payment. The decline in the relative importance of official grants in the international flow of development finance since the early 1960s is unfortunate. The mild tendency for official grants to expand faster than official loans that can now be discerned needs to be sharply accentuated.

The terms on which official loans are provided to developing countries vary widely. Some are given on market or near market terms. Such loans are also, however, geared to projects which do not normally attract private funds from abroad. For example, the loans offered by IBRD and the regional development banks for economic and social infrastructure, ranging all the way from electricity generation to education, are usually of this type. While such loans will no doubt continue to be important, there is now a growing need for loans on softer terms. To the extent that such assistance is given as loans, account should be taken of the specific economic circumstances of the borrowing country and thus the loans should be on the easiest possible terms with regard to interest rate as well as maturity and grace periods. A growing part of the multilateral assistance needs to be given at low rates of interest. Especially important in this connexion are the loans provided by the International Development Association and the new lending facility--the "third window"--offered by IBRD.

The analysis of trends in the international flow of development finance contained in the preceding sections has shown that the distribution of this flow among developing countries has been highly inequitable. If it remains unchecked, this lop-sided distribution will continue contributing to a widening of economic disparities among developing countries. Such a state of affairs could hardly be considered tolerable. Indeed, there is an urgent need to devise ways and means of bringing about a relative shift in the international flow of development finance in favour of low-income developing countries. The components of development finance that are amenable to such a shift are naturally the flows of grants and loans provided by aid-giving countries and international institutions. In the framework of international economic co-operation designed to reduce economic inequalities prevailing in the world, it is important to direct a substantial share of the international flow of concessional economic assistance to the poorer members of the world economy.

The external-debt problem of developing countries has not been examined in the present paper. The fact remains, however, that this problem is a very serious one. Analyses made in the United Nations, the World Bank and other international organizations with regard to the burden of external indebtedness in the years immediately ahead suggest an even more sombre picture than the one discernible from the information pertaining to the recent past.

External Finance for Development 359

The upshot of such projections analyses is that the core of the debt problem does indeed lie in the lower-income developing countries. These analyses emphasize that measures are required to cope with the problem not only as it stands but also to avoid its pitfalls in the future.[11] The latter aspect reinforces the argument that official development assistance should, by and large, be in the form of grants. A reorientation of the international aid policy is, thus, more urgent than ever.

NOTES

[1] Based on such information, an analysis of the distribution of international economic assistance--that is, official grants and concessional loans--among developing countries in recent years is provided in a companion paper. See "Foreign aid and development needs" in the present issue of the Journal of Development Planning.

[2] On the average, 1 SDR equalled $1.00298 in 1971, $1.08571 in 1972, $1.19213 in 1973 and $1.20248 in 1974. See International Monetary Fund, International Financial Statistics (Washington, D.C., September 1975), p. 392.

[3] Data for Pakistan throughout the present paper refer to that country as it was prior to the establishment of Bangladesh (the former East Wing of Pakistan) and for the period ending in 1971.

[4] International Monetary Fund, Balance of Payments Manual, third edition (Washington, D.C., 1961), para. 351.

[5] All foreign loans received or given by the banking institutions of the reporting country are included in this column. Some of these transactions may be for a maturity period of more than one year, and such transactions should strictly be included in estimates of long-term capital. However, for most developing countries, the available information does not make it possible to distinguish between the short-term and long-term external transactions of banking or monetary institutions. The broad policy conclusions yielded by the analysis contained in the present paper are not likely to be affected by this discrepancy.

[6] Regarding the data contained in the penultimate column of table 1, it should be noted that, in accounting terms, a net addition to a country's international reserves is equivalent to a net outflow of funds and is therefore recorded with a negative sign. Conversely, a net decline of reserves, being equivalent to a net inflow of funds, is recorded without a sign.

The combined international reserves of all developing

countries and areas increased from about SDR 13 billion at the end of 1967 to nearly SDR 35.5 billion at the end of 1973--that is, annually on the average by about SDR 3.7 billion. (See International Monetary Fund, International Financial Statistics (Washington, D.C.), May 1972 and September 1975). A substantial part of this annual increase was accounted for by petroleum--exporting developing countries; among them, the Libyan Arab Republic and Saudi Arabia added annually to their international reserves to the tune of nearly SDR 1 billion. It will also be recalled that table 1 does not cover all developing countries and areas; such countries as Kuwait and the United Arab Emirates, which could not be included in the table because of lack of data, are reported to have made sizable additions to their international reserves. Moreover, in addition to short-term capital movements, the data in the penultimate column of table 1 include "errors and omissions".

[7] It should be noted that the net outflow of one component of development finance from Saudi Arabia during 1971-1973, namely, long-term private capital, is reported to have included a large increase in the accrued taxes and royalties payable to the Government of that country. See International Monetary Fund, Balance of Payments Yearbook, 1969-1973 (Washington, D.C., 1974-1975), vol. 26, country pages for Saudi Arabia.

[8] Both the Libyan Arab Republic and Saudi Arabia were not importers of development finance in 1961-1963. If these two countries are included in the data shown in table 4 for both the early 1960s and the early 1970s--that is, the sample is enlarged to cover 44 countries--the net annual flow of development finance received by these 44 countries from the rest of the world shows an increase of 131 per cent, from SDR 3.8 billion in 1961-1963 to SDR 8.8 billion in 1971-1973; and the share of official donations shows a steep decline, from 27 to 9 per cent.

[9] It should be stressed that these examples are based on absolute amounts of the net flow of official donations and long-term official capital received from abroad. The economic significance of large or moderately large absolute receipts of such funds, however, varied enormously among the eight countries mentioned in the text above. For example, on a per capita basis, the net annual receipts of these official funds in 1971-1973 amounted to SDR 65 in Jordan, SDR 11 in Egypt, SDR 10 in Chile, SDR 5 in Sri Lanka, SDR 3 in Uganda, and SDR 1 in Burma and India. The question of the economic significance or contribution of the component of the flow of development finance is discussed in the next section.

In the context of the offsetting role of official funds, in terms of the statistical comparison made in the text above, mention should also be made of the Philippines, Venezuela, Zambia, Iraq and Gabon (see table 7). While most of these countries are prominent exporters of petroleum or other minerals, a different interplay of forces is reflected in them. The net outflow of private capital from Iraq and Zambia was strongly influenced by the nationalization of certain activities in these countries; in Gabon and Venezuela, the repayment of loans by the private sector to external institutions shaped the outcome. Moreover, the large or moderately large net flow of official funds received by these countries did not really represent economic assistance; a substantial part of the flow in fact consisted of loans obtained by their Governments and official institutions from external sources on commercial or near commercial terms, including loans from the Euro-currency market. Of course, as will be pointed out in the text above, a number of other countries also received such loans. The rationale for citing India, Egypt, Jordan, Chile, Sri Lanka, Uganda and Burma as the countries where official capital did play an offsetting role of some significance is that these countries received little or no loan capital from the Euro-currency market or other comparable foreign private institutions during 1971-1973; for these countries, the offsetting role that is discernible was largely played by official development assistance.

[10] In 1973, nearly 76 per cent of the exports of developing countries went to the developed market economies and about 4 per cent to the centrally planned economies; the remaining 20 per cent represented trade among the developing countries themselves. See United Nations, Monthly Bulletin of Statistics, vol. XXIX, No. 7 (July 1975).

[11] For a discussion of relevant policies, see Gamani Corea, "The debt problem of developing countries" in Journal of Development Planning, No. 9 (United Nations publication, Sales No. E.76.II.A.3).

The Production Structure and the Dynamics of Development

GERARD FICHET
NORBERTO GONZALEZ

I. INTRODUCTION

Most of the Latin American countries are faced with controversy on the development strategy which should be followed, and are discussing, among other fundamental aspects, the role that should be played in it by import substitution policies and policies to promote the export of manufactures.

This papers sets out to show that the time has come to consider such policies as complementary elements of a development strategy for Latin America. The common fallacy that the two policies are in opposition is the result of a mistaken over-simplification and only confuses the search for appropriate solutions.

This confusion has above all militated against Latin American cooperation in the industrial and commercial spheres. Import substitution is often erroneously regarded as a policy which can only be applied in the limited context of each national market. Nor has the export manufactures, mainly from the economically largest countries of the region, been carried out with sufficient attention to the important role that Latin American trade can play as an instrument for securing these countries a better foothold in the world economy. There is, in consequence, a tendency to assume that it is possible to pass directly from the historical stage of highly-protected national industrialization to the conquest of international markets, envisaging the Latin American market merely as a part of the world market, without assigning an important role to the co-operation between the Latin American countries, and thus disregarding the possibilities of import substitution at the level

From **CEPAL REVIEW**, 1976, (163-202), reprinted by permission of the publisher.

The Production Structure and the Dynamics of Development   363

of the regional market.

These erroneous concepts acquire particular significance in the context of the period of difficulties and radical change through which both the world economy and that of Latin America are now passing. Latin America, without losing its identity as a member of the developing world, is becoming more and more individualized as a region whose characteristics, problems and potentialities distinguish it from the rest of the Third World. Because of its higher per capita income it has been increasingly excluded from the international mechanisms of financial co-operation. Its degree of industrial development, which is on an average higher than that of the countries of Africa and Asia, allows it to assign a more prominent role to the manufacturing sector in both the growth of exports and the solution of the domestic problems of absorbing labour and overcoming mass poverty, without detracting from the continuing importance of exports of primary commodities and simple manufactures. Many Latin American countries are already exporting significant quantities not only of simple manufactures but also of capital goods and other products entailing a fairly advanced technology, manufactured by the metal-transforming industries. It is clearly essential to define a new role for Latin America and a new mode of incorporation of the Latin American countries in world trade and industry.

As will be shown later, regional co-operation[2] must play a primary role in securing this new position and in the achievement of a satisfactory balance between import substitution and the conquest of external markets.

The following section analyses the relation which exists, for the industries producing capital and intermediate goods, between the size of the domestic market and the possibilities of increasing production and trade in the countries of the Organisation for Economic Co-operation and Development (OECD), which have competitive economies. It will be appreciated that if competitive conditions in Latin America were similar to those of the OECD economies, the opportunity of operating in a market of regional size would considerably broaden the possibilities of change in the structure of domestic production and of trade; this is true even of the more developed and larger countries of Latin America.

Sections 2 and 3 set forth some strategy options and study the prospects for Latin American development on the assumption that it will continue to be based entirely on the domestic market and the isolated effort of each country to conquer external markets; it will be seen that these prospects are decidedly restricted, since in such conditions only very limited changed in the production and trade structures would be feasible.

Section 4 briefly analyses a hypothesis of co-operation based on the promotion of the metal-transforming and chemical industries and of regional trade in their output. The results could be very significant, since such a course would not only appreciably speed up the rate of development, but would also help to overcome the chronic backwardness of these sectors, inasmuch as conditions of international competition would prevail and their exports to the rest of the world might expand considerably.

Lastly, some of the instruments which could serve to implement regional co-operation strategy are outlined in brief.

II. LATIN AMERICA'S ROLE IN WORLD TRADE AND INDUSTRY: PAST AND PRESENT

The foreign trade and industrial production structures of Latin America show serious deficiencies in comparison with those of the industrially advanced countries, as is evidenced both in trends over the last twenty-five years and in the current situation.

(a) Trends Over the Last 25 Years

An analysis of trends in the external sector and in industry reveals some characteristics which will have marked repercussions on the future economic development of the region.

The important substitution process has been very intensive over the last 25 years, particularly towards the mid-1960s, and since then there has been an unprecedented expansion of exports, and a parallel increase in imports. It should however be pointed out that:

(i) Import substitution is making very unequal progress; not only are some countries more backward than others in this respect, but even in those that are more advanced some industrial sectors of great strategic importance for development (intermediate and capital goods) are lagging behind, and still show quite high import coefficients;

(ii) The growth rate of Latin American imports, which up to 1964 was only 0.4 times that of the product, is now 1.3 times the latter rate, and in some countries almost twice as high. Among the main causes of this phenomenon it should be particularly noted that as per capita income rises there is a more rapid increase in demand for goods with a higher import content (intermediate goods and production equipment), since the region's technological backwardness and low capacity for innovation make it necessary to import many of the new goods. Secondly, in many countries more and more liberalization of imports has been among the effects of the rapid increase in export values and of access to external financing.

(iii) During the period 1963-1972, in Latin America as a whole the manufacturing sector grew faster than in the industrialized countries, but its production structure still differs greatly from that observable in the latter. (See figure 1.) In the Latin American industrialization process the production of consumer goods has been given priority over that of capital and intermediate goods.

(iv) About half the Latin American population is almost

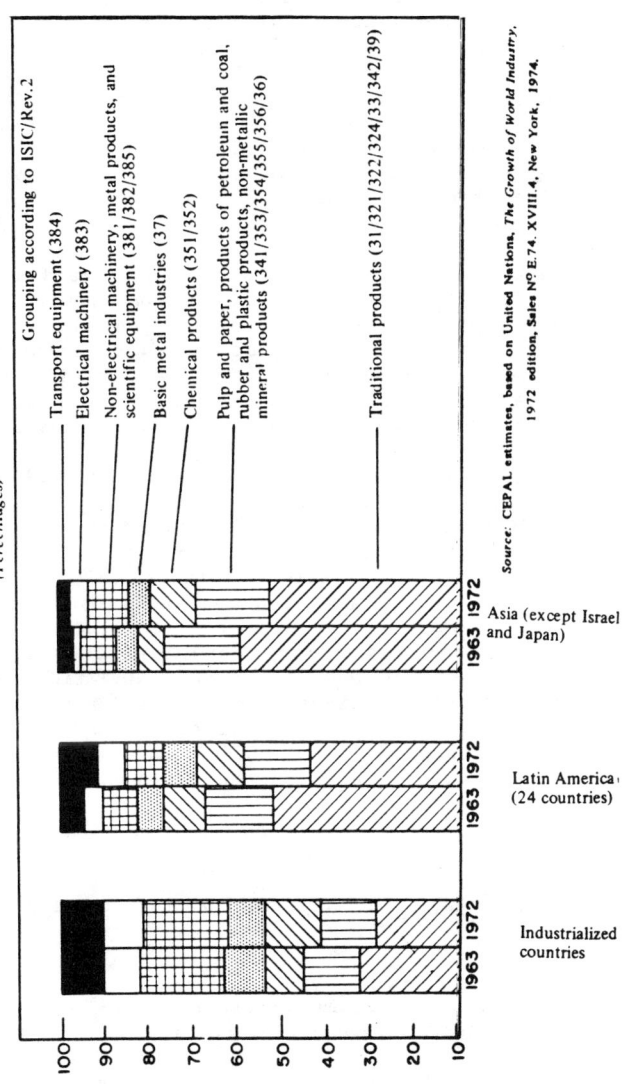

Figure 1
STRUCTURE OF INDUSTRIAL PRODUCTION, 1963 AND 1972
(Percentages)

entirely cut off from participating in demand for manufactures, and only a fifth of the total population contributes to creating a market for industry and serves as a basis for its expansion abroad. The low income strata affected by unemployment and under-employment make no contribution to demand. At the other extreme there is a small social sector, with very diversified and refined patterns of consumption, which orients industrialization. The small size of the real markets, attributable to this factor and to the lack of inter-country integration, goes a long way towards accounting for the backwardness of those industrial sectors which are more dynamic and of greater significance for development, such as the producers of capital and intermediate goods; in small markets it is difficult to produce on a competitive scale, and this limits the possibilities of exporting manufactures, a handicap which in turn helps to determine the peculiar nature of the region's present role in the world economy.

(v) Exports of manufactures increased rapidly from 1970 onwards in several countries of the region. However, they still represent only just over a fifth of total exports,[3] and consequently afford no certainty of a rapid increase in the total volume of exports. Furthermore, 75 per cent of industrial exports are concentrated in the three economically largest countries. Intra-regional trade is very important, especially in industrial sectors; in 1974 the area absorbed 70 per cent and 46 per cent, respectively, of the products of the metal-transforming industries exported by Argentina and Brazil.

(vi) In recent years the trade-balance deficit has come to be the fundamental hindrance to development. The prices of raw materials, which rose temporarily, has fallen (with exceptions such as petroleum), and are again showing their usual trends. The growth rate of exports of manufactures has slackened, because of the problems besetting the economies of the industrialized countries. In contrast, because of world inflation import prices are rising, and will continue to do so, at least for a time, and foreign debt servicing is also increasing sharply. Hence it is reasonable to suppose that for the next few years the balance of payments will tend to condition the development of many of the countries of the region.

(b) Current Deficiencies of Industrial and Trade Structures

The products of the metal-transforming and intermediate industries predominate in Latin American imports. Some 40 per cent of the region's total imports of goods are metal-transforming products, whereas the proportion is much lower in Japan (14 per cent) and in the United States.

The difference is even clearer in the case of exports, for while 45 per cent of the two industrialized countries' total exports of goods consisted of metal-transforming products in 1970, in Latin America the corresponding proportion is now only 6 per

Table 1

STRUCTURE OF FOREIGN TRADE

(Percentages of total exports and imports)

Groupings according to ISIC/Rev.1	Japan (1970)		United States (1970)		Latin America (in the mid-1970s)	
	Exports	Imports	Exports	Imports	Exports [a]	Imports
Primary products [b]	3.7	52.3	20.8	20.4	44.8	17.1
Traditional industries [c]	24.3	16.7	13.0	26.7	24.6	9.1
Intermediate industries [d]	26.7	17.1	19.8	22.9	25.1	33.8
Engineering industries [e]	45.3	13.9	46.4	30.0	5.5	40.0

Source: United Nations, *Yearbook of International Trade Statistics 1972-1973* (Sales Nº: E.74.XVII.6), and CEPAL estimates for Latin America.

[a] In this table goods which in the UNCTAD classification are correctly considered as primary and semi-manufactured products are included under the traditional and intermediate industries. This explains the difference between the proportion of manufactures to the total according to this table, and that of just over a fifth of the total of manufactures in the strict sense previously mentioned in the text.

[b] Divisions 01 to 19 of ISIC/Rev.1.
[c] Divisions 20 to 26 and 28, 29 and 39, of ISIC/Rev.1.
[d] Divisions 27 and 30 to 34 of ISIC/Rev.1.
[e] Division 35 to 38 of ISIC/Rev.1.

Table 2

STRUCTURE OF INDUSTRIAL PRODUCTION

(Percentages of total production)

	Japan (1970)	European Economic Community [a] (1972)	United States (1970)	Latin America (in the mid-1970s)
Traditional industries [b]	25.6	29.0	36.6	38.5
Intermediate industries [c]	29.5	34.0	27.4	37.8
Engineering industries [d]	44.9	37.0	36.0	23.7

Source: United Nations, *The Growth of World Industry*, 1972 edition, *op. cit.*, Volume I, "General Industrial Statistics, 1962-1971", and CEPAL estimates for Latin America.

[a] Comprising nine countries.
[b] Divisions 20 to 26, 28, 29 and 39 of ISIC/Rev.1.
[c] Divisions 27 and 30 to 34 of ISIC/Rev.1.
[d] Divisions 35 to 38 of ISIC/Rev.1.

Table 3

IMPORTS AND EXPORTS OF SOME STRATEGIC SECTORS

(Billions of dollars)

Sector	United States [a] (1970)		European Economic Community [a] [b] (1972)		Latin America (in the mid-1970s) [c]	
	Imports	Exports	Imports	Exports	Imports	Exports
Chemical products	1.6	4.3	12.6	16.5	4.3	2.6
Non-electrical machinery	3.0	8.4	15.2	24.9	5.0	0.5
Electrical machinery	2.3	3.0	8.1	10.9	2.1	0.8
Transport equipment	5.9	6.5	11.4	20.1	3.0	0.4
Sub-total of these sectors	*12.8*	*22.2*	*47.3*	*72.4*	*14.4*	*4.3*
Other goods	27.2	21.0	106.8	81.2	14.4	26.0
Total goods	*40.0*	*43.2*	*154.1*	*153.6*	*28.8*	*30.3*

Source: United Nations, *Yearbook of International Trade Statistics, 1972-1973, op. cit.,* and CEPAL estimates for Latin America.

[a] At current prices.
[b] Comprising nine countries.
[c] At 1973 prices.

cent. The disparity is much more marked in absolute terms: the value of Latin America's exports of these goods (from several countries) was some 2,000 million dollars; that of Japan's, 9,000 million; and that of the United States', 20,000 million. At the same time, a high proportion of Latin American exports consists of primary commodities (45 per cent), while the share of such products in the exports of Japan and the United States is much lower. (See table 1.)

In Latin America there is very markedly assymetry in foreign trade caused by the difference in the relative importance of products of the metal-transforming industry and of primary commodities in total imports and exports; this asymmetry is not found in the developed countries. Furthermore, the proportions represented by traditional goods in imports and in exports are more similar in the United States than in Latin America. The heavy imbalance observable in Japan's foreign trade in primary commodities is due to its shortage of natural resources.

Latin America's manufacturing production is very different in structure from that of Japan or the United States. (See table 2). In Latin America the relative share of the metal-transforming industry in total production is considerably lower than in the two industrialized countries, as will be seen clearly farther on, when the components of the capital goods sector are studied in more detail. The production of traditional and intermediate goods predominates in the region.[4]

Thus, in comparison with other countries Latin America is lagging behind in the production of capital goods and basic intermediate goods, and this is reflected in the asymmetric structure of its foreign trade.

The metal-transforming products which have a lower percentage share in Latin American production (23.7) and whose relative significance in imports of industrial goods is greatest (48.3 per cent) are precisely those in which the volume of world trade is growing most rapidly: 10.7 per cent a year over the period 1965-1973. In Latin American exports, however, the predominant products are those in which world trade is growing at a slower rate; during the same period the volume of world exports of agricultural goods increased by only 3.7 per cent yearly.[5]

These shortcomings in the production and trade structures make for a more rapid increase in import requirements than in exports, and thus lead to external bottlenecks.

A more detailed analysis of the absolute participation of the chemical and metal-transforming sectors in total trade reveals that it is in these areas that Latin America is most backward. Table 3 shows that imports of chemical products, non-electrical and electrical machinery and transport equipment amount to 14,400 million dollars (50 per cent of total Latin American imports) and exports to only 4,300 million dollars (12 per cent of the total). In the United States and the European Economic Community (EEC), on the other hand, the relative share of these goods in imports is lower than in exports (30 and 50 per cent, respectively).

In each of the sectors considered there is a manifest imbalance. The industrialized countries export much more than they import, because they sell these types of goods to the developing countries, while among themselves they buy and sell products of similar sectors. In Latin America, on the other hand, the asymmetry is very marked and highly unfavourable; the ratio between imports and regional sales of non-electrical machinery is ten to one, and in the case of transport equipment, seven to one.

In recent years the gross value of per capita production in the chemical industries has been only a quarter as much in Latin America as in France, one-fifth as much as in Japan, one-sixth as much as in West Germany and one-seventh as much as in the United States. In the metal-transforming industries the difference is far greater; in terms of value, the region's per capita production is equivalent to one-third of that of Italy, one-sixth of that of the Netherlands, one-tenth of that of West Germany, the United Kingdom and Japan, and one-thirteenth of Sweden's.

Since Latin America's total per capita product is smaller than that of the developed countries, it is only to be expected that in each of the sectors the region is lagging behind in comparison. It should however be noted that the backwardness of the four strategic sectors included in table 3 is much greater than that of the rest of the economy. In table 4 is can be seen that the gap between Latin America's total gross domestic product per capita and that of the developed countries is substantially less than the difference noted in the previous paragraph for these industrial sectors.

(c) Relation Between Market Size, Specialization And Foreign Trade In Competitive Economies

All that has been said so far is important because, as will be seen below, the smaller the size of a country, the more it needs to export in order to achieve a scale of industrial production which will enable it to compete in world markets. This leads each country to specialize its exports intra-sectorally and therefore to import from other countries the goods that it cannot manufacture on competitive terms. This can be seen very clearly in the small European countries, where the global ratio of imports to the gross domestic product is high and on the increase and at the same time exports are rising. In the OECD countries the economies are very open in order to be competitive. The system of preferences existing between these same countries also plays an important role. Thus, in the early stages of the operation of the European Economic Community the external tariff was much higher than the internal, so that the industries were able to produce on a regional scale; once this objective had been attained, they were in a position to compete in the outside world.

Another way of expressing the same phenomenon is afforded by the relation between the proportion of demand supplied by imports (import coefficient) and the domestic size of demand. The greater the size of a market, the lower the import coefficient can be. This in fact occurs in each of the major industrial sectors of the countries which can compete at the world level, as can be seen in

Figure 2

OECD COUNTRIES:[a] COEFFICIENT OF IMPORTS WITH RESPECT TO SIZE OF DOMESTIC DEMAND IN SOME INDUSTRIAL SECTORS, IN VARIOUS YEARS[b]

(Natural scale)

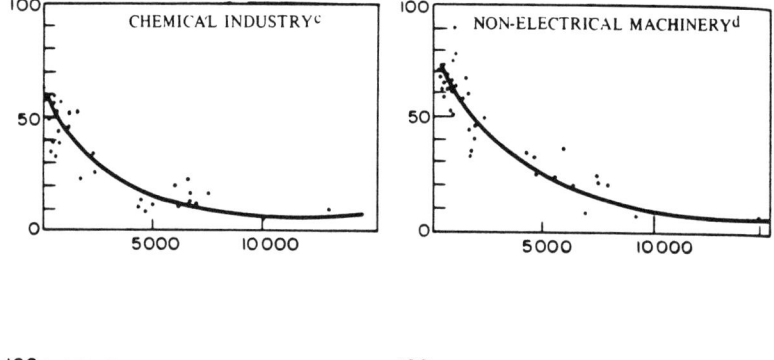

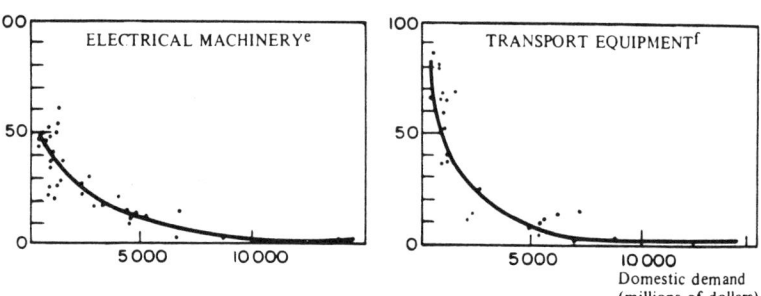

Domestic demand
(millions of dollars)

Source: CEPAL, on the basis of OECD, *The Chemical Industry* and *The Engineering Industries in North America-Europe-Japan,* various issues.

[a] Excluding the United States in all cases, since its domestic demand is excessively large compared with that of the other countries.

[b] The following formula was used: $\log M/D_i = a + b \log D_i + c (\log D_i)^2$.

[c] $\log M/D_i = -0.4642 + 1.7523 \log D_i -0.3511 (\log D_i)^2$ years 1963-1968-1970
(0.7663)   (0.1172)
$R^2 = 0.8423$

[d] $\log M/D_i = -1.9714 + 2.7685 \log D_i -0.5039 (\log D_i)^2$ years 1966-1967-1969
(0.5923)   (0.0892)
$R^2 = 0.8557$

[e] $\log M/D_i = -4.2845 + 4.3063 \log D_i -0.7796 (\log D_i)^2$ years 1966-1967-1969
(0.7492)   (0.1160)
$R^2 = 0.8627$

[f] $\log M/D_i = -0.0043 + 2.0896 \log D_i -0.4972 (\log D_i)^2$ years 1966-1967-1969
(1.6157)   (0.2360)
$R^2 = 0.9256$

Figure 3

OECD COUNTRIES: PATTERN OF EXPORTS AS A PROPORTION OF IMPORTS IN RELATION TO DOMESTIC DEMAND IN THE CHEMICAL INDUSTRY, 1971

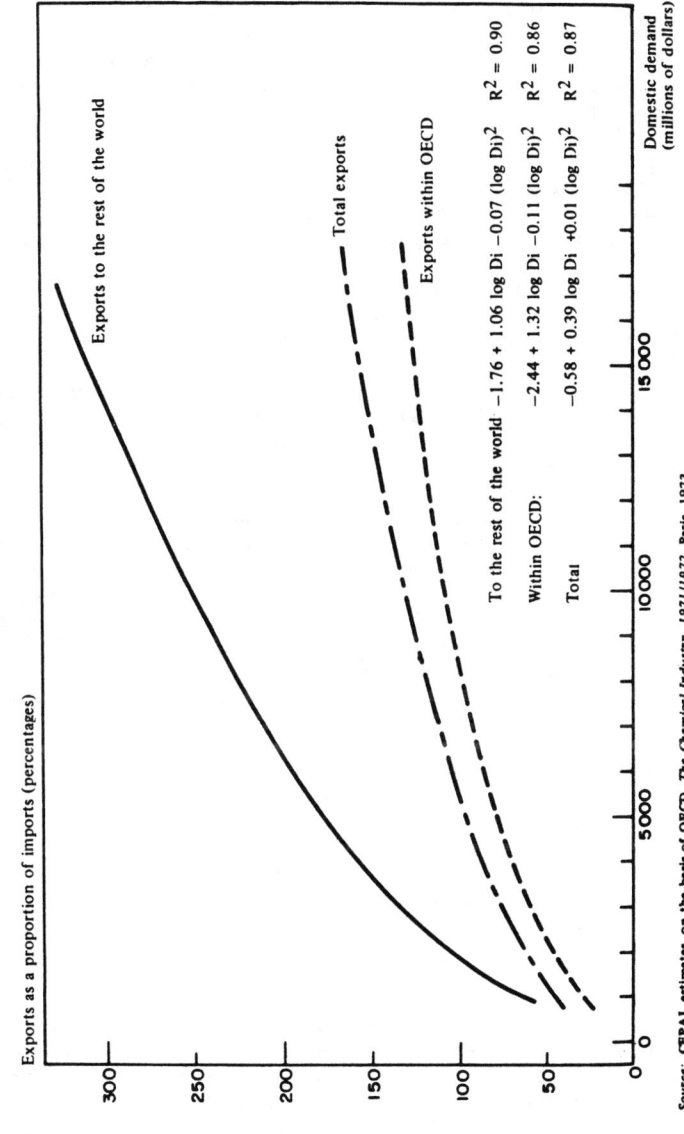

Source: CEPAL estimates, on the basis of OECD, *The Chemical Industry, 1971/1972*, Paris, 1973.

figure 2. As the size of the national market increases, the need to import diminishes in relative terms, since the industries of each of these sectors can operate on a competitive basis with low costs and high efficiency, by virtue of the greater size of the national market, plus exports on a relatively more modest scale. The countries with smaller markets, however, have a high import coefficient to avoid producing goods under inefficient conditions. Because of the dimensions of their markets, the smaller countries of Europe, such as the Scandinavian countries, Switzerland, Belgium, the Netherlands, etc., have specialized in the production of certain goods in each sector and import other parts or goods pertaining to the same sector which they cannot produce on competitive terms.[6]

This specialization is reflected in a high proportion of exports in relation to production, and of imports in relation to demand.

It is thus to be expected that, within each of these basic industrial sectors, the total generated by exports of some goods would be similar to that represented by imports of those which are not manufactured by domestic industry. If this occurred it would be very important, as it would make competitive production compatible with a diversified production structure including the different types of metal-transforming and chemical products that are so important for development. If the relation between the exports and imports of each of the above-mentioned sectors in the OECD countries is observed, it can be seen that in each of them there is in fact this equivalence between imports and exports, and in every case the situation of the countries becomes more favourable as the magnitude of domestic demand increases. The larger countries are in a better position to produce these types of goods internally; thus their requirements respecting imports of goods from each sector are proportionally less, and are more than offset by exports.

In a small country, on the other hand, import requirements are proportionally greater in relation to demand and may not be totally counterbalanced by exports of goods from the same sector, since the national market is not large enough to promote domestic production to the required extent. Figure 3, shows that for countries which trade in competitive conditions, such as those of the OECD, a correlation exists between the size of national demand and the proportion of exports to imports in the chemical industries.[7] The bigger the country, the larger are its exports in comparison to imports. It can also be seen in figure 3 that the OECD countries have a consistent tendency to export more to the developing countries than they import from them, a disadvantageous situation for the latter which must be remedied, since as matters stand the developing world is helping the industrialized countries to step up their industrial development, and, in particular, allowing the smaller OECD countries to obtain partial compensation for their unfavourable position in trade with the larger countries of the Organization.

In the case of Latin America, figure 4 makes it plain that in the chemical and metal-transforming sectors, imports from OECD countries are very high and exports to them are almost

Figure 4

TRADE BALANCES OF THE OECD COUNTRIES WITH LATIN AMERICA IN SOME INDUSTRIAL SECTORS, 1969-1974

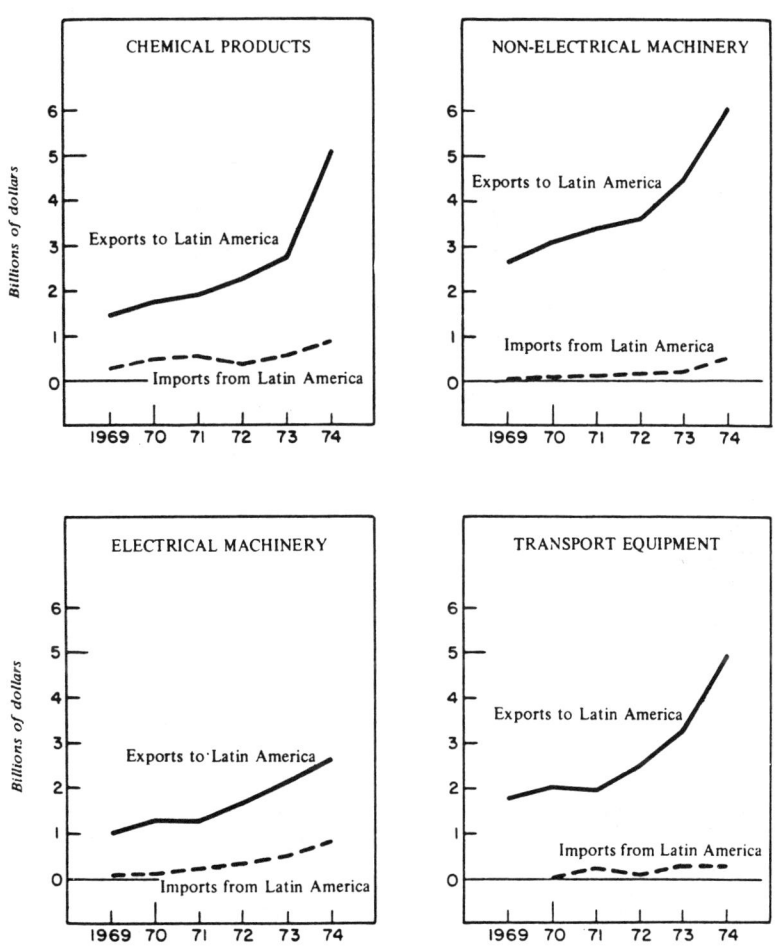

Source: CEPAL, on the basis of OECD, *Trade by Commodities. Market Summaries: Exports*, series C, Vol. I, various issues.

Figure 5

OECD COUNTRIES AND LATIN AMERICA: COEFFICIENTS OF IMPORTED SUPPLY OF TRANSPORT EQUIPMENT IN RELATION TO THE DOMESTIC DEMAND OF THE SAME INDUSTRIAL SECTOR[a]

(Natural scale)

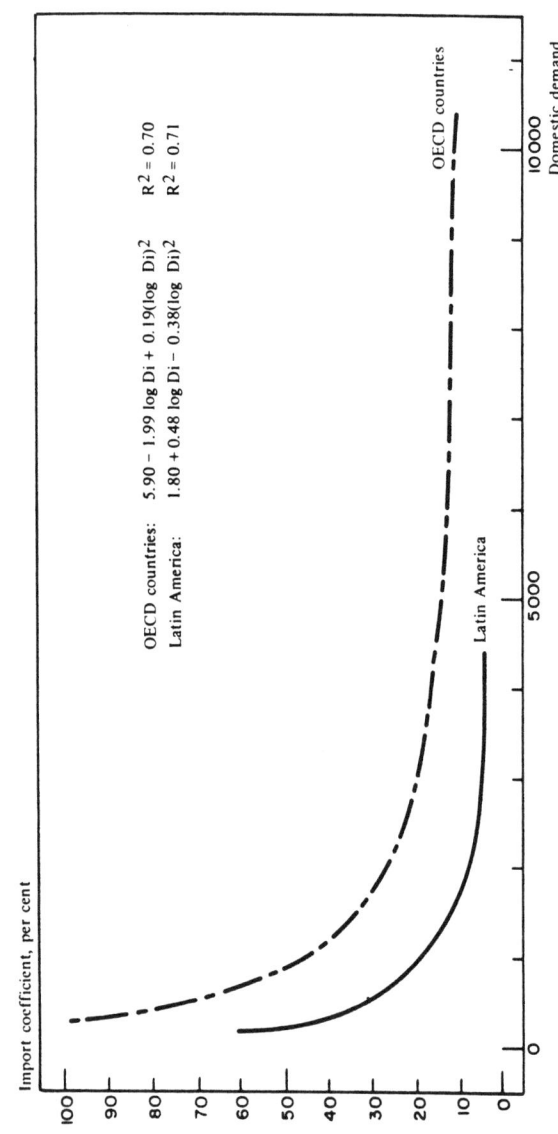

Source: CEPAL estimates, based on OECD, *The Engineering Industries, 1969/1970,* volume I, Paris, 1971.
[a] OECD figures for 1969, Latin American figures for 1970.

non-existent. In 1973 some 45 per cent of the OECD countries' total exports to Latin America consisted of metal-transforming products, while 95 per cent of their imports from the region were primary commodities.

(d) Relation Between Market Size And Foreign Trade In Latin America

What is the situation of the Latin American countries in respect of the relation between the size of their national markets and the foreign trade of their metal-transforming and chemical sectors?

From figure 5 it can be seen that the transport equipment industries of Latin America as a whole also show the relation noted in the OECD countries between import coefficient and market size: the largest countries to the region need to import proportionally less to function with a degree of efficiency similar to that of the smaller countries. But it is likewise clearly apparent that the Latin American curve is consistently lower than that of the OECD countries; that is, the import coefficients in Latin America fall short of those which would be appropriate to the sizes of its markets if they functioned competitively. This is due to the fact that in the Latin American countries industry is highly protected and has a low level of efficiency. Furthermore, since integration among the Latin American countries is almost non-existent today, the size of each national market, and not that of the regional market, is what determines the coefficient in competitive trade.

Thus, for example, in 1972 the Brazilian market for transport equipment was slightly larger than that of Italy in 1969; but the proportion of demand supplied by imports was 11.2 per cent, as against 25 per cent in Italy. In 1972 the size of the chemical products market in Spain and Argentina was very similar, but the import coefficient in the former was 17.5 per cent and in the latter, 9.5 per cent. In the same year, domestic demand for non-electrical machinery in Mexico was much the same as in the Netherlands in 1969, but while the Mexican import coefficient was 52 per cent, that of the Netherlands amounted to 68 per cent. Similarly, there are important differences in costs between the Latin American and OECD countries.

So what would happen if Latin America were considered as a whole, that is, as a single integrated market for the operation and development of these sectors? Taking into account the size of the region's market, the import coefficient could be much lower than it is at present, and even then these sectors would function competitively at the international level, that is, in much better conditions than at present. Of course in this case each individual country would have a higher import coefficient than at present, since in addition to imports from the rest of the world there would be those obtained from other Latin American countries. It may be recalled that total Latin American demand for non-electrical machinery was equivalent in 1972 to that of West Germany in 1969, but that the import coefficient for the region as a whole amounted to around 44 per cent, while that of Germany was only 24 per cent.

In the OECD countries there is also a relation between exports, production and demand; in fact an import-production-export cycle exists, which reflects the economic vitality of these countries in importing to export. In contrast, the low export production coefficient reflects the backwardness of the Latin American countries which do not export all that they should in order to produce competitively in accordance with their size.

In Latin America there is not yet a well-established export pattern. Exports of manufactures are developing steadily but are still not very systematic and are well below imports of industrial goods. Several countries of the region, and particularly those of greater economic size -- which are precisely those whose exports reach a proportionally higher total, although their volume of production is similar to that of some European countries -- have a very low export/production coefficient. The gross value of output of transport equipment in Argentina and Brazil in 1972-1973 was similar to the corresponding figure for Italy in 1969, but the export coefficient was only about 3 per cent, whereas in Italy it was 40 per cent.

III. FUTURE OUTLOOK

As was seen in the preceding section, great strides have been made in the industry and trade of the Latin American countries over the last few quinquennia: the growth rates of exports have been significantly higher than in the past, the degree of competitiveness of industry has gradually improved and protection policies have been rationalized.

These changes have not been intensive enough, however, to prevail over some of the fundamental development handicaps of the Latin American countries. From the end of the 1960s onwards it was increasingly felt that the external bottleneck problems chronically afflicting these countries had greatly decreased in importance. During 1973 and the first half of 1974 this impression was strengthened by the short-lived increase in the prices of many raw materials. In the second half of 1974, however, events made it plain that these hopes of growth without major external obstacles were merely an illusion. During that year and in 1975 heavy trade deficits were shown; in the latter year, the non-petroleum-exporting countries of Latin America, taken together, had a trade-balance deficit of 11,000 million dollars, equivalent to 44 per cent of their exports. They met this situation with very high short-term foreign borrowing, which greatly increased the impact of debt-servicing on the balance of payments. The deficit on current account of these same countries amounted to 16,400 million dollars, that is, 66 per cent of exports.[8]

In these circumstances, the discussion on possible development strategies and policy options has been resumed in many countries.

The Production Structure and the Dynamics of Development 379

The reduction of the growth rate experienced in 1975 as a result of the difficulties of the external sector cannot be considered as a valid policy option for the forthcoming years, but must be seen as a temporary situation which must be overcome as soon as possible. Were such a reduction to be prolonged, it would seriously jeopardize the possibilities of overcoming the domestic problems of marginality, unemployment and inequitable income distribution, and would aggravate the social and political tensions which are already causing great concern to the governments of the region.

It is therefore necessary to devise an industrialization and foreign trade strategy which would make a sufficiently high and steady growth rate viable and would thus complement the internal employment and income distribution policies needed to overcome those problems.

The economic forces and policy orientations in the countries of the region, have combined two elements in varying proportions: the export of manufactures from existing sectors, and import substitution through the promotion of some of the industries which have been lagging behind. Development policies have been devised on the basis of one or other of these elements as if they were mutually exclusive options.

When the emphasis is placed on the export of manufactures -- the course followed up to now by some Latin American countries -- the aim is to establish a competitive economy which would permit specialization in exports from certain branches of industry on which the development effort was to be concentrated. There would thus be an open import policy, with very low protection vis-a-vis the rest of Latin America and the world at large. These industries which did not prove competitive by the criterion of international prices would be likely to undergo transformation or to cease production, and a purely supplementary role would be assigned to regional integration and co-operation. In keeping with what was said in discussing the relation between market size and proportion of exports in the developed countries, even the economically largest countries of Latin America would have to export a very high proportion of their output in order to be able to produce new intermediate and capital goods on competitive terms. The smaller countries would have to export most of the output of many of their sectors in order to attain scales of production comparable to international standards. Thus the establishment of new industries would essentially depend on the external markets, which would mean that the risk would be very high. All this suggests that increases in exports would derive more from industries already in existence than from genuinely new economic activities which by their growth would help to overcome the backwardness of the domestic production structure. The diversification of foreign trade, which would make it possible to lessen the predominance of primary products in exports, would not, however, prevent exports from continuing to be based on a limited variety of traditional industries, whose products would not be among those in which world trade is growing most rapidly.

The policy which lays the emphasis on import substitution also aims at continuing a course followed up to now by some countries of the region. It seeks to overcome the shortcomings of the industrial structure in the countries concerned through progress in the backward metal-transforming and chemical sectors, but to that end has to rely mainly on each national market alone, together with some supplementary exports on a small scale. Even without reverting to the policies which were followed until the mid-sixties, the degree of protection would probably have to be high for a long period, and the production of many goods would only be possible in inefficient conditions; the role assigned to regional co-operation with a view to this development of industry and trade would also be limited.

If these two alternatives, instead of being regarded as mutually exclusive, were combined, the results would be a third and different option which would depart substantially from the lines of policy so far followed by all the Latin American countries. It would consist in a policy of co-operation at the Latin American level, implemented through formal integration agreements and complementary arrangements which would allow each country to specialize on the basis of the regional market with the aim of branching out abroad to conquer foreign markets. The support which the regional market would give to the development of each industrial sector would make it possible to reduce external protection and compete in an increasingly widening range of sectors and products, in a broad and energetic combination of exports of manufactures with import substitution and the incorporation of new sectors. Thus the establishment of new sectors for the production of capital goods and basic intermediate goods would be undertaken not only to meet the need for import substitution in each domestic market but also to export to the Latin American and world markets. Exports would not be augmented mainly by goods from existing industries, as is now the case, but also by the products of new industries which in turn would take the place of imports. The diversification of the trade structure would be a great deal more radical than in the case of the other options, and industrial export and import substitution policies would be much more rationally and genuinely harmonized and combined.

All these policy measures should go hand in hand with the broadening of the domestic market, a vigorous impulse being given to employment and income redistribution, in order to incorporate the sectors that are marginal today. These domestic policies, which are outside the scope of the present paper, should have a central role in development strategy.

Two hypotheses will be considered in the rest of this paper in order to analyse the possible repercussions of the various policy options. The first, in the nature of a prognosis, assumes that the policy orientations and forces which have been operating in the countries of the region will continue to do so. Although it postulates exports of manufactures and import substitution, it assumes that both would be carried out without the support of regional co-operation or the market of the Latin American countries in the aggregate. In this way import substitution and exports of manufactures would benefit different manufacturing sectors. Substitution would take place in respect of capital and intermediate goods, in each national market, and with little or no export trade. Exports would come from sectors already in existence in the domestic production structure. Import substitution and the export of manufactures would be undertaken in various sectors at the same time, but would not be combined in any one sector. The results of this hypothesis are summarized in section 3 below.

The second hypothesis postulates a significant change in current trends and a policy with very different bases from those of the prognosis hypothesis: it is assumed that the Latin American countries would agree to put into effect a resolute regional co-operation policy aimed at the industrial development of the metal-transforming and chemical sectors, which would effectively combine the export of manufactures with import substitution in each of these sectors and would give vigorous impetus to exports of goods produced by sectors already in existence. This second hypothesis will be considered in section 4 below.

IV. WHERE ARE THE CURRENTLY OPERATIVE FORCES LEADING?

Supposing that the forces which have been in play, and which seem likely to predominate over the next few years in view of the current policy orientations, continue to operate; that the policy changes which are already being implemented and those which are clearly on the way are brought to completion; and that the trends visible in the world economy produce their effect; what influence would all this have on the structure of the economy and evolution of the Latin American countries up to the middle of the next decade?[9] That is the question we shall now consider.

In respect of imports, we have assumed that the rate of substitution in each sector will continue to evolve in accordance with the trends recently observed; this would mean that in industries whose current development plans continued to be applied and improved, import coefficients would maintain their downward movement; in cases in which a policy of greater liberalization of imports have contributed, in recent years, to an increase in import coefficients, we have assumed stablization at their current level. We have also posited changes in the structure of domestic demand resembling those recorded in the past, expressed in terms of sectoral elasticity coefficients similar to those of the last ten years.

For the purposes of this exercise, we have considered separately the behaviour pattern of each country's imports from Latin America separately from that of its imports from the rest of the world, taking into account both the different composition and the differing rates of development of the two categories of imports in recent years.

As regards exports, we have assumed that all the policies adopted and the expansion plans being formulated will be implemented and will have the favourable results envisaged.

With respect to primary commodities, we have considered the growth of world demand, the expansion of sales deriving from programmes to increase production in each country, and possible exports of new agricultural commodities. We have assumed that exports of manufactures will grow at a high rate, though slightly lower than the average annual rate for the last few years; that the share of exports of manufactures in the total will continue to increase until it doubles the present proportion in the middle of the next decade; that the effort to export manufactures begun in many Latin American countries in about 1965 will continue; and that the policies and programmes in force both in the major Latin American countries and in the countries of the Andean sub-region will have successful results.

Given these assumptions, total exports of goods and services to the rest of the world would grow at an annual rate of 6.7 per cent over the next 10 years.

If the growth rates of the product were the same as in the past, or slightly higher, and if the above assumptions were realized, machinery and metal manufactures and chemical products would continue to account for the lion's share of imports. The proportion represented by these goods in total imports of manufactures from outside the region would rise from the present 65 per cent to about 75 per cent within the next 10 years (see table 5). Therefore, the predominance of capital goods and basic intermediate products in Latin America's imports would be accentuated. The structure of imports would not improve and would reflect ever-increasing external dependence in terms of the operation and growth of the Latin American economies.

Intra-area trade would still continue to play a fairly limited role and to represent a small proportion of the total, not much higher than 10 per cent.

By the mid-1980, 40 per cent of extraregional exports would be composed of primary commodities proper; to these should be added primary products with some degree of processing by the traditional industries. Exports of manufactured goods produced by non-traditional industries would double their share, reaching one-fifth of the total within 10 years, but although the proportion of these exports would increase appreciably, it would still be much lower than in mature economies (see figure 6).[10]

The composition of the exports and imports of the Latin American countries as a whole towards the middle of the next decade would continue to show considerable asymmetry, with the more advanced industries still playing a limited role in exports and imports consisting of essential goods. Latin America would continue to be dependent upon exports for which world demand is growing slowly, to finance rapidly increasing import requirements.

From a more thorough examination of the performance of extraregional exports and imports in some particularly important sectors of Latin American industry it may be observed that their respective shares would continue to be very different. It should be remembered that the OECD countries export various goods produced by each sector to a value approximately equal to or even higher than that of the goods they import. In Latin America, in contrast, exports of chemical products and capital goods represent a tiny fraction of the corresponding imports from the same sectors. According to the prognostical hypothesis under consideration, the

The Production Structure and the Dynamics of Development 383

same situation would still be found in Latin America in 10 years' time. Table 6 shows that in the mid-1960s the region's exports of machinery and metal manufactures represented only 9 per cent of its imports of these same goods; in 10 years' time the proportion would reach only 12 per cent. It should be recalled that in recent years, the extra-regional exports of machinery and metal manufactures of the OECD countries as a whole amounted to 10 times their imports of these items.

This clearly shows that, according to the prognostical hypothesis, the basic structural shortcomings of the system of production and foreign trade, which are fundamental obstacles to sustained growth without bottlenecks, would persist in Latin America for a long time.

These problems would also be reflected in the persistence of the chronic propensity to systematic trade and balance-of-payments deficits, which, far from being overcome, is more likely to be accentuated in the next 10 years.

Let us briefly examine this point. As the product grows, the structure of demand changes, since requirements in terms of goods with a higher import content expand more rapidly,[11] so that imports tend to increase faster than the gross domestic product. Moreover, if economic growth accelerates -- i.e., if the growth rate of the product rises -- the ratio of the growth of imports to that of the product becomes even higher. In fact, from the mid-1960s up to the present time, with the Latin American product growing at an annual rate of 6.3 per cent, imports increased by 8.4 per cent annually, or 1.34 times faster than the product. A simple exercise shows that if the assumptions regarding the performance of the economy referred to at the beginning of this section were maintained, and if the aim were to attain a growth rate of around 8 per cent of the Latin American countries,[12] the ratio of the growth rate of imports to that of the product would be about 1.7, which means that imports would have to increase by over 13 per cent annually. This growth rate of around 8 per cent for the product is approximately the rate established as a target for the Second United Nations Development Decade. it is also similar to that required in order to be able to deal successfully with the problems of redundant manpower and marginality in the countries of the region.[13]

If such were the evolution of imports and if exports were to grow in the manner described above, it would not be feasible to obtain the historical growth rate of 6.3 per cent for the product, since in that case the trade deficit would amount to about half the value of exports, which is obviously unrealistic. It would be even more impossible to attain growth rates for the product similar to the targets for the Second United Nations Development Decade, since in this case the trade deficit would be much greater still in proportion to exports. On the basis of these same assumptions, if an attempt were made to keep the trade deficit within manageable proportions, the economic growth rate that would be feasible for the Latin American countries as a whole would be no higher than just under 5 per cent annually in the period considered. Clearly, this rate would be insufficient for dealing with the serious economic and social problems affecting the various countries.

In short, the continuance and intensification of the present industrial development and foreign trade model would bring Latin America to a dead end, with an increasingly limited growth rate and an accentuation of the basic structural shortcomings hitherto observed. It is desirable, therefore, to examine a different hypothesis not only postulating a higher growth rate but also assigning regional economic co-operation a fundamental role in the spheres of trade and industry, with a view to developing the basic sectors manufacturing capital goods and chemical products.

V. A NEW FORM OF LATIN AMERICAN PARTICIPATION IN THE WORLD ECONOMY

(a) The Role Of Regional Co-Operation In Industry And Trade

A different form of participation for Latin America in world trade and industry is an essential requisite for ensuring dynamic development, facilitating the attainment of full employment with better manpower training, and obtaining a fairer distribution of income, while at the same time achieving a structural change in the economy that will enable it to grow steadily, unhampered by constant bottlenecks. A strategy with these fundamental objectives must be the framework for external policies, the new role of Latin America in the world economy, and regional co-operation in industry and trade, which will be more specifically considered here.

A major component of such a policy is the sustained growth of exports of manufactures both from existing sectors and from new sectors which at the same time would substitute domestic production for imports. This would permit industrial establishments, plants and enterprises to reduce their costs and improve the quality of their products, as well as to achieve the economic and financial capacity necessary for a more creative and autochtonous adaptation of their technology, and for the improvement of their bargaining power. In this way, the industries of the region, particularly those owned by Latin American capital and confined to the narrow sphere of domestic markets composed of minority sectors of the population, could overcome the present disadvantages.

Exports of manufactures must also contribute to the development of a group of industrial sectors which will gradually constitute an adequate manufacturing infrastructure. It is not enough to develop only some sectors of industry, virtually isolated from the rest of the economy, producing almost exclusively for export to other regions, and thus constituting new examples of enclaves; rather, an industrial network should be promoted through which exports will in addition produce effects that will make themselves felt in the rest of the economy, help to increase the product in other sectors supplying inputs or capital goods, and facilitate the dissemination of technology and the improvement of quality in a wide range of production activities. A mature economy of which exports of manufactures are a substantial component specializes in the production of certain goods in each sector, but at the same time carries on a number of activities which are supplementary to its export activities proper. In addition to essentially manufacturing industries, it is also necessary to establish an infrastructure comprising energy, transport and efficient services that will contribute to the satisfactory development of all activities directly or indirectly associated with exports.

Industrial development in conjunction with a thriving foreign trade requires economic units of adequate size and potential. This means that the countries of the region, as well as seeking to specialize, should promote close co-operation in the production and trade areas. Such a policy is analysed below.

(b) What Kind Of Regional Co-Operation Policy Could Be Adopted?

The hypothesis of a new industrial and trade policy, which was introduced in summarized form in section 2, will be developed here.

Let us suppose that the Latin American countries adopt a regional programme for industrial and trade co-operation aimed at developing, on the basis of their joint market, a group of key industries producing chemicals, electrical and non-electrical machinery and transport equipment. Of course, none of the countries would abandon the industries they already have in these sectors, but they would each co-ordinate the production increase that should take place in the future. Installed production capacity would be gradually rationalized with a view to improving its competitive potentialities and achieving a certain degree of specialization.

A regional co-operation programme in the fields of industry and trade requires a clearly-defined scientific and technological policy, which would include among its basic objectives the satisfaction of industrial development needs. Since the resources available to the countries in the field of science and technology are very limited, it is essential to establish priorities and guidelines for their use in harmony with those needs. As the aim would be to establish an industry which could compete at the world level with the help of the regional market, basic elements that would have to be taken into account in order to attain that goal would be the introduction of technological innovations and the reduction of costs. Better advantage could be taken of the countries' individual efforts if in respect of technology too a policy of speicalization and regional co-operation were adopted that would take into consideration the objectives and guiding principles of the region and of each individual country.

This co-operation, effected through formal integration processes and supplementary measures, would presuppose a more selective and specialized industrial development policy implemented along such lines that sectors of great industrial and technological importance for the regional market would be developed in each and

Table 4

COMPARISON OF SOME VARIABLES, 1972

(With respect to the average for Latin America)

Countries or groups of countries	Per capita gross domestic product	Per capita product of the goods-producing sectors	Per capita manufacturing product	Population
Latin America (19 countries)	1.0	1.0	1.0	1.00
Argentina	1.9	2.0	2.5	0.09
Brazil	0.8	0.8	0.8	0.36
Mexico	1.4	1.3	1.4	0.19
Andean Group (6 countries)	0.9	1.0	0.8	0.25
West Germany	6.2	7.1	10.8	0.22
Belgium	5.4	4.7	6.8	0.03
Canada	7.0	4.9	6.1	0.08
Spain	2.0	1.8	1.8	0.12
United States	8.2	6.0	8.8	0.74
France	5.8	6.1	8.3	0.18
Italy	3.2	3.2	4.3	0.18
Japan	4.0	4.1	5.8	0.38
United Kingdom	3.9	3.0	4.4	0.20
Sweden	7.6	6.0	8.0	0.03

Source: United Nations, *Monthly Bulletin of Statistics,* July 1975, and estimates of CEPAL and of the Latin American Demographic Centre (CELADE) for Latin America.

Note: The variables for the industrialized countries are expressed in current prices of the year 1972, while for Latin America they are in 1970 prices. The absolute values for Latin America in 1972 are as follows: gross domestic product, 680 dollars; product of the goods-producing sectors, 350 dollars; manufacturing product, 160 dollars; population, 282.2 million.

Table 5

LATIN AMERICA: PERCENTAGE STRUCTURE OF IMPORTS OF INDUSTRIAL GOODS

Sectors of industry	Mid-1970s			Forecast for the mid-1980s [a]		
	Intra-regional	Extra-regional	Total	Intra-regional	Extra-regional	Total
Traditional sectors	24.3	9.7	11.0	14.6	6.5	7.0
Intermediate sectors	54.2	39.4	40.7	53.7	33.8	35.3
Chemicals	11.7	18.6	18.0	12.5	18.0	17.6
Engineering industries	21.5	50.9	48.3	31.7	59.7	57.7
Non-electrical machinery	13.8	23.2	22.4	22.5	32.2	31.5
Electrical machinery	2.6	9.6	9.0	4.4	13.1	12.4
Transport equipment	2.7	13.6	12.6	2.7	11.1	10.5
Total for industry as a whole	100.0	100.0	100.0	100.0	100.0	100.0
Subtotal for chemical products, electrical machinery, other machinery and transport equipment	30.8	65.0	62.0	42.1	74.4	72.0

Source: CEPAL estimates.
[a] Hypothesis of an 8 per cent annual growth rate of the gross domestic product.

all of the Latin American countries. Since industries would be established to meet the needs of the regional market instead of those of each separate domestic market, their costs and investment requirements would be commensurate with the larger size of the regional market. In each case, as much progress would be made as was possible in internationally competitive conditions, in line with the behaviour of the import and export coefficients indicated above for the OECD countries which trade on a competitive footing in the world market.

Thus, Latin American industrial development policy at the regional level could in these new sectors combine the substitution of domestic production for imports from the rest of the world with extra-regional exports of manufactures, since the new plants would operate in conditions enabling them to compete on a world basis. The region as a whole and each individual country would go in for specialization within each of the sectors under discussion. Import and export coefficients in the advanced industries might be a great deal lower for Latin America as a whole than they would be for each of the national markets operating singly; however, each individual country would have a much higher trade coefficient, since in addition to trade with the rest of the world there would be the vigorous regional trade created by increased specialization.

Current extra-regional imports in the four sectors covered by the regional co-operation policy (the chemical, electrical machinery, other machinery, and transport equipment industries) still represent approximately 65 per cent of total imports of manufactured goods. If the past and present trends were to continue, they would constitute about 75 per cent of that total by the mid-1980s (see table 5). In other words, these sectors primarily producing basic intermediate products and capital goods are not only of great importance for the structure of industry and investment, but they also exercise a decisive influence on present and future imports.

It will also be recalled[14] that for each of these sectors the import coefficients are still high, even in the Latin American countries which have made most progress in industrialization, as will be seen in table 7. The situation is even clearer in the case of specific goods or small groups of goods. For example, in investment goods in the sector producing machinery other than electrical, various stages of advancement in the production process may be distinguished, depending on the degree of technological complexity. The production of simple machinery (pumps, elevators and compressors) has made great strides, even in the medium-sized countries. As regards the production of machine-tools, experience shows a predominance of import substitution in the case of multipurpose machines which are more suitable for maintenance and for use in general workshops. The manufacture of more complex machinery of key importance for development and capital formation, such as specialized machines, is in its infancy, even in the larger and more advanced countries of Latin America.[15] Progress in the production of these specialized machines calls for a better knowledge of the technology of the sector in which they are to be used, and capacity for creative adaptation so as to be able to introduce innovations and compete.

Figure 6

LATIN AMERICA: COMPARATIVE STRUCTURE OF EXPORTS, IMPORTS, GROSS VALUE OF PRODUCTION AND DOMESTIC DEMAND IN THE MID-1970s AND MID-1980s, BY INDUSTRIAL ORIGIN

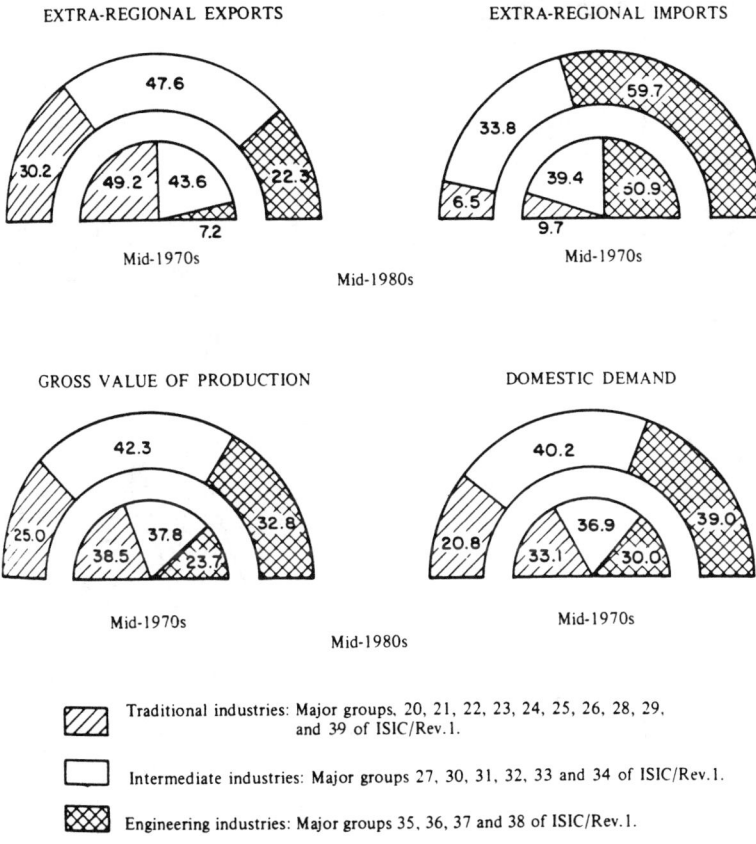

Traditional industries: Major groups, 20, 21, 22, 23, 24, 25, 26, 28, 29, and 39 of ISIC/Rev.1.

Intermediate industries: Major groups 27, 30, 31, 32, 33 and 34 of ISIC/Rev.1.

Engineering industries: Major groups 35, 36, 37 and 38 of ISIC/Rev.1.

Source: CEPAL estimates.

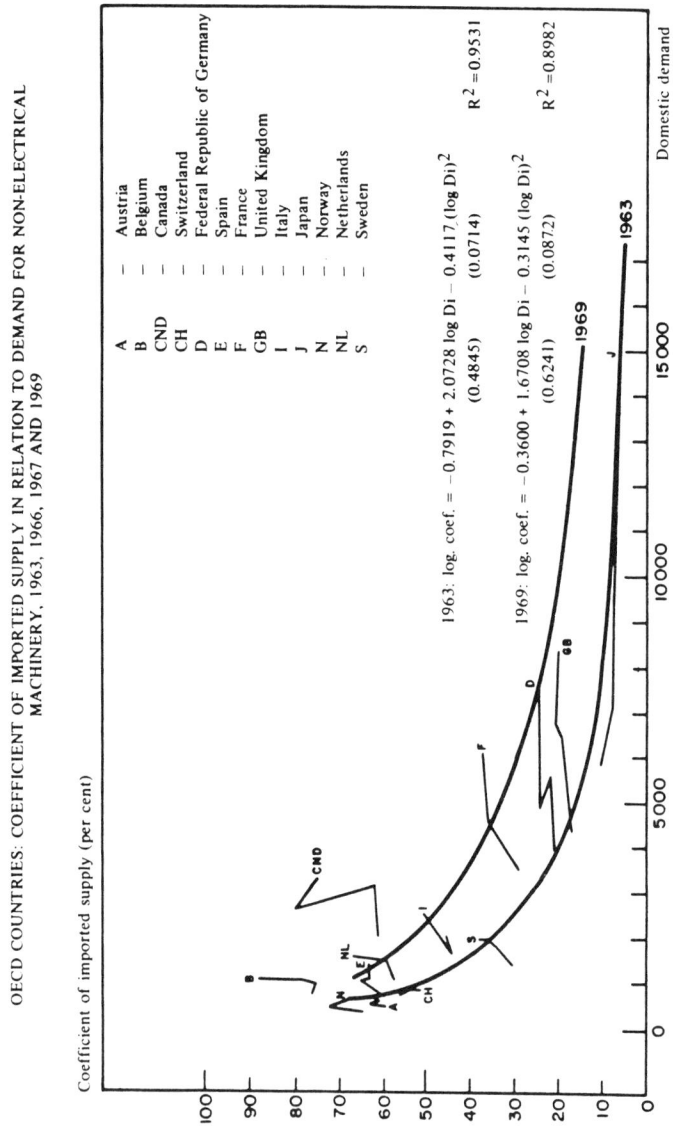

Figure 7

OECD COUNTRIES: COEFFICIENT OF IMPORTED SUPPLY IN RELATION TO DEMAND FOR NON-ELECTRICAL MACHINERY, 1963, 1966, 1967 AND 1969

Source: CEPAL estimates, on the basis of OECD, *The Engineering Industries in 1963-1970*, vol. I, 1971.

Another aspect of the problem which makes it necessary to take particular care in evaluating the advances made in production concerns the prices of domestically-produced machines compared with those of machines imported from outside the region. owing to the protection which has prevailed hitherto, the prices of those manufactured locally are higher than the international prices and, therefore, the proportion of total demand covered by domestic production appears higher than it actually is.

The conclusions are fairly clear: technology and market size play a fundamental role in the possible future progress of the metal-transforming industries. It will necessarily be linked with the production of capital goods, which have a powerful impact on the balance of payments and on the possibilities of freeing investment from the external bottleneck. Hitherto, import substitution in these industries has been markedly "consumer-type"; it is only in recent years that a start has been made on the production of more investment goods, and among these more headway has been made in the production of simple goods than of those with a more important role in development. Demand for the latter is growing very rapidly; in consequence, despite all that has been achieved in import substitution, the external bottleneck, far from being eased, is being aggravated.

The Latin American co-operation programme presented in this study would therefore consist in the concerted development of the metal-transforming and chemical industries, making full use of the regional market. Both the individual Latin American countries and the region as a whole would seek to attain for each of these sectors trade coefficients similar to those of open and competitive economies like the countries of the OECD. In view of the relatively small size of the domestic markets, each country's trade with Latin America would be highly intensive as a result of specialized progress in these sectors; however, as indicated above, each country would import and export goods produced by each of these sectors, thereby diversifying its production and trade structures. Thanks to the larger size of the regional market, the extra-regional trade coefficients of Latin America as a whole would, in contrast, be much lower, without loss of efficiency. On the other hand, the region as a whole would also gradually achieve a certain degree of specialization within each sector vis-a-vis the outside world, and would move towards applying a low level of protection would be assigned to the new sectors from the outset, while that established for existing production would gradually approach the same levels.

This means that the coefficient of imports from the rest of the world would tend to diminish, so that imports would be kept within limits which could be covered by exports and a reasonable amount of external financing. The coefficient of each country's imports from the rest of the region would tend to rise, and these larger intra-regional imports would be paid for with more intra-regional exports. Altogether, the total import coefficient would increase for each country.

The trade coefficients of the larger OECD countries have followed a different trend from those of the smaller countries. Figure 7 shows the change in the import coefficients in the

Table 6

OECD COUNTRIES AND LATIN AMERICA: DEGREE OF COVERAGE OF EXTRA-REGIONAL IMPORTS BY EXPORTS TO THE REST OF THE WORLD

(Percentages)

Sectors	OECD countries in 1972	Latin America Mid-1970s	Latin America Mid-1980s [a]
Traditional goods	...	340	149
Food	...	2 203	1 633
Textiles	103	109	165
Clothes and footwear	25	149	340
Miscellaneous manufactures	...	15	8
Intermediate goods	...	74	45
Pulp and paper	927	2	3
Chemical products	545	44	30
Petroleum products	17	153	71
Metals	...	108	74
Metal manufactures and machinery	1 001	9	12
Non-electrical machinery	2 006	6	7
Electrical machinery	385	19	17
Transport equipment	1 605	9	12
Subtotals			
Including petroleum exports			
Primary sector	...	340	175
Manufacturing sector	...	67	32
Total goods	94	106	52
Excluding petroleum exports			
Primary sector	...	126	49
Manufacturing sector	...	57	33
Total goods	...	69	34

Source: CEPAL estimates.

[a] Hypothesis of an 8 per cent annual growth rate of the gross domestic product.

Table 7

LATIN AMERICA: COEFFICIENTS OF IMPORTED SUPPLY IN RELATION TO TOTAL DEMAND IN THE MID-1970s

(Percentages)

Sector	Relatively more developed countries	Countries with insufficient markets	Relatively less developed countries
Chemicals	15.8	35.7	73.6
Non-electrical machinery	43.3	77.1	90.7
Electrical machinery	21.8	41.3	78.5
Transport equipment	12.7	40.9	82.0

Source: CEPAL estimates.

Table 8

LATIN AMERICA: PROPORTION OF DEMAND SUPPLIED EXTERNALLY AND ANNUAL GROWTH RATES OF THE INDUSTRIAL SECTORS COVERED BY THE REGIONAL PROGRAMME OF INDUSTRIAL AND TRADE CO-OPERATION

(Percentages)

Sector	Coefficients of imported supply of total demand [a]			Average annual growth rate of production		
	In the mid-1970s	In the mid-1980s		1960-1970 [b]	In the mid-1980s	
		Continuation of past trend (forecast)	Regional co-operation programme		Continuation of past trend (forecast)	Regional co-operation programme
Chemical	18.9	16.9	6.0	10.4	15.4	16.7
Non-electrical machinery	49.2	46.2	15.0	7.4	19.9	25.6
Electrical machinery	25.7	24.9	8.0	10.0	18.6	20.8
Transport equipment	18.2	18.9	1.0	9.9	12.7	14.2
Total manufacturing sector	*16.2*	*19.2*	*9.1*	*6.7*	*11.8*	*13.0*

Source: CEPAL estimates.

Note: The differences between the growth rates for the period 1960-1970 and the historical trends of the projections are due to the increase in the growth rate of the gross domestic product.
[a] Includes only imports from the rest of the world.
[b] At constant 1960 prices.

non-electrical machinery sector of each OECD country over the period 1963-1969. It may be observed that the import coefficients for the larger countries (Federal Republic of Germany, France, United Kingdom and Japan) did not increase, but rather remained fairly stable during the period, while the scale of domestic demand increased with the growth process. In contrast, the coefficients for the smaller countries (all the rest included in figure 7) rose sharply, even though domestic demand expanded. This would be explained by the fact that competition with the larger countries compels the rest to intensify their specialization, devoting themselves more thoroughly to the production of certain goods within each sector, and trading more and more vigorously with third countries. It will also be seen from figure 7, therefore, that the curve showing the relationship between the size of each domestic market and the import coefficient gradually shifts in time, taking on a form which reflects this different evolution in the various countries according to the magnitude of their domestic demand.

In preparing the regional programme for Latin America it has been assumed that the countries of the region would follow a similar trend, approximating to the trade coefficients (and, therefore, the degrees of specialization) of the mature economies, in accordance with the size of the market of each country and of the region as a whole.

It should be noted that at the present time the trade coefficient of each of the Latin American countries is lower than it would be if the economy were as open as that of an OECD country. (See Figure 8). However, the trade coefficient of Latin America as a whole is higher than it would be with respect to the outside world if the region operated as a single integrated market; in that case and in accordance with the trends corresponding to the OECD countries, the size of the regional market would make it possible to reduce the import coefficient while maintaining international competitiveness. Today, when only a limited degree of regional integration exists, each of the Latin American economies is, in practice, more integrated with economies of developed countries than with the rest of the region. Since Latin America does not function as a single large market, intra-regional trade is on a very small scale, and most of the imports, especially of products of the metal-transforming and chemical industries, come from outside the area. Thus the possibilities of reducing the trade coefficient are determined by the size of each national market. This programme, in contrast, assumes that due advantage is taken of the size of the regional market and thus that the relative importance of extra-regional imports would tend to diminish, while on the other hand that of intra-regional imports would increase as a result of the regional co-operation policy. Thus each country's overall trade coefficient would rise very substantially, and at the same time the trade coefficient of the region as a whole in respect of the exterior would diminish considerably, in accordance with the trend corresponding to the OECD countries, up to the middle of the next decade.

These are the lines on which the regional co-operation programme has been formulated; the ten years it covers, however, might prove insufficient to overcome Latin America's current technological backwardness entirely. Although it is implicitly assumed that in carrying out this industrial and trade co-operation the region would make a special effort to bring its economic and technological potential nearer to that of the OECD countries, it would probably be unable to make up the whole of its leeway. Thus in preparing the programme it has been assumed that at the end of the ten years there would still be a difference, although proportionally much smaller than at present, between the Latin American countries and developed OECD countries with economies similar in size to those of the region. This would mean that Latin America would have to import from the rest of the world a higher proportion of goods than would correspond to the size of its market, so as to be able to incorporate the new goods created by technical progress, which the Latin American countries would not be able to produce for lack of innovatory capacity. For this reason it has been assumed in the projections made that in the region as a whole, the import coefficients of the sectors included in the programme would be somewhat higher at the end of the period than they would have been if the economy had developed exactly like an OECD economy, in accordance with the size of its market.

This would probably mean that the intra-regional trade and the real degree of integration between the Latin American countries in the sectors covered by the programme would be somewhat lower than would be necessary to achieve rather closer linkage with economies of greater technical capacity; at all events, however, the degree of co-operation for development and the intensity of real integration in these sectors would be much greater than at present, as will be seen later in the context of the projection of intra-regional trade.

By reducing the extra-regional import coefficient of the region as a whole to a figure situated between the level which it might reach within a decade if the current inertia continued to prevail and that it would attain if this regional co-operation policy were applied, it is possible to determine the additional growth potential of Latin American industry in the metal-transforming and chemical sectors.

(c) Effects Of This Policy

The likely effects of this policy are shown in table 8. In the non-electrical machinery sector, for example, the coefficient of extra-regional imports with respect to total Latin American demand would pass from the current 49.2 per cent to 46.2 per cent by the middle of the next decade if past trends persist, but if the regional co-operation programme were applied the coefficient would drop to 15 per cent by the same date. The table also shows the great differences between these two hypotheses as regards the projected coefficients of imports by the region as a whole from the rest of the world.[16] Similarly, the table shows that the growth rates of regional production in these ten years would differ

Table 9

LATIN AMERICA: IMPORTS OF GOODS AND NON-FINANCIAL SERVICES IN THE MID-1980s

	Past trends (forecast)				Regional co-operation programme			
	Billions of 1973 dollars		Percentage composition		Billions of 1973 dollars		Percentage composition	
	Intra-regional	Extra-regional	Intra-regional	Extra-regional	Intra-regional	Extra-regional	Intra-regional[a]	Extra-regional
Primary goods [b]	3.7	11.5	32.2	11.1	3.7	11.5	6.4	19.6
Manufactured goods [c]	6.7	84.9	58.3	81.9	52.6	40.1	91.7	68.2
Chemicals	0.9	15.3	7.8	14.8	16.0	5.4	27.9	9.2
Non-electrical machinery	1.5	27.3	13.0	26.4	17.1	8.9	29.8	15.1
Electrical machinery	0.3	11.1	2.7	10.7	7.5	3.6	13.1	6.1
Transport equipment	0.2	9.5	1.7	9.1	8.1	0.5	14.1	0.9
Subtotal	(2.9)	(63.2)	(25.2)	(61.0)	(48.7)	(18.4)	(84.9)	(31.3)
Non-financial services	1.1	7.2	9.5	7.0	1.1	7.2	1.9	12.2
Total goods and services	11.5	103.6	100.0	100.0	57.4	58.8	100.0	100.0

Source: CEPAL estimates.

[a] The intra-regional trade shown here is based on the hypothesis that the additional production would be distributed between the participating countries in proportion to the demand for these goods in each of them.
[b] Divisions 01 to 19 of ISIC/Rev.1.
[c] Divisions 20 to 39 of ISIC/Rev.1.

considerably depending on whether the regional co-operation programme were applied or current trends persisted, especially in the group of non-electrical machinery industries.

Table 9 shows the amounts and composition of imports (both intra-regional and extra-regional) for the two hypotheses. The extra-regional imports of the four sectors covered by the proposed co-operation would greatly diminish if the programme were applied and there would also be a significant change in the composition of imports, since the share of these sectors -- which produce mainly intermediate and capital goods, so vital for the functioning of the economy and development -- in the total purchases of goods and services from abroad would fall from 61.0 per cent to 31.3 per cent. This would mean a more favourable import structure, as its composition would not include such a large proportion of goods whose purchase abroad is difficult to restrict. Even so, imports of such goods from outside the region would still amount to a very significant absolute value, because Latin America would develop along the lines of an economy which was fairly open towards the exterior and would in no way tend to close its economy any more than was needed to allow it to attain a scale of market permitting the achievement of competitive efficiency.

As regards Latin America's possibilities of exporting goods from these four industries beyond the region, the discussion in section 2 on the behaviour of open, efficient and mature economies should be recalled. In that section it was shown that the OECD countries' exports of these types of products are similar in amount to their imports of similar goods. Since under the co-operation policy assumed here the Latin American countries would achieve a level of economic and technical efficiency and capacity not very far behind that of the developed countries, it can be supposed that this policy, likewise, would enable them at the end of the ten years, to export a volume of chemical products and capital goods similar to the figures shown in table 9 for their imports from the rest of the world.

Another aspect which calls for comment is the effect of the co-operation policy on intra-regional trade. Table 9 shows that this trade, including the reciprocal imports between the countries of each group and the trade between groups, would come to represent almost half the total imports of goods and services. Thus a high level of interdependence would gradually be attained, reflecting the increasing momentum that the co-operation itself could gain as integration became more effective. At the end of the ten years, the trade in chemical and mechanical goods as a whole within Latin America would represent 72 per cent of the total purchases of these products, i.e., a similar percentage to that achieved in the trade in these types of goods among the OECD countries, which amounted to 74 per cent in 1972. If the hypothesis which assumes no regional co-operation (section 3) is compared with the hypothesis assuming the application of a policy of intensive integration of the countries, it can be seen that the global ratios of imported supply to internal Latin American demand in these four sectors, would not be very different at the end of the periods as table 10 shows. The main difference between the two hypotheses would lie in the geographical origin of these purchases. If past trends continue,

The Production Structure and the Dynamics of Development 399

the supply of these industrial sectors in the region as a whole would depend almost entirely on the exterior, with very little intra-regional trade. On the other hand, if Latin America operated as a highly integrated economy in competitive conditions similar to those prevailing internationally (thus needing a level of protection not much higher than that of the OECD countries) it could greatly lessen its external dependence and at the same time each country could begin to obtain high proportions of its needs from the rest of the region. The fact that this intra-regional trade would represent only about 10 per cent of total imports by 1985 if past trends continue, but almost 50 per cent under the co-operation policy, shows the vigorous impulse which can be provided by collaboration and negotiation between the Latin American countries.

The regional co-operation programme would also have very important effects in respect of the external bottleneck, as it would help to reduce the trade deficit with the rest of the world. If this policy were applied, the increased growth rate of the mechanical and chemical industries would make possible a very substantial reduction in the requirements for imports of these goods from outside the region and thus diminish by more than nine-tenths the deficit which would arise if the forces currently in operation persisted. This means that the co-operation policy would have such an impact on the external bottleneck that a growth rate of nearly 8 per cent a year over the next ten years could be perfectly feasible for Latin America as a whole since the effective trade deficit would be of very manageable size, and it would appear that it could be overcome by the net inflows of external financing.

(d) Sub-Regional And Regional Co-Operation

A final aspect to be considered is that of the geographical extension of co-operation within Latin America. Two hypotheses can be analysed. According to the first hypothesis, co-operation would be carried out exclusively between the countries of particular groups, so that strong ties of trade and co-operation would exist between the members of each sub-regional group, but there would be very few links between groups: this is what has been happening to some extent in Latin America.

In the second hypothesis, co-operation would extend to all Latin America, and even if there were some more intensive processes of sub-regional integration, there would at the same time be strong links between the different processes. We must now ask ourselves whether the results would be similar or very different in each case.

In the case of co-operation limited to sub-regional spheres, progress would apparently be easier, as it would involve attempting to link fewer countries and those with a similar degree of development could be grouped together, thus entailing fewer potential problems of imbalance. It may be seen from figure 8 that

Table 10

LATIN AMERICA: COEFFICIENTS OF IMPORTED SUPPLY OF TOTAL DEMAND

(Percentages)

Sector	Mid-1970s			Mid-1980s					
				Continuation of past trend			Regional co-operation [a]		
	Total	Rest of the world	Intra-regional	Total	Rest of the world	Intra-regional	Total	Rest of the world	Intra-regional
Chemical	20.1	18.9	1.2	17.8	16.9	0.9	23.6	6.0	17.6
Non-electrical machinery	52.1	49.2	2.9	48.8	46.2	2.6	43.9	15.0	28.9
Electrical machinery	26.4	25.7	0.7	25.6	24.9	0.7	24.8	8.0	16.8
Transport equipment	18.5	18.2	0.3	19.3	18.9	0.4	17.1	1.0	16.1
Total manufacturing	17.8	16.2	1.6	20.7	19.2	1.5	20.9	9.1	11.8

Source: CEPAL estimates.

[a] Also includes the allocation of benefits in accordance with sectoral demand.

Figure 8

LATIN AMERICA: IMPORT COEFFICIENTS WITH RESPECT TO DOMESTIC DEMAND IN SELECTED SECTORS OF INDUSTRY AND THEIR RELATIVE POSITION WITH RESPECT TO THE REFERENCE CURVE OF THE OECD COUNTRIES

(Natural scale)

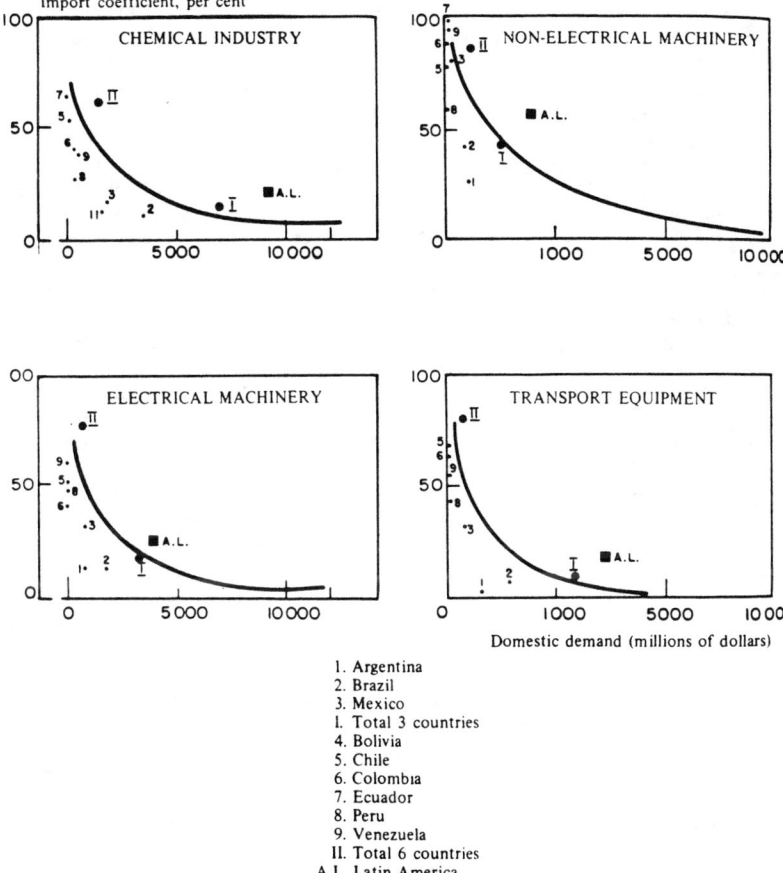

1. Argentina
2. Brazil
3. Mexico
I. Total 3 countries
4. Bolivia
5. Chile
6. Colombia
7. Ecuador
8. Peru
9. Venezuela
II. Total 6 countries
A.L. Latin America

Source: CEPAL estimates.

this co-operation could give considerably better results than if there were no sub-regional or regional co-operation; the figure shows that the import coefficients of these four sectors in each of the countries of the Andean sub-region are at present lower than would correspond to the size of each country's market if they operated as open and competitive economies; the market of the group of countries taken as a whole, however, would allow the average outward trade coefficient of the sub-region to be lower than at present, in similar conditions of specialization and competitiveness to those of the OECD countries. This is also true in the case of the three economically largest countries of Latin America (Argentina, Brazil and Mexico). Each of them, according to figure 8, currently has a lower import coefficient than would correspond to a competitive economy of similar size, but the grouping together of the three would create a size of market which would have a smaller import coefficient than they have at present. These two sub-regional groups, which are shown here merely by way of example, are of course chosen only to illustrate the kind of results that could be gained from such sub-regional schemes. It may be concluded from the foregoing that it is better that there should be co-operation, even within the limited context of sub-regional groups, than that there should be none, or very little, as has been the case up to now.

The same figure also shows that co-operation is far more beneficial if it is not only carried out within the restricted sphere of each of the sub-regional groups but also extended between them. It can also be seen that the extra-regional trade coefficient, in relation to the total size of the Latin American market and on similar conditions of specialization and competitiveness as those found in the OECD countries, is considerably lower than that of each of the two sub-regional groups; thus, for example, in the case of non-electrical machinery, the import coefficients of a competitive economy in the Andean sub-region and in the group made up of the three largest countries of Latin America would be 62 per cent and 46 per cent respectively. For Latin America as a whole, however, according to the same assumption of a competitive economy, the import coefficient would be only 35 per cent.

It can thus be said that although co-operation limited to sub-regional groups is better than a situation of national isolation, it attains much more limited results than co-operation extending to all the Latin American countries, even if there continue to be very strong links within each group. The benefit of broad co-operation, of regional scope and not limited to sub-regions, is greater for the intermediate and small countries than for the large countries. This is clearly shown by the figures and is due to the fact that in the intermediate and small countries the market sizes are further away from the sizes recorded for the region as a whole.

If there are strong links within the sub-regions, and solid co-operation between them, it is necessary to promote the productive specialization of each of the sub-regions or each of the groups of countries with a similar level of development, so as to arrive at a balanced situation in which all of them attain results that satisfy them.

This raises the problem of establishing a balance between countries of initially unequal development which are seeking integration.

In the past, traditional instruments such as trade liberalization, common external tariffs, free movement of factors, etc., have tended to accentuate the imbalances in distribution when applied indifferently to all the countries. If a policy of regional co-operation like that analysed above were implemented and the distribution of the new industries were left to the free play of the market forces, the countries which started in a more advantageous position would probably obtain a higher proportion of the net additional benefits.

The largest countries are most attractive when considering the location of a new industry, because they have a larger domestic market, a greater degree of industrialization with the accompanying infrastructure, greater capacity for domestic financing, greater capacity for domestic financing and foreign borrowing, more labour and managerial capacity, more developed technology, etc.

Another way of approaching this problem so as not to leave the situation at the mercy of the free play of the market forces would be to complement the system of markets with a policy aimed at securing a more equitable distribution of the benefits of this programme between the countries by modifying the initial disparities during the integration process.

The study of the balanced distribution of benefits raises theoretical and practical difficulties partly attributable to the fact that the approach to the problem is subject to circumstantial negotiations, appraisals and effects. The considerations involved are not only commercial, although the distribution can be expressed in each country in terms of foreign trade which is balanced both in global amounts and in structure. It is necessary to take into account, among other aspects, the effects of co-operation on the general development of each country, its production structure and its possibilities of dealing more adequately with excess labour and marginality and alleviating the problem of the external bottleneck.

An adequate distribution of the benefits and costs of the programme cannot, of course, resolve the economic development problems of the less advanced countries unless it is complemented with a vigorous domestic effort. At all events, however, a policy aimed at securing regional balance is a very important element in the development of these countries.

(e) Instruments For Co-Operation

This study has discussed some of the main possible characteristics of a development strategy aimed at certain objectives of growth and transformation of the production structure. In order to carry out such a strategy, it would be necessary to apply instruments and policies which need to be analysed at length. Although such an analysis is outside the scope of this paper, it is worth noting some particularly important aspects.

One of the instruments for co-operation is the formation of multinational Latin American enterprises. There are various factors which may induce countries to undertake co-operation activities through multinational enterprises. These include taking advantage of economies of scale, of the improved efficiency deriving from specialization, of the economies gained in the provision of supplies domestically or in third countries, of the advantages of better and more adequate marketing in association with third countries, of the better conditions for securing technology and, in general, of the strengthening of the position of the countries and regional enterprises with respect to the transnational enterprises. Although the development of multinational Latin American enterprises is still a recent phenomenon, there are notable cases of entities of this nature and of associations between Latin American national enterprises for industrial production and for the exploitation of natural resources (mainly hydroelectric) or the operation of public services.[17] In general, these ventures involve capital from only two countries, although in the Andean sub-region the activity of these enterprises has effects on the markets of other countries (sectoral programmes of industrial integration); such Latin American binational or plurinational enterprises can be mixed or totally private.

Other forms of governmental co-operation are also being developed in the region: the economic co-operation agreement signed in 1974 between Argentina and Uruguay; the general treaty of friendship, co-operation and trade, signed in 1975 between Brazil and Uruguay; the participation of Venezuela in the Andean Development Corporation, in the Central American Economic Integration Bank and the Caribbean Development Bank, and the special financial resources which it has provided for the Central American countries; the formation of the Union of Banana-Exporting Countries; and the programmes of export credit established in Argentina and Brazil to facilitate their sales of machinery to other Latin American countries.

The treatment extended to transnational enterprises is also important in regional co-operation. The essential objectives are to increase the negotiating power of the Latin American countries, to fix norms of conduct which are compatible with the interests of these countries and acceptable to the transnational enterprises themselves, and to establish development plans to which the transnational enterprises should adopt their activities so as to better serve the long-term needs of the countries. The joint action would be more effective if it succeeded in establishing and enforcing a set of regional and national objectives to which the foreign firms should adhere, and negotiating specific agreements within the guidelines thus fixed. This would help the relations between the transnational enterprises and the Latin American countries to be more stable, as they would rest on a more satisfactory foundation.

Co-operation between developing countries, and in particular regional co-operation realized through integration schemes and complementary agreements, should serve as one of the instruments for securing a new role for Latin America in world industry and trade.

Bilateral agreements and agreements between limited groups of countries can be useful as instruments for securing the creation of a network of effective trade interrelations between the Latin American countries. Both types of agreements have limitations, however, because they do not provide scope for a sufficiently big expansion of trade and co-operation to enable industrial production to attain dimensions corresponding to large enough installations to permit it to compete at the world level. For this reason, these limited agreements must be considered in relation to broader schemes of co-operation between the Latin American countries.

The world economy is now ruled by large economic blocs, and there is no room in it for isolated countries or small groups of countries. Even the developed countries tend to combine in very large units -- such as the EEC, which contains 9 countries -- and to intensify the relations between blocs on multilateral bases. The markets of the Latin American countries, which are already limited because broad sectors of the population do not have access to them and because of the low average per capita income, are still much more isolated from each other. Because of this, the countries of the region have to limit their objectives even more than the shortage of available investment resources and their balance-of-payments restrictions would otherwise make necessary. The main part of the effort to overcome the problems of poverty and backwardness must be made by the developing countries themselves. In the next few years international financial co-operation must play an important role, but it can only be complementary to these internal efforts and cannot replace them or become the centre of the economic policies. The efforts at regional financial co-operation can contribute much, however, to maintaining the balance of payments, the systems of payments designed to promote mutual trade, the financing of projects of common interest, and the heightening of the region's negotiating power abroad.

Side by side with its efforts to intensify regional co-operation, Latin America must participate actively in the creation of a new economic framework for development, through co-operation within the Third World. Within the context of collective autodependence, co-operation entails a great increase in the horizontal links between Third World countries in many aspects of economic activities. These links should be much more diversified and go far beyond traditional economic integration to include measures in the spheres of trade and industrial development, monetary policy, international financing, and technology.

A number of the instruments of Latin American co-operation -- physical infrastructure projects, bilaterl agreements between various countries, the creation of binational or plurinational enterprises, the exploration and exploitation of renewable and non-renewable resources, financial co-operation -- would make it possible to put into effect the regional programme of industrial and trade co-operation referred to in section 4. It is only through decisions like these that the economic integration of Latin America can make progress, since they give the process coherence and rationality.

NOTES

[1] The authors are grateful to Juan Ayza for his assistance in carrying out the analysis of the relationship between the development potential of the more dynamic industrial sectors and the dimensions of national demand, which occupies an important place in the central argument of this article.

[2] The hypotheses presented here are merely illustrative and refer to a group of countries comprising Argentina, Bolivia, Brazil, Chile, Colombia, Ecuador, Mexico, Peru and Venezuela; since only limited statistical information was available on the other countries of Latin America they were not included in these hypotheses, but co-operation should of course extend to the whole of the region.

[3] CEPAL, Exports of manufactures in Latin America, E/CEPAL/L.128, January 1976, shows that sales of traditional manufactures represent almost half of total industrial exports.

[4] The industries producing intermediate goods include the basic non-ferrous metal industries, which are very important in Latin America.

[5] General Agreement on Tariffs and Trade (GATT), International trade in 1973/1974, Sales No.: GATT/1974-4, Geneva, 1974.

[6] The size of demand is not of course the only determinant of the possibilities of industrial progress. The availability of other factors -- including skilled labour -- is also an important element. However, the size of demand conditions specialization and the possibilities of tackling industries of these types.

[7] A similar situation is found in the metal-transforming industries, where, although the statistical correlation is less stable, a clear relation can be noted between the size of the national markets and the ratio between the totals of imports and exports.

[8] CEPAL, Economic Survey of Latin America 1975, E/CEPAL/1014, mimeographed version, June 1976.

[9] For this exercise a ten-year period has been taken, as it seems suitable for identifying the effects of a particular policy orientation. However, in order to interpret the results of the

analysis correctly, this period should not be considered as rigorously exact but as an approximate time-span starting when the new orientations begin to take effect (after the stage of preparation and implementation of decisions and new projects) and ending in the second half of the following decade.

[10] Attention is drawn again to the footnote to table 1 regarding the different definitions that may be adopted to classify manufactures. In the present case a strict definition, much more so than UNCTAD's, is adopted and only manufactures produced by non-traditional sectors are considered. If goods produced by the more traditional industries (such as textiles, footwear, etc.) are added, the share of manufactures in total exports in the last few years is just over one-fifth.

[11] See J. Ayza, G. Fichet and N. Gonzalez, America Latina, integracion economica y sustitucion de importaciones, CEPAL, Fondo de Cultura Economica, Mexico, 1975.

[12] The annual rate of 7.7 per cent estimated for Latin America is based on the growth targets for each country established in the respective development plans. This rate has been used in the projections for both the prognosis and the co-operation programme.

[13] See Raul Prebisch, Change and Development, IDB, Washington, D.C., 1970.

[14] See J. Ayza, G. Fichet and N. Gonzalez, op. cit., particularly the figures in the annex, which show the evolution of import coefficients, at the sectoral level and by country, between 1950 and 1970.

[15] Instituto de Planejamento Economico e social, A Industria de Maquinas-Ferramenta no Brasil, Brasilia, 1974.

[16] For the hypothesis of the persistence of current trends, the projected import coefficient of Latin America as a whole is greater than in the mid-seventies, mainly because of the imports of petroleum which would have to be made.

[17] In the infrastructural field, mention may be made of the hydroelectric plants at Itaipu (Brazil-Paraguay), Salto Grande (Argentina-Uruguay) and Yariceta-Apipe (Argentina-Paraguay). In transport, there is the Flota Mercante Grancolombiana, the Caribbean Multination Shipping Company, and the construction of the trans-Amazon highway. Finally, in the industrial area, the Bolivian-Argentinian pesticide plant, the Ecuatoriana de Atun (Childe-Ecuador) and Monomeros Colombo-Venezolanos are worthy of note.

Third World Countries: Problems of Economic Development and Ways of Solving Them

MAI VOLKOV

The third world is vast and varied. It embraces more than 100 countries, with varying social and economic structures, political orientations, and per capita national incomes. This differentiation among third world countries is growing each year. Hence the variety of problems faced by the third world and the impossibility of offering identical recipes to all countries for coping with these problems.

At the same time, there is a certain identity of conditions and problems that warrants grouping the apparently dissimilar Asian, African and Latin American countries under the heading of the third world and giving serious consideration to a common strategy for their economic development. These common features include economic backwardness and economic dependence upon scientific, technical and industrial centres in North America, Western Europe and Japan.

The third world countries' economic backwardness and dependence are due to the origins of these countries. It was not until after the Second World War that most of them gained political independence, with the latest of them obtaining it merely a year or two ago. And despite rapid economic growth since independence they have still retained a primarily colonial economic structure. The world market mechanism, which offers automatic advantages to partners with sophisticated technology, modern scientific and technical know-how and a well ramified economic infrastructure and which places the third world countries at a disadvantage, makes the countries more backward and more dependent, and increases the gap between them and the industrialised countries. It is not fortuitous that in recent years the restructuring of the system of international economic relations has become such an urgent task.

From **INTERNATIONAL DEVELOPMENT REVIEW**, 1977/3, (17-20), reprinted by permission of the publisher.

I. GOAL—TO OVERCOME BACKWARDNESS

This goal is faced by all developing countries, because it is otherwise impossible to solve the most immediate problems: providing a rapidly growing population with adequate food, eliminating appalling mass poverty, wiping out epidemics and diseases caused by unsanitary conditions, increasing employment, reducing unemployment, achieving universal literacy and creating conditions for the flowering of national cultures. The third world cannot reconcile itself to the fact that while comprising 82 per cent of all nonsocialist countries and 73 per cent of their population it accounts only for some 15 per cent of the GNP, 10 per cent of the industrial production, and one per cent of the scientific and technical potential (in numbers of patents) while, on the other hand, it accounts for almost 97 per cent of the totally and partially unemployed.

A mere redistribution of income among countries will not solve these problems. Those of the third world oil-producing countries which, as a result of higher oil prices and exports to industrialized countries, now have higher per capita national incomes than say, the USA, still continue to be among the developing countries, although cars of latest models speed along their roads, their armies are equipped with the last word in weaponry and their safes contain shares of Western corporations.

The majority of the developing countries, however, containing the bulk of the third world population, find themselves in increasingly difficult conditions. Their debts are growing and have now reached 190,000 million dollars and, adding short-term commercial indebtedness, even 250,000 million dollars. The chronic balance of payments deficit and the scale of inflation are becoming increasingly critical.

Needless to say, vast changes have taken place in the newly emergent countries during the period of their independent development. Many of them have embarked upon the path of industrialization and created new industrial centres and whole developed regions on their territory. On the whole, the pace of economic growth in the third world has greatly quickened compared with the colonial period. The pace is also well ahead of the rate of growth in the industrialized countries of the West. Also increased is the rate of accumulation which is approaching the level typical of industrially-developed countries.

But the more intensive the process of technical modernization in the economies of the third world countries and the higher the rates of growth, the more acute becomes the contradiction between this growth and the social and economic structure of these countries, dominated by small-scale natural or semi-commodity production and characterised by outmoded forms of land holding and tenure. So the backwardness of the third world countries cannot be overcome without carrying through deep-going reforms in the social and economic sphere as well.

II. NEW ROLE FOR THE STATE

The industrialization experience of the third world countries suggests that the nation state has a far more active role to play in this process than it had in the now industrially developed Western countries during their industrialization. Is this fortuitous?

We think that the new role played by the state in the industrialization of the developing countries is quite natural. It stems both from objective conditions and from the ideological concepts embraced by heads of these countries. Both these factors are closely intertwined, because ideological concepts are a form of subjective evaluation of objective conditions. Besides, leader of the developing countries enjoy a possibility that was denied to Western leaders in the period of industrialization, namely, that of comparing two types of industrialization -- the capitalist and the socialist, of comparing their results, and drawing appropriate lessons from them.

Now, with the October Revolution approaching its 60th anniversary, the results achieved by the first socialist state within a comparatively short span of history, including some 20 years of wars, economic dislocation and post-war rehabilitation, cannot but exercise an important influence on public opinion in the developing countries, as does the possibility of using for industrialization purposes the scientific, technical and economic cooperation with the socialist countries.

Economically and technically, the gap between the industrialized countries of the West and the young states of Asia, Africa and Latin America is so deep that its bridging in a relatively short period of time, historically speaking, will require special measures to protect the national economies of these states and the introduction by them of a system of incentives to encourage industrial development and scientific and technical progress.

Asian, African and Latin American countries possess great resources, the tapping of which could substantially accelerate their economic advance and industrialization. But can they be tapped by private enterprise which constitutes the principal form of decentralized industrialization? They can, but on a very limited scale and not always in the spheres of industrialization that meet the interests of the whole nation. The largest iron and steel works, for example, badly needed by every developing economy, have been built by the state in such different third world countries as India and Brazil because private interests seek and find spheres of investment which, although more profitable, are less important for the establishment of a modern economy.

Private capital, as it forms in the developing countries, often leaves not only the production sphere, but even these countries themselves. While the young states are hard pressed for investment, private capital flows abroad, mainly to the industrialized Western countries. This applies not only to "petrodollars", but also to money accumulated by so-called "poor" countries, including those of South and South-East Asia.

Private enterprise restricts its activity only to "chosen" industries with the shortest possible period of capital recoupment and the highest rate of profit. Yet, even there, its activities often clash with the interests of the whole nation. Indicative in this respect is the situation in India's textile industry. This is a big industry with some 700 factories employing more than a million workers. Traditionally, all textile enterprises in India are privately-owned. But in 1974, 100 factories were nationalised. The reason was not the ideological concepts of the government at the time, but objective necessity. The manufacturers were curtailing the production of cheap fabrics needed by the bulk of the population in order to create a shortage on the market and raise prices. Tens of thousands of textile workers found themselves without jobs. The state had to nationalize part of the enterprises in that branch.

If the third world countries that have scored great successes in establishing and developing their national industry had oriented themselves on decentralized industrialization, they would also not now have their own iron and steel industry, modern heavy industry, or the core of the modern scientific and technical potential. National development and the development of the public sector are becoming synonymous for the public in the third world.

III. INTERDEPENDENCE OR ECONOMIC INDEPENDENCE

The external factor is of particular importance for the economic development of the newly-free countries. This is due to two circumstances. First, in the period of the scientific and technological revolution, an important role begins to be played in economic development by new sophisticated techniques, and scientific and technical knowledge which can be acquired by the developing countries only from abroad. Secondly, during the period of colonialism the economic structure of the now independent countries was often adapted by coercive, non-economic means to suit the needs of the conquerers. To this day distinguishing marks of this structure are its lop-sidedness, excessive development of industries manufacturing goods for markets in the industrialized Western countries, and the lack of many industries necessary to the young states themselves.

Selling raw materials and farm produce remains the principal way of obtaining foreign currency. The deepening international division of labour, which is a natural tendency in the development of the world productive forces, makes production increasingly international. The economic isolation of any country from the outside world more and more limits the possibilities for its technical modernization and economic growth. This undoubted reality is reflected in the now widespread concept in the West of the interdependence of nations. This concept maintains that multinational corporations, which provide the backward countries with capital, the latest technology and technical expertise, are now the basic motive force in world economic development. It further claims that in these new conditions national sovereignty becomes an obstacle to economic progress and should be sacrificed to the interests of the economic health of nations.

The concept of the interdependence of nations, however, omits the fact that the interconnected nations hold far from equal stations in the world economy. Some of them, because of their economic might, high levels of science and technology and their possession of a well-ramified network of world economic infrastructure (banks, insurance companies, merchant marine, communication and mass media, trading mechanism, etc.) derive constant advantages from their external economic ties, while others that are economically backward are suffering losses, even if they are rich in natural resources. Herein lies the kernel of the major contradiction in the development of the third world countries: on the one hand, they cannot get along without maintaining intensive economic contacts with the industrialized Western countries and without drawing on the colossal reserves of capital and latest technology owned by the multinational corporations, but on the other hand these ties, owing to the unequal status of the developing countries in the world economy, are constantly depriving these countries of a portion of their national income and, therefore, stand in the way of economic progress.

The developing countries seek a way out of this contradiction through establishing a new international economic order. One of its fundamental principles is recognition of the absolute sovereignty of these countries over all natural and economic resources located on their territory. This sovereignty also forms the basis of economic independence, which is sought by countries that have already won their political independence. The interdependence-of-nations concept fully rejects the economic independence of third world countries as a principle supposedly incompatible with the deepening international division of labour and the expanding participation of developing countries in the world economy.

But economic independence is not equivalent to economic isolation, not at all. It presupposes the inclusion of a country into the world economy, but in a way in which this country can vigorously uphold its national interests, pursue an independent foreign economic policy, bar foreign interference in its economic affairs, enjoy full sovereignty over its natural and economic resources, create a highly developed modern economy, set itself goals in the context of its own set of values, and choose for itself a social and economic system without any outside influence.

In the ultimate analysis, the actual economic independence of the newly-free countries can bring benefits to the industrialized countries too. Industrialization, technical progress and higher living standards in the third world will open up new markets for the industry of the developed countries and provide employment for many workers in the West. The role of the West in the economic development of the third world will be largely determined by what will prevail in its actions -- a desire for an immediate rise in profits at all costs or a wise and farsighted view of mutual benefits and interests.

PART II
STATISTICAL INFORMATION AND SOURCES

Main purpose of this section is to provide a current bibliography of data sources and statistical data for various indicators of international development, as they relate to economic policy and planning with special reference to the developing countries. An attempt is made to provide the reader with an overview of global trends, based on an analysis of the country data, as it is sometimes difficult to form any such general impression when faced with a general body of highly detailed data.

I. BIBLIOGRAPHY OF INFORMATION SOURCES

AFRICAN STATISTICAL YEARBOOK, UN

Presents data arranged on a country basis for 44 African countries for the years 1965-1978. Available statistics for each country are presented in 48 tables: population; national accounts; agriculture, forestry, and fishing industry; transport and communications; foreign trade; prices; finance; and social statistics: education and medical facilities.

ASIAN INDUSTRIAL DEVELOPMENT NEWS, UN, Sales no. E.74.II.F.16

In four parts: (a) brief reports on the ninth session of the Asian Industrial Development Council and twenty-sixth session of the Committee on Industry and Natural Resources; (b) articles on multinationals and the transfer of know-how, acquisition of technology for manufacturing agro-equipment, fuller utilization of industrial capacity; (c) report of Asian Plan of Action on the Human Environment; and (d) statistical information on plywood, transformers, and transmission cables.

Banks, Arthur S., et al., eds.
ECONOMIC HANDBOOK OF THE WORLD: 1981. New York; London; Sydney and Tokyo: McGraw-Hill Books for State University of New York at Binghamton, Center for Social Analysis, 1981.

Descriptions, in alphabetical order, of all the world's independent states and a small number of non-independent but economically significant areas (such as Hong Kong). Data are current as of 1 July 1980 whenever possible. Summary statistics for each country include: area, population, monetary unit, Gross National Product per capita, international reserves (1979 year end), external public debt, exports, imports, government revenue, government expenditure, and consumer prices. Principal economic institutions, financial institutions, and international memberships are listed at the end of each description.

BULLETIN OF LABOUR STATISTICS. Quarterly, with supplement 8 times per year. Approx. 150 p.

Quarterly report, with supplements in intervening months, on employment, unemployment, hours of work, wages, and consumer prices, for 130-150 countries and territories. Covers total, nonagricultural, and manufacturing employment; total unemployment and rate; average nonagricultural and manufacturing hours of work per week, and earnings per hour, day, week, or month; and food and aggregate consumer price indexes.

COMPENDIUM OF SOCIAL STATISTICS, 1977. 1980, UN, Sales No. E-F.80.XVII.6.

Contains a collection of statistical and other data aimed at describing social conditions and social change in the world. In four parts. Part 1 includes estimates and projections for the world, macroregions, and regions. Part 2 comprises data for countries or areas that represent key series describing social conditions and social change. Part 3 consists of general statistical series for countries or areas. Part 4 is devoted to information for cities or urban agglomerations. Includes a total of 151 tables, covering population, health, nutrition, education, conditions of work, housing and environmental conditions, etc. Provides an overall view of the world social situation and future trends.

DEMOGRAPHIC YEARBOOK, 1978. (ST-ESA-STAT-SER.R-7) 1979, UN, Sales No. E-F.79.XIII.I.

--Vol. 1. viii, 463 p. This volume contains the general tables giving a world summary of basic demographic statistics, followed by tables presenting statistics on the size distribution and trends in population, natality, fetal mortality, infant and maternal mortality, general mortality, nuptiality, and divorce. Data are also shown by urban/rural residence in many of the tables.
--Vol. 2: Historical supplement.

DEVELOPMENT FORUM BUSINESS EDITION. DESI/DOP, UN, Palais des Nations, CH-1211 Geneva 10, Switzerland. 24 times a yr. 16 p.

A tabloid-size paper, published jointly by the United Nations Department of Information's Divison for Economic and Social Information and the World Bank. Presents articles on all aspects of the development work of the United Nations, with emphasis on specific development problems encountered by the business community. Contains notices referring to goods and works to be procured through international competitive bidding for projects assisted by the World Bank and the International Development Association (IDA). It also includes a Supplement of the World Bank, entitled "Monthly Operational Summary", and a similar supplement of the Inter-American Development Bank (IDB), once a month, which provide information about projects contemplated for financing by the World Bank and IDB, respectively.

DEVELOPMENT FORUM GENERAL EDITION

A tabloid-size paper, published jointly by the United Nations Department of Public Information's Division for Economic and Social Information and the World Bank, having as objective the effective mobilization of public opinion in support of a number of major causes to which the United Nations is committed. Presents articles reporting on the activities of various UN agencies concerned with development and social issues (health, education, nutrition, women in development). Includes a forum for nongovernmental organizations (NGO's) and book reviews.

DEVELOPMENT AND INTERNATIONAL ECONOMIC CO-OPERATION: LONG-TERM TRENDS IN ECONOMIC DEVELOPMENT. Report of the Secretary-General. Monograph. May 26, 1982.

Report analyzing world economic development trends, 1960's-81, with projections to 2000 based on the UN 1980 International Development Strategy, and on alternative low and medium economic growth assumptions. Presents data on GDP, foreign trade, investment, savings, income, population and labor force, housing, education, food and energy supply/demand, and other economic and social indicators.

DIRECTORY OF INTERNATIONAL STATISTICS: VOLUME 1. 1982 Series. Sales No. E.81.XVII.6

Vol. 1 of a 2-volume directory of international statistical time series compiled by 18 UN agencies and selected other IGO's. Lists statistical publications, and machine-readable data bases of economic and social statistics, by organization and detailed subject category. Also includes bibliography and descriptions of recurring publications, and technical descriptions of economic/social data bases.

VOLUME 2: INTERNATIONAL TABLES. Sales No. E.82.XVII.6, Vol. II

Presents analytical summary of major income and product accounts for approximately 160 countries, by country and world region.

ECONOMIC AND SOCIAL PROGRESS IN LATIN AMERICA: 1980-81 REPORT. 1981, IDB.

Provides a comprehensive survey of the Latin America economy since 1970, with particular emphasis on 1980 and 1981. Part One is a regional analysis of general economic trends, the external sector, the financing of development from internal and external sources, regional economic integration, and social development trends (women in the economic development of Latin America). Part Two contains country summaries of socioeconomic trends for 24 States members of IDB. Statistical appendix includes data on population, national accounts, public finance, balance of payments, primary commodity exports, external public debt, and hydrocarbons.

ECONOMIC AND SOCIAL SURVEY OF ASIA AND THE PACIFIC, 1977. The International Economic Crises and Developing Asia and the Pacific. 1978, UN, Sales No. E.78.II.F.1.

In two parts: (a) review of recent economic developments and emerging policy issues in the ESCAP region, 1976-1977; and (b) the impacts of the international economic crises of the first half of the 1970's upon selected developing economies in the ESCAP region and the market and policy response thereto. Topics discussed include: the food crisis; the breakdown of the international monetary system; fluctuations in the international market economy comprising the primary commodities export boom, the associated inflation and the subsequent recession, and, finally the sharp rise in the price of petroleum.

ECONOMIC AND SOCIAL SURVEY OF ASIA AND THE PACIFIC, 1979. Regional Development Strategy for the 1980's. 1981, UN, Sales No. E.80.II.F.1.

Analyzes recent economic and social development in the UN ESCAP region, as well as related international developments. Focuses on economic and social policy issues and broad development strategies. In two parts: (a) recent economic developments, 1978-1979, covering the second oil price shock economic performance of the developing countries of the ESCAP region, inflation, and external trade and payments; and (b) findings of a two-year study dealing with regional developmental strategies, covering economic growth, policies for full employment and equity, energy, technology, implementation systems, international trade, shipping, international resource transfers, and intraregional cooperation.

ECONOMIC SURVEY OF ASIA AND THE FAR EAST, 1973. 234 p. (also issued as <u>Economic Bulletin for Asia and the Far East</u>, vol. 24, no. 4), 1974, UN, Sales No. E.74.II.F.1.

Contains a general summary followed by Part One, which covers: education and employment--the nature of the problem; population, labor force and structure of employment and underemployment in the ECAFE [ESCAP] region; the role of location--assumptions underlying the education policies of developing countries in the ECAFE region; momentum and direction of expansion of education; structuring the flow of workers into the modern science of education for self employment--the traditional and informal sectors; and the search for new policies--a review of current thinking. Part Two covers: current economic developments--recent economic developments and emerging policy issues in the ECAFE region, 1972/73; and current economic developments and policies in 28 countries of the ECAFE region.

ECONOMIC SURVEY OF LATIN AMERICA. Series.

Series of preliminary annual reports analyzing recent economic trends in individual Latin American countries. Each report presents detailed economic indicators, including GDP by sector, agricultural and industrial production by commodity, foreign trade, public and private sector finances, and prices. Also includes selected data on employment and earnings.

THE ECONOMIST. THE WORLD IN FIGURES. Third edition. New York: Facts on File, Inc., 1980.

Compendium of figures on economic, demographic, and sociopolitical aspects of over 200 countries of the world. The first part is a world section with information on population, national income, production, energy, transportation, trade, tourism, and finance. The second part is organized by country (grouped by main region), containing statistics on location, land, climate, time, measurement systems, currency, people, resources, production, finance and external trade, and politics and the economy. The data, from many sources, cover through 1976. Country name and "special focus" indices.

FACTS OF THE WORLD BANK. Monthly (current issues).

A compilation of figures on World Bank lending, giving cumulative amounts and amounts for the current fiscal year of commitments by number of projects and by sector, as well as for each country by region. Also gives figures on sales of parts of Bank loans and IDA credits and on World Bank borrowings by currency of issue, original and outstanding amounts, and number of issues.

IMF SURVEY. Biweekly.

Biweekly report on international financial and economic conditions; IMF activities; selected topics relating to exchange rates, international reserves, and foreign trade; and economic performance of individual countries and world areas.

MAIN ECONOMIC INDICATORS: HISTORICAL STATISTICS, 1960-1979. 1980, OECD, Sales No. 2750 UU-31 80 20 3.

Bilingual: E-F. Replaces previous editions. Base year for all indicators is 1970. Arranged in chapters by country, the tables cover the period 1960 to 1979, and are followed by short notes describing some major characteristics of the series, and, where applicable, indicating breaks in continuity. Note: Supplements the monthly bulletin Main Economic Indicators.

MONTHLY BULLETIN OF STATISTICS. Monthly.

Monthly report presenting detailed economic data including production, prices, and trade; and summary population data; by country, with selected aggregates for world areas and economic groupings, or total world. Covers population size and vital statistics; employment; industrial production, including energy and major commodities; construction activity; internal and external trade; passenger and freight traffic; manufacturing wages; commodity and consumer prices; and money and banking. Each issue includes special tables, usually on topics covered on a regular basis but presenting data at different levels of aggregation and for different time periods. Special tables are described and indexed in IIS as they appear.

POPULATION AND VITAL STATISTICS REPORT. Quarterly.

Quarterly report on world population, births, total and infant deaths, and birth and death rates, by country and territorial possession, as of cover date. Also shows UN population estimates for total world and each world region.

QUARTERLY BULLETIN OF STATISTICS FOR ASIA AND THE PACIFIC. Quarterly.

Quarterly report presenting detailed monthly and quarterly data on social and economic indicators for 38 ESCAP member countries. Includes data on population; births and deaths; employment; agricultural and industrial production; construction; transportation; foreign trade quantity, value, and direction; prices; wages; and domestic and international financial activity.

1978 REPORT ON THE WORLD SOCIAL SITUATION. 1979, UN, Sales No. E.79.IV.1.

Deals with the global issues of population trends and employment; growth and distribution of income and private consumption; the production and distribution of social services; and changing social concerns. A supplement reviews the patterns of recent governmental expenditures for social services in developing countries, developed market economies, and centrally planned economies.

STATISTICAL INDICATORS FOR ASIA AND THE PACIFIC. Quarterly.

Quarterly report presenting selected economic and demographic indicators for 26 Asian and Pacific countries. Covers, for most countries, population size, birth and death rates, family planning methods, industrial and agricultural production, construction, transport, retail trade, foreign trade, prices, money supply, currency exchange rate, and GDP.

STATISTICAL YEARBOOK, 1979/80. 1981, UN, Sales No. E/F.81.XVII.1.

A comprehensive compendium of the most important internationally comparable data needed for the analysis of socioeconomic development at the world, regional and national levels. Includes tables (200) grouped in two sections: (a) world summary by regions (17 tables); and (b) remaining tables of country-by-country data, arranged in chapters: population; manpower; agriculture; forestry; fishing; industrial production; mining and quarrying; manufacturing; construction; development assistance; wholesale and retail trade; external trade; international tourism; transport; communications; national accounts; wages and prices; consumption; finance; energy; health; housing; science and technology; and culture. For this first time, this issue contains three new tables on industrial property: patents, industrial designs, and trademarks and service marks. Note: This issue is a special biennial edition, covering data through mid-1980, and in some cases for 1980 complete.

STATISTICAL YEARBOOK FOR ASIA AND THE PACIFIC, 1978. 1979, UN, Sales No. E-F.79.II.F.4.

Eleventh issue. Contains statistical indicators for the ESCAP region and statistics for period up to 1978 available at the end of 1978 for 34 countries and territories members of ESCAP, arranged by country, covering, where available: population; manpower; national accounts; agriculture, forestry, and fishing; industry; consumption; transport and communication; internal and external trade; wages, prices, and household expenditures; finance; and social statistics.

STATISTICAL YEARBOOK FOR LATIN AMERICA, 1979. 1981, UN, Sales No. E/S.80.II.G.4.

In two parts. Part 1 presents indicators of economic and social development in Latin America for 1960, 1965, 1970 and 1975-1978, including: population; demographic characteristics; employment and occupational structure; income distribution; living levels; consumption and nutrition; health; education; housing; global economic growth; agricultural activities; mining and energy resources; manufacturing; productivity; investment; saving; public financial resources; public expenditure; structure of exports and imports; intra-regional trade; transport services; tourist services; and external financing. Part 2 contains historical series in absolute figures for the years 1960, 1965 and 1970-1978 on population; national accounts; domestic prices; balance of payments; external indebtedness; external trade; natural resources and production of goods; infrastructure services; employment; and social conditions.

SURVEY OF ECONOMIC AND SOCIAL CONDITIONS IN AFRICA, 1980-81 AND OUTLOOK FOR 1981-82: SUMMARY

Examines growth in GDP, agricultural and industrial production, trade and balance of payments, resource flows, energy production/consumption, and selected other economic indicators, 1979-80, with outlook for 1981-82 and trends from 1960's.

TECHNICAL DATA SHEETS

Provides up-to-date information about projects as they are approved for World Bank and IDA financing. In addition to a description of the project, its total cost, and the amount of Bank financing, each technical data sheet describes the goods and services that must be provided for the project's implementation and gives the address of the project's implementing organization. On the average, 250 such sheets will be issued annually. Requests for sample copies are to be addressed to: Publications Distribution Unit, World Bank, 1818 H St., N.W., Washington, D.C. 20433, U.S.A.

UNESCO STATISTICAL YEARBOOK, 1978-79, 1266 p. 1980, UNESCO.

Composite: E/F/S (introductory texts). Presents statistical and other information for 206 countries on education; science and technology; libraries; museums and related institutions; theater and other dramatic arts; book production; newspapers and other periodicals; film and cinema; radio broadcasting; and television. In this edition, the summary tables relating to culture and communications, previously given in the introduction to each of the corresponding chapters, have been grouped together in a separate chapter.

World Bank. ANNUAL REPORT, 1982. 1982, WBG.

Presents summary and background of the activities of the World Bank Group during the fiscal year ended 30 June 1982, covering: the International Bank for Reconstruction and Development (IBRD); the International Development Association (IDA); and the International Finance Corporation (IFC). Chapters cover: brief review of Bank operations in fiscal 1982; a global perspective of the economic situation; Bank policies, activities and finances for fiscal 1982; 1982 regional perspectives; and Executive Directors. Lists projects approved for IBRD and IDA assistance in fiscal 1982 by sector, region and purpose. Also reviews trends in lending by sector for 1980-82 and includes statistical annex.

WORLD BANK COUNTRY STUDIES. Series.

Series of studies, prepared by World Bank staff, on development issues and policies, and economic conditions in individual developing countries. Studies may focus on specific economic sectors or issues, or on general economic performance of the country as a whole.

The World Bank.
WORLD DEVELOPMENT REPORT, 1978. August 1978.

First volume in a series of annual reports designed to provide a comprehensive, continuing assessment of global development issues. After an overview of development in the past 25 years, the report discusses current policy issues and projected developments in areas of the international economy that influence the prospects of developing countries. Analyzes the problems confronting policy makers in developing countries, which differ in degree and in kind, affecting the choice of appropriate policy instruments, and recognizes that development strategies need to give equal prominence to two goals: accelerating economic growth and reducing poverty. Reviews development priorities for low-income Asia, sub-Saharan Africa, and middle-income developing countries.

The World Bank.
WORLD DEVELOPMENT REPORT, 1979. Washington, D.C.

Second in a series of annual reports designed to assess global development issues. Focuses on development in the middle income countries, with particular emphasis on policy choices for industrialization and urbanization. Part one assesses recent trends and prospects to 1990 and discusses capital flows, and energy. Part two focuses upon structural change and development policy relevant to employment, the balance between agriculture and industry, and urban growth. Part three reviews development experiences and issues in three groups of middle income countries: semi-industrialized nations; mineral primary-producing countries; and predominantly agricultural primary-producing countries. Maintains that progress toward expanding employment and reducing poverty in developing countries lies not only in internal policy choices but also in a liberal environment for international trade and capital flows.

The World Bank.
WORLD DEVELOPMENT REPORT, 1980. New York: Oxford University Press for the World Bank, 1980.

Third in a series of annual reports. Parts one examines economic policy choices facing both developing and developed countries and their implications for national and regional growth. Projects, to the year 2000 but particularly to the mid to late 1980's, growth estimates for oil-importing and oil-exporting developing countries; and analyzes the fundamental issues of energy, trade, and capital flows. Part two focuses on the links between poverty, growth, and human development. It examines the impact of education, health, nutrition, and fertility on poverty; reviews some practical lessons in implementing human development programs; and discusses the trade-offs between growth and poverty and the allocation of resources between human development and other activities. Stresses the views that growth does not obviate the need for human development and that direct measures to reduce poverty do not obviate the need for economic expansion. Concludes that world growth prospects have deteriorated in the past year, but higher oil prices have impoved the outlook [for the first half of the 1980's] for the fifth of the developing world's population that lives in oil-exporting countries; however, the four-fifths that live in oil-importing countries will experience slower growth for the first half of the decade. Includes a statistical appendix to part one; a bibliographical note; and a very lengthy annex of World Development Indicators.

The World Bank.
WORLD DEVELOPMENT REPORT, 1981. New York: Oxford University Press for the World Bank, 1981.

With the major focus on the international context of development, examines past trends and future prospects for international trade, energy, and capital flows and the effects of these on developing countries. Presents two scenarios for the 1980's, one predicting higher growth rates than in the 1970's and one lower. Analyzes national adjustments to the international economy, presenting in-depth case studies. Concludes that countries pursuing outward-oriented policies adjusted more easily to external shocks. Contends that whichever scenario prevails, income differentials will increase between the industrial and developing countries. Low income countries have fewer options and less flexibility of adjustment, therefore requiring continued aid from the more affluent countries. Advocates policies to channel increased resources to alleviate poverty.

The World Bank.
WORLD DEVELOPMENT REPORT, 1982.

The Report this year focuses on agriculture and food security. As in previous years there is also a section on global prospects and international issues, as well as the statistical annex of World Development indicators.

The World Bank.
WORLD TABLES 1980: FROM THE DATA FILES OF THE WORLD BANK. Second edition. Baltimore and London: Johns Hopkins University Press for the World Bank, 1980.

A broad range of internationally comparable statistical information drawn from the World Bank data files. Includes historical time series for individual countries in absolute numbers for most of the basic economic indicators for selected years (1950-77 when available); also presents derived economic indicators for selected periods of years and demographic and social data for selected years. Although the number of social indicators is fewer than those in the 1976 edition the quality of the data has been improved through the use of more uniform definitions and concepts, greater attention to population statistics, and better statistics on balance of payments and central government finance. Includes an index of country coverage.

WORLD ECONOMIC OUTLOOK: A SURVEY BY THE STAFF OF THE INTERNATIONAL MONETARY FUND. 1980, IMF.

An in-depth forecast of the world economy in 1980 and a preliminary summary for 1981. Chapters discuss: a profile of current situation and short-term prospects; global perspectives for adjustment and financing; industrial countries; developing countries--oil-exporting and non-oil groups; and key policy issues. Appendixes include country and regional surveys; technical notes on the world oil situation, estimated impact of fiscal balances in selected industrial countries, and monetary policy and inflation; and statistical tables.

WORLD ECONOMIC OUTLOOK: A SURVEY BY THE STAFF OF THE INTERNATIONAL MONETARY FUND. [1982 ed.] 1982, IMF.

A comprehensive analysis of economic developments, policies, and prospects through June 1981 for industrial, oil exporting and non-oil developing countries. It highlights persistent imbalances in the world economy, high inflation, rising unemployment, excessive rates of real interest, and unstable exchange rates. Appendix A includes supplementary notes providing information on selected topics in greater depth or detail than in the main body of the report: country and regional surveys; medium-term scenarios; fiscal development; monetary and exchange rate development; world oil situation; growth and inflation in non-oil developing countries; developments in trade policy; and commodity price developments and prospects. Appendix B presents statistical tables on: domestic economic activity and prices; international trade; balance of payments; external debt; medium-term projections; and country tables.

The World Bank.
WORLD BANK ATLAS. Fourteenth edition. 1979. Annual.

Presents estimates of gross national product (GNP) per capita (1977), GNP per capita growth rates (1970-77), and population (mid-1977), with population growth rates (1970-77) for countries with populations of one million or more in three global maps; a computer-generated map shows GNP per capita (1977) by major regions. Six regional maps give the same data for 184 countries and territories, as well as preliminary data for 1978. The base years 1976-78 have been used for the conversion of GNP for both 1977 and 1978. A Technical Note explains in detail the methodology used.

The World Bank.
WORLD DEVELOPMENT INDICATORS. June 1979. 71 pages.

A volume of statistics prepared in conjunction with and constituting the Annex to the World Development Report, 1979 to provide information of general relevance about the main features of economic and social development, reporting data for a total of 125 countries whose population exceeds one million. Countries are grouped in five categories and ranked by their 1977 per capita gross national product (GNP) levels. The volume contains 24 tables covering some 110 economic and social indicators. The choice of indicators has been based on data being available for a large number of countries, the availability of historical series to allow the measurement of growth and change, and on the relevance of data to the principal processes of development.

The World Bank.
WORLD ECONOMIC AND SOCIAL INDICATORS. Quarterly (current issues).

Presents most recent available data on trade, commodity prices, consumer prices, debt and capital flows, industrial production, as well as social indicators and select annual data (by countries where applicable). Each issue contains an article on topics of current importance. Strategies for improving the access to education of the disadvantaged rural poor by serving areas out of range of existing schools are discussed and programs in four projects financed by the World Bank are described.

WORLD ECONOMIC OUTLOOK: A SURVEY BY THE STAFF OF THE INTERNATIONAL MONETARY FUND. Annual. April 1982. (Occasional Paper No. 9)

Annual report on economic performance of major industrial and oil exporting and non-oil developing countries, 1970's-81 and forecast 1982-83, with some projections to 1986. Includes analysis of economic indicators for selected industrial countries, world economic groupings, and world areas, primarily for IMF member countries. Covers domestic economic activity, including prices, GNP, and employment; international trade; balance of payments; and foreign debt. Also includes financial indicators for selected industrial countries, including government budget surpluses and deficits, savings, money supply, and interest rates.

WORLD ECONOMIC SURVEY. 1978, UN, Sales No. E.78.II.C.1.

Provides an overview of salient developments in the world economy in 1977 and the outlook for 1978. Focuses on policy needs for improving the tempo of world production and trade. Examines in detail the course of production and trade and related variables in the developing economies, the developed market economies, and the centrally planned economies.

WORLD ECONOMIC SURVEY 1979-80. 1980, UN, Sales No. E.80.II.C.2.

A survey of current world economic conditions and trends, with chapters on salient features and policy implications; the growth of world output, 1979-80; the accelerating pace of inflation; world trade and international payments; world economic outlook, 1980-1985; and adjustment policies in developing countries. Annexes cover external factors and growth in developing countries--the experience of the 1970's; supply and price of petroleum in 1979 and 1980; and prospective supply and demand for oil.

YEARBOOK OF NATIONAL ACCOUNTS STATISTICS, 1980. Annual. 1982.

Annual report presenting national income and product account balances for approximately 170 countries, and for world areas and economic groupings, selected years 1970-79, often with comparisons to 1960 and 1965. Data are compiled in accordance with the UN System of National Accounts (SNA) for market economies, and the System of Material Product Balances (MPS) for centrally planned economies. SNA data include GDP final consumption expenditures by type; production, income/outlay, and capital formation accounts, by institutional sector; and production by type of activity. MPS data include material and financial balances, manpower and resources, and national wealth and capital assets.

STATISTICAL NEWSLETTER. Quarterly.

Quarterly newsletter on ESCAP statistical programs and activities, and major statistical developments in ESCAP countries. Includes brief descriptions of meetings, working groups, upcoming international statistical training programs, and regional advisory services; and an annotated bibliography of recent ESCAP and UN statistical publications.

1976 FAO TRADE YEARBOOK. Vol. 30. FAO Statistics Series, no. 8. Rome: Food and Agriculture Organization; distributed by Unipub, New York, 1977.

Annual summation of world trade in agricultural products for the calendar year 1976. The 182 tables provide information on: trade index numbers for the aggregate agricultural and aggregate food products; quantities and values of trade for agricultural products and requisites; and present value summaries by Standard International Trade Classification divisions for selected countries. Data acquired for national publications of the respective governments and/or FAO questionnaires. This edition is shorter than previous editions due to the reduction of the General and Commodity Notes.

HANDBOOK OF INTERNATIONAL TRADE AND DEVELOPMENT STATISTICS, 1979. New York: United Nations, 1979.

Compilation of data drawn from existing international and national sources related to world trade and development. Tables, covering various time periods since 1950, with countries and territories classified: according to economic type and geographic area, developed market economies, socialist countries of Asia, and developing countries and territories. In eight parts: value of world trade by regions and countries 1950-78; volume, unit value, and terms of trade index numbers by regions, commodity prices, and consumer price indices, networks of world trade; exports and imports for individual countries by commodity structure, major exports of developing countries, and LDC imports of manufactured goods and imports from LDC's of semi-manufactured goods; balance of payments, financial resource flows, and external indebtedness of LDC's; basic indicators of development; special studies; and shipping statistics.

WORLD DEBT TABLES. December 28, 1979.

A compilation of data on the external public and publicly guaranteed debt of 96 developing countries, 1972-78 from the World Bank Debtor Reporting System (DRS). Volume I contains five parts. Parts A, C, and D describe the nature, content, and coverage of the data. Part B gives a review of external debt of 96 countries through 1978. Part E contains statistical tables supporting the review given in Part B. Volume II contains tables on external public debt outstanding, commitments, disbursements, service payments, and net borrowing of 96 developing countries, by country and category of lender, 1972-85.

FOREIGN TRADE STATISTICS OF ASIA AND THE PACIFIC. UN, 1977.

Detailed regional commodity trade statistics (imports and exports) for the calendar year 1974 of the countries and territories of the region (18) which reported to the UN Economic and Social Commission for Asia and the Pacific (ESCAP). Data are reported by sections and groups of the Standard International Trade Classification. Revised (SITC), in matrix form.

UNESCO YEARBOOK ON PEACE AND CONFLICT STUDIES. 1980. 1981, Greenwood Press/UNESCO.

Reflecting UNESCO's long-term commitment to supporting, disseminating and exchanging the findings of peace researchers, this first volume of a projected series investigates a wide range of topics relevant to the study of conflict and conflict prevention by groups, societies, and the world at large. New approaches to the study of war--from societal, political, and economic and statistical points of view--are examined in detail, utilizing new research in psychology, philosophy, military affairs, international relations, and other fields. Also reviews new methods of processing and documenting data on peace and war and recent institutional developments in the field of peace studies.

HANDBOOK OF INTERNATIONAL TRADE AND DEVELOPMENT STATISTICS: SUPPLEMENT 1980. UN, 1981.

Provides, on an interim basis, a revised and updated version of the Handbook of International Trade and Development Statistics,

1979. It is planned to issue the Handbook in its entirety for the next session of UNCTAD, tentatively scheduled for 1983, in seven parts: (a) value of world trade by regions and countries, 1950, 1960, 1970-1979; (b) volume, unit value, and terms of trade index numbers by regions; commodity prices; consumer price indexes; (c) network of world trade--summary by selected regions of origin and destination and structure of exports and imports by selected commodity groups; (d) exports and imports for individual countries by commodity structure, and major exports of developing countries by leading exporters; (e) balance of payments, financial resource flows and external indebtedness of developing countries.

EXTERNAL DEBT STATISTICS FOR DEVELOPING COUNTRIES: LATEST TRENDS. OECD, 1980.

This document presents, in a short commentary, the latest available data and the historical trend of the external indebtedness of developing countries, by type, origin and destination. Sources, coverage and definitions of these data are described in a technical note.

BALANCE OF PAYMENTS YEARBOOK: VOL. 31. Ed. by Werner Danneman and Arie C. Bouter. IMF, 1980.

Each monthly issue of the yearbook consists of a booklet containing annual, half-yearly, or quarterly balance of payments data in the form of an analytic presentation for those countries that have provided new data during the preceding month. Notes and additional tables to complete each country section of the Year book will not be published until the annual issue is prepared at the end of the year. Note: a subscription covers eleven monthly booklets and a copy of the annual issue. In addition, each subscriber will receive a copy of a supplement giving a world summary of international transactions within a framework of categories of transactions, which are then analyzed by country.

DIRECTORY OF UNITED NATIONS INFORMATION SYSTEMS. IOB for UN, 1980.

Vol. 1: Information Systems and Data Bases. This volume gives particulars of United Nations family organizations and their information systems, together with the practical details, such as the address to contact for information, the conditions of access, the type of services that can be obtained. Details are provided on where to obtain bibliographies, indexes and other publications which are frequently available in several languages. The information systems covered include libraries, referral centres, clearing-houses, data banks, statistical information systems and other data collections, computerized or manual.
Vol. 2: Information Sources in Countries. Gives information by country, to facilitate contact between users and organizations' systems and services. More than 2,500 addresses in 167 countries are given. The addresses include organizations' offices, centres contributing information or serving as contact points to the various systems, and depository libraries where the publications

or organizations can be found. Information is given on the publications and papers of the different organizations held in depository libraries and in United Nations Information Centres, and on the related services provided.

COMMODITY TRADE STATISTICS. Series.

Series of annual reports on foreign trade on individual countries with the rest of world, by country, world area and economic grouping; by SITC 1- to 4-digit commodity. Each report covers imports, exports, and sometimes re-exports, by country, for 1 or several countries. Data sources: National government records. Format and data presentation: (a) Index and explanatory notes; (b) 2-3 import/export tables arranged by SITC classification, repeated for each country covered in report. All tables show trade values in US$ and, frequently, quantities traded. All tables show country of origin or destination for each commodity group.

II. STATISTICAL TABLES AND FIGURES

This section focuses attention on some of the major economic and social indicators from a global and developing country perspective. It's aim is to highlight some generalizations made in the first part of this book as pointers to needed policies. The limited extent to which statistical information is cited in this book is solely for illustrative purposes. Most of the statistical information in the following pages have been reproduced from the following sources:

WORLD TABLES 1980: FROM THE DATA FILES OF THE WORLD BANK, Baltimore: Johns Hopkins University Press for the World Bank, 1980, (Reprinted by permission of the World Bank and Johns Hopkins University Press).

WORLD ECONOMIC AND SOCIAL INDICATORS, October 1978. Report No. 700/78/04. Washington, D.C.: WORLD BANK.

432 Statistical Information and Sources

GLOBAL INDICATORS

TABLE 1. SOCIAL INDICATORS BY INCOME GROUP OF COUNTRIES

(ADJUSTED COUNTRY GROUP AVERAGES)

INDICATOR	DEVELOPING COUNTRIES EXCLUDING CAPITAL SURPLUS OIL EXPORTERS									INTERMEDIATE MIDDLE INCOME		
	LOW INCOME			LOWER MIDDLE INCOME			INTERMEDIATE MIDDLE INCOME					
	1960	1970	MOST RECENT ESTIMATE	1960	1970	MOST RECENT ESTIMATE	1960	1970	MOST RECENT ESTIMATE	1960	1970	MOST RECENT ESTIMATE
GNP PER CAPITA (IN CURRENT US $)	67.4	107.4	162.0	136.1	239.6	398.6	225.6	410.9	817.9			
POPULATION												
GROWTH RATE (%) - TOTAL	2.2	2.4	2.4	2.7	2.7	2.6	2.7	2.7	2.5			
- URBAN	5.3	4.7	4.7	4.7	4.4	9.8	5.4	4.9	5.1			
URBAN POPULATION (% OF TOTAL)	10.4	14.0	14.8	17.7	21.6	26.1	33.7	41.4	46.1			
VITAL STATISTICS												
CRUDE BIRTH RATE (PER 1000)	47.5	46.9	45.2	47.1	45.5	42.6	44.6	41.2	38.2			
CRUDE DEATH RATE (PER 1000)	26.1	21.7	18.2	21.4	16.1	12.7	18.6	13.5	11.1			
GROSS REPRODUCTION RATE	2.9	3.1	3.1	3.4	3.2	3.3	3.0	2.8	2.6			
EMPLOYMENT AND INCOME												
DEPENDENCY RATIO - AGE	0.8	0.9	0.9	0.9	0.9	0.9	0.9	0.9	0.9			
- ECONOMIC	1.0	1.1	1.1	1.3	1.4	1.4	1.6	1.6	1.5			
LABOR FORCE IN AGRICULTURE (% OF TOTAL)	65.4	62.0	59.3	70.4	65.9	62.5	62.8	54.5	47.0			
UNEMPLOYED (% OF LABOR FORCE)	4.7	4.0	3.1	6.3	8.4	5.3	6.1	6.0	5.8			
INCOME RECEIVED BY - HIGHEST 5%	24.5	23.3	20.3	25.1	23.1	25.5	31.5	27.0	19.3			
- LOWEST 20%	4.6	5.1	6.5	4.8	4.9	4.8	4.4	3.9	5.7			
HEALTH AND NUTRITION												
DEATH RATE (PER 1000) AGES 1-4 YEARS	43.6	33.0	33.0	9.3	6.8	7.5	8.5	3.6	2.7			
INFANT MORTALITY RATE (PER 1000)	129.0	121.3	102.8	84.6	79.9	58.4	88.6	65.8	55.0			
LIFE EXPECTANCY AT BIRTH (YRS)	39.2	43.8	46.0	45.0	50.8	53.2	51.1	57.0	59.1			
POPULATION PER - PHYSICIAN	21790.7	15219.9	13235.9	16767.4	11977.3	10586.0	3299.7	2549.2	2412.7			
- NURSING PERSON	8472.3	5215.0	4830.9	4078.2	1921.9	1683.8	3394.0	2205.1	1502.1			
- HOSPITAL BED	1386.7	1267.8	1236.2	1037.6	815.3	793.1	721.8	629.2	507.1			
PER CAPITA PER DAY SUPPLY OF:												
CALORIES (% OF REQUIREMENTS)	89.8	91.5	94.5	85.1	93.3	102.3	94.4	101.8	103.9			
PROTEIN (GRMS) - TOTAL	50.5	51.6	53.9	47.4	53.0	56.9	54.4	58.7	60.6			
- FROM ANIMALS & PULSES	14.9	14.4	16.4	17.7	18.1	18.8	21.8	22.1	23.0			
EDUCATION												
ADJ. ENROLLMENT RATIOS - PRIMARY	37.4	48.4	59.0	60.7	74.0	92.7	77.8	95.3	99.9			
- SECONDARY	4.8	10.3	13.9	4.8	12.7	22.6	14.5	26.7	29.4			
FEMALE ENROLLMENT RATIO (PRIMARY)	34.6	39.0	43.3	45.6	75.0	77.5	65.8	87.8	87.6			
ADULT LITERACY RATE (%)	24.4	32.0	33.8	41.0	60.0	63.0	49.8	57.8	62.3			

TABLE 1. Social Indicators by Income Group of Countries (Continued).

(ADJUSTED COUNTRY GROUP AVERAGES)

INDICATOR	DEVELOPING COUNTRIES EXCLUDING CAPITAL SURPLUS OIL EXPORTERS									
	LOW INCOME			LOWER MIDDLE INCOME			INTERMEDIATE MIDDLE INCOME			
	1960	1970	MOST RECENT ESTIMATE	1960	1970	MOST RECENT ESTIMATE	1960	1970	MOST RECENT ESTIMATE	
HOUSING										
PERSONS PER ROOM - URBAN	2.5	2.0	2.8	2.6	2.5	2.2	2.3	2.2	1.6	
OCCUPIED DWELLINGS WITHOUT WATER	62.2	69.8	..	68.7	64.6	67.8	74.6	64.2	58.9	
ACCESS TO ELECTRICITY (%) - ALL	..	..	..	17.3	23.3	40.4	28.4	49.6	71.9	
- RURAL	..	..	..	..	..	..	5.6	26.7	34.1	
CONSUMPTION										
RADIO RECEIVERS (PER 1000 POP.)	4.5	14.4	23.1	11.9	62.3	70.4	48.8	96.2	102.6	
PASSENGER CARS (PER 1000 POP.)	1.3	2.5	3.0	3.0	6.5	8.6	4.2	7.5	11.1	
ENERGY (KG COAL/YR PER CAPITA)	62.0	83.4	104.8	99.6	220.1	265.2	258.7	489.2	586.2	
NEWSPRINT (KG/YR PER CAPITA)	0.2	0.4	0.3	0.6	0.8	0.8	1.1	1.8	2.4	

INDICATOR	DEV'G CTRIES. EXCL. CAP. SURP. OIL EXP.											
	UPPER MIDDLE INCOME			HIGH INCOME			CAP. SURP. OIL EXP.			INDUSTRIALIZED COUNTRIES		
	1960	1970	MOST RECENT EST.	1960	1970	MOST RECENT EST.	1960	1970	MOST RECENT EST.	1960	1970	MOST RECENT EST.
GNP PER CAPITA (IN CURRENT US $)	401.2	817.1	1648.7	689.4	1564.2	2911.1	1054.3	2858.9	5710.5	1417.4	3096.8	5297.7
POPULATION												
GROWTH RATE (%) - TOTAL	1.6	1.3	1.5	2.1	3.1	2.9	4.5	2.4	2.7	0.9	0.9	0.9
- URBAN	3.3	3.4	2.8	4.5	3.9	3.5	..	5.8	6.8	1.6	1.3	1.3
URBAN POPULATION (% OF TOTAL)	43.4	51.1	53.1	63.0	82.1	88.6	24.6	20.0	39.0	66.1	70.5	73.8
VITAL STATISTICS												
CRUDE BIRTH RATE (PER 1000)	26.2	28.5	20.8	41.7	37.4	33.6	48.3	49.4	45.0	21.3	20.0	18.7
CRUDE DEATH RATE (PER 1000)	10.4	9.1	8.9	9.6	8.3	8.0	21.2	22.8	14.7	9.7	9.0	8.8
GROSS REPRODUCTION RATE	1.7	1.8	1.8	2.3	2.5	1.8	..	3.5	3.3	1.3	1.3	1.2

TABLE 1. Social Indicators by Income Group of Countries (Continued)

(ADJUSTED COUNTRY GROUP AVERAGES)

INDICATOR	DEV'G CTRIES, EXCL. CAP. SURP. OIL EXP. UPPER MIDDLE INCOME			CAP. SURP. OIL EXP. HIGH INCOME			CAP. SURP. OIL EXP.			INDUSTRIALIZED COUNTRIES		
	1960	1970	MOST RECENT EST.	1960	1970	MOST RECENT EST.	1960	1970	MOST RECENT EST.	1960	1970	MOST RECENT EST.
EMPLOYMENT AND INCOME												
DEPENDENCY RATIO - AGE	0.7	0.7	0.6	0.8	0.6	0.6	0.9	0.9	0.9	0.5	0.6	0.4
- ECONOMIC	1.3	1.7	1.6	1.2	1.2	1.2	1.8	1.7	1.7	0.9	0.9	0.8
LABOR FORCE IN AGRICULTURE (% OF TOTAL)	48.5	42.5	36.3	26.1	17.8	21.0	54.7	44.5	29.0	19.8	13.2	10.0
UNEMPLOYED (% OF LABOR FORCE)	7.4	3.3	4.0	9.0	5.4	5.1	7.4	2.0	3.0	2.1	1.5	1.9
INCOME RECEIVED BY - HIGHEST 5%	32.5	28.2	21.3	18.9	16.1	..	13.3	..	..	19.3	14.0	15.5
- LOWEST 20%	4.2	3.8	4.7	5.8	6.6	..	10.1	..	..	4.2	7.0	5.7
HEALTH AND NUTRITION												
DEATH RATE (PER 1000) AGES 1-4 YEARS	4.8	2.9	1.9	..	1.3	..	..	3.6	3.6	1.2	0.9	0.8
INFANT MORTALITY RATE (PER 1000)	74.4	51.3	37.9	44.9	27.8	23.2	..	134.3	80.3	27.9	17.0	15.0
LIFE EXPECTANCY AT BIRTH (YRS)	64.6	67.3	68.4	66.2	64.0	68.2	45.4	44.9	52.9	69.5	71.4	72.5
POPULATION PER - PHYSICIAN	1625.8	957.5	718.2	1117.5	888.9	756.9	9833.7	6323.4	1260.0	895.2	825.6	656.0
- NURSING PERSON	1690.7	1279.6	1028.5	1165.0	605.9	683.5	5140.0	2856.8	460.0	279.6	194.6	167.1
- HOSPITAL BED	209.9	180.4	185.8	170.0	162.5	170.0	1093.2	727.5	230.0	96.1	86.0	81.9
PER CAPITA PER DAY SUPPLY OF:												
CALORIES (% OF REQUIREMENTS)	104.5	114.4	111.5	106.3	107.2	113.6	83.9	90.3	104.9	118.7	118.7	119.5
PROTEIN (GRMS) - TOTAL	75.5	84.9	77.8	78.5	79.2	89.9	53.6	57.0	65.1	90.3	94.1	94.8
- FROM ANIMALS & PULSES	27.0	29.0	27.5	33.0	40.1	48.0	11.0	14.8	18.2	49.7	55.0	54.9
EDUCATION												
ADJ. ENROLLMENT RATIOS - PRIMARY	94.6	97.9	95.7	104.4	120.1	107.6	18.2	47.1	145.0	106.7	104.3	103.3
- SECONDARY	22.7	36.6	46.7	18.1	40.1	46.2	3.1	12.4	47.0	59.5	79.1	79.8
FEMALE ENROLLMENT RATIO (PRIMARY)	89.7	87.9	86.1	100.2	100.0	102.0	3.5	31.6	40.4	111.4	104.6	104.0
ADULT LITERACY RATE (%)	51.4	67.8	66.1	81.8	86.2	87.2	25.2	17.1	..	98.0	99.0	99.0
HOUSING												
PERSONS PER ROOM - URBAN	1.4	1.2	..	1.1	..	..	..	1.9	..	0.8	0.7	0.9
OCCUPIED DWELLINGS WITHOUT WATER	59.1	75.3	67.1	57.1	20.0	..	..	69.0	..	7.2	3.1	4.3
ACCESS TO ELECTRICITY (%) - ALL	50.6	47.4	59.8	79.3	91.0	..	..	24.0	..	97.3	98.9	99.1
- RURAL	26.9	..	..	57.0	58.0	..	..	..	..	91.4	95.2	94.8
CONSUMPTION												
RADIO RECEIVERS (PER 1000 POP.)	76.3	137.2	200.4	170.7	174.3	185.6	13.8	17.5	18.4	277.1	359.7	379.3
PASSENGER CARS (PER 1000 POP.)	11.2	29.2	42.3	14.1	41.3	54.4	7.6	16.6	113.7	90.7	233.3	266.5
ENERGY (KG. COAL/YR PER CAPITA)	676.2	1426.1	1618.7	798.4	1755.1	2467.6	302.5	1003.1	1419.4	2624.7	4575.2	4997.3
NEWSPRINT (KG/YR PER CAPITA)	1.4	1.9	2.3	3.5	8.7	6.6	0.2	0.2	0.1	16.4	22.3	22.2

TABLE 2. SOCIAL INDICATORS BY GEOGRAPHIC AREAS (DEVELOPING COUNTRIES)
(ADJUSTED COUNTRY GROUP AVERAGES)

INDICATOR	EUROPE			LATIN AMERICA & CARIBBEAN			N. AFRICA & MIDDLE EAST		
	1960	1970	MOST RECENT ESTIMATE	1960	1970	MOST RECENT ESTIMATE	1960	1970	MOST RECENT ESTIMATE
GNP PER CAPITA (IN CURRENT US $)	496.6	1018.0	2070.3	362.0	626.8	1015.6	307.7	579.0	1290.3
POPULATION									
GROWTH RATE (%) - TOTAL	1.0	0.8	0.9	2.5	2.7	2.6	2.7	2.9	3.0
- URBAN	3.8	2.8	2.1	4.2	4.1	4.2	6.4	4.5	5.1
URBAN POPULATION (% OF TOTAL)	32.1	40.7	38.7	48.3	54.3	58.5	33.8	39.6	44.3
VITAL STATISTICS									
CRUDE BIRTH RATE (PER 1000)	23.3	20.5	19.2	40.9	39.0	36.8	48.3	47.2	45.7
CRUDE DEATH RATE (PER 1000)	10.5	9.0	9.0	14.1	10.9	9.2	22.6	18.0	15.3
GROSS REPRODUCTION RATE	1.4	1.3	1.3	2.7	2.6	2.6	2.3	3.4	3.4
EMPLOYMENT AND INCOME									
DEPENDENCY RATIO - AGE	0.6	0.6	0.4	0.9	1.0	0.9	0.9	1.0	1.0
- ECONOMIC	1.0	1.1	1.0	1.6	1.5	1.7	1.6	2.0	1.9
LABOR FORCE IN AGRICULTURE (% OF TOTAL)	47.9	31.8	27.4	48.3	41.0	36.9	52.6	43.4	42.9
UNEMPLOYED (% OF LABOR FORCE)	3.0	4.0	6.0	7.6	6.2	8.8	6.3	3.4	4.1
INCOME RECEIVED BY - HIGHEST 5%	21.8	24.5	25.0	37.1	30.4	31.7	24.0	25.0	21.0
- LOWEST 20%	5.4	3.9	3.9	3.9	3.5	2.0	4.4	4.2	5.2
HEALTH AND NUTRITION									
DEATH RATE (PER 1000) AGES 1-4 YEARS	4.7	2.8	1.7	10.6	7.7	6.6		6.0	
INFANT MORTALITY RATE (PER 1000)	60.4	39.7	34.5	77.4	67.3	56.2	127.8	111.6	97.8
LIFE EXPECTANCY AT BIRTH (YRS)	65.8	68.6	69.1	55.8	60.6	62.5	45.5	50.3	52.8
POPULATION PER - PHYSICIAN	1004.0	821.3	694.4	2058.1	1866.8	1796.9	5690.8	5760.2	4724.7
- NURSING PERSON	1343.2	653.9	339.2	4542.1	3389.5	280.5	3286.6	2564.7	2383.1
- HOSPITAL BED	190.5	168.0	170.5	444.1	392.3	405.6	670.8	661.6	700.0
PER CAPITA PER DAY SUPPLY OF:									
CALORIES (% OF REQUIREMENTS)	109.3	118.0	118.0	97.6	103.2	105.5	80.9	91.0	96.0
PROTEIN (GRMS) - TOTAL	85.9	90.7	90.0	63.7	59.8	60.7	54.5	58.3	63.1
- FROM ANIMALS & PULSES	27.0	29.0	33.0	29.0	28.0	28.2	17.5	15.0	15.6
EDUCATION									
ADJ. ENROLLMENT RATIOS - PRIMARY	105.0	102.1	104.3	85.0	101.7	105.1	51.5	75.6	80.5
- SECONDARY	25.5	50.5	49.2	15.0	27.6	36.0	10.3	20.4	22.2
FEMALE ENROLLMENT RATIO (PRIMARY)	98.9	99.4	100.4	85.6	98.3	98.1	30.8	50.2	52.3
ADULT LITERACY RATE (%)	64.9	75.0	88.2	61.4	74.6	75.7	17.7	26.9	40.6
HOUSING									
PERSONS PER ROOM - URBAN	1.4	1.5	1.4	1.9	1.3	2.1	1.8	2.3	3.0
OCCUPIED DWELLINGS WITHOUT WATER	67.0	63.3	59.5	65.5	67.0	66.4	62.2	77.1	90.5
ACCESS TO ELECTRICITY (%) - ALL	51.4	46.3	57.9	44.4	54.2	53.1	40.1	31.0	39.1
- RURAL	18.1	20.9	33.8	9.3	12.5	12.6	..	..	..

436 Statistical Information and Sources

TABLE 2. Social Indicators by Geographic Areas (Developing Countries), Continued

(ADJUSTED COUNTRY GROUP AVERAGES)

INDICATOR	AFRICA SOUTH OF SAHARA			SOUTH ASIA			EAST ASIA AND PACIFIC		
	1960	1970	MOST RECENT ESTIMATE	1960	1970	MOST RECENT ESTIMATE	1960	1970	MOST RECENT ESTIMATE
GNP PER CAPITA (IN CURRENT US $)	94.9	137.0	207.4	54.1	88.2	131.4	141.8	290.0	568.3
POPULATION									
GROWTH RATE (%) - TOTAL	2.2	2.4	2.6	2.2	2.6	2.1	3.0	2.8	2.3
- URBAN	5.6	6.0	6.0	5.2	4.1	4.3	5.4	5.0	5.2
URBAN POPULATION (% OF TOTAL)	9.1	12.5	13.5	7.8	9.8	12.4	28.1	27.1	38.1
VITAL STATISTICS									
CRUDE BIRTH RATE (PER 1000)	48.8	48.1	47.1	47.4	45.8	45.1	42.3	40.7	32.0
CRUDE DEATH RATE (PER 1000)	26.7	23.7	21.2	26.4	21.4	17.3	19.2	12.4	8.7
GROSS REPRODUCTION RATE	2.9	3.1	3.0	3.2	3.0	2.9	3.0	2.5	2.3
EMPLOYMENT AND INCOME									
DEPENDENCY RATIO - AGE	0.9	0.9	0.9	0.8	0.8	0.8	0.9	0.9	0.7
- ECONOMIC	1.1	1.1	1.1	1.5	1.4	1.2	1.4	1.4	1.3
LABOR FORCE IN AGRICULTURE (% OF TOTAL)	79.8	75.0	73.1	61.8	60.8	63.0	67.9	59.5	48.4
UNEMPLOYED (% OF LABOR FORCE)	5.1	4.6	5.1			11.0	5.1	5.1	4.1
INCOME RECEIVED BY - HIGHEST 5%	28.2	26.4	25.7	24.6	23.2	18.6	22.7	20.5	19.8
- LOWEST 20%	5.2	3.9	5.7	4.6	5.2	7.8	5.5	5.8	6.6
HEALTH AND NUTRITION									
DEATH RATE (PER 1000) AGES 1-4 YEARS								3.4	2.0
INFANT MORTALITY RATE (PER 1000)	153.9	129.6	127.5	136.2	124.3	104.0	61.2	31.1	27.4
LIFE EXPECTANCY AT BIRTH (YRS)	36.9	41.5	43.4	40.6	45.2	48.1	52.5	59.1	61.6
POPULATION PER - PHYSICIAN	31866.1	21906.5	21616.5	9920.9	8519.2	7412.6	3429.3	2268.9	2208.9
- NURSING PERSON	4558.4	3088.7	2496.5	14566.1	9168.6	8339.3	3096.6	1935.5	1465.5
- HOSPITAL BED	1234.7	819.9	799.9	2885.8	1998.5	1908.0	1270.8	921.7	662.1
PER CAPITA PER DAY SUPPLY OF:									
CALORIES (% OF REQUIREMENTS)	89.6	90.7	91.9	89.1	97.6	96.0	90.0	99.4	106.5
PROTEIN (GRMS) - TOTAL	56.6	59.0	60.6	47.8	53.2	50.8	48.1	53.4	55.6
- FROM ANIMALS & PULSES	19.2	19.8	23.1	15.0	16.0	15.5	19.0	22.1	22.1
EDUCATION									
ADJ. ENROLLMENT RATIOS - PRIMARY	27.7	42.4	50.0	36.9	47.9	55.2	95.0	105.7	110.0
- SECONDARY	1.9	5.6	6.9	9.1	15.5	20.0	17.3	26.9	51.1
FEMALE ENROLLMENT RATIO (PRIMARY)	21.7	37.4	43.2	22.2	53.8	44.5	88.5	102.0	104.7
ADULT LITERACY RATE (%)	9.8	17.4	18.4	16.0	20.0	21.0	47.7	66.4	72.6
HOUSING									
PERSONS PER ROOM - URBAN	2.7	2.4	1.7				2.5	2.3	
OCCUPIED DWELLINGS WITHOUT WATER							83.7	69.5	60.3
ACCESS TO ELECTRICITY (%) - ALL							22.6	40.7	50.5
- RURAL							12.0	20.1	23.4

GLOBAL INDICATORS

TABLE 3. COMPARATIVE SOCIAL INDICATORS FOR DEVELOPING COUNTRIES (BY GEOGRAPHIC AREA AND COUNTRY)

AREA AND COUNTRY	POPULATION & VITAL STATISTICS				EMPLOYMENT AND INCOME			HEALTH & NUTRITION				EDUCATION (MOST RECENT ESTIMATE)		
	POP. GROWTH RATE % (65-75)	URBAN POP. % OF TOTAL	CRUDE BIRTH RATE (/000)	CRUDE DEATH RATE (/000)	LABOR IN AGR. % OF TOTAL	INCOME RECD BY HIGHEST 5% HH	INCOME RECD BY LOWEST 20% HH	LIFE EXPECT. YRS AT BIRTH	CALORIE SUPPLY %/CAP REQD.	PROTEIN SUPPLY GR/DAY /CAP	PRIMARY SCHOOL ENROLL RATIO %	FEMALE ENROLL. RATIO PRIMARY	ADULT LITERACY RATE % OF TOTAL
EUROPE													
CYPRUS	0.6	42.2	22.2	6.8	34.0	12.1	7.9	71.4	113.0	86.0	71.0	72.0	85.0
GREECE	0.6	64.8	15.4	9.4	34.0	18.7	6.3	71.8	132.0	102.0	106.0	104.0	82.0
MALTA	0.2	94.3	17.5	9.0	6.0	..	..	69.6	114.0	89.0	109.0	109.0	87.0
PORTUGAL	0.3	28.8	19.2	10.5	32.5	56.3	7.3	68.7	118.0	85.0	116.0	94.0	70.0
ROMANIA	1.2	43.0	19.7	9.3	36.0	..	..	69.1	118.0	90.0	109.0	109.0	98.0
SPAIN	1.0	59.1	19.5	8.3	23.0	18.5	6.0	72.1	135.0	94.1	115.0	115.0	94.0
TURKEY	2.6	42.6	39.4	12.5	52.5	28.0	3.5	56.9	113.0	75.7	104.0	94.0	55.0
YUGOSLAVIA	0.9	38.7	18.2	9.2	39.0	25.1	6.6	68.0	137.0	97.5	97.0	93.0	85.0
ALL COUNTRIES - MEDIAN	0.8	42.8	19.4	9.3	34.0	18.6	6.5	69.4	118.0	89.5	107.5	99.0	85.0
LATIN AMERICA & CARIBBEAN													
ARGENTINA	1.4	80.0	21.8	8.8	15.0	21.4	5.6	68.3	129.0	107.1	108.0	109.0	93.0
BAHAMAS	3.6	57.9	22.4	5.7	7.0	20.7	3.4	66.7	100.0	87.0	135.0	..	93.0
BARBADOS	0.4	-3.7	21.6	8.9	18.0	19.8	6.8	69.1	133.0	82.5	117.0	116.0	97.0
BOLIVIA	2.7	34.0	44.0	19.1	65.0	36.0	4.0	46.8	77.0	48.5	74.0	65.0	40.0
BRAZIL	2.9	59.1	37.1	8.8	37.8	35.0	3.0	61.4	105.0	62.1	90.0	90.0	64.0
CHILE	1.9	83.0	27.9	9.2	19.0	31.0	4.8	62.6	116.0	78.3	119.0	118.0	90.0
COLOMBIA	2.8	70.0	40.6	8.8	39.0	27.2	5.2	60.9	94.0	47.0	105.0	108.0	81.0
COSTA RICA	2.8	40.6	31.0	5.8	36.4	22.8	5.4	69.1	113.0	60.8	109.0	109.0	89.0
DOMINICAN REPUBLIC	2.9	45.9	45.8	11.0	53.8	26.3	4.3	57.8	98.0	45.4	104.0	105.0	51.0
ECUADOR	3.4	41.6	41.8	9.5	43.5	..	..	59.6	93.0	47.4	102.0	100.0	69.0
EL SALVADOR	3.4	39.4	42.2	11.1	55.0	38.0	2.0	65.0	84.0	50.3	75.2	69.0	63.0
GRENADA	1.0	..	27.4	6.8	30.8	..	..	..	89.0	57.0	93.0	..	85.0
GUATEMALA	3.2	37.3	42.8	13.7	56.0	35.0	5.0	54.1	91.0	52.8	62.0	56.0	47.0
GUYANA	2.1	40.0	32.4	5.9	30.9	18.8	4.3	67.9	104.0	58.0	114.0	114.0	85.0
HAITI	1.6	23.1	35.8	16.3	77.0	..	..	50.0	90.0	39.0	70.0	37.0	20.0
HONDURAS	2.7	31.4	49.3	14.6	60.3	28.0	2.5	53.5	90.0	56.0	90.0	88.0	53.0
JAMAICA	1.7	37.1	32.2	7.1	26.9	30.2	2.2	69.5	118.0	68.9	111.0	112.0	86.0
MEXICO	3.5	63.3	42.0	8.6	41.0	27.9	3.4	64.7	117.0	66.9	112.0	109.0	76.0
NICARAGUA	3.6	48.0	48.3	13.9	48.0	42.4	3.1	52.9	105.0	68.4	85.0	87.0	57.0
PANAMA	3.2	49.6	36.2	7.1	30.0	22.2	4.6	66.5	105.0	61.0	124.0	120.0	82.2

TABLE 3. COMPARATIVE SOCIAL INDICATORS FOR DEVELOPING COUNTRIES (BY GEOGRAPHIC AREA AND COUNTRY) Continued

AREA AND COUNTRY	POPULATION & VITAL STATISTICS					EMPLOYMENT AND INCOME				HEALTH & NUTRITION				(MOST RECENT ESTIMATE) EDUCATION		
	POP. GROWTH RATE % (65-75)	URBAN POP. % OF TOTAL	CRUDE BIRTH RATE (/000)	CRUDE DEATH RATE (/000)		LABOR IN AGR. % OF TOTAL	INCOME RECD BY HIGHEST 5% HH	INCOME RECD BY LOWEST 20% HH	LIFE EXPECT. YRS AT BIRTH	CALORIE SUPPLY %/CAP REQD.	PROTEIN SUPPLY GR/DAY /CAP		PRIMARY SCHOOL ENROLL RATIO %	FEMALE ENROLL. RATIO PRIMARY	ADULT LITERACY RATE % OF TOTAL
PARAGUAY	2.6	37.4	39.8	8.9		49.0	30.0	4.0	61.9	118.0	74.5		106.0	102.0	81.0
PERU	2.9	55.3	41.0	11.9		40.0	28.8	3.1	55.7	100.0	61.7		111.0	106.0	72.0
TRINIDAD & TOBAGO	1.0	25.1	27.3	5.9		13.5			69.5	114.0	66.0		111.0	111.0	90.0
URUGUAY	0.4	80.6	20.4	9.3		13.2	19.0	4.4	69.8	116.0	98.1		95.0	94.0	94.0
VENEZUELA	3.3	75.7	36.1	7.0		21.0	21.8	3.6	66.4	98.0	63.1		96.0	96.0	82.0
ALL COUNTRIES - MEDIAN	2.7	43.7	36.2	8.9		37.8	27.9	4.0	63.0	104.0	61.7		105.0	105.0	81.0
NORTH AFRICA & MIDDLE EAST															
ALGERIA	3.3	39.9	48.7	15.4		42.8			53.3	88.0	57.2		77.0	72.0	35.0
BAHRAIN	3.3	78.1	49.6	18.7					44.5						
EGYPT	2.4	44.6	37.8	14.0		43.9	21.0	5.2	52.4	113.0	70.7		72.0	55.0	40.0
IRAN	2.9	43.0	45.3	15.6		41.0	29.7	4.0	51.0	98.0	56.0		90.0	67.0	50.0
IRAQ	3.3	62.0	48.1	14.6		51.0	35.1	2.1	52.7	101.0	60.4		93.0	63.0	26.0
JORDAN	3.4	42.0	47.6	14.7		19.0			53.2	90.0	65.0		83.0	77.0	62.0
KUWAIT	7.7	88.0	45.4			2.0	26.0		64.0				90.0	86.0	55.0
LEBANON	2.8	60.1	39.8	9.9		17.8	13.3	4.0	63.3	101.0	67.9		132.0	125.0	68.0
LIBYA	4.2	30.5	45.0	14.7		19.5	20.0	10.1	52.9	117.0	62.0		145.0	135.0	27.0
MOROCCO	2.4	40.1	46.2	15.7		50.0		4.0	53.0	108.0	70.5		61.0	44.0	28.0
OMAN	3.1	5.0	49.6	18.7		48.0			47.0				44.0		20.0
QATAR	10.5	85.0											112.0		21.0
SAUDI ARABIA	1.9	17.9	50.2	24.4		61.0			42.0	86.0	56.0		34.0	27.0	15.0
SYRIAN ARAB REP.	3.1	46.2	45.4	15.4		49.9	17.0	5.0	56.0	104.0	66.7		102.0	81.0	40.0
TUNISIA	2.3	47.0	40.0	13.8		37.4			54.1	102.0	67.4		95.0	75.0	55.0
UNITED ARAB EMIRATES	13.1	80.0											75.0		21.0
YEMEN ARAB REP.	1.7	7.0	49.6	20.6		73.0			37.0	83.0	58.3		25.0	6.0	10.0
YEMEN PEOP. DEM. REP.	3.1	35.3	49.6	20.6		42.9			44.8	84.0	57.0		78.0	48.0	27.1
ALL COUNTRIES-MEDIAN	3.1	43.8	46.9	15.6		42.9	21.0	4.0	52.8	101.0	62.0		83.0	70.5	28.0
AFRICA SOUTH OF SAHARA															
BENIN PEOP. REP.	2.7	13.5	49.9	23.0		47.5	31.4	5.5	41.8	87.0	56.0		44.0	28.0	20.0
BOTSWANA	2.1	10.7	45.6	23.0		83.0	28.1	1.6	43.5	85.0	65.0		85.0	93.0	25.0
BURUNDI	2.0	3.7	48.0	24.7		86.0			39.0	99.0	62.0		23.0	17.0	10.0
CAMEROON	1.9	28.5	40.4	22.0		82.0			41.0	102.0	59.0		111.0	97.0	6.0
CENTRAL AFRICAN EMPIRE	2.2	35.9	43.4	22.5		91.0			41.0	102.0	49.0		79.0	53.0	15.0

Statistical Tables and Figures 439

TABLE 3. COMPARATIVE SOCIAL INDICATORS FOR DEVELOPING COUNTRIES (BY GEOGRAPHIC AREA AND COUNTRY) Continued (MOST RECENT ESTIMATE)

AREA AND COUNTRY	POPULATION & VITAL STATISTICS				EMPLOYMENT AND INCOME			HEALTH & NUTRITION			EDUCATION		ADULT LITERACY RATE % OF TOTAL
	POP. GROWTH RATE % (65-75)	URBAN POP. % OF TOTAL	CRUDE BIRTH RATE (/000)	CRUDE DEATH RATE (/000)	LABOR IN AGR. % OF TOTAL	INCOME REC'D BY HIGHEST 5% HH	INCOME REC'D BY LOWEST 20% HH	LIFE EXPECT. YRS AT BIRTH	CALORIE SUPPLY %/CAP REQD.	PROTEIN SUPPLY GR/DAY /CAP	PRIMARY SCHOOL ENROLL RATIO %	FEMALE ENROLL. RATIO PRIMARY	
CHAD	2.0	13.9	44.0	24.0	90.0	21.5	7.7	38.5	75.0	60.2	37.0	20.0	15.0
CONGO PEOP. REP.	2.3	38.0	45.1	20.8	56.0	..	..	43.5	98.0	44.0	153.0	140.0	50.0
EQUATORIAL GUINEA	1.3	..	..	..	..	..	..	..	..	..	..	..	..
ETHIOPIA	2.5	11.2	49.4	25.8	85.0	..	..	41.0	82.0	58.9	23.0	14.0	7.0
GABON	1.5	32.0	32.2	22.2	58.0	45.3	3.2	41.0	98.0	49.3	199.0	197.0	12.0
GAMBIA	2.3	14.0	43.3	24.1	79.6	..	..	40.0	98.0	64.0	32.0	21.0	10.0
GHANA	2.6	32.4	48.8	21.9	52.0	..	..	43.5	101.0	53.4	60.0	53.0	25.0
GUINEA	2.8	19.5	44.6	22.9	84.1	..	..	41.0	84.0	42.7	28.0	..	7.0
IVORY COAST	4.1	34.3	45.6	20.6	80.0	30.9	9.0	43.5	113.0	64.5	86.0	64.0	20.0
KENYA	3.4	13.0	48.7	16.0	84.0	20.2	3.9	50.0	91.0	59.6	109.0	101.0	40.0
LESOTHO	2.2	3.1	39.0	19.7	90.0	..	..	46.0	109.0	67.6	121.0	144.0	40.0
LIBERIA	3.3	27.6	43.6	20.7	72.0	61.7	5.3	43.5	87.0	39.0	62.0	44.0	15.0
MADAGASCAR	2.9	14.5	50.2	21.1	83.0	41.0	5.2	43.5	105.0	57.0	85.0	80.0	40.0
MALAWI	2.5	6.4	47.7	23.7	86.0	29.5	5.7	41.0	103.0	68.4	61.0	48.0	25.0
MALI	2.2	13.4	50.1	25.9	88.7	..	..	38.1	75.0	64.0	22.0	16.0	10.0
MAURITANIA	2.6	23.1	44.8	24.9	85.0	..	..	38.5	81.0	63.2	17.0	9.0	10.0
MAURITIUS	1.4	48.3	25.1	7.8	30.3	31.0	4.5	65.5	108.0	55.8	80.0	78.0	80.0
MOZAMBIQUE	2.2	55.0	43.3	21.4	73.0	..	..	41.0	94.0	41.0	46.0	..	..
NIGER	2.7	9.4	52.2	25.5	91.0	23.0	6.0	38.5	78.0	62.1	17.0	12.0	5.0
NIGERIA	2.5	26.0	49.3	22.7	62.0	..	..	41.0	88.0	46.3	49.0	39.0	25.0
RWANDA	2.8	3.8	50.0	23.6	93.0	..	..	41.0	90.0	51.3	58.0	54.0	23.0
SENEGAL	2.7	38.8	47.6	23.9	73.0	36.8	3.2	40.0	97.0	67.1	43.0	33.0	10.0
SIERRA LEONE	2.3	15.0	44.7	20.7	73.0	36.2	1.1	43.5	97.0	50.9	35.0	28.0	15.0
SOMALIA	2.4	28.3	47.2	21.7	77.0	..	..	41.0	79.0	55.1	58.0	41.0	50.0
SUDAN	2.2	13.2	47.8	17.5	66.5	20.9	5.1	48.6	88.0	60.4	40.0	27.0	15.0
SWAZILAND	3.2	14.3	49.0	21.8	83.0	..	..	43.5	89.0	..	103.0	102.0	50.0
TANZANIA	2.8	7.3	47.0	20.1	83.1	33.5	2.3	44.5	86.0	47.1	57.0	46.0	49.0
TOGO	2.7	15.0	50.6	23.3	75.0	..	..	41.0	96.0	52.1	98.0	68.0	12.0
UGANDA	3.1	8.4	45.2	15.9	86.0	20.0	6.2	50.0	90.0	54.0	44.0	43.0	25.0
UPPER VOLTA	2.2	12.1	48.5	25.8	89.0	..	..	38.0	78.0	59.2	14.0	11.0	7.0
ZAIRE	2.7	26.4	45.2	20.5	77.0	..	..	43.5	85.0	32.0	88.0	87.0	15.0
ZAMBIA	2.9	36.3	51.5	20.3	52.0	23.0	3.8	44.5	89.0	58.8	88.0	86.0	43.0
ALL COUNTRIES-MEDIAN	2.5	14.8	47.4	22.1	82.5	30.9	4.5	41.0	90.0	57.0	58.0	47.0	15.0

TABLE 3. COMPARATIVE SOCIAL INDICATORS FOR DEVELOPING COUNTRIES (BY GEOGRAPHIC AREA AND COUNTRY) Continued

(MOST RECENT ESTIMATE)

AREA AND COUNTRY	POPULATION & VITAL STATISTICS					EMPLOYMENT AND INCOME			HEALTH & NUTRITION			EDUCATION		
	POP. GROWTH RATE % (65-75)	URBAN POP. % OF TOTAL	CRUDE BIRTH RATE (/000)	CRUDE DEATH RATE (/000)		LABOR IN AGR. % OF TOTAL	INCOME RECD BY HIGHEST 5% HH	INCOME RECD BY LOWEST 20% HH	LIFE EXPECT. YRS AT BIRTH	CALORIE SUPPLY %/CAP RECD.	PROTEIN SUPPLY GR/DAY /CAP	PRIMARY SCHOOL ENROLL RATIO %	FEMALE ENROLL. RATIO PRIMARY	ADULT LITERACY RATE % OF TOTAL
SOUTH ASIA														
AFGHANISTAN	2.2	14.3	51.4	30.7		52.9	..	..	40.3	83.0	61.5	23.0	7.0	14.0
BANGLADESH	2.3	8.8	49.5	28.1		78.0	16.7	7.9	45.0	93.0	58.5	73.0	51.0	23.0
BURMA	2.2	22.3	39.5	15.8		67.8	14.6	8.0	50.1	103.0	58.0	85.0	81.0	67.0
INDIA	2.2	20.6	37.0	17.0		69.0	25.0	4.7	49.5	89.0	48.0	65.0	52.0	36.0
NEPAL	2.1	4.8	42.9	20.3		94.4	..	..	43.6	95.0	50.0	59.0	10.0	19.2
PAKISTAN	2.9	26.0	47.4	16.5		54.8	17.3	8.4	49.8	93.0	54.0	51.0	31.0	21.0
SRI LANKA	2.0	24.3	28.2	7.9		55.0	18.6	7.3	67.8	97.0	48.0	77.0	77.0	78.1
ALL COUNTRIES--MEDIAN	2.2	20.6	42.9	17.0		67.8	17.3	7.9	49.5	93.0	54.0	65.0	51.0	23.0
EAST ASIA & PACIFIC														
CHINA REP.	2.6	51.1	23.0	4.7		35.0	13.3	8.8	68.6	111.0	68.0	104.0	..	82.0
FIJI	2.2	38.5	25.0	4.3		43.3	19.0	5.1	70.0	..	43.8	111.0	110.0	75.0
INDONESIA	2.3	18.2	42.9	16.9		69.0	33.7	6.8	48.1	98.0	75.7	81.0	75.0	62.0
KOREA	2.1	48.5	28.8	8.9		44.6	18.1	7.2	68.0	115.0	58.0	109.0	109.0	92.0
LAO P.D.R.	2.7	15.0	44.6	22.8		85.0	..	..	40.4	94.0	58.0	57.0	47.0	20.0
MALAYSIA	2.7	30.2	31.7	6.7		45.2	28.3	3.5	59.4	115.0	56.5	93.0	91.0	60.0
PAPUA NEW GUINEA	2.5	12.9	40.6	17.1		83.0	..	..	47.7	98.0	48.2	59.0	44.0	31.0
PHILIPPINES	2.9	29.8	43.8	10.5		52.6	28.8	5.5	58.5	87.0	50.0	105.0	103.0	87.0
SINGAPORE	1.7	90.2	21.2	5.2		2.8	..	..	89.5	122.0	74.7	111.0	108.0	75.0
THAILAND	3.1	16.5	37.6	9.1		76.0	22.0	5.6	58.0	107.0	50.0	78.0	75.0	82.0
VIET NAM	2.6	..	..	6.7		67.0	..	..	58.0	100.0	52.7	91.0	..	97.8
WESTERN SAMOA	1.9	21.5	36.9	8.9		52.6	22.0	5.6	58.5	103.5	53.6	93.0	91.0	75.0
ALL COUNTRIES--MEDIAN	2.6	29.8	36.9											

COMPARATIVE ECONOMIC DATA
TABLE 4. Selected Economic Development Indicators: Population and Production
(Average annual real growth rates)

Income group/ region/country	Population			Gross domestic product				GDP per capita			
	1950-60	1960-65	1965-70	1970-77	1950-60	1960-65	1965-70	1970-77	1950-60	1960-65	1965-70	1970-77
Developing countries	2.2	2.4	2.5	2.4	4.9	5.6	6.4	5.7	2.7	3.1	3.8	3.2
Capital-surplus oil-exporting countries	2.3	3.2	3.7	4.1	..	..	11.0	6.7	..	..	7.2	3.0
Industrialized countries	1.2	1.2	0.9	0.8	3.8++	5.3	4.9	3.2	2.5++	4.0	4.0	2.4
Centrally planned economies	1.7	1.8	1.6	1.4	..	6.2+	7.7+	6.4+	..	4.8+	6.7+	5.6+
A. Developing countries by income group												
Low income	2.0	2.4	2.4	2.2	3.8	3.8	5.3	4.0	1.8	1.4	2.8	1.7
Middle income	2.4	2.5	2.5	2.5	5.3	6.1	6.6	6.0	2.8	3.5	4.0	3.4
B. Developing countries by region												
Africa south of Sahara	2.3	2.5	2.5	2.7	3.6	5.0	4.9	3.7	1.3	2.4	2.3	0.9
Middle East and North Africa	2.4	2.6	2.7	2.7	5.1	6.4	9.4	7.1	2.6	3.7	6.5	4.3
East Asia and Pacific	2.4	2.6	2.5	2.2	5.2	5.5	8.0	8.0	2.8	2.8	5.4	5.7
South Asia	1.9	2.4	2.4	2.2	3.8	4.3	4.9	3.2	1.8	1.9	2.4	1.0
Latin America and the Caribbean	2.8	2.8	2.7	2.7	5.3	5.2	6.1	6.2	2.4	2.3	3.3	3.4
Southern Europe	1.5	1.4	1.4	1.5	6.1	7.5	6.5	5.3	4.5	6.0	5.0	3.8
C. Developing countries by region and country												
Africa south of Sahara												
Angola	1.6	1.5	1.6	2.3	..	5.9	3.2	-9.4	..	4.3	1.6	-11.5
Benin	2.2	2.5	2.7	2.9	..	3.1	2.7	2.7	..	0.6	0.0	-0.1
Botswana	1.7	1.9	1.9	1.9	2.9	4.2	9.8	15.7	1.2	2.2	7.8	13.5
Burundi	2.0	2.3	2.4	1.9	-1.3	2.8	5.8	2.3	-3.2	0.5	3.3	0.4
Cameroon	1.4	1.7	1.9	2.2	1.7	2.9	7.3	3.4	0.3	1.2	5.3	1.2
Cape Verde	3.1	3.1	2.7	2.1	..	..	..	..	..	..	..	..
Central African Republic	1.4	2.2	2.2	2.2	2.6	0.4	3.5	3.1	1.1	-1.7	1.3	0.9
Chad	1.4	1.8	1.9	2.2	..	0.5	1.6	1.2	..	-1.3	-0.3	-0.9
Comoros	3.0	3.2	3.3	3.8	..	9.5	3.2	-1.5	..	6.1	-0.1	-5.2
Congo, People's Republic of the	1.6	2.1	2.2	2.5	1.1	2.7	3.4	3.9	-0.5	0.6	1.2	1.4
Equatorial Guinea	1.5	1.7	1.9	2.2	..	13.8	2.0	-3.0	..	11.8	0.1	-5.0
Ethiopia	2.1	2.3	2.4	2.5	3.9	5.1	3.7	2.6	1.7	2.7	1.2	0.1
Gabon	0.2	0.5	0.7	0.9	11.5	3.9	5.3	9.1	11.3	3.3	4.6	8.1

TABLE 4. COMPARATIVE ECONOMIC DATA (Continued)

Income group/ region/country	Population			Gross domestic product				GDP per capita			
	1950-60	1960-65	1965-70	1970-77	1950-60	1960-65	1965-70	1970-77	1950-60	1960-65	1965-70	1970-77
Gambia, The	2.0	3.3	3.2	3.1	1.3	5.2	4.3	8.2	-0.7	1.9	1.1	4.9
Ghana	4.5	2.7	2.1	3.0	4.1	3.3	2.5	0.4	-0.4	0.6	0.4	-2.5
Guinea	2.2	2.7	3.0	3.0	.	3.9	3.0	5.4	.	1.2	0.0	2.4
Guinea-Bissau	0.2	-1.1	-0.2	1.6	.	.	.	.	.	.	.	.
Ivory Coast	2.1	3.7	3.8	6.0	3.6	10.1	7.4	6.5	1.5	6.1	3.5	0.5
Kenya	3.3	3.4	3.5	3.8	4.0	3.6	8.6	4.8	0.7	0.2	4.9	1.0
Lesotho	1.5	1.8	2.2	2.4	4.4	8.7	2.1	8.0	2.8	6.7	-0.1	5.5
Liberia	2.8	3.1	3.2	3.4	10.5	3.1	0.4	2.7	7.4	0.0	3.1	-0.6
Madagascar	1.8	2.1	2.3	2.5	2.3	1.4	4.9	-0.7	0.5	-0.7	2.5	-3.2
Malawi	2.4	2.7	2.9	3.1	.	3.3	4.5	6.3	.	0.6	1.5	3.1
Mali	2.1	2.5	2.4	2.5	3.2	3.2	2.9	4.7	1.0	0.7	0.5	2.1
Mauritania	2.2	2.5	2.6	2.7	.	9.9	4.6	2.2	.	7.2	2.0	-0.5
Mauritius	3.3	2.7	1.9	1.3	0.1	5.4	-0.3	8.2	-3.0	2.7	-2.2	6.8
Mozambique	1.4	2.1	2.3	2.5	3.1	2.3	8.3	-3.7	1.7	0.2	5.9	-6.1
Namibia	.	2.4	2.6	2.8	.	.	.	.	.	.	.	.
Niger	2.3	4.0	2.7	2.8	.	6.6	-0.3	1.2	.	2.5	-2.9	-1.5
Nigeria	2.4	2.5	2.5	2.6	4.1	5.3	4.5	6.0	1.6	2.7	1.9	3.3
Réunion	.	3.3	2.5	1.8	.	.	.	.	.	.	.	.
Rhodesia	4.1	4.2	3.7	3.3	.	3.2	6.1	3.2	.	-0.9	2.4	-0.1
Rwanda	2.3	2.5	2.7	2.9	1.0	-2.9	8.5	5.2	-1.2	-5.3	5.6	2.2
Senegal	2.2	2.4	2.5	2.6	.	3.6	1.3	2.8	.	1.1	-1.2	0.2
Sierra Leone	1.8	2.1	2.3	2.5	3.6	4.3	3.9	1.5	1.8	2.1	1.6	-1.0
Somalia	2.0	2.4	2.5	2.3	12.8	-0.5	3.4	1.2	10.6	-2.8	0.9	-1.1
South Africa	3.0	2.5	2.7	2.7	2.9	6.6	5.9	4.0	-0.1	4.0	3.1	1.2
Sudan	1.9	2.2	2.4	2.6	5.5	1.5	1.3	5.4	3.5	-0.7	-1.0	2.7
Swaziland	2.0	2.3	2.1	2.5	8.4	13.6	6.3	6.2	6.3	11.0	4.1	3.7
Tanzania, United Republic of	2.2	2.6	2.8	3.0	6.0	5.2	5.9	5.2	3.7	2.6	3.1	2.1
Togo	2.2	2.7	2.7	2.6	1.3	8.4	6.7	4.0	-0.9	5.6	3.9	1.4
Uganda	2.8	3.8	3.7	3.0	3.3	5.7	5.9	0.5	0.5	1.8	2.2	-2.4
Upper Volta	1.9	1.6	1.6	1.6	1.6	2.7	3.3	0.5	-0.3	1.0	1.6	-1.0
Zaire	2.3	1.9	2.1	2.7	3.4	3.7	4.3	1.0	1.1	1.7	2.2	-1.7
Zambia	2.4	2.8	2.9	3.0	5.0	5.4	2.8	2.8	3.1	2.6	-0.1	-0.2

TABLE 4. COMPARATIVE ECONOMIC DATA (Continued)

Income group/ region/country	Population			Gross domestic product				GDP per capita			
	1950-60	1960-65	1965-70	1970-77	1950-60	1960-65	1965-70	1970-77	1950-60	1960-65	1965-70	1970-77
C. Developing countries by region and country (cont.)												
Middle East and North Africa												
Algeria	2.1	2.0	3.7	3.2	6.5	0.8	8.1	5.4	4.4	-1.2	4.2	2.2
Bahrain	3.5	4.2	2.9	7.1				10.7[d]				3.2[d]
Egypt, Arab Republic of	2.4	2.5	2.1	2.1	3.3	7.6	3.2	6.4	0.9	4.9	1.1	4.2
Iran	2.5	2.7	2.8	3.0	5.9	9.2	12.6	7.4	3.3	6.3	9.5	4.3
Iraq	2.8	3.1	3.2	3.4	9.9	7.7	4.1	8.1[e]	6.9	4.5	0.9	4.7[e]
Jordan	3.2	3.0	3.2	3.3				7.0[f]				3.6[f]
Lebanon	2.6	3.0	2.8	2.5								
Morocco	2.7	2.5	2.9	2.7	2.0	4.2	5.7	6.4	-0.7	1.7	2.8	3.6
Syrian Arab Republic	2.7	3.1	3.3	3.3		8.8	5.6	9.6		5.4	2.3	6.2
Tunisia	1.8	1.9	2.1	2.0		5.2[c]	4.9	8.5		3.3[c]	2.8	6.4
Yemen, Arab Republic of	2.0	2.1	1.5	1.9				8.4				6.4
Yemen, People's Democratic Republic of.	1.9	1.9	1.9	1.9				6.8[d]				4.8[d]
East Asia and Pacific												
Fiji	3.1	3.3	2.3	1.8	2.8	3.7	7.4	5.0	-0.3	0.3	5.0	3.1
Hong Kong	4.5	3.7	1.3	2.0	9.2	11.7	8.0	8.0	4.5	7.7	6.6	5.9
Indonesia	2.1	2.2	2.2	1.8	4.0	1.6	7.5	8.0	1.9	-0.6	5.2	6.1
Korea, Republic of	2.0	2.6	2.2	2.0	5.1	6.7	10.3	9.9	3.1	4.0	7.9	7.8
Malaysia	2.5	2.9	2.9	2.7	3.6	6.8	5.9	7.8	1.0	3.7	2.9	4.9
Papua New Guinea	1.8	2.3	2.4	2.4	4.8	6.4	5.7	5.0	2.9	4.0	3.3	2.5
Philippines	2.7	3.0	3.1	2.7	6.5	5.2	5.2	6.3	3.6	2.2	2.1	3.5
Singapore	4.8	2.8	2.0	1.6		5.5	13.0	8.6		2.6	10.7	6.9
Solomon Islands	2.6	2.6	2.6	3.5	10.7	3.7	2.5	5.4	7.9	1.1	-0.1	1.8
Taiwan	3.5	3.0	2.4	2.0	7.6	8.9	9.2	7.7	4.0	5.8	6.7	5.6
Thailand	2.8	3.0	3.1	2.9	5.7	7.4	8.4	7.1	2.8	4.2	5.1	4.0
South Asia												
Afghanistan	1.5	2.2	2.2	2.2		1.7	2.3	4.5		-0.4	0.2	2.2
Bangladesh	2.4	2.8	3.0	2.5		4.6	3.4	2.3		1.8	0.4	-0.1

TABLE 4. COMPARATIVE ECONOMIC DATA (Continued)

Income group/ region/country	Population				Gross domestic product				GDP per capita			
	1950-60	1960-65	1965-70	1970-77	1950-60	1960-65	1965-70	1970-77	1950-60	1960-65	1965-70	1970-77
Bhutan	.	1.9	2.1	2.3	.	.	.	.	.	.	.	.
Burma	1.9	2.1	2.2	2.2	.	4.4	2.3	3.6	.	2.2	0.1	1.4
India	1.9	2.3	2.4	2.1	3.8	4.0	5.0	3.1	1.9	1.7	2.6	1.0
Nepal	1.2	1.9	2.2	2.2	2.4	2.7	2.2	2.6	1.2	0.8	0.0	0.4
Pakistan	2.3	2.7	2.9	3.1	2.4	7.2	6.9	3.8	0.1	4.4	3.8	0.7
Sri Lanka	2.6	2.5	2.3	1.7	3.9	4.0	5.8	2.9	1.3	1.5	3.4	1.1
Latin America and the Carribbean												
Argentina	1.9	1.5	1.4	1.3	2.8	3.6	4.5	2.8	0.9	2.0	3.1	1.5
Bahamas	3.6	4.8	4.4	2.7	.	.	.	.	.	.	.	.
Barbados	0.9	0.3	0.3	0.5	5.9	4.5	7.9	2.0	4.9	4.1	7.6	1.4
Belize	3.1	2.8	2.8	0.9	.	.	.	6.0	.	.	.	5.0
Bolivia	2.1	2.5	2.6	2.7	.	5.0	4.8	5.9	.	2.5	2.1	3.1
Brazil	3.1	2.9	2.9	2.9	6.9	4.0	8.0	9.9	3.7	1.1	5.0	6.8
Chile	2.2	2.3	1.9	1.7	4.0	4.9	3.6	0.1	1.8	2.6	1.7	-1.8
Colombia	3.1	3.3	2.8	2.1	4.6	4.7	5.9	5.7	1.5	1.4	2.9	3.6
Costa Rica	3.7	3.7	3.2	2.5	.	5.3	6.9	6.0	.	1.5	3.6	3.3
Dominican Republic	2.9	2.9	2.9	3.0	5.8	4.6	6.6	8.0	2.8	1.6	3.6	4.9
Ecuador	2.9	3.0	3.0	3.0	.	.	5.8	9.2	.	.	2.7	6.0
El Salvador	2.8	3.4	3.5	3.1	4.4	6.7	4.3	5.3	1.5	3.2	0.7	2.1
Honduras	3.3	3.5	2.8	3.3	3.1	4.9	4.2	3.2	-0.2	1.4	1.4	-0.1
Jamaica	1.5	1.6	1.2	1.7	8.1	3.7	5.1	0.0	6.5	2.1	3.9	-1.7
Mexico	3.2	3.3	3.3	3.3	5.6	7.4	6.8	4.9	2.4	3.9	3.5	1.5
Netherlands Antilles	1.7	1.7	1.4	1.2	.	.	.	.	.	.	.	.
Nicaragua	2.9	3.0	3.0	3.3	5.2	10.4	4.1	5.8	2.2	7.2	1.1	2.4
Panama	2.9	3.1	3.1	3.1	4.9	7.9	7.8	3.5	1.9	4.7	4.6	0.4
Paraguay	2.6	2.6	2.7	2.9	2.7	4.5	4.3	7.0	0.1	1.9	1.6	4.0
Peru	2.6	2.9	2.9	2.8	4.9	7.1	4.3	4.5	2.2	4.1	1.4	1.7
Puerto Rico	0.6	1.6	1.3	2.8	5.3	8.1	7.0	3.6	4.7	6.5	5.6	0.7
Trinidad and Tobago	2.8	3.0	1.1	1.2	.	4.7	3.3	2.2	.	1.6	2.2	1.0
Uruguay	1.4	1.2	1.0	0.2	1.7	0.6	1.9	1.6	0.3	-0.0	1.0	1.3
Venezuela	4.0	3.6	3.3	3.4	8.0	7.4	4.9	5.6	3.8	3.7	1.6	2.2

Statistical Tables and Figures   445

TABLE 4. COMPARATIVE ECONOMIC DATA (Continued)

Income group/ region/country	Population			Gross domestic product				GDP per capita			
	1950-60	1960-65	1965-70	1970-77	1950-60	1960-65	1965-70	1970-77	1950-60	1960-65	1965-70	1970-77
C. Developing countries by region and country (cont.)												
Southern Europe												
Cyprus	1.5	0.6	0.8	0.7	4.0	3.7	8.1	1.0	2.5	3.0	7.2	0.3
Greece	1.0	0.5	0.6	0.7	6.0	7.7	7.2	4.6	5.0	7.2	6.6	3.9
Israel	5.3	3.9	3.0	2.8	11.3	9.8	8.7	5.0	5.6	5.6	5.5	2.2
Malta	0.5	-0.6	0.5	0.3	3.3	0.3	9.0	11.4	2.7	0.9	8.5	11.1
Portugal	0.7	0.2	-0.2	0.8	4.1	6.4	6.4	4.6	3.4	6.1	6.6	3.7
Spain	0.8	1.0	1.1	1.0	6.2	8.0	6.3	4.7	5.3	7.5	5.1	3.6
Turkey	2.8	2.5	2.5	2.5	6.3	5.3	6.3	7.3	3.4	2.8	3.7	4.6
Yugoslavia	1.2	1.1	0.9	0.9	5.6	6.6	6.2	6.2	4.4	5.4	5.2	5.2
D. Capital-surplus oil-exporting countries												
Kuwait	0.2	11.1	9.6	6.2		4.7[h]	5.7	-0.1		-5.8	-3.5	-6.0
Libyan Arab Republic	2.7	3.8	4.2	4.1								
Oman	2.0	2.5	2.7	3.2		5.7	39.7	6.8		3.2	36.0	3.5
Qatar	2.4	7.1	6.9	10.3								
Saudi Arabia	2.0	2.5	2.8	3.0			9.1	12.7			6.1	9.4
United Arab Emirates	2.4	9.3	13.7	16.7				12.5[f]				-2.1[f]
E. Industrialized countries												
Australia	2.3	2.0	1.9	1.7	4.7[j]	5.3	6.2	3.3	2.3[j]	3.2	4.2	1.6
Austria	0.2	0.6	0.5	0.2	5.6	4.3	5.1	4.0	5.4	3.7	4.6	3.8
Belgium	0.6	0.7	0.4	0.3	3.1[j]	5.2	4.8	3.7	2.5[j]	4.5	4.4	3.4
Canada	2.7	1.9	1.7	1.2	4.0[j]	5.8	4.8	4.7	1.3[j]	3.8	3.0	3.4
Denmark	0.7	0.8	0.7	0.4	3.6[j]	5.1	4.5	2.8	2.9	4.3	3.7	2.4
Finland	1.0	0.6	0.2	0.4	4.9	5.0	5.1	3.4	3.9	4.4	4.9	3.0
France	0.9	1.3	0.8	0.7	4.8	5.9	5.3	3.8	3.8	4.5	4.5	3.1
Germany, Federal Republic of	1.0	1.3	0.6	0.2	7.3[j]	4.8	4.5	2.4	6.3[j]	3.5	3.9	2.2
Iceland	2.1	1.8	1.2	1.3		7.1	1.1	4.6		5.2	-0.2	3.2
Ireland	-0.5	0.3	0.5	1.2		4.0	5.3	3.4		3.7	4.7	2.3
Italy	0.7	0.7	0.7	0.7	5.5[g]	5.0	6.1	2.9	4.8[g]	4.3	5.4	2.2

TABLE 4. COMPARATIVE ECONOMIC DATA (Continued)

Income group/ region/country	Population				Gross domestic product				GDP per capita			
	1950-60	1960-65	1965-70	1970-77	1950-60	1960-65	1965-70	1970-77	1950-60	1960-65	1965-70	1970-77
Japan	1.3	1.0	1.1	1.2	8.0ᶦ	10.1	12.4	5.0	6.6ᶦ	9.0	11.2	3.7
Luxembourg	0.6	1.1	0.4	0.8	:	3.3	3.6	2.3	:	2.2	3.2	1.5
Netherlands, The	1.3	1.4	1.2	0.9	4.7	4.9	5.7	3.2	3.3	3.5	4.4	2.3
New Zealand	2.2	2.1	1.4	1.7	:	5.0	2.6	2.9	:	2.9	1.2	1.2
Norway	0.9	0.8	0.8	0.6	3.4ᶦ	5.1	4.8	4.8	2.5ᶦ	4.3	3.9	4.1
Sweden	0.6	0.7	0.8	0.4	3.4	5.3	3.9	1.7	2.7	4.6	3.1	1.3
Switzerland	1.3	2.1	1.1	0.2	4.6	5.2	4.2	0.2	3.2	3.0	3.1	0.0
United Kingdom	0.4	0.7	0.3	0.1	2.8	3.2	2.5	1.9	2.3	2.4	2.2	1.7
United States	1.7	1.5	1.1	0.8	3.3	4.7	3.2	2.8	1.5	3.2	2.1	1.9
F. Centrally planned economies⁺⁺												
Albania	2.8	3.0	2.8	2.5	:	:	:	:	:	:	:	:
Bulgaria	0.8	0.8	0.7	0.6	:	7.0	8.6	7.5	:	6.2	7.8	6.9
China	1.9	2.0	1.8	1.6	:	:	:	:	:	:	:	:
Cuba	2.6	2.1	1.9	1.6	:	:	:	:	:	:	:	:
Czechoslovakia	1.0	0.7	0.3	0.7	:	:	6.6ᵃ	5.2	:	:	6.3ᵃ	4.5
German Democratic Republic	-0.6	-0.3	0.0	-0.2	:	2.7ᶦ	5.5ᶦ	5.1ᶦ	:	5.9	5.5	5.3
Hungary	0.7	0.3	0.4	0.4	:	4.5	6.8	6.2	:	4.2	6.4	5.8
Korea, Democratic People's Republic of	0.8	2.8	2.8	2.6	:	:	:	:	:	:	:	:
Mongolia	2.2	2.8	3.1	3.0	:	:	:	:	:	:	:	:
Poland	1.8	1.3	0.6	1.0	:	6.0	6.0	8.7	:	4.6	5.4	7.6
Romania	1.2	0.7	1.4	0.9	:	8.8	7.7	10.7	:	8.0	6.2	10.1ᵐ
Union of Soviet Socialist Republics	1.8	1.5	1.0	0.9	:	6.6	8.2	6.1	:	5.0	7.1	5.5ᵐ

+ Weighted average of the country growth rates; GDP in US dollars were used as weights; these are not strictly comparable to other group averages. ++ 1955-60. a. 1966-70. b. 1967-70. differences in national accounting system. l. Based on NMP index (1960=100) constructed from 1975 constant price series. m. 1970-76.

TABLE 4. COMPARATIVE ECONOMIC DATA (Continued)

	Gross production							
	Agriculture				Manufacturing			
	1950-60	1960-65	1965-70	1970-77	1950-60	1960-65	1965-70	1970-77
Developing countries	3.9	2.6	3.4	2.7	4.9	7.6	7.5	7.4
Capital-surplus oil-exporting countries	..	..	2.2	4.4	..	..	..	..
Industrialized countries	2.3+	2.0	2.2	2.1	6.1+	5.9	5.8	2.8
Centrally planned economies	..	..	3.2+	2.4+	..	8.0+	8.3+	7.4+
A. Developing countries by income group								
Low income	..	1.6	4.1	2.2	..	8.4	3.3	5.2
Middle income	4.5	3.1	3.0	3.0	4.7	7.5	7.9	7.2
B. Developing countries by region								
Africa south of Sahara	4.8	2.6	2.4	1.3	..	8.3	6.0	5.6
Middle East and North Africa	..	1.3	3.0	2.8	..	10.0	6.9	12.1
East Asia and Pacific	4.8	4.6	3.4	4.1	..	4.8	11.9	11.6
South Asia	3.2	1.1	4.7	2.1	6.4	8.8	3.5	4.3
Latin America and the Caribbean	..	3.5	2.8	3.3	4.0	5.6	6.7	5.8
Southern Europe	4.4	3.2	3.2	3.1	8.4	11.4	9.3	6.1
C. Developing countries by region and country								
Africa south of Sahara								
Angola	..	3.2	2.0	-3.4	..	..	..	..
Benin	3.3	1.9	5.2	1.5	..	..	..	..
Botswana	..	2.4	0.4	4.5	..	..	..	..
Burundi	-1.5	1.7	1.7	2.0	..	..	..	..
Cameroon	3.7	7.2	4.4	1.8	..	..	10.7ª	6.2
Cape Verde	..	..	..	..	..	..	..	..
Central African Republic	..	-1.2	3.3	2.1	..	4.1	8.1	6.0
Chad	..	0.9	-0.3	0.2	..	..	2.0ᵇ	5.7
Comoros	..	..	..	..	..	..	..	..
Congo, People's Republic of the	..	0.0	2.9	2.8	..	3.4	7.7	2.3
Equatorial Guinea	..	4.8ᶜ	-3.1	-4.9	..	..	..	..
Ethiopia	4.1	1.8	1.9	-0.1	..	..	..	..
Gabon	..	3.2ᶜ	1.9	1.3	..	..	..	..

Statistical Tables and Figures   447

TABLE 4. COMPARATIVE ECONOMIC DATA (Continued)

Gross production

	Agriculture			Manufacturing		
	1950-60	1960-65	1965-70	1970-77	1950-60	1960-65	1965-70	1970-77
Gambia, The	0.4	7.1	-0.3	1.7	..	3.1	8.9	4.3
Ghana	7.0	3.5	3.8	-0.4	4.6	10.8	12.5	-1.9
Guinea	2.7	1.9	3.5	0.0	..	..	..	..
Guinea-Bissau	..	..	..	..	..	..	..	..
Ivory Coast	9.3	11.3	3.7	4.5	..	14.2	8.0	7.5
Kenya	4.7	2.9	1.1	3.0	..	..	..	..
Lesotho	..	0.1	1.5	2.0	..	..	..	..
Liberia	2.6	3.0	3.0	2.3	..	..	14.1	5.5
Madagascar	3.9	4.1	1.6	2.7	..	..	..	1.2
Malawi	..	3.8	3.4	3.8	..	..	..	10.6
Mali	1.8	2.3	3.2	2.7	..	..	4.0	9.2
Mauritania	..	3.4	2.2	-3.3	..	..	35.1	2.9
Mauritius	..	3.1	-1.4	2.6	..	..	..	..
Mozambique	..	0.8	4.4	-1.6	..	..	..	..
Namibia	..	..	..	..	..	..	..	..
Niger	5.5	5.2	0.6	0.4	..	14.6	8.8	8.6
Nigeria	5.1	2.1	1.7	1.7	..	11.1	10.4	8.1
Réunion	..	..	..	..	..	..	..	..
Rhodesia	..	2.9	0.0	3.9	5.0	6.2	7.5	3.8
Rwanda	..	-1.6	8.4	3.6	..	..	..	..
Senegal	4.8	4.1	-4.5	5.0	..	0.4	1.2	8.2
Sierra Leone	0.3	4.7	2.2	2.0	..	..	2.7	3.6
Somalia	..	2.7	1.9	0.0	..	..	..	..
South Africa	4.1	1.5	3.9	2.2	5.0	8.4	6.7	3.2
Sudan	-0.4	5.4	0.0	2.3	..	..	..	..
Swaziland	..	4.6	7.0	3.6	..	17.1[c]	21.9	7.3
Tanzania, United Republic of	6.9	2.9	3.0	1.2	..	..	..	..
Togo	9.3	31.3	1.4	-5.5	..	..	6.7	11.3
Uganda	6.9	1.4	4.2	0.8	..	..	..	..
Upper Volta	-0.2	7.2	2.2	1.0	..	..	3.8[h]	7.1
Zaire	1.0	-2.2	2.3	1.9	..	..	0.3	1.1
Zambia	..	1.2	1.9	4.7	..	12.1	8.6	1.7

TABLE 4. COMPARATIVE ECONOMIC DATA (Continued)

	Agriculture			Gross production		Manufacturing		
	1950-60	1960-65	1965-70	1970-77	1950-60	1960-65	1965-70	1970-77

C. Developing countries by region and country (cont.)

Middle East and North Africa

Algeria	-0.5	-2.2	4.1	0.4	..	..	..	..
Bahrain	..	..	1.6	4.0	..	..	..	6.3
Egypt, Arab Republic of	3.4	3.6	3.5	0.7	8.8	20.0	3.8	16.0
Iran	2.1	2.7	4.1	4.2	..	9.5	13.4	..
Iraq	1.5	4.0	4.0	-2.3	..	..	..	..
Jordan	..	20.7	-15.3	-1.6	..	..	..	..
Lebanon	5.0	9.1	0.7	-0.5	5.2	3.3	5.8	6.5
Morocco	3.0	5.1	4.1	-2.0	6.3	9.2	4.8	8.3
Syrian Arab Republic	2.1	10.8	-1.7	9.8	..	2.9	4.8	5.6
Tunisia	4.5	3.6	-0.5	5.0	..	..	..	..
Yemen, Arab Republic of	..	1.2	-4.3	3.1	..	..	..	..
Yemen, People's Democratic Republic of	..	2.6	1.2	3.8	..	..	..	..

East Asia and Pacific

Fiji	..	11.2c	3.3	-0.4	..	..	5.4	3.0
Hong Kong	..	0.9	-0.3	-10.3	..	12.4	18.6	4.0
Indonesia	2.6	3.9	3.3	3.1	..	1.0	7.9	12.5
Korea, Republic of	5.5	6.3	3.1	4.9	16.4	13.9	25.6	23.5
Malaysia	0.9	5.2	6.4	4.3	..	..	11.5	12.6
Papua New Guinea	..	4.2	2.8	3.1	9.7g	..	..	..
Philippines	3.3	2.8	3.2	5.8	..	6.2	4.4	5.2
Singapore	..	1.4	15.8	1.0	..	7.7	15.8	11.2
Solomon Islands	..	1.4	0.9	1.9	..	..	..	..
Taiwan	4.8	4.8	2.9	3.1	15.4	13.6	21.0	13.3
Thailand	3.8	6.6	3.1	4.7	6.4	10.8	10.2	11.8

South Asia

Afghanistan	..	1.6	1.0	4.0	..	..	8.0	9.3
Bangladesh	..	3.1	3.1	1.8	..	5.8	7.4	5.7

TABLE 4. COMPARATIVE ECONOMIC DATA (Continued)

	Gross production						
	Agriculture			Manufacturing			
	1950-60	1960-65	1965-70	1970-77	1950-60	1960-65	1965-70	1970-77
Bhutan								
Burma	2.5	3.1	3.1	1.6		5.6	1.7	4.4
India	3.2	0.5	4.9	2.1	6.6	9.0	2.8	4.6
Nepal		0.9	1.7	1.2				
Pakistan		4.6	5.9	2.6		12.1	9.4	2.6
Sri Lanka	2.3	3.6	2.1	2.4	-0.9	6.1	5.6	2.7
Latin America and the Carribean								
Argentina		3.0	3.0	3.3	0.4	3.9	6.1	3.0
Bahamas								
Barbados		3.6	-2.5	-2.7			1.6*	6.5
Belize		13.7	5.4	2.6				
Bolivia		4.1	4.2	4.4	1.3	7.0	3.4	7.1
Brazil	4.5	3.2	2.7	4.4	9.1	3.7	10.4	9.6
Chile	2.9	2.2	2.5	1.7	5.7	6.7	1.5	-4.4
Colombia		2.8	3.6	3.9	6.5	5.7	6.2	6.5
Costa Rica		3.4	5.6	3.5		9.2	8.0	8.1
Dominican Republic		-2.7	5.9	2.0	5.0	1.5	11.4	8.8
Ecuador		5.8	3.0	3.5			7.2	10.6
El Salvador		2.9	0.4	3.3	5.7	17.0	5.0	8.3
Honduras		4.5	5.3	1.3	7.0	3.0	4.9	5.6
Jamaica	2.9	3.2	-1.3	1.1		7.6	3.0	0.6
Mexico	5.4	5.9	2.0	2.1	7.0	9.6	8.4	5.9
Netherlands Antilles		1.2	3.1	9.7				
Nicaragua	1.1	13.0	1.2	5.0				
Panama		4.3	6.5	3.5	10.7	12.6	9.6	1.2
Paraguay		4.9	2.4	4.6		3.5	5.9	3.1
Peru	3.6	2.4	2.3	0.7	7.3	9.7	6.7	5.8
Puerto Rico								
Trinidad and Tobago		2.8	1.4	-0.5			6.1	-1.1
Uruguay	0.3	2.3	3.1	0.4	3.2	1.0	2.4	2.7
Venezuela		5.6	5.7	2.2	13.0	9.5	3.6	5.6

TABLE 4. COMPARATIVE ECONOMIC DATA (Continued)

	Agriculture			Gross production			Manufacturing		
	1950-60	1960-65	1965-70	1970-77	1950-60	1960-65	1965-70	1970-77	
C. Developing countries by region and country (cont.)									
Southern Europe									
Cyprus	3.8	7.7	5.4	0.8	..	2.5	10.1	1.4	
Greece	4.7	6.5	2.4	3.8	7.9	7.9	8.7	7.7	
Israel	12.0	8.1	5.8	4.9	11.8	13.6	11.8	6.1	
Malta	..	2.7	6.7	0.4	..	..	..	..	
Portugal	2.1	3.7	1.1	-1.1	6.7	8.7	8.9	1.2	
Spain	2.9	2.6	3.3	3.4	8.8	12.0	10.1	7.9	
Turkey	4.7	2.9	4.0	3.7	8.6	12.7	11.6	10.1	
Yugoslavia	6.2	2.5	3.1	4.0	10.4	11.7	6.1	8.2	
D. Capital-surplus oil-exporting countries									
Kuwait	..	..	3.0	1.5	..	..	..	..	
Libyan Arab Republic	3.9	7.2	-2.0	11.4	..	..	..	..	
Oman	..	..	2.8	2.1	..	..	..	..	
Qatar	..	..	..	..	..	..	..	..	
Saudi Arabia	..	2.8	2.9	2.8	..	..	11.9	4.0	
United Arab Emirates	..	..	..	..	..	..	..	..	
E. Industrialized countries									
Australia	3.8	0.5	3.6	1.9	6.3	6.1	4.9	1.3	
Austria	4.7	0.7	3.6	1.9	7.5	4.5	6.4	3.3	
Belgium	1.3	0.7	4.3	0.9	4.1	6.3	6.0	2.6	
Canada	2.5	5.0	-1.2	2.8	3.5	6.3	4.9	3.7	
Denmark	1.5	0.8	-1.1	1.2	3.5	6.9	4.6	1.8	
Finland	3.4	2.4	1.4	1.4	6.4	6.2	7.5	3.3	
France	3.2	2.7	1.6	1.3	6.8	5.5	9.6	2.8	
Germany, Federal Republic of	3.3	0.8	3.7	0.4	9.8	5.7	6.5	1.0	
Iceland	..	..	..	3.2	..	..	..	..	
Ireland	2.2	0.3	3.2	3.9	3.0	6.6	7.1	4.1	
Italy	2.2	3.0	2.4	1.0	9.3	6.3	7.3	3.0	

TABLE 4. COMPARATIVE ECONOMIC DATA (Continued)

	Gross production						
	Agriculture			Manufacturing			
	1950-60	1960-65	1965-70	1970-77	1950-60	1960-65	1965-70	1970-77
Japan	2.4	3.2	3.3	2.1	18.3	11.5	16.3	2.9
Luxembourg	1.3	0.7	4.5	0.9	4.4	1.8	4.5	0.0
Netherlands, The	2.9	0.1	6.6	3.0	5.9	6.2	7.4	2.1
New Zealand	3.0	3.0	2.2	1.0	..	..	..	..
Norway	0.6	-0.8	0.8	1.6	4.8	5.8	4.2	2.2
Sweden	-0.2	0.3	0.7	2.5	3.0	7.4	4.9	2.0
Switzerland	1.1	-0.9	2.5	1.9	6.0	5.1	5.8	-1.0
United Kingdom	2.7	3.1	1.1	0.8	3.5	3.4	3.0	0.5
United States	1.8	1.7	1.5	3.1	3.4	6.3	3.8	3.3
F. Centrally planned economies								
Albania	..	..	4.2	3.4	..	..	..	..
Bulgaria	..	..	1.5	1.6	..	..	..	8.4
China	..	..	2.5	3.0	..	11.0	11.0	..
Cuba	..	..	4.0	0.0	..	..	..	..
Czechoslovakia	..	..	3.8	2.9	..	4.5	6.8	6.7
German Democratic Republic	..	..	1.2	3.6	..	5.7	6.4	6.3
Hungary	..	..	2.7	3.7	..	7.7	5.9	6.2
Korea, Democratic People's Republic of	..	..	2.1	6.7	..	..	..	..
Mongolia	..	..	-2.0	2.3	..	..	..	..
Poland	..	..	1.6	1.3	..	8.7	8.9	10.7
Romania	..	..	-0.4	6.9	..	..	..	..
Union of Soviet Socialist Republics	..	..	4.1	1.8	..	8.4	8.6	7.2

c. 1961-65. d. 1973-77. e. 1970-75. f. 1972-77. g. 1951-60. h. 1962-65. i. 1952-60. j. 1953-60. k. GDP data are not strictly comparable to those of other countries because of

COMPARATIVE ECONOMIC DATA
TABLE 5. Selected Economic Development Indicators: Expenditure
(average annual growth rates)

Income group/ region/country	Consumption									Gross domestic investment		
	Private				General government							
	1960-60	1960-65	1965-70	1970-77	1960-60	1960-65	1965-70	1970-77		1960-60	1960-65	1965-70	1970-77
Developing countries	..	5.0	6.0	5.5	..	5.2	6.9	8.5	..	7.7	7.9	8.1
Capital-surplus oil-exporting countries	..	..	..	..	..	..	..	..	..	..	9.3	42.8
Industrialized countries	..	5.0	4.8	3.7	..	4.1	3.9	2.8	..	7.3	5.9	0.9
Centrally planned economies	..	..	..	..	..	..	..	..	..	..	..	..
A. Developing countries by income group												
Low income	..	3.1	5.3	3.3	..	4.5	5.2	5.0	..	7.8	5.6	5.5
Middle income	..	5.5	6.1	5.9	..	5.4	7.3	9.1	..	7.7	8.3	8.4
B. Developing countries by region												
Africa south of Sahara	..	3.9	3.7	2.9	..	7.8	7.9	6.5	..	8.2	6.0	6.5
Middle East and North Africa	..	6.3	7.1	8.7	..	6.9	11.5	15.4	..	-0.6	13.0	18.4
East Asia and Pacific	..	4.5	7.4	6.8	..	2.0	7.6	8.5	..	11.0	14.3	10.3
South Asia	..	..	..	..	..	..	..	..	..	9.1	4.2	4.3
Latin America and the Caribbean	4.9	5.0	5.8	6.4	6.9	4.1	6.8	8.3	7.0	4.7	8.2	7.9
Southern Europe	5.6	7.1	6.8	5.4	4.4	5.4	6.1	6.7	7.5	12.3	6.1	5.3

TABLE 5 (Continued) Selected Economic Development Indicators: Expenditure

	Exports of goods and N.F.S.			Imports of goods and N.F.S.		
	1950-60	1960-65	1965-70	1970-77	1950-60	1960-65	1965-70	1970-77
Developing countries	..	6.4	8.3	5.2	..	5.9	8.7	9.0
Capital-surplus oil-exporting countries	..	..	7.4	..	..	..	10.5	..
Industrialized countries	..	6.9	9.4	6.7	..	7.8	9.4	5.1
Centrally planned economies	..	..	..	..	..	..	..	..
A. Developing countries by income group								
Low income	..	2.1	5.8	6.0	..	3.9	3.7	6.5
Middle income	..	7.1	8.6	5.1	..	6.2	9.4	9.3
B. Developing countries by region								
Africa south of Sahara	..	5.9	6.5	3.9	..	6.1	6.1	7.5
Middle East and North Africa	..	5.0	10.6	2.5	..	-2.4	10.6	19.7
East Asia and Pacific	..	6.1	11.5	11.7	..	4.9	14.0	11.3
South Asia	..	4.6	2.5	5.1*	..	5.1	-1.4	-2.5*
Latin America and the Caribbean	4.4	6.0	5.4	3.1	5.0	3.8	7.5	6.0
Southern Europe	10.8	11.8	10.8	5.1	6.0	15.4	9.9	6.5

COMPARATIVE ECONOMIC DATA
TABLE 6. Economic Structure Indicators: Expenditure (percentage of GDP at current market prices)

Income group/ region/country	Gross domestic investment					General government consumption				
	1955	1960	1965	1970	1977	1955	1960	1965	1970	1977
Developing countries	..	19.0	20.2	21.9	24.5	..	10.2	10.6	11.9	13.1
Capital-surplus oil-exporting countries	..	..	18.5	16.0	24.7	..	..	15.4	17.9	23.9
Industrialized countries	25.5	22.5	23.6	24.2	22.1	14.3	14.8	15.1	15.9	17.1
Centrally planned economies	..	26.1	24.4	28.3	27.0	..	2.6	3.5	3.6	..
A. Developing countries by income group										
Low income	..	14.0	16.1	17.2	19.7	..	9.2	9.9	10.7	11.1
Middle income	..	20.4	21.1	22.9	25.4	..	10.4	10.8	12.1	13.4
B. Developing countries by region										
Africa south of Sahara	..	16.2	19.5	20.2	24.0	..	9.8	11.2	13.2	15.4
Middle East and North Africa	..	22.6	17.6	22.1	35.3	..	13.0	14.6	16.3	19.5
East Asia and Pacific	..	12.8	16.6	22.0	24.6	..	11.6	9.8	11.1	12.2
South Asia	..	16.0	18.1	17.9	20.9	..	7.6	9.7	9.7	9.8
Latin America and the Caribbean	17.4	20.7	19.5	21.5	21.9	9.1	9.9	9.7	10.3	10.9
Southern Europe	22.9	22.4	25.8	25.7	25.6	11.9	10.9	11.0	13.0	14.2

TABLE 6 (Continued) Economic Structure Indicators : Expenditure

	Exports of goods and N.F.S.					Imports of goods and N.F.S.				
	1965	1960	1965	1970	1977	1965	1960	1965	1970	1977
Developing countries	..	15.2	15.4	16.2	20.8	..	16.6	16.5	18.0	23.0
Capital-surplus oil-exporting countries	..	..	60.6	61.6	69.2	..	..	27.0	27.5	34.0
Industrialized countries	11.7	13.4	13.1	14.9	18.1	11.1	12.8	12.6	14.3	18.3
Centrally planned economies	..	..	..	..	..	..	..	..	..	..
A. Developing countries by income group										
Low income	..	11.2	9.6	9.8	13.0	..	13.0	11.7	11.8	14.1
Middle income	..	16.3	16.7	17.6	22.2	..	17.5	17.6	19.3	24.6
B. Developing countries by region										
Africa south of Sahara	..	24.9	24.8	23.5	28.9	..	25.1	25.6	24.4	30.0
Middle East and North Africa	..	21.8	19.6	21.7	29.5	..	23.0	17.3	23.6	32.6
East Asia and Pacific	..	22.6	22.5	28.4	40.2	..	24.9	25.4	32.3	39.8
South Asia	..	6.3	5.1	5.0	6.9	..	9.4	8.0	6.6	8.9
Latin America and the Caribbean	13.0	13.8	13.7	12.9	14.9	12.3	14.4	12.8	13.6	16.0
Southern Europe	7.0	10.1	12.7	14.0	15.2	10.4	11.7	16.6	18.2	21.1

COMPARATIVE ECONOMIC DATA
TABLE 7. Economic Structure Indicators : Product (percentage of GDP at current factor cost)

Income group/ region/country	Agriculture					Manufacturing				
	1955	1960	1965	1970	1977	1955	1960	1965	1970	1977
Developing countries	..	30.1	27.1	22.7	19.4	..	18.6	19.7	20.2	21.5
Capital-surplus oil-exporting countries	..	..	5.7	3.7	1.0	..	..	5.7	5.5	3.5
Industrialized countries	..	6.4	5.3	4.2	3.8	..	30.6	30.1	29.4	27.0
Centrally planned economies	..	21.5	22.1	20.6	16.4	..	51.8	52.7	51.8	52.5
A. Developing countries by income group										
Low income	..	49.9	47.7	45.3	39.2	..	11.5	12.4	12.4	13.3
Middle income	..	24.6	22.1	17.7	15.5	..	20.6	21.4	21.9	23.2
B. Developing countries by region										
Africa south of Sahara	..	40.5	35.5	31.5	28.2	..	10.3	12.3	13.1	13.3
Middle East and North Africa	..	26.0	24.4	19.4	12.6	..	12.4	14.0	14.9	13.2
East Asia and Pacific	..	38.0	36.2	29.6	23.4	..	13.5	15.4	16.3	20.7
South Asia	..	49.4	45.9	46.3	40.8	..	13.2	14.3	13.9	15.5
Latin America and the Caribbean	21.0	18.0	16.9	12.7	12.8	23.8	24.1	24.6	24.7	26.5
Southern Europe	26.1	24.8	20.6	16.2	14.6	23.5	25.0	25.1	24.7	26.2

TABLE 7 (Continued) Economic Structure Indicators : Product

	Other industry					Services				
	1965	1960	1965	1970	1977	1965	1960	1965	1970	1977
Developing countries	..	9.5	10.3	12.1	14.6	..	41.8	43.0	45.1	44.4
Capital-surplus oil-exporting countries	..	..	58.4	61.7	74.7	..	..	30.2	29.1	20.7
Industrialized countries	..	10.4	10.4	10.2	10.5	..	52.5	54.2	56.1	58.8
Centrally planned economies	..	9.9	9.2	10.3	11.2	..	16.8	16.0	17.2	19.8
A. Developing countries by income group										
Low income	..	6.0	6.5	7.9	11.9	..	32.6	33.5	34.4	35.8
Middle income	..	10.5	11.2	13.0	15.2	..	44.3	45.3	47.4	46.2
B. Developing countries by region										
Africa south of Sahara	..	11.8	12.9	14.4	20.2	..	37.4	39.3	40.9	38.3
Middle East and North Africa	..	18.6	19.3	23.7	34.6	..	42.9	42.4	42.0	39.5
East Asia and Pacific	..	6.9	7.9	8.6	13.7	..	41.7	40.5	43.5	42.2
South Asia	..	5.6	6.5	7.0	8.1	..	31.8	33.3	32.8	35.8
Latin America and the Caribbean	6.6	8.7	8.3	10.9	11.0	48.7	49.2	50.1	51.7	49.8
Southern Europe	10.6	9.9	11.5	12.3	11.4	39.8	40.3	42.8	46.8	47.9

COMPARATIVE ECONOMIC DATA
TABLE 8. Foreign Trade Structure: Export Composition
(percentage of total merchandise exports)

Income group/ region/country	Food and beverages				Nonfood agriculture				Fuels, minerals, and metals			
	1960[a]	1965	1970	1977	1960[a]	1965	1970	1977	1960[a]	1965	1970	1977
Developing countries	36.0	38.4	28.7	21.4[c]	17.6	13.3	12.1	6.0[c]	31.0	30.8	33.4	41.2[c]
Capital-surplus oil-exporting countries	3.1	0.1	0.3	0.2[c]	0.8	0.1	..	..	96.0	99.5	96.2	97.5[c]
Industrialized countries	14.7	14.4	11.5	11.2	7.5	6.5	4.7	3.9	9.5	9.2	9.4	8.9
Centrally planned economies	18.0	15.1	12.3	10.4	11.7	11.4	6.3	2.4	19.6	17.6	18.2	6.8
A. Developing countries by income group												
Low income	43.3	41.9	33.8	27.6[c]	26.3	19.5	16.8	10.9[c]	10.6	11.6	22.5	39.4[c]
Middle income	34.6	37.9	28.1	20.6[c]	15.9	12.4	11.5	5.3[c]	34.9	33.5	34.9	41.4[c]
B. Developing countries by region												
Africa south of Sahara	50.5	40.9	34.4	26.5[c]	22.1	16.9	12.1	5.3[c]	14.3	30.1	38.7	65.3[c]
Middle East and North Africa	10.5	14.2	14.1	3.7[c]	13.5	14.9	9.2	2.7[c]	70.9	63.5	66.6	88.6[c]
East Asia and Pacific	25.7	29.0	18.4	15.8[c]	32.6	22.9	23.3	10.5[c]	17.9	15.7	17.9	22.5[c]
South Asia	45.4	38.7	30.9	33.8[c]	20.9	19.3	14.1	5.9[c]	4.9	6.8	9.1	7.4[c]
Latin America and the Caribbean	36.6	47.2	38.5	37.6[c]	10.1	7.8	6.3	3.4[c]	48.3	39.6	44.4	43.4[c]
Southern Europe	44.1	39.0	30.1	21.7	10.9	8.8	7.5	5.0	9.9	8.9	10.2	7.4

TABLE 8 (Continued) Foreign Trade Structure: Export Composition

	Machinery and equipment				Other manufactures			
	1960[a]	1965	1970	1977	1960[a]	1965	1970	1977
Developing countries	2.0	2.3	4.9	8.0[c]	13.4	15.2	20.9	23.4[c]
Capital-surplus oil-exporting countries	...	0.3	0.4	0.7[c]	...	...	1.1	1.5[c]
Industrialized countries	31.2	31.5	35.9	38.5	37.2	38.4	38.5	37.6
Centrally planned economies	16.5	21.1	25.4	44.6	34.2	34.8	37.8	35.8
A. Developing countries by income group								
Low income	0.4	0.7	2.5	2.3[c]	19.4	26.2	24.4	19.7[c]
Middle income	2.4	2.5	5.2	8.8[c]	12.2	13.7	20.4	23.9[c]
B. Developing countries by region								
Africa south of Sahara	1.5	1.3	2.3	0.4[c]	11.6	10.8	12.4	2.5[c]
Middle East and North Africa	0.0	0.3	1.3	0.6[c]	5.0	7.1	8.9	4.4[c]
East Asia and Pacific	3.5	4.1	6.9	12.7[c]	20.3	28.3	33.5	38.5[c]
South Asia	0.5	1.0	4.2	4.9[c]	28.3	34.3	41.7	48.1[c]
Latin America and the Caribbean	0.5	0.6	2.4	4.9[c]	4.5	4.8	8.4	10.6[c]
Southern Europe	8.5	10.0	13.7	19.8	26.7	33.3	38.6	46.1

COMPARATIVE ECONOMIC DATA
TABLE 9. Foreign Trade Structure: Import Composition
(percentage of total merchandise imports)

Income group/ region/country	Food and beverages				Nonfood agriculture				Fuel and lubricants			
	1960[f]	1965	1970	1977	1960[f]	1965	1970	1977	1960[f]	1965	1970	1977
Developing countries	16.4	16.7	13.8	12.3[c]	6.8	6.2	5.4	4.7[c]	10.8	8.8	8.0	17.5[c]
Capital-surplus oil-exporting countries	11.5	20.3	24.5	11.6[c]	1.4	1.5	1.6	1.5[c]	3.8	2.2	1.6	1.8[c]
Industrialized countries	21.7	19.8	15.8	13.4	11.1	9.4	6.6	4.7	11.6	10.8	10.3	22.0
Centrally planned economies	12.8	20.0	16.9	11.3	9.6	7.2	6.6	5.9	4.9	4.4	5.0	14.1
A. Developing countries by income group												
Low income	17.3	20.5	18.8	17.5[c]	5.2	4.7	4.1	5.2[c]	7.7	5.3	6.6	18.2[c]
Middle income	16.2	16.0	13.2	11.8[c]	7.2	6.4	5.6	4.7[c]	11.5	9.5	8.2	17.4[c]
B. Developing countries by region												
Africa south of Sahara	16.3	11.7	11.3	12.6[c]	2.7	2.7	2.2	0.7[c]	7.2	5.9	5.8	5.8[c]
Middle East and North Africa	26.7	24.3	17.2	15.6[c]	6.2	5.8	5.6	3.5[c]	10.0	8.2	3.6	3.1[c]
East Asia and Pacific	20.3	20.8	16.1	12.2[c]	11.4	9.5	7.8	7.5[c]	9.6	8.6	7.8	17.3[c]
South Asia	18.2	22.3	22.9	20.2[c]	6.9	5.6	6.3	7.2[c]	7.7	4.8	6.7	22.0[c]
Latin America and the Caribbean	12.0	12.1	10.8	8.2[c]	3.5	4.3	3.5	2.0[c]	15.0	13.3	11.1	28.8[c]
Southern Europe	16.6	17.2	12.6	11.9	10.5	9.1	7.3	5.8	10.4	8.4	8.7	20.7

TABLE 9 (continued) Foreign Trade Structure : Import Composition

	Nonfuel minerals and metals				Machinery and equipment				Other manufactures			
	1960[a]	1965	1970	1977	1960[a]	1965	1970	1977	1960[a]	1965	1970	1977
Developing countries	3.9	3.7	3.9	3.1[c]	29.5	29.6	32.4	31.5[c]	32.6	35.0	36.5	30.9[c]
Capital-surplus oil-exporting countries	0.7	1.0	0.8	0.7	40.1	34.1	32.8	41.6[c]	42.5	40.8	38.7	42.8[c]
Industrialized countries	9.0	9.5	9.5	5.3	18.2	19.3	24.9	23.7	26.3	31.2	32.9	30.8
Centrally planned economies	6.5	4.9	4.3	8.2	33.8	31.1	32.6	35.7	32.3	32.3	34.5	24.7
A. Developing countries by income group												
Low income	7.7	4.0	4.1	3.4[c]	29.7	31.9	26.3	27.2[c]	32.4	33.7	38.1	28.5[c]
Middle income	3.0	3.7	3.8	3.1[c]	29.4	29.1	32.9	32.0[c]	32.7	35.2	36.3	31.1[c]
B. Developing countries by region												
Africa south of Sahara	2.8	2.9	1.8	1.5[c]	28.6	34.2	37.6	42.9[c]	42.4	42.6	41.3	36.6[c]
Middle East and North Africa	2.1	1.7	2.3	1.6[c]	24.9	24.6	31.5	41.5[c]	30.0	35.5	39.8	34.6[c]
East Asia and Pacific	3.2	3.0	3.3	3.1[c]	18.9	21.0	27.6	27.6[c]	36.7	37.1	37.4	32.3[c]
South Asia	9.4	5.0	6.3	4.5[c]	31.4	33.3	25.1	20.3[c]	26.3	29.0	32.7	25.8[c]
Latin America and the Caribbean	2.6	3.7	3.5	3.1[c]	36.2	32.5	35.5	30.2[c]	30.7	34.1	35.8	27.6[c]
Southern Europe	4.2	5.0	6.4	4.5	30.6	29.0	32.4	28.6	27.8	31.2	32.5	28.5

COMPARATIVE ECONOMIC DATA
TABLE 10. Capital Flows

Income group/ region/country	Current account balance (millions of U.S. dollars) (- indicates deficit)				Current account balance as percentage of exports of goods and N.F.S. (percent)			
	1960	1965	1970	1977	1960	1965	1970	1977
Developing countries	-1945.0	-4889.2	-10645.9	-25166.8	-9.3	-12.6	-16.0	-9.0
Capital-surplus oil-exporting countries	...	...	716.0	20464.3	...	...	14.6	29.6
Industrialized countries	2200.4	4193.4	10705.0	-8856.7	2.0	2.5	3.6	-1.0
A. Developing countries by income group								
Low income	-856.2	-2057.4	-1697.9	-1140.5	-35.3	-41.0	-22.4	-5.8
Middle income	-1088.8	-2831.8	-8948.0	-24026.3	-5.9	-8.4	-15.2	-9.2
B. Developing countries by region								
Africa south of Sahara	...	-1069.9	-1871.1	-1572.3	...	-18.0	-15.9	-4.0
Middle East and North Africa	-114.3	-185.6	-958.5	-327.3	-4.2	-5.4	-12.0	-0.7
East Asia and Pacific	...	-738.9	-1805.3	-870.2	...	-12.2	-16.8	-1.4
South Asia	-856.2	-1727.9	-515.3	-969.2	-35.3	-51.7	-17.9	-23.8
Latin America and the Caribbean	-1070.9	-290.4	-3444.5	-11165.5	-10.9	-2.1	-17.4	-16.0
Southern Europe	294.4	-877.2	-1384.3	-10262.6	11.6	-14.1	-11.0	-22.0

TABLE 10 (Continued) Capital Flows

Financing of current surplus or deficit (millions of U.S. dollars)

	Direct investment (net)				Long-term capital (net)				Short-term capital (net)			
	1960	1965	1970	1977	1960	1965	1970	1977	1960	1965	1970	1977
Developing countries	774.9	1452.5	2427.7	6679.4	1616.5	3478.0	7101.9	34672.4	147.1	75.9	1858.2	-4699.5
Capital-surplus oil-exporting countries			159.0	274.4			73.0	-11066.9			-76.0	-2966.7
Industrialized countries	1656.4	-3906.6	-4646.5	-11583.5	-1355.2	-2595.4	-988.3	7693.0	74.5	370.8	1091.3	6832.0
A. Developing countries by income group												
Low income	7.3	50.0	193.4	344.6	671.7	1640.9	997.4	2898.1	-12.8	94.6	101.9	-432.6
Middle income	767.6	1402.5	2234.3	6334.8	944.8	1837.1	6104.5	31774.3	159.9	-18.7	1756.3	-4266.9
B. Developing countries by region												
Africa south of Sahara		359.2	452.6	433.7		328.6	907.2	1911.5		74.4	339.5	-701.4
Middle East and North Africa	29.1	231.0	130.0	1230.7	71.8	243.8	607.4	5899.8	2.3	-0.7	155.7	-3885.9
East Asia and Pacific		131.3	418.4	1502.8		461.8	944.7	4378.4		-25.0	482.4	-1503.4
South Asia	7.3	-2.7	5.7	14.0	671.7	1352.1	609.1	1078.1	-12.8	122.0	34.7	-21.0
Latin America and the Caribbean	468.8	535.1	1072.3	2950.4	341.6	451.2	2198.5	14107.0	95.7	-266.2	702.6	-2452.1
Southern Europe	152.5	198.6	348.7	547.9	231.7	620.5	1835.0	7497.6	51.0	171.4	143.3	3664.2

COMPARATIVE ECONOMIC DATA
TABLE 11. Selected Economic Indicators – I

Income group/ region/country	International reserves as months of imports of goods and N.F.S.			
	1960	1965	1970	1977
Developing countries	3.9	3.5	3.5	4.7
Capital-surplus oil-exporting countries	5.0	8.4	9.6	12.3
Industrialized countries	5.9	4.5	3.2	3.6
A. Developing countries by income group				
Low income	4.0	2.2	2.9	5.2
Middle income	3.8	3.8	3.5	4.7
B. Developing countries by region				
Africa south of Sahara	..	2.6	2.9	2.8
Middle East and North Africa	3.6	2.9	2.7	5.8
East Asia and Pacific	3.7	4.5	4.2	3.8
South Asia	3.8	2.6	3.7	7.7
Latin America and the Caribbean	3.4	3.2	3.3	5.7
Southern Europe	5.4	4.9	3.8	4.3

TABLE 11 (Continued) Selected Economic Indicators – I

	External public debt service ratio			Deficit or surplus on current account as a percentage of GDP[b] (– indicates deficit)			
	1960	1965	1970	1977	1960	1965	1970	1977
Developing countries	..	..	9.5	9.0	-1.1	-1.3	-2.3	-2.0
Capital-surplus oil-exporting countries	..	..	..	..	..	..	14.8	22.8
Industrialized countries	..	..	..	..	0.2	0.3	0.5	-0.2
A. Developing countries by income group								
Low income	..	..	13.8	10.1	-1.9	-1.1	-1.4	-0.4
Middle income	..	..	8.9	8.8	-0.8	-1.4	-2.6	-2.3
B. Developing countries by region								
Africa south of Sahara	..	..	5.4	7.7	..	..	-3.9	-1.8
Middle East and North Africa	..	..	10.8	6.4	-1.3	-3.3	-2.7	-0.5
East Asia and Pacific	..	..	6.0	5.2	-0.4	-0.7	-4.2	-0.3
South Asia	..	..	25.2	11.1	-2.3	-2.5	-0.9	0.0
Latin America and the Caribbean	..	..	13.3	18.0	-1.5	-0.4	-2.1	-2.7
Southern Europe	..	..	7.1	6.4	0.4	-1.6	-1.7	-3.9

COMPARATIVE ECONOMIC DATA
TABLE 12. Selected Economic Indicators – II

Income group/ region/country	Total per capita consumption index (1970=100)				Food consumption per capita (calories per day)			
	1960	1965	1970	1977	1960	1966	1970	1977
Developing countries	75.3	84.6	100.0	125.7	2213.7	2144.4	2253.7	2290.2
Capital-surplus oil-exporting countries	...	...	...	...	2063.5	2171.8	2233.4	2716.7
Industrialized countries	70.5	83.7	100.0	121.6	3183.8	3201.1	3317.7	3376.5
Centrally planned economies	...	...	...	...	2265.3	3217.0	3323.2	3434.3
A. Developing countries by income group								
Low income	86.1	88.9	100.0	110.0	2059.3	1915.9	2062.0	2051.2
Middle income	72.8	83.5	100.0	128.6	2397.9	2430.6	2493.0	2583.8
B. Developing countries by region								
Africa south of Sahara	89.9	93.4	100.0	111.4	2276.6	2190.9	2266.1	2235.1
Middle East and North Africa	66.0	77.4	100.0	160.4	2161.5	2293.6	2336.6	2703.9
East Asia and Pacific	73.9	79.9	100.0	138.9	2037.4	2026.4	2169.8	2231.3
South Asia	87.7	90.3	100.0	102.9	2052.9	1896.2	2055.5	2036.1
Latin America and the Caribbean	77.0	85.9	100.0	125.0	2420.0	2487.0	2530.3	2565.3
Southern Europe	60.6	78.1	100.0	131.2	2927.5	2940.3	2978.1	3156.8

TABLE 12 (Continued)   Selected Economic Indicators – II

	Energy consumption per capita (kilograms of coal equivalent)			Average national savings rate (percent)			
	1960	1965	1970	1977	1960	1965	1970	1977
Developing countries	260.8	315.8	396.3	506.9	16.8	17.9	19.0	20.1
Capital-surplus oil-exporting countries	701.9	899.1	1740.9	3251.4	:	41.1	39.4	58.3
Industrialized countries	4451.4	5245.4	6598.9	7048.7	23.3	24.3	25.0	22.2
Centrally planned economies	1379.3	1437.7	1706.8	2103.3	:	:	:	:
A. Developing countries by income group								
Low income	115.3	132.8	141.7	155.1	11.4	12.9	13.8	17.0
Middle income	434.6	532.9	696.8	945.2	18.3	19.1	20.2	20.8
B. Developing countries by region								
Africa south of Sahara	227.5	262.2	286.0	352.7	13.8	16.7	16.4	20.7
Middle East and North Africa	269.9	313.1	489.3	792.2	22.8	15.7	21.0	24.1
East Asia and Pacific	148.1	194.0	291.9	465.9	9.7	13.3	17.6	23.7
South Asia	126.0	154.3	162.5	154.0	12.5	14.2	14.7	17.6
Latin America and the Caribbean	592.3	681.7	850.8	1076.7	18.8	18.8	19.5	18.5
Southern Europe	582.9	800.8	1116.0	1654.8	20.9	22.2	22.4	20.5

TABLE 13 Growth of Population, GNP and GNP per Person, 1960-90

(average annual percentage growth rates)

Country group	Population				GNP[a]				GNP per person[a]			
	1960-70	1970-80	1980-85	1985-90	1960-70	1970-80	1980-85	1985-90	1960-70	1970-80	1980-85	1985-90
Low-income countries	2.4	2.3	2.3	2.2	4.2	4.0	4.5	4.7	1.8	1.7	2.1	2.5
Sub-Saharan Africa	2.5	2.8	3.0	2.7	4.2	3.0	3.1	3.8	1.7	0.2	0.1	1.1
Asia	2.4	2.2	2.2	2.1	4.2	4.2	4.7	4.9	1.8	2.0	2.4	2.7
Middle-income countries	2.5	2.5	2.5	2.3	6.0	5.6	5.2	5.8	3.5	3.1	2.7	3.4
East Asia and Pacific	2.8	2.3	2.1	2.0	7.7	8.0	7.0	7.3	4.9	5.7	4.8	5.2
Latin America and Caribbean	2.8	2.6	2.6	2.4	5.7	5.8	5.5	6.3	2.9	3.2	2.9	3.8
Middle East and North Africa	2.5	2.6	2.7	2.5	3.6	6.4	5.1	5.3	1.1	3.8	2.4	2.7
Sub-Saharan Africa	2.5	2.9	3.2	2.8	4.8	4.5	4.9	4.3	2.3	1.6	1.7	1.4
Southern Europe	1.4	1.4	1.3	1.2	7.0	4.6	3.8	3.7	5.6	3.2	2.5	3.4
Oil-importing developing countries	2.4	2.3	2.3	2.2	5.6	5.1	4.7	5.5	3.1	2.7	2.4	3.2
Low-income countries	2.5	2.4	2.4	2.2	4.1	3.3	4.1	4.6	1.6	0.9	1.7	2.4
Sub-Saharan Africa	2.5	2.8	3.0	2.7	4.2	3.0	3.1	3.8	1.6	0.2	0.1	1.1
Asia	2.4	2.3	2.3	2.1	4.1	3.4	4.3	4.8	1.6	1.1	2.0	2.6
Middle-income countries	2.4	2.3	2.3	2.1	6.1	5.5	4.9	5.7	3.6	3.1	2.6	3.5
East Asia and Pacific	2.8	2.3	2.1	2.0	7.8	8.0	6.9	7.3	4.9	5.6	4.7	5.2
Latin America and Caribbean	2.6	2.5	2.4	2.3	5.4	6.0	5.0	6.2	2.7	3.5	2.6	3.8
Middle East and North Africa	2.4	2.6	3.1	3.1	2.3	3.0	3.7	3.9	-0.2	0.4	0.6	0.8
Sub-Saharan Africa	2.5	2.9	3.0	2.7	4.9	3.9	4.6	4.2	2.4	0.9	1.6	1.4
Southern Europe	1.5	1.3	1.3	1.2	7.0	4.6	3.8	4.7	5.4	3.2	2.5	3.4
Oil-exporting developing countries[c]	2.6	2.5	2.7	2.5	5.5	6.1	6.3	5.9	2.8	3.5	3.5	3.4
All developing countries	2.5	2.4	2.4	2.2	5.6	5.3	5.1	5.6	3.1	2.8	2.6	3.3
Industrialized countries	1.0	0.7	0.5	0.4	5.0	3.1	3.3	4.0	3.9	2.4	2.9	3.5
Capital-surplus oil exporters	3.0	3.1	2.8	3.0	10.5	8.4	5.3	5.8	7.3	5.0	2.8	2.8
Centrally planned economies	1.7	1.3	1.2	1.1	..	5.2	4.6	4.5	..	3.8	3.4	3.3

Sources: World Bank estimates; High-case projections of *World Development Report, 1980.*
a. 1977 prices.
b. Estimates for oil-exporting developing countries are based on analysis of 11 major oil exporters.

TABLE 14 Capital Flows and Debt of the Developing Countries and Oil Exporters, 1975-90
(billions of current dollars)

Item	Oil importers						Oil exporters					
	1975	1977	1980	1985	1990		1975	1977	1980	1985	1990	
Current account deficit before interest payments[a]	32.9	16.8	42.7	43.4	42.2		6.8	7.8	-11.1	4.0	30.2	
Interest payments	6.7	8.1	18.3	35.0	62.0		2.0	4.1	8.8	11.8	17.5	
Changes in reserves and short-term debt	-9.1	9.9	-4.4	6.8	23.5		6.2	5.8	20.2	8.4	2.6	
Total to be financed	30.6	34.8	56.6	85.2	127.7		15.0	17.7	18.0	24.2	50.2	
Financed by medium- and long-term capital												
From public sources	12.5	13.2	21.7	41.1	66.6		5.4	6.0	7.3	11.2	16.6	
From private sources	18.1	21.7	34.9	44.0	61.2		9.6	11.7	10.7	13.0	33.6	
Private direct investment	4.2	3.9	6.5	9.6	16.4		2.7	2.1	3.5	5.8	8.2	
Private loans	13.9	17.7	28.4	34.4	44.7		6.9	9.6	7.2	7.2	25.4	
Total net capital flows												
Current dollars	30.5	34.8	56.6	85.2	127.7		15.0	17.7	18.0	24.2	50.2	
Constant 1977 dollars	34.2	34.8	40.0	42.1	47.2		16.8	17.7	12.7	12.0	18.5	
Outstanding medium- and long-term debt												
Public sources	57.7	77.5	100.4	212.9	397.1		16.2	24.3	48.8	79.6	130.0	
Private sources	72.5	108.9	187.1	343.4	558.5		24.7	43.9	66.5	97.5	175.4	
Total debt												
Current dollars	130.3	186.4	287.5	556.3	955.6		40.9	68.2	115.3	177.1	305.4	
Constant 1977 dollars	146.4	186.4	203.5	275.0	352.9		46.0	68.2	81.6	87.5	112.8	
Debt service												
Interest payments	6.7	8.1	18.3	35.0	62.0		2.0	4.1	8.8	11.8	17.5	
Debt amortization	12.7	18.9	28.6	65.0	114.2		3.6	6.5	12.2	23.6	40.1	
Interest payments as percentage of GNP	0.9	0.8	1.2	1.2	1.3		1.0	1.6	2.7	1.3	1.1	
Price deflator	89.3	100.0	141.3	202.3	270.8		89.3	100.0	141.3	202.3	270.8	

Source: High-case projections of *World Development Report*.
a. Excludes official transfers.

TABLE 15 Investment and Savings Ratios, Developing Countries, 1976 and 1990

(Percentage of gross domestic product at 1975 prices)

Country	Gross domestic investment		Gross domestic savings		Net flows of external resources	
	1976	1990	1976	1990	1976	1990
Low-income countries	17.8	25.0	15.7	21.2	2.1	3.8
Africa	16.0	22.1	8.8	11.4	7.2	10.7
Asia	18.0	25.3	16.7	22.4	1.3	3.0
Middle-income countries	26.1	26.0	23.1	23.9	3.0	2.1
East Asia and the Pacific	27.0	30.9	25.5	31.1	1.5	-0.2
Latin America and the Antilles	23.7	26.0	22.3	24.8	1.4	1.2
Middle East and North Africa	31.4	25.1	29.0	20.0	2.4	5.1
Africa south of the Sahara	27.0	24.4	25.1	21.0	1.9	3.4
Southern Europe	26.2	23.8	19.0	21.1	7.2	2.7
Developing countries as a whole	24.8	25.8	21.9	23.5	2.9	2.3

Source: World Bank, *World Development Report, 1979* (New York, Oxford University Press, 1979).

TABLE 16 Net Disbursements of Medium and Long-term Capital to Developing Countries, by Type of Capital and Country Income Group, 1970-85
(Percentages)

	Low Income Countries			Middle Income Countries			All Developing Countries		
	1970	1975	1985	1970	1975	1985	1970	1975	1985
A. Distribution of Capital by Category									
Official Grants	38	28	39	13	12	11	20	16	16
Concessional Loans	42	39	52	17	14	11	23	19	18
Loans at Market Terms	15	29	8	71	74	78	57	64	66
Official	11	1	7	12	11	9	12	9	9
Private	4	28	1	59	63	68	45	56	57
Total	100	100	100	100	100	100	100	100	100
B. Distribution of Capital by Income Group[a]									
Official Grants	50	38	42	50	63	58	100	100	100
Concessional Loans	46	43	48	54	56	52	100	100	100
Loans at Market Terms	7	10	2	92	91	98	100	100	100
Official	23	3	13	69	100	87	100	100	100
Private	2	11	—	98	89	100	100	100	100
Total	25	21	17	74	79	83	100	100	100

Note: Totals may not add due to rounding.
— Negligible.
[a] The distribution of concessional capital by income group is highly sensitive to the criterion used in classifying countries into Low and Middle Income groups.

TABLE 17 Developing Countries : Structure of Production, 1975 and 1990
(Percentages of gross domestic product, at 1975 prices)

	Agriculture		Industry[a]		Services	
	1975	1990	1975	1990	1975	1990
Low Income Countries	41	30	23	28	36	42
Africa	41	33	17	20	42	47
Asia	41	30	24	29	35	41
Middle Income Countries	15	10	38	41	48	49
East Asia and Pacific	22	12	31	39	47	49
Latin America and Caribbean	12	9	36	40	52	51
Middle East and North Africa	12	8	51	50	37	42
Sub-Saharan Africa	22	17	37	37	41	46
Southern Europe	15	11	36	39	49	50
All Developing Countries	19	14	35	39	46	47

Note: Sectoral shares may not add to 100 percent, due to rounding.
[a]Industrial production in all tables in this report refers to value added in manufacturing, mining, construction and public utilities.

TABLE 18 Growth of Merchandise Exports, by Product Category and Country Group, 1960–77 and 1977–90

(average annual percentage growth rates, 1977 prices)

Product category	1960–77			1977–90[a]		
	World	Industrialized countries	Developing countries	World	Industrialized countries	Developing countries
Fuels and energy	6.4	4.4	6.6	1.8	3.3	3.0
Other primary products	4.5	5.6	3.3	3.8	4.0	3.6
Food and beverages	4.6	6.3	2.8	4.1	4.3	3.9
Nonfood agricultural products	4.7	6.0	3.2	2.8	2.9	2.2
Minerals and nonferrous metals	4.1	3.6	5.2	4.1	4.0	3.8
Manufactures	8.9	8.8	12.3	6.8	6.5	9.7
Machinery and transport equipment	9.6	9.6	16.8	7.2	6.8	14.2
Other manufactures	8.3	8.0	11.3	6.5	6.2	7.7
Total merchandise[b]	7.2	7.7	6.0	5.4	5.9	6.0

Sources: World Bank; UN, Yearbook of International Trade Statistics, various issues; UNCTAD, Handbook of International Trade and Development Statistics, various issues.
a. High-case projections.
b. Excludes gold.

TABLE 19 Shares of Regions in World Exports of Goods

(Percentage in 1970 prices)

Region	Year	Scenario[a]	Agriculture	Mineral resources	Light industry	Machinery and equipment	Materials	Invisibles[b]	Total exports
Developed market economies[c]	1970		46.0	43.5	75.2	83.9	85.0	75.0	68.7
	2000	X	47.5	16.4	69.6	73.2	77.4	76.3	64.7
	2000	M	41.4	16.4	66.7	73.2	77.6	74.1	63.2
Centrally planned economies	1970		10.5	12.4	7.5	13.0	6.4	0	9.3
	2000	X	9.8	6.2	9.1	20.2	8.6	0	12.0
	2000	M	8.5	6.2	8.6	20.1	8.5	0	11.7
Developing market economies	1970		32.7	39.3	12.8	1.5	5.1	12.3	16.2
	2000	X	31.6	75.0	13.8	2.7	7.1	11.9	17.2
	2000	M	40.5	75.0	17.4	2.7	7.1	14.4	19.1
Latin America	1970		12.7	10.8	1.2	0.4	1.7	6.2	5.1
	2000	X	12.9	15.6	1.9	0.9	2.7	5.7	4.6
	2000	M	24.0	15.6	2.2	0.9	2.7	7.0	5.5
Asia and the Middle East	1970		12.9	23.8	9.9	1.0	2.6	4.5	8.5
	2000	X	12.1	51.9	11.2	1.7	3.9	4.6	11.0
	2000	M	10.7	52.1	14.4	1.8	3.9	5.6	11.9
Africa (non-oil)	1970		7.1	4.8	1.7	0.1	0.8	1.6	2.5
	2000	X	6.6	7.5	0.7	0.1	0.5	1.6	1.8
	2000	M	5.8	7.4	0.8	0.1	0.5	1.8	1.8

[a] For 2000, X and M indicate names of two scenarios with different assumptions. Scenario M is analysed in the balance-of-payments section.
[b] Including services and transportation.
[c] Not including medium-income regions.

TABLE 20 Regional Structure of Exports of Developing Regions

(Percentage of total exports from each region, based on 1970 prices)

Region	Agriculture	Resources[a]	Light industry	Machinery and equipment	Materials[b]	Invisibles[c]	Subtotals Agriculture and resources	Subtotals Manufacturing
Latin America (medium-income)								
1970	49.4	18.1	3.8	3.4	4.0	21.4	67.5	11.2
2000	21.6	34.9	9.0	11.1	8.6	14.7	56.5	28.7
Latin America (low-income)								
1970	31.6	52.0	2.3	0.7	2.4	10.9	83.6	5.4
2000	17.0	56.0	6.5	2.2	7.6	10.7	73.0	16.3
Middle East								
1970	8.6	84.7	1.2	0.5	0.7	4.3	93.8	2.4
2000	1.9	88.0	4.4	1.6	2.3	1.8	89.9	8.3
Asia (low-income)								
1970	40.3	11.2	26.9	6.5	5.3	9.9	51.5	38.7
2000	16.6	9.3	44.0	13.2	8.7	8.2	25.9	63.9
Africa (arid)								
1970	47.2	14.2	17.2	3.4	5.4	12.6	61.4	26.0
2000	36.3	9.8	23.2	4.0	8.8	17.9	46.1	36.0
Africa (tropical)								
1970	46.7	37.5	5.3	1.0	2.4	7.1	84.2	8.7
2000	23.2	62.8	3.7	0.7	2.3	7.3	86.0	6.7

[a] Resources in this and other tables relating to foreign trade include exports of petroleum, refining products and primary metals.
[b] Materials (manufactured) in this and other tables relating to foreign trade exclude exports of petroleum-refining products and primary metals.
[c] Including services and transportation.

TABLE 21 Shares of Regions in World Imports

(Percentage in 1970 prices)

Region	Year	Scenario[a]	Agriculture	Mineral resources	Light industry	Machinery and equipment	Materials	Invisibles[b]
Developed market economies[c]	1970		63.5	70.6	70.5	63.2	63.8	79.0
	2000	X	43.1	56.0	59.4	45.8	44.5	62.5
	2000	M	43.0	55.8	60.1	47.2	45.8	62.4
Developing market economies	1970		15.3	10.7	16.2	18.8	20.4	13.9
	2000	X	39.4	19.3	22.2	34.0	39.6	27.0
	2000	M	39.4	19.4	20.9	33.5	37.8	27.0
Latin America	1970		3.5	3.5	3.7	6.4	7.0	7.0
	2000	X	7.5	8.2	4.4	12.0	8.9	12.5
	2000	M	8.0	8.2	4.1	10.7	8.1	12.7
Asia and the Middle East	1970		9.3	5.7	9.4	9.3	10.0	5.0
	2000	X	28.6	10.3	15.1	22.0	28.4	12.7
	2000	M	28.3	10.3	14.3	21.3	27.6	12.6
Africa (non-oil)	1970		2.4	1.5	3.1	3.0	3.4	2.0
	2000	X	3.2	0.9	2.7	1.7	2.3	1.8
	2000	M	3.2	0.9	2.5	1.6	2.1	1.7

[a] X and M indicate names of two scenarios with different assumptions. Scenario M is analysed in the balance-of-payments section.
[b] Including services and transportation.
[c] Not including medium-income regions.

TABLE 22 Import Dependence of Developing Regions

(Ratio of import to total requirements, percentage based on 1970 prices)[a]

Region	Year	Scenario	Agriculture	Mineral resources	Light industry	Machinery and equipment	Materials
Latin America (medium-income)	1970		3.0	24.0	4.0	27.0	15.0
	2000	X	3.0	30.0	5.0	24.0	13.0
	2000	M	3.0	28.0	4.0	18.0	9.0
Latin America (low-income)	1970		8.0	12.0	17.0	61.0	37.0
	2000	X	7.0	3.0	19.0	50.0	32.0
	2000	M	7.0	3.0	19.0	50.0	32.0
Middle East	1970		15.0	7.0	27.0	80.0	64.0
	2000	X	12.0	3.0	23.0	36.0	44.0
	2000	M	12.0	3.0	23.0	36.0	44.0
Asia (low-income)	1970		9.0	34.0	16.0	50.0	29.0
	2000	X	10.0	49.0	15.0	40.0	27.0
	2000	M	10.0	47.0	11.0	30.0	20.0
Africa (arid)	1970		8.0	26.0	11.0	31.0	22.0
	2000	X	8.0	15.0	28.0	33.0	26.0
	2000	M	8.0	15.0	21.0	24.0	19.0
Africa (tropical)	1970		7.0	19.0	28.0	80.0	50.0
	2000	X	7.0	13.0	55.0	47.0	59.0
	2000	M	7.0	13.0	55.0	47.0	59.0

[a] Total requirements are the sum of internal consumption and exports.

TABLE 23 Regional Structure of Imports of Developing Regions

(Percentage of total imports of goods into each region, based on 1970 prices)

Region	Agriculture	Resources[a]	Light industry	Machinery and equipment	Materials	Invisibles	Subtotals	
							Agriculture and resources	Manufacturing
Latin America (medium-income)								
1970	10.6	13.1	6.7	37.2	13.6	18.1	23.7	57.5
2000	5.0	17.1	6.4	46.6	11.3	13.5	22.1	64.4
Latin America (low-income)								
1970	11.7	8.4	11.9	37.0	13.2	17.6	20.1	62.1
2000	6.1	1.5	12.6	51.3	14.5	14.0	7.6	78.4
Middle East								
1970	13.9	11.8	12.2	40.0	12.8	9.3	25.7	65.0
2000	7.3	2.1	14.2	47.5	22.7	6.2	9.4	84.4
Asia (low-income)								
1970	21.1	11.6	15.6	31.8	12.2	7.9	32.7	59.6
2000	14.6	13.7	15.6	35.4	13.8	6.9	28.3	64.8
Africa (arid)								
1970	21.0	9.0	15.0	31.3	13.3	10.6	30.0	59.6
2000	13.1	3.1	26.8	30.1	18.2	18.7	16.2	75.1
Africa (tropical)								
1970	13.4	9.7	15.6	37.8	13.2	10.2	23.1	66.6
2000	9.9	7.4	25.3	33.2	14.1	10.1	17.3	72.6

[a] Including services and transportation.

TABLE 24 Trade in Manufactures Among Developing Countries, 1976

From \ To	Destination of Manufactured Exports (percentage of total)						Total Manufactured Exports Traded Among Developing Countries (billion current US dollars)
	East and South Asia	Latin America and Caribbean	Middle East and North Africa	Other Africa	Southern Europe	All Developing Countries	
East and South Asia	26.6[b]	2.3	11.8	5.5	1.3	47.6	9.0
Latin America and Caribbean	0.4	13.9	0.3	1.0	0.6	16.1	3.1
Middle East and North Africa[a]	0.9	0.2	7.6[b]	0.2	0.4	9.3	1.8
Other Africa	0.4	0.4	0.5	3.0	0.5	4.8	0.9
Southern Europe	2.4	4.9	7.2	5.0	2.8	21.2	4.2
All Developing Countries	30.7	21.7	27.4	14.6	5.6	100.0	19.0

Note: Capital surplus oil exporters are included with developing countries in this table, while trade in manufactures excludes SITC 9. Totals may not add due to rounding.

[a] Includes the capital surplus oil exporters; excludes Algeria and Morocco which are counted in "Other Africa".
[b] Includes substantial re-exports of goods manufactured elsewhere.

Sources: Computed from United Nations Yearbook of International Trade Statistics, 1977, Vol. 1, Table B (New York: United Nations, UN Statistical Office), and United Nations Commodity Trade Statistics, Series D (New York: United Nations, UN Statistical Office) for individual countries.

PART III
RESOURCE BIBLIOGRAPHY

This bibliography is entirely restricted to publications in English language and covers the literature since 1970. In a bibliography of this nature, it is essential that the material be as contemporary as possible, while at the same time it was thought desirable to provide a balanced weight of materials discussed over the last decade.

With respect to classification of the material, a bibliographic subject index by item number has been provided at the end of this section.

First part of this bibliography entitled, DEVELOPMENT (GENERAL) has been classified for the general reader, according to the following categories. This classification is arbitrary, however, much cross indexing has been done in the bibliographic subject index following this section of the book.

    A. Problems, Issues and Trends;
    B. Analytical Methods;
    C. Strategies and Policies; and
    D. Country Studies.

Many of the annotations in this section have been compiled from the Journal of Economic Literature, World Bank Publications, IMF-IBRD Joint Library Periodicals, Finance and Development, U.N. Documents and Publisher's Book Promotion Pamphlets.

I. BOOKS

DEVELOPMENT (GENERAL)

01   Abraham, M. Francis
A B   PERSPECTIVES ON MODERNIZATION: TOWARD A GENERAL THEORY OF THIRD WORLD DEVELOPMENT
            Washington, D.C.: University Press of America, 1980.

02   Adelman, Irma and Morris, Cynthia Taft
B   ECONOMIC GROWTH AND SOCIAL EQUITY IN DEVELOPING COUNTRIES
            Stanford, Calif.: Stanford University Press, 1973.

            A quantitative investigation of the interactions among economic growth, political participation, and the distribution of income in noncommunist developing nations. The study is based on data (presented in the earlier study, <u>Society, politics, and economic development</u>) from 74 countries which is given in the form of 48 qualitative measures of the [countries] social, economic, and political characteristics, and it includes the use of discriminant analysis in an examination of the forces tending to increase political participation and the use of a stepwise analysis of variance technique in analyzing the distribution of income.

03   Albin, Peter S.
A B   PROGRESS WITHOUT POVERTY; SOCIALLY RESPONSIBLE ECONOMIC GROWTH
            New York: Basic Books, 1978.

            Examines the relationship among important social tendencies, growth processes, and growth policies and argues for the return of the growth economy, with the caveat that social objectives and policy directions be reformulated to avert ecological disaster and to improve economic welfare. Using a dualistic imbalance framework, explores the style and impact of unbalanced growth in modern industrial capitalism, focusing on educational policy, income distribution, and the control of technology, poverty, and urban decay. Concludes with policy recommendations for a program of social and technical advance that is geared to the intelligent management of a growth economy and the renovation of its distributive mechanisms. An appendix presents a dualistic-imbalance model of modern industrial growth.

04   Alexander, Robert J.
A B C   A NEW DEVELOPMENT STRATEGY
         Maryknoll, N.Y.: Orbis Books, 1976.

Focusing on the demand side of the development equation, this monograph concerns itself with an economic development strategy of import substitution where industries are established to manufacture products for which a home market has already been created by imports. Analyzing the effect on development of this assured demand, and exploring the limit to which this strategy can be used, the author, looks in detail at the prerequisites for the use of this method (substantial imports and protection for newly created industries) and discusses the priorities for private and public investment in this phase. Contends that this process provides a basis for developing countries to decide which projects should be undertaken first and which can be postponed until later.

05   Alvarez, Francisco Casanova
A C   NEW HORIZONS FOR THE THIRD WORLD
         Washington, D.C.: Public Affairs Press, 1976.

Presents the factors leading to approval of the Charter of Economic Rights and Duties of States by the United Nations General Assembly on 12 December 1974. Shows that the charter, with the main objective of overcoming the injustice prevailing in economic relations between nations and [elimination of] the dependence of Third World countries on industrial nations, owes its origin and adoption to President Luis Echeverria of Mexico. Argues that the developing nations remain essentially colonized and dependent entities of the industrialized world. Concludes that the future world will be less unjust and less ridden with anxiety, more secure and better able to care for its own if we respect the principles of the charter.

06   Anell, Lars and Nygren, Birgitta
A B C   THE DEVELOPING COUNTRIES AND THE WORLD ECONOMIC ORDER
         New York: St. Marin's Press, 1980.

Explores the possible form, functioning, and enforcement of a New International Economic Order (NIEO). Provides an account of the demands of developing countries for a better allocation of the world's resources and considers the early cooperation between developing and developed countries, particularly resolutions passed at various U.N. General Assembly sessions. Also analyzes and comments on the central NIEO demands. Among the possible actions the authors suggest developing countries could take are: (1) force industrialized countries to increase the flow and quality of aid by threatening trade discrimination; (2) establish a list of honest consultancy firms and a file of information on technology procurement; and (3) feel free to steal patents from big corporations and make use of copyrights without compensation.

07 Angelopoulos, Angelos T.
A C FOR A NEW POLICY OF INTERNATIONAL DEVELOPMENT
New York: Praeger, 1977.

08 Angelopoulos, Angelos T.
A C THE THIRD WORLD AND THE RICH COUNTRIES;
PROSPECTS FOR THE YEAR 2000
Translated by N. Constantinidis and C. R. Corner
New York: Praeger, 1972.

An examination and projection of the gap in incomes between the developed and underdeveloped countries of the world. The author brings data on and discusses the indicators of poverty, the population explosion in the developing world, the main causes of economic backwardness, the "myth" of development aid, the need for a new international development strategy, various strategies of development financing, precipitating factors in the emergence of the Third World, economic growth and forecasts of world income in the year 2000, and the possibilities of China becoming the spokesman for the Third World.

09 Arkhurst, Frederick S., ed.
B C D AFRICA IN THE SEVENTIES AND EIGHTIES;
ISSUES IN DEVELOPMENT
New York and London: Praeger in cooperation with the Adlai Stevenson Institute of International Affairs, 1970.

Eleven experts in various fields express their views in a symposium "Africa in the 1980's" which met in Chicago in early 1969 under the auspices of the Adlai Stevenson Institute of International Affairs. The purpose...was to attempt to draw a portrait of Africa in the 1980's on the basis of the experience of the past decade and, also, on the basis of current trends in the area of politics, economic development, population, agriculture, trade, education and law - all viewed as composite and interactive factors in the development process.

10
A B C
Arndt, H. W., et al.
THE WORLD ECONOMIC CRISIS: A COMMONWEALTH PERSPECTIVE
London: Commonwealth Secretariat, 1980.

Report of a group of experts from Commonwealth countries on obstacles to structural change and sustained economic growth, with recommendations for specific measures by which developed and developing countries might act to reduce or eliminate such constraints. Focuses on the implications of the world economic crises - inflation, slowdown of economic growth, and staggering disequilibria in balance of payments - for the developing countries of the Third World. Stresses the need for collective action in view of the interdependence of the world economy.

11
A C D
Bairoch, Paul
THE ECONOMIC DEVELOPMENT OF THE THIRD WORLD SINCE 1900
Translated from the fourth French edition by Cynthia Postan
Berkeley: University of California Press, 1975.

The author covers a wide range of factors important to development, namely population, agriculture, extractive industry, manufacturing industry, foreign trade, education, urbanization, the labor force and employment, and macroeconomic data. Particular attention is devoted to the development of agriculture. Comparison is drawn between the economic progress of Third World countries and developed countries at a similar stage of industrialization. Twenty-four countries were selected for the analysis, representing 80 percent of the population of the Third World. These include seven countries from each of Africa, Latin-America, and Asia respectively, and three countries from the Middle East.

12
A B
Bairoch, Paul and Levy-Leboyer, Maurice, eds.
DISPARITIES IN ECONOMIC DEVELOPMENT SINCE THE INDUSTRIAL REVOLUTION
New York: St. Martin's Press, 1981.

Collection of thirty-five previously unpublished essays presented at the 7th International Economic History Congress in Edinburgh in August 1978. Main theme deals with disparities in economic development. Concerns differences in income at micro-regional and international levels. In four parts: (1) discussing economic disparities among nations (two papers on international disparities: ten on the Third World and five on the developed world); (2) covering regional economic disparities (eight essays on northern, western, and central Europe; three on France; two on Southern Europe and one on the Third World); (3) detailing relations between regional and national disparities (two papers); and (4) discussing the methodological aspects of measurement of economic disparities (two papers).

13   Baldwin, Robert E.
B C   ECONOMIC DEVELOPMENT AND GROWTH
        New York, London, Sydney and Toronto: John Wiley and
        Sons, Inc., 1972.

        This short text seeks to provide "an analysis of economic
        development that in terms of breadth and sophistication
        lies between the usual elementary and advanced approaches
        to the development topic." It is organized around three
        themes, i.e., what the nature of growth problem is, what
        the main theories of growth and development are, and
        what the main policy issues facing less developed countries
        are. Therefore, the chapters deal with the characteristics
        of poverty, various classical development theories
        relatively more recent contributions to development theory,
        national and sectoral policies for growth, and issues
        in the financing of development.

14   Bauer, P.T.
B C   DISSENT ON DEVELOPMENT. STUDIES AND DEBATES IN DEVELOPMENT
        ECONOMICS
        Cambridge, Mass.: Harvard University Press, 1972.

        A collection of previously published articles, essays,
        and book reviews, some of which have been rewritten and
        expanded, dealing with various theoretical and empirical
        issues in economic development. Part One ("Ideology
        and Experience") examines general problems of concept
        method, analysis, historical experience and policy in
        economic development, such as the vicious circle of
        poverty, the widening gap, central planning, foreign
        aid, Marxism, etc. Part Two ("Case Studies") features
        five of the author's studies on developing countries,
        particularly Nigeria and India. Part Three ("Review
        Articles") brings book reviews on such well known books
        as W. Arthur Lewis' The Theory of Economic Growth, Benjamin
        Higgins' Economic Development, Walt W. Rostow's The Stages
        of Economic Growth, Thomas Balogh's The Economics of
        Poverty, and other volumes by Gunnar Myrdal, John Pincus,
        Harry G. Johnson, E.A.G. Robinson, B.K. Madan and Jagdish
        Bhagwati.

15   Bauer, P.T.
A B   EQUALITY, THE THIRD WORLD AND ECONOMIC DELUSION
        Cambridge, Mass.: Harvard University Press, 1981.

        Critique of methods and finding of contemporary economics,
        particularly development economics, arguing that there
        is a hiatus between accepted opinion and evident reality.
        All but four chapters are extended and/or revised versions
        of previously published articles. In the three parts:
        equality, the West and the Third World, and the state
        of economics. Criticizes economics and especially
        development economics for disregard of personal qualities

and social and political arrangements as determinants of economic achievement and for ignoring the role of external contracts in extending markets. Notes that the benefits of mathematical economics have been bought at the cost of an uncritical attitude, which has led to inappropriate use and in some cases to an emphasis on form rather than substance.

16   Berry, Leonard and Kates, Robert W., eds.
A C   MAKING THE MOST OF THE LEAST
      New York: Holmes and Meier Publishers, 1979.

The poverty faced by Third World countries today seriously challenges the stability of the world order. The contributors look torward the restructuring of the present economic order by establishing "harmonious linkages" between the industrialized and nonindustrialized worlds. A welcome addition to the literature on economic development.

17   Bhatt, V. V.
A B C   DEVELOPMENT PERSPECTIVES: PROBLEM, STRATEGY AND POLICIES
        Oxford; New York: Sydney and Toronto: Pergamon Press, 1980.

Discusses the dynamics of the socioeconomic system in terms of the cumulative and cyclical changes in economic institutions, ideologies, and technology. Stresses the importance of: upgrading traditional technology and adapting modern technology to given situations; the financial system, since it affects savings and shapes the pattern of resource allocation; and upgrading of agricultural organization and technology. Sets forth as necessary for the development process: the stability of the international currencey and the international monetary system, which the author proposes be linked to prices of primary products; the shaping of the international monetary-financial-trade system to be consistent with LDC's development strategy; and viewing the process of socioeconomic development as an integral part of nation-building and of building the international community.

18   Brown, Lester R.
A C   THE GLOBAL ECONOMIC PROSPECT: NEW SOURCES OF ECONOMIC STRESS
      Worldwatch Paper no. 20
      Washington, D.C.: Worldwatch Institute; New York, 1978.

Considers the relationship between the expanding global economy and the earth's natural systems. Discusses the increase in fuel costs, suggesting that the world is running out of cheap energy; diminishing returns in grain production and to fertilizer use; overfishing; global inflation; capital shortages; unemployment; and the changing growth prospect. Concludes that future economic policies must shift from growth to sustainability; not advocating abandonment of growth as a goal, but with concern for carrying capacities of biological system. Fisheries, forests, grasslands, and croplands, require development of alternative energy sources and population policies consistent with resource availability.

19 Chenery, Hollis and Syrquin, Moises
A B C   PATTERNS OF DEVELOPMENT, 1950-1970
Assisted by Hazel Elkington
New York and London: Oxford University Press, 1975.

Examines principal changes in economic structure that normally accompany economic growth, focusing on resource mobilization and allocation, particularly those aspects needed to sustain further growth. These aspects are treated in a uniform econometric framework to provide a consistent description of a number of interrelated types of structural change and also to identify systematic differences in development patterns among countries that are following different development strategies. The major aim of the research is to separate the effects of universal factors affecting all countries from particular characteristics. The authors use data for 101 countries in the period 1950 to 1970. Countries are grouped into three categories: large country, balanced allocation; small country, industry specialization. Chapter 5 compares the results obtained from time-series data with those observed from cross-sectional data. Results are obtained from regression techniques, where income level and population are treated as exogenous variables. The demographic variables show how the movement of population from rural to urban areas and lowering of the birth rate and death rate have influenced demand and supply of labor. A technical appendix discusses the methods used, the problems encountered, and all the regression equations specified in this study.

20 Chenery, Hollis B., et al., eds.
A B C   STUDIES IN DEVELOPMENT PLANNING
Cambridge, Mass.: Harvard University Press, 1971.

Attempts to bring together the contributors' varied backgrounds in both field work and the use of quantitative techniques and show how modern methods can be used in operational development planning.

21 Chodak, Szymon
A B   SOCIETAL DEVELOPMENT: FIVE APPROACHES WITH CONCLUSIONS FROM COMPARATIVE ANALYSIS
New York: Oxford University Press, 1973.

A sociologist analyzes the development and change of societies using five different conceptual approaches, attempting to view the processes of development in society from a multidimensional synthesizing perspective. These five approaches are called: "Evolutionary Theories," "Development - The Growing Societal Systemness," "Development and Innovation in the Search for Security," "Economic and Political Development," and "Modernization." The author gives references to the societal development which has taken place in various parts of the world and under different political systems.

22 Colman, David and Nixson, Frederick
A B C ECONOMICS OF CHANGE IN LESS DEVELOPED COUNTRIES
New York: Wiley, Halsted Press, 1978.

Analyzes the changes that are occurring in the less-developed countries (LDC's); considers the problems generated by change; and examines the agents of change. Emphasizes the internal (rather than the international) aspects of development and focuses on economic inequality within LDC's and the impact on the development process in agriculture and industry of different income distributions. Although recognizing the impact of transnational corporations on the nature and characteristics of development within the LDC's, the authors argue that it is the LDC government that is responsible for the economic policies pursued. Also outlines the concepts and measurement of development, and reviews the literature on economic theorizing about development. A final chapter discusses inflation and migration in LDC's. Authors note that too often policy recommendations ignore political acceptability and recommend that the economist should cooperate with the political scientist in the study of inflation and with the sociologist in the study of rural urban migration.

23 Corbet, Hugh and Jackson, Robert, eds.
A B C IN SEARCH OF A NEW WORLD ECONOMIC ORDER
New York and Toronto: Wiley, Halsted Press, 1974.

Focuses on the reform of the international commercial systems for further liberalizations of world trade. Papers are grouped into four categories: (1) introduction, (2) general factors affecting negotiations, (3) outside issues of significance, (4) issues on the agenda.

24 Fields, Gary S.
A B C D POVERTY, INEQUALITY, AND DEVELOPMENT
New York and London: Cambridge University Press, 1980.

Focuses on the distributional aspects of economic development and explores the impact of the rate and type of growth on poverty and inequality in poor countries. Findings show that in general growth reduces poverty, but a high aggregate growth rate is neither necessary nor sufficient for reducing absolute poverty or relative inequality. Uses case studies of distribution and development in Costa Rica, Sri Lanka, India, Brazil, the Phillippines, and Taiwan to examine which combinations of circumstances and policies led to differential performance. Concludes that a commitment to developing to help the poor does not guarantee progress, but it helps a great deal. In its absence, the flow of resources to the haves, with only some trickle down to the have-nots, will be perpetuated.

25 Finger, J. M.
A B D INDUSTRIAL COUNTRY POLICY AND ADJUSTMENT TO IMPORTS FROM DEVELOPING COUNTRIES
World Bank Staff Working Paper no. 470, July 1981.

A background study for World Development Report 1981. Reviews and interprets recent analyses of the policies established by industrial countries in response to increasing imports from developing countries.

26 Finger, Nachum
A C D THE IMPACT OF GOVERNMENT SUBSIDIES ON INDUSTRIAL MANAGEMENT: THE ISRAELI EXPERIENCE
New York: Praeger, 1971.

27 Fitzgerald, E. V.
A B PUBLIC SECTOR INVESTMENT PLANNING FOR DEVELOPING COUNTRIES
New York: Holmes and Meier, 1978.

28 Florence, P. Sargant
A B C ECONOMICS AND SOCIOLOGY OF INDUSTRY: A REALISTIC ANALYSIS OF DEVELOPMENT
Baltimore, Md.: Johns Hopkins University Press, 1969.

29 Frank, Andre Gunder
A B C CRISIS IN THE THIRD WORLD
New York: Holmes and Meier, 1981.

30 Frank, Andre Gunder
A B DEPENDENT ACCUMULATION AND UNDERDEVELOPMENT
New York and London: Monthly Review Press, 1979.

Explains underdevelopment by an analysis of the production and exchange relations of dependence. Distinguishes the three main stages or periods in this world embracing process of capital accumulation and capitalist development: mercantilist (1500-1770), industrial capitalist (1770-1870), and imperialist (1870-1930). Analyzes each period in terms of history, trade relations between the metropolis and the periphery, and transformation of the modes or relations of production, and the development of underdevelopment in the principal regions of Asia, Africa, and the Americas.

31   Frank, Charles R., Jr., and Webb, Richard C., eds.
A B D INCOME DISTRIBUTION AND GROWTH IN THE LESS-DEVELOPED COUNTRIES
Washington, D.C.: Brookings Institution, 1977.

Fourteen previously unpublished essays representing part of the results of a project undertaken jointly by the Brookings Institution and the Woodrow Wilson School of Public and International Affairs at Princeton University, dealing with the relation between income distribution and economic growth in the developing countries. The first two articles present an overview of income distribution policy and discuss the causes of growth and income distribution in LDC's, respectively. The next nine examine the relation between income distribution and different economic policies and factors, including: industrialization, education, population, wage, fiscal, agricultural, public works, health and urban land policies.

32   Gant, George F.
A B   DEVELOPMENT ADMINISTRATION - CONCEPTS, GOALS, METHODS
Madison, Wisconsin: The University of Wisconsin Press, 1979.

Growth and modernization in the less developed countries (LDC's) during the past three decades has frequently depended upon the state's ability to plan and manage a range of developmental activities. Gant's study of development administration looks at some of the issues that could be of concern to managers in LDC's: in particular, coordination, budgeting, the selection of personnel, training, etc. He also delves into the administrative side of certain specific governmental concerns, such as family planning and education, drawing on examples from a number of Asian countries. This is not a book which goes into much technical detail. Nor does it tell one how to design an efficient administrative setup. Primarily for the general reader interested in an overview of these topics.

33   Garbacz, Christopher
A B D INDUSTRIAL POLARIZATION UNDER ECONOMIC INTEGRATION IN LATIN AMERICA
Austin, Texas: Bureau of Business Research, Graduate School of Business, The University of Texas, 1971.

The author discusses the problem of increased disparities in the levels of regional economic development that tend to come about as a result of economic integration. The political and economic implications of industrial polarization are studies within the context and experience of the Central American Common Market and the Latin American Free Trade Association. Finally, the author considers the problem in the light of the planned Latin American Common Market, discussing the various measures that could be taken as well as the implications for the future.

34   Garzouzi, Eva
A B C   ECONOMIC GROWTH AND DEVELOPMENT: THE LESS DEVELOPED COUNTRIES
        New York: Vantage Press, 1972.

Essays to consolidate into one readable text the whole of the economics of growth and development. Part I discusses the meaning and theories of economic development, outlines historical patterns of development, and summarizes the impact of capital, agriculture, industry, monetary and fiscal policies, international trade, and foreign aid on economic growth. Part II presents comparative analyses of developing regions, including Latin America, the Middle East and North Africa, Africa south of the Sahara, and Southeast Asia.

35   Geithman, David T., ed.
A B C D   FISCAL POLICY FOR INDUSTRIALIZATION AND DEVELOPMENT IN LATIN AMERICA
          Gainesville: University Presses of Florida.

Collection of 10 previously unpublished papers (and related comments) presented at the Twenty-First Annual Latin American Conference held in February 1971. Central theme of the conference was the analysis and evaluation of the interaction among fiscal problems, fiscal tools, and fiscal systems in the industrializing economies of Latin America.

36   Ghai, D. P.
A B C   THE BASIC-NEEDS APPROACH TO DEVELOPMENT: SOME ISSUES REGARDING CONCEPTS AND METHODOLOGY
        ILO, Geneva, 1977.

Contains five papers which discuss issues which arise in the formulation of criteria and approaches for the promotion of employment and the satisfaction of the basic needs of a country's population. Presents the first results of the research and conceptual work initiated by the ILO to help countries implement the basic needs-oriented strategy recommended by the World Employment Conference in 1976.

37 Gianaris, Nicholas V.
A B C ECONOMIC DEVELOPMENT: THOUGHT AND PROBLEMS
North Quincy, Mass.: Christopher Publishing House, 1978.

Part one examines the process of development, the historical perspective, mathematical models, and modern theories of development; part two considers domestic problems of development, specifically land and other natural resources, human resources (particularly the role of education), capital formation and technological change, the allocation of resources, and the role of government and planning; part three discusses the international aspects of development (foreign trade, aid, investment, and multinationals) and current issues such as environmental problems, the status of women, income inequalities, and discrimination.

38 Giersch, Herbert, ed.
A B C D INTERNATIONAL ECONOMIC DEVELOPMENT AND RESOURCE TRANSFER: WORKSHOP 1978
Tubingen, Germany: J. C. B. Mohr, 1979.

Twenty-four previously unpublished papers from a workshop held in June 1978 at the <u>Institut</u> <u>fur</u> <u>Weltwirtschaft</u>, Kiel University. Contributions organized under ten headings: Rural Industrialization, Employment and Economic Development; Choice of Techniques and Industries for Growth and Employment; Agricultural Patterns and Policies in Developing Countries; Hypotheses for the Commodity Composition of East-West Trade; The Relationship Between the Domestic and International Sectors in Economic Development; Patterns of Trade in Services and Knowledge, Changes in Industrial Interdependencies and Final Demand in Economic Development; Public Aid for Investment in Manufacturing Industries; Institutional and Economic Criteria for the Choice of Technology in Developing Countries; and Problems of Measuring the Production and Absorption of Technologies in Developing Countries.

39 Gierst, Friedrich and Matthews, Stuart R.
A B C GUIDELINES FOR CONTRACTING FOR INDUSTRIAL PROJECTS IN DEVELOPING COUNTRIES
New York: United Nations Publications, 1975.

Designed to serve public and private organizations in developing countries as a guide in preparing contracts concerned with industrial investment projects. Examines various stages involved in the preparation of an industrial project and discusses the basic types of contacts involved (i.e. those with financial institutions, with consultants and with contractors).

40 Gill, Richard T.
A B C ECONOMIC DEVELOPMENT: PAST AND PRESENT

Third Edition. Foundations of Modern Economics. Englewood Cliffs, N.J.: Prentice-Hall, 1973.

Third edition of an introductory textbook with revisions of the discussions. The Green Revolution, two-gap analysis of foreign aid, Denison-Jorgenson-Griliches studies of factors affecting United States economic growth and Leibenstein's "X-efficiency" concept have been added. Statistical tables have been updated to include figures on Chinese economic growth. Six chapters cover: 1) General factors in economic development, 2) Theories of development, 3) Beginnings of development in advanced countries, 4) Growth of the American economy, 5) Problems of underdeveloped countries, and 6) Development in China and India.

41 Goulet, Denis
A B C THE CRUEL CHOICE: A NEW CONCEPT IN THE THEORY OF DEVELOPMENT
Cambridge, Mass.: Center for the Study of Development and Social Change, Atheneum, 1971.

This work is intended to probe moral dilemmas faced by economic and social development. Its central concern is that philosophical conceptions about the "good life" and the "good society" should be of more profound importance in assessing alternative paths to development than economic, political, or technological questions. The theoretical analysis is based on two concepts: "vulnerability" and "existence rationality." Vulnerability is defined as exposure to forces that can not be controlled, and is expressed in the failure of many low-income countries to attain their development goals, as well as in manifestations of mass alienation in certain societies where prosperity has already been achieved. Existence rationality denotes those strategies used by all societies to possess information and to make practical choices designed to assure survival and satisfy their needs for esteem and freedom. These strategies vary with a country's needs and are conditioned by numerous constraints.

42 Griffin, Keith
A B C INTERNATIONAL INEQUALITY AND NATIONAL POVERTY
New York: Holms & Meier, 1978.

Nine essays, seven previously published between 1970 and 1978. Challenges the classical assumption that unrestricted international intercourse will reduce inequality and poverty. Argues that forces creating inequality are automatic, and not due to malevolence of developed nations or corporations, but that the motor of change in the contemporary world economy is technical innovation. Since the advances tend to be concentrated in the developed countries where they are applicable to their technology, rich countries are able to extract supra-normal profits and rents from the poor countries through trade. The high level of factor earnings in rich countries attract the most valuable financial and human resources of the poor countries through induced international migration. Divided into two parts, part one deals with international inequality and discusses: the international transmission of inequality; multinational corporations; foreign capital, domestic savings, and economic development; emigration, and the New International Economic Order. The essays in part two focus on national poverty, discussing the facts of poverty in the Third World, analyzing models of development, and assessing the Chinese system of incentives.

43
A B C
Griffin, Keith B. and Enos, John L.
PLANNING DEVELOPMENT
Reading, Mass.; Don Mills, Ontario; Sydney; London; and Manila: Addison-Wesley, 1971.

Part of a series intended to serve as guidebooks on development economics, this book deals with practical problems of planning and economic policy in underdeveloped countries. Consists of four parts: 1) the role of planning, 2) quantitative planning techniques, 3) sector policies, and 4) planning in practice with reference to Chile, Columbia, Ghana, India, Pakistan and Turkey.

44
A B C
Hagen, Everett E.
THE ECONOMICS OF DEVELOPMENT
Revised Edition. The Irwin Series in Economics.
Homewood, Ill.: Irwin, 1975.

Revised edition with two new chapters added, one dealing with the earth's stock of minerals and economic growth, and the other on the relationships between economic growth and the distribution of income. Chapters on population and economic planning have been extensively revised, with the former focusing on the relationship of food supply to continued world growth. Additional changes include: reorganization of the discussion of growth theories; a considerably augmented discussion of entrepreneurhsip; and a reorganization of the chapters on import substitution versus export expansion and external finance.

45
B C
Helleiner, G. K., ed.
A WORLD DIVIDED: THE LESS DEVELOPED COUNTRIES IN THE INTERNATIONAL ECONOMY
Perspectives on Development, no. 5
New York; London and Melbourne: Cambridge University Press, 1976.

Twelve papers discussing the new policies and instruments needed if the interests of poor nations are to be met. Within the realm of trade, consideration is given to the possibility of increased cooperation through: supply management schemes; bargaining capacity and power; closer ties with other less developed countries; and the development of alternative marketing channels and joint sales efforts. Relations between the less developed countries and transnational firms is then considered with special attention given to the factors affecting the bargaining position of the countries. Issues in international finance and monetary policy are: the borrowing of Eurodollars by less developed countries, internationally agreed upon principles for an honorable debt default, and interests of less developed countries in a new international monetary order. Another paper considers means by which a self-reliant but poor country can seek to conduct its economic affairs in the face of a most inhospitable and uncertain international environment. The concluding paper considers the implication of the new mood in the less developed countries for future international organisation.

46   Hermassi, Elbaki
A C D   THE THIRD WORLD REASSESSED
        Berkeley: University of California Press, 1980.

47   Horowitz, Irving Louis, ed.
A B C   EQUITY, INCOME, AND POLICY: COMPARATIVE STUDIES IN THREE
        WORLDS OF DEVELOPMENT
        New York and London: Praeger, 1977.

Ten previously unpublished papers by sociologists and economists on the multiple ideologies of development and the drive toward equity congruent with different social systems. Six essays address the problems of the "First World," i.e. those types of societies dominated by a free market and an open society, where the main problem would seem to be how to maintain growth and development while providing distributive justice. Two papers look at the "Second World" of socialism; these assume the central role of state power as imposing its will to produce equity. The remaining papers consider the Third World, examining in particular income distribution in Tanzania and economic equality and social class in general.

48   Jalan, Bimal
A B C   ESSAYS IN DEVELOPMENT POLICY
        Delhi: S. G. Wasani for Macmillan of India, 1975.

A common theme of the 11 essays (some previously published) is the explicit reference to political philosophies involved in the choices of means and objectives of development and social change. Essays include: discussion of self-reliance objectives; trade and industrialization policies; distribution of income; the project evaluation manual of Professors Little and Mirrlees; UNIDO guidelines for project evaluation; criteria for determination of appropriate terms of aid assistance; the definition and assessment of performance in developing countries; the history of the United Nations Capital Development Fund, the World Bank, and the International Development Association; and an analysis of the principal recommendations of the Pearson Commission Report (1969).

49 Jumper, Sidney R.; Bell, Thomas L. and Ralston, Bruce A.
B C ECONOMIC GROWTH AND DISPARITIES: A WORLD VIEW
Englewood Cliffs, N.J.: Prentice-Hall, 1980.

The authors emphasize understanding of real world differences in levels of human development, rather than sophisticated analytical procedures. In seven parts: geographical concepts; the factors influencing variations in levels of development; world food supplies; minerals; factors affecting intensity of manufacturing development; the service industries; and a summary of the role of geographers in facing these development problems.

50 Kahn, Herman
A B C WORLD ECONOMIC DEVELOPMENT: 1979 AND BEYOND
With the Hudson Institute.
Boulder: Westview Press, 1979.

Examines economic prospects focusing on the period 1978-2000, and particularly the earlier part of the period. In two parts, part one presents the general historical framework, concepts, and perspectives on economic growth and cultural change. Part two examines the major trends and problems of the real world, focusing on the elements of change and continuity in both the advanced and developing economies. Rejects attempts by some to stop the world and argues for and suggests strategies for rapid worldwide economic growth, for Third World industrialization, and for the use of advanced (or at least appropriate) technology.

51 Kasdan, Alan R.
A B C THE THIRD WORLD: A NEW FOCUS FOR DEVELOPMENT
Cambridge, Mass.: Schenkman Publishing, 1973.

52 Kindleberger, Charles P. and Herrick, Bruce
B ECONOMIC DEVELOPMENT
Third Edition. Economics Handbook Series.
New York; London; Paris and Tokyo: McGraw-Hill, 1977.

Textbook that survey[s] the present panorama of international poverty, the applications to it of economic analysis, and the policies for improvement that the analysis implies. This edition which has been completely rewritten and updated, includes new chapters on: population, urbanization, collective international action, employment, income distribution, and the theories of economic development.

53
A B C

Leipziger, Danny M., ed.
BASIC NEEDS AND DEVELOPMENT
Foreword by Paul P. Streeten
Cambridge, Mass.: Oelgeschlager, Gunn & Hain, 1981.

Five previously unpublished essays discuss the potential contribution of the basic needs approach to developmental theory and practice. Michael J. Crosswell gives his views in two essays on a development planning approach and on growth, poverty alleviation, and foreign assistance. Maureen A. Lewis discusses sectional aspects of the linkages among population, nutrition, and health. Danny M. Leipziger writes about policy issues and the basic human needs approach. Martha de Melo presents a case study of Sri Lanka focusing on the effects of alternative approaches to basic human needs. The authors are all economists.

54
A B C

Leontief, Wassily, et al.
THE FUTURE OF THE WORLD ECONOMY: A UNITED NATIONS STUDY
New York: Oxford University Press, 1977.

Investigates the interrelationships between future world economic growth and availability of natural resources, pollution, and the impact of environmental policies. Includes a set of alternative projections of the demographic, economic, and environmental states of the world in the years 1980, 1990, and 2000 with a comparison with the world economy of 1970. Constructs a multiregional input-output economic model of the world economy. Investigates some of the main problems of economic growth and development in the world as a whole, with special accent on problems encountered by the developing countries. The findings include: (1) target rates of growth of gross product in the developing regions...are not sufficient to start closing the income gap between the developing and the developed countries; (2) the principal limits to sustained economic growth and accelerated development are political, social and institutional in character rather than physical; (3) the necessary increased food production is technically feasible, but dependent on drastically favorable public policy measure; (4) pollution is not an unmanageable problem.

55   Lin, Ching-Yuan
A C D DEVELOPING COUNTRIES IN A TURBULENT WORLD: PATTERNS OF ADJUSTMENT SINCE THE OIL CRISIS
New York: Praeger, 1981.

Examines national authorities' policy reactions to changes in the world economy since 1973, to determine whether differences in national economic performances can be explained in terms of differences in their policy reactions. Investigates global patterns of absorption, production, and adjustment since the oil crisis; global expenditure flows before and after the crisis; and international bank transactions and world trade. Reviews the experiences of developing countries during the period, focusing on non-oil countries. Finds that collectively the non-oil developing countries experienced a much milder contraction of domestic demand and real ouput than the more developed countries after the disturbances in 1973-75, although individual experiences varied; however, inflation remains persistent. Argues that most developing countries did not pursue demand management policies early enough to counteract sharp changes in external demand.

56   Madhava, K. B., ed.
A B C D INTERNATIONAL DEVELOPMENT, 1969: CHALLENGES TO PREVALENT IDEAS ON DEVELOPMENT
Dobbs Ferry: Oceana for Society for International Development, 1970.

Contains the proceedings of the 11th World Conference of the Society for International Development held in 1969 in New Delhi. The theme "Challenges to Prevalent Ideas on Development" was carried out through roundtable discussions centering on: the redefinition of goals; foreign aid; manpower, education, and development; population communication; social communication; political and social-cultural requisites; and challenges to theorists and strategists.

57   May, Brian
A C D THE THIRD WORLD CALAMITY
London and Boston: Routledge & Kegan Paul, 1981.

Assessment of social conditions, politics, economics, and cultural barriers in the Third World, with particular reference to India, Iran, and Nigeria. Contends that the "chronic socio-economic stagnation" that characterizes these countries is not attributable to Western imperialism, maintaining that fundamental change in Third World countries was and is blocked by psychological and cultural facts. Compares relevant factors in Europe and in the three countries to show the constraints that block significant socioeconomic change.

58   McGreevey, William Paul, ed.
A B C   THIRD-WORLD POVERTY: NEW STRATEGIES FOR MEASURING
         DEVELOPMENT PROGRESS
         Lexington, Mass.: Heath, Lexington Books, 1980.

Five previously unpublished papers on the problems of measuring progress in alleviating poverty in the Third World, originally part of a series of seminars (1976-79) sponsored by the Agency for International Development. Editor McGreevey reviews the development progress from both a human capital and poverty alleviation standpoint; Gary S. Fields looks at absolute-poverty measures (i.e., those not depending on income distribution considerations); Harry J. Bruton considers the use of available employment and unemployment data in assessing government poverty policy, and G. Edward Schuh and Robert L. Thompson discuss measures of agricultural progress and government commitment to agricultural development. The fifth paper by Nancy Birdsall is a summary of discussion in two seminars on time-use surveys and networks of social support in LDC's.
The authors find in part that: (1) existing data are inadequate to judge progress; (2) the best data gathering method is multipurpose household surveys; and (3) networks of social support are important (and unmeasured) means of income transfer between households.

59   McHale, John and McHale, Magda C.
A B C   BASIC HUMAN NEEDS: A FRAMEWORK FOR ACTION
         New Brunswick, N.J.: Rutgers University, Transaction
         Books, 1978.

60   Meadows, Dennis L., ed.
A B C   ALTERNATIVES TO GROWTH--I: A SEARCH FOR SUBSTAINABLE
         FUTURES: PAPERS ADAPTED FROM ENTRIES TO THE 1975 GEORGE
         AND CYNTHIA MITCHELL PRIZE AND FROM PRESENTATIONS BEFORE
         THE 1975 ALTERNATIVES TO GROWTH CONFERENCE, HELD AT
         THE WOODLANDS, TEXAS
         Cambridge, Mass.: Lippincott, Ballinger, 1977.

Seventeen previously unpublished interdisciplinary papers on the transition from growth to a steady-state society, i.e., a society with a constant stock of physical wealth and a constant stock of people. In four parts: the relation between population and food or energy; economic alternatives; the rationales, mechanisms, and implications of various long-term planning proposals; and analysis of the determinants, nature, and implications of current paradigms, norms, laws, and religion.

61   Melady, Thomas Patrick and Suhartono, R. B.
A B   DEVELOPMENT -- LESSONS FOR THE FUTURE
         Maryknoll, New York: Orbis Books, 1973.

Investigation of what determines, economically, which countries are developing, based on examination of characteristics of nations agreed to be undergoing this experience. The study examines such facets of development as the nonhomogeneity of the developing countries; factors affecting economic growth, the sectoral aspect of growth (industry and agriculture), measurements of the phenomenon, and the applicability of economic theory in this work; and the effects of economic development on man and his role in society.

62 Morawetz, David
A B D TWENTY-FIVE YEARS OF ECONOMIC DEVELOPMENT, 1950 TO 1975
Johns Hopkins University Press for IBRD, 1977.

Assesses development programs of developing countries and global development targets adopted by international organizations over the past 25 years. Chapters cover: a) changing objectives of development; b) growth in GNP per capita, population and the gap between rich and poor countries; c) reduction of poverty including employment, income distribution, basic needs, nutrition, health, housing and education; d) self-reliance and economic independence; and e) conclusions, hypotheses, and questions.

63 Morgan, Theodore
B C ECONOMIC DEVELOPMENT: CONCEPT AND STRATEGY
New York and London: Harper & Row, 1975.

Textbook in economic development with emphasis on policy, its appropriate definition, its targets, and its improvement of application. Diverts focus from GNP and average income growth rates and into issues such as income distribution, nutrition, disease, climate, and population increases and their effects on development. Surveys existing theoretical literature. Discusses development planning and the importance of the statistical foundation of decision-making, and planning techniques such as cost-benefit analysis. Provides sporadic data for less-developed countries, mostly for the post-World War II period, on various national variables.

64 Ramati, Yohanan, ed.
A B C ECONOMIC GROWTH IN DEVELOPING COUNTRIES--MATERIAL AND HUMAN RESOURCES: PROCEEDINGS OF THE SEVENTH REHOVOT CONFERENCE
Praeger Special Studies in International Economics and Development
New York and London: Praeger in cooperation with the Continuation Committee of the Rehovot Conference, 1975.

Collection of 49 papers presented in September 1973. The papers are grouped into five sections following the

structure of the conference. Part I includes papers
setting the framework to analyze natural and human
resources as factors in development and problems of
planning and the quality of life. Part II includes papers
on resources, technology, and income distribution. Part
III deals with external constraints on development. Part
IV examines planning and implementation. Part V contains
the very brief closing addresses by Simon Kuznets and
Abba Eban. Participants included 99 experts and policy
makers for developing countries in Africa, Latin America,
and Southeast Asia.

65   Rubinson, Richard, ed.
A B   DYNAMICS OF WORLD DEVELOPMENT
            Political Economy of the World-System Annuals, vol. 4
            Beverly Hills and London: Sage, 1981.

Twelve previously unpublished papers, almost all by
sociologists, presented at the Fourth Annual Political
Economy of the World-System conference at Johns Hopkins
University, June 1980. Papers are based on the assumption
that the world's history is the history of capitalist
accumulation; and that capitalist development is the
development of a single...modern world-system. Papers
cover: development in peripheral areas; development
in semiperipheral states; development and state
organization; cycles and trends of world system
development; theooretical issues; and dynamics of
development of the world economy.

66   Sachs, Ignacy
A C   THE DISCOVERY OF THE THIRD WORLD
            Cambridge, Mass., and London: M. I. T. Press, 1976.

Focusing on a redefinition of development theory, discusses
the role of ethnocentrism and domination by European
and Western ideas in such areas as science, technology,
and economics. Argues that discussions regarding economic
development strategies attempt to apply Western theories
and ignore the fact that Third World growth, unlike
capital-intensive European growth, must be based on the
use of labor. Proposes a general development theory to
bridge the gap between European theory and Third World
practice and discusses problems such as economic surplus
and economic aid. Recommends that the U.N. assess Western
nations and funnel the money to Third World nations on
a "no-strings" basis.

67   Shafei, Mohamed Z.
A B   THREE LECTURES ON ECONOMIC DEVELOPMENT
            Beirut, Lebanon: Beirut Arab University, 1970.

The first lecture focuses on the characteristics of
developing countries. The second traces the process

of economic development in the U.A.R. (Egypt) since 1952. The third is on the foreign assistance needs of developing countries.

68 Singer, H. W.
A C THE STRATEGY OF INTERNATIONAL DEVELOPMENT: ESSAYS IN THE ECONOMICS OF BACKWARDNESS
Edited by Sir Alec Cairncross and Mohinder Puri
White Plains, N.Y.: International Arts and Sciences Press, 1975.

A collection of 13 papers by the author, all published in past years, dealing with some of the central problems of economic development and development policy. Papers cover such issues as gains distribution among borrowing and investing countries, dualism, international aid, trade and development, employment problems, income distribution, science and technology transfers, etc. Introduction to the author's work and career by editor Sir Alec Cairncross.

69 Singer, Hans W. and Ansari, Javed A.
A   RICH AND POOR COUNTRIES
Baltimore and London: Johns Hopkins University Press, 1977.

Examines the changes that are required if the relationship between rich and poor countries is to make a more effective contribution to the development of the poor countries. Part one describes the structure of international economy and the nature of development process. Part two discusses the importance of the international trade sector to development in the poorer countries and reviews the trade policies of the rich and poor countries. Part three deals with the role of aid in the development process; and part four is concerned with international factor movement. Stresses the need for the formulation of an international development strategy...by the rich countries (both old and new), providing assistance in an increasing flow of resources through trade, aid capital and the transfer of skills and technology to the poor countries. Argues that such a strategy first must provide for some discrimination in international trade in favor of poor countries to provide more resources and secondly to enable the importation of more appropriate technologies.

70 Spiegelglas, Stephen and Welsh, Charles J., eds.
A B ECONOMIC DEVELOPMENT; CHALLENGE AND PROMISE
Englewood Cliffs, N.J.: Prentice-Hall, 1970.

A collection of 33 reprinted readings, each representing an outstanding contribution, controversial issue, or synthesis of ideas in economic development. Major sections include: an introduction; nature and techniques of planning; strategy and policy; and trade or aid. The selection of topics in these sections reflects recent increased emphasis on practical development problems, particularly on human resources development and the need to create exportable manufactured goods. A matrix showing how each selection fits into the scheme and sequence of the seven widely used development textbooks is included.

71   T. N. Srinivasan
A B C D   DEVELOPMENT, POVERTY, AND BASIC HUMAN NEEDS: SOME ISSUES
World Bank Reprint Series, 76
IBRD, 1977.

Reprinted from Food Research Institute Studies, vol. XVI, no. 2 (1977), pp. 11-28. Deals with the raising of standard of living of the poorest sections of the population in developing countries. Discusses aid problems, distributional aspects of economic growth, employment goals, and the new perceptions of development.

72   Stein, Leslie
A C D   ECONOMIC REALITIES IN POOR COUNTRIES
Sydney, London and Singapore: Angus and Robertson, 1972.

This book surveys the problems of growth faced by the developing countries of the world. The first part of the book describes the economic and social characteristics of Third World countries and presents some theories of development, including Baran's Marxian view, W. W. Rostow's non-Marxist alternative, balanced growth theory, and Myrdal's view which considers non-economic as well as economic factors of growth. Succeeding chapters discuss population growth, problems of education, the role of agriculture and industrial development, obstacles to trade, and government plans which have been used in developing countries. Designed for use as a text or for the layman.

73   Streeten, Paul
A B D   DEVELOPMENT PERSPECTIVES
New York: St. Martin's Press, 1981.

A combination of 17 previously published articles and 7 new chapters, in five parts: concepts, values, and methods in development analysis; development strategies; transnational corporations; the change in emphasis from the growth approach to the basic needs approach; and two miscellaneous chapters on taxation and on Gunnar Myrdal. Newly written chapters cover: the results of development strategies for the poor, alternatives in development, the New International Economic Order, the basic needs approach, human rights and basic needs, the search for a basic-needs yardstick (with Norman Hicks), and transnational corporations and basic needs.

74 Thomson, W. Scott, ed.
A C THE THIRD WORLD: PREMISES OF U.S. POLICY
San Francisco: Institute for Contemporary Studies, 1978.

75 Tinbergen, Jan
A B THE DESIGN OF DEVELOPMENT
The Johns Hopkins University Press, 1958.

Formulates a coherent government policy to further development objectives and outlines methods to stimulate private investments.

76 Todaro, Michael P.
A B C ECONOMIC DEVELOPMENT IN THE THIRD WORLD: AN INTRODUCTION TO PROBLEMS AND POLICIES IN A GLOBAL PERSPECTIVE
London and New York: Longman, 1977.

In four parts: Part one discusses the nature of underdevelopment and its various manifestations in the Third World, and parts two and three focus on major development problems and policies, both domestic (growth, income distribution, population, unemployment, education, and migration) and international (trade, balance of payments, and foreign investment). The last part reviews the possibilities and prospects for Third World development.

77 Todaro, Michael P
A B DEVELOPMENT PLANNING: MODELS AND METHODS
Series of undergraduate teaching works in economics, Volume V.
London, Nairobi, and New York: Oxford University Press, 1971.

This is the last in a series of undergraduate teaching works in economics developed at Makere University, Uganda. This book is an introduction to development planning, with emphasis on plan formulation rather than implementation.

78 United Nations Department of Economic and Social Affairs
THE INTERNATIONAL DEVELOPMENT STRATEGY: FIRST OVER-ALL REVIEW AND APPRAISAL OF ISSUES AND POLICIES. REPORT OF THE SECRETARY-GENERAL
New York: United Nations, 1973.

Deals with the issues and policies in the field of economic and social development...of prime concern in the first two years of the Second United Nations Development Decade. Emphasis is upon changes in the following areas: priorities of objectives, techniques of production, trade and aid relationships, and the external environment in which economic and social development takes place.

79
A C
United Nations Department of Economic and Social Affairs
SHAPING ACCELERATED DEVELOPMENT AND INTERNATIONAL CHANGES
New York: United Nations Publications, 1980.

Contains views and recommendations of the UN Committee for Development Planning relating to the international development strategy for a third UN development decade. Chapters cover general premises and basic objectives; priority areas for action; means and implementation; and key goals and needed changes.

80
A C
United Nations Department of Economic and Social Affairs
DEVELOPMENT IN THE 1980'S: APPROACH TO A NEW STRATEGY; VIEWS AND RECOMMENDATIONS OF THE COMMITTEE FOR DEVELOPMENT PLANNING
New York: United Nations Publications, 1978.

Reviews development issues for the 1980's with a discussion of the current situation and preliminary comments relating to a development strategy for the 1980's. Discusses economic cooperation among developing countries, covering trade, economic integration and other arrangements for economic cooperation.

81
A B C
United Nations Industrial Development Organization
INDUSTRIALIZATION FOR NEW DEVELOPMENT NEEDS
New York: United Nations Publication, 1974.

Emphasizes the reshaping of industrial development in the light of new development needs that the pervasive problems of unemployment, maldistribution of income, and poverty in general have brought to the fore in the developing countries.

82
A B C
UNRSID
THE QUEST FOR A UNIFIED APPROACH TO DEVELOPMENT
UNRSID: 1980.

Provides background information on UNRSID's efforts to formulate a unified approach to development analysis and planning, an approach which would bring together all the different aspects of development into a set of feasible objectives and policy approaches. Chapters cover: styles of development--definitions and criteria; strategies; the findings of the Expert Group; an assessment by Marshall Wolfe, former Chief of the Social Development Division of UN ECLA; and an annex containing the final report on the project by the UN Commission for Social Development, covering questions of diagnosis, monitoring, indicators, and planning and capicitation.

83   Uri, Pierre
A B C   DEVELOPMENT WITHOUT DEPENDENCE
        New York: Praeger for the Atlantic Institute for
        International Affairs, 1976.

        Monograph on foreign aid. Contends that the aid programs
        of the 1950's and 1960's were lopsided and failed to
        address the needs of the truly poor. According to Bundy,
        the author argues that although effective transfer of
        resources and skill remains a vital part of the need...such
        nation-to-nation aid...can only help to foster the very
        feelings of dependence...that are the deepest grievance
        of the developing world. Discusses control of population
        growth, the role and necessary scale of official foreign
        aid, stabilization of the raw materials market so as
        to assist consumers and producers alike, and the types
        of industries the developing countries should strive
        to build as a part of a rational world division of labor.
        Examines the control and regulation of multinational
        corporations and, focusing on Latin America, the extent
        to which regional cooperation can be developed. Recommends
        that development planning be based on future population
        growth and distribution.

84   Varma, Baidya Nath
A B C   THE SOCIOLOGY AND POLITICS OF DEVELOPMENT: A THEORETICAL
        STUDY
        International Library of Sociology Series
        London and Boston: Routledge & Kegan Paul, 1980.

        The author critically examines theories of development
        and presents his own theory. Considers general criteria
        used for evaluating the modernization process; describes
        a model for a general paradigm of modernization; surveys
        other models encompassing ideological, social scientific,
        anthropological and activistic theories; and discusses
        theoretical problems of planning and national
        reconstruction. Summarizes views of theorists in various
        social science disciplines and features of modernization
        in terms of guidance provided for economic, political,
        educational, and bureaucratic decision-making in a
        developing country. Concludes that both the socialist
        and capitalist systems of modernization are viable models
        for Third World countries.

85   Vogeler, Ingolf and De Souza, Anthony R., eds.
A C   DIALECTICS OF THIRD WORLD DEVELOPMENT
        Montclair: Allanheld, Osmun, 1980.

        Collection of previously published (some revised) papers
        designed for use by students of economics, political
        science, and development. Representing a variety of
        ideas and arguments relevant to Third World
        underdevelopment, the readings discuss climate and

resources, cultural traditions, European colonialism (i.e., plantation agriculture), population, tourism, and imperialism. An appendix provides "awareness" exercises.

86 Wallman, Sandra, ed.
A B PERCEPTIONS OF DEVELOPMENT
New York: Cambridge University Press, 1977.

87 Ward, Richard J.
A C DEVELOPMENT ISSUES FOR THE 1970'S
New York and London: Dunellen, 1973.

An assessment of key issues and problems which emerged from the Decade of Development and which will continue to absorb the attention of students of development in the present decade. The author, former Chief of Planning of the U.S. Agency for International Development, presents much data which has not been previously released and which is unavailable elsewhere. The book is divided into three parts: "Food and Human Welfare," "Development Problems for This Decade," and "Planning Programs and Strategies." The chapters specifically discuss such issues as labor absorption in agriculture, means of population control, the burden of debt service, the role of foreign aid, big-push development, etc.

88 Waterston, Albert
A B DEVELOPMENT PLANNING; LESSONS OF EXPERIENCE
The Johns Hopkins University Press, 1979.

Analyzes the success of the development planning experience in over 100 countries in Asia, Africa, Europe, and the Americas. In two parts. Part 1 describes and analyzes the problems associated with the implementation of planning programs, the provision of basic data, the role of national budget, and administrative obstacles. Part 2 contains an extensive and comparative discussion of the experience of the countries under review in setting up organizations and administrative procedures for preparing and implementing development projects; the distribution of planning functions, types of central planning agencies, and subnational regional and local planning bodies.

89 Watts, Nita, ed.
A B ECONOMIES OF THE WORLD
New York: Oxford University Press.

The purpose of this new series is to provide a brief review of economic development during the post-war period in each of a number of countries which are of obvious importance in the world economy, or interesting because of peculiarities of their economic structure or experience, or illustrative of widespread economic development problems. The series will be of interest to economists in universities, and in business and government.

90 Wilber, Charles K., ed.
A B THE POLITICAL ECONOMY OF DEVELOPMENT AND UNDERDEVELOPMENT
New York: Random House, 1973.

Emphasis in approach and content is on political economy in the sense of attempting to incorporate such noneconomic influences as social structures, political systems, and cultural values as well as such factors as technological change and the distribution of income and wealth. Readings are radical in that they are willing to question and evaluate the most basic institutions and values of society. Divided into eight groups concerned with methodological problems, historical perspective, trade and imperialism, agricultural and industrial institutions and strategies, comparative models of development, the human cost of development, and indications for the future.

91 Worsley, Peter
A C THE THIRD WORLD
Chicago: University of Chicago Press, 1972.

92 Wriggins, W. Howards and Adler-Karlsson, Gunnar
A C REDUCING GLOBAL INEQUALITIES
New York: McGraw-Hill, 1978.

Two papers, plus an introduction on the role that developing countries themselves take to reduce the gap between rich nations and poor and to eliminate mass poverty within their own societies. W. Howard Wriggins, U.S. ambassador to Sri Lanka and formerly professor of political science at Columbia University, analyzes the various bargaining strategies open to developing countries such as developing commodity or regional coalitions, or a variety of threats to developed countries. The future is likely to see continued efforts at coalition building, but also periodic outbreaks of irregular violence against local opponents, neighbors, or Northern centers of power.

93 Zuvekas, Clarence, Jr.
A B C ECONOMIC DEVELOPMENT: AN INTRODUCTION
New York: St. Martin's Press, 1979.

Text written from an interdisciplinary perspective stressing policy and empirical findings rather than an overall development theory. Aims at balance between theory and policy, including historical development and empirical evidence. After discussing the terminology of and the obstacles to development, the author examines population growth, trade and development, and the role of government. Also covers: the problems of agriculture and industry, income distribution, employment, mobilization of domestic and foreign savings, manipulation of trade to the advantage of the developing country, and with the limits to growth controversy. Presumes acquaintance with basic macro and micro theory.

ECONOMIC POLICY AND PLANNING IN THIRD WORLD DEVELOPMENT

94   Adelman, Irma and Robinson, Sherman
INCOME DISTRIBUTION POLICY IN THE DEVELOPING COUNTRIES: A CASE STUDY OF KOREA
Standford University Press, Stanford, California, 1977.

Seeks to answer the question of how much can actually be done to improve income distribution in developing countries, by means of a dynamic general equilibrium model for investigating the potential impact of standard policy instruments and programs intended to improve the relative and absolute incomes of the poor. The model is rooted in the actual economy of the Republic of Korea. Concludes that current standard policy instruments are largely ineffective but also indicates that a government can achieve the stated goal by making antipoverty policy the major focus of its development strategy.

95   Adelman, Irma, ed.
ECONOMIC GROWTH AND RESOURCES: PROCEEDINGS OF THE FIFTH WORLD CONGRESS OF THE INTERNATIONAL ECONOMIC ASSOCIATION HELD IN TOKYO, JAPAN, 1977. VOLUME 4, NATIONAL AND INTERNATIONAL POLICIES
New York: St. Martin's Press, 1979.

Thirteen previously unpulblished papers on North-South relations and on the nature of economic growth in the industrially developed world. Part one on national policies includes papers by: Lionel Stoleru, Jergen H. Gelting, J.O.N. Perkins, Tibor Scitovsky, Marian Ostrowski and Zdzislaw Sadowsky, and Paul Streeten; part two on international policies includes papers by: Suklamoy Chakravarty, Josef Pajestka, Rikard Lang, Hla Myint, Bela Balassa, William M. Corden, and Jean C. Benard. Specific topics include: the moral and philosophical bases for a new international economic order; the potential effectiveness of various technical proposals for reform; problems of inflation, employment, social consensus; and international equilibrium facing developed nations.

96 ADP
TRENDS IN DEVELOPING ASIA: NO. 10: APRIL 1979
ADP, 1979.

Contains charts (52) prepared by the AsDB Economic Office covering data on area and population; national accounts; production; transport; money supply and consumer prices; public finance; financial flow; balance of payments and foreign trade; social indicators; AsDB loans and technical assistance. Prepared for the 1979 Annual Meeting of the Board of Governors.

97 Ady, Peter, ed.
A C PRIVATE FOREIGN INVESTMENT AND THE DEVELOPING WORLD
New York: Praeger, 1971.

98 Aharoni, Yair
MARKETS, PLANNING AND DEVELOPMENT: THE PRIVATE AND PUBLIC SECTORS IN ECONOMIC DEVELOPMENT
Cambridge, Mass.: Lippincott, Ballinger, 1977.

Examines the roles played by the private and public sectors in the process of economic development. Is concerned with what level of output of each sector is optimal under the current conditions of less developed economies, rather than with the issue of whether private or public ownership of the means of production is best. The first four chapters establish the framework of analysis by detailing the dimensions of interrelationship and contrast between the two sectors. The following chapter reviews the recent history of economic development in the LDC's, particularly with regard to investment and governental forced savings, to import substitutions, and to exchange rate policy. The last five chapters comprise a detailed analysis of entrepreneurship, direct foreign investment, multinational enterprises, and state-owned enterprises.

99 Ahluwalia, Montek S., Carter, Nicholas G. and Chenery, Hollis B.
GROWTH AND POVERTY IN DEVELOPING COUNTRIES (REVISED)
World Bank, Washington, D.C., 1979.

States that despite impressive economic growth in developing countries over the past 25 years, the poorest countries have only grown slowly and the income of the poor in those countries increased much more slowly than the average. Using a quantitative framework for examining global poverty for 36 developing countries, which together account for 80 percent of the population of the developing world, the paper concludes that the elimination of poverty by the year 2000 is highly unlikely unless policies are combined to speed growth of GNP, slow population growth, and provide more equity in poor countries.

100   Ahmed, Raisuddin
        AGRICULTURAL PRICE POLICIES UNDER COMPLEX SOCIOECONOMIC AND NATURAL CONSTRAINTS: THE CASE OF BANGLADESH. RESEARCH REPORT NO. 27
        Washington, D.C.: International FOOD Policy Research Institute, 1981.

        Analyzes rice pricing policy in Bangladesh from the perspective of three policy objectives: efficiency in resource allocation to achieve and optimum increase in agricultural production; recognition of indirect effects of agricultural prices on nonagricultural activities; and welfare of the poor. Analyzes interrelationships between rice and jute. Recommends removing the current export tax on jute and implementing policies that indirectly support food grain prices, such as policies to increase the spending power of low-income households and development of a marketing system that reduces the instability of rice prices.

101   Ainley, E.M.
        THE IMF: PAST, PRESENT AND FUTURE. BANGOR OCCASIONAL PAPERS IN ECONOMICS, NO. 15
        Cardiff, Wales: University of Wales Press, 1979.

        Examines the need for a stronger IMF and possible ways in which it may be strengthened. Outlines the structure and working of the IMF, its shortcomings from 1945-71, the failure of the reforms of 1972-76, and prospective developments in international adjustments up to 1982. Examines IMF influence on members' future adjustment policies, via consultation, sanctions, exchange rate supervision, and lending conditions; current financing efforts; and two alternative proposals for improving the effectiveness of the IMF--establishment of a new lending institution to aid the IMF and closer links between the IMf and commercial banks. Finds that: (1) the chances of a new lending institution are slim; (2) the growing practice among commercial banks to link loans informally to IMF agreements; (3) the bases for extending IMF influence already exist; and (4) despite the IMF's track record and the serious implications for the medium term with respect to international adjustments, "it seems unlikely at present that individual governments will have the vision to allow the IMF th fullfill its potential."

102   Aksoy, M. Ataman
        STRUCTURAL ASPECTS OF TURKISH INFLATION: 1950-1979
        World Bank Staff Working Paper No. 540, 1982.

        Inflation has been one of the major problems of the Turkish economy during the postwar period. This paper develops alternative inflation models and analyzes their performance in light of the Turkish experience in order to provide a framework on which a more realistic macro model can be developed.

103 Alamgir, Mohiuddin
BANGLADESH: A CASE OF BELOW POVERTY LEVEL EQUILIBRIUM TRAP
Dacca, Bangladesh: Bangladesh Institute of Development Studies, 1978.

A case study of PIFD (poverty, inequality, famine, and death) and the concept of "Below Poverty Level Equilibrium Trap," a level of existence that occurs between poverty and famine. Examines real income, poverty, and inequality in Bangladesh; analyzes the social forces and historical processes that have produced PIFD in Bangladesh; and critically evaluates development strategy for the area. Concludes that "traditional teachings of economic development do not provide solutions" and argues that the situation in Bangladesh "cannot ...improve until an end is brought to the dominance of the comprador bourgeoisie and other classes representing basically semi-feudal/semi-colonial interests."

104 Alamgir, Mohiuddin and Berlage, Lodewijk J.J.B.
BANGLADESH: NATIONAL INCOME AND EXPENDITURE 1949/50-1969/70.
RESEARCH MONOGRAPH NO. 1
Dacca: Bangladesh Institute of Development Studies, 1974.

A comprehensive and previously unpublished presentation of national income and expenditures data for Bangladesh for the 1950's and 1960's. The authors provide estimates for the long-run behavior of many major economic aggregates (including taxes and subsidies) and then perform some econometric analyses, seeking to discover the more important structural changes which have taken place in Bangladesh during the past two decades.

105 Al-Bashir, Faisal Safooq
A STRUCTURAL ECONOMETRIC MODEL OF THE SAUDI ARABIAN ECONOMY: 1960-1970
New York: Wiley, Wiley-Interscience, 1977.

Formulates and estimates a model of Saudi Arabian economy, which differs from most models in three aspects: (1) oil, and not the country's aggregate demand, is the generator of economic growth; (2) government expenditures are identified as endogenous variables; and (3) the model has no export sector because oil's income constitutes all the exports. Discusses the oil and other sectors of the economy, the consumption function, imports, and investment. Finds that the oil sector affects almost the whole economy, that most government and private investment went to construction activities, and that there is a great dependency on imports.

106   Allen, G.C.
JAPAN'S ECONOMIC POLICY
New York: Holmes & Meier, 1980.

Ten previously published essays written over a fifty-year period and presented here in revised form. Some topics include the relationship of Japan's foreign exchange, banking, and monetary policies to her economic development in the nineteen twenties; industrial organization and manufacturing in the thirties; the complex of factors responsible for industrial expansion after the Second World War; and the important role of the state in modern Japan's economic growth. A newly written introduction previews some of the volume's various themes--the West's underestimation of Japan's capacity for industrialization, economic resilience, and the crucial role of business leadership in Japan's accomplishments.

107   Allen, Loring
VENEZUELAN ECONOMIC DEVELOPMENT: A POLITICO-ECONOMIC ANALYSIS. CONTEMPORARY STUDIES IN ECONOMIC AND FINANCIAL ANALYSIS, VOL. 7
Greenwich, Conn.: JAI Press, 1977.

Survey of Venezuelan development over the period 1945-75. Topics include: the evolution of democracy, petroleum policy, economic policy; economic growth, the public sector, human resources, money and banking, trade, agriculture, petroleum development, and industry. Finds an impressive transformation of the economy, stemming from "petroleum plus innovative, nationalistic petroleum policies...[and] economic policies that have helped to develop and diversify the economy and to distribute its benefits more equitably." The political transformation reflects the taming of the military and the installation of a party-based political system. Concludes, therefore, that "Venezuela will be one of the first less developed countries to attain developed-country status, only a few years from now." Includes 36 tables of related macroeconomic data.

108   Altimir, Oscar
THE EXTENT OF POVERTY IN LATIN AMERICA
World Bank Staff Working Paper No. 522, 1982.

This work originated in a research project for the measurement and analysis of income distribution in the Latin American countries; undertaken jointly by the Economic Commission for Latin America and the World

Bank. Presents estimates of the extent of absolute poverty for ten Latin American countries and for the region as a whole in the 1970s.

109 Amin, Samir
ACCUMULATION ON A WORLD SCALE: A CRITIQUE OF THE THEORY OF UNDERDEVELOPMENT. 2 VOLS. TRANSLATED BY BRIAN PEARCE
New York and London: Monthly Review Press, 1974.

An English translation of the 1971 French second edition. It is a critique of current economic theory (marginalism) and an attempt to extend Marxist analysis to deal explicitly with "underdeveloped" countries. A basic thesis of the book is that all countries are integrated into a worldwide system of commercial and financial relations, but that current economic theory is inapplicable for the analysis of these relations. The author's analysis of accumulation on a world scale leads to the conclusion that the interaction of capitalist and pre-capitalist modes of production leads to a transfer of value to capitalist accumulation due to the mechanism of "primitive accumulation" in periphery areas.

110 Amin, Samir
UNEQUAL DEVELOPMENT: AN ESSAY ON THE SOCIAL FORMATIONS OF PERIPHERAL CAPITALISM. TRANSLATED BY BRIAN PEARCE
New York and London: Monthly Review Press, 1976.

Translation of Le Developpement inegal. Develops a theory of underdevelopment based on the relations between the developed "center" and the undeveloped "periphery" of the woeld capitalist system. Chapters one and two review the genesis of preceptitalist systems and the laws of capitalism, respectively. Chapter three reviews the theory of "unequal exchange" between center and periphery. Chapter four is detailed analysis of center-periphery relations, and chapter five discusses capitalist and precapitalist formations in the periphery. Some empirical evidence is presented.

111 Amuzegar, Jahangir
COMPARATIVE ECONOMICS: NATIONAL PRIORITIES, POLICIES, AND PERFORMANCE
Cambridge, Mass.: Winthrop, 1981.

Approach is to combine analysis of the principles of economic problem-solving in the real world and in the application to real world economics. The conceptual part lays out five principal mechanisms of decisionmaking and the descriptive application to market-oriented advanced industrial countries (U.S., U.K., and Japan); centrally directed economies (U.S.S.R., Peoples' Republic of China, and Yugoslavia); and the LDCs (Brazil, India, and Nigeria).

112   Anand, Sudhir
        INEQUALITY AND POVERTY IN MALAYSIA: MEASUREMENT AND DECOMPOSITION
        Oxford University Press, 1982.

        An account of income inequalities and poverty in Malaysia. The research is policy oriented and the findings, to which the author's statistical technique is applied, are thoroughly discussed. A range of issues in covered, from data problems to conceptual questions arising with respect to measurement.

113   Anderson, Dennis
        SMALL INDUSTRY IN DEVELOPING COUNTRIES: SOME ISSUES
        World Bank Staff Working Paper, No. 518, 1982.

        The role of small industries in the development process has been the subject of a large number of studies over the past thirty years. This paper examines changes in the size structure of industry, by region; it discusses entrepreneurship and argues that, while small and large firms alike are highly responsive to the growth of markets, the entrepreneurial response is neither as full nor as efficient as is desirable; and it analyzes small industry programs and their relation to development policy.

114   Anderson, Dennis and Khambata, Farida
A C D   SMALL ENTERPRISES AND DEVELOPMENT POLICY IN THE PHILIPPINES: A CASE STUDY
        World Bank Staff Working Paper No. 468, July 1981.

        Presents an ex post evaluation of the small and medium industries program introduced in the Philippines in 1974, and reassesses the assumptions behind the programs. One of a series of case studies and surveys being financed by the World Bank's Research Committee.

115   Anderson, Dennis and Khambata, Farida
A C   FINANCING SMALL-SCALE INDUSTRY AND AGRICULTURE IN DEVELOPING COUNTRIES: THE MERITS AND LIMITATIONS OF "COMMERCIAL" POLICIES
        World Bank Staff Working Paper No. 519, May 1982.

        A discussion of how two factors lead to an unwillingness of financial institutions of finance small-scale industry and agriculture in developing countries: (a) controls in interest rates and (b) the initially high risks and administrative costs involved. Notes that most economists appeal for a relaxation of the controls, but shows that this policy alone will not achieve an efficient flow of finance to small-scale activities. Draws on observations made during the course of project work in several countries and outlines ways to reduce risks and administrative costs over time.

116 Agarwal, A.N.
INDIAN ECONOMY: NATURE, PROBLEMS AND PROGRESS
Delhi: Vikas; distributed by International Publications Service, New York, 1975.

A comprehensive survey of the Indian economy as a whole. Intended as a textbook for courses at Indian universities and as reference for national civil service candidates. Begins with an overall perspective of possibilities and provides a historical background for the economy, both before the Independence and since 1947. The main features discussed are: national income measurement; its size and composition; distribution, consumption, and poverty; population and its relation to economic development; occupational structure; unemployment; capital formation; natural resources; several chapters on agriculture and industry; the public sector, monopoly, and concentration; foreign trade; the balance of payments; planning objectives, strategy, and financing; foreign aid; price trends and policy; and a progress evaluation on the economy as a whole. Data are as of July 1975.

117 Arian, Asher, ed.
ISRAEL--A DEVELOPING SOCIETY. THE PINHAS SAPIR CENTER FOR DEVELOPMENT CONFERENCE SERIES
Assen, The Netherlands: Van Gorcum, 1980.

Fifteen previously unpublished papers and discussion from an April 1978 conference held at Tel Aviv University in celebration of the thirtieth anniversary of the founding of the State of Israel. Participants were economists, political scientists, historians, anthropologists, public officials, a professor of law, and bankers. Topics include: international relations--both foreign policy and strategic problems; politics and ideology; immigrant absorption; and economic development--balance of payments and exchange rate policy, fiscal policy, and the Israeli economy in comparative perspective.

118 Aronson, Jonathan David, ed.
DEBT AND THE LESS DEVELOPED COUNTRIES. WESTVIEW SPECIAL STUDIES IN INTERNATIONAL ECONOMICS AND BUSINESS
Boulder, Colo.: Westview Press, 1979.

Twelve articles by political scientists, economists, a sociologist and government practitioners. Part one describes the extent and distribution of the current international debt situation, analyzes the policies of major public creditors, and examines the place of debt in the maintenance and management of a stable international monetary system. Part two explores the role of both domestic and external debt in the development process, with special reference to Latin America. Part three focuses upon the changing interactions among developed and developing countries, private bank lenders, and the International Monetary Fund, and examines debtor, creditor renegotiations in light of recent developments in the international debt market.

119   Aronson, Jonathan David
MONEY AND POWER: BANKS AND THE WORLD MONETARY SYSTEM. PREFACE BY SUSAN STRANGE. SAGE LIBRARY OF SOCIAL RESEARCH, VOL. 66
Beverly Hills and London: Sage, 1977.

Examines the nature and scope of the roles and power of private American banks in the international monetary system since 1958. Specifically questions "whether bank behavior exerts pressure on government decision-makers to adopt policies or take decisions which they do not favor." In addition, considers the impact of banks' actions on monetary outcomes and begins to assess the "appropriate relationship between public and private actors in the international economic system."

120   Asfour, Edmund and others
TURKEY: PROSPECTS AND PROBLEMS OF AN EXPANDING ECONOMY
The Johns Hopkins University Press, February, 1975.

Explores a remarkably consistent development strategy by which the country has modernized in the last fifty years through emphasis on industrialization and self-sufficiency, and analyzes medium- and long-term growth perspectives. Based on the findings of an economic mission to Turkey, April-May 1973.

121   Atta, Jacob K.
A MACROECONOMETRIC MODEL OF A DEVELOPING ECONOMY: GHANA (SIMULATIONS AND POLICY ANALYSIS)
Washington, D.C.: University Press of America, 1981.

Constructs a macroeconomic model of the Ghanian economy, based on 1958-68 data; emphasizes the supply side in presenting a model of a small open economy. Using simulation, examines the impacts of alternative government policies on key economic aggregates. The findings include: (1) high nominal wages (initiated by minimum wage regulation) can be partially blamed for the past stagflation in Ghana; (2) the most promising policy for economic growth may be export promotion.

122   Attia, Mona Fouad
TARIFF PROTECTION AND GROWTH IN DEVELOPING COUNTRIES: A MULTISECTORAL ANALYSIS APPLIED TO PERU

The Netherlands: Rotterdam University Press, 1976.

Examines the effects of tariff protection on the development and growth of emerging economies, explicitly recognizing both the costs and benefits within a general equilibrium framework. The role of the tariff in the Peruvian economy is simulated from 1968 to 1980 using a multisectoral programming model. The effects of tariff are evaluated by comparing projected GDP and employment in Peru in 1980 under the existing tariff structure with the same achievements under a simulated hypothetical nontariff situation.

123 Ayhan, Cilingiroglu
A C MANUFACTURE OF HEAVY ELECTRICAL EQUIPMENT IN DEVELOPING COUNTRIES
World Bank Staff Paper, No. 9, 1969.

Analyzes growth and competitiveness, comparing prices and costs with those in the international market.

124 Ayre, P.C.I.
FINANCE IN DEVELOPING COUNTRIES
Frank Cass and Co., Ltd., London, England, 1977.

A collection of essays which first appeared in a special issue of finance in developing countries in the Journal of Development Studies.

125 Bachmann, Heinz B. and others
SENEGAL: TRADITION, DIVERSIFICATION, AND ECONOMIC DEVELOPMENT
The Johns Hopkins University Press, October 1974.

Traces the development of the country's economy from independence to date, discusses its growth experience and its markedly improved economic performance during the last five years, its prospects, and creditworthiness. Based on the findings of an economic mission to Senegal in February-March 1972.

126 Baer, Werner
A C D THE BRAZILIAN ECONOMY: ITS GROWTH AND DEVELOPMENT
Columbus, Ohio: Grid, 1979.

Traces the historical evolution of the Brazilian economy, focusing upon the process, methods, and impact of its industrialization in the twentieth century. Examines the institutional structure of Brazil's current mix of private and state capitalism and analyzes some aspects of its economic policies and system, which "account for the persistence of underdevelopment in the midst of economic growth."

Part one offers the historical perspective, while part two deals with contemporary problems of foreign trade, inflation, regional imbalances, and agricultural growth and stagnation.

127 Bain, Joe S., ed.
ESSAYS ON ECONOMIC DEVELOPMENT. ROYER LECTURES/UNIVERSITY OF CALIFORNIA
Berkeley: University of California for the Institute of Business and Economic Research, 1970.

Contains four lectures given from 1967 to 1969 as part of the Royer Program in Political Economy at the University of California (Berkeley) on contemporary problems of economic development in both well developed and underdeveloped countries. Includes: "Foreign Investment, Trade and Industrial Growth" (Richard E. Caves); "Western European Integration: Status and Prospects" (Bart Landheer); "Politics and Economic Development, With Special Reference to India: (Charles E. Lindblom); and "The Poor Countries' Development Policies and the Rich Countries' Responsibility" (Tibor Scitovsky).

128 Baird, Mark, Mission leaders and others
UGANDA: COUNTRY ECONOMIC MEMORANDUM
1982.

Outlines the priority areas for further action and the implications of the balance-of-payments outlook for aid requirements. A more detailed review of the problems and issues in five major sectors--agriculture, industry, transport, energy and education--is also discussed.

129 Balassa, Bela and Associates
THE STRUCTURE OF PROTECTION IN DEVELOPING COUNTRIES
Baltimore and London: Johns Hopkins Press for the International Bank for Reconstruction and Development and the Inter-American Development Bank, 1971.

Uses the "effective protection measure" to appraise the effects of the existing system of protection in six developing countries--Brazil, Chile, Mexico, West Malaysia, Pakistan, and the Philippines; for purposes of comparison, there is also a study of Norway. Furthermore, the authors provide criteria for evaluating systems of protection and offer guidelines for future policy formulation. Five appendices supplement the study mathematically and descriptively.

130 Balassa, Bela
STRUCTURAL ADJUSTMENT POLICIES IN DEVELOPING ECONOMIES
World Bank Staff Working Paper No. 464, July 1981.

Examines structural adjustment policies (policy responses to external shocks, such as the quadrupling of oil prices and the world recession of the 1970s) of developing countries. Considers reforms in production incentives, incentives to save and to invest, public investments, sectoral policies, and monetary policies, and comments on the interdependence on the various policy measures and on the international environment in which they operate.

131 Balassa, Bela
A C THE NEWLY INDUSTRIALIZING COUNTRIES IN THE WORLD ECONOMY
Pergamon Press, New York, 1981.

The newly industrializing countries, or NICs as they are called in the current jargon, are a small number of developing countries that have become important exporters of manufactured goods and therefore competitors with the industrial countries on world markets, largely in the last 15 years. Their rapid growth in the face of the difficult international economic circumstances of the 1970s has led both developed countries and other developing countries to study the economic plans and policies behind their growth.

132   Balassa, Bela and Associates
A C D DEVELOPMENT STRATEGIES IN SEMI-INDUSTRIAL ECONOMIES
The Johns Hopkins University Press, 1982.

This book provides an analysis of development strategies in semi-industrial economies that have established an industrial base. It endeavors to quantify the systems of incentives that are applied in six of these economies: Argentina, Colombia, Israel, Korea, Singapore, and Taiwan, and to indicate the effects of the systems on the allocation of resources, international trade, and economic growth.

133 Baldwin, George B.
PAPUA NEW GUINEA: ITS ECONOMIC SITUATION AND PROSPECTS FOR DEVELOPMENT: REPORT OF A MISSION SENT TO PAPUA NEW GUINEA BY THE WORLD BANK: ASSISTED BY SWADESH R. BOSE, ALICE C. GALENSON, AND PAUL C. MOULIN
A World Bank Country Economic Report. Washington, D.C.: World Bank, 1978.

Focuses upon Papua New Guinea's present and prospective financial self-reliance as it manages the transition to "economic identity and independence" subsequent to its political independence in late 1975.

134 Bandyopadhyaya, Kalyani
A B INDUSTRIALIZATION THROUGH INDUSTRIAL ESTATES: A PATTERN OF ECONOMIC DECENTRALIZATION
Patna: Bookland Private, 1969.

A study examining how far and under what conditions industrial estates, in absolute terms and compared to industries outside the industrial estates, can be a useful and potent tool for industrial development. Using the Indian economy as a framework, the author examines its industrial estates and planning and bases much of her findings on case studies of West Bengal.

135 Banks, Arthur S., et al., eds.
ECONOMIC HANDBOOK OF THE WORLD: 1981
New York: McGraw Hill, 1981.

136 Batscha, Robert
THE EFFECTIVENESS OF DISSEMINATION METHODS FOR SOCIAL AND ECONOMIC DEVELOPMENT RESEARCH
OECD, 1976.

In five chapters: (a) review of the dissemination and research process; (b) dissemination methods employed by the OECD Development Assistance Committee (DAC) Member countries (Canada, U.K., Germany, Sweden, U.S.A., France, Switzerland and Austria); (c) dissemination methods employed by selected multilateral organizations and research institutes (IBRD, OECD Development Centre, UNCTAD, World Employment Programme (ILO) and Institute for Development Studies (University of Sussex)); (d) international comparison of methods of dissemination of institutes concerned; and (e) discussion of the need for additional research.

137 Bauer, Peter T.
EQUALITY, THE THIRD WORLD AND ECONOMIC DELUSION
Cambridge, Mass.: Harvard University Press, 1981.

138 Bautista, Romeo M.; Hughes, Helen; Lim, David; Morawetz, David; and Thoumi, Francisco E.
CAPITAL UTILIZATION IN MANUFACTURING: COLOMBIA, ISRAEL, MALAYSIA, AND THE PHILLIPPINES
Oxford University Press, 1982.

The authors surveyed 1,200 manufacturing firms in four developing countries to establish actual levels of capital utilization. The information collected was the first and remains the only data base available for the study of capital utilization. It was found that capital utilization is not as low as had been supposed. The study is concerned with factors that cause differences in levels of capital utilization and the policies that might be used to increase it.

139 Beckerman, Wilfred
MEASURES OF LEISURE, EQUALITY AND WELFARE
OECD, 1978.

Examines how much difference would be made to the relative growth rates of "Measurable Economic Welfare" of thirteen countries, when this is taken to mean GNP adjusted for leisure and income distribution.

140 Behrman, Jere R.
MACROECONOMIC POLICY IN A DEVELOPING COUNTRY: THE CHILEAN EXPERIENCE. CONTRIBUTIONS TO ECONOMIC ANALYSIS NO. 109
New York: Elsevier North-Holland; Amsterdam and Oxford: North-Holland, 1977.

An empirical study of the economic structure and the impact of macroeconomic policies in Chile during the postwar period (1946-70). Provides a historical and institutional analysis of major postwar Chilean stabilization attempts; estimates the sectoral relationships and discusses their practical equilibrium implications; and analyzes the complete model of the Chilean economy and simulates the policy alternatives.

141 Bell, Frederick W. and Canterbery, E. Ray
AQUACULTURE FOR THE DEVELOPING COUNTRIES: A FEASIBILITY STUDY
Cambridge, Mass.: Lippincott, Ballinger, 1976.

Tests the economic feasibility of transferring existing aquaculture technologies (the farming of aquatic animals and plants) to developing countries, with emphasis on the small farmer. Evaluates aquaculture protein sources compared with alternative sources and appraises the research and development requirements for aquaculture enterprises in LDC's. Develops and applies a bioeconomic model, for simulation purposes, to 14 aquacultured species in 90 developing countries, examined as potential recipients.

142 Bennathan, Esra and Walters, A.A.
PORT PRICING AND INVESTMENT POLICY FOR DEVELOPING COUNTRIES
New York; London; Toronto and Hong Kong: Oxford University Press for the World Bank, 1979.

Focuses primarily on the principles of pricing or tariff policy in port economies for developing countries; covers only the outline and general direction of investment planning. Advocates making short-run marginal costs the basis of all port tariffs and applies marginal costs principles to analyses of ship size, port time, competition among ports, and economies of scale in ports.

143 Benoit, Emile
DEFENSE AND ECONOMIC GROWTH IN DEVELOPING COUNTRIES. STUDIES IN INTERNATIONAL DEVELOPMENT AND ECONOMICS
Lexington, Mass., Toronto and London: Heath; Lexington Books, 1973.

A study of the effects of national defense budgets on growth in developing countries exclusively. The author uses multiple regression analysis on 1950-65 data for 44 countries. Results are checked through partial regression analysis. The findings suggest that the size of defense spending relative to GDP is positively, rather than inversely, correlated to the rate of growth of the economy. Many statistical and data tables.

144 Bergsman, Joel
A B C GROWTH AND EQUITY IN SEMI-INDUSTRIALIZED COUNTRIES
World Bank Staff Paper No. 351, August, 1979.

A background study for World Development Report, 1979. Analyzes economic growth, income distribution, and the extent of poverty in semi-industrialized, middle-income developing countries (such as Brazil, Republic of Korea, Mexico, Philippines, Turkey, and Yugoslavia) over the last few decades. Different results are related to differences in policies and social and economic conditions. Policies to promote economic growth and alleviate poverty.

145 Bergsten, C. Fred
THE WORLD ECONOMY IN THE 1980S: SELECTED PAPERS OF C. FRED BERGSTEN, 1980
Lexington, Mass., and Toronto: Heath, Lexington Books, 1981.

An appraisal of developing countries in the world economy within the perspective of U.S. policy; the role of the International Monetary Fund and multilateral development banks; the pursuit of a general agreement on tariffs and trade (GATT) for investment; and the growing international roles of Saudi Arabia, Brazil, and Mexico. Proposes specific measures to improve international economic relations for the decade of the 1980s.

146 Bergsten, C. Fred
MANAGING INTERNATIONAL ECONOMIC INTERDEPENDENCE: SELECTED PAPERS OF C. FRED BERGSTEN, 1975-1976
Lexington, Mass., and Toronto: Heath, Lexington Books, 1977.

Twenty-four papers--12 previously published in books or journals and the rest consisting of congressional testimony and government reports. The articles discuss "economic interdependence, the need to anticipate international economic problems well in advance, the demonstrable value of international rules and institutions in limiting economic conflict...and the essentiality of effective leadership...to deal with these issues." In seven parts: an overview of the world economy; toward a new international monetary system; international trade;

multinational corporations; raw materials; the U.S. and developing countries; and organizing international economic policy.

147 Bernstein, Edward M., et al.
REFLECTIONS ON JAMAICA. ESSAYS IN INTERNATIONAL FINANCE, NO. 115
Princeton, N.J.: Princeton University; International Finance Section, 1976.

Series of eight previously unpublished essays commenting on the agreements reached at the meeting of the Interim Committee of the Board of Governors of the International Monetary Fund in Kingston, Jamaica, January 7-8, 1976. The essays all revolve around the effects of the Jamaican agreement on the international monetary system, monetary reform, exchange-stability, international relations, and developing countries.

148 Berry, R. Albert and Soligo, Ronald, eds.
ECONOMIC POLICY AND INCOME DISTRIBUTION IN COLOMBIA
Boulder, Colo.: Westview Press, 1980.

Assess the distributional impact of a variety of economic policies pursued in Colombia. An introduction by the editors previews the descriptive evidence on income inequality in Colombia and surveys earlier studies on the determinants of income distribution. The remaining papers discuss the distributive effects of: the 1974 Colombian tax reform; local government finances; the post-1970 inflation; educational policy; "new exports" (i.e. agricultural exports other than coffee, minerals other than petroleum, and manufactures); tourism; subsidized farm mechanization; agricultural price supports; urban building; and low income housing development.

149 Betancourt, Roger and Clague, Christopher
CAPITAL UTILIZATION: A THEORETICAL AND EMPIRICAL ANALYSIS
Cambridge University Press, New York, 1981.

A useful contribution to the theory of production, this book surveys the existing knowledge on the topic of capital utilization and, with the help of international data and econometric tests, explores the determinants of shift work as well as its productive and distributive effects.

150 Beveridge, Andrew A. and Oberschall, Anthony R.
AFRICAN BUSINESSMEN AND DEVELOPMENT IN ZAMBIA
Princeton, N.J.: Princeton University Press, 1979.

Explores the role of indigenous entrepreneurs in the Third World, focusing upon (1) the structural sources and patterns of individual characteristics and experiences that contributed to the growth of African business enterprise in Zambia, (2) the effect of government policies on business growth and the Africanization of Zambia's private sector, and (3) the impact of African businesses and businessmen on Zambian society.

151   Beyer, John C.
      BUDGET INNOVATIONS IN DEVELOPING COUNTRIES: THE EXPERIENCE OF NEPAL
      New York: Praeger, 1973.

152   Bhalla, Surjit S.
      THE ROLE OF SOURCES OF INCOME AND INVESTMENT OPPORTUNITIES IN RURAL SAVINGS
      World Bank, Washington, D.C., 1978.

      Investigates the effects that sources of income and investment opportunities have on the savings behavior of farm households in rural India. Shows that income variability rather than investment opportunities can account for differences in the propensity to save out of different sources of income, and observes that the effect of investment opportunities on savings depends importantly on capital market conditions.

153   Bhanoji, Rao, V.V. and Ramakrishnan, M.
      INCOME INEQUALITY IN SINGAPORE: IMPACT OF ECONOMIC GROWTH AND STRUCTURAL CHANGE, 1966-1975
      Singapore: Singapore University Press, 1980.

      Analyzes changes in the distribution of personal income and in the degree of income inequality in Singapore during the 1966-75 decade of rapid economic growth and structural change. Considers the effect of growth and structural changes as well as taxation and government expenditures for public housing and family planning.

154   Bharier, Julian
      ECONOMIC DEVELOPMENT IN IRAN, 1900-1970
      New York, London, and Toronto: Oxford University Press, 1971.

      "The aim of this book is to document the changes which have occurred in Iran since the beginning of the twentieth century, both in the economy as a whole and in individual sectors, and to assess their effects on development." Starting with a composite picture of the Iranian economy in 1900, it discusses development of the economy as a whole, the role of the state, the problems and issues of various sectors, and concludes with a discussion of the state of the economy in 1970 and the prospect for the seventies.

155   Bhatt, Vinayak V.
      SOME ASPECTS OF FINANCIAL POLICIES AND CENTRAL BANKING IN DEVELOPING COUNTRIES

World Bank, Washington, D.C., 1974.

Studies the importance of a sound and well-integrated financial system to any development strategy, and the dual role of central banks in promoting and regulating this system.

156 Bhatt, Vinayak V. and Khatkhate, Deena R.
CENTRE-STATES FINANCIAL RELATIONS IN THE CONTEXT OF PLANNED DEVELOPMENT
World Bank, Washington, D.C., 1978.

Discusses the broad lines on which Federal-States financial relations have evolved in India; discusses rational principles of allocations; suggests a new institutional device for the rational use of borrowed resources by the Federal government and the States; and indicates the broad principle according to which such problems need to be tackled in a country with a democratic framework of government.

157 Bhatt, Vinayak V. and Roe, Alan R.
CAPITAL MARKET IMPERFECTIONS AND ECONOMIC DEVELOPMENT
World Bank, Washington, D.C.

Consists of two papers. The first paper, "Interest Rate, Transaction Costs and Financial Innovations," seeks to provide an overall perspective for research on how and through what means the capital market in developing countries becomes integrated, with attendant effects on savings, investment, output, and income distribution. The second paper, "Some Theory concerning the Role and Failings of Financial Intermediation," analyzes the impact of transaction costs, identifies negative policy interventions, and suggests areas for policy action.

158 Bhattasali, B.N. and Bhattasali, G.
A B PRODUCTIVITY AND ECONOMIC DEVELOPMENT
Tokyo: Asian Productivity Organization, 1972.

159 Bienen, Henry and Diejomaoh, V.P., eds.
THE POLITICAL ECONOMY OF INCOME DISTRIBUTION IN NIGERIA.
POLITICAL ECONOMY OF INCOME DISTRIBUTION IN DEVELOPING COUNTRIES SERIES, NO.2
New York and London: Holmes & Meier, 1981.

Thirteen previously unpublished case studies on income distribution as related to growth in Nigeria, a country experiencing an oil boom, massive rural migration to urban areas, rapid growth in its manufacturing sectors, and poor growth of the rural economy. Based on national survey data and major published and unpublished sources, papers present an extensive picture of industrial sector income distributions, including intraindustry wage differentials and occupational incomes, and compare formal and informal urban sector incomes.

160 Bienen, Henry, General Editor
POLITICAL ECONOMY OF INCOME DISTRIBUTION IN DEVELOPING COUNTRIES
N.Y.: Holmes & Meier Publishers, 1980.

This new series examines in detail the economies of Turkey, Nigeria, Egypt, and Mexico and the problems inherent in growth, planning, and distribution of wealth. Based on microsurveys and aggregate data. The series is a joint effort of the Research Program in Development Studies of the Woodrow Wilson School of International Affairs, Princeton University, and of scholars and experts from the developing world.

161 Billerbeck, K. and Yasugi, Y.
PRIVATE DIRECT FOREIGN INVESTMENT IN DEVELOPING COUNTRIES
World Bank, Washington, D.C., 1979.

A background study for World Development Report, 1979. Discusses the changing characteristics of private direct foreign investment in developing countries in relation to home and host country policies. Examines the changed environment in developing countries for transnational corporations, reviews policy issues for developing countries that wish to attract foreign investment and for the industrialized countries that are the principal sources of such flows, and discusses the role of international institutions in private investment.

162 Binswanger, Hans P.
A B C THE ECONOMIC OF TRACTORS IN SOUTH ASIA: AN ANALYTICAL REVIEW
New York: Agricultural Development Council; Hyderabad, India: International Crops Research Institute for the Semi-arid Tropics, 1978.

Surveys the literature on the economic effects of tractors on agriculture in South Asia, making findings of the studies comparable across agroclimatic zones. Compares agricultural results using tractors as opposed to bullocks and discusses the cost advantage of tractors. Finds in part that: (1) the literature fails "to provide evidence that tractors are responsible for substantial increases in intensity, yields, timeliness, and gross returns on farms in India, Pakistan, and Nepal"' (2) many of the cost-benefit studies may have overestimated the private and social benefits of tractors; and (3) although tractor farms tend to use the same amount of labor as bullock farms, the output of the former tends to be greater due to the level of capitalization.

163   Bird, Richard M. and Oldman, Oliver, eds.
        READINGS ON TAXATION IN DEVELOPING COUNTRIES. THIRD EDITION
        Baltimore and London: Johns Hopkins University Press, 1975.

        An edited collection of 41 previously published papers dealing with many forms, targets, and applications of taxation in a development context. Only seven of the selections appeared in the previous two editions in 1964 and 1967. Major areas dealt with are: fiscal policy and economic development, taxation and the external sector, taxation of income and wealth, taxation of consumption, taxation and incentives, agricultural taxation, urban finance, and tax administration. Sporadic taxation data for various countries and years in some of the selections.

164   Bird, Richard
        INTERGOVERNMENTAL FISCAL RELATIONS IN DEVELOPING COUNTRIES
        World Bank, Washington, D.C., 1978.

        Considers a broad range of issues relating to intergovernmental fiscal relations in developing countries, particularly their implications for the provision of urban services. In view of the extremely complex political, economic, and administrative issues, the paper emphasizes the need for an explicit recognition of potentially conflicting goals of fiscal policy, and for a careful analysis of the institutions of the country or city for which policy recommendations are to be made. Special attention is paid to the organizational structure of the public sector, direct controls by government over local authorities, urban tax policy, and intergovernmental transfers.

165   Birla Institute of Scientific Research, Economic Research
A B   Division
        STRUCTURAL TRANSFORMATION AND ECONOMIC DEVELOPMENT
        New Delhi: Arnold-Heinemann, 1980.

        Explores the process of structural transformation occurring in developing countries, focusing on the experiences of India and its problems of stagnation in terms of the persistent primacy of agriculture in employment and output. Discusses the historical shifts of labor from primary to secondary activities in the developed countries, examines the structure of output and employment in eight Asian countries, and analyzes in detail India's agricultural, industrial, and service-related structures.

166   Blaikie, Piers; Cameron, John and Seddon, David
        NEPAL IN CRISIS: GROWTH AND STAGNATION AT THE PERIPHERY
        Oxford and New York: Oxford University Press, Clarendon Press, 1980.

Investigates the economic and social effects of three road construction projects in West-Central Nepal, a predominantly agricultural economy. Explains why these construction projects have had minimal effect in developing agricultural production and why the Nepalese State was unable to postpone the growing ecological crisis. Details background on the crisis and underdevelopment in Nepal; and discusses growth and stagnation at the periphery, concentrating on the West-Central region. Emphasizes the dependency theory explanation of Nepal's condition, characterized as stagnation that is a product of partial incorporation in India.

167 Blase, Melvin G. and Goodwin, Joseph B., eds.
READINGS IN INTERNATIONAL AGRICULTURAL ECONOMIC DEVELOPMENT
New York: MSS Educational Publishing Company, 1970.

Compilation (presumably for teaching purposes) of 14 previously published articles by leading agricultural economists. Subjects cover both theory and empirical findings in the field of international agricultural economic development, the latter placing emphasis on research in Indian agriculture.

168 Blitzer, Charles R.
DEVELOPMENT AND INCOME DISTRIBUTION IN A DUAL ECONOMY: A DYNAMIC SIMULATION MODEL FOR ZAMBIA
Working Paper No. 292; Washington, D.C.: World Bank, 1978.

Discusses medium-term development prospects for Zambia by carrying out the analysis in terms of a dual-economy model, modified to capture key aspects of the Zambian economy. Simulations are carried out on the basis of governmental expenditure, investment, and taxation policies with special attention to sectoral employment and income distribution.

169 Blitzer, Charles R., Clark, Peter B. and Taylor, Lance, eds.
ECONOMY-WIDE MODELS AND DEVELOPMENT PLANNING
New York; London; Melbourne and Singapore: Oxford University Press for World Bank, 1975.

Twelve essays surveying the specification and uses of economy-wide planning models for developing countries, with attention focused on a medium-term and perspective planning. Designed to aid both practical planners and potential model builders by providing a summary of techniques and a discussion of the performance of the models. The material is organized into three parts: (1) concerned with general planning issues, data collection and estimation, and the theoretical bases of economy-wide planning models; (2) deals with the application of models to specific policy problems such as investment planning, income distribution, and foreign trade; and (3) covers methodological problems such as how to model economies of scale, factor substitution, and regional interactions in the national economy.

170 Bos, H. C.; Sanders, Martin and Secchi, Carlo
PRIVATE FOREIGN INVESTMENT IN DEVELOPING COUNTRIES. A QUANTITATIVE STUDY ON THE EVALUATION OF THE MACRO-ECONOMIC EFFECTS
Boston and Dordrecht, Holland: D. Reidel, 1974.

Quantitative, macroeconomic study of a particular aspect of development. In four parts, the analysis reviews the literature concerning the evaluation of private foreign investment and suggests the need for an appropriate methodology, develops the principles and techniques for such a methodology, presents an empirical application of the criteria to data for five developing countries (India, the Philippines, Ghana, Guatemala, and Argentina), and considers the appraisal of projects financed through foreign investment and discusses the special features of social benefit-cost analysis of such projects.

171 Boserup, Ester
WOMAN'S ROLE IN ECONOMIC DEVELOPMENT
New York: St. Martin's Press, 1970.

Investigates the changes in the traditional division of labor between the sexes; contends the changes were initiated by the development process and conditioned by the socio-cultural milieu of the area in transition. This study reflects the experience of some 34 countries in Africa, the Mid-East, South and East Asia, and Latin America. The patterns of these changes and their impact in development are examined.

172 Bosson, Rex and Benison, Varon
THE MINING INDUSTRY AND THE DEVELOPING COUNTRIES
New York: Oxford University Press, 1978.

Provides an overview of the world mining industry: its structure and operation, and the major factors bearing on them, such as the characteristics of mineral resources, economies of scale, capital requirements, lead time, and economic risk; production, consumption, and trade; the behavior of mineral prices; and its impact on economic growth with particular reference to the developing countries.

173 Bottomley, Anthony
FACTOR PRICING AND ECONOMIC GROWTH IN UNDERDEVELOPED RURAL AREAS
London: Crosby Lockwood, 1971.

A study of the ways in which traditional marginal factor pricing must be reinterpreted within the context of underdeveloped rural areas. Such reinterpretations include emphasis on the relationship between marginally higher wages and marginally higher output at subsistence levels where wage increases directly improve nutrition and thus, physical strength of labor supply. Also, the case of hidden unemployment is interpreted as part of an institutional framework obligating the owners of land and capital to provide labor employment.

174 Brenner, Y. S.
LOOKING INTO THE SEEDS OF TIME: SOCIAL MECHANISMS IN ECONOMIC DEVELOPMENT
Assen, The Netherlands: Van Gorcum, 1979.

Analyzes the mechanisms of economic progress and attempts to show that such progress (the augmentation of freedom of choice) is functionally related to mankind's increasing ability to satisfy its material needs more fully and with less effort. Discusses economic development from both the historian's and economist's perspectives, demand stimulated growth, the changing socio-cultural landscape of Europe from the eve of the Reformation to the rise of egalitarian society following World War II. Sees alternatives for the future of industrial society as: decline and fall, a command economy, or democratic participation. Trusts that mankind will substitute social for individualistic rationality if the struggle against the masters of the new industrial feudalism is not lost.

175 Broehl, Wayne G., Jr.
THE VILLAGE ENTREPRENEUR: CHANGE AGENTS IN INDIA'S RURAL DEVELOPMENT
Cambridge, Mass. and London: Harvard University Press, 1978.

Starting from the assumption that change is the sine qua non [sic] of development, the study focuses upon the village entrepreneur in India as an important change agent in rural economic development. Presents an entrepreneurial system model, which defines the nature and locus of entrepreneurship in less developed countries and explores the entrepreneurial role by observing the attitude and behavior of the fertilizer distributor and the rice miller. Examines economic activities in two community development blocks in the south of India.

176 Brown, Christopher P.
THE POLITICAL AND SOCIAL ECONOMY OF COMMODITY CONTROL
New York: Praeger, 1980.

An attempt to identify the principal economic, political and organizational factors that fashioned the Integrated Program for Commodities worked out by the United Nations

Conference on Trade and Development. A useful guide to recent international efforts in the field of commodity stabilization with a bibliography.

177 Brown, Gilbert T.
KOREAN PRICING POLICIES AND ECONOMIC DEVELOPMENT IN THE 1960'S
Baltimore and London: The Johns Hopkins University Press, 1973.

Assessment of the relationship between major shifts in economic policy and rapid economic growth in the Republic of Korea since 1963. Topics dealt with in eleven chapters include: Fiscal Policy and Governmental Saving, Government Product Pricing, Agricultural Price and Marketing Programs, Exchange Rate and Trade Policy Reform, Interest Rate Reform and Domestic Saving, Foreign Credit Inflows, Stabilization Planning and Monetary Policy.

178 Bruckmann, Gerhart, ed.
INPUT-OUTPUT APPROACHES IN GLOBAL MODELING: PROCEEDINGS OF THE FIFTH IIASA SYMPOSIUM ON GLOBAL MODELING, SEPTMEBER 26-29, 1977
Oxford; New York; Toronto and Frankfurt: Pergamon, 1980.

Sixteen papers (some of which have been published in some form or delivered at meetings) in addition to comments and conference addresses surveying the role that input-output techniques can play in global modeling, the conference was methodologically oriented rather than model oriented. Modeling work treated includes the Leontief "Future of the World Economy" model, the Japanese "Future of Global Interdependence" model, and modeling work in the Soviet Union and Poland. Other contributions consider the use of adaptive mechanisms in global modeling, energy-oriented models, software concepts, and general methodological concerns.

179 Brun, Ellen and Hersh, Jacques
SOCIALIST KOREA: A CASE STUDY IN THE STRATEGY OF ECONOMIC DEVELOPMENT
New York and London: Monthly Review Press, 1976.

Presentation of the development of the Democratic People's Republic of Korea establishing a basis for understanding the scope of the socioeconomic transformation of Korean Society. Divided into three parts, the first describes the historical development; the second part identifies the forces and laws behind the process of rapid development as revealed by the Korean example; and the last part explores the problems of a transitional society.

180 Bryden, John M.
TOURISM AND DEVELOPMENT: A CASE STUDY OF THE COMMONWEALTH CARIBBEAN

New York and London: Cambridge University Press, 1973.

A case study of the political and social, but primarily economic, implications of tourism for the economic development process of the Commonwealth Caribbean. There is a review of the importance of tourism in the world economy and of the measurement problems of estimating the impact of tourism on a nation's economy.

181   Burstein, M. L.
      NEW DIRECTIONS IN ECONOMIC POLICY
      New York: St. Martin's Press, 1978.

Examination of new perceptions and new theories (particularly rational expectations) of economic events from both a philosophical and a policy perspective. Contends that economic policy has turned in new directions because of both the fundamental ideological transformations and objective shifts in observation, integration, and interpretation. Arguing that acts of perception create that which appears to be perceived and that "the economy" is as much the creation of economic theory as it is its field of study, the analysis focuses on pronounced shifts in perception of cause-and-effect in economic policy. Shifts in perception of banking, the definition and control of money supply, policy focus on inflation versus unemployment, share-price formation, and LDC's are seen to have occurred within recent years. In a treatment of shifts in the perception of economics, the author provides a nonmathematical explanation of the rational expectations theory of market behavior.

182   Buttari, Juan J., ed.
      EMPLOYMENT AND LABOR FORCE IN LATIN AMERICA: A REVIEW
      AT NATIONAL AND REGIONAL LEVELS
      OAS: ECIEL, 1979.

Offers a vision of the overall employment situation in Latin America, and provides a statistical and conceptual frame of reference for further studies. For various countries and the region as a whole, describes and analyzes population and labor force characteristics, migration flows, sectorial distribution of product and employment, labor productivity differentials, levels of unemployment, and characteristics of the unemployed.

183   Caiden, Naomi and Wildavsky, Aaron
      PLANNING AND BUDGETING IN POOR COUNTRIES
      New Brunswick, NJ and London: Transaction Books, 1980.

Analyzes the budgetary and economic planning processes of over eighty developing nations with per capita GNP's of less than $800 a year. Surveys the lessons drawn from theories of economic growth and development and

and analyzes the nature of poverty and uncertainty that characterizes the economic and political environments of poor countries.

184 Cairncross, Alec and Puri, Mohinder, eds.
EMPLOYMENT, INCOME DISTRIBUTION AND DEVELOPMENT STRATEGY: PROBLEMS OF THE DEVELOPING COUNTRIES: ESSAYS IN HONOUR OF H. W. SINGER
New York: Holmes & Meier, 1976.

A collection of 17 essays, only one previously published, examining the economic and social problems confronting the developing countries. The book begins with a piece by Singer in which he recounts his upbringing as an economist. The first six papers deal with the distribution of income and development or the related issue of employment opportunities. The next seven discuss various aspects of development strategy including industrialization, the role of capital goods, collective self-reliance, and population policy.

185 Camps, Miriam and Gwin, Catherine
COLLECTIVE MANAGEMENT: THE REFORM OF GLOBAL ECONOMIC ORGANIZATIONS
New York: McGraw-Hill, 1981.

This study of the major global economic problems has well-documented chapters on the roles and evolving structures of the IMF and the World Bank as well as an authoritative discussion of key issues now subject to international discussion and negotiation. It is a central argument of the book that more of the weight of management of world economic problems gradually shift to a few strong and efficiently organized global institutions.

186 Camps, Miriam
THE MANAGEMENT OF INTERDEPENDENCE: A PRELIMINARY VIEW
New York: Council on Foreign Relations, Inc., 1974.

Study concerned with the political institutions (both formal structures and informal rules, practices, and associations) which become necessary as interdependence increases among modernized and modernizing societies. Investigation is concerned with future problems of management in four major areas: security, management of the international economy, development, and management and conservation of natural resources.

187 Candler, Wilfred and Norton, Roger D.
MULTI-LEVEL PROGRAMMING AND DEVELOPMENT POLICY
Working Paper No. 258; Washington, D.C.: World Bank, 1977.

Presents a new algorithm making possible the simultaneous

treatment of two related subproblems of economic policy: the "behavioral" problem of forecasting the economy's reactions to policy changes, and the "policy" problem of choosing among alternative outcomes. For illustrative purposes, the procedure is applied to a model of Mexican agriculture.

188 Cardoso, Fernando Henrique and Faletto, Enzo
DEPENDENCY AND DEVELOPMENT IN LATIN AMERICA
Berkeley and London: University of California Press, 1978.

Analysis of the economic dependency of Latin America stressing "the socio-political nature of the economic relations of production" in the tradition of Marx. Seeks to identify the processes through which the domination of Latin American economies by European and American capitalism is sustained and to identify the possibilities for change.

189 Carey-Jones, N. S.; Patankar, S. M. and Boodhoo, M. J.
POLITICS, PUBLIC ENTERPRISE AND THE INDUSTRIAL DEVELOPMENT AGENCY
London: Croom Helm, 1974.

190 Chandy, K. T.
FACTORS WHICH HINDER OR HELP PRODUCTIVITY IMPROVEMENT: COUNTRY REPORT: INDIA
APO, 1980.

This study represents India's contribution to the 1979/80 APO Basic Research Project on the factors affecting the growth of productivity in the Asian region. Chapters cover: nature, scope and coverage of the study; the economic set up in India; productivity in the power sector and fertilizer, cement and cotton textile industries; assessment of experiences of India's National Productivity Council.

191 Chaudhuri, Pramit
THE INDIAN ECONOMY: POVERTY AND DEVELOPMENT
New York: St. Martin's Press, 1979.

Discusses economic growth during the past twenty-five years; examines questions of resource mobilization, stability, and self-reliance; and assesses economic performance in Indian agriculture and industry. Part two explores the structure of poverty and the state of the poor. Part three focuses on the role of the state in the formulation and execution of economic policy.

192 Cheetham, Russel J.; Gupta, Syamaprasad and Schwartz, Antoine
THE GLOBAL FRAMEWORK
Working Paper No. 355; Washington, D.C.: World Bank, 1979.

A background study for World Development Report, 1979. Describes the main features of the global model system used in preparing the report. The system provides a quantitative basis for the study of growth prospects in developing countries in the context of the world economy, and has been used to make projections for the period 1975-90.

193   Cheetham, Russel J. and Hawkins, Edward K.
THE PHILIPPINES: PRIORITIES AND PROSPECTS FOR DEVELOPMENT: REPORT OF A MISSION SENT TO THE PHILIPPINES BY THE WORLD BANK
Washington, D.C.:   The World Bank, 1976.

Comprehensive report on the economy of the Philippines. Attention is given to: agriculture, urban and rural development, agrarian reform, industry, power, and human resources. Also examines financial resource aspects of the development process, quantifying the financial requirements of growth and development. Argues that dependence on foreign inflows can be diminished only if sufficient attention is paid to export promotion and prudent management of the balance of payments.

194   Chelliah, R. J.
FISCAL POLICY IN UNDERDEVELOPED COUNTRIES
New York: Allen and Unwin.

Now a standard reference work in the field, this study has made a distinct contribution by reorienting the theory of fiscal policy originally developed in the economically advanced countries to the problems, requirements and institutional structure of an underdeveloped, over-populated country with a mixed enterprise system.

195   Chen, Edward K. Y.
HYPER-GROWTH IN ASIAN ECONOMIES: A COMPARATIVE STUDY OF HONG KONG, JAPAN, KOREA, SINGAPORE AND TAIWAN
New York: Holmes & Meier, 1979.

This study of export-led growth in five East Asian countries attempts to identify common patterns of development, causes of rapid growth, and the consequences of economic expansion particularly on income distribution. A number of hypotheses are tested empirically, using time-series data for the period 1955-70.

196   Chenery, Hollis
STRUCTURAL CHANGE AND DEVELOPMENT POLICY
New York; Oxford; Toronto and Melbourne: Oxford University Press for the World Bank, 1979.

A four-part study of the management of structural change and the development of feasible combinations of market forces and government intervention for market development. Part one consists of a general introduction to the analysis of structural change. Part two focuses on the changing allocation of production, foreign exchange, investment, and labor by sector in the course of transition from traditional to modern forms of economic organization.

197   Chenery, Hollis B.
TRANSITIONAL GROWTH AND WORLD INDUSTRIALIZATION
World Bank Reprint No. 61, 1978.

Examines the uneven spread of industry among countries from two points of view: first, as a central feature of the internal transformation required by a developing economy, and then as part of the process by which a rapidly growing country has to readjust the structure of its trade in response to its changing comparative advantage and external market conditions. Analyzes the nature of transitional growth and of the countries that are completing the transition; alternative strategies of industrialization and their impact on individual industrial sectors; and the changes in factor proportions and comparative advantage associated with different development patterns and their effect on trade in manufactures.

198   Chenery, Hollis B.; Ahluwalia, Montek S.; Bell, C. L. G.; Duloy, Johns H. and Jolly, Richard
REDISTRIBUTION WITH GROWTH
New York: Oxfrod University Press, 1974.

Essays developed from an investigation by members of the Institute of Development Studies at the University of Sussex (United Kingdom) and the Development Research Center of the Bank. Part One: Reorientation of Policy. Describes the existing inequality in incomes in developing countries and proposes a reorientation of development policy aimed at achieving a more equitable distribution, focusing on separate target groups. Part Two: Quantification and Modeling. Part Three: Annex and Bibliography. Some Country Experience.

199   Choksi, Armeane M.
STATE INTERVENTION IN THE INDUSTRIALIZATION OF DEVELOPING COUNTRIES: SELECTED ISSUES
Working Paper No. 341; Washington, D.C.: World Bank, 1979.

A background study for World Development Report, 1979. Attempts to clarify and analyze the economic implications of state intervention in public sector enterprises, industrial licensing and price controls, and industrial planning. Concludes that a selective role can be played by the state and the private sector in the process of industrialization, and suggests some policy options for developing countries to permit greater interaction of the state with market forces and promote cooperation between the private and public sectors.

200 Cleron, Jean Paul
     SAUDI ARABIA 2000: A STRATEGY FOR GROWTH
     New York: St. Martin's Press, 1978.

     Assesses, within a planning framework, long-term strategies of development on the basis of assumptions referring to policy decisions, structural changes, and behavioral patterns. Uses a dynamic simulation model incorporating mechanisms that both favor and constrain economic development. Results providing projections to 2025 are briefly presented and discussed. Appendix gives computer program of model.

201 Cline, William R.
     POTENTIAL EFFECTS OF INCOME REDISTRIBUTION ON ECONOMIC GROWTH: LATIN AMERICAN CASES
     New York and London: Praeger, 1972.

     This book examines the "theoretical arguments concerning income redistribution's predicted effect on economic growth and uses simulation analysis for Latin American cases to estimate the empirical importance of each major influence proposed on a basis of theory."

202 Cline, William R., et al.
     WORLD INFLATION AND THE DEVELOPING COUNTRIES
     Washington, D.C.: Brookings Institution, 1981.

     Eight previously unpublished articles on the problem of inflation in Third World economics. Discusses the dimensions of the worldwide inflation and recession of 1972-75, its transmission, and its real economic effects on large numbers of developing countries. Presents case studies on: Brazil's aggressive response to external shocks and policy response to external fluctuations, India's closed economy and world inflation, Central American accomodation to external disruptions, and Malaysian growth and price stabilization.

203 Cline, William R. and Weintraub, Sidney, eds.
     ECONOMIC STABILIZATION IN DEVELOPING COUNTRIES
     Washington, D.C.: Brookings Institution, 1981.

     Twelve papers analyze inflation and balance of payments difficulties persistently facing some developing countries in Latin America, Africa, and South Asia. Stabilization programs and policies are studied in detail; includes comments on each paper by economics experts from U.S. and Canadian universities, the United Nations, the Worth Bank, and Bank of America. The editors note agreement on several new patterns of stabilization: (1) inflation has proved more difficult to handle than balance of payments problems; (2) both international and domestic factors caused problems in the seventies; (3) a government's credibility affects stabilization prospects; (4) early action is crucial to successful stabilization; and (5) Asian countries have been more successful.

204 Coats, Warren L. and Khatkhate, Deena R.
MONEY AND MONETARY POLICY IN LESS DEVELOPED COUNTRIES: A SURVEY OF ISSUES AND EVIDENCE
Oxford: Pergamon Press, 1980.

This collection of readings, edited by two IMF staff economists, contains nearly fifty journal papers on monetary analysis in less-developed countries. Each group of papers is accompanied by a bibliography. The articles cover the role of money in the development process, the implementation of monetary policy and econometric models; and they include both classic pieces and newer work by younger economists. The scope is confined, however, to the monetarist canon, and little is presented from other viewpoints, whether Keynesian or structuralist.

205 Codoni, Rene
THE INTERNATIONAL DIVISION OF LABOR IN VIEW OF THE SECOND DEVELOPMENT DECADE
Zurich: Swiss Federal Institute of Technology, Center for Economic Research, 1974.

Examines a deliberate change or improvement in the international division of labor, such that a rise in semi-manufactured and manufactured exports from developing countries would result. The first two chapters discuss the international planning mechanisms adopted by UNCTAD for its "Second Development Decade," which seek to reduce trade gaps of LDC's. The final three chapters examine the international division of labor as in a global context as an operational concept and policy issue. Suggests division of labor analysis could be improved by including institutional aspects and capital transfers.

206 Cody, John; Hughes, Helen and Wall, David, eds.
POLICIES FOR INDUSTRIAL PROGRESS IN DEVELOPING COUNTRIES
New York: Oxford University Press, 1980.

Provides an analysis of the principal policy issues that influence the course and pace of industrialization in the developing countries. It differs from previous writing on the subject in its broad coverage and presentation in a form accessible to nonspecialist readers and complements the existing literature on planning and project evaluation.

207 Colclough, Christopher and McCarthy, Stephen

THE POLITICAL ECONOMY OF BOTSWANA: A STUDY OF GROWTH AND DISTRIBUTION
New York: Oxford University Press, 1980.

Politico-economic history of Botswana, focusing on the post-colonial period after 1966. Traces the growth of total output and analyzes its impact on the incomes and productive capacity of the population. Following material on the general historical, political, and economic situation, the text is arranged by sector: government and planning; agriculture, mining, and industry; migration, employment, and income distribution; education and social policy; and infrastructure. Finds in general that aggregate increases in output are per se less important than their structural composition, and in particular that: (1) while the general population has benefited from growth in output, the growth is the result of sustained good weather, which could easily be reversed; (2) the fundamental productive capacity of the rural population, a key sector, has remained unchanged; and (3) income distribution has become worse and will continue to worsen unless policies are changed.

208 Collins, Paul, ed.
ADMINISTRATION FOR DEVELOPMENT IN NIGERIA
Lagos: African Education Press, 1980.

209 Committee on Economics Teaching Material for Asian Universities
THE ECONOMICS OF DEVELOPMENT
New Delhi: Wiley Eastern, 1976.

A collection of supplementary readings designed to accompany a standard introductory textbook in economic development. Contains 11 articles, all previously published. They provide empirical studies and results from the development experience of various Asian countries, illustrating the main concepts in the study of economic development, such as: poverty and inequality, dimensions of growth, agriculture and development, capital accumulation, foreign trade, education, projections and development planning, and an overview of the Asian economic scene. Provides case studies for Taiwan, Singapore, India, and Indonesia.

210 Cooper, Richard N.
CURRENCY DEVALUATION IN DEVELOPING COUNTRIES
Princeton, NJ: International Finance Section, Department of Economics, Princeton University, 1971.

Briefly summarizes the theoretical effects of devaluation, and the modification of the theory for less developed countries. The author interprets the experience from studies of 36 devaluations between 1953 and 1970 in the light of the theoretical discussions.

211	Coreux, Louis M. with contributions by Penny Davis and Rene Vaurs
	INTERDEPENDENCE IN PLANNING: MULTILEVEL PROGRAMMING STUDIES OF THE IVORY COAST
	Baltimore, MD: Johns Hopkins University Press for IBRD, 1977.

	Presents a system of economic models which permit independent analysis of each economic component, taking into account the interdependence of component parts whenever necessary. The system is applied in this study to the economy of the Ivory Coast.

212	Cornelisse, Peter A.
	PRICE CONSISTENCY IN DEVELOPMENT PLANNING
	Croningen: Academic Book Services for Rotterdam University Press, 1973.

	One in a series of quantitatively designed studies which examines both the danger of an inconsistency between market prices and prices inherently assumed in a development program and the procedures and their statistical requirements which can correct the problem. In addition, an optimum, price-equilibrium programming problem for Turkey is presented to illustrate the practical problems in applying these procedures.

213	Crotty, Raymond
	CATTLE, ECONOMICS AND DEVELOPMENT
	Slough, England: Commonwealth Agricultural Bureaux, 1980.

	A text on the "principles of pastoral resource exploitation," for agronomists, anthropologists, geographers, economists, sociologists, and veterinarians. Presents a mathematical model of decision-making by cattle owners, and using the model examines six types of grazing situations in Western Europe and North America (post World War II), South America, Africa, South East Asia, and India. Maintains that pastoral production is limited because of misuse of available resources and that there is currently widespread gross misuse.

214	Culbertson, John M.
	ECONOMIC DEVELOPMENT: AN ECOLOGICAL APPROACH
	New York: Alfred A. Knopf, 1971.

	Descriptive exposition of the determinants of the standard of living and the "relation of population growth and environmental destruction" to this standard. A chapter in the book surveys and examines inter alia Rostow's important theory of economic development.

215	Damachi, Ukandi, G. and Ewusi, Kodwo, eds.

MANPOWER SUPPLY AND UTILISATION IN GHANA, NIGERIA, AND SIERRA LEONE
IILS, 1979.

This volume brings together the results of separate and independent studies carried out by various scholars in the West African region on employment and industrial relations. It analyzes the problems of manpower development and utilization that the West African states are facing and makes various policy recommendations.

216   Damachi, Ukandi G. and Seibel, Hans Dieter, eds.
SOCIAL CHANGE AND ECONOMIC DEVELOPMENT IN NIGERIA
New York and London: Praeger, 1973.

Collection of fourteen essays (only one previously published) concentrating on the interplay between social change and economic development in Nigeria. The first four essays deal with general social aspects of economic development, and the next four examine manpower and trade unions in their relationship to economic development. The three essays in the third section of the book concentrate on schools and universities and the final group examines the political framework for economic development.

217   Danjo, Kunio and Sonoda, Richi
IMPROVING MANAGEMENT IN PROCESS, PARTS AND MANUFACTURING INDUSTRIES
Tokyo: Asian Productivity Organization, 1971.

218   Das, Amritananda
FOUNDATIONS OF GANDHIAN ECONOMICS
New York: St. Martin's Press, 1979.

Argues that Gandhi saw mass poverty to be the result of two decision errors: attempts to modernize faster than the conditions of the economy permits and the use of international trade in an "accumulationist" fashion that increases capital intensity; the errors result in insufficient generation of new employment. Noting the misconception that affluence can be attined by poor countries using "modern economic growth," Gandihian economics holds that India must opt out of the international development game; only then can growth be structured around a semi-autarkic pattern where trade is used as a means to obtain minimum advantages starting from a domestically-balanced growth policy.

219   Das, Nabagocal
THE INDIAN ECONOMY UNDER PLANNING
Calcutta: World Press Private Ltd., 1972.

Written by an Indian economist with wide government experience, this is a study and appraisal of India's planning experience, particularly its Fourth Five Year Plan. The author discusses the constraints on Indian economic growth, the history and practice of planning in India, the various economic and social problems planners have had to consider, and the many socio-political and economic issues that India has yet to resolve.

220   Dasgupta, Ajit K.
AGRICULTURE AND ECONOMIC DEVELOPMENT IN INDIA
New Delhi: Associated Publishing House; distributed in the U.S. and Canada by International Scholarly Book Services, 1973.

The pattern of growth of output, employment and productivity of labor in agriculture in India is analyzed and compared with the growth of output and employment in the non-farm sector.

221   Dasgupta, P. S. and Hela, G. M.
ECONOMIC THEORY AND EXHAUSTIBLE RESOURCES
New York: Cambridge University Press, 1980.

On the basis, first, of a simple model of price formation for an exhaustible resource, and then a variety of more complex models, the authors analyze the consequences of resource depletion for capital formation, economic growth, and equity among generations; the impact of alternative forms of market structure and of taxation on the pace of depletion; and finally the effects of uncertainty on the production of exhaustible resources.

222   Datta, Jayati
THE CAPITAL GOODS SECTOR IN LDC'S: A CASE FOR STATE INTERVENTION?
Working Paper No. 343; Washington, D.C.: World Bank, 1979.

A background study for World Development Report, 1979. Sets out the rationale for capital goods manufacture in a range of semi-industrialized developing countries, delineates the principal features of machinery production as distinguished from consumer goods or process industries, and identifies the constraints to efficient operations in the sector. The emerging threefold typology of constraints underlines the case for state intervention in the sector.

223   Day, Richard H. and Singh, Inderjit
ECONOMIC DEVELOPMENT AS AN ADAPTIVE PROCESS: THE GREEN REVOLUTION IN THE INDIAN PUNJAB
Cambridge; London; New York and Melbourne: Cambridge Unviersity Press, 1977.

Describes and projects the transition of traditional agriculture to modern farming in the Indian Punjab through the use of an analytical approach that emphasizes three important features: the strategic details of technology conditioning change; imperfect decision-making rules that approximate actual practice, and disequilibrium mechanisms.

224   Dayal, R.
A QUANTITATIVE VIEW OF FUTURE WORLD ECONOMIC DEVELOPMENT
Diessenhofen, Switzerland: Ruegger, 1980.

Analyzes past trends (1960-80) and presents projections to the year 2000 for four major regions of the world: the OECD countries, the developing countries, and the socialist countries of Europe and of Asia. Based on an analysis of past trends and employing a type of full equilibrium model of world trade and development incorporating the recursive approach used in two-gap models, studies five sectors separately (agriculture, mining, machinery and equipment, other manufactures, and services) for each region. Also considers international financial flows; savings, consumption, and intermediate flows; and suggests a new institutional framework (to work alongside the existing one) to handle large amounts of external financial flows and financial assets and liabilities and to facilitate financing arrangements for Third World countries. The approach in the study is in the context of the New International Economic Order Development Strategy.

225   de Kadt, Emanuel, et al.
TOURISM: PASSPORT TO DEVELOPMENT? PERSPECTIVES ON THE SOCIAL AND CULTURAL EFFECTS OF TOURISM IN DEVELOPING COUNTRIES
New York; Oxford; Toronto and Tokyo: Oxford University Press for the World Bank and UNESCO, 1979.

Background paper by Professor de Kadt and 13 previously unpublished contributions to a December 1976 seminar on the impacts of tourism on developing countries sponsored by the World Bank and UNESCO. Broad areas covered include: the effects of tourism on the economy; tourism's effect on tourists, hosts, and the host culture; and specific case studies. Policy recommendations adopted by the seminar are included in an appendix. Concludes that tourism can make substantial contributions to economic and social development, but that its development should be a carefully planned part of the national development program.

226   Dell, Sidney
THE INTER-AMERICAN DEVELOPMENT BANK: A STUDY IN DEVELOPMENT FINANCING
New York and London: Praeger, 1972.

A study of the Bank's organization and administration, resources, lending policies, and the geographical and sectoral distribution of funds for the purpose of assessing its performance in relation to its objectives.

227 Dell, Sidney and Lawrence, Roger
THE BALANCE OF PAYMENTS ADJUSTMENT PROCESS IN DEVELOPING COUNTRIES
New York; Oxford; Toronto and Paris: Pergamon in cooperation with the United Nations, 1980.

Examines the manner in which the burden of adjustment to balance-of-payments disequilibrium in the 1970's was distributed between developed and developing countries. Draws on specially prepared case studies for Brazil, India, Indonesia, Ivory Coast, Jamaica, Kenya, the Republic of Korea, Peru, Philippines, Sri Lanka, the United Republic of Tanzania, Uruguay, and Zambia.

228 Dervis, Kemal; de Melo, Jaime and Robinson, Sherman
A GENERAL EQUILIBRIUM ANALYSIS OF FOREIGN EXCHANGE SHORTAGES IN A DEVELOPING ECONOMY
Working Paper No. 443; Washington, D.C.: World Bank, 1981.

Examines the consequences of alternative adjustment mechanisms to foreign exchange shortages in semi-industrial economies. Compares devaluation to two forms of import rationing and finds that adjusting by rationing is much more costly in terms of lost gross domestic product.

229 Deutsch, Karl, ed.
ECOSOCIAL SYSTEMS AND ECOPOLITICS: A READER ON HUMAN AND SOCIAL IMPLICATIONS OF ENVIRONMENTAL MANAGEMENT IN DEVELOPING COUNTRIES
Paris: UNESCO; distributed by Unipub, New York, 1977.

Nineteen selections, eighteen previously published, about "the growing interplay of mankind's social and economic activities and its natural environment, and about the political challenges and decisions which this growing interplay produces or requires," for the use of political decision-makers, social and economic planners and businessmen.

230 Diamond, William
DEVELOPMENT BANKS
Baltimore, MD: Johns Hopkins University Press, 1957.

A detailed examination of operating experiences to serve as a practical guide for developing countries, with a selected list and summary description of some development banks.

231 Diamond, William and Raghavan, V. S., eds.
ASPECTS OF DEVELOPMENT BANK MANAGEMENT
Baltimore, MD: Johns Hopkins University Press.

This is the first book to deal exclusively with the management of development banks--with their problems and the various ways of tackling them. The book comprises eight sections, each focusing on one aspect of management. Each section opens with an introduction by the editors that highlights the relations affecting the various issues confronting management and the role of management in dealing with them.

232   Diamond, William, ed.
DEVELOPMENT FINANCE COMPANIES: ASPECTS OF POLICY AND OPERATION
Baltimore, MD: Johns Hopkins University Press, 1968.

Review of subjects discussed at a 1965 conference of chief executives of eighteen development finance companies in Europe, Africa, Latin America, and Asia.

233   Diebold, William, Jr.
INDUSTRIAL POLICY AS AN INTERNATIONAL ISSUE
New York: McGraw-Hill, 1980.

Economic policies pursued in one country often clash with those of another, resulting in disputes in areas such as trade and employment. The author discusses why these problems persist, and makes specific proposals for improving the way governments can deal with structural change at the national and international level without damaging the world economy and international cooperation.

234   Donges, Juergen B.; Stecher, Bernd and Wolter, Frank
INDUSTRIAL DEVELOPMENT POLICIES FOR INDONESIA
Kieler Studien 126. Germany: J.C.B. Mohr, 1974.

Research results of a five-month fieldwork study in Indonesia in 1973. Discusses the long-run relative advantage--due to natural riches--in promoting industrializaton through export potential manufacturing activities. Choice of industries, location, and economic policy instruments are analyzed.

235   Dopfer, Kurt
THE NEW POLITICAL ECONOMY OF DEVELOPMENT: INTEGRATED THEORY AND ASIAN EXPERIENCE
New York: St. Martin's Press, 1980.

The author takes a much-needed interdisciplinary approach in this analysis of Asian development in the period 1950 to 2000. He proposes a systems framework that delineates the causal relationships among population dynamics, the socioeconomic and political systems, nonrenewable resources, and the carrying capacity of ecosystems.

236   Dornbusch, Rudiger

EXCHANGE RATE POLICIES FOR DEVELOPING COUNTRIES
Seoul: Korea International Economic Institute, 1981.

This lecture is part of a seminar series on alternative exchange rate policy for developing countries experiencing accelerated inflation, large current account deficits, structural excesses in exports capacity, and constraints on policy options. Also includes questions posed by participants and answers by the author. Suggests three policy measures: an exchange rate regime of a stable real exchange rate pegged on a mini-basket; a social security tax on wages; and an export subsidy substantial enough to combat the export problem.

237 Dorner, Peter
LAND REFORM AND ECONOMIC DEVELOPMENT
Baltimore; Middlesex, England and Ringwood, Victoria, Australia: Penguin, 1972.

Discusses the role which land reform can play within a development strategy, reviews the diversity of existing land tenure systems and approaches to reform, analyzes the realignments of power and income which result from land reform, and discusses the effect of land reform on agricultural employment, investment, and productivity.

238 Dubey, Vinod and Faruqi, Shakil (and others)
TURKEY: POLICIES AND PROSPECTS FOR GROWTH
Washington, D.C.: World Bank, 1980.

States that overall economic growth during the 1960's and most of the 1970's was good compared with other developing countries. Concludes, however, that the recent sharp increase in oil prices had an unfavorable impact on the country and that resumption of sustainable growth depends on the adoption of an export-oriented strategy; on policies aimed at increasing domestic savings and at keeping aggregate demand for resources in line with aggregate supply; and on the support for these policies by various donors and the financial community.

239 Due, John F.
INDIRECT TAXATION IN DEVELOPING ECONOMIES: THE ROLE AND STRUCTURE OF CUSTOMS DUTIES, EXCISES, AND SALES TAX
Baltimore and London: Johns Hopkins Press, 1970.

The purpose of this study is to determine the manner in which a government can make a selective use of indirect taxation during progressive stages of economic growth. The three principal indirect taxes considered are: customs duties, excise taxes, and sales taxes. Although the study is based on the tax structures of some countries in Latin America, Africa, and Asia.

240   Dunn, Edgar S., Jr.
ECONOMIC AND SOCIAL DEVELOPMENT: A PROCESS OF SOCIAL LEARNING
Baltimore and London: Johns Hopkins Press for Resources for the Future, Inc., 1971.

An economist's analysis of "human problem solving seen as a process of social learning." The author reviews the principal characteristics of the modern synthetic theory of evolution while establishing the sense in which it functions as a learning system; he then attempts to identify the peculiarities of social evolution and development, hoping to reach an understanding of the components of social learning. Social learning concepts are then applied to the problems of regional and national development, and their implications for social science research are then discussed.

241   Eaton, Jonathan and Gersovitz, Mark
POOR-COUNTRY BORROWING IN PRIVATE FINANCIAL MARKETS AND THE REPUDIATION ISSUE
Princeton, NJ: Princeton University, Department of Economics, International Finance Section, 1981.

Discusses the effect on capital flows among rich and poor countries, due to a fear of debt repudiation. Explains how the possibility of debt repudiation by LDC's affect the functioning of international financial markets and the development prospects of LDC's, potentially limiting capital mobility. Examines guidelines for risk analysis by lenders and assesses the attempt to develop statistical models to predict defaults.

242   ECLA
ECONOMIC AND SOCIAL DEVELOPMENT AND THE EXTERNAL ECONOMIC RELATIONS OF LATIN AMERICA
New York: UN, 1979.

--Vol. 1. Discusses the evolution of Latin American economy. Coverage includes: (a) long-term evolution: towards a new stage of economic development; (b) the 1970's: rise and fall of the economic growth rate; (c) the agricultural sector; (d) the industrial sector; (e) the energy sector; (f) income distribution and poverty situations; (g) social development; structural changes and transformations.

243   Edwards, Edgar O., ed.
EMPLOYMENT IN DEVELOPING NATIONS: REPORT ON A FORD FOUNDATION STUDY
New York and London: Columbia University Press, 1974.

Collection of 20 previously unpublished papers selected from among the papers prepared for three international seminars in 1973 on employment problems in developing nations. The papers approach the employment problem from the points of view of policy, technology, rural development, international issues, and education. Four papers dealing with country experiences are included.

244   Elliott, Charles, ed.
CONSTRAINTS ON THE ECONOMIC DEVELOPMENT OF ZAMBIA
New York, Nairobi and London: Oxford University Press, 1971.

A book of twelve readings about constraints on economic development in Zambia. Seven of the articles deal with general constraints: manpower, industrial relations, wages, financial, fiscal, markets, and foreign exchange. Five of the articles deal with constraints on individual industries: mining, agriculture, manufacturing, transport, and construction. Many of the authors are associated with the University of Zambia either permanently or as visiting scholars. Contains an introduction by Elliott which outlines the basic features of the Zambian economy and their implications for its economic policy, and which gives the history of economic planning in Zambia and the emergence of a strategy for development immediately before and after the achievement of political independence in 1964.

245   Elliott, Charles
PATTERNS OF POVERTY IN THE THIRD WORLD: A STUDY OF SOCIAL AND ECONOMIC STRATIFICATION
New York: Praeger, 1975.

246   El Mallakh, Ragaei
THE ECONOMIC DEVELOPMENT OF THE UNITED ARAB EMIRATES
New York: St. Martin's Press, 1981.

Traces the process of economic integration fostered by the political federation of the seven Trucial coast emirates in 1971, showing how within the span of 20 years the Arab sheikhdoms were transformed from among the poorest to among the richest nations of the world. Presents basic economic data on the United Arab Emirates (UAE); delineates and analyzes the conceptual problems in the economy; exmaines the UAE developmental process; and describes the social and economic infrastructures. Notes that the UAE as a relatively low absorber of foreign funds, recycles its surplus funds by investing abroad, extending bilateral aid to less-developed nations, and contributing to multinational organizations. Also describes the foreign trade sector, the financial sector, and patterns and opportunities for business relations with the UAE.

247   Enthoven, Adolf J. H.

ACCOUNTANCY SYSTEMS IN THIRD WORLD ECONOMIES
North Holland Publishing Co., N.Y., 1977.

The book discusses the various aspects of enterprise, government, and national accounting systems and the problems encountered in their implementation in the developing world. It also provides detailed case studies of six African and nine Asian countries, dealing, among other things, with the status of the accounting profession in both the public and private sectors, training programs offered in these sectors, and recent efforts at improving accounting systems.

248 FAO
TRAINING HOME ECONOMISTS FOR RURAL DEVELOPMENT: REPORT OF A GLOBAL STUDY ON THE DEVELOPMENT OF CRITERIA FOR ESTABLISHING TRAINING INSTITUTIONS FOR HOME ECONOMICS STAFF IN RURAL DEVELOPMENT. (FAO ECONOMIC AND SOCIAL DEVELOPMENT PAPER, 6)
FAO, Rome, 1978.

Suggests guidelines for organizing training programs for home economists employed in rural development programs. Identifies four aspects of rural development of new institutions for training home economists and other staff serving rural development: (a) improving the quality of human resources as a part of rural development; (b) increasing recognition of women as a significant human resource; (c) increasing understanding of the role of the family in human resource development; and (d) improving the skills of home economists and other staff working in family-oriented rural programs.

249 Farley, Rawle
A B THE ECONOMICS OF LATIN AMERICA. DEVELOPMENT PROBLEMS
C D IN PERSPECTIVE
New York and London: Harper & Row, 1972.

A comprehensive and over-all look at the economic development problems of Latin America, reviewing the current conditions, past achievements, and the issues yet to be successfully dealt with. The author discusses such varied topics as demography, housing, education, agricultural development, land tenure, industrialization, capital formation, external financing, economic integration, and the political varibles in Latin American economic development.

250 Feder, Gershon
ECONOMIC GROWTH, FOREIGN LOANS AND DEBT SERVICING CAPACITY OF DEVELOPING COUNTRIES
World Bank, Washington, D.C., 1978.

A simple aggregate model of growth and external debt is linked with an empirical formula for debt-servicing capacity. Using data of two groups of developing countries, the underlying conditions and pattern of debt-servicing problems that emerge from simulations of patterns and policies for the alleviation of problems are examined. The study raises doubts about the applicability of accepted beliefs and rules related to external debt management.

251 Fei, John C.H., Ranis, Gustav and Kuo, Shirley W.K.
GROWTH WITH EQUITY: THE TAIWAN CASE. ASSISTED BY YU-YUAN BIAN AND JULIA CHANG COLLINS. A WORLD BANK RESEARCH PUBLICATION
New York: Oxford; Melbourne and Delhi: Oxford University Press for the World Bank, 1979.

Develops a policy-oriented theory of the link between economic growth and family income distribution in a labor surplus economy. While noting that ideal equity is equality of opportunity, not necessarily equality of income, the authors maintain that a more equal distribution increases the equality of opportunity in each generation. Part one focuses first on the case of Taiwan generally for the period of the 1950's and then in depth for the period after 1964 when better data are available. Examines the relation between growth and distribution by factor components as well as wage, economic structure, and taxation considerations. Finds that "it is possible for economic growth to be compatible with an improved distribution of income during every phase of the transition from colonialism to modern growth," and that given an initial distribution that is not too unfavorable, growth can equitably be achieved by affecting the basic growth path, not by direct government intervention.

252 Fields, Gary S.
POVERTY, INEQUALITY, AND DEVELOPMENT
New York: Cambridge University Press, 1980.

253 Fitzgerald, E.V.K.
THE STATE AND ECONOMIC DEVELOPMENT: PERU SINCE 1968. UNIVERSITY OF CAMBRIDGE DEPARTMENT OF APPLIED ECONOMICS OCCASIONAL PAPER 49
Cambridge; New York and Melbourne: Cambridge University Press, 1976.

Study of the political economy of Peru between 1960 and 1975, emphasizing the state intervention in surplus mobilization and allocation since 1968. Thus, deals with policy options open to a "nationalist, reforming regime within a dependent developing economy" to reduce the degree of external dependency without committing itself to pure socialism.

254 Fleming, Alex
PRIVATE CAPITAL FLOWS TO DEVELOPING COUNTRIES AND THEIR

554 Resource Bibliography

DETERMINATIONS: HISTORICAL PERSPECTIVE, RECENT EXPERIENCE, AND FUTURE PROSPECTS
World Bank Staff Working Paper No. 484, 1981.

A background study for World Development Report 1981. Discusses the nature and determination of recent private capital flows to developing countries. Focuses on those flows passing through the international banks and examines the prospects for and constraints on developing countries' continuing access to the international capital markets.

255   Fletcher, Lehman B.; Graber, Eric; Merrill, William C. and Thorbecke, Eric
GUATEMALA'S ECONOMIC DEVELOPMENT: THE ROLE OF AGRICULTURE
Ames, Iowa: Iowa State University Press, 1971.

A study carried out by the authors with the help of the United States A.I.D. Mission in Guatemala and the government of Guatemala. It "analyzes the present role of agriculture in the economic development of Guatemala and suggests short- and medium-term policies conducive to economic development." Treats in detail the structure and the working of the agricultural sector.

256   Foldi, Tamas, ed.
ECONOMIC DEVELOPMENT AND PLANNING: SELECTED STUDIES
Budapest: Akademiai Kiado, 1973.

The third English publication of research papers from the Hungarian Academy of Sciences. Based on two former collections in Hungarian, this collection os six monographs by staff members of the institute of Economics contains works dealing with problems of long-range socialist economic planning, income and price elasticities of demand, budgetary equilibrium, industrial development strategies in developing countries, and agricultural development both in Hungary and in capitalist economies.

257   Frobel, Folker
CURRENT DEVELOPMENT OF THE WORLD ECONOMY
UNU, Tokyo, 1980.

Studies the developmental tendencies which characterized the political and economic model of accumulation of the economic boom decades after the Second World War.

258   Foxley, Alejandro, ed.
INCOME DISTRIBUTION IN LATIN AMERICA
Cambridge; New York and Melbourne: Cambridge University Press, 1976.

Eleven papers, six previously published, dealing with the distributional effects of economic growth in the following Latin American countries: Argentina, Brazil,

Chile, Colombia, Cuba, Mexico, Puerto Rico, Peru, and Venezuela. Recent distributive tendencies in several of the countries and factors explaining those tendencies are exmained in the first half of the book. Papers in the second half deal with the development of policies designed to make economic growth and redistributive objectives compatible.

259 Frank, Andre Gunder
ON CAPITALIST UNDERDEVELOPMENT
Bombay; New York; London and Hong Kong: Oxford University Press, 1975.

Represents an early exposition of the "dependence" theory of underdevelopment. Underdevelopment is seen as a result of the historical process of capitalist development, an outgrowth of colonization processes undertaken by the developed nations. The bulk of the essay is a historical analysis of the genesis of capitalism, it's relation to feudalism, and its colonial aspects. While the author looks at capitalism as a worldwide phenomenon, special attention is paid to Latin America. Underdeveloped nations are seen as creations of the developed nations and are therefore dependent upon them for their development.

260 Franko, Laurence G. and Seiber, Mariyn J., eds.
DEVELOPING COUNTRY DEBT. PERGAMON POLICY STUDIES ON SOCIO-ECONOMIC DEVELOPMENT, NO. 36
New York; Oxford; Toronto and Sydney: Pergamon Press, 1979.

Part one presents the situation of developing country debt, and part two provides case studies on debt in the Philippines, Jamaica, Turkey, Portugal, Peru, and Egypt and the bankers' view of debt. Part three presents some alternative approaches to the debt problem as well as actions that could be taken by the United States and the International Monetary Fund, and part four examines the debt situation in a global context. The editor notes that "contrary to the view that LDC's in general are profligate wastrels, most borrowing countries, most of the time, supported not just growth in current consumption, but growth in investment for future growth." Concludes in part that while the LDC's have coped well with the OPEC oil-price revolution, the structure of financial market interactions between developed countries and non-oil LDC's has created two trade problems for the advanced countries: a rapid growth of exports of manufactures from borrower LDC's--helping lenders yet hurting small business and labor--and a slow growth of OECD exports to the non-oil LDC's.

261 Friedman, Irving S.
THE EMERGING ROLE OF PRIVATE BANKS IN THE DEVELOPING

556 Resource Bibliography

WORLD. FORWARD BY G.A. COSTANZO
New York: Citicorp, Public Affairs Department, 1977.

Discusses the borrowing needs of the developing countries and the increasing lending by private banks to these countries. Argues that the facts do not support theories of imprudent lending by private banks or impending default by developing countries, and that the American banking system has not been endangered by its loans to these countries. Suggests some guidelines for both borrowers and lenders and concludes that the prerequisite for any successful approach is the productive use of the funds borrowed from private banks.

262 Friedman, Irving S.
INFLATION: A GROWING WORLD-WIDE DISASTER
Garden City, New York: Anchor Press/Doubleday, 1975.

Examines the international inflationary experience, especially from the second World War through 1972 and analyzes the factors and policies responsible for its creation and preservation. Focuses particularly on the problem of "persistent inflation," its economic signs and effects and its social and political effects world-wide. Discusses the balance-of-payments crises that have occurred in the United Kingdom and the United States, and the more general impact of inflation on the international monetary system. Suggests guidelines for national economic policies to combat inflation and predicts world inflationary trends with and without these policies.

263 Friedman, Milton
MONEY AND ECONOMIC DEVELOPMENT. THE HOROWITZ LECTURES OF 1972. PRAEGER SPECIAL STUDIES IN INTERNATIONAL ECONOMICS AND DEVELOPMENT
New York and London: Praeger, 1973.

A transcript of the Horowitz Lectures delivered by the author in Jerusalem and Tel Aviv during April of 1972. One of the lectures is a survey of the evidence for monetarism together with a review of the key propositions of the monetarist approach to macroeconomics. The second lecture is on monetary policy in developing countries, with comments on inflation and development, money creation as a source of government revenue, and other issues in monetary management.

264 Frisch, Ragnar
ECONOMIC PLANNING STUDIES: A COLLECTION OF ESSAYS. EDITED WITH AN INTRODUCTION BY FRANK LONG. PREFACE BY JAN TINBERGEN. INTERNATIONAL STUDIES IN ECONOMICS AND ECONOMETRICS, VOL. 8
Dordrecht, Holland and Boston: Reidel, 1976.

A collection of five previously published essays by the late Ragnar Frisch. "From Utopian Theory to Practical Applications: The Case of Econometrics"; "Co-operation between Politicians and econometricians on the Formalization of Political Preferences"; "Preface to the Oslo Channel Model"; "An Implementation System for Optimal National Economic Planning without Detailed Quantity Fixation from a Central Authority"; "Economic Planning and the Growth Problem in Developing Countries."

265   Fry, Maxwell J.
      THE AFGHAN ECONOMY. MONEY, FINANCE, AND THE CRITICAL CONSTRAINTS TO ECONOMIC DEVELOPMENT
      Leiden, Netherlands: E.J. Brill, 1974.

      Comprehensive analysis of the economic structure of Afghanistan. The author provides an introduction to the economic, social, and geographic characteristics of Afghanistan and then focuses his attention on an examination of resource mobilization under recent development plans, the structure and role of the country's financial sector, its public finances, its foreign trade sector, and recent monetary and fiscal policies.

266   Fryer, Donald W.
      EMERGING SOUTHEAST ASIA: A STUDY IN GROWTH AND STAGNATION
      New York and Toronto: Wiley, Halsted Press, [1970] 1979.

      "Part one is a generalized discussion of Southeast Asia in the modern world; the land and its utilization; and urbanization, industrialization, and modernization. Part two discusses countries that have progressed in the post-World War II period and presents individual examinations of the economic conditions and prospects of Thailand, the Philippines, and Malaysia, and Singapore. Part three, assesses the economies of Indonesia, Burma, and Vietnam, Laos, and Cambodia, which have not progressed. Part four considers the region's prospects for economic growth and regional cooperation and integration."

267   Furness, Eric L.
      MONEY AND CREDIT IN DEVELOPING AFRICA
      London: Heineman.

      A general work on monetary economics with special reference to developing economies and to African countries in particular. It is concerned more with analysis than with institutional description, though an account is given of a selection of African banking systems.

268   Furtado, Celso
      ECONOMIC DEVELOPMENT OF LATIN AMERICA: HISTORICAL BACKGROUND AND CONTEMPORARY PROBLEMS. SECOND EDITION. TRANSLATED BY SUZETTE MACEDO. CAMBRIDGE LATIN AMERICAN STUDIES, NO. 8

New York; London and Melbourne: Cambridge University Press, 1976.

Introductory survey in eight parts: early history of Latin America up to the formation of nation-states; entry into the system of international division of labor; traditional structural pattern; industrialization process characteristics; recent reorganization of development; international relations; intraregional relations; and structural reconstruction policies. Many of the chapters in this edition have been rewritten "to give greater depth to the study of the institutional framework which is the basis of the structural matrix prevailing in the region" and to update the material. Includes data on trade and development indicators.

269   Garcia-Zamor, Jean-Claude and Sutin, Stewart E., eds.
        FINANCING DEVELOPMENT IN LATIN AMERICA. PRAEGER SPECIAL STUDIES--PRAEGER SCIENTIFIC
        New York: Praeger, 1980.

        Eighteen previously unpublished papers, written from the standpoint of "lenders or detached observers," on issues of finance, banking, and the capital needs of developing countries in Latin America.

270   Germidis, Dimitri, ed.
        INTERNATIONAL SUBCONTRACTING: A NEW FORM OF INVESTMENT
        OECD, 1980.

        This analysis of international subcontracting is divided in four parts. Part 1 looks at the problems and perspectives of the international subcontracting and industrialization of the Third World. Part 2 describes the state-of-the-art of subcontracting. Part 3 contains country case studies from Haiti, Morocco, Tunisia, and Sri Lanka. Part 4 consists of regional case studies illustrating the impact of international subcontracting on the integration of the Caribbean and Asian countries.

271   Ghai, Dharam, ed.
        ECONOMIC INDEPENDENCE IN AFRICA
        Nairobi, Kampala, and Dar es Salaam: East African Literature Bureau, 1973.

        Collection of ten revised papers which were originally presented at a conference held at the University of Nairobi in February, 1971. Papers deal with different facets of economic independence including a general survey of issues, concepts and strategies, its international aspects, its interaction with economic cooperation, its relationship to development of the state sector, its political aspect and case studies of Kenya, Zambia, Egypt and the Sudan.

272   Ghatak, Subrata
        MONETARY ECONOMICS IN DEVELOPING COUNTRIES
        New York: St. Martin's Press, 1981.

        Highlights applicability to LDC's of theoretical views by Keynesians and monetarists. Presents a brief introduction on the special characteristics of financial markets and monetary institutions in LDCs. Also discusses theories of money and economic growth; the Polak model to analyze the effect of imports, exports, and money supply within the circualr flow model; the role of monetary policy in developing countries; and international liquidity; and SDRs (special drawing rights). Concluding chapter suggests reform of the International Monetary System from point of view of LDCs.

273   Ghatak, Subrata
        DEVELOPMENT ECONOMICS. MODERN ECONOMICS SERIES
        London and New York: Longman, 1978.

        Aims at "strik[ing] a greater balance between the theory and the practice" than existing texts, assessing the relevance of existing theories of growth and development to the economic realities of the less developed countries (LDC's) and also quantifying available evidence.

274   Ghosh, A.
        DEVELOPMENT PLANNING IN SOUTH-EAST ASIA. AN INPUT-OUTPUT APPROACH. IN COLLABORATION WITH D. CHAKRAVARTI AND H. SARKAR. FOREWORD BY J. TINBERGEN
        The Netherlands: Rotterdam University Press; distributed in the United States and Canada by International Scholarly Book Services, 1974.

        Demonstrates the use of input-output modeling and regression analysis techniques as they were applied to long-range development planning in South-East Asia--mainly in Taiwan, Korea, Malaysia, and Ceylon. This monograph provides a model and guide for planners in other countries at a similar stage of economic development. Projections are made for outputs (1960-1980) and sectoral employment.

275   Ghosh, Santikumar
        DEVELOPMENT PERFORMANCE AND STAGFLATION
        Calcutta: World Press, 1974.

        Traces the course of planned economic development in India during the three Five Year Plans. Examines the nature and extent of the achieved cultural transformation and the stagflation phenomenon in the mid-sixties. Data for 1960 to 1973 and projections on the effects of the fourth plan.

276 Ginneken, Wouter Van
SOCIO-ECONOMIC GROUPS AND INCOME DISTRIBUTION IN MEXICO
N.Y.: St. Martin's Press, 1980.

This study shows how Mexico's relatively high and steady level of income inequality differs from the pattern predicted by the Kuznets hypothesis and offers an innovative analysis of the unique economic, social, and political characteristics of Mexican income distribution within the framework of a basic economic model.

277 Girvan, Norman
FOREIGN CAPITAL AND ECONOMIC UNDERDEVELOPMENT IN JAMAICA
Jamaica: Institute of Social and Economic Research, University of the West Indies, 1971.

Deals with foreign investment in Jamaica, choosing the bauxite industry as a specific example. Studies the determination of the industry's output, the industry's impact on development plans, the country's financial system, and the national economy in general.

278 Goh, Keng Swee
THE ECONOMIC OF MODERNIZATION AND OTHER ESSAYS
Singapore: Asian Pacific Press and Detroit, Mich.: Cellar Book Shop, 1972.

279 Goodland, Robert
TRIBAL PEOPLES AND ECONOMIC DEVELOPMENT: HUMAN ECOLOGIC CONSIDERATIONS
World Bank, Washington, D.C., 1982.

At the current time, approximately 200 million tribal people live in all regions of the world and number among the poorest of the poor. This paper describes the problems associated with the development process as it affects tribal peoples; it outlines the requisites for meeting the human ecologic needs of tribal peoples; and presents general principles that are designed to assist the Banks staff and project designers in incorporating appropriate procedures to ensure the survival of tribal peoples and to assist with their development.

280 Gordon, David L., coordinating author
EMPLOYMENT AND DEVELOPMENT OF SMALL ENTERPRISES
Washington, D.C.: World Bank, 1978.

Suggests that efficient substitution of labor for capital is possible in a broad spectrum of small-scale manufacturing and other activities which can absorb a rapidly growing labor force in developing countries, particularly in the larger towns and cities, and often help nurture intrepreneurial talent and technological innovation. Examines the potential role of the World Bank in encouraging developing countries to assist small enterprises.

281 Goreux, Louis M.
INTERDEPENDENCE IN PLANNING: MULTILEVEL PROGRAMMING STUDIES OF THE IVORY COAST
Baltimore and London: Johns Hopkins University Press for the World Bank, 1977.

Designs and tests a dynamic, optimizing system composed of independent models relating to specific projects or sectors and a central model that integrates the sectoral components of the economy of the Ivory Coast.

282 A B C D Gouverneur, J.
PRODUCTIVITY AND FACTOR PROPORTIONS IN LESS DEVELOPED COUNTRIES: THE CASE OF INDUSTRIAL FIRMS IN THE CONGO
New York:: Oxford University Press, 1971.

Discusses optimal techniques and long-run changes in input coefficients and factor proportions and the qualifications necessary for studies of these variables in LDCs. Basic data collected by the author is used to measure long-run changes in the labor coefficient, capital intensity, capital coefficient, and the ratios of Europeans to Africans and to output.

283 Griffiths, B.
MEXICAN MONETARY POLICY AND ECONOMIC DEVELOPMENT. PRAEGER SPECIAL STUDIES IN INTERNATIONAL ECONOMIC AND DEVELOPMENT
New York and London: Praeger, 1972.

A case study in the use of macroeconomic policy to achieve both economic stability and economic growth. Analyzes the role of monetary, fiscal, and balance of payments policies in the performance of the Mexican economy from 1940 to 1967, a period distinguished by high rate of economic growth and low rate of inflation.

284 Griffin, Keith, ed.
FINANCING DEVELOPMENT IN LATIN AMERICA. PROBLEMS IN FOCUS SERIES
London: Macmillan; New York: St. Martin's Press, 1971.

A collection of eight original essays on Latin America's development finance, focused on domestic rather than foreign investment. After an introduction by Keith Griffin, the essays examine development finance in relation to basic principles, surplus and the budget, the public sector activities, agricultural taxation, private savings, inflation, and foreign capital. The main thesis is that a large proportion of the economic surplus is diverted into relatively "unproductive" uses.

285 Griffin, Keith
UNDERDEVELOPMENT IN SPANISH AMERICA
New York: Allen and Unwin.

An interpretation of economic backwardness in the Spanish speaking countries of South America, an analysis of the forces restraining progress and suggestions for a development strategy which would combine growth with equity.

286 Griffin, Keith and James, Jeffrey
A C D THE TRANSITION TO EGALITARIAN DEVELOPMENT: ECONOMIC POLICIES FOR STRUCTURAL CHANGE IN THE THIRD WORLD
New York: St. Martin's Press, 1981.

Examines policies that may be adopted and issues that may arise in the Third World countries during transition from an inegalitarian to an egalitarian growth strategy. Advocates rapid redistribution of income and wealth to alleviate poverty by transformations in output composition, in ownership of productive assets, and in the manner of government organization. Includes case studies of the contemporary experiences of Chile (1970-73), Cuba, and China. Concludes that a strategy for egalitarian development differs from the typical government intervention in that it requires a reorientation of government policy in favor of the poor and a realignment of political forces. Stresses that major institutional and structural changes are a sine qua non for egalitarian development.

287 Griffin, Keith and Khan, Azizur Rahman, eds.
GROWTH AND INEQUALITY IN PAKISTAN
London: Macmillan, 1972.

A collection of ten articles (only one, the chapter by the editors, not previously published), dealing with economic growth and inequality in Pakistan. The articles are grouped into four sections: I, Post-Independence Development and Strategy; II, Stagnation and Growth in Agriculture; III, Industry and Trade; IV, Wages, Income Distribution, and Savings.

288 Guha, Ashok S.
AN EVOLUTIONARY VIEW OF ECONOMIC GROWTH
Oxford: Clarendon Press, 1981.

The author argues that economic growth is an extension of organic evolution, and that development is best interpreted as the adaptation of social structures inherited from the past to the pressures of population, military competition and so on. Thus development should be assessed not as an increase in welfare but rather in terms of the capacity of a society to support human life.

289 Guindey, Guillaume
THE INTERNATIONAL MONETARY TANGLE: MYTHS AND REALITIES
N.Y.: M.E. Sharpe, Inc., 1977.

This summary of international monetary developments from 1944 to 1976 provides a rounded defense of the Bretton Woods charter as the basis for world monetary cooperation by a senior French finance official who served as Director General of the Bank for International Settlements from 1958 to 1963.

290 Gupta, Suraj B.
MONETARY PLANNING FOR INDIA
Delhi; Oxford University Press, 1979.

Theoretical and empirical analysis of the sources of changes in the money supply and the activities of the monetary authorities in controlling money growth in India. Focusing on the period 1950/51 to 1976/77, the author discusses the aims of monetary policy from a mormative standpoint and examines the sources of change in the supply of money in general and high-powered money in particular.

291
A B
C D
Gupta, Syamaprasad
A MODEL FOR INCOME DISTRIBUTION, EMPLOYMENT, AND GROWTH: A CASE STUDY OF INDONESIA. WORLD BANK PAPER, NO. 24
Baltimore: Johns Hopkins University Press for the World Bank, 1977.

Presents a comparatively disaggregated general equilibrium model, consisting of a set of nonlinear equations, which explores the trade-offs between growth and equity, growth and employment, and growth and poverty in Indonesia within the long-term context of various development strategies. Based on official data, 1967-72, the author finds that a strategy that achieves growth through distributive-neutral policy measures is preferable in the long run, since it helps bring about a more rapid transition for the country; this policy, however, will raise income inequality to a high level during the transition. Also includes growth projections to 1985. Data on population, employment, and principal macroeconomic indicators (1967-72) included.

292 Gutkind, Peter C.W. and Walerstein, Immanuel, eds.
THE POLITICAL ECONOMY OF CONTEMPORARY AFRICA. SAGE SERIES ON AFRICAN MODERNIZATION AND DEVELOPMENT, VOL. 1
Beverly Hills, Calif., and London: Sage, 1976.

Authors consider topics such as: African involvement in the world economy, the African peasantry, rural political economy, evolution of the class structure, the congruence of political economies and ideologies, the effects of foreign investment.

293 Hale, William
THE POLITICAL AND ECONOMIC DEVELOPMENT OF MODERN TURKEY
New York: St. Martin's Press, 1981.

Traces the historical evolution of the Turkish Republic from its foundation in 1923 to the present. Briefly describes the pre-1960 period and concentrates on the years 1960-80. Focuses on the relationship of Turkey's economic growth to political change.

294   Hansen, John R., Chief of Mission, et al.
      GUATEMALA: ECONOMIC AND SOCIAL POSITION AND PROSPECTS
      Washington, D.C.: World Bank, 1978.

A working document based on a mission to Guatemala in November 1976. Concludes that, despite current problems because of the fall in coffee prices which occurred after the final work on the report had been done, the economy is financially sound and has good future growth prospects. Recommends that the Government's tax system be reformed to strengthen its fiscal position in order to attack the root causes of poverty, which particularly affects the large indigenous Indian population.

295   Harbison, Frederick H.; Maruhnic, Joan and Resnick, Jane
A B   R.
      QUANTITATIVE ANALYSES OF MODERNIZATION AND DEVELOPMENT
      Princeton: Industrial Relations Section, Princeton University, 1970.

In this work the three authors set out quantitative indicators of development and modernization. Various methods are used in ranking, classifying, and comparing countries or regions within countries. Development, it is claimed, cannot be measured only by indicators of economic growth; the cultural, educational, health, and political aspects of a country must be accounted for. Hence, the term "modernization" is used to better describe the progress of the world's nations. These quantitative indicators, while not resulting in an accurate measure of growth or progress, are useful as a point of departure for more definitive investigation by analysis in the developing countries who might desire to use these methods of data analyses.

296   Harper, Malcolm and Tan Thiam Soon
A B   SMALL ENTERPRISES IN DEVELOPING COUNTRIES: CASE STUDIES
C D   AND CONCLUSIONS
      London: Intermediate Technology Publications, 1979.

297   Hartland-Thunberg, Penelope
A C D BOTSWANA: AN AARICAN GROWTH ECONOMY
      Boulder, Colo.: Westview Press, 1978.

Describes and analyzes the structure of the Botswanan economy in an effort to uncover the factors responsible for Botswana's relative economic success. Examines the traditional and modern sectors of the economy, including the transportation, agricultural, mineral, manufacturing, and service sectors.

298   Hassan, Mostafa E.
ECONOMIC GROWTH AND EMPLOYMENT PROBLEMS IN VENEZUELA: AN ANALYSIS OF AN OIL BASED ECONOMY. PRAEGER SPECIAL STUDIES IN INTERNATIONAL ECONOMICS AND DEVELOPMENT
New York and London: Praeger, 1975.

Examines the relations between Venezuela's high rate of economic growth in the post World War II period and her simultaneous high rates of unemployment. Part I analyzes the factors contributing to that economic growth--the oil industry, investment value, and the international environment. Part II examines factors affecting unemployment such as capital-intensive production methods, labor policies, education, and agricultural development. The final part analyzes the Venezuelan planning process, assessing it in terms of its success in meeting growth and employment targets.

299   Hawkins, Robert G.; Ness, Walter L., Jr. and SaKong, Il.
IMPROVING THE ACCESS OF DEVELOPING COUNTRIES TO THE U.S. CAPITAL MARKET. BULLETIN 1975-4
New York: Graduate School of Business Administration, Center for the Study of Financial Institutions, New York University, 1975.

Examines three alternative proposals for facilitating borrowing in the capital market of the United States by the governments of developing countries. Specifically, the intent of each scheme is to provide a means to increase the acceptability of LDC long-term debt issue. The plans are as follows: (1) the U.S. government would pay a portion of the interest payment on LDC bonds; (2) the U.S. government would guarantee to the investor the interest and amortization payments on LDC government bond issues; (3) an agency of the U.S. government would purchase the bonds of LDC governments. Concludes by comparing each plan in light of six assumed objectives: (a) increasing gross capital inflows to LDC's; (b) reducing the LDC debt-service burden; (c) transition to borrowing-without-subsidy; (d) minimizing thr impact on the U.S. federal budget; (e) minimizing the U.S. balance-of-payments impact; and (f) minimizing administrative complexity.

300   Hawrylyshyn, Oli, et al.
PLANNING FOR ECONOMIC DEVELOPMENT: THE CONSTRUCTION AND USE OF A MULTI-SECTORAL MODEL FOR TUNISIA. PRAEGER SPECIAL STUDIES IN INTERNATIONAL ECONOMICS AND DEVELOPMENT
New York and London: Praeger, 1976.

Describes the construction and use of one mathematical planning tool--PST, a dynamic multi-sectoral simulation model of the Leontief closed type, in the economic planning process in Tunisia, 1970-73. Discusses the model's application to planning in terms of the development of Tunisia's Fourth Medium-Term Development Plan (1973-76) and Second Long-Term Development Plan (1972-81). The model is put into the broader planning framework, and its use made clear by delineating the procedure by which (1) the model is specified, (2) the data are collected, and (3) the model is refined and used.

301 Hellawell, Robert, ed.
UNITED STATES TAXATION AND DEVELOPING COUNTRIES. COLUMBIA UNIVERISTY CENTER FOR LAW AND ECONOMIC STUDIES SERIES
New York: Columbia University Press, 1980.

U.S. tax policy as related to investment and other operations of multinationals in LDC's, originally presented in preliminary form at a symposium sponsored by the Columbia University Center for Law and Economic Studies, held in November 1978. Papers examine the effect of multinational investment on U.S. employment, the tax systems in other capital-exporting countries, and the U.S. tax system from the standpoint of the development of the LDC involved.

302 Helmers, F.L.C.H.
PROJECT PLANNING AND INCOME DISTRIBUTION. STUDIES IN DEVELOPMENT AND PLANNING, VOL. 9
Boston; The Hague and London: Martinus Nijhoff, 1979.

Study incorporating income distribution consideration into traditional project planning for developing countries. Part one examines conventional methods of investment assessments, including valuation of benefits and costs, the rules for maximizing net benefits of a single project, and miscellaneous and external considerations. Part two focuses on income distribution.

303 Hewlett, Sylvia Ann
THE CRUEL DILEMMAS OF DEVELOPMENT: TWENTIETH-CENTURY BRAZIL
New York: Basic Books, 1980.

Investigates through a case study of Brazil, the human, the political, and the economic trade-offs in the contemporary development process. Part one traces the evolution of Brazil's economic structure and characterizes its political and ideological framework. Part two analyzes the dominant economic issues in Brazil's development--inflation, the state, and the multinational corporation. Part three examines the social and political consequences of Brazil's development experience. The central thesis is that Brazil's impressive economic performance has been made at great social cost and has "depended upon massive poverty and political repression."

304 Heyer, Judith; Maitha, J.K. and Senga, W.M., eds.
AGRICULTURAL DEVELOPMENT IN KENYA: AN ECONOMIC ASSESSMENT
Nairobi; New York; London and Hong Kong: Oxford University Press, 1976.

Ten previously unpublished papers by economists dealing with the subject from the colonial era to the post-independence period of the early 1970's. Topics covered include: the agricultural sector and its achievement; agricultural development policy; land tenure reform; the development of small farms, large farms, and the land range areas; water supplies and irrigation; and the marketing system.

305 Hirschman, Albert O.A.
A BIAS FOR HOPE. ESSAYS ON DEVELOPMENT AND LATIN AMERICA
New Haven and London: Yale University Press, 1971.

A collection of 16 of the author's previously published essays on the interaction of economic and political forces in the process of economic development and social change in the developing Latin American countries. These short essays, written within the span of 18 years, are reproduced without change and are divided into three parts: 1) elaboration of the strategy of economic development, 2) critique and appeals addressed to the rich countries, and 3) addressed to the developing countries.

306   Ho, Samuel P.
A B   ECONOMIC DEVELOPMENT OF TAIWAN, 1860-1970
C D   New Haven, CT.: Yale University Press, 1978.

307 Hodder, B.W.
ECONOMIC DEVELOPMENT IN THE TROPICS. 3RD EDITION
New York: Methuen, 1980.

308 Hoogvelt, Ankie M.M.
THE SOCIOLOGY OF DEVELOPING SOCIETIES
Atlantic Highlands, N.J.: Humanities Press, 1976.

Combines, for the purpose of defining thr socio-logical structure of contemporary developing countries, the perspectives of two schools--the "highly abstract--indeed a historical structural functionalist model of societal evolution" and the "Marxist historical interpretation of international processes of development and underdevelopment."

309 Hope, Nicholas C.
DEVELOPMENTS IN AND PROSPECTS FOR THE EXTERNAL DEBT OF THE DEVELOPING COUNTRIES: 1970-80 AND BEYOND
World Bank Staff Working Paper No. 488, 1981.

This background study for World Development Report 1981 analyzes the debt situation and its implications for future borrowing.

310 Horowitz, Irving L.
     EQUITY, INCOME AND POLICY: COMPARATIVE STUDIES IN THREE WORLDS OF DEVELOPMENT
     New York: Praeger, 1977.

311 Howe, James W., et al.
     THE U.S. AND THE DEVELOPING WORLD: AGENDA FOR ACTION 1974
     New York and London: Praeger for the Overseas Development Council, 1974.

     A collection of eight original essays by the ODC staff, dealing with the urgent need for a revised U.S. foreign policy, especially with regard to the less-developed world, and stating in essence that "a cooperative global effort is essential to counter the threat of a severe and sustained global economic slowdown and to maintain momentum in the developing countries, where the human toll of poverty is most severe." Includes statistical annexes on the development gap, trade between developed and developing countries; energy, raw materials and food; and total resource transfers from developed to developing countries.

312 Hunter, John M. and Foley, James W.
     ECONOMIC PROBLEMS OF LATIN AMERICA
     Boston and London: Houghton Mifflin, 1975.

     The problem of population is discussed first, showing how it influences the agricultural sector. Attention is then focused on the industrial sector, showing the role of foreign investment and public finance, and discussing the causes and implications of inflation. The final sections of the book are concerned with the role of education and the scope of future planning, both in terms of social capital and foreign assistance. The emphasis is on the nature of the problems of underdevelopment and the requirements for their solution.

313 Ichimura, Shinichi, ed.
     THE ECONOMIC DEVELOPMENT OF EAST AND SOUTHEAST ASIA
     Honolulu: University Press of Hawaii for East-West Center, 1975.

     Previously published articles on eight countries: Indonesia, Singapore, Thailand, the Philippines, Hong Kong, Taiwan, and Korea., In addition, as an appendix to Chapter Seven, Wan-Yong Kuo discusses technical change, foreign investment and growth in the manufacturing industries of Taiwan, 1952-1970. The papers were first presented at the International Conference on Economic Development of Southeast Asia. Because of the end of The Vietnam War, the normalization of China-Japan relations, and the oil crisis, the editor and authors "hope to revise the book in the near future."

314   ILO
        ORGANISATIONS OF RURAL WORKERS AND THEIR ROLE IN ECONOMIC AND SOCIAL DEVELOPMENT
        ILO, 1975.

        Report IV (1). 1974. Preliminary report covers proposals for a Recommendation concerning organizations of rural workers and their role in economic and social development. Report includes a questionnaire addressed to governments. Report IV (2). 1975. Summarizes replies of 72 governments, with brief commentaries, to the questionnaire accompanying Part 1 of the Report.

315   Institute of Developing Economies
        NEW DIRECTIONS OF ASIA'S DEVELOPMENT STRATEGIES
        Tokyo: Institute of Developing Economies, 1980.

        These are the proceedings of a symposium held at the IDE to discuss the economic achievements of the past two decades in South-east Asia and suggest strategies for the next.

316   International Bank for Reconstruction and Development
        WORLD BANK OPERATIONS. SECTORAL PROGRAMS AND POLICIES.
        Baltimore and London: Johns Hopkins University Press for the IBRD, 1972.

        A collection of what were originally internal working papers on the aggregation of World Bank operations by sectors of economic activity. The papers describe the distinctive economic and developmental characteristics of each sector and review the approach and scale of Bank operations in each field. The sectors which are analyzed are the following: agriculture, industry, transportation, telecommunication, electric power, water supply and sewerage, education, population planning, tourism and urbanization.

317   International Labour Office
        FISCAL MEASURES FOR EMPLOYMENT PROMOTION IN DEVELOPING COUNTRIES
        Geneva: ILO, 1972.

        A collection of papers, most of which were presented at the 1971 conference held in Geneva as part of the "International Labour Office's World Employment Programme." The writings deal with the question of how fiscal policy, through influencing the product mix and the choice of techniques, promotes greater employment.

318   International Monetary Fund
        VOLUME 5: SURVEYS OF AFRICAN ECONOMIES: BOTSWANA, LESOTHO,
        SWAZILAND, BURUNDI, EQUATORIAL GUINEA, AND RWANDA
        Washington, D.C.: IMF, 1973.

        One of a series of economic surveys on individual countries done by IMF staff specialists. Contains trade, tax, national accounts, and some specific industry data pertaining mostly to the period 1966-71, including earlier data when relevant and later when available.

319   International Monetary Fund
        VOLUME 6: SURVEYS OF AFRICAN ECONOMIES: THE GAMBIA, GHANA, LIBERIA, NIGERIA, AND SIERRA LEONE
        Washington, D.C.: IMF, 1975.

        Studies five English-speaking countries on the West African coast. Like the previous five volumes of the series, this book is based mainly on published data sources, supplemented by IMF data as gathered from central banks and government authorities. Covers for each country the general setting; structure of the economy; economic development and planning; prices, wages, and employment; government finance; money and banking; balance of payments; and exchange and trade control system. The economic data are drawn mainly from the 1969 to 1973 period.

320   International Monetary Fund
        VOLUME 7: SURVEYS OF AFRICAN ECONOMIES: ALGERIA, MALI, MOROCCO, AND TUNISIA
        Washington, D.C.: IMF, 1977.

        Reviews developments in each of the 4 countries primarily for the 1970-74 period covering: the general setting, structure of the economy, economic development and planning, prices and employment; government finance, money and banking, the balance of payments, and exchange and trade control systems.

321   Islam, Nurul, ed.
        AGRICULTURAL POLICY IN DEVELOPING COUNTRIES
        New York and Toronto: Halsted Press, 1974.

        A collection of twenty previously unpublished papers presented at a 1972 conference. There are four papers on the interrelations between agriculture and national economic growth, three articles on the interrelations among technological progress, population growht, and food supplies, three essays on the role of trade in agricultural commodities, and five papers on the employment effects of agricultural policy.

322   Jallade, Jean-Pierre
        PUBLIC EXPENDITURES ON EDUCATION AND INCOME DISTRIBUTION IN COLOMBIA

World Bank Staff Occasional Papers, No. 18. Baltimore, MD: Johns Hopkins University Press, 1974.

Focuses on the impact of education expenditures on income distribution, examines the allocation of educational benefits among various population groups, and also considers the distributional effects on taxes that pay for public subsidies in general.

323 Janossy, Ferenc
THE END OF THE ECONOMIC MIRACLE. APPEARANCE AND REALITY IN ECONOMIC DEVELOPMENT
White Plains, NY: International Arts and Sciences Press, 1971.

Analyzes the "miracles" of economic development which have occurred since World War II and generalizes the results of the analysis in a theory which recognizes the development of man himself as the basic vehicle of economic development.

324 Jha, Prem Shankar
INDIA: A POLITICAL ECONOMY OF STAGNATION
Bombay: Oxford University Press, 1980.

Argues that Indian economic stagnation between 1966 and 1976 had its roots in politics, not economics, and was linked to the rise of an intermediate class comprising peasant proprietors, small manufacturers, traders, and other self-employed groups, all of whom had a vested interest in the perpetuation of the stagnation. Employing Marxist sociological concepts, the author discusses the activities of this class in reinforcing a regime of economic controls on industry, applying a brake to employment, and industrial output.

325 Johnson, Walter L. and Kamerschen, David R.
READINGS IN ECONOMIC DEVELOPMENT
Cincinnati, Ohio and Brigton, England: South-Western Publishing Co., 1972.

A selection of 29 articles (two of them previously not published) that is designed to provide depth to the chosen textual materials in economic development at the undergraduate levels. The readings cover a wide range of aspects of development: methodology, dimensions and characteristics of LDC's, measurement and theories of growth/development, ingredients of development and policy issues involved.

326 Joshi, Vijay
INTERNATIONAL ADJUSTMENT IN THE 1980'S
Working Paper No. 485; Washington, D.C.: World Bank, 1982.

A background study for World Development Report 1981.

Analyzes the macroeconomics of international adjustment. Highlights potential market failure and areas for intervention.

327 Jud, Gustav Donald
INFLATION AND THE USE OF INDEXING IN DEVELOPING COUNTRIES
New York and London: Praeger, 1978.

Divided into four parts. Part one considers the theory of indexation relevant to both the domestic economy and to international trade in primary commodities. Part two examines the domestic experience of indexation in Brazil, Chile, Argentina, and Colombia. Part three assesses the proposals put forth by Third World countries for the indexation of primary commodity trade for the purpose of stabilizing real export proceeds and transferring income and wealth. Part four summarizes the study's conclusion, some of which are (1) indexation is not a cure for inflation, (2) indexing's principal virtue is "as a sedative for the painful misallocations produced by inflation," and (3) policies other than commodity indexation are better suited for transferring resources to poor countries.

328 Kadar, Bela
PROBLEMS OF ECONOMIC GROWTH IN LATIN AMERICA
New York: St. Martin's Press, 1980.

Part one focuses on the main trends and phases in Latin American development, discussing the heritage of Pre-Columbian Society and of colonization, the different characteristics of agricultural and industrial development in the various countries, the external economic sector including trade patterns and financial and capital relations, and regional cooperation in Latin America. Part two examines the characteristic features of the economic growth process in five countries, Peru, Argentina, Brazil, Colombia, and Mexico. Discusses the successes and failure of the various policies adopted, the nationalization of the decision-making centers, and the switchover from import-substituting growth to export-oriented economic development.

329 Kalecki, Michal
ESSAYS ON DEVELOPING ECONOMIES
Hassocks, England: Harvester Press; Atlantic Highlands, NJ: Humanities press, 1976.

A collection of eleven essays (mostly written in the 1960's). They cover three areas: (1) economic problems of underdeveloped non-Socialist economies; (2) financing economic development; (3) case studies of specific problems in Israel, Cuba, Bolivia, and the Third World.

330 Kakwani, Nanak C.

INCOME INEQUALITY AND POVERTY: METHODS OF ESTIMATION AND POLICY APPLICATIONS
New York: Oxford University Press for the World Bank, 1980.

Theoretical and empirical analysis of the size distribution of income. Discusses the various distribution functions and methods for determining income distribution and examines the measurement of inequality, expenditure systems, and the effect of relative price changes on inequality of income, as well as the Lorenz curve and its applications to economic analysis. Explores the government's role in alleviating inequality and the impact of two policy instruments: progressive taxation and the negative income tax. Also includes a section on the measurement of poverty.

331   Kamarck, Andrew M.
        THE ECONOMICS OF AFRICAN DEVELOPMENT
        New York: Praeger, 1971.

A revised edition of a well-received study of the problems and prospects of African development. The original conclusions and forecasts are reexamined in the light of actual experience, and the course of African development is forecast to the year 2000.

332   Kamarck, Andrew M.
        THE TROPICS AND ECONOMIC DEVELOPMENT: A PROVOCATIVE INQUIRY INTO THE POVERTY OF NATIONS
        Baltimore, MD: Johns Hopkins University Press, 1976.

Presents a nontechnical examination, outlining major characteristics of the tropical climates that are significant to economic development, the adverse effects of tropical climate on agriculture and mineral exploration, and the widespread extent and impact of tropical diseases the directly affect man's economic activity. Explores the first systematic international efforts now under way to cope with these effects.

333   Kanet, Roger E. and Bahry, Donna, eds.
        SOVIET ECONOMIC AND POLITICAL RELATIONS WITH THE DEVELOPING WORLD
        New York and London: Praeger, 1975.

General surveys of Soviet policy toward developing countries are presented in three essays comprising Part I. Part II contains two papers assessing the relevance of the Soviet economic development model for developing countries. Two papers in Part III deal with Soviet policy in the Middle East, and five essays in the final section evaluate Soviet policy in South and East Asia.

334   Karunathlake, H. N. S.

ECONOMIC DEVELOPMENT IN CEYLON
New York: Praeger, 1971.

An analysis of economic development in Ceylon from 1950 through 1970. Gives a detailed account of public policy and progress in the agricultural, industrial, and manpower sections.

335 Kasper, Wolfgang
MALAYSIA: A STUDY IN SUCCESSFUL ECONOMIC DEVELOPMENT
Washington, D.C.: American Enterprise Institute for Public Policy Research, 1974.

A case study in development economics. The author describes the structure, overall economic performance, policy framework, industrialization policies, and other major aspects of the Malaysian economy. He attempts to explain how and why, since it gained independence fifteen years ago, Malaysian national output has grown at more than 6 percent annually; industrial output has expanded at about 11 percent; up to 1972, the price level remained extremely stable; and there have been none of the balance-of-payments crises typical of so many other developing countries.

336 Katz, Jeffrey A.
CAPITAL FLOWS AND DEVELOPING COUNTRY DEBT
Working Paper No. 352; Washington, D.C.: World Bank, 1979.

A background study for World Development Report, 1979. Reviews the growth and changing structure of the external debt of developing countries, including their private, nonguaranteed debt, during the period 1970 through 1977. Discusses these developments in relation to other economic changes during this period, as well as the growth of external assets. Also reviews trends in debt service and the cost of debt, along with a prospective look at patterns of debt amortization.

337 Kautsky, John H.
THE POLITICAL CONSEQUENCES OF MODERNIZATION
New York: John Wiley, 1972.

338 Keegan, Warren J.
CASE STUDIES IN THE MANAGEMENT OF ECONOMIC DEVELOPMENT
London: Oxford University Press.

These case studies provide a systematic and rational approach to the solution of administrative problems in developing countries; they describe actual cases of problems in Eastern African public administration and would be suitable material for trainees in this field.

339	Kenessey, Zoltan
THE PROCESS OF ECONOMIC PLANNING
New York: Columbia University Press, 1978.

Designed around eight major topics involved in planning in the market-oriented economy: (1) the possibilities and limitations of planning; (2) institutional aspects; (3) aims, strategies, and policies of development planning; (4) the elaboration of development plans; (5) scientific and quantitative evidence; (6) techniques of planning; (7) plan implementation; and (8) planning and politics in the United States. Discussion involves two basic assumptions: (1) the ultimate goals of plans are not adequately studied or embedded in the planning process and (2) relatively nondetailed planning linked with greater use of market forces is preferable to planning in great detail, exercised by the use of extreme controls. Maintains that planning in this sense is not antagonistic to the market concept, but both planning and market activities are necessary for solutions to current problems. Emphasizes preparatory steps and advocates a systematic integration of those steps into the planning process.

340	Khan, Azizur Rahman
THE ECONOMY OF BANGLADESH
New York: St. Martin's Press, 1972.

This is a study of the current status and problems of the newly created country. Provides analysis and data on that country's population, labor force, standard of living, agricultural and industrial sectors, external trade, private and public savings, etc. An important part of the book (almost half) is dedicated to "Planning for the Future," which is the author's view of what needs to be done in terms of sectoral priorities, land reform, industrialization, financing economic development, and other issues in development policy and strategy.

341	Khan, Mohammad Shabbir
PLANNING AND ECONOMIC DEVELOPMENT IN INDIA
New York: Asia, 1970.

Contains four lectures (and a postscript) given during a recent tour of American universities. The lectures focus on: (1) the strategy of planning in India; (2) a review of the first three economic plans, noting the problems created by the emphasis on the heavy industries; (3) the role of foreign aid in Indian development; and (4) an examination of the draft of the Fourth Five Year Plan.

342	Khan, Qamar Uddin
THE ECONOMIC CONTEXT OF DEVELOPMENT IN ASIA
IILS, 1977.

Topics covered: sectoral growth rates; consumption of energy; world trade; international flows; transfer of technology; prices and international reserves position; transnational corporations; and labor force and employment.

343   Kilby, Peter
INDUSTRIALIZATION IN AN OPEN ECONOMY: NIGERIA 1945-1966
New York: Cambridge University Press, 1969.

A detailed study of how manufacturing and processing industries have developed in the largest country in West Africa, examined within its historical framework. Dr. Kilby shows that the experience of Nigeria's industrialization challenges conventional development theory.

344   Kilby, Peter, ed.
ENTREPRENEURSHIP AND ECONOMIC DEVELOPMENT
New York: The Free Press, 1971.

A collection of 17 articles outlining the major theories of the role of entrepreneurship in economic development and empirical studies that support or contradict them.

345   Kim, Seung Hee
FOREIGN CAPITAL FOR ECONOMIC DEVELOPMENT: A KOREAN CASE STUDY
New York: Praeger, 1970.

The two gap (internal and external) analysis is applied in this study which includes efforts of import substitution policies and future debt service payments in estimating the needs for foreign capital during the next decade. Describes the process by which Korea's utilization of both U.S. economic and military aid propelled the country from a capital importer to a net capital exporter. The incremental capital-output ration is used to estimate the contribution of foreign capital in economic growth.

346   King, J. R.
STABILIZATION POLICY IN AN AFRICAN SETTING: KENYA 1963-73
London; Nairobi and Lusaka: Heinemann Educational Books, 1979.

Examination of prices, unemployment, and the balance of payments and how they are influenced or controlled by government policies. Comparing the income-expenditure models with the monetary theory of the balance of payments, finds that the latter provides a more comprehensive picture of the economy and yields a much closer approximation to the real world.

347   Kirsch, Henry W.
INDUSTRIAL DEVELOPMENT IN A TRADITIONAL SOCIETY: THE CONFLICT OF ENTREPRENEURSHIP AND MODERNIZATION IN CHILE

Gainesville: University Presses of Florida, 1977.

Examines the social and economic development of Chile from the late nineteenth century to the Great Depression. Argues that Chilean industrialization was fully active by the late nineteenth century and attempts to explain the failure of Chilean industry to fulfill the developmental role.

348 Kobrin, Stephen Jay
FOREIGN DIRECT INVESTMENT, INDUSTRIALIZATION AND SOCIAL CHANGE
Greenwich, Conn.: JAI Press, 1977.

Investigates the effects of foreign direct investment and resultant industrialization on social modernization in developing countries. Tests the theory of a strong and positive relationship against data for Mexico and Venezuela.

349 Korea Development Institute
LONG-TERM PROSPECT FOR ECONOMIC AND SOCIAL DEVELOPMENT 1977-91
Honolulu: University Press of Hawaii, 1978.

The English version, slightly modified and updated, of a study for the Economic Planning Board, published in Korean in 1978. Identifies the major tasks facing the Korean economy and indicates priority policy objectives for the next 15 years. Anticipates continued rapid growth, substantial changes in the industrial structure, improved labor productivity, social development, and improved equity of income distribution.

350 Kravis, Irving B.; Heston, Alan and Summers, Robert
PHASE III: WORLD PRODUCT AND INCOME: INTERNATIONAL COMPARISONS OF REAL GDP
Baltimore, MD: Johns Hopkins University Press, 1982.

This report restates and extends the methodology set out in the first two volumes. Particular attention is given to the problem of comparing services and to the conflicting demands of regional and global estimates. Comparisons are given of prices, real per capita quantities, and final expenditure components of GDP for thirty-four countries for 1975. By relating the results to certain widely available national income accounting data and related variables, the authors develop extrapolating equations to estimate per capita GDP for the thirty-four countries for 1950 to 1978. In addition, the 1975 distribution of world product by region and per capita income class is estimated.

351 Kuhnen, Frithjof

PROBLEMS OF EMPLOYMENT PROMOTION IN PAKISTAN
Geneva: International Labour Office, 1971.

352 Lakshmanan, M. S.
ECONOMIC DEVELOPMENT IN INDIA
Delhi: Hindustan, 1974.

A study of India's recent economic growth experience since 1951 with particular emphasis on the role of the foreign sector.

353 Lal, Deepak
APPRAISING FOREIGN INVESTMENT IN DEVELOPING COUNTRIES
New York: Homes & Meier; London; Toronto; Johannesburg and New Delhi: Heinemann Educational Books, 1975.

Appraisal of private overseas investment (POI) in developing countries from the host country's standpoint; to aid in formulating decision rules on the social profitability of particular foreign investments.

354 Landau, Luis
DOMINICAN REPUBLIC: ITS MAIN ECONOMIC DEVELOPMENT PROBLEMS
Baltimore, MD: Johns Hopkins University Press, 1978.

Based on the findings of a mission to the Dominican Republic in October-November 1976. Despite its accomplishments in the way of savings, foreign investment, tourism, exports, and growth of gross domestic product (GDP), the Dominican Republic still faces severe poverty and unemployment.

355 Lee Hock Lock
HOUSEHOLD SAVING IN WEST MALAYSIA AND THE PROBLEM OF FINANCING ECONOMIC DEVELOPMENT
Kuala Lumpur, Malaysia: Khee Meng Press, 1971.

Draws a profile of the Malaysian saver and analyzes the factors affecting the volume and structure of household savings in West Malaysia; with an aim toward mobilizing greater household saving for development purposes, the study then assesses the efficiency of the existing system of financial intermediareis as users and collectors of household savings. Finds that not all the savings that go through financial intermediaries become available for development and suggests specific policy recommendations to increase the rate of saving and to improve the efficiency of financial intermediaries.

356 Lees, Francis A. and Brooks, Hugh C.
THE ECONOMIC AND POLITICAL DEVELOPMENT OF THE SUDAN
London: Macmillan Press; Boulder, CO: Westview Press, 1977.

Study of the progress and problems encountered in the

development process of the Sudan. Provides an economic overview and examines the following sectors: population and manpower; agriculture and forestry; transport, power and industry; and financial intermediaries.

357   Lewis, Stephen R., Jr.
ECONOMIC POLICY AND INDUSTRIAL GROWTH IN PAKISTAN
Cambridge, MA: MIT Press, 1969.

358   Lewis, W. Arthur
SOME ASPECTS OF ECONOMIC DEVELOPMENT
New York: Allen and Unwin.

Professor Lewis's Aggrey-Fraser-Guggisberg Memorial Lectures delivered at the University of Ghana. Here he sets out forthrightly the lessons, concerned with aspects of economic development, which have been learned in the years since the end of colonialism. His discussion is not restricted to West Africa, but ranges over the whole underdeveloped world.

359   Lim, Chong-Yah
ECONOMIC DEVELOPMENT IN SOUTHEAST ASIA
Singapore: Federal Publications, 1981.

360   Lim, David, ed.
READINGS ON MALAYSIAN ECONOMIC DEVELOPMENT
Kuala Lumpur; London; New York and Melbourne: Oxford University Press, 1975.

Following a look at the overall picture of the problems of Malaysia and a discussion of the export sector, agricultural development and industrialization programs are examined in detail. Also considers unemployment, income distribution inequity, and money and finance; an entire section is devoted to noneconomic factors of development such as cultural, psychological, sociological, and institutional factors.

361   Lindblom, Charles E.
POLITICS AND MARKETS: THE WORLD'S POLITCAL-ECONOMIC SYSTEMS
New York: Basic Books, 1977.

A broad-gauged economic-political comparative analysis of the workings of the Russian, United States, and Chinese systems in a searching examination of the options facing the world community. The author regards questions about government-market realtions to be at the core of both political and economic analysis for planned and market-oriented systems. The work aims to dissect and to compare the fundamental characteristics of the dominant systems in the world economy today.

362 Lioi, Vittorio Corbo
INFLATION IN DEVELOPING COUNTRIES: AN ECONOMETRIC STUDY OF CHILEAN INFLATION
New York: American Elsevier, 1974.

An attempt toward building a macroeconomic model to study the interaction among the main macroeconomic variables in the creation of inflation in a developing country. The first part deals with monetarism, structuralism, and past studies of Chilean inflation. The second part discusses a quarterly model for industrial prices, industrial wages, and inflation. The last part is devoted to the specification, estimation, and simulation of an annual econometric model of the Chilean economy.

363 Lipton, Michael
WHY POOR PEOPLE STAY POOR: URBAN BIAS IN WORLD DEVELOPMENT
Cambridge, MA: Harvard University Press, 1976.

Examines the conflict of interest between the urban and rural sectors of developing countries. Discusses how, why, and with what effects the rural sector is "squeezed," both by transfers of resources from it and by prices that are turned against it. Surveys ideologies of rural and urban development, including discussion of Classical and Marginalist economies.

364 Little, I. M. D. and Mirrlees, J. A.
PROJECT APPRAISAL AND PLANNING FOR DEVELOPING COUNTRIES
New York: Basic Books, 1974.

In this work, the shadow wage is more explicitly dependent on income distribution, and several additions of material are noted--a lengthier discussion of the organization of project planning and evaluation and of its relationship to sectoral and macroeconomic planning, more concern with agricultural and infrastructural projects, more work with the measurement of production benefits of non-traded goods and services, more treatment of income distribution, a more detailed application of the principles to private investment, particularly private overseas investment.

365 Livingstone, Ian, ed.
DEVELOPMENT ECONOMICS AND POLICY: READINGS
London; Boston and Sydney: Allen & Unwin, 1981.

Includes several surveys of the field and many heavily-used articles from reading lists in development courses at British universities. Topics cover: causal factors and theories of development; population, labor, and employment; trade and investment; industrialization strategy; investment choice and project appraisal; agricultural development; and money and finance.

366 Loehr, William and Powelson, John P., eds.
ECONOMIC DEVELOPMENT, POVERTY, AND INCOME DISTRIBUTION
Boulder, CO: Westview Press, 1977.

In three parts: Part one is an examination of income distribution from both the theoretical and empirical perspectives; part two addresses the question of defining the poor; and the last part surveys a range of policies proposed for the elimination of poverty. The editors note some of the following findings: (1) the poor comprise such a heterogeneous group that few generalizations are valid; (2) the heavy rural-to-urban migration is associated with increasing inequality and poverty; (3) foreign assistance may have caused increasing income inequality by stimulating capital-intensive growth in the urban areas; and (4) the poor quality of available data impedes progress on the problem.

367 Loehr, William and Powelson, John P.
THE ECONOMICS OF DEVELOPMENT AND DISTRIBUTION
New York: Harcourt Brace Jovanovich, 1981.

Analyzes the economic development of Europe and considers the applicability to today's LDC's in Asia, Africa, and Latin America, concluding that strong forces other than those normally considered by economists may underlie a country's rate of economic development. Maintains that the study of development must be broadened and the areas of ignorance defined. Describes development as a process, not as theory, arguing that there are thresholds and cumulative effects but also unexplained reversals.

368 Looney, Robert E.
THE ECONOMIC DEVELOPMENT OF PANAMA: THE IMPACT OF WORLD INFLATION ON AN OPEN ECONOMY
London: Praeger, 1976.

Examination of the effect of the Panama Canal and the treaty with the United States on the economy of the Republic of Panama. Adopts a two-gap macroeconomic approach, which involves the estimation for an assumed rate of growth of the difference between investment requirements and potential saving and the difference between import requirements and potential export of goods and services.

369 Looney, Robert E.
MEXICO'S ECONOMY: A POLICY ANALYSIS WITH FORECASTS TO 1990
Boulder, CO: Westview Press, 1978.

An analysis of Mexican economic policy, focusing upon trends, particularly since 1970; examines forces underlying high growth rate of 1960's/early 1970's to determine whether economic expansion can be resumed in the 1980's;

discusses economic policies pursued by the Echeverria and the Lopez Portillo administrations, the causes of the 1976 crises culminating in the devaluation of the peso, and long-term development strategy.

370   Looney, Robert E.
INCOME DISTRIBUTION POLICIES AND ECONOMIC GROWTH IN SEMI-INDUSTRIALIZED COUNTRIES: A COMPARATIVE STUDY OF IRAN, MEXICO, BRAZIL AND SOUTH KOREA
New York: Praeger, 1975.

371   Lowe, Adolph
THE PATH OF ECONOMIC GROWTH
New York: Cambridge University Press, 1976.

In contrast to the conventional approach to economic growth where the main preoccupation is with equilibrium dynamics, this work concerns typical disequilibria as they arise under the impact of changes in labor supply, the supply of natural resources, and technology.

372   Maane, Willem and others
LESOTHO: A DEVELOPMENT CHALLENGE
Baltimore, MD: Johns Hopkins University Press, 1975.

Reviews Lesotho's economic development since independence in 1966, and examines its development constraints, agricultural potential, and current and future employment and investment opportunities. Based on economic missions in June-July 1973 and March 1974.

373   Mabro, Robert
THE EGYPTIAN ECONOMY 1952-1972
London: Oxford University Press, Clarendon Press, 1974.

Reviews the country's historical and political background and then analyzes changes in population, resource utilization, land tenure, land use, institutions, industry, infrastructure, employment, income distribution, and related aspects.

374   MacEwan, Arthur
REVOLUTION AND ECONOMIC DEVELOPMENT IN CUBA
New York: St. Martin's Press, 1981.

Examines the progress and continuing problems in the Cuban economy, focusing on changes in Cuban agriculture since the revolution in 1959 when agrarian reform was initiated, through the 1970's and relates these changes to Cuba's economy generally. Interprets Cuban experience viewed from the perspective of socialist development in terms of changing social organization and class relations.

375   Maddison, Angus
ECONOMIC PROGRESS AND POLICY IN DEVELOPING COUNTRIES
New York: Allen and Unwin.

Assessing the successes and failures of economic policy in the developing world in the past two decades, this study contains a wealth of comparative historical data on gross national product, industrial and agricultural production, employment, productivity, physical and human resource investment, external finance, trade, taxation and prices in 22 countries. It also explains the reasons for the post-war acceleration in growth and for the wide variation in growth rates.

376   Mahajan, V. S.
PLANNING, DEVELOPMENT AND ECONOMIC POLICY IN INDIA
Delhi: Kalyani Publishers, 1974.

Shows the influence of planning in different sectors of the economy, giving particular attention to the Fifth Plan strategy. Details are given on agricultural development, industrial policy, the growth of the public sector and the emergence of monopoly control over industry. Discussion covers the relation of development to the problems of industrial finance and banking. Examination is also made of India's foreign trade and need for foreign currency.

377   Maiss, Otto
YEMEN ARAB REPUBLIC: DEVELOPMENT OF A TRADITIONAL ECONOMY
Baltimore, MD: Johns Hopkins University Press, 1979.

Based on the findings of two economic missions during 1977. Outlines the far-reaching changes, in a short period of time, in the socioeconomic and political structure of the Yemen Arab Republic since the 1962 Revolution, the creation of essential government institutions, and the development of the public and private sectors, largely aided by foreign technology and capital. Discusses major development issues, foremost among which is a manpower shortage as a result of labor migration to neighboring states, inflation, and a rational allocation of growing investment resources, during the period 1969-77 and looking toward the early 1980's.

378   Maitra, Priyatosh
THE MAINSPRING OF ECONOMIC DEVELOPMENT
New York: St. Martin's Press, 1980.

Based on two papers presented at conferences in 1976 and 1978, the book combines examination of the basic force behind the Industrial Revolution of the nineteenth and twentieth centuries and of the basic characteristics of both successful and unsuccessful cases of imported industrialization. Concludes that economic development depends on the generation of indigenous technology, which necessitates fundamental changes in agrarian organization; that dependence on imported technology by mid-twentieth century underdeveloped countries leaves indigenous resources idle and unproductive, thereby perpetuating problems of underdevelopment and overpopulation.

379   Makdisi, Samir A.
FINANCIAL POLICY AND ECONOMIC GROWTH: THE LEBANESE EXPERIENCE New York: Columbia University Press, 1979.

Assesses Lebanon's economic and financial performance during the period 1945-74; discusses the role that government policy positions played in the national economy; and, considering the disruption of the 1975-76 civil war, evaluates the past and possible future roles of financial planning in the economic development of the country.

380   Mallon, Richard D. and Sourrouille, Juan V.
ECONOMIC POLICYMAKING IN A CONFLICT SOCIETY: THE ARGENTINE CASE
Cambridge, MA and London: Harvard University Press, 1975.

Based upon the Argentine experience, the authors seek a policy approach appropriate for constitutional democratic governments in pluralistic conflict societies. Focuses on balance-of-payments and anti-inflationary stabilization policies, but is not confined to the discipline of economics. Analyzes the structural and institutional problems of policy making, using Argentina as the example.

381   Mandi, Peter
EDUCATION AND ECONOMIC GROWTH IN THE DEVELOPING COUNTRIES
Budapest: Academiai Kiado, 1981.

A study in Hungarian of the role, position, and development of education in the Third World. Discusses the theory of the economics of education, arguing that there is a reciprocal causal relationship between education and economic growth and that a macroeconomic approach to educational planning is more applicable to developing countries than a human capital approach based on individuals. Discusses planning methods used in educational development in socialist countries and several developing countries, and manpower planning. Examines educational policy in developed countries and discusses policy considerations for developing countries. Finds that 20 to 30 percent literacy has been sufficient historically for modern development to commence. Concludes that to launch modern economic development and industrialization in Third World countries will not require a European-type education of the population as a whole, but rather an educational plan based on a national economic plan that determines the distribution of workplaces and jobs.

382 Markham, J. W. and Papanek, Gustav F., eds.
INDUSTRIAL ORGANIZATION AND ECONOMIC DEVELOPMENT: IN HONOR OF E. S. MASON
Boston, MA: Houghton Mifflin, 1970.

383 Marzouk, G. A.
ECONOMIC DEVELOPMENT AND POLICIES: CASE STUDY OF THAILAND
Rotterdam: Rotterdam University Press, 1972.

A broad analytical coverage of the factors contributing to Thailand's sustained (two decades) high rate of economic growth, containing a theoretical framework as well as considerable detailed statistical data. Discusses ad seriatum demography, trends in income growth and distribution, the rice economy and other agricultural activities, agricultural productivity and efficiency, changes in the manufacturing sector and the policies affecting it, foreign trade and exchange topics, domestic monetary policy and events, fiscal policy, and planning methods and their implementation.

384 Mason, Edward S., et al.
THE ECONOMIC AND SOCIAL MODERNIZATION OF THE REPUBLIC OF KOREA
Cambrdige: Harvard University Press, 1980.

Presents the historical record of the rapid growth of the Korean economy during the period 1945-75 and the distribution of the fruits of that growth, with an analysis of the importance of American assistance and the sources of economic growth. Covers, as do the underlying studies, macro changes in the structure of the economy, the foreign sector, development of the financial and fiscal systems, rural development, urbanization and urban problems, education, and health and social development.

385 Mazur, Michael P.
ECONOMIC GROWTH AND DEVELOPMENT IN JORDAN
Boulder, CO: Westview Press, 1979.

An analysis of the economies of pre-1967 Jordan and the post-1967 East Bank. Presents a primarily statistical evaluation of the economic development of Jordan for the period between the unification of the two banks and the 1967 Middle East war; a survey of economic change in Jordan, 1967-75, which includes a critical evaluation of data available for that period; and an examination of government development policies in the areas of agriculture, industry, and general planning, with special emphasis on the Five-Year Development Plan for 1976-80.

386 McDiarmid, Orville John
UNSKILLED LABOR FOR DEVELOPMENT: ITS ECONOMIC COST
Baltimore, MD: Johns Hopkins University Press, 1977.

Focuses on the problem of estimating the economic cost of unskilled labor by examining the labor market conditions that cause a significnat spread between the economic and market wages and other determinants, such as the intensity of employment, the relative cost of labor and capital, and indirect costs and benefits, with special attention to the effect of fiscal and monetary policies.

387 McGranahan, D. V.; Richard-Proust, C.; Sovani, N. V. and Subramanian, M.
CONTENTS AND MEASUREMENT OF SOCIOECONOMIC DEVELOPMENT
New York and London: Praeger, 1972.

A staff study by the United Nations Research Institute for Social Development, this is an attempt to examine the nature of development and particularly the interrelations of its social and economic aspects through a comparative (cross-national) analysis using social and economic indicators available as of 1960. Drawing on a set of 73 developmental variables for 115 countries with populations over one million, the authors prepare a general index of socioeconomic development containing 18 core indicators for the 58 countries for which sufficient data were available; they are then ranked and compared with gross national product per capita, the usual development measure.

388 Meeraus, Alexander and Stoutjesdijk, Ardy, eds.
THE PLANNING OF INVESTMENT PROGRAMS
Baltimore, MD: Johns Hopkins University Press, 1979.

Series consisting of a number of volumes that describe a systematic approach to investment planning, relying primarily on mathematical programming techniques. Includes both general methodological volumes and studies dealing with specific industrial subsectors, such as fertilizer, forestry and forest industries, steel, and so forth. Each volume is designed as a self-contained treatment of its subject matter, and no prior knowledge is required of either mathematical programming or the specific set of industrial activities under consideration.

389 Mehmet, Ozay
ECONOMIC PLANNING AND SOCIAL JUSTICE IN DEVELOPING COUNTRIES New York: St. Martin's Press, 1978.

Argues that regular economic planning is an effective, non-violent alternative path to development with social justice. Critically reviews post-war growth and planning in LDC's; examines the influence of elites on economic planning and policy through case studies of Malaysia,

Liberia, Pakistan, Brazil, and Uganda; and explains the appropriateness of egalitarian planning and reform of LDC's. Calls for decentralized, pro-rural egalitarian planning, which will aim at land reform and maximization of job creation and employment income for the short and medium term, and investment in human capital in the longer term. Recommends restructuring of international trade and aid.

390   Mehta, J. K.
ECONOMICS OF GROWTH
New York: Asia Publishing House, 1970.

391   Meier, Gerald M.
PRICING POLICY FOR DEVELOPMENT MANAGEMENT
Baltimore, MD: Johns Hopkins University Press, 1983.

Presupposing no formal training in economics, it explains the essential elements of a price system, the functions of prices, the various policies that a government might pursue in cases of market failure, and the principles of public pricing of goods and services provided by government enterprises. It also provides the would-be practitioner with an appreciation of the underlying logical structure of cost-benefit project appraisal. To give substance to the applied and policy dimensions, many of the readings are drawn from the experience of development practitioners and relate to such important sectors as agriculture, industry, power, urban services, foreign trade, and employment. The principles outlined are therefore relevant to a host of development problems.

392   Meier, Gerald M., ed.
LEADING ISSUES IN ECONOMIC DEVELOPMENT
New York: Oxford University Press, 1976.

The editor emphasizes the interrelatedness of the readings selected on each issue, with the leadings issues now coalescing in a central theme: "policies which are designed to eradicate poverty, reduce inequality, and deal with problems of employment." Replaces the earlier readings selections so as to reflect the central theme and adds several new chapters. Also includes new sections to raise the level of theoretical analysis and provide more empirical relationships. More than 100 selections, reprinted from various sources, discuss the history of development, various theories of development, industrialization, agriculture, trade, human resources, and planning.

393   Mellor, John W.
THE NEW ECONOMICS OF GROWTH: A STRATEGY FOR INDIA AND THE DEVELOPING WORLD
Ithaca and London: Cornell University Press, 1976.

Advocates a "rural-led, employment-oriented strategy of economic growth...for India and many other countries as well." While concerned that absolute income rises for the poor will not improve their relative position, the author believes that this strategy improving agricultural output, will have a consequent multiplier effect on growth and will thereby expand employment opportunities. Urges abandoning high technology for industry, accepting open trade arrangements, accepting foreign technical advice, and supporting minimum capital-intensive but maximum labor-intensive projects.

394   Mishan, E. J.
THE ECONOMIC GROWTH DEBATE: AN ASSESSMENT
London and Reading, MA: Allen & Unwin, 1977.

Deals with the question of the social desirability of continued economic growth. Argues that economic analysis is of little use and that consequences of technological and economic growth should be assessed in the light of the constituents of the good life. In the latter he includes: food and shelter, health, leisure, enjoyment of nature, love and trust, security, freedom, etc. Examines the dangers of continued technological development.

395   Mitra, Ashok
ECONOMIC THEORY AND PLANNING: ESSAYS IN HONOUR OF A. K. DAS GUPTA
London: Oxford University Press.

396   Morawetz, David
TWENTY-FIVE YEARS OF ECONOMIC DEVELOPMENT: 1950 TO 1975
Washington, D.C.: World Bank; distributed by Johns Hopkins University Press, Baltimore, 1977.

Broad assessment of efforts, since the early 1950's to establish targets for the economic grwoth of poor countries, to formulate and implement rational development plans, and to assure international cooperation. Discusses the changing objectives of development and evaluates economic growth, the reduction of poverty, and the move towards self-reliance and economic independence. Contends that although the developing countries have on balnce been remarkably successful in achieving growth (3.4 percent per year 1950-1975), the distribution of its benefits among and within countries has been much less satisfactory. Concludes that the years in question clearly demonstrate that there is more than one feasible route to equitable growth and development and that regardless of political philosophy, a decentralized system of decision-making relies heavily for success upon the response of the local functionaries to centrally determine incentives. Includes substantial statistical data on GNP per capita, life expectancy, unemployment, public debt, growth of GNP, and other macroeconomic indicators.

397   Morris, Arthur
        LATIN AMERICA: ECONOMIC DEVELOPMENT AND REGIONAL DIFFERENTIATION
        Totowa, NJ: Barnes & Noble Books, 1981.

        Historical analysis of the regional development processes in Latin America, traced from the colonial through the neo-colonial and modern periods. About one-half the book deals with the modern period. Also examines, within a spatial context, the proposition that a combination of centrally-organized and regional institutions is the best compromise for harmonious dynamic development. Describes four major types of current regional planning policy. Discusses sets of economic measures appropriate to different types of regions: metropolitan, urbanized developing, international and national export-base, and resource and traditional. Argues that for some problems some kind of government intervention in terms of national aims is desirable.

398   Mouly, J. and Costa, E.
        EMPLOYMENT POLICIES IN DEVELOPING COUNTRIES
        London: George Allen and Unwin.

        A systematic account of the problems which face developing countries in the field of employment is provided in this book. The authors, specialists of the International Labour Office, have drawn upon the resources of the ILO's World Employment Programme to present a broad survey of measures taken to alleviate or solve these problems, and of the results achieved.

399   Myint, H.
        ECONOMIC THEORY AND THE UNDERDEVELOPED COUNTRIES
        New York: Oxford University Press, 1971.

400   Newlyn, W. T.
        THE FINANCING OF ECONOMIC DEVELOPMENT
        Oxford: Oxford University Press, Clarendon Press, 1977.

        An inquiry into the ways the potential national surplus of developing countries can be maximized and channeled into "capacity-creating" expenditures and also into the role that foreign finance can play in this process. The first half of the study considers themajor policy issues of intermediation and credit creation, government finance, and foreign finance; and then integrates them into a macro-model for fifteen developing countries. The second half examines the financing of economic development in three South Asian countries (India, Malaysia, and Thailand), in Ghana (1960-69), and in Nigeria (1950-71); also presents case studies of "Company Savings in Kenya's Manufacturing Sector" and the mining industry in Zambia. Concluding chapter makes specific domestic and international recommendations (e.g., develop domestic financial systems; funds; improve international cooperation to ease the trade constraint and to increase the resources of the U.N. Development System.)

401 North-South Institute
THIRD WORLD DEFICITS AND THE DEBT CRISIS
Ottawa: North-South Institute, 1977.

Second report of a series on Canada's relations with the Third World. Outlines the dimensions of the developing country debt burden; summarizes the debt-relief debate; discusses the likely agenda for an International Conference on Debt Problems, which has already been agreed to in principle by Canada and most other industrial nations; and considers the adequacy of existing financing facilities.

402 Nyilas, Jozsef, ed.
THEORY AND PRACTICE OF DEVELOPMENT IN THE THIRD WORLD
Budapest: Akademiai Kiado; distributed by Sijthoff, Leyden, 1977.

Three analyses by Marxists on the characteristics, causes, and consequences of economic underdevelopment and the problems of growth and planning in the Third World. One theme is that the economic lagging of Third World nations is consciously planned; hence the nineteenth century experience of now developed nations is irrelevant.

403 O'Brien, Richard
PRIVATE BANK LENDING TO DEVELOPING COUNTRIES
Working Paper No. 482; Washington, D.C.: World Bank, 1981.

A background study for World Development Report 1981. Describes the evolution of relationships between private banks and developing countries.

404 OECD
INTERNATIONAL ASPECTS OF INFLATION: THE HIDDEN ECONOMY: THE WORLD CURRENT ACCOUNT DISCREPANCY
Paris: OECD, 1982.

Gives the findings of OECD's Economics and Statistics Department on three topics of current concern to economic analysts: (a) international aspects of inflation, including commodity prices, import and export prices and inflation, and international competitiveness and profitability; (b) the hidden economy and the national accounts; and (c) world current account discrepancy.

405 OECD
EXTERNAL DEBT OF DEVELOPING COUNTRIES
Paris: OECD, 1981.

This document sets out, with a short commentary, the latest available data and the historical trend of the external indebtedness of developing countries, by type, origin and destination. It includes, where possible, preliminary figures for 1980 and estimates for 1981. Covers the largest debtors; the cost of foreign finance; debt renegotiations; and debt and debt service of individual developing countries.

406   Ohkawa, Kazushi and Key, Bernard, eds.
ASIAN SOCIOECONOMIC DEVELOPMENT: A NATIONAL ACCOUNTS APPROACH
Honolulu: University Press of Hawaii, 1980.

Twelve essays, one appendix essay, and two additional remarks, arranged in three parts: National Accounts Framework for LDC's, Measurement of Social Accounts, and Income Distribution.

407   Okita, Saburo
THE DEVELOPING ECONOMIES AND JAPAN: LESSONS IN GROWTH
Tokyo: University of Tokyo Press; distributed by Columbia University Press, New York, 1980.

Collection of author's essays written during the 1970's on economic development and planning with particular reference to the Third World economics; some essays have been previously published, while others were speeches, conference or working papers. Many of the essays draw heavily on Japanese historical experience as a developing nation. In 3 parts: developing countries in the world economy, the Japanese example, and Japan's relations with the developing world.

408   Packer, Arnold H.
MODELS OF ECONOMIC SYSTEMS: A THEORY FOR THEIR DEVELOPMENT AND USE
Cambridge, MA: MIT Press, 1972.

409   Papanek, Gustav F.; Schydlowski, Daniel M. and Stern, Joseph J.
DECISION MAKING FOR ECONOMIC DEVELOPMENT: TEXT AND CASES
Boston: Houghton Mifflin, 1971.

This textbook uses the case study method to analyze development problems based on first-hand experiences in Pakistan, Colombia, and Peru. The 13 cases, which are simplified for class room work, deal with issues of: 1) investment decision, 2) policies for the external sector, 3) short-term fiscal and monetary policy, or 4) long-term problems of macroeconomic planning. A brief text and set of appropriate statistical data accompanies each case.

410   Payer, Cheryl
        THE DEBT TRAP: THE IMF AND THE THIRD WORLD
        New York and London: Monthly Review Press, 1974.

        This book is about the efforts of poor nations to gain some control over their own economies [toward autonomous national development], and the role of the IMF in frustrating those efforts by their control of all of the major sources of credit in the developed capitalist world. The first two chapters develop a model of foreign-exchange and balance-of-payments crises and suggest alternative solutions as well as the ones favored by the IMF and their sociopolitical effects. The remaining chapters are a collection of case studies. The countries examined are: the Philippines, Indonesia, Indochina, Yugoslavia, Brazil, India, Chile, Ghana, and North Korea. Discusses their foreign-exchange needs and resources and the policies used to resolve their payments crises.

411   Peacock, Alan and Shaw, G. K.
        FISCAL POLICY AND THE EMPLOYMENT PROBLEM IN LESS DEVELOPED COUNTRIES
        Paris: OECD, 1971.

        In this report, the authors' primary goal is to provide an analysis of the use of public finance as a policy instrument designed to influence the level of employment in developing countries. The basic assumptions on which this study is based revolve about those developing countries where population growth, and therefore the growth in the labor force, is rapid with severe limitations in the growth of capital stock. Personal consumption cannot be reduced to release resources for increasing the stock of capital, and imports of capital equipment are subject to the constraint of available foreign exchange.

412   Pfeffermann, Guy Pierre and Webb, Richard C.
        THE DISTRIBUTION OF INCOME IN BRAZIL
        Working Paper No. 356; Washington, D.C.: World Bank, 1979.

        Examines whether growth has been widely shared and, in particular, whether it has raised the absolute incomes of the poorest groups in Brazil. Covering the period 1960-77, new sources--a national household budget survey and the 1976 household employment survey--have made possible a reexamination of previous sources and a clearer separation in the analysis of income trends before and during the fast growth period between 1968 and 1974.

413   Pinell-Siles, Armando
        DETERMINANTS OF PRIVATE INDUSTRIAL INVESTMENT IN INDIA
        Working Paper No. 333; Washington, D.C.: World Bank, 1979.

        Analyzes the behavior of private industrial investment

in India over time and some of the factors influencing it, such as sales, profitability, taxation, and financial resources, based on financial data compiled by the Reserve Bank of India from large samples of predominantly manufacturing companies for the period 1960/61 to 1975/76. Reveals that a significant deceleration in the rate of growth of the fixed capital stock has taken place to which inadequate growth of industrial demand and a decline in real rates of return on nonfinancial assets have contributed. Also briefly discusses recent investment developments and prospects.

414 Potholm, Christian P.
SWAZILAND: THE DYNAMICS OF POLITICAL MODERNIZATION
Berkeley: University of California Press, 1972.

415 Priest, A. R.
PUBLIC FINANCE IN UNDER-DEVELOPED COUNTRIES
New York: John Wiley, 1972.

Covers taxes, public expenditure issues, legislative and administrative aspects, and regional financial issues; "...the main thrust of the changes [in this edition] has been to concentrate more exclusively than before on public finance in the narrower sense and not to attempt to cover such subjects as debt policy, foreign aid, development plan formulation, and the like." The major additions are a discussion of revenue sources other than the usual types of taxes, and an emphasis on regional financial issues.

416 Pyatt, Graham and Roe, Alan
SOCIAL ACCOUNTING FOR DEVELOPMENT PLANNING WITH SPECIAL REFERENCE TO SRI LANKA
London; New York and Melbourne: Cambridge University Press, 1977.

Rearranges and extends the United Nations Standard System of National Accounts so as to provide a useful data base to be used in economic analyses of the economic conditions of Sri Lanka. Presents aggregated figures from this system for 1970 and analyzes quantitatively issues such as investment strategy, protection policy, resource allocation, and the distributional effects of fiscal policy. Information on the compilation of the social-accounting matrix appended.

417 Ramachandran, N.
ROLE OF PRODUCTIVITY IN ASIAN ECONOMIC GROWTH
Tokyo: Asian Productivity Organization, 1970.

418 Ramos, Joseph R.
LABOR AND DEVELOPMENT IN LATIN AMERICA
New York: Columbia University Press, 1970.

419 Ranis, Gustav, ed.
GOVERNMENT AND ECONOMIC DEVELOPMENT
New Haven and London: Yale University Press, 1971.

A collection of papers, early versions of which were originally presented at a 1968 Economic Growth Center Conference on "The Role of Government in Economic Development." Fourteen articles (grouped into 5 sections) on the development of different countries are given, each with separate commentaries. Part I examines the government as goal setter; Part II treats the government as producer; Part III--the government as regulator; Part IV--the government as fiscal agent; and Part V--some comparative studies. The countries on which development articles were written are Colombia, Malaysia, Turkey, Africa (Gold Coast and Ghana), Chile, Argentina, Israel, Japan, Mexico, and Peru.

420 Rees, Elfan and Ademicael, Berhanykun
NON-GOVERNMENTAL ORGANIZATIONS IN ECONOMIC AND SOCIAL DEVELOPMENT
UNITAR, 1975.

Summarizes not only the discussions held in Schloss Herstein from 13-17 July 1975 but also written comments of additional members of non-governmental organizations (NGO) outside Europe. In trying to explain recent setbacks in the UN Economic and Social Council consultative process for NGO's and to explore further avenues for positive contribution by NGO's in partnership with the UN system, the participants have sought to define the main problems and have suggested some remedies.

421 Reuber, Grant L.
PRIVATE FOREIGN INVESTMENT IN DEVELOPMENT
New York: Oxford University Press, 1973.

422 Reynolds, Lloyd G.
IMAGE AND REALITY IN ECONOMIC DEVELOPMENT
New Haven and London: Yale University Press, 1977.

Outlines the current perceptions of the economics of development, defining the core of the field as the author sees it. Part one sets out the theoretical concepts of development, including discussion of agriculture; a model of a closed economy; and growth, trade, and technological and capital transfer in an open economy. The focus then turns, in Part two, to development experience, both past and present. Discusses in particular: Japan, 1868-1905; contemporary developing economies; the agricultural, industrial, and governmental sectors; patterns of development; growth under socialism; and development policy.

423   Richter, Lothar
       LABOUR MARKET INFORMATION IN DEVELOPING COUNTRIES: A GENERAL REVIEW
       Geneva: ILO, 1978.

       Reviews the current situation and main problems of labor market information in developing countries. Examines the needs for such information and suggests ways and means of improving existing labor market information activities which at present are almost exclusively concerned with modern, relatively small labor markets. It also proposes a new low-cost complementary approach to manpower information collection in the large informal sectors.

424   Robinson, Austin
       ECONOMIC PROSPECTS OF BANGLADESH
       London: Overseas Development Institute, 1973.

425   Robinson, Joan
       FREEDOM AND NECESSITY
       New York: Allen & Unwin.

       A brilliant survey, based on the wide reading of specialists in their fields, of the developments of the structures of the world's economies and of the ideas which underlie them--a short tour through economic history.

426   Roemer, Michael and Stern, Joseph J.
       CASES IN ECONOMIC DEVELOPMENT: PROJECTS, POLICIES AND STRATEGIES
       Boston; London and Sydney: Butterworths, 1981.

       Presents case studies in an imaginary country (Beracia) to give students simulated planning experience in economic development, divided into cases on project analysis, sectoral planning, and macroeconomic policies. The cases cover mining, agriculture, manufacturing, transport, education, and health. Exercises are designed to illustrate investment planning and policy analysis applied by economists in the Third World.

427   Rothchild, Donald and Curry, Robert L., Jr.
       SCARCITY, CHOICE, AND PUBLIC POLICY IN MIDDLE AFRICA
       Berkeley and London: University of California Press, 1978.

       An interdisciplinary (political science and economics) examination of the policy alternatives available to African decision-makers and the implementation of public policies toward achieving political, social, and economic goals. Emphasizes the elements of choice in relation to political and economic resources, and presents a model of policy analysis oriented toward problem-solving.

428   Rothwell, Kenneth J., ed.
      ADMINISTRATIVE ISSUES IN DEVELOPING ECONOMIES
      Lexington, MA: Heath, Lexington Books, 1972.

429   Sabot, Richard H., ed.
      MIGRATION AND THE LABOR MARKET IN DEVELOPING COUNTRIES
      Boulder, CO: Westview Press, 1982.

      A collection of largely conceptual papers by a World Bank economist on issues in urban unemployment and rural-urban migration, the contributions to this technically rich volume do not offer much hope for policymakers faced with deteriorating rural economies and burgeoning labor forces in the cities of the developing world.

430   Sadowski, Zdzislaw
      CONCEPT OF RATIONALITY AND THE MACRO-INDICATORS OF GOAL ATTAINMENT IN SOCIO-ECONOMIC DEVELOPMENT
      Tokyo: UNU, 1980.

      This paper discusses measuring the effectiveness of overall development by encompassing all the social effects of all development activities of the society.

431   Salem, Elie Adib
      MODERNIZATION WITHOUT REVOLUTION: LEBANON'S EXPERIENCE
      Bloomington, Ind. and London: Indiana University Press, 1973.

      Written by a Lebanese political scientist, this is an interpretation of the politics of modernization and economic development in Lebanon since the early 1920's. A study of the forces of change in that country, a review of modernization problems, a description of planning and decision-making, and of the role of bureaucracy-planning-economic development interrelationships.

432   Sayigh, Yusif A.
      THE ECONOMIES OF THE ARAB WORLD: DEVELOPMENT SINCE 1945--VOLUME 1; THE DETERMINANTS OF ARAB ECONOMIC DEVELOPMENT--VOLUME 2.
      New York: St. Martin's Press, 1978.

      Volume 1 records the developmental achievements and failures of twelve Arab countries--Iraq, Kuwait, Saudi Arabia, Jordan, Syria, Lebanon, Egypt, Sudan, Libya, Tunisia, Algeria, and Morocco--from the time of their independence, mostly in 1946, to the early 1970's. Placed in a broad socio-political context, economic development is examined through economic and social indicators such as national product, sectoral structure, education and manpower development, changes in the socioeconomic (and political) system and the degree of seriousness of planning. Concludes with a survey of the trends and issues of regional development, focusing upon the impact of petroleum and the matter of cooperation among the Arab countries. The companion volume discusses the conceptual and methodological issues of the determinants of development and examines the specific economic, political and administrative, and socio-cultural determinants operating in the region. The final chapter (in the second volume) assesses the prospects for development over the next 25 years, concluding that the outlook for the region's real economic growth is bright, although the rates of growth will probably vary widely, say between 5 and 10 per cent.

433 Schatz, Sayre P., ed.
SOUTH OF THE SAHARA: DEVELOPMENT IN AFRICAN ECONOMIES
Philadelphia: Temple University Press, 1972.

Published here are seventeen papers presented at a conference on African economic development held at Temple University at the end of the 1960's. Written by economists with extensive research experience in Africa, the papers deal with various issues related to the growth and development experience of the Black African nations.

434 Seidman, Ann
PLANNING FOR DEVELOPMENT IN SUB-SAHARAN AFRICA
New York and London: Praeger, 1974.

A comprehensive study of economic underdevelopment and of policy options to promote the economic growth and development of the area. The author analyzes the external constraints to export expansion, the role of class structure in economic development, and the basic requirements for successful economic planning in Africa. She then examines the pattern of industrial and agricultural growth and the basic aspects of industrial strategy and of reform in the agricultural sector; next she discusses the role of foreign trade in African development and of alternative commerical policies. Finally, there is a section on the fiscal, monetary, and income policies necessary to further African economic development.

435 Seolwsky, Marcelo
WHO BENEFITS FROM GOVERNMENT EXPENDITURE? A CASE STUDY OF COLOMBIA
New York: Oxford University Press, 1979.

With the help of a specially designed country-wide survey, this research attempts to identify the main beneficiaries of government services. This more clearly identifies which income groups benefit from public expenditures.

436	Sen, Sudhir
	THE UNITED NATIONS ECONOMIC DEVELOPMENT: A NEED FOR A NEW STRATEGY
	Dobbs Ferry, NY: Oceana Publications, 1969.

437	Sewell, John W. and the Staff of the Overseas Development Council
	THE UNITED STATES AND WORLD DEVELOPMENT: AGENDA 1980
	New York: Praeger for ODC, 1980.

	Assesses the global economic situation, stressing the need for urgent action (1) to revive effort to reform the international economic system in ways that serve both rich and poor nations and (2) to initiate an international effort to meet the basic needs of all people. Part one reviews developments in the North and the South during the past decade and discusses missed opportunities in U.S. relations with the Third World. Part two explores the major challenges to both the North and the South during the 1980's and beyond. Part three lays the groundwork for the development of a long-term, comprehensive U.S. development cooperation policy and suggests a program for immediate action that includes (1) reform of the world's monetary system, (2) sustaining world trade, (3) improving world food security, (4) increasing energy security, and (5) meeting existing development assistance and emergency relief commitments.

438	Shaw, Edward S.
	FINANCIAL DEEPENING IN ECONOMIC DEVELOPMENT
	New York, London and Toronto: Oxford University Press, 1973.

	A book on the role which financial markets can play in the economic development process. The emphasis is on financial deepening, i.e., the accumulation of financial assets at a pace faster than accumulation of non-financial wealth. The author discusses the importance of financial deepening, the wealth and debt-intermediation views on money, finance, and capital accumulation, financial repression and reform, coordination of fiscal and financial strategies, financial deepening in open economies, and instability in lagging economies.

439	Singer, Hans W.
	THE STRATEGY OF INTERNATIONAL DEVELOPMENT: ESSAYS IN THE ECONOMICS OF BACKWARDNESS
	White Plains, NY: International Arts and Sciences Press, 1975.

440	Sofranko, Andrew J. and Bealer, Robert C.
	UNBALANCED MODERNIZATION AND DOMESTIC INSTABILITY: A COMPARATIVE ANALYSIS
	Beverly Hills, CA: Sage Publications, 1972.

441   Squire, Lyn
        EMPLOYMENT POLICY IN DEVELOPING COUNTRIES: A SURVEY
        OF ISSUES AND EVIDENCE
        New York: Oxford University Press, 1981.

        Low rates of growth in industrial employment, high rates
        of unemployment among new entrants to the urban labor
        market, and low levels of labor productivity and
        remuneration are the three issues addressed in this study.
        The author identifies the important determinants of labor
        demand and supply and the extent to which the growth
        of labor demand has been constrained--and labor supply
        advanced--by appropriate policies. On the demand side,
        industrial trade policy, agricultural growth, and the
        operation of capital markets are discussed; on the supply
        side, attention is focused on population and education
        policy.

442   Squire, Lyn
        LABOR FORCE, EMPLOYMENT AND LABOR MARKETS IN THE COURSE
        OF ECONOMIC DEVELOPMENT
        Working Paper No. 336; Washington, D.C.: World Bank, 1979.

        A background study for World Development Report, 1979.
        Addresses the issues of low rates of industrial employment
        growth, high rates of unemployment for new entrants to
        the labor market, and low levels of labor productivity
        and remuneration. Attempts to identify the more important
        determinants of labor demand, by discussing industrial
        trade policy, agricultural growth, and the operation
        of capital markets, and of labor supply by focusing on
        population and education policy.

443   Standing, Guy
        LABOUR FORCE PARTICIPATION AND DEVELOPMENT
        Geneva: ILO, 1978.

        Examines economic determinants of labor force participation
        in low-income industrializing countries. Concentrates
        on factors influencing the changing role of women and,
        to a lesser extent, on those influencing young men and
        the elderly. Presents a critical examination of the
        neoclassical household decision-making model of labor
        force participation and reviews evidence from both
        industrialized and non-industrialized countries.
        Determinants studied are primarily observed correlates
        of economic growth, such as changing patterns of fertility,
        the growing need for cash income, the structure of
        employment, rising unemployment, rural-urban migration,
        and the spread of education.

444   Stein, Leslie
        ECONOMIC REALITIES IN POOR COUNTRIES
        Sydney, Australia: Angus and Robertson, 1972.

445   Sternlieb, George and Listokin, David, eds.
       NEW TOOLS FOR ECONOMIC DEVELOPMENT: THE ENTERPRISE ZONE, DEVELOPMENT BANK, AND RFC
       Piscataway, NJ: Rutgers University, Center for Urban Policy Research, 1981.

       Six papers (three previously published) discuss some of the approaches that are under review or have been advocated during the past years to spur urban economic development in industrialized countries in recognition of the deterioration of the central city as a source of jobs and a place to live. Stresses that the revitalization of the central city requires a broad cased constructive partnership between government at all levels and private industry. Discusses three strategies: the Enterprise Zone, a National Development Bank, and the Reconstruction Finance Corporation. These consider, respectively, entrepreneurial islands within urban areas that we are given preferential tax and regulatory treatment, financing for capital-short distressed areas, and financial aid and other support to aging basic industries.

446   Stevens, Christopher, ed.
       EEC AND THE THIRD WORLD: A SURVEY
       New York: Holmes & Meier, 1981.

       First of a projected series of annual surveys on major developments in the EEC, this volume contains six previously unpublished papers on the EEC's economic relations with the Third World during 1979-80. Topics include: trade protectionism; the collapse of negotiations on the international wheat agreement; the effects of oil price rises on non-agricultural, raw materials questions; and the concern of the EEC for the long-term security of its mineral supplies, principally in Africa.

447   Stewart, Frances, ed.
       EMPLOYMENT, INCOME DISTRIBUTION AND DEVELOPMENT
       London: Frank Cass and Forest Grove, Ore.: ISBS, 1975.

448   Sutcliffe, R. B.
       INDUSTRY AND UNDERDEVELOPMENT
       London: Addison-Wesley, 1980.

       The author discusses the arguments for and against industrialization in detail, stressing in particular the differences in the argument's applicability to "market" and "centrally-planned" economies throughout the world. He sees industrialization as a major historical process involving great changes in whole societies, and not merely changes in economic structure.

449   Sweet, Morris L.

INDUSTRIAL LOCATION POLICY FOR ECONOMIC REVITALIZATION: NATIONAL AND INTERNATIONAL PERSPECTIVES
New York: Praeger, 1981.

Examines government policies and programs affecting the locational pattern of industry in industrial democracies, and their effects on industrial development and the formulation of industrial policy. Analyzes the locational impact of controls on national, regional, and sub-regional industrial development, particularly their effect on the recovery of declining economies within the framework of industrial policy or reindustrialization; also examines the economic impact on private sector locational decisions. Discusses direct and indirect controls, the latter including codetermination and plant closing legislation, comparing the United States and various developed countries.

450 Swerdlow, Irving
THE PUBLIC ADMINISTRATION OF ECONOMIC DEVELOPMENT
New York and London: Praeger, 1975.

The thesis is that government administrators are an important element in expediting or slowing down the pace of economic development in LDC's. The author argues that successful economic planning requires public administrators to understand the planning process. The main determinants of growth are discussed, showing the role of government in improving income distribution. There is considerable discussion of planning operations, administration of economic policies, and processes of administration.

451 Swift, Jeannine
ECONOMIC DEVELOPMENT IN LATIN AMERICA
New York: St. Martin's Press, 1978.

Views issues in Latin American development as problems rooted in the history and institutional setting of each country. Emphasizes the notion of underdevelopment as a process rather than as a stage of growth, and thereby examines the forces that in some cases lead to distorted growth or deterioration. Author views radical social change in political institution as a necessary correlate of economic development that will benefit the masses of people. Topics include a discussion of the usefulness of models of development in Latin America, a treatment of the formation and consolidation of the conditions of underdevelopment, multinational corporations and the quesiton of economic dependence, appropriate technology, employment, income distribution, agrarian reform, and inflation.

452 Szentes, Tamas
THE POLITICAL ECONOMY OF UNDERDEVELOPMENT

Budapest: Akademiai Kiado, 1971.

A Marxist economist presents a perceptive analysis of the causes, substance, and the laws of motion of underdevelopment. He surveys various theories of underdevelopment, investigates the heterogeneous social structure as an internal factor of the system of underdevelopment, and summarizes the prospects for overcoming the problems from an international and single national economy viewpoint; author also discusses the peculiarities and prospects of state capitalism in underdeveloped economies.

453 Taylor, Charles Lewis, ed.
INDICATOR SYSTEMS FOR POLITICAL, ECONOMIC, AND SOCIAL ANALYSIS
Cambridge, MA: Oelgeschlagwe, Gunn & Hain; Konigstein/Ts., West Germany: Anton Hain, 1980.

Twelve papers (two previously published) and an introduction by the editor examining the development, analysis, and use of political, demographic, and economic indicators. Contributions are from a 1978 conference sponsored by the International Institute for Comparative Social Research and held in 1978 in Berlin. Specific topics include: the value of indicators, theoretical and concrete views of the systematization of indicators, the compilation of data by organs of the United Nations, and specific indicators of development, government repression, detente, and dependency.

454 Taylor, John G.
FROM MODERNIZATION TO MODES OF PRODUCTION: A CRITIQUE OF THE SOCIOLOGIES OF DEVELOPMENT AND UNDERDEVELOPMENT
Atlantic Highlands, NJ: Humanities Press, 1979.

A two-part treatise on the analysis of the structure, reproduction, and future development of Third World societies. Part one assesses critically the theory of the Sociology of Development and its theoretical alternative--the Sociology of Underdevelopment. Part two develops a new general framework, using concepts of historical materialism and recent advances in the theory of modes of production, for analyzing the non-capitalist societies that preceded colonialism, the effects of different forms of capitalist penetration on them, and the consequent emergence of a form of capitalist development particular to these societies.

455 Taylor, Lance
MACRO MODELS FOR DEVELOPING COUNTRIES
New York; London; Montreal and Paris: McGraw-Hill, 1979.

Draws together macro models designed for examining the difficulties faced by LDC's. Deals first with short-run models. Reviews national-accounting frameworks, applying particular ones to Portugal and Egypt and discusses three models incorporating markup pricing and designed with inflationary shifts in mind. Moves to medium- and long-run models that deal with growth and inflation and discusses applications of two flexible-price models to Brazil.

456 Temu, Peter
FROM POVERTY TO PROSPERITY
London: Oxford University Press.

This introduction to economics relates economic theory to particular aspects of the East African economy; it tries to answer basic questions about government services and use of funds which are frequently asked in developing countries.

457 Thirlwall, A. P.
GROWTH AND DEVELOPMENT: WITH SPECIAL REFERENCE TO DEVELOPING ECONOMIES
London: Macmillan, 1977.

Following an introduction, the material is divided into five parts: factors of production; obstacles to development; planning and resource allocation; financing development; and the international aspects of development. The entire text has been rewritten for this edition, and includes new material on: production function studies in developing countries; supply response of agricultural output; the population problem; the thesis of circular and cumulative causation; input-output analysis; the trade versus aid controversy; and the potential of Special Drawing Rights.

458 Tims, Wouter
NIGERIA: OPTIONS FOR LONG-TERM DEVELOPMENT
Baltimore and London: Johns Hopkins University Press, 1974.

One in a series of country economic reports which reviews the major trends and policies that have characterized economic development to date and examines in more detail the current position of the economy, its prospects during the remaining period of the Second National Development Plan (1972/73-1973/4) and the longer-term outlook through the early 1980's.

459 Toye, J. F. J., ed.
TAXATION AND ECONOMIC DEVELOPMENT
London and Totowa, NJ: Frank Cass, 1978.

Twelve papers (10 previously published) on assessing the tax performance of a developing country in relation to the growth and distribution functions. Part one looks at some "simple-minded" approaches to the measurement of tax capacity and tax effort; part two considers tax revenue as related to economic growth; and part three examines tax policy as it affects income distribution.

460 Tullis, F. LaMond
POLITICS AND SOCIAL CHANGE IN THIRD WORLD COUNTRIES
New York, London, Sydney, and Toronto: Wiley, 1973.

The book reviews the literature and ideas on the political and social aspects of modernization, introduces the reader to the use of analytical tools and quantitiatve analysis as well as to the formulation of testable hypotheses, and provides three case studies (Brazil, Libya, and Peru) as examples of differing models of modernization and political change.

461 Turnham, David
THE EMPLOYMENT PROBLEM IN LESS DEVELOPED COUNTRIES: A REVIEW OF EVIDENCE
Paris: OECD, 1971.

The first in a series of studies concerning the employment problem in less developed countries. Chapters deal with the labor force and the structure of employment in less developed countries; unemployment in less developed countries; income distribution, nutrition and working efficiency; and employment growth: trends and prospects.

462 UN Economic and Social Council
INDUSTRIALIZATION FOR NEW DEVELOPMENT NEEDS: VIEWS AND RECOMMENDATIONS
New York: UN Publications, 1974.

Emphasizes reshaping industrial development in developing countries in light of pervasive problems of unemployment, maldistribution of income, and poverty in general.

463 UN Department of Economic and Social Affairs
WORLD ECONOMIC SURVEY, 1973: PART TWO; CURRENT ECONOMIC DEVELOPMENTS
New York: Author, 1974.

Second part of a two part survey (the first deals with population and development) reviewing current trends in the world economy. First chapter presents an overview of world production and trade and then examines from a global point of view for 1973: the rise in commodity prices, the world food situation, and the world energy situation. The remaining chapters focus upon how recent economic developments have affected the supply and use of resources and the state of internal and external balance in the developed market economies, the centrally planned economies, and the developing countries.

464   UN Economic Commission for Latin America
        DEVELOPMENT PROBLEMS IN LATIN AMERICA
        Austin and London: University of Texas Press for the
        Institute of Latin American Studies, 1970.

        A compendium of publications issued by the ECLA (Economic
        Commission for Latin America) over the past twenty years;
        these publications cover factors and questions not only
        of an economic but also of social and political nature.
        Features a 1968 address delivered by Mr. Carlos Quintana,
        Executive Secretary of ECLA, at the second session of
        the United Nations Conference on Trade and Development.
        Also contains two articles by Raul Prebisch--"Economic
        Development or Monetary Stability" and "Toward a Dynamic
        Development Policy for Latin America."

465   Untied Nations
        WORLD INDUSTRY IN 1980
        New York: UN, 1981.

        Central theme of this issue is the restructuring of world
        industry. Topics discussed: the restructuring process;
        current trends in world industry; the export performance
        of developing countries--dynamic changes in comparative
        advantage; trends and prospects in selected
        branches--chemicals, iron and steel, engineering goods,
        food processing; energy requirements in the manufacturing
        sector; and the transnational corporation as an agent
        for industrial restructuring.

466   United Nations
        POLICIES AND TECHNIQUES FOR MOBILIZING PERSONAL SAVINGS
        IN DEVELOPING COUNTRIES
        New York: UN, 1977.

        Summarizes the discussions and recommendations of the
        Workshop. Topics covered: conceptual and policy context;
        institutional framework for mobilizing personal savings;
        safeguarding the value of savings; interest rates as
        savings incentive; increasing return on savings through
        tax measures; increasing rates on savings through premiums;
        incentives through promise of future credits; mobilization
        of savings in rural areas; and facilitating access to
        credit by farmers, craftsmen and small business.

467   United Nations
        SURVEY OF CHANGES AND TRENDS IN PUBLIC ADMINSITRATION
        AND FINANCE FOR DEVELOPMENT, 1975-77
        New York: UN, 1978.

        Discusses inter alia, the changing demands on public
        administration and finance; the organization of public
        administration for planned development; administrative
        machinery and processes for planning; human resources

for public services; government budgeting and financial management; and trends and responses in the 1980s.

468 UNESCO
THE USE OF SOCIO-ECONOMIC INDICATORS IN DEVELOPMENT PLANNING
Paris: UNESCO Press; distributed by Unipub, New York, 1976.

Eight previously unpublished essays by economists and other social scientists, presented at two Unesco meetings, 1973 and 1974. Includes: two papers on social indicators, one theoretical and methodological and the other on application, two case studies on the use of indicators in development planning (India and France); three case studies on the use of indicators in development planning (India and France); three case studies concerned with the development of indicators of distribution (Kenya, Zambia, and Asian countries); and a closing essay on a new approach to the construction of social models.

469 UNESCO
SOCIO-ECONOMIC INDICATORS FOR PLANNING: METHODOLOGICAL ASPECTS AND SELECTED EXAMPLES
UNESCO, Paris, 1981.

Contains four papers which discuss the applicability of socioeconomic indicators to planning: (a) use of social indicators for planning; (b) identification of socioeconomic indicators for use in integrated social and economic planning; (c) socioeconomic indicators for development planning in Africa; and (d) identification of social concerns and social indicators relevant to development planning Africa.

470 United Nations Industrial Development Organization
A C INDUSTRIAL PRIORITIES IN DEVELOPING COUNTRIES
N.Y.: United Nations Publications, 1979.

Focuses on the way five major developing countries--Brazil, India, Mexico, Republic of Korea, and Turkey--have selected industrial priorities in recent years (up to around 1975). Discusses: s system operated by and for the business community; economic rationale in decision making; commercial profitability; use of programming models in decision making; and the ad hoc nature of decision making.

471 United Nations Industrial Development Organization
A C D INDUSTRIALIZATION IN AFRICA
N.Y.: United Nations Publications, 1973.

Conference sponsored by the Economic Commission for Africa (ECA), the Organization of African Unity (OAU) and UNIDO. Annex contains the recommendations of the First Meeting on the Follow-up Committee on Industrialization in Africa,

Addis Ababa, September 1974.

472 United Nations Industrial Development Organization
A B C WORLD INDUSTRY SINCE 1960: PROGRESS AND PROSPECTS: SPECIAL ISSUE OF THE INDUSTRIAL DEVELOPMENT SURVEY FOR THE THIRD GENERAL CONFERENCE OF UNIDO, NEW DELHI, INDIA, 21 JANUARY-8 FEBRUARY 1980
New York: United Nations, 1979.

Documents and analyzes the basic trends in world production, trade, employment, technology, and finance for the period 1960-2000 and evaluates the progress made by developing countries in achieving the long-term objectives stated in the Lima Declaration and Plan of Action on Industrial Development and Co-operation. The main theme is world interdependence and its implications for a restructured world ecoonomy that recognizes the need for international solutions to world problems that are consistent with the economic goals and potential of both the developing and the developed countries. Some specific topics include current international issues; the changing pattern of industrial production; industrial development at the branch and commodity levels; strategies and policies; the relationship of trade to the industrialization process; the processing of natural resources; rural development; financing industrial development; and the role of the public sector.

473 Uphoff, Norman T. and Ilchman, Warren F., eds.
THE POLITICAL ECONOMY OF DEVELOPMENT: THEORETICAL AND EMPIRICAL CONTRIBUTIONS
Berkeley and London: Univeristy of California Press, 1972.

Edited by two political scientists, this is a collection of previously published articles on important political and economic issues in economic development. Forty-three articles deal with such issues as the role of social science in the development process, the political environment of development, observations on the process of development (with Latin America as the case-study), the role of leadership, and the political economy of land reform, education, employment, political and administrative infrastructure, and economic policy.

474 Usher, Dan
THE MEASUREMENT OF ECONOMIC GROWTH
N.Y.: Columbia Univeristy Press, 1980.

Economists have long known that such commonly used measures of economic welfare as changes in gross national product had serious shortcomings, but the systematic investigation of these deficiencies and attempts to construct alternative measures of social welfare are relatively recent. Usher presents the theory that growth can be determined mainly by measuring technical changes in the means of production. This very useful book goes some way toward bridging the gap between national income texts and technical articles analyzing various measures of growth.

475 Van De Laar, Aart
THE WORLD BANK AND THE POOR. INSTITUTE OF SOCIAL STUDIES SERIES ON THE DEVELOPMENT OF SOCIETIES
Boston: The Hague and London: Marinus Nijhoff, 1980.

Assesses the World Bank's response to the challenge of redirecting its activities toward the low-income strata, i.e., the poorest 40 percent, of the total population in all developing countries. Part one reviews the growth and evolution of both the International Bank for Reconstruction and Development and the International Development Association, and disucsses the finances of the Bank and the recruitment, organization, and geographical composition of its staff. Part two focuses on the possibilities for new deployment of Bank resources.

476 Varon, Bension, Chief of Mission, and others
ZAIRE: CURRENT ECONOMIC SITUATION AND CONSTRAINTS
May 1980.

Presents an integrated analysis of the difficulties experienced by the Zairian economy between 1975 and the first half of 1979 and suggests that the country needs to revamp its institutions and its system of incentives and adopt policies that will lay the foundation for a development pattern that will render it less vulnerable to changes in the world economy.

477 Virmani, Arvind
THE NATURE OF CREDIT MARKETS IN DEVELOPING COUNTRIES: A FRAMEWORK FOR POLICY ANALYSIS
World Bank Staff Working Paper No. 524, 1982.

The central purpose of the paper is to analyze various forms of government intervention in the loan market in terms of their effect on efficiency.

478 Wai, U. Tun
FINANCIAL INTERMEDIARIES AND NATIONAL SAVINGS IN DEVELOPING COUNTRIES. PRAEGER SPECIAL STUDIES IN INTERNATIONAL ECONOMICS AND DEVELOPMENT
New York: Praeger, 1972.

The book deals with the evolution of net national savings in developing countries, financial intermediation, the relevance of existing theories of savings for developing countries, come econometric approaches to financial intermediation and national savings, and attempts to build an integrated theory of savings.

479 Westphal, Larry E.
A B PLANNING INVESTMENTS WITH ECONOMIES OF SCALE
Amsterdam and London: North-Holland, 1971.

A highly technical book on planning investment projects in less developed economies. Includes a glossary of symbols on capital accumulation path modesl to assist the reader in better understanding of the book's content. The study provides a model incorporating important elements in development (input-output relationships, sectoral competition for scarce resources, and changing comparative costs related to changes in available resources).

480 Whynes, David K.
THE ECONOMICS OF THE THIRD WORLD MILITARY EXPENDITURE
Austin: University of Texas Press, 1979.

Analyzes the impact on Third World economic development of military expenditure. Examines LDC defense expenditure data to determine the causes of the growth in military spending, assesses the real resource costs by focusing on interface between the military and civilian economy, and discusses the specific issues of military aid and military intervention. Concludes that current levels of defense spending "impose considerable economic and social costs onto the Third World." Provides a review of possible methods of effectively reducing the burden of military expenditure while maintaining internal and external security.

481 Willett, Thomas D.
INTERNATIONAL LIQUIDITY ISSUES
Washington, D.C.: American Enterprise Institute for Public Policy Research, 1980.

Analyzes international liquidity issues in the new international monetary environment. Part one, an analytic history of major international liquidity concepts and developments, focuses on the similarities and differences between the effects on economic behavior of changes in national monetary aggregates and changes in international reserve aggregates.

482 Wionczek, Miguel S., ed.
LDC EXTERNAL DEBT AND THE WORLD ECONOMY
Mexico, D.F.: El Colegio de Mexico and Center for Economic and Social Studies of the Third World, 1978.

Fifteen previously unpublished papers on North-South financial relations. Papers were originally presented at a private international conference in Mexico City in October 1977 sponsored by El Colegio de Mexico and the Center for Economic and Social Studies of the Third World. Includes final report from the meeting. Consensus was that LDC debt should be handled in the general framework of international economic relations and not separated from such issues as trade policies, development assistance, etc.; that this external debt is the joint responsibility of the borrower and lender.

483   Wolfson, Dirk J.
PUBLIC FINANCE AND DEVELOPMENT STRATEGY
Baltimore, MD: Johns Hopkins University Press, 1979.

484   World Bank
LESOTHO: A DEVELOPMENT CHALLENGE. A WORLD BANK COUNTRY ECONOMIC REPORT
Washington: Author; distributed by Johns Hopkins Press, Baltimore.

Examination of the economic situation in Lesotho, located in Southern Africa. Discusses the economic setting, trends in the economy, operations of the government, and various sectors of the economy and provides an outlook for development. Finds that the country is very poor and desperately short of natural resources and that economic indicators point to poverty and stagnation over a long period of time, reflecting the lack of resources and past economic development.

485   World Bank
CHAD: DEVELOPMENT POTENTIAL AND CONSTRAINTS
Washington, D,C,: Author, 1974.

Report prepared by an economic mission on the Chad economy covering economic structure, development potential and problems, development constraints, planning and growth prospects, financial prospects, and aid outlook.

486   World Bank
ACCELERATED DEVELOPMENT IN SUB-SAHARAN AFRICA: AN AGENDA FOR ACTION
Washington, D.C.: World Bank, 1981.

In the fall of 1979, the African Governors of the World Bank addressed a memorandum to the Bank's president expressing their alarm at the dim economic prospects for the nations of sub-Saharan Africa and asking that the Bank prepare a "special paper on the economic development problems of these countries" and an appropriate program for helping them. This report, building on the Lagos Plan of Action, is the response to that request.

487   Wriggins, Howard W. and Adler-Karlsson, Gunnar
REDUCING GLOBAL INEQUITIES
New York: McGraw-Hill, 1978.

II. SELECTED PERIODICAL ARTICLES

488   Abban, J.B.
        "Aggregate Economic Performance in the Context of Innovations in Monetary Policy in Ghana, 1960-67." GHANA SOCIAL SCIENCE JOURNAL 2 (May 1972): 66-85.

489   Abeysekera, Gamini
        Economic growth, employment and income distribution; lessons from Sri Lanka's experience. CENTRAL BANK OF CEYLON, STAFF STUDIES (COLOMBO) 6:133-48, April 1976.

        For an "underdeveloped economy Sri Lanka has a remarkably low income inequality and moreover, it has significantly reduced the level of income disparities over a period of twenty years. Yet, economic growth performance of Sri Lanka has not been very impressive and the unemployment problem of the country has not found satisfactory solutions.

489a   Acharya, Shankar N.
        Fiscal financial intervention, factor prices and factor proportions; a review of issues. THE BANGLADESH DEVELOPMENT STUDIES (DACCA) 3:429-64, Oct. 1975.

        Outlines four main types of limitations to the "scope for factor-price intervention to shift to efficient factor combinations with more employment perunit of capital in the economy."

489b   Adams, John
        The economic development of African pastoral societies; a model. KYKLOS (BASLE) 28, No. 4:852-65, 1975.

        "Uses a diagrammatic framework to discuss the development of African pastoral societies through three phases: the traditional, colonial and modern."

489c   Adams, John
        Regional patterns of development in Karnataka. JOURNAL OF DEVELOPING AREAS (MACOMB, ILL.) 12:439-48, July 1978.

        Examines the economic structure and development of Karnataka (formerly Mysore) in 1971.

489d   Adelman, Irma
        Economic development and political change in developing countries. SOCIAL RESEARCH (NEW YORK) 47:213-34, Summer 1980.

489e   Adelman, I.
        "On the State of Development Economics." JOURNAL OF DEVELOPMENT ECONOMICS 1 (June 1974).

489f Adelman, Irma
Development economics; a reassessment of goals. AMERICAN ECONOMIC REVIEW, PAPERS AND PRODEEDINGS (NASHVILLE) 65:302-309, May 1975.

Reviews some recent work on this topic, then proposes a minimum humanistic goal for development and, finally, suggests development strategies that may permit achievement of that goal.

489g Adelman, Irma
Growth, income distribution and equity-oriented development strategies. WORLD DEVELOPMENT (OXFORD) 3:67-76, Feb./March 1975.

"Suggests that equitable growth requires a radical re-orientation of development strategies."

489h Adeyokunnu, T.O.
"Agriculture and Nigeria's Economic Development." QUARTERLY JOURNAL OF ADMINISTRATION 6 (October 1971): 17-28.

489i Adler, John H.
Development strategy; the political economy of delinking. INTERECONOMICS, REVIEW OF INTERNATIONAL TRADE AND DEVELOPMENT (HAMBURG) No. 3:136-43, May/June 1980.

Gives an account of the arguments for delinking which is followed by an evaluation of these arguments and a discussion of the policy implications for industrial countries. Finally, an attempt is made to evaluate what contribution the proponents of delinking have made to the understanding of the development process and the normative implications of that knowledge.

489j AFRICAN DEVELOPMENT 8 (March 1974): N1-72. "Nigerian Economic Survey."

490 AFRICAN DEVELOPMENT (January 1973), pp. 1-40. "Sudan Economic Survey."

491 AFRICAN DEVELOPMENT (September 1972), pp. 1-24. "Zaire Economic Survey."

492 Aftab, Khalid
Does education accelerate economic growth? An assessment of McClelland's hypothesis. PAKISTAN ECONOMIC AND SOCIAL REVIEW (LAHORE) 15:127-51, Autumn/Winter 1977.

493 Afxentiou, P.C.
"Fiscal Policy and Economic Development." DEVELOPING ECONOMIES 14 (June 1976): 164-78.

494 Ajayi, S. IBI

"An Econometric Case Study of the Relative Importance of Monetary and Fiscal Policy in Nigeria." BANGLADESH ECONOMIC REVIEW 2 (April 1974): 559-76.

495 Alamgir, Mohiuddin
"Some Analysis of Distribution of Income, Consumption, Saving and Poverty in Bangladesh." BANGLADESH DEVELOPMENT STUDIES 2 (October 1974): 737-818.

496 Alamgir, Mohiuddin and Horton, Susan
Model of rural household economy in a developing country: application to Bangladesh data. HARVARD INSTITUTE FOR INTERNATIONAL DEVELOPMENT, DEVELOPMENT DISCUSSION PAPER (CAMBRIDGE, MASS.) No. 90:1-33, March 1980.

497 Alamgir, Mohiuddin and Ahmad, Sadiq
Poverty and income distribution in Bangladesh: evidence and policies. HARVARD INSTITUTE FOR INTERNATIONAL DEVELOPMENT, DEVELOPMENT DISCUSSION PAPER (CAMBRIDGE, MASS.) No. 119:1-58, July 1981.

498 Alauddin, Talat
Mass poverty in Pakistan; a further study. PAKISTAN DEVELOPMENT REVIEW (ISLAMABAD) 14:431-50, Winter 1975.

"This study measures poverty not only in terms of real consumption expenditure but also in terms of real income. The use of income levels has shown that the problem of poverty is much more severe than portrayed by an analysis based on expenditures only."

499 Anderson, Lascelles
Manpower and economic planning; a linear programming model for Tanzania. SOCIAL AND ECONOMIC STUDIES (MONA, JAMAICA) 24:15-46, March 1975.

"The model developed and analysed in this study is a fairly simple model. One of the objecives of the formulation of this type model was to demonstrate how meaningful programming models can be for the range of questions in manpower planning which face developing countries like Tanzania, and yet remain fairly simple."

500 Andreano, Ralph L. and North, Douglass C.
"Institutional Change and Economic Growth." JOURNAL OF ECONOMIC HISTORY 31 (March 1971): 126-34.

501 Aoki, Masanso
On decentralized stabilization policies and dynamic assignment problems. JOURNAL OF INTERNATIONAL ECONOMICS (AMSTERDAM) 6:143-71, May 1976.

Illustrates by a simple example involving two countries, a type of analysis one could perform to evaluate

502 Areskoug, Kaj
"Private Foreign Investment and Capital Formation in Developing Countries." ECONOMIC DEVELOPMENT AND CULTURAL CHANGE 24 (April 1976): 539-47.

503 Ariff, K.A.
"Economic Development of Malaysia: Pattern and Perspective." DEVELOPING ECONOMIES 11 (December 1973): 371-91.

504 Arndt, H.W.
Economic development: a semantic history ECONOMIC DEVELOPMENT AND CULTURAL CHANGE (CHICAGO) 29:457-66, April 1981.

505 Arnold, Wolfgang
Growth, distribution and motivation in LDCs. INTERECONOMICS, REVIEW OF INTERNATIONAL TRADE AND DEVELOPMENT (HAMBURG) No. 6:298-303, Nov./Dec. 1979.

Examines various alternative explanations of the personal distribution of income to answer the question how the distribution objective can be attained and what effect certain measures of distribution policy have on growth.

506 Assael, Hector
The internationalization of the Latin American economies; some reservations. CEPAL REVIEW (SANTIAGO DE CHILE) p. 41-55, Apr. 1979. Spanish version in REVISTA DE LA CEPAL (SANTIAGO DE CHILE) p. 43-57, Apr. 1979.

507 Aubey, Robert; Kyle, John and Strickon, Arnold
"Investment Behavior and Elite Social Structures in Latin America." JOURNAL OF INTERAMERICAN STUDIES AND WORLD AFFAIRS 16 (February 1974): 73-95.

508 Axinn, George H.
The development cycle; new strategies from an ancient concept. INTERNATIONAL DEVELOPMENT REVIEW (WASHINGTON) 19, NO. 4:9-15, 1977.

Defines a development cycle as an alternative assessment of development that places each human group somewhere on a cycle moving at their own pace to a follow-up stage.

509 Bacha, Edmar L. and Taylor, Lance
Brazilian income distribution in the 1960s; 'Facts', model results and the controversy. JOURNAL OF DEVELOPMENT STUDIES (LONDON) 14:271-97, April 1978.

"Discusses a number of hypotheses that have been put

forward to explain apparently unequalising changes in Brazilian income distribution in the 1960s.

510 Bachir, S. Ben
"The National and Economic Regionalization: The Moroccan Experience." AFRICAN ADMINISTRATIVE STUDIES (July 1974), pp.157-68.

511 Baer, W.
Paraguayan economic condition: past and current obstacles to economic modernization. INTERNATIONAL AMERICAN ECONOMIC AFFAIR 29:49-63, Summer 1975.

512 Bagi, Faqir Singe
Economic development with surplus labor: a welfare criterion. INDIAN JOURNAL OF ECONOMICS (ALLAHABAD) 61:61-74, July 1980.

513 Bahl, Roy W. and Velayudhan Pillai
The allocative effects of intergovernmental flows in less developed countries; a case study of India. PUBLIC FINANCE (THE HAGUE) 31, No. 1:73-89, 1976.

Estimates the fiscal responsiveness of local governments to formal intergovernmental flows, in aggregate and by type of central government assistance, in a less developed country setting. The model developed here is tested in terms of a case study of intergovernmental relations in India.

514 Balakrishnan, N.
Economic policies and trends in Sri Lanka. ASIAN SURVEY (BERKELEY, CALIF.) 20:891-902, Sept. 1980.

515 Balassa, B.
Structural adjustment policies in developing economics. WORLD DEVELOPMENT 10:23-38, Jan. 1982.

516 Baier, Stephen
"Economic History and Development: Drought and the Sahelian Economies of Niger." AFRICAN ECONOMIC HISTORY 1 (Spring 1976): 1-16.

517 Baily, Mary Ann
The effect of differential shift costs on capital utilization. JOURNAL OF DEVELOPMENT ECONOMICS (AMSTERDAM) 3:27-47, March 1976.

"This paper presents the results of a micro study of the influence of the shift differential factor on utilization rates in Kenyan manufacturing."

518 Ballentine, J. Gregory and Soligo, Ronald

Consumption and earnings patterns and income distribution. ECONOMIC DEVELOPMENT AND CULTURAL CHANGE (CHICAGO) 26:693-708, July 1978.

The authors use data from a 1968 closed input-output model of Colombian economy developed by UNAID.

519 Barkay, Richard M.
"National Accounting as a Planning Tool in Less Developed Countries: Lessons of Experience." REVIEW OF INCOME AND WEALTH (December 1975).

520 Barnabas, A.P.
"Sociological Implications of Multi-level Planning." INDIAN JOURNAL OF PUBLIC ADMINISTRATION 19 (July-September 1973): 357-62.

521 Batscha, Robert M.
"Dissemination of Research on Economic and Social Development." INTERNATIONAL SOCIAL SCIENCE JOURNAL 26 (1974): 525-29.

522 Behrman, Jere R.
"Sectoral Investment Determination in a Developing Economy." AMERICAN ECONOMIC REVIEW 62 (December 1972): 825-84.

523 Beigie, Carl E.
"An Economic Overview of Barriers to Trade Liberalization." BUSINESS ECONOMICS (January 1971).

524 Beim, David O.
Rescuing the LDCs [debt accumulation by the less-developed countries; emphasis on the large sums owed to commercial banks]. FOREIGN AFFAIRS 55:717-31, July 1977.

525 Beitz, C.R.
Economic rights and distributive justice in developing societies. WORLD POLITICS 33:321-46, April 1981.

526 Bergsten, C. Fred; Keohane, Robert O. and Nye, Joseph S., Jr.
"International Economics and International Politics: A Framework for Analysis." INTERNATIONAL ORGANIZATION 29 (1975): 3-36.

527 Berry, Roger
Redistribution, demand structure and factor requirements: the case of India. WORLD DEVELOPMENT (OXFORD) 9:621-35, July 1981.

Suggests that even 'radical' redistributions of private consumption expenditure would have no significant impact on the level of employment, either directly through increasing labour requirements or indirectly through reducing scarce resource requirements.

528   Berry, Sara A.
        "Economic Development with Surplus Labour: Further Complications Suggested by Contemporary African Experience." OXFORD ECONOMIC PAPERS (July 1970).

529   Berry, Sara
        Capitalism and underdevelopment in Africa: a critical essay. BOSTON UNIVERSITY. AFRICAN STUDIES CENTER. WORKING PAPERS (BOSTON) No. 49:1-33, 1981.

530   Berry, Sara S. and Eckstein, Peter
        "An Econometric Model of Development: Comment." AMERICAN ECONOMIC REVIEW (March 1970).

531   Bessonov, S.A.
        Economic Planning in the Developing Countries of Africa. BUDAPEST: CENTER FOR AFRO-ASIAN RESEARCH OF THE HUNGARIAN ACADEMY OF SCIENCES, 1974.

532   Betz, H.K. and Hunt, E.K.
        "Methodological Problems in Contracting Economic Systems." AMERICAN JOURNAL OF ECONOMICS AND SOCIOLOGY 29 (October 1970).

533   Beyer, John C.
        "High Growth, Unemployment, and Planning in Venezuela: Some Observations." ECONOMIC DEVELOPMENT AND CULTURAL CHANGE 18 (January 1970): 267-73.

534   Bhalla, Surjit S.
        The measurement of permanent income and its application to savings behavior. JOURNAL OF POLITICAL ECONOMY (CHICAGO) 88:722-44, Aug. 1980.

        Attempts to test the savings-income relationship of rural households, using data collected by the National Council for Applied Economic Research (1974) on some 2,000 households in rural India.

535   Bhargava, P.K.
        Economic planning in India: failure or success? LONG RANGE PLANNING (OXFORD) 15:87-96, Feb. 1982.

536   Bhatia, D.P.
        Savings, growth and distribution in India; an empirical investigation. MARGIN: QUARTERLY JOURNAL OF THE NATIONAL COUNCIL OF APPLIED ECONOMIC RESEARCH (NEW DELHI) 12:93-103, Oct. 1979.

537   Bhatt, V.V.
        Economic development; an analytic-historical approach. WORLD DEVELOPMENT (OXFORD) 4:583-92, July 1976.

538   Bird, Graham
        Some proposals for increasing the size and improving the nature of financial flows to developing countries. RIVISTA INTERNAZIONALE DI SCIENZE ECONOMICHE E COMMERCIALI (MILAN) 27:1038-52 O/N 1980.

539   Blades, Derek W.
        Subsistence activities in the national accounts of developing countries with special reference to Latin America. REVIEW OF INCOME AND WEALTH (NEW HAVEN) SERIES 21, No. 4:391-410, Dec. 1975.

        "Presents some preliminary findings from a research study by the OECD Development centre into the treatment of subsistence activities in national accounts. It summarizes the results of a questionnaire on country practices, and reports on the findings with respect to shares of non-monetary production in GDP, methods of estimation, and usefulness of the resulting estimates."

540   Blake, David
        Investment; the key to world recovery. TIMES (LONDON) p. 17, July 22, 1982.

        Discusses economic policy and the obstacles to world growth.

541   Blanchart, Olivier Jean
        Debt and the current account deficit in Brazil. HARVARD INSTITUTE OF ECONOMIC RESEARCH, DISCUSSION PAPER (CAMBRIDGE, MASS.) No. 865:1-17, December 1981.

        Suggests that from the point of view of solvency, the current account deficit is not a major problem, and that, if Brazil does not want to accumulate high levels of debt, the reduction in the deficit should come mostly from consumption rather than from investment.

542   Blaug, Mark
        "Economic and Educational Planning in Developing Countries." PROSPECTS 2 (Winter 1972): 431-41.

543   Blitzer, Charles R.
        Development and income distribution in a dual economy: a dynamic simulation model for Zambia. JOURNAL OF DEVELOPMENT ECONOMICS (AMSTERDAM) 6:407-29, Sept. 1979.

        Discusses medium-term development prospects for Zambia. The analysis is carried out in terms of a modified dual economy model. Special attention is paid to sectoral employment and income distribution implications.

544   Blumle, Gerold
        Economic development and personal income distribution

in developing countries. ECONOMICS (TUBINGEN) 20:52-65, 1979.

545   Bognar, Jozsef
      Global economic security and growth; world economic prospects for the eighties and nineties. NEW HUNGARIAN QUARTERLY (BUDAPEST) 21:9-24, Autumn 1980.

546   Boisier, Sergio
      Towards a social and political dimension of regional planning. CEPAL REVIEW (SANTIAGO DE CHILE) p. 93-123, April 1981.

547   Bomberger, W.A. and Makinen, G.E.
      Inflation, unemployment, and expectations in Latin America; some simple tests. SOUTHERN ECONOMIC JOURNAL (CHAPEL HILL, N.C.) 43:1112-23, Oct. 1976.

      Examines the relationship between inflation and capacity utilization.

548   Boserup, Ester
      "Women's Role in Economic Development." DEVELOPMENT DIGEST 9 (April 1971): 97-122.

549   Boulier, Bryan L.
      The effects of demographic variables on income distribution. PRINCETON UNIVERSITY. WOODROW WILSON SCHOOL OF PUBLIC AND INTERNATIONAL AFFAIRS. RESEARCH PROGRAM IN ECONOMIC DEVELOPMENT. DISCUSSION PAPER (PRINCETON) No. 61:1-16, May 1975.

      "The purpose of this article is to suggest that empirically observed relationships between fertility and income distribution may be generated by an entirely different mechanism. In particular, high fertility and rapid rate of population growth may be the sources of a less equitable distribution of income."

550   Boulier, Bryan L.
      Income distribution and fertility decline: a skeptical view. PRINCETON UNIVERSITY. WOODROW WILSON SCHOOL OF PUBLIC AND INTERNATIONAL AFFAIRS. RESEARCH PROGRAM IN DEVELOPMENT STUDIES. DISCUSSION PAPER (PRINCETON) No. 97:1-32, Aug. 1981.

      The author reviews previous empirical research on the relations between income distribution and fertility, and presents some additional tests of the hypothesis using household data from the Philippines. He concludes that there is no persuasive evidence for the proposition that reductions in income inequality would induce declines in fertility.

551   Bourguignon, Francois
        General equilibrium analysis of the Colombian income distribution: applications to rural development, wage and income policies. INTERNATIONAL LABOR OFFICE. WORLD EMPLOYMENT PROGRAMME RESEARCH. INCOME DISTRIBUTION AND EMPLOYMENT PROGRAMME, WORKING PAPERS (GENEVA) WP No. 68:1-109, June 1978.

552   Brada, Josef C. and others
        The optimal rate of industrialization in developed and developing centrally-planned economics: a general equilibrium approach. WORLD DEVELOPMENT 9:991-1004, S/O 1981.

553   Brannon, Russell H.
        Employment, Poverty, and Income Distribution in Asia: A Rural Focus. LEXINGTON: UNIVERSITY OF KENTUCKY, COLLEGE OF AGRICULTURE, 1976.

554   Brett-Crowther, M.R.
        Economic development: theory v. practice [review article]. ROUND TABLE no. 283:280-8, July 1981.

555   Brock, William A. and Mirman, Leonard J.
        "Optimal Economic Growth and Uncertainty: The Discounted Case." JOURNAL OF ECONOMIC THEORY (June 1972).

556   Brunner, Karl
        Economic development, Cancun and the western democracies [analysis of proposals for a New International Economic Order; based on lecture]. WORLD ECONOMY (LONDON) 5:61-84, March 1982.

557   Bruton, Henry J.
        "The import-Substitution Strategy of Economic Development Survey." PAKISTAN DEVELOPMENT REVIEW 10 (Summer 1970): 123-46.

558   Buira Seira, Ariel
        Recession, inflation and the international monetary system. WORLD DEVELOPMENT (OXFORD) 9:1115-28, Nov./Dec. 1981.

        Outlines the likely course of the world economy during the decade now beginning, and proposes an agenda for reform of the international monetary system.

559   Butler, Arthur and Della Valle, Philip
        "'Surprise' Inflation, Economic Growth and Employment." INTERNATIONAL LABOUR REVIEW 104 (December 1971): 489-504.

560   Caiden, N.
        Budgeting in poor countries: ten common assumptions re-examined.
        PUBLIC ADMINISTRATION REVIEW 40:40-6, Jan. 1980.

561 World recession and policies for recovery. CAMBRIDGE ECONOMIC POLICY REVIEW (FARNBOROUGH, ENG.) No. 5:8-23, April 1979.

562 Cameron, David R.
On the limits of the public economy. AMERICAN ACADEMY OF POLITICAL AND SOCIAL SCIENCE, ANNALS (PHILADELPHIA) 459:49-62, Jan. 1982.

Presents a systematic analysis of the relationships among 19 nations between increases in spending and lower rates of economic growth, higher unemployment, increases in deficits, and inflation, and concludes that, contrary to the conventional macroeconomic wisdom, high levels of spending and large increases in spending have not caused stagflation.

563 Cardozo, Ovidio C.
Flexible exchange rates, inflation and economic development. WORLD DEVELOPMENT (OXFORD) 4:613-26, July 1976.

Content: I. Introduction. II. Inflation and the stages of economic development. III. Inflation and devaluation in less developed countries; two alternatives.

564 Carlberg, Michael
A Leontief model of interregional economic growth. ANNALS OF REGIONAL SCIENCE (BELLENGHAM) 14:30-40, Nov. 1980.

565 Cartier, Robert
Noneconomic factors in the study of economic development. RICE UNIVERSITY. PROGRAM OF DEVELOPMENT STUDIES (HOUSTON) PAPER. NO. 61:1-34, Winter 1975.

566 Carvajal, M.J. and Geithman, David T.
Income distribution and economic development; some intra-country evidence. SOUTHERN ECONOMIC JOURNAL (CHAPEL HILL, N.C.) 44:922-28, April 1978.

567 Champion, Madeleine
Bolivia; continued economic progress. BANK OF LONDON & SOUTH AMERICA REVIEW (LONDON) 10:308-16, June 1976. Reviews Bolivia's economic development.

568 Chandavarkar, Anand G.
"Interest Rate Policies in Developing Countries." FINANCE AND DEVELOPMENT 7 (March 1970): 19-27.

569 Chandavarkar, Anand G.
"How Relevant Is Finance for Development?" FINANCE AND DEVELOPMENT 10 (September 1973): 14-16.

570 Chang, K.S.
Economic conditions of Taiwan and its prospects for

development. INDUSTRY OF FREE CHINA (TAIPEI) 51:11-16, May 25, 1979.

571 Charle, Edwin
"Political Systems and Economic Performance in Some African Societies." ECONOMIC DEVELOPMENT AND CULTURAL CHANGE 18, pt. 1 (July 1970): 575-97.

572 Chase-Dunn, Christopher
"The Effects of International Economic Dependence on Development and Inequality: A cross-national Study." AMERICAN SOCIOLOGICAL REVIEW 40 (1975): 720-38.

573 CHASE MANHATTAN BANK, INTERNATIONAL FINANCE (NEW YORK) 17: p. 1, July 19, 1982. Slower growth in the developing economies.

574 Chelliah, Raja J.
"Trends in Taxation in Developing Countries." INTERNATIONAL MONETARY FUND STAFF PAPERS (July 1971).

575 Chen, Sun
The trend of economic development and productivity in Taiwan. INDUSTRY OF FREE CHINA (TAIPEI) 45:2-19, March 1976.

Content: I. The hypothesis. II. Growth of GDP per capita and labor productivity in Taiwan. III. Productivity and wage rate in the manufacturing industry. IV. Growth wages and structural change. V. Concluding remarks.

576 Chichilnisky, Graciela and Cole, Sam
Growth of the North and growth of the South; some results on export led policies. HARVARD INSTITUTE FOR INTERNATIONAL DEVELOPMENT, DEVELOPMENT DISCUSSION PAPER (CAMBRIDGE, MASS.)No. 42:1018, Sept. 1978.

577 Chiswick, Barry R.
"Earnings Inequality and Economic Development." QUARTERLY JOURNAL OF ECONOMICS 85 (February 1971): 21-39.

578 Chossudovsky, Michel
Capital accumulation in Chile and Latin America. ECONOMIC AND POLITICAL WEEKLY (BOMBAY) 13:955-62, June 10, 1978.

Reviews economic policy in Chile since 1973, then analyzes changes in the pattern of development in Chile and their implications for Latin America.

579 Christakis, Alexander N.
"The Limits of Systems Analysis in Economic and Social Development Planning." EKISTICS 34 (July 1972): 37-42.

580 Christensen, Laurits R. and Cummings, Dianne
Economic growth, 1947-1973; an international comparison.
HARVARD INSTITUTE OF ECONOMIC RESEARCH, DISCUSSION PAPER SERIES (CAMBRIDGE, MASS.) No. 521: 1-130, Dec. 1976.

581 Clark, Colin
Economic development in communist China. JOURNAL OF POLITICAL ECONOMY (CHICAGO) 84:239-64, April 1976.

"This text is an extension of a previous study covering the period from the 1930s to 1959, published by the present writer in 1965. The results of the earlier study are included in the final table."

582 Cleveland, H. Van B. and Bhagavatula, R.
Continuing world economic crisis. FOREIGN AFFAIRS 59 No. 3:594-616, 1981.

583 Cline, William R.
International economic reform and income distribution. CEPAL REVIEW (SANTIAGO DE CHILE) No. 10:103-12, April 1980.

584 Coats, Warren L., Jr. and Khatkhate, Deena R.
Money and monetary policy in less developed countries; survey of issues and evidence. ECONOMIC AND POLITICAL WEEKLY (BOMBAY) 14:1881-1900, Nov. 17, 1979.

The introductory chapter of a forthcoming book "Readings in money and monetary policy in LDCs" edited by the authors.

585 Cole, William E. and Sanders, Richard D.
"Income Distribution, Profits and Savings in the Recent Economic Experience of Mexico." INTER-AMERICAN ECONOMIC AFFAIRS 24 (1970): 49.

586 Colladay, Frederick L. and Adelman, Irma
"Socio-Economic Policy Alternatives in National Development: A Parametric Programming Analysis." BEHAVIORAL SCIENCE 17 (March 1972): 204-20.

587 Collier, D.
Timing of economic growth and regime characteristics in Latin America. COMP POL 7:331-59, April 1975.

588 Collins, Joseph and Lappe, Moore Frances
Whom does the World Bank serve? ECONOMIC AND POLITICAL WEEKLY (BOMBAY) 14:853-56, May 1979.

The authors show how the Bank has become a major force shaping the economic policies of various countries and critically examine some of its policies.

589 COMERCIO EXTERIOR (MEXICO) 23:247-51, July 1977. Latin America; economic growth and social inequality.

Concludes that latin American economic development is not matched in the region by social progress of similar intensity.

590 Correa, Hector
Quantitative analysis of the implementation of economic plans in Latin America. ECONOMICS OF PLANNING (BIRMINGHAM, ENG.) 14, No. 1:31-43, 1976.

Presents a statistical analysis of the idea that the characteristics of an economic planning process influence the degree of implementation of the plan's targets. Data from 17 Latin American countries are used.

591 Coussement, Andre M.
Why the bond market should open up for developing countries. EUROMONEY (LONDON) p. 117-27, Aug. 1980.

Examines the various sources of external financing open to the developing countries, including the syndicated credit market, the external bond markets and the IMF.

592 Crockett, Andrew D.
Stabilization policies in developing countries: some policy considerations. STAFF PAPERS, INTERNATIONAL MONETARY FUND (WASHINGTON) 28:54-79, March 1981.

593 DaCosta, Michael
How bank lending helps the LDCs [less developed countries]. BANKER (LONDON) 130:47, 1980.

594 Dadzie, K.K.S.
Economic development. SCIENTIFIC AMERICAN (NEW YORK) 243:59-65, Sept. 1980.

Describes how the nations of the impoverished three-fourths of mankind press for the creation of a new economic order to redress the asymmetry in relations between the developed countries and developing ones.

595 David, W.L.
Alternative paradigms in economics and the study of development and underdevelopment. BLACK POLITICS ECONOMICS 6:72-89, Fall, 1975.

596 Davis, Russell
With a view to the future; tracing broad trends and planning. HARVARD INSTITUTE FOR INTERNATIONAL DEVELOPMENT, DEVELOPMENT DISCUSSION PAPER (CAMBRIDGE, MASS.) No. 61:1-44, June 1979.

597 Deger, Saadet
Investment, defence and growth in less developed countries. BIRKBECK COLLEGE. DEPT. OF ECONOMICS. DISCUSSION PAPERS IN ECONOMICS No. 105:1-20, Oct. 1981.

598 De Gregori, Thomas R.
Prodigality or parsimony: the false dilemma in economic development theory. JOURNAL OF ECONOMIC ISSUES (June 1973).

599 de Janvry, Alain
The political economy of rural development in Latin America; an interpretation. AMERICAN JOURNAL OF AGRICULTURAL ECONOMICS 57:490-99, Aug. 1975.

Extends the theory of unequal exchange between center and periphery to provide an interpretation of rural underdevelopment in Latin America. This theory provides a framework to analyze the political economy of rural development programs.

600 Diamond, J.
Econometric modelling of development processes. HARVARD INSTITUTE FOR INTERNATIONAL DEVELOPMENT, DEVELOPMENT DISCUSSION PAPER No. 81:1-42, Oct. 1979.

601 Diamond, J.
The analysis of structural constraints in developing economies: a case study. OXFORD BULLETIN OF ECONOMICS AND STATISTICS (May 1974).

602 Dickinson, Richard D. N.
Some ethical perspectives on a just economic order. INDIAN JOURNAL OF ECONOMICS 62:17-33, July 1981.

603 Diejomaoh, V. P. and Orimalade, W. A. T.
Unemployment in Nigeria: an economic analysis of scope, trends, and policy issues. NIGERIAN JOURNAL OF ECONOMIC AND SOCIAL STUDIES 13 (July 1971): 127-60.

604 Ding, Chen
The economic development of China. SCIENTIFIC AMERICAN 243:152-65, Sept. 1980.

605 Divatia, V. V.
Inequalities in asset distribution of rural households. RESERVE BANK STAFF OCCASIONAL PAPERS 1:1-45, June 1976.

Quantifies and analyzes the prevailing inequalities in the distribution of rural household assets in India and also examines the distributions of total value of assets according to broad categories of assets.

606 Dolan, Michael B. and Brain W. Tomlin

First world-Third world linkages; external relation and economic development. INTERNATIONAL ORGANIZATION 34:41-63, Winter 1980.

The authors first examine the impact that external economic ties have upon economic growth, income distribution, and structural imbalance of the economy in underdeveloped countries. Then they explore the negative impact of investment on economic growth. Finally they attempt to sort out the contrary immediate and long-term impacts of foreign investment on economic growth.

607 Dubner, Howard E. and Weinkle, Julian
The economic impact of an externally financed loan program. JOURNAL OF INTER-AMERICAN STUDIES AND WORLD AFFAIRS 12 (April 1970): 205-16.

608 Duff, Declan
The dangers of Third World debt defaults. EUROMONEY (May 1975).

609 Dwyer, D. J.
Economic development: development for whom? GEOGRAPHY 62:325-34, November 1977.

610 Eaton, Jonathan and Mark Gersovits
LDC participation in international financial markets, debt and reserves. JOURNAL OF DEVELOPMENT ECONOMICS 7:3-21, March 1980.

The authors analyze LDC borrowing and reserve-holding behavior as part of a general equilibrium portfolio problem. Estimates of LDC debt and reserve demand and credit supply suggest that debt, along with reserves, serves a transactions role. Another finding is that most LDC borrowers are credit constrained.

611 Edel, Matthew
Innovative supply: a weak point in economic development theory. SOCIAL SCIENCE INFORMATION 13 (June 1970).

612 Elias, Victor Jorge
Sources of economic growth in Latin American countries. REVIEW OF ECONOMICS AND STATISTICS 60:362-70, Aug. 1978.

613 Elliott, Edward L.
Accounting and economic development in Latin America. INTERNATIONAL JOURNAL OF ACCOUNTING 8 (Fall 1972): 89-98.

614 Enthoven, Adolf J.
Standardized accounting and economic development. FINANCE AND DEVELOPMENT 10 (March 1973): 28-33.

615 Eshag, E.
The relative efficacy of monetary policy in selected industrial and less-developed countries. ECONOMIC JOURNAL 81 (June 1971): 294-305.

616 Esser, Klaus
Key countries in the Third world; a challenge to the industrialised countries. INTERECONOMICS, REVIEW OF INTERNATIONAL TRADE AND DEVELOPMENT No. 5:224-31, Sept./Oct. 1981.

The authors define a group of "key countries" which are of strategical importance for the world economy and outline the development risks facing these countries. They suggest that the OECD countries would be better advised to follow a policy of cooperation with these key countries rather than the "man mind thyself" policies which are presently gaining in popularity.

617 Etherington, Dan M.
Economies of scale and technical efficiency: a case study in tea production. EAST AFRICAN JOURNAL OF RURAL DEVELOPMENT 4 (1971): 72-87.

618 Fajana, Olufemi F.
The evolution of skill wage differentials in a developing economy: the Nigerian experience. DEVELOPING ECONOMIES 13 (June 1975): 150-67.

619 Falero, Frank, Jr.
Foreign investment and the balance of payments: some negative implications for developing countries. INTER-AMERICAN ECONOMIC AFFAIRS 28 (Autumn 1974): 77-85.

620 Farek, Jiri
Inflation in developing countries. ECONOMIC PAPERS (WARSAW) No. 11:44-63, 1980.

621 Feder, G.
Economic growth, foreign loans and debt servicing capacity of developing countries. JOURNAL OF DEVELOPMENT STUDIES 16:352-68, April 1980.

622 Fields, G. S.
Who benefits from economic development?--a reexamination of Brazilian growth in the 1960's. AMERICAN ECONOMIC REVIEW 67:570-82, Sept. 1977.

623 Fields, Gary S.
Poverty, inequality, and development: a distributional approach. JOURNAL OF POLICY MODELING 3:295-315, Oct. 1981.

624 Fields, Gary S.

A welfare economic approach to growth and distribution in the dual economy. QUARTERLY JOURNAL OF ECONOMICS 93:325-53, Aug. 1979.

The author explores the similarities and differences between the absolute income and poverty and relative inequality approaches for a general dualist development model and for three stylized special cases. Finally, he attempts to determine who received the benefits of growth in two less developed countries--Brazil and India.

625 Fields, Gary S.
Poverty, inequality, and the measurement of development performance. YALE UNIVERSITY. ECONOMIC GROWTH CENTER. CENTER DISCUSSION PAPER No. 273:1-93, Dec. 1977.

Presents evidence on the extent of improvement in economic position of the poor in six less developed countries--Costa Rica, Sri Lanka, India, Brazil, the Philippines, and Taiwan--and explores the reasons for the differential performances.

626 Fields, Gary S.
More on changing income distribution and economic development in Brazil. YALE UNIVERSITY. ECONOMIC GROWTH CENTER. CENTER DISCUSSION PAPER No. 244:1-18, April 1976.

627 Fields, Gary S.
Higher education and income distribution in a less developed country. OXFORD ECONOMIC PAPERS N.S., 27:244-59, July 1975.

Examines Kenya's higher education system with the goal of testing among three alternative hypotheses: that the higher education system redistributes income from rich to poor, that it redistributes income from poor to rich, or that it has no important effect on the distribution of income.

628 Fields, Gary S.
On inequality and economic development. YALE UNIVERSITY. ECONOMIC GROWTH CENTER. CENTER DISCUSSION PAPER No. 233:1-61, Aug. 1975.

629 Filgueira, Carlos
Consumption in the new Latin American models. CEPAL REVIEW (SANTIAGO DE CHILE) No. 15:71-110, Dec. 1981.

630 Fincham, R.
Economic dependence and the development of industry in Zambia. JOURNAL OF MODERN AFRICAN STUDIES 18:297-313, June 1980.

631 Findlay, Ronald
Economic development and the theory of international trade. AMERICAN ECONOMIC REVIEW, PAPERS AND PROCEEDINGS 69:186-90, May 1979.

632 Fishlow, A.
Debt remains a problem. FOR POL No. 30:133-43, Spring 1978.

633 Foxley, Alejandro
Stabilization policies and stagflation: the cases of Brazil and Chile. WORLD DEVELOPMENT 8:887-912, Nov. 1980.

634 Foxley, Alejandro
Redistribution of consumption; effects on production and employment. JOURNAL OF DEVELOPMENT STUDIES 12:171-90, April 1976.

In section II, some theoretical hypotheses concerning the relationship between redistribution, growth, consumption and employment are discussed. Section III deals with the measurement of the basic consumption threshold for Chile. In section IV, results for the effects of redistribution on production and employment are given. Section V deals with an empirical analysis of the concept of "minimum growth rates" in redistribution strategies. The final section gives the conclusions of the study.

635 Frank, Andre Gunder
The political economic response to crisis in the West. UNIVERSITY OF EAST ANGLIA. DEVELOPMENT STUDIES DISCUSSION PAPER. No. 44:1-93, April 1980.

636 Frank, Andre Gunder
The new economic crisis in the West. UNIVERSITY OF EAST ANGLIA. DEVELOPMENT STUDIES DISCUSSION PAPER. No. 42:1-95, April 1980.

637 Galbis, Vicente
Financial intermediation and economic growth in less developed countries; a theoretical approach. JOURNAL OF DEVELOPMENT STUDIES 13:58-72, Jan. 1977.

638 Gerstenfeld, Arthur and Lawrence H. Wortzel
Strategies for innovation in developing countries. SLOAN MANAGEMENT REVIEW 19:57-68, Fall 1977.

639 Ghandour, Marwan M.
Dualistic development: a new approach. DEVELOPING ECONOMIES 13 (September 1975): 243-51.

640 Gillis, M.
Role of state enterprises in economic development. SOC

RES 47:248-89, Summer 1980.

641 Gilpin, Robert
Three models of the future. INTERNATIONAL ORGANIZATION 29:37-60, Winter 1975.

Presents and evaluates three models of the future drawn from current writings on international relations. These models are really representative of the three prevailing schools of thought on political economy: liberalism, marxism, and economic nationalism.

642 Glezakos, Constantine
Inflation and growth; a reconsideration of the evidence from the LDC's. JOURNAL OF DEVELOPING AREAS 12:171-82, Jan. 1978.

The contention of this study is that economic growth is affected more by the pattern of price changes than by the rate of inflation per se.

643 Gobalet, J. G. and L. J. Diamond
Effects of investment dependence on economic growth. INTERNATIONAL STUDIES QUARTERLY 23:412-44, S 1979.

644 Goldstone, Leo
Improving social statistics in developing countries. INTERNATIONAL SOCIAL SCIENCE JOURNAL 29, No. 4:756-71, 1977.

Discusses the general characteirstics of social statistics in developing countries, the need for an integrated approach, the importance of designing a realistic minimum programme, and the emphasis on output of publications.

645 Gonzalez Casanova, Pablo
The economic development of Mexico. SCIENTIFIC AMERICAN 243:192-204, Sept. 1980.

646 Goodman, D. E.
The Brazilian economic "miracle" and regional policy; some evidence from the urban Northeast. JOURNAL OF LATIN AMERICAN STUDIES 8, Pt. 1:1-27, May 1976.

Attempts only a partial, exploratory treatment of this complex topic and concentrates on employment, earnings and income distribution in the urban sector of the Northeast region since 1960.

647 Gray, Clive and Andre Martens
The political economy of the "recurrent cost problem" in the East African Sahel. HARVARD INSTITUTE FOR INTERNATIONAL DEVELOPMENT, DEVELOPMENT DISCUSSION PAPER. No. 128:1-40, February 1982.

648 Greer, Douglas F.
The economic benefits and costs of trademarks; lessons for the developing countries. WORLD DEVELOPMENT 7:683-704, July 1979.

649 Griffin, Keith
Economic development in a changing world. WORLD DEVELOPMENT 9:221-26, March 1981.

650 Gross, B.
Management strategy for economic and social development: III. POLICY SCIENCES 3 (1972): 1-25.

651 Grosse, Scott
A skeptical perspective on income redistribution and poverty reduction in Sri Lanka. UNIVERSITY OF MICHIGAN. CENTER FOR RESEARCH ON ECONOMIC DEVELOPMENT. DISCUSSION PAPER No. 91:1-27, May 1981.

652 Grosser, Gunter and Gunter Weinert
World economy on the down-track. INTERECONOMICS, REVIEW OF INTERNATIONAL TRADE AND DEVELOPMENT No. 1:48-52, Jan./Feb. 1981.

653 Grove, John D.
The effect of economic development and growth on ethnic income mobility; a cross-cultural study. STUDIES IN COMPARATIVE INTERNATIONAL DEVELOPMENT 15:22-36, Fall 1980.

654 Guisinger, Stephen E. and Mohammad Irfan
Inter-industry differentials in wages and earnings in Pakistan's manufacturing sector. PAKISTAN DEVELOPMENT REVIEW 14:274-95, Autumn 1975.

Explores just one facet of the wage structure in Pakistan: the pattern of inter-industry wage differentials in the large-scale manufacturing sector.

655 Gulati, Umesh C.
Effect of capital imports on savings and growth in less developed countries. ECONOMIC INQUIRY 16:563-69, Oct. 1978.

Examines some of the arguments of the critics of foreign aid and other capital inflows to LDC's and finds that the critics lack sufficient evidence on the supposedly adverse effect of capital transfers to LDC's on their savings and growth of incomes.

656 Hagen, Everett E.
Why economic growth is slow. WORLD DEVELOPMENT 8:291-98, April 1980.

Presents a general theory of economic progress in the

LDC's: that increase in productivity is slow because, for techno-economic reasons economic growth can proceed only in stages and requires a high degree of innovational talent, which is scarce in any country.

657   Hainsworth, Geoffrey B.
       Economic growth and poverty in Southeast Asia: Malaysia, Indonesia and the Philippines. PACIFIC AFFAIRS 52:5-41, Spring 1979.

658   Hamm, Walter
       Inflation and economic growth in LDC's. INTERECONOMICS (June 1973), pp. 183-86.

659   Hammond, Peter J.
       Dual interpersonal comparisons of utility and the welfare economics of income distribution. JOURNAL OF PUBLIC ECONOMICS 7:51-71, Feb. 1977.

       Considers the implications of interpersonal comparisons of the utility of income for ethical preferences regarding the distribution of income.

660   Handwerker, W. Penn.
       Productivity, marketing efficiency, and price-support programs: alternative paths to rural development in Liberia. HUMAN ORGANIZATION 40:27-39, Spring 1981.
       Using the example of Liberia, the author attempts to show that government-sponsored price-support programs are shortsighted solutions which often defeat the central purpose of economic development, namely enabling people to enjoy increased material standards of living.

661   Hanson, James A.
       The short-run relation between growth and inflation in Latin America: a quasi-rational or consistent expectations approach. AMERICAN ECONOMIC REVIEW 70:972-89, Dec. 1980.

662   Harberger, Arnold C.
       Issues concerning capital assistance to less-developed countries. ECONOMIC DEVELOPMENT AND CULTURAL CHANGE 20 (July 1972): 631-40.

663   Hay, Alan M.
       Notes on the economic basis for periodic marketing in developing countries. GEOGRAPHICAL ANALYSIS (October 1971), pp. 393-401.

664   Hazaray, M. R.
       Economic development trends in India. INTERECONOMICS (November 1972), pp. 350-52.

665   Helleiner, G. K.
       Relief and reform in Third world debt. WORLD DEVELOPMENT 7:113-24, Feb. 1979.

666 Heller, Peter S.
A model of public fiscal behavior in developing countries: aid, investment, and taxation. AMERICAN ECONOMIC REVIEW 65 (June 1975): 429-45.

667 Hemmer, Hans-Rimbert
The limitations of the market economy as a regulating concept for economic policies in developing countries. ECONOMICS (TUBINGEN) 14:31-49, 1976.

668 Henry, Paul-Marc
Economic development, progress and culture. DEVELOPMENT No. 3/4:17-25, 1981.

669 Hensley, Roy J.
Two approaches to economic development. JOURNAL OF INTER-AMERICAN STUDIES AND WORLD AFFAIRS 13 (July-Oct. 1971): 517-23.

670 Hernadi, Andras
Development strategies and economic policy in the Pacific region. ASIA PACIFIC COMMUNITY (TOKYO) No. 13:68-93, Summer 1981.

671 Hewlett, Sylvia Ann
Human rights and economic realities in developing nations. WOODROW WILSON INTERNATIONAL CENTER FOR SCHOLARS, LATIN AMERICAN PROGRAM. WORKING PAPERS No. 13:1-41, 1978.

672 Hickman, Bert G. and Stefan Schleicher
The interdependence of national economies and the synchronization of economic fluctuations; evidence from the LINK project. WELTWIRTSCHAFTLICHES ARCHIV (KIEL) 114, No. 4:642-708, 1978.

The authors present and interpret evidence from Project LINK concerning the international transmission of economic fluctuations and inflation.

673 Hilhorst, Jos G. M.
National development strategies and regional planning in Latin America: some reflections. DEVELOPMENT AND CHANGE (THE HAGUE) 12:525-45, Oct. 1981.

674 Hindle, T., ed.
Multipurpose for the less developed? ECONOMIST 278:survey 92, March 14-20, 1981.

675 Hirono, Ryokichi
Changing patterns of economic interdependence in Asia. DEVELOPING ECONOMIES 11 (December 1973): 325-62.

676 Hisao, Kanamori
The economics of growth rate acceleration. JAPAN INTERPRETER 7 (Winter 1971): 26-35.

677 Ho, Yhi-Min
Income redistribution and its effects on factor demand in Taiwan; a simulation approach. SOUTHERN ECONOMIC JOURNAL 43:1017-30, Oct. 1976.

In this paper attempts have been made to test the factor intensity of consumption hypothesis and to measure through simulations the impact of income redistribuiton on factor demand in the context of the experience in Taiwan.

678 Hobsbawm, E. J.
The development of the world economy. (Review article) CAMBRIDGE JOURNAL OF ECONOMICS 3:305-18, Sept. 1979.

679 Hodd, Michael
Income distribution in Kenya, 1963-72. JOURNAL OF DEVELOPMENT STUDIES 12:221-28, April 1976.

Computes two measures of income distribution for Kenya, compares the Kenyan distribution with those of other countries, seeks possible causes for changes in the Kenyan distribution and explores the effect of changes in income distribution on the Kenyan economy.

680 Hoffman, Lutz and Bernhard Weber
Economies of scale, factor intensities and substitution; macro estimates for Malaysia's manufacturing industries. WELTWIRTSCHAFTLICHES ARCHIV (KIEL) 112, No. 1:111-35, 1976.

In Malaysia the possibilities for substitution between labor and capital appear to be rather limited in most industries. However, with rising capital intensity, the scope for substitution seems to increase.

681 Hoffman, Lutz and Kurt von Rabenau
Distribution policy in developing countries: the aspect of growth. ECONOMIC (TUBINGEN) 20:22-51, 1980.

682 Hogan, Warren P.
Capital allocation in less developed economies. DEVELOPING ECONOMIES 8 (Sept. 1970): 299-316.

683 Holsen, John A.
Notes on the "LDC debt problem." WORLD DEVELOPMENT 7:145-59, Feb. 1979.

Reviews trends in trade, payments and debt of the non-oil developing countries in the 1974-77 period.

684 Holzner, L.
Development, distribution and character of the manufacturing industry in southern Africa. GEOGRAPHISCHE ZEITSCHRIFT (1972), pp. 181-218.

685   Hopkins, M. J. D.
      A global forecast of absolute poverty and employment.
      INTERNATIONAL LABOUR REVIEW 119:565-77, Sept./Oct. 1980.

      Gives some rough estimates of absolute poverty, under the hypothesis that existing trends continue, for the years 1974, 1982, 1987 and 2000. Two poverty lines are used, one based on the methodology used by the World Bank and the other on a definition used by the author in another paper.

686   Horn, R. V.
      Social indicators for development planning and analysis [in LDC's]. INTERNATIONAL LABOUR REVIEW 111:483-506, June 1975.

687   House, William J. and Henry Rempel
      The determinants of and changes in the structure of wages and employment in the manufacturing sector of the Kenyan economy, 1967-1972. JOURNAL OF DEVELOPMENT ECONOMICS 3:83-98, March 1976.

      Considers explicitly the structure of both employment and earnings in the manufacturing sector of the Kenyan economy. Also, the responsiveness of the structure of wages and employment to changes in industry demand for labour is considered.

688   Huber, Richard L.
      Brazil's formula for economic growth. COLUMBIA JOURNAL OF WORLD BUSINESS (March-April 1972).

689   Humphries, Jane
      Causes of growth. ECONOMIC DEVELOPMENT AND CULTURAL CHANGE 24 (Jan. 1976): 339-53.

690   Ichiro, Nakayama
      Growth and inflation. JAPAN QUARTERLY 20 (Oct.-Dec. 1973): 382-87.

691   Ingham, B. and C. Simmons, eds.
      Two world wars and economic development [symposium]. WORLD DEVELOPMENT 9:701-802, August 1981.

692   Islam, Nurul
      The relevance of development models to economic planning in developing countries. ECONOMIC BULLETIN FOR ASIA AND THE FAR EAST (June-Sept. 1970).

693   Iyoha, Milton A.
      The relation between employment and growth in developing countries; an econometric analysis. SOCIAL AND ECONOMIC STUDIES (MONA, JAMAICA) 27:69-84, March 1978.

694 Iyoha, M. A.
Inflation and openness in less developed economies: a cross country analysis. ECONOMIC DEVELOPMENT AND CULTURAL CHANGE 22:31-38, October 1973.

695 Jameson, Kenneth
Development patterns and regional imbalance in Brazil. REVIEW OF ECONOMICS AND STATISTICS 57:361-64, Aug. 1975.

696 Jao, Y. C.
Financial deepening and economic growth; a cross-section analysis. MALAYAN ECONOMIC REVIEW 21:47-57, April 1976.

Presents a cross-section study of the relationship between financial development and economic growth covering a farily large sample of countries and a very recent historical period.

697 Jao, Y. C.
Trade and economic development in Taiwan. INTERECONOMICS, MONTHLY REVIEW OF INTERNATIONAL TRADE AND DEVELOPMENT No. 6:172-76, June 1976.

Analyses the country's economic development and appraises its future prospects.

698 Johnson, E. G.
An economic analysis of corrupt government, with special application to less developed countries. KYKLOS 28, 1975.

699 Johnson, Omotunde and Joanne Salop
Stabilization programs and income distribution. FINANCE AND DEVELOPMENT 17:28-31, Dec. 1980.

The authors look at programs implemented with Fund support in Bolivia, Ghana, Indonesia, and the Philippines and review the short-run impact of the adjustment measures on the earnings of different income groups.

700 Kakazu, Hiroshi
Market distortions and economic development. DEVELOPING ECONOMIES 14:109-31, June 1976.

The main objective of the article is the reformulation of conventional development theories with special emphasis on the financial markets by bringing explicitly the market distortions into the analysis.

701 Kaldor, Nicholas
Structural causes of the world economic recession. MONDES EN DEVELOPPEMENT (PARIS) No. 22:254-63, 1978.

702 Kamarck, Andrew M.
The appraisal of country economic performance. ECONOMIC DEVELOPMENT AND CULTURAL CHANGE 18:153-65, Jan. 1970.

703 Kapur, Basant K.
Alternative stabilization policies for less-developed economies. JOURNAL OF POLITICAL ECONOMY 84 (Aug. 1976).

704 Karunatilake, H. N. S.
Income and wealth distribution strategies in Sri Lanka. CENTRAL BANK OF CEYLON, STAFF STUDIES (COLOMBO) 6:173-202, April 1976.

The use of conventional statistical indicators such as growth rates and per capita income to assess Sri Lanka's progress seems to be inadequate in the light of achievements in social welfare and income distribution.

705 Katz, B. S.
Mexican fiscal and subsidy incentives for industrial development. AMERICAN JOURNAL OF ECONOMICS AND SOCIOLOGY 31 (Oct. 1972): 353-61.

706 Kawaguchi, Hiroshi
Nature and causes of contemporary inflation. DEVELOPING ECONOMIES 10 (Dec. 1972): 410-30.

707 Kawata, Tadashi
The Asian situation and Japan's economic relations with the developing Asian countries. DEVELOPING ECONOMIES 9 (June 1971): 133-53.

708 Kelley, Allen C.
Savings, demographic change, and economic development. ECONOMIC DEVELOPMENT AND CULTURAL CHANGE 24:683-93, July 1976.

Examines several connections between population growth and the supply of savings for investment. Attention is centered on the relationship between family size and the rate of household saving.

709 Kelley, Allen C. and Williamson, Jeffrey
Modeling economic development and general equilibrium histories. AMERICAN ECONOMIC REVIEW 63 (May 1973): 450-58.

710 Kenya: economic problems and prospects. AFRICA INSTITUTE BULLETIN 15 (1975): 135-42.

711 Khalaf, N. G.
Country size and economic growth and development. JOURNAL OF DEVELOPING STUDIES 16:67-72, Oct. 1979.

712 Khan, M. Zubair
The responsiveness of tax yield to increases in national income. PAKISTAN DEVELOPMENT REVIEW 12 (Winter 1973): 416-32.

713 Khatkhate, Deena R.
Analytic basis of the working of monetary policy in less developed countries. INTERNATIONAL MONETARY FUND STAFF PAPERS (November 1972).

714 Killick, Tony
The IMF and economic management in Kenya. OVERSEAS DEVELOPMENT INSTITUTE. WORKING PAPER No. 4:1-62, July 1981.

Draft chapter of a study of the IMF and economic management in developing countries being conducted under the auspices of the Overseas Development Institute.

715 Killick, Tony
Trends in development economics and their relvance to Africa. JOURNAL OF MODERN AFRICAN STUDIES 18:367-86, Sept. 1980.

716 Kim, Sungwoo
Internal labor migration and economic development: a case study of Korea. ASIAN FORUM 4:39-51, Oct.-Dec. 1972.

717 Kincaid, G. R.
Inflation and the external debt of developing countries. FINANCE AND DEVELOPMENT 18:45-48, December 1981.

718 Kitamura, Hiroshi
Challenges of development economics--relevance of economic theory to contemporary development problems. DEVELOPING ECONOMIES 13:3-21, March 1975.

719 Knight, J. B.
Devaluation and income distribution in less-developed economies. OXFORD ECONOMIC PAPERS N.S., 28:208-27, July 1976.

720 Knight, J. B.
Explaining income distribution in less developed countries; a framework and an agenda. OXFORD BULLETIN OF ECONOMICS AND STATISTICS 38:161-77, Aug. 1976.

Provides a general framework for such explanation and an agenda for further research.

721 Kobrin, S. J.
Foreign direct investment, industrialization, and social change. JOURNAL OF CONFLICT RESOLUTION 20:497-522, S 1976.

722 Kojima, Kiyoshi
Direct foreign investment to developing countries: the issue of over-presence. HITOTSUBASHI JOURNAL OF ECONOMICS 19:1-15, Dec. 1978.

Investigates the proper role of direct foreign investment in developing countries and the behaviour of foreign firms and their expatriates in the host country with special reference to Japanese direct foreign investments.

723 Koopman, J.
Economic planning and decision making. QUARTERLY JOURNAL OF ADMINISTRATION 8 (July 1974): 427-35.

724 Kravis, Irving B. and Alan W. Heston
Real GDP per capita for more than one hundred countries. ECONOMIC JOURNAL (LONDON) 88:215-42, June 1978.

The purpose of this paper is to fill, in an approximate way, a gap in the world statistical system arising from the absence of comparative data on "real" GDP per capita (i.e. gross domestic product per capita adjusted for differences in the purchasing power of currencies).

725 Krieger, Ronald A.
Inflation and growth: the case of Latin America. COLUMBIA JOURNAL OF WORLD BUSINESS (Nov.-Dec. 1970).

726 Kurian, Rachel
Income distribution, poverty and employment. INSTITUTE OF SOCIAL STUDIES, OCCASIONAL PAPERS (THE HAGUE) No. 73:1-55, Sept. 1979.

Examines the marginalization of women in theory and in reality, with examples from studies carried out in Sri Lanka and Yugoslavia.

727 Kuznets, Simon
Modern economic growth: findings and reflections. AMERICAN ECONOMIC REVIEW 63 (June 1973): 247-58.

728 Kuznets, Simon
Demographic aspects of the size distribution of income; an exploratory essay. ECONOMIC DEVELOPMENT AND CULTURAL CHANGE 25:1-94, Oct. 1976.

Content: 1) Introduction; 2) The recipient unit; 3) Differences in size of family or household; 4) Size of family and the life cycle; 5) Family or unit size and income differentials by age of head; 6) Cross-section differentials by age of head and lifetime income; 7) Concluding comments.

729 Lakshman, W. D.

Income and wealth distribution in Sri Lanka: an examination of evidence pertaining to post-1960 experience. INTERNATIONAL DEVELOPMENT CENTER OF JAPAN. IDCJ WORKING PAPER SERIES No. 16:1-42, Dec. 1980.

730 Lal, Deepak
Shadow pricing and wage and employment issues in national economic planning. THE BANGLADESH DEVELOPMENT STUDIES 6, No. 3:233-56, 1978.

731 Lall, Sanjaya
Transfer pricing and developing countries; some problems of investigation. WORLD DEVELOPMENT 7:59-71, Jan. 1979.

Reviews some of the main problems which arise for developing host countries in the investigation of transfer pricing of commodity trade by transnational corporations in manufacturing industry.

732 Lampert, Heinz
Economic policy and social policy. INTERECONOMICS (Nov. 1970), pp. 351-54.

733 Lateef, K. Sarwar
China and India: economic performance and prospects. Communications series 118. Brighton, U.K.: Institute of Development Studies, 1976. 42 pp.

734 Lecaillon, Jacques and Dimitrios Germidis
Income differentials and the dynamics of development. INTERNATIONAL LABOUR REVIEW (GENEVA) 114:27-42, July/Aug. 1976.

Attempts to investigate if there is a close correlation between the distribution of income and the use to which it is put. The investigation is based on information from a number of countries in French-speaking black Africa, particularly the United Republic of Cameroon, the Ivory Coast, Madagascar and Senegal.

735 Leeds, Roger S.
Co-financing for development: why not more? OVERSEAS DEVELOPMENT COUNCIL, WASHINGTON, D.C. DEVELOPMENT PAPER No. 29:1-56, April 1980.

736 Leeds, R. S.
External financing of development: challenges and concerns. JOURNAL OF INTERNATIONAL AFFAIRS 34:19-39, Spring 1980.

737 Leff, Nathaniel H.
Entrepreneurship and economic development; the problem revisited. JOURNAL OF ECONOMIC LITERATURE 17:46-64, March 1979.

The author considers both private and state entrepreneurship in the LDC's. The discussion is confined, however, to the uncertainty- and risk-bearing features of entrepreneurship, which affect the capacity for investment and innovation.

738 Leibenstein, Harvey
Issues in development economics: an introduction. SOCIAL RESEARCH 47:204-12, Summer 1980.

Examines some of the main problems of economic development and indicates some areas in which economists have contributed through their study of the development experience.

739 Leontief, Wassily
The future of the world economy. SOCIETE D'ETUDES ET D'EXPANSION, REVUE (LIEGE) 76:505-21, July/Sept. 1977.

740 Leontief, W.
Structure of the world economy: outline of a simple input-output formulation. AMERICAN ECONOMIC REVIEW 64:823-34, December 1974.

741 Levy, Emanuel
International transfers and economic performance analysis. REVIEW OF INCOME AND WEALTH 22, No. 2:187-98, June 1976.

Examines the treatment of international transfers in the United Nations system of national accounts, and assesses the impact of this treatment on the adequacy of the derived estimates of national saving and external current account surplus for country performance analysis.

742 Li, K. T.
Problems of economic development and their countermeasures in Asia in the 1980's. INDUSTRY OF FREE CHINA 55:2-14, March 25, 1981.

743 Li, K. T.
Mainland China's economic modernization; an evaluation based on Taiwan's development experience. INDUSTRY OF FREE CHINA 51:2-10, May 25, 1979.

744 Li, K. T.
Thirty years of economic development in Asia. INDUSTRY OF FREE CHINA 54:2-13, Nov. 25, 1981.

745 Libby, Ronald T.
External co-optation of a less developed country's policy making; the case of Ghana, 1969-1972. WORLD POLITICS 29:67-89, Oct. 1976.

Advances the thesis that the World Bank, the International Monetary Fund, and creditor countries structured the context in which their client, Ghana--a less developed country--formulated its economic policy between 1969 and 1972.

746 Lim, David
On the measurement of capital utilization in less developed countries. OXFORD ECONOMIC PAPERS (March 1976).

747 Limqueco, Peter and Bruce McFarlane
Problems of economic planning for underdeveloped socialist countries. JOURNAL OF CONTEMPORARY ASIA 9, No. 1:5-26, 1979.

Examines the actual problems of countries like Vietnam which have neither the geographical nor the cultural peculiarities which have impinged on Soviet and Chinese planning practice and ideology.

748 Lind, Joan D.
The long view of economic development; new theories. DEVELOPMENT AND CHANGE (BEVERLY HILLS, CA) 9:667-81, Oct. 1978.

749 Lindbeck, Assar
Economic dependence and interdependence in the industrialized world. UNIVERSITY OF STOCKHOLM. INSTITUTE FOR INTERNATIONAL ECONOMIC STUDIES. REPRINT SERIES No. 90:59-86, 1978.

750 Lindholm, Richard W.
A tested program for third world economic development. AMERICAN JOURNAL OF ECONOMICS AND SOCIOLOGY 36:165-70, April 1977.

Critical of American and international financial institution advisers who recommend principles of economic growth distilled out of Keynesian recipes for an over-saving Western society of the 1930's, and out of aspects of American experience with no applicability elsewhere.

751 Lippit, Victor D.
Economic planning in Japan. JOURNAL OF ECONOMIC ISSUES (March 1975).

752 Lipson, Charles
The international organization of Third world debt. INTERNATIONAL ORGANIZATION 35:603-31, Autumn 1981.

753 Lohani, Prakash C.
Nepal's economy in retrospect and its prospects for the 1980's. ECONOMIC BULLETIN FOR ASIA AND THE PACIFIC 31, No. 1:66-93, June 1980.

754 Lotz, Joergen R.
Patterns of government spending in developing countries. MANCHESTER SCHOOL OF ECONOMIC AND SOCIAL STUDIES (June 1970).

755 Luxton, P.
A new look at the "two-gap" approach to economic development. INDIAN JOURNAL OF ECONOMICS 59:267-88, Jan. 1979.

756 Mabogunje, Akin L.
The perceptual dimension in regional economic development: two African examples. INTERNATIONAL SOCIAL DEVELOPMENT REVIEW (1973), pp. 20-27.

757 MacDougall, Sir Donald
Economic growth and social welfare. SCOTTISH JOURNAL OF POLITICAL ECONOMY 24:193-206, Nov. 1977.

Concludes that just as economic growth requires a basic infra-structure of social welfare, so social welfare depends fundamentally upon economic growth.

758 Maddison, Angus
Explaining economic growth. BANCA NAZIONALE DEL LAVORO QUARTERLY REVIEW (Sept. 1972), pp. 211-62.

759 Makki, M. F. and A. Qayum
Prospects for Egyptian economic development. ECONOMIA INTERNAZIONALE (GENOA) 28:157-76, Feb./May 1975.

760 Mannur, H. G.
Development economics and economic development--old theories and new perspectives. INDIAN JOURNAL OF ECONOMICS 62:35-64, July 1981.

761 Marglin, Stephen A.
To gain the whole world; the ends and means of economic development. HARVARD INSTITUTE OF ECONOMIC RESEARCH, DISCUSSION PAPER SERIES No. 813:1-32, Jan. 1981.

762 Martin, Ricardo
Immiserizing growth for a tariff-distorted, small economy; further analysis. JOURNAL OF INTERNATIONAL ECONOMICS 7:323-28, Nov. 1977.

Derives an exact criterion for deciding if capital accumulation in a small, open economy where the only distortion is a tariff on imports will result in a loss of welfare.

763 Marzouk, M. S.
The Brazilian economy: trends and prospects. ORBIS 18 (Spring 1974).

764 Mathieson, John A.
The advanced developing countries: emerging actors in the world economy. OVERSEAS DEVELOPMENT COUNCIL, WASHINGTON, D.C. DEVELOPMENT PAPER No. 28:1-67, Nov. 1979.

765 Mayer, Lawrence A.
The world economy: inflation everywhere--but some real growth, too. FORTUNE (August 1970).

766 McGinn, Noel and Donald Snodgrass
A typology of implications of planning education for economic development. HARVARD INSTITUTE FOR INTERNATIONAL DEVELOPMENT, DEVELOPMENT DISCUSSION PAPER No. 62:1-38, June 1979.

767 McGowan, Patrick J.
Economic dependence and economic performance in black Africa. JOURNAL OF MODERN AFRICAN STUDIES 14:25-40, March 1976.

Content: Research design and policy implications; A first text of the dependency theory; A second test of the dependency theory; Discussion; Technical problems in this study; Substantive problems of the dependency theory.

768 McGowan, Patrick J. and Dale L. Smith
Economic dependency in black Africa; an analysis of competing theories. INTERNATIONAL ORGANIZATION 32:179-235, Winter 1978

The authors find that there is need for much caution in attempting to transfer to tropical Africa Latin American based theories of development. They conclude that the best endowed African states will register the best economic performances.

769 McIntosh, James
The econometrics of growth and underdevelopment; a test of the dual hypotheses. REVIEW OF ECONOMIC STUDIES 45:285-98, June 1978.

Tests a general equilibrium version of the dual model as a set of simultaneous structural equations using time series data from Taiwan over the period 1951-1969.

770 Meacock, D. M.
A new strategy for India in new era. ECONOMIC AFFAIRS 22:184-92, 208, May 1977.

Recommends a new combined monetary-economic strategy which will ensure stability in wages and prices, and a monetary stability for maximum economic expansion.

771   Meacock, Michael
      Ground rules for economic development. ECONOMIC AFFAIRS 25:109-20, Apr./June 1980.

772   Mensah, J. H.
      Some unpleasant truths about debt and development. DEVELOPMENT DIALOGUE 1 (1973): 3-16.

773   Meyer-Krahmer, Frieder
      Overall economic planning in Brazil. INTERECONOMICS, MONTHLY REVIEW OF INTERNATIONAL TRADE AND DEVELOPMENT No. 10:287-90, Oct. 1976.

      In Brazil economic policy planning, with its beginning in the early fifties, has been undertaken for a relatively long period already. Just this fact makes it possible to analyse development, contents, significance, limitations, and chances of this planning and its realisation over a prolonged period.

774   Mincer, Jacob
      Human capital and economic growth. NATIONAL BUREAU OF ECONOMIC RESEARCH. WORKING PAPER SERIES No. 803:1-28, Nov. 1981.

775   Mirman, Leonard J. and Itzhak Zilcha
      On optimal growth under uncertainty. JOURNAL OF ECONOMIC THEORY 11:329-39, Dec. 1975.

776   Misra, R. P.
      Critical analysis of the traditional cost-benefit approach to economic development. DEVELOPMENT No. 3/4:51-5, 1981.

777   Mitra, Pijush Kanti
      Debt-servicing in developing countries. JOURNAL OF WORLD TRADE LAW 4 (March-April 1970): 383-400.

778   Modigliani, F. and Tarantelli, E.
      A generalization of the Phillips curve for a developing country. REVIEW OF ECONOMIC STUDIES (April 1973).

779   Mohabbat, Khan A.
      Economic development with surplus labor. PHILIPPINE ECONOMIC JOURNAL 14, No. 4:449-62, 1975.

      Develops three theoretical models dealing with the elimination of surplus labor under various assumptions of intersectoral mobility.

780   Morawetz, David
      Twenty-five years of economic development. FINANCE AND DEVELOPMENT 14:10-13, Sept. 1977.

      The author reviews the experience of the past twenty-five

years and highlights some of the lessons that may be learned and some of the questions that arise from that experience.

781 Morgan, Theodore
Economic diversification in less developed countries; a framework for evaluation. MALAYAN ECONOMIC REVIEW 21:26-35, Oct. 1976.

782 Morley, Samuel A. and Williamson, Jeffrey G.
Demand, distribution, and employment: the case of Brazil. ECONOMIC DEVELOPMENT AND CULTURAL CHANGE 23 (Oct. 1974): 33-60.

783 Mueller, M. G.
Economic development and the world income gap. CO-EXISTENCE 10 (1973): 76-79.

784 Mullins, D. and Scheepers, C. F.
A proposed method to quantify the possible impact of alternative sectoral economic development strategies on certain socioeconomic objectives. FINANCE & TRADE REVIEW 14:13-30, June 1980.

785 Murphy, John M.
Economic development and future prospects of the Republic of Korea. JOURNAL OF SOCIAL AND POLTIICAL AFFAIRS (April 1976), pp. 165-74.

786 Murrell, Peter
Optimal growth models as economic planning tools. ECONOMICS OF PLANNING 16, No. 2:92-101, 1980.

787 Musgrove, Philip
Household size and composition, employment, and poverty in urban Latin America. ECONOMIC DEVELOPMENT AND CULTURAL CHANGE 28:249-66, Jan. 1980.

Seeks to separate the effects of household size, family composition, and the employment status of household members on relative poverty in 10 cities in five Andean countries.

788 Mutharika, Bingu W.
Export credit financing as a development policy. FINANCE AND DEVELOPMENT 13 (June 1976): 29-33.

789 Myrdal, Gunnar
The Western view vs. the Asian view in economic growth. SOLIDARITY 8:3-9, Sept. 1973.

790 Myrdal, Gunnar
Need for reforms in underdeveloped countries. UNIVERSITY OF STOCKHOLM. INSTITUTE FOR INTERNATIONAL ECONOMIC STUDIES. REPRINT SERIES No. 161:501-25, 1981.

791 Nakagane, Katsuji
Notes on the Chinese model of economic development--its impact on and influence from foreing economic systems. DEVELOPING ECONOMIES 12 (March 1974): 23-40.

792 Nakayama, Ichiro
Future direction of economic growth. DEVELOPING ECONOMIES 10 (Dec. 1972): 329-39.

793 Narasimhulu, M.
Fiscal policy for planned development. INDIAN JOURNAL OF PUBLIC ADMINISTRATION 18 (July-Sept. 1972): 414-25.

794 Nayar, Baldev R.
Political mainsprings of economic planning in the new nations: the modernization imperative versus social mobilization. COMPARATIVE POLITICS 6 (1974): 341-66.

795 Ndongko, Wilfred A.
The financing of economic development in Cameroon. AFRICA DEVELOPMENT (DAKAR) 2:59-76, July/Sept. 1977.

796 Nishikawa, Jun
Toward economic independence of Southeast Asia. DEVELOPING ECONOMIES 11 (Dec. 1973): 466-85.

797 Nitsch, Manfred
Social policy measures and the distribution of wealth and income--as exemplified by Brazil. ECONOMICS (TUBINGEN) 21:65-90, 1980.

798 Nordhaus, William D.
Economic policy in the face of declining productivity growth. COWLES FOUNDATION FOR RESEARCH IN ECONOMICS. YALE UNIVERSITY. DISCUSSION PAPER No. 604:1-34, Sept. 1981.

799 Nugent, Jeffrey, B. and Pan A. Yotopoulos
What has orthodox development economics learned from recent experience. WORLD DEVELOPMENT (OXFORD) 7:541-54, June 1979.

The authors suggest that the processes which generate the backwash effects of development are endogenous to the system. They conclude that if their analysis is correct, the appropriateness of the market as an important foundation of orthodox economics for the context of LDC's must be called into question.

800 Nwaneri, V. C.
Income distribution criteria for the analysis of development projects. FINANCE AND DEVELOPMENT 10 (March 1973): 16-19.

801 Odetola, T. O.
Economic development and the structure and process of economic decision making. NIGERIAN JOURNAL OF ECONOMIC AND SOCIAL STUDIES 17:139-50, March 1975.

802 O'Herlihy, C. St. J.
Capital/labour substitution and the developing countries: a problem of measurement. BULLETIN OF THE OXFORD UNIVERSITY INSTITUTE OF ECONOMICS AND STATISTICS (August 1972).

803 Ojo, Oladeji
The demand for money; evidence from an underdeveloped money market. NIGERIAN JOURNAL OF ECONOMIC AND SOCIAL STUDIES 16:235-42, July 1974.

804 Palmer, Michael
Economic and social challenges for developing nations: a review of problems and policies as observed from abroad. COLO BUSINESS REVIEW 54:2-4, S 1981.

805 Papanek, Gustav F.
Economic growth, income distribution, and the political process in less developed countries. BOSTON UNIVERSITY, DEPT. OF ECONOMICS. DISCUSSION PAPER No. 7:1-25, June 1977.

806 Papanek, Gustav F.
Pakistan, India, Bangladesh, Indonesia; real wages, growth, inflation, income distribution and politics. (Special report) PAKISTAN ECONOMIST 19;13-30, Sept. 22, 1979.

807 Parker, I. C.
Ideological and economic development in Tanzania. AFRICAN STUDIES REVIEW 15 (April 1972): 43-78.

808 Parmer, S. L.
What good is economic betterment? CERES 3:21-25, July-Aug. 1970.

809 Pashardes, Panos
Income distribution, the structure of consumer expenditure and development policy. JOURNAL OF DEVELOPMENT STUDIES 16:224-45, Jan. 1980.

Investigates the employment and import substitution implications of different kinds of income redistribution, with special reference to the case of Greece.

810 Paszynski, Marian
Models of the export sector in the African economy. AFRICANA BULLETIN (1971), pp. 119-44.

811 Paukert, Felix and Jiri Skolka
Income distribution by size, structure of the economy

and employment: a comparative study for four Asian countries. INTERNATIONAL LABOR OFFICE. WORLD EMPLOYMENT PROGRAMME RESEARCH. INCOME DISTRIBUTION AND EMPLOYMENT PROGRAMME. WORKING PAPER No. 72:1-27, March 1979.

812   Paukert, Felix
Income distribution at different levels of development: a survey of evidence. INTERNATIONAL LABOUR REVIEW 108 (Aug.-Sept. 1973): 97-125.

813   Payer, C.
Third world debt problems: the new wave of defaults. MONTHLY REVIEW 28:1-22, September 1976.

814   Phongpaichit, Pasuk
Accounting for development. CAMBRIDGE JOURNAL OF ECONOMICS 4:245-58, Sept. 1980.

Introduces a way of tabulating data on an economy which is attempting to achieve rapid economic growth. The tabulation was devised for a study on post-second world war Thailand, and data from that study are used to illustrate how the table may be composed and what information they convey.

815   Pierson, Gail
Money in economic growth. QUARTERLY JOURNAL OF ECONOMICS (August 1972).

816   Pinches, Christine Rider
Economic development; the need for an alternative approach. ECONOMIC DEVELOPMENT AND CULTURAL CHANGE 26:139-46, Oct. 1977.

817   Powelson, John P.
Income distribution within the developing countries. CULTURES ET DEVELOPPEMENT (LOUVAIN) 8, No. 1:119-36, 1976.

Despite the exceptions in certain countries, it is becoming increasingly clear that economic growth does not bring with it an automatic increase in the incomes of all. The author proposes a remedy for "planning from below."

818   Prybyla, Jan S.
The economy of Taiwan; a study in development. ASIAN AFFAIRS, AN AMERICAN REVIEW 3:347-63, July/Aug. 1976.

819   Pyatt, G.
Economic strategies for growth with equity. ECONOMIC DEVELOPMENT AND CULTURAL CHANGE 25:581-87, April 1977.

820   Pyatt, Graham and Jeffrey I. Round
Social accounting matrices for development planning.

REVIEW OF INCOME AND WEALTH Series 23, No. 4:339-64, Dec. 1977.

The paper reports experience in constructing social accounting matrices (SAM's) for three national economies, viz, Iran, Sri Lanka and Swaziland. The SAM's focus particularly on the distribution of income.

821 Rajaraman, Indira
Data sources on income distribution in Bangladesh, India, Pakistan and Sri Lanka: an evaluation. REVIEW OF INCOME AND WEALTH Series 22, No. 3:223-38, Sept. 1976.

This paper examines the data base available in four South Asian countries, India, Pakistan, Bangladesh, and Sri Lanka, for the examination of trends in real inequality and poverty.

822 Randall, Laura
Income distribution and investment in Argentina. LATIN AMERICAN RESEARCH REVIEW 12, No. 3:136-53, 1977.

823 Ranis, Gustav
Technology choice and the distribution of income. AMERICAN ACADEMY OF POLITICAL AND SOCIAL SCIENCE, ANNALS 458:41-53, Nov. 1981.

Attempts to define and analyze the relations between technology and the distribution of income in the typical LDC setting.

824 Ranis, Gustav
Economic development and financial institutions. YALE UNIVERSITY. ECONOMIC GROWTH CENTER. CENTER DISCUSSION PAPER No. 236:1-34, Sept. 1975.

825 Rao, V. V. Bhanoji and M. K. Ramakrishnan
Economic growth, structural change and income inequality, Singapore, 1966-1975. MALAYAN ECONOMIC REVIEW 21:92-122, Oct. 1976.

Focuses on the trends in the degree of inequality in the personal income distribution of Singapore over the 1966-75 period.

826 Reynolds, Clark W.
Why Mexico's "stabilizing development" was actually destabilizing (with some implications for the future). WORLD DEVELOPMENT 6:1005-18, July/Aug. 1978.

827 Rimmer, Douglas
Some origins of development economics. IDS BULLETIN, INSTITUTE OF DEVELOPMENT STUDIES AT THE UNIVERSITY OF SUSSEX 10:33-37, July 1979.

Looks at the period from about 1935 to 1945, when fairly evident harbingers of development economics can be found in reports of international agencies, writings of students of international economic relations, and policies and pronouncements of some national governments.

828 Roberts, David L.
Trends and prospects for the debt burden of developing countries. FEDERAL RESERVE BANK OF NEW YORK RESEARCH PAPER No. 8011:1-23, Nov. 1980.

Examines some of the problems of defining and measuring debt burden, then looks at the trends in debt burden in the period since 1973, concentrating on the experience of Latin American countries.

829 Robinson, Sherman
Toward an adequate long-run model of income distribution and economic development. AMERICAN ECONOMIC REVIEW, PAPERS AND PROCEEDINGS 66:122-27, May 1976.

This paper has two purposes. The first is to present a strategy for constructing long-run, economy-wide models of developing countries. Second, the paper will outline the components of one possible long-run model which includes the distribution of income.

830 Roemer, Michael
Economic development; a goals-oriented synopsis of the field. HARVARD INSTITUTE FOR INTERNATIONAL DEVELOPMENT, DEVELOPMENT DISCUSSION PAPER No. 51:1-34, Jan. 1979.

831 Roemer, Michael
Economic development in Africa; performance since independence and a strategy for the future. HARVARD INSTITUTE FOR INTERNATIONAL DEVELOPMENT, DEVELOPMENT DISCUSSION PAPER No. 121:1-41, Sept. 1981.

832 Roemer, Michael
Resource-based industrialization in the developing countries; a survey of the literature. HARVARD INSTITUTE FOR INTERNATIONAL DEVELOPMENT, DEVELOPMETN DISCUSSION PAPER No. 21:1-74, Jan. 1977.

833 Rondinelli, Dennis A.
Why development projects fail: problems of project management in developing countries. PROJECT MANAGEMENT QUARTERLY 7:10-15, March 1976.

834 Rondinelli, Dennis A.
Administrative decentralisation and economic development: the Sudan's experiment with devolution. JOURNAL OF MODERN AFRICAN STUDIES 19:595-624, Dec. 1981.

835 Rubinson, R. and Holtzman, D.
Comparative dependence and economic development. JOURNAL OF CONTEMPORARY SOCIOLOGY 22:86-101, March/June 1981.

836 Rwegasira, Delphin
Inflation and economic development; some lessons from the Tanzanian experience. AFRICAN DEVELOPMENT 2:29-50, July/Sept. 1977.

Attempts to identify the major forces that led to the failure to achieve financial stability during the Second Five-Year Plan, which was launched in 1969.

837 Rymalov, V.
Newly-free countries: problems of economic development. INTERNATIONAL AFFAIRS p. 48-59, July 1978.

838 Sachs, Ignacy
Development, maldevelopment and industrialization of Third World countries. DEVELOPMENT AND CHANGE 10:635-46, Oct. 1979.

839 Sarmad, Khwaja
Characteristics of economic planning in developing countries. PAKISTAN ECONOMIC AND SOCIAL REVIEW 18:45-55, Spring/Summer 1980.

840 Sastry, S. A. R.
Poverty: concepts and measurement. INDIAN JOURNAL OF ECONOMICS 61:147-60, Oct. 1980.

841 Schweitzer, Pierre-Paul
On the financing problems of the Third World. EUROMONEY (March 1976).

842 Sen, A. K.
On the development of basic income indicators to supplement GNP measures. ECONOMIC BULLETIN FOR ASIA AND THE FAR EAST 24:1-11, Sept./Dec. 1973.

843 Shah, Sukhdev
Developing an economy--Nepal's experience. ASIAN SURVEY 21:1060-79, Oct. 1981.

844 Shaw, Timothy M. and Malcolm J. Grieve
The political economy of resources; Africa's future in the global environment. JOURNAL OF MODERN AFRICAN STUDIES 16:1-32, March 1978.

The authors analyze the impact of the global environment on Africa's development prospects--and examine different projections of its future problems and opportunities.

845 Sicat, Gerardo P.

Economic independence: the dilemma of the third world [conference paper]. JOURNAL OF PHILIPPINE DEVELOPMENT 3:181-94, second semester 1976.

846 Silber, Jacques
Incorporating the distribution of income and the duration of life into a measure of economic growth: some new suggestions. YALE UNIVERSITY. ECONOMIC GROWTH CENTER. DISCUSSION PAPERS No. 420:1-17, July 1982.

847 Singer, H. W. and R. A. Mahmood
Is there a poverty trap for developing countries? Polarization: reality or myth. WORLD DEVELOPMENT 10:19-22, Jan. 1982.

848 Singh, Ram D.
Labour migration and its impact on employment and income in a small farm economy. INTERNATIONAL LABOUR REVIEW 116:331-41, Nov./Dec. 1977.

849 Situation and prospects of the world economy. INTERECONOMICS, REVIEW OF INTERNATIONAL TRADE AND DEVELOPMENT Nos. 11/12:309-12, Nov./Dec. 1978.

850 Smith, Lawrence D.
Aspects of the employment problem: a case study of Kenya. ROUND TABLE 63:105-14, Jan. 1973.

851 Smyth, Douglas C.
The global economy and the Third world; coalition or cleavage? WORLD POLITICS 29:584-609, July 1977.

Positions taken by delegations in the U.N. General Assembly during debates of the Sixth and Seventh Special Sessions are analyzed to determine clustering on economic issues and their sources.

852 Snower, Dennis J.
Economic planning and intersectoral fiscal policies. JOURNAL OF ECONOMIC ISSUES 14:371-89, June 1980.

Explores the use of intersectoral fiscal policies as instruments of economic planning in mature, capitalist systems, focusing on their function in dealing with the joint problems of inflation and unemployment.

853 Sobhan, Rehman
Bangladesh and the world economic system: the crisis of external dependence. DEVELOPMENT AND CHANGE 12:327-47, July 1981.

854 Soehoed, A. R.
Commodities and viable economic sectors--a possible basis for development planning. INDONESIAN QUARTERLY 5:46-70, Jan 1977.

This paper has outlined the main features of a long-term strategy for the development of the national economy. The strategy places emphasis upon the role of specific commodities and sectors that possess vital and reliable growth potential.

855 Srivastava, M. P.
Where is economic power concentrated? YOJANA 15:5-40, April 1971.

856 Stewart, F. ed.
Special issue on employment, income distribution and development. JOURNAL OF DEVELOPMENT STUDIES 11:1-86, Jan. 1975.

857 Stoneman, Colin
Foreign capital and the prospects for Zimbabwe. WORLD DEVELOPMENT 4:25-58, Jan. 1976.

Investigates the role played by foreign capital in Rhodesia's development, and the growth of domestic capital in its shadow.

858 Streeten, Paul
Linking money and development. INTERNATIONAL AFFAIRS (Jan. 1970).

859 Stuckey, Barbara
Spatial analysis and economic development. DEVELOPMENT AND CHANGE (THE HAGUE) 6:89-106, Jan. 1975.

860 Sundararajan, V. and Subhash Thakur
Public investment, crowding out, and growth: a dynamic model applied to India and Korea. STAFF PAPERS, INTERNATIONAL MONETARY FUND 27:814-55, Dec. 1980.

The model is used to investigate the magnitude and the dynamic time path of the effect of public investment on private investment and growth in India (1960-76) and Korea (1958-76).

861 Sundrum, R. M.
Aspects of economic inequality in developing countries. BANGLADESH ECONOMIC REVIEW 2:445-68 (Jan. 1974).

862 Symposium on income distribution. JOURNAL OF DEVELOPMENT STUDIES 14:271-396, April 1978.

The first two articles in this issue are revised versions of papers submitted to the Workshop on analysis of distributional issues in development planning, Bellagio, May 1977. The next 3 papers were submitted independently, and the remaining 4 were written in response to previous articles in the Journal.

863 Syrquin, M.
Application of multidimensional scaling to the study of economic development. QUARTERLY JOURNAL OF ECONOMICS 92:621-39, Nov. 1978.

864 Taake, Hans-Helmut
The implementation of development plans; organization and policies. DEVELOPING ECONOMIES (TOKYO) 13:22-33, March 1975.

Planning is not only the efficient determination of optimal target-instrument relations, but essentially a "politico-economic process that draws together the techniques of economic analysis and the forces of consensus-building, decision-making and action-taking. In order to show the relevance of these elements the author draws on the medium-term development plans of Taiwan, South Korea, and Indonesia."

865 Thirsk, Wayne R.
Aggregation bias and the sensitivity of income distribution to changes in the composition of demand: the case of Colombia. JOURNAL OF DEVELOPMENT STUDIES 16:50-66, Oct. 1979.

866 Thoburn, J. T.
Exports and economic growth in West Malaysia. OXFORD ECONOMIC PAPERS (March 1973).

867 Thon, Dominique
Income inequality and poverty: some problems. REVIEW OF INCOME AND WEALTH Series 27 No. 2:207-10, June 1981.

868 Thorbecke, E.
Agriculture and economic development. SOC RESEARCH 47:290-304, Summer 1980.

869 Tinbergen, Jan
The target of twenty-five per cent for the third world. INDUSTRY AND DEVELOPMENT No. 3:7-16, 1979.

Discusses the possibility of achieving the target set at the second General Conference of UNIDO of increasing the developing countries' share of total industrial production to 25 per cent of world industrial added value by the year 2000.

870 Tun, Wai, U.
Some economic concepts and policy issues in developing countries. FINANCE AND DEVELOPMENT 12:27-30, June 1975.

871 Turner, Jonathan H.
A cybernetic model of economic development. SOCIOLOGICAL QUARTERLY (Spring 1971), pp. 191-203.

872   Turnham, David
      The employment problem in less developed countries. OECD OBSERVER (December 1970), pp. 6-10.

873   Tyler, William G.
      Growth and export expansion in developing countries; some empirical evidence. JOURNAL OF DEVELOPMENT ECONOMICS 9:121-30, Aug. 1981.

      Employing data from 55 middle income developing countries for the period 1960-1977, bivariate tests revealed significant positive associations between growth and various other economic variables including the growth of manufacturing output, investment, total exports, and manufacturing exports.

874   Uathavimul, Phaichitr
      Integrated social and economic development planning: national and sub-national problems and policy. INTERNATIONAL SOCIAL DEVELOPMENT REVIEW (1973), pp. 73-83.

875   United Nations. Centre for development planning, projections and policies.
      Economic growth and major streams of production; some basic problems in hardcore developing countries. JOURNAL OF DEVELOPMENT PLANNING No. 10:131-65, 1976.

      Focuses on some of the problems of underdevelopment in South Asia and Africa and the policy issues posed by these problems.

876   Vaitsos, Constantine V.
      Foreign investment policies and economic development in Latin America. JOURNAL OF WORLD TRADE LAW 7 (Nov.-Dec. 1973): 619-65.

877   Van de Laar, Aart J. M.
      The World Bank and the world's poor. WORLD DEVELOPMENT 4:837-61, Oct./Nov. 1976.

      Analyzes the Bank policy statements and investigates how the Bank thinks it can implement this new strategy.

878   van Heemst, Jan
      Some issues in connection with the improvement of the social accounting systems of developing countries. INSTITUTE OF SOCIAL STUDIES, OCCASIONAL PAPERS (THE HAGUE) No. 78:1-27, Dec. 1979.

      Suggests that the reason why the social accounting system of developing countries are generally inadequate for purposes of analysis and planning is because they are more or less copies of those used in the industrialized countries.

879   Volkov, Mai
        Third world countries; problems of economic development and ways of solving them. INTERNATIONAL DEVELOPMENT REVIEW 19, No. 3:17-20, 1977.

        The author considers that the Western concept of the interdependence of nations omits the fact that the interconnected nations hold far from equal stations in the world economy.

880   Volkov, N.
        The developing countries and international economic relations. INTERNATIONAL AFFAIRS p. 57-67, S 1976.

881   von Furstenberg, George M.
        Inflation, taxes, and welfare in LDC's. PUBLIC FINANCE 35, No. 2:183-212, 1980.

        This paper shows that inflation does not induce a large decline in fiscal revenues or explicit taxes. The author suggests that even at low levels of inflation the excess burdens of inflation become so large as to overwhelm any alleged excesses of public over private sector spending efficiency. This makes inflation extremely unattractive compared with other taxes.

882   Walker, A.
        Tackling world economic problems. ROUND TABLE No. 267:220-24, July 1977.

883   Warwick, Donald
        Analyzing the transactional context for planning. HARVARD INSTITUTE FOR INTERNATIONAL DEVELOPMENT, DEVELOPMENT DISCUSSION PAPER No. 65:1-56, June 1979.

        Begins with the assumption that successful planning requires careful attention to bureaucratic and political contexts, and presents a framework for assessing those contexts. Then the discussion turns to a specific case in which the suggested approach was applied to the analysis of the context for educational planning.

884   Watanabe, Susumu
        Minimum wages in developing countries: myth and reality. INTERNATIONAL LABOUR REVIEW 113:345-58, May-June 1976.

885   Weinstein, John M.
        Economic development and the quality of life: a structural analysis of the modernizer's dilemma. STUDIES IN COMPARATIVE INTERNATIONAL DEVELOPMENT 16:108-26, Fall/Winter 1981.

886   White, M.
        Kalecki's theories of economic growth and development. JOURNAL OF CONTEMPORARY ASIA 7, No. 3:298-331, 1977.

887 Whitworth, C. H.
Economic policy and third world poverty; postwar theory and practice. DEVELOPING ECONOMIES 14:179-89, June 1976.

Discusses first why the economic problems of the poor nations were so long neglected and then traces the evolution of economic research and policy advice in the years since the end of World War II. After a review of some newer policy emphases, tries to draw some conclusions about the lessons economists may have learned in their approach to Third World poverty.

888 Wiesebach, Horst Paul
Mobilization of development finance; promises and problems of automaticity. DEVELOPMENT DIALOGUE (UPPSALA) No. 1:5-28, 1980.

889 Williamson, Robert B.
The role of exports and foreign capital in Latin American economic growth. SOUTHERN ECONOMIC JOURNAL 45:410-20, Autumn 1978.

Attempts to provide some new statistical evidence on the relationships between economic growth and the underlying investment levels on the one hand and exports and foreign capital flows on the other for Latin American countries for the period of the 1960's and early 1970's.

890 Winston, G. C.
Capital utilisation in economic development. ECONOMIC JOURNAL 81:36-60, March 1971.

891 Wolfson, Dirk J.
The fiscal policy aspect of development strategy. INTERNATIONAL DEVELOPMENT REVIEW 15:7-12, 1973.

892 Woodfield, Alan and John McDonald
On the relation between savings, distribution and inflation. JOURNAL OF DEVELOPMENT STUDIES 14:357-65, April 1978.

A model of inflation, distribution and savings analysed by Thirlwall is evaluated...It is shown that in general very large inflation changes are required to raise savings through redistribution.

893 Wright, Charles L.
Income inequality and economic growth: examining the evidence. JOURNAL OF DEVELOPING AREAS 13:49-66, Oct. 1979.

894 Yunker, James A.
A world economic equalization program; results of a simulation. JOURNAL OF DEVELOPING AREAS 10:159-79, Jan. 1976.

The numerical results from this simulation model clearly suggest that very substantial equalization could be achieved, over a relatively limited period of time, and without imposing excessive and intolerable sacrifices on the populations of the richer regions.

895 Zuvekas, Clarence
Economic planning in Ecuador: an evaluation.
INTER-AMERICAN ECONOMIC AFFAIRS 25:39-69, Spring 1972.

III. SPECIALIZED PUBLICATIONS
(REPORTS, DOCUMENTS AND DIRECTORIES)

896 Administration for Development: A Comparative Perspective on the Middle East and Latin America, edited by Jack W. Hopkins, contains six papers presented at a meeting on the above theme, held at Indiana University in May 1976. Copies are available from the School of Public and Environmental Affairs, Indiana University, Bloomington, Indiana 47401, USA.

897 Agricultural Development and the Rural Poor, edited by Guy Hunter, is based on an international seminar in May 1978 sponsored by the Overseas Development Institute. The meeting considered the need for a radical review of both the policies and implementation of agricultural development in the Third World. Copies are available from ODI Sales, Montagu House, Huntingdon, Cambridgeshire, United Kingdom.

898 Black Africa--A Comparative Handbook, by Donald G. Morrison, offers country profiles for the 32 independent black African nations. In addition, the reference provides comparative profiles in the fields of demography, ecology and pluralism, social and economic development, political development, security systems and stability, international linkages, and urban and ethnic patterns. The document is available from the Free Press, 866 Third Avenue, New York, New York 10022, USA. Maps and bibliographies are included for each country profile.

899 Criteria for Evaluation of Development Projects Involving Women was prepared by the Subcommittee on Women in Development of the Committee on Development Assistance, American Council of Voluntary Agencies for Foreign Service. The criteria are set forth and then tested against six sample development projects. The booklet is available from the Technical Assistance Information Clearing House, ACVAFS, 200 Park Avenue South, New York, New York 10003.

900 The Development of Development Thinking is the theme of the OECD Development Centre's Liaison Bulletin--1977/1.

The report contains papers and discussion summaries of the First Inter-Regional Meeting on Development Research, Communication and Education, organized by the OECD Development Centre and Institute of Development Studies in 1976. "New Development Strategies," "Collective Self-Reliance," and "Inter-Regional Co-operation" are the major subject areas. Copies are available from OECD Publications, 2, rue Andre-Pascal, 75775 Paris Cedex 16, France, or from any OECD sales agent.

901 Development Planning in Ecuador, by R. J. Bromley, presents a picture of Ecuador in the first half of 1976 against a background of historical trends and with short-term projections into the future. Copies are available from Grant & Cutler Ltd., 11 Buckingham Street, London WC2N 6DQ, England.

902 Development Studies--United Kingdom Research Register 1976, edited by G. E. Gorman, is a guide to current development studies research in Great Britain. The 450 projects listed represent a wide range of institutions and agencies involved in development research. Copies are available from IDS Communications, Institute of Development Studies, University of Sussex, Brighton, Sussex BN1 9RE, United Kingdom.

903 Directory of Activities of International Voluntary Agencies in Rural Development in Africa (Third Edition) contains description of thirty-seven agencies and their rural development projects in Africa. Copies may be obtained from the Voluntary Agencies Bureau, Social Development Division, U.N. Economic Commission for Africa, P.O. Box 3001, Addis Ababa, Ethiopia.

904 Directory of Economic and Social Development Research and Training Units in OECD Member Countries/1976--No. 3-4 describes some 300 economic and social development research and training institutions in OECD Member Countries. All information is valid as of January 1977. Copies of the Directory are available from any OECD Sales Office or from OECD Publications, 2, rue Andre-Pascal, 75775 Paris Cedex 16, France.

905 Directory of Financial Aids for International Activities contains information on 231 sources of grants to individuals for study abroad. The guide includes geographic, subject, type, and level of eligibility indexes. Copies are available from the Office of International Programs, University of Minnesota, 201 Nolte West, Minneapolis, Minnesota 55455.

906 A Directory of Institutional Resources: U.S. Centers of Competence for International Development describes the resources and services of U.S. universities that

Specialized Publications 661

are involved in overseas development programs. The directory is available from TA/PPU/EUI, Room 2669, Agency for International Development, U.S. Department of State, Washington, D.C. 20523.

907 A Directory of Non-Commercial Organisations in Britain Actively Concerned with Overseas Development and Training is the third edition prepared by the British Overseas Development Institute. Some 200 agencies are described in the new edition. Copies are available from ODI Sales, Montagu House, High Street, Huntingdon, Cambs. PE18 6EP, England.

908 Directory of Social Research and Training Units--Africa was prepared by the OECD Development Centre. The document, with introductions in French and English, contains a descriptive listing of institutions in some thirty-seven African countries. Also included are a subject index, index of directors and list of institution periodicals. Copies of the document are available from OECD Publications, 2, rue Andre-Pascal, 75775 Paris Cedex 16, France.

909 A Directory of Social Science Research and Training UNITS--Latin America updates a previous listing prepared by the OECD Development Centre. The directory contains descriptive summaries of institutions classified by country and also provides an alphabetical list of institutions, index of directors, subject index, and periodical guide. It is available from OECD Publications, 2, rue Andre Pascal, 75775 Paris Cedex 16, France.

910 The Directory of United Nations Information Systems and Services lists all the information activities of the United Nations system. It contains details on more than 100 information sources, and covers subjects ranging from human rights to industry. Also listed are some 2500 addresses of local offices of organizations and information centers in 155 countries. Copies are available to organizations, universities and libraries from the Director, IOB Secretariat, Palais des Nations, CH-1211 Geneva 10, Switzerland.

911 Dissertation Abstracts Relating to International Agricultural and Rural Development, Volumes I, II, II and IV, compiled by N. S. Peabody, III contain abstracts of participants in Cornell University's Program in International Agriculture. Single copies are available from the New York State College of Agriculture and Life Sciences, Cornell University, Ithaca, New York 14850.

912 Education and Training for Public Sector Management in Developing Countries, edited by Laurence D. Stifel, James S. Coleman, and Joseph E. Black, contains nine papers

on various aspects of training for development administration. Copies may be obtained from The Rockefeller Foundation, 1133 Avenue of the Americas, New York, New York 10036.

913   Employment in Developing Countries, by Edgar O. Edwards, is based on a Ford Foundation study. The report discusses the nature of the employment problem, environmental factors which limit the choice of employment programs, and various strategies for handling the problem, including program options for donor agencies. The document is available from the Ford Foundation, Office of Reports, 320 East 43rd Street, New York, New York 10017.

914   The European Community and the Third World describes in depth all the European Community programs on behalf of the developing countries. The booklet is available from the Commission of the European Communities, Rue de la Loi 200, 1049 Brussels, Belgium, or any Community press/information offices around the world.

915   Family Farms in Rural Development: A Comparative Study of Japan and Developing Countries in Asia, by Masakatsu Akino, Kazushi Ohkawa, and Saburo Yamada, is available from the International Development Center of Japan, Daini Shuwa Toranomon Bldg., 20 Sakuragawa-cho, Nishikubo, Shiba, Minato-ku, Tokyo 105, Japan.

916   Financial Resources for Industrial Projects in Developing Countries gives information on some 200 industrial development financing institutions in 100 countries, and on international banking and aid-giving institutions. The directory was compiled by the Investment Cooperative Programme Office of UNIDO. The document is available from this office, UNIDO, P.O. Box 707, A-1011, Vienna, Austria.

917   Glossary of Institutions Concerned with Latin America, 2nd Edition, is a reference guide to some 244 international, regional, governmental and private institutions concerned with Latin America and the Caribbean. The Glossary is available from the Information Centre, Canadian Association for Latin America, 42 Charles Street East, Toronto, Canada M4Y 1T4.

918   Government Finance Statistics Yearbook--1977, prepared by the International Monetary Fund, provides current data on the finances of IMF member governments. Material for each country is organized in three parts: the statistical tables, institutional tables, and where information is available, a derivation table followed by a statement on the coverage of the central government statistics. Copies of the Yearbook are available from the International Monetary Fund, Washington, D.C. 20431.

Specialized Publications 663

919 A Guide to the Economic Appraisal of Projects in Developing Countries is a publication of the British Ministry of Overseas Development. The Guide is designed to provide a practical basis for the economic appraisal of projects financed by the public sector and for screening private sector projects subject to public sector approval. Copies are available from Her Majesty's Stationery Office, 49 High Holborn, London WC1V 6HB, England.

920 Higher Education and Social Change--Volume 2, edited by Kenneth W. Thompson, Barbara R. Fogel, and Helen E. Danner, contains twenty-five case studies and seven special reports on higher institutions in the Third World and their approaches to development problems. The publication is available from Praeger Publishers, New York, Washington and London.

921 The Integration of Women in Development: Why? When? How?, by Ester Boserup and Christina Liljencrantz, explains how and why women's participation in development presents special problems, and makes proposals for resolving these problems. The booklet is designed for decision makers, leaders and training personnel concerned with the role of women in development. Copies are available from Room CN-300, United Nations Development Programme, New York, New York 10017.

922 A Management Approach to Project Appraisal and Evaluation with Special Reference to Non-Directly Productive Projects, by N. Imboden, is addressed to officials concerned with the management of development programs. The book is based on the premise that appraisal/evaluation frameworks must be adapted in the socio-economic situation of a given country. It is available from OECD Publications, 2, rue Andre-Pascal, 75775 Paris Cedex 16, France, or from any OECD Sales Office.

923 National Objectives and Project Appraisal in Developing Countries, by Hartmut Schneider, analyzes whether and how national objectives are or might be taken into account in making project appraisals in developing countries. Major subject headings are: (1) Interrelations between national objectives; (2) Linking project appraisal to national objectives; and (3) Towards a new framework for project appraisal. Copies of the study are available from OECD Publications, 2, rue Andre-Pascal, 75775 Paris Cedex 16, France.

924 On the Strategy of Industrialization in Developing Countries and Experiences in Economic and Social Development in Socialist Countries (Parts I and II) contains papers presented at the 14th International Summer Seminar sponsored by the University of Economic Science "Bruno Leuschner" in Berlin in 1977. Both documents

are available from the Institute for the Economy of Developing Countries, University of Economic Science "Bruno Leuschner", Hermann-Duncker-Strasse 8, 1157 Berlin, German Democratic Republic.

925 The Process of Development in the Middle East: Goals and Achievements is a summary of the 30th Annual Conference of The Middle East Institute, held in Washington, D.C., October 15-16, 1976. Copies are available from The Middle East Institute, 1761 N Street, N.W., Washington, D.C. 20036.

926 Promotion of Small-Scale Industries in Developing Countries, by Dr. Karl Wolfgang Menck is a report published by HWWA--Institut fur Wirtschaftforschung--Hamburg. It contains 57 abstracts of books and articles which are concerned with various aspects of promotion of small-scale industries. Copies are available from HWWA--Institut fur Wirtschaftsforschung--Hamburg, Public Relations, Neuer Jungsfernstein 21, 2000 Hamburg 36, Germany.

927 Public Administration Training for the Less Developed Countries, edited by Irving Swerdlow and Marcus Ingle, reports on a conference sponsored by the Maxwell School of Citizenship and Public Affairs, held at Syracuse University, New York, April 18-19, 1974. The panels discussed such topics as "Agricultural Administration Training," "Public Administration and Public Enterprises," "Criteria for Improving Public Administration Training," "Urban and Rural Works Programs," and "Public Management and Development Assistance." Copies of the document may be obtained from the Maxwell School of Citizenship and Public Affairs, Syracuse University, Syracuse, New York 13210.

928 The 1978/79 Publications List of Third World Publications contains over 300 titles of pamphlets, books and teaching materials about the Third World. The listing is free from Third World Publications, Ltd., 151 Stratford Road, Birmingham B11 1RD, England.

929 Register of Development Research Projects in Africa notes 226 current development research projects in 21 African countries, classified by country and institution. It contains project descriptions as well as indexes of researchers, institutions and financial sponsors. The OECD Development Centre prepared the Register, and is also working on similar volumes for Latin America and Asia. For more information contact the OECD Development Centre, 94, rue Chardon Lagache, 75016 Paris, France.

930 Register of Research Projects in Progress in Development Studies in Selected European Countries was prepared by the Centre for Development Studies of the University

of Antwerp at the request of The European Association of Development Research and Training Institutes. Copies are available from the Centre, St. Ignatius Faculties, University of Antwerp, 13 Prinsstraat, 2000 Antwerp, Belgium.

931   Report to Congress on Women in Development, prepared by the Office of Women in Development of the U.S. Agency for International Development, assesses the impact of U.S. development aid programs on the integration of women into the developing economies of countries receiving assistance. The report contains five parts: Summary and evaluation; Introduction; Specific projects in Africa, Asia, Latin America, and the Near East plus activities in the area of population; data section; and description of AID programs in the area of women in development. Copies are available from Office of Women in Development, Room 3243 NS, Agency for International Development, U.S. Department of State, Washington, D.C. 20523.

932   Resources for Development: Organizations and Publications, edited by David A. Tyler, notes agencies and publications in the U.S., Africa, Asia and Latin America that would be useful to Peace Corps field workers in coordinating their programs with other local development efforts. Copies are available from the Office of Multilateral and Special Programs, Action/Peace Corps, 806 Connecticut Avenue, N.W., Washington, D.C. 20525.

933   The Role of Rural Women in Development is based on a conference sponsored by the Agricultural Development Council, held in Princeton, New Jersey, December 2-4, 1974. The report summarizes the meeting and lists the participants and major papers presented. Copies are available from the Agricultural Development Council, 1290 Avenue of the Americas, New York, NY 10019.

934   Rural Development Planning in Zambia: Objectives, Strategies and Achievements, by Joachim Luhring, is a socioeconomic analysis with special reference to problems of administration and regional planning. The monograph is available from the African Training and Research Centre in Administration for Development (CAFRAD), P.O. Box 310, Tangier, Morocco.

935   Social Development and the International Development Strategy is a brief paper prepared by the staff of the United Nations Research Institute for Social Development. Copies may be obtained from the Institute, Palais des Nations, 1211 Geneva 10, Switzerland.

936   Social and Economic Development Plans--Microfiche Project is a cumulative catalogue listing the holdings of Inter Documentation Company AG on social and economic development

plans around the world. About 1400 plans from over 180 countries are included. Copies of the catalogue and other catalogues of IDC's microfiche projects are free on request from Inter Documentation Company AG, Poststrasse 14, 6300 Zug-Switzerland.

937 Systems Approaches to Developing Countries contains the proceedings of the First IFAC/IFORS (International Federation of Automatic Control and International Federation of Operational Research Societies) Symposium on the topic, held in May 1973, in Algiers, Algeria. The sixty-six papers in the book were written by authorities representing twenty countries. The papers present the systems engineering approach for the following applications: Management and Development Policies; Agriculture and Food; Power Generation; Water and Pollution Control; Urban Planning, Transport and Communications; Gas, Oil and Cement Industries; Methodology; Education and Health; Human Resources; and International Cooperation and Development. The document is available from the Instrument Society of America, Publications Department, 400 Stanwix Street, Pittsburgh, Pennsylvania 15222.

938 Third World Deficits and the "Debt Crisis," prepared by the North-South Institute, is a comprehensive analysis of the debt problem of developing countries with suggestions for action in debt relief. Copies of the booklet are available from the North-South Institute, 185 Rideau Street, Ottawa, Canada K1N 5X8.

939 The United States and the Developing Countries is a report of the Atlantic Council Working Group on the United States and the Developing Countries. The report reviews U.S. development policy and suggests some guidelines for future action. Copies are available from Westview Press, Inc., 1898 Flatiron Court, Boulder, Colorado 80301.

940 The University Center for Cooperatives has issued a new Directory of International Training Programs, a listing of programs which it is offering at the University of Wisconsin. Copies are available from the University Center for Cooperatives, 524 Lowell Hall, 610 Langdon Street, Madison, Wisconsin 53706.

941 Women and World Development, edited by Irene Tinker and Michele Bo Bramsen, contains twelve essays prepared as background papers for the American Association for the Advancement of Science Seminar on Women in Development, held in Mexico City, June, 1975. Also included are the Proceedings of the Seminar. Copies are available from the Overseas Development Council, 1717 Massachusetts Avenue, N.W., Washington, D.C. 20036.

942 The World Directory of Social Science Institutions:

Research, Advanced Training, Documentation and Professional Bodies has been updated by Unesco. For copies write to Unesco, 7 Place de Fontenoy, 75700 Paris, France.

IV. BIBLIOGRAPHIC SUBJECT INDEX

ADJUSTMENT POLICIES, 130, 227, 515

AFGHANISTAN, 265

AFRICA, 9, 150, 267, 271, 292, 331, 346, 427, 433, 434, 471, 481, 486, 529, 531, 571, 647, 684, 715, 756, 768, 810, 831, 844

AGRICULTURE, 100, 141, 167, 220, 304, 321, 868

AID, 666

ALGERIA, 320

ALTERNATIVE STABILIZATION POLICIES, 703

ARAB ECONOMIC DEVELOPMENT, 432

ARGENTINA, 380, 822

ASIA, 96, 162, 195, 235, 266, 273, 274, 313, 315, 342, 359. 406, 417, 555, 657, 675, 707, 744, 796

BANGLADESH, 100, 103, 104, 340, 424, 495, 496, 497, 806, 821, 853

BANKS, 230, 321, 261, 403, 593

BASIC NEEDS, 36, 53, 59, 71

BOLIVIA, 567

BOTSWANA, 297, 318

BURUNDI, 318

CAMEROON, 795

CAPITAL, 149, 254, 345, 517, 655, 662, 682, 746, 802, 890

CAPITALISM, 110, 259, 529

CEYLON, 334

CHAD, 485

CHILE, 140, 362, 578, 633

CHINA, 581, 604, 733, 743, 791

COLLECTIVE MANAGEMENT, 185, 186

COLOMBIA, 322, 435, 551, 865

COMMODITY CONTROL, 176

CONGO, 282

Bibliographic Subject Index   669

CREDIT, 267, 477

CUBA, 374

CURRENCY, 210

DEBT, 309, 336, 401, 405, 410, 482, 524, 608, 621, 632, 665, 683, 717, 772, 777, 813, 828

DEFENSE, 143

DEPENDENCE, 572, 749, 767, 835

DEVELOPMENT, 14, 17, 19, 20, 41, 43, 44, 45, 51, 61, 71, 75, 79, 82, 83, 86, 87, 132, 169, 187, 196, 209, 212, 148, 257, 273, 275, 295, 367, 387, 402, 439, 454, 457, 488, 508, 530, 586, 595, 623, 625, 639, 686, 711, 718, 734, 735, 736, 854, 856, 858, 864

DEVELOPMENT ADMINISTRATION, 32

DEVELOPMENT PERSPECTIVES, 73

DEVELOPMENT PLANNING, 77, 88, 468, 579, 820

DEVELOPMENT STRATEGY, 4, 78, 80

DOMINICAN REPUBLIC, 354

ECONOMIC DEVELOPMENT, 11, 12 13, 37, 38, 40, 50, 52, 62, 63, 64, 67, 70, 76, 93, 98, 127, 136, 157, 158, 168, 171, 174, 223, 225, 240, 246, 256, 263, 268, 279, 283, 314, 323, 325, 338, 349, 358, 366, 378, 383, 392, 396, 400, 409, 419, 420, 422, 426, 430, 438, 445, 463, 483, 485, 504, 512, 521, 537, 548, 556, 557, 563, 565, 577, 594, 598, 609, 611, 614, 628, 640, 649, 653, 668, 669, 691, 700, 708, 709, 711, 742, 748, 750, 755, 758, 760, 761, 766, 771, 780, 816, 824, 837, 863, 871, 874, 879

ECONOMIC GROWTH, 2, 34, 49, 288, 371, 379, 394, 474, 500, 564, 580, 621, 656, 474, 727, 774, 792, 805, 815

ECONOMIC INTERDEPENDENCE, 146

ECONOMIC PLANNING, 264, 339, 389, 692, 724, 747, 838

ECONOMIC POLICY, 148, 181, 286, 375, 667, 732, 798, 870

ECONOMICS, 22, 89, 111, 135, 203, 221, 272, 273, 390, 804

EDUCATION, 381, 492, 542, 627

EGYPT, 373, 759

EMPLOYMENT, 184, 243, 280, 317, 398, 441, 447, 461, 634, 685, 693, 726, 730, 850, 856, 872

ENTREPRENEURSHIP, 344, 737

ENVIRONMENT, 229

EQUALITY, 15, 137, 139

EQUITY, 47, 310, 819

EQUITORIAL GUINEA, 318

FINANCE, 124, 155, 156, 226, 232, 241, 269, 415, 467, 478, 843, 569, 610, 841, 888

FISCAL POLICY, 35, 194, 411, 493, 793, 852, 891

FISCAL RELATIONS, 164

FOREIGN EXCHANGE, 228

FOREIGN INVESTMENT, 97, 161, 170, 348, 353, 421, 502, 619, 721, 722

FOREIGN LOANS, 250

GAMBIA, 318

GHANA, 121, 319, 488, 745

GUATEMALA, 255

INCOME DISTRIBUTION, 31, 94, 160, 258, 276, 301, 366, 370, 486, 518, 534, 544, 549, 550, 553, 566, 583, 659, 699, 704, 720, 726, 800, 809, 812, 817, 823, 829, 846, 856, 862

INDIA, 116, 175, 190, 191, 219, 220, 290, 324, 341, 352, 376, 393, 413, 513, 527, 535, 536, 664, 733, 770, 806, 821, 860

INDONESIA, 234, 291, 806

INDUSTRIAL POLICY, 25

INDUSTRIALIZATION, 28, 81, 113, 114, 115, 131, 134, 144, 197, 199, 206, 217, 233, 234, 343, 347, 382, 448, 449, 462, 465, 470, 472, 552, 616, 721, 832

INEQUALITIES, 92

INFLATION, 202, 262, 327, 404, 547, 559, 563, 620, 642, 658, 690, 694, 706, 717, 818, 892

INTERDEPENDENCE, 672

INTEREST RATE, 568

INTERNATIONAL DEVELOPMENT, 7, 56, 68

INTERNATIONAL SUBCONTRACTING, 270

INVESTMENT, 27, 142, 152, 388, 413, 479, 522, 540, 597, 643, 666

IRAN, 154

ISRAEL, 26, 117

IVORY COAST, 211, 281

JAMAICA, 147, 277

JAPAN, 106, 195, 407, 707, 751

JORDON, 385

KOREA, 94, 117, 179, 195, 384, 710, 785, 860

KENYA, 304, 679, 687, 714, 850

LABOR, 205, 386, 423, 442, 443, 528, 716, 779, 848

LAND REFORM, 237

LATIN AMERICA, 33, 35, 108, 182, 188, 201, 242, 249, 258, 268, 269, 284, 305, 312, 328, 397, 418, 451, 464, 506, 507, 539, 547, 587, 589, 590, 599, 612, 613, 629, 661, 673, 725, 787, 876, 889

LEBANON, 431

LESOTHO, 318, 372, 484

LIBERIA, 319

MALAYSIA, 112, 335, 355, 360, 503, 680, 866

MALI, 320

MANAGEMENT, 833

MEXICO, 276, 283, 369, 585, 645, 705, 826

MIGRATION, 429

MILITARY EXPENDITURE, 480

MINING, 172

MODERNIZATION, 1

MONETARY PLANNING, 290

MONETARY POLICY, 204, 558, 584, 615, 713

MOROCCO, 320, 510

MULTI-LEVEL PLANNING, 520

NEPAL, 151, 166, 753, 843

Bibliographic Subject Index   671

NEW GUINEA, 133

NIGER, 516

NIGERIA, 208, 216, 319, 458, 487, 489, 494, 603, 618

PAKISTAN, 287, 357, 498, 654, 806, 821

PANAMA, 368

PARAGUAY, 511

PERU, 122, 253

PHILIPPINES, 193

POLITICS, 84, 90, 189, 361, 453, 460, 473, 526, 546

POVERTY, 3, 24, 42, 58, 71, 99, 108, 112, 245, 252, 366, 456, 555, 623, 625, 685, 840, 847, 867, 887

PRICING POLICY, 391

PRODUCTIVITY, 660, 875

PROTECTION, 129

RECESSIONS, 101

RWANDA, 318

SAUDI ARABIA, 105, 200

SENEGAL, 125

SIERRA LEONNE, 319

SINGAPORE, 153, 195, 825

SOCIETAL DEVELOPMENT, 21

SOCIAL WELFARE, 757

SRI LANKA, 416, 489, 514, 651, 704, 821

SUDAN, 356, 490, 834

SWAZILAND, 318, 414

TAIWAN, 195, 251, 306, 570, 575, 677, 818

TANZANIA, 499, 807, 836

TAXATION, 163, 239, 459, 574, 666, 712

TEA, 617

TOURISM, 180, 225

TRADE, 523, 576, 631, 697

TROPICS, 307, 332

TUNISIA, 300, 320

TURKEY, 102, 120, 238, 293

UGANDA, 128

UNDERDEVELOPMENT, 30, 109, 285, 452, 454, 595, 769

UNITED NATIONS, 54, 436

URBAN BIAS, 363

USA, 74, 299, 301, 311, 437

USSR, 333

VENEZUELA, 107, 298, 533

WAGES, 884

WORLD BANK, 316, 475, 588, 877

WORLD DEVELOPMENT, 65

WORLD ECONOMIC ORDER, 6, 23

WORLD ECONOMY, 145, 739, 740, 764, 765

WORLD INCOME GAP, 783

WORLD MONETARY SYSTEM, 119

YEMEN, 377

ZAMBIA, 168, 244, 543, 630

ZAIRE, 476, 491

ZIMBABWE, 857

PART IV
DIRECTORY OF INFORMATION SOURCES

I. UNITED NATIONS INFORMATION SOURCES

AUDIO MATERIALS LIBRARY
United Nations, Department of Public Information, Radio and Visual Services Division, United Nations Plaza, New York, NY 10017.

COMPREHENSIVE INFORMATION SYSTEM ON TRANSNATIONAL CORPORATIONS
United Nations, Information Analysis Division, Centre of Transnational Corporations, 605 Third Avenue, New York, NY 10017.

BIBLIOGRAPHY ON TRANSNATIONAL CORPORATIONS
United Nations, Centre of Transnational Corporations, Information Analysis Division, 605 Third Avenue, New York, NY 10017.

CORPORATE PROFILE SYSTEM
United Nations Centre on Transnational Corporations, Information Analysis Division, United Nations, New York, NY 10017.

DAG HAMMARSKJOLD LIBRARY
United Nations, Department of Conference Services, United Nations Plaza, New York, NY 10017.

UNITED NATIONS BIBLIOGRAPHIC INFORMATION SYSTEM
United Nations, Department of Conference Services Dag Hammarskjold Library, United Nations Plaza, New York, NY 10017.

UNBIS DATA BASE
United Nations, Department of Conference Services, Dag Hammarskjold Library, United Nations Plaza, New York, NY 10017.

DEVELOPMENT INFORMATION SYSTEM
United Nations, Department of International Economic and Social Affairs, Information Systems Unit, Room DC 594, New York, NY 10017.

DEVELOPMENT INFORMATION SYSTEM DATA BASE
United Nations, Department of Internaitonal Economic and Social Affairs, Information Systems Unit, Room DC 594, New York, NY 10017.

676   Directory of Information Sources

REFERENCE UNIT OF THE OFFICE FOR DEVELOPMENT RESEARCH AND POLICY ANALYSIS
United Nations, Department of International Economic and Social Affairs, Office for Development Research and Policy Analysis, New York, NY 10017.

MACRO-ECONOMIC DATA BANK AND TABLE PROCESSING SYSTEM
United Nations, Department of International Economic and Social Affairs, Office for Development Research and Policy Analysis, New York, NY 10017.

MACRO-ECONOMIC DATA BANK AND TABLE PROCESSING SYSTEM DATA BASE
United Nations, Department of International Economic and Social Affairs, Office for Development Research and Policy Analysis, New York, NY 10017.

REFERENCE UNIT OF THE OFFICE FOR SCIENCE AND TECHNOLOGY
United Nations, Department of International Economic and Social Affairs, Office for Science and Technology, New York, NY 10017.

UNITED NATIONS PHOTO LIBRARY
United Nations, Department of Public Information, Radio and Visual Services Division, United Nations Plaza, New York, NY 10017.

POPULATION INFORMATION NETWORK
United Nations, Department of International Economic and Social Affairs, Population Division, New York, NY 10017.

REFERENCE CENTRE OF THE POPULATION DIVISION
United Nations, Department of International Economic and Social Affairs, Population Division, New York, NY 10017.

EXTERNAL TRADE STATISTICS
United Nations, Department of International Economic and Social Affairs, Statistical Office, New York, NY 10017.

GENERAL INDUSTRIAL STATISTICS
United Nations, Department of International Economic and Social Affairs, Statistical Office, New York, NY 10017.

INTEGRATED STATISTICAL INFORMATION SYSTEM
United Nations, Department of International Economic and Social Affairs, Statistical Office, New York, NY 10017.

UNITED NATIONS VISUAL MATERIALS LIBRARY
United Nations, Department of Public Information, Radio and Visual Services Division, United Nations Plaza, New York, NY 10017.

WORLD ENERGY SUPPLIES SYSTEM
United Nations, Department of International Economic and Social Affairs, Statistical Office, New York, NY 10017.

WORLD STATISTICS IN BRIEF
United Nations, Department of International Economic and Social Affairs, Statistical Office, New York, NY 10017.

United Nations Information Sources

HABITAT LIBRARY AND DOCUMENTATION CENTRE
United Nations, Centre for Human Settlements (HABITAT), Division of Information, Documentation and Audio-Visual, P.O. Box 30030, Kenyatta Conference Centre, Nairobi, Kenya.

UNCHS-HABITAT FILM LIBRARY
United Nations, Centre for Human Settlements (HABITAT), Division of Information, Documentation and Audio-Visual, P.O. Box 30030, Kenyatta Conference Centre, Nairobi, Kenya.

UNCRD LIBRARY AND DOCUMENTATION SERVICES
United Nations Centre for Regional Development, Marunouchi 2-4-7, Naku-ku, Nagoya 460, Japan.

UNRISD LIBRARY AND DOCUMENTATION UNIT
United Nations Research Institute for Social Development, Palais des Nations, CH-1211 Geneva 10, 16 Avenue Jean Trembley, 1209 Geneva, Switzerland.

CAFRAD LIBRARY AND DOCUMENTATION CENTRE
United Nations, African Training and Research Centre in Administration for Development (CAFRAD), B.P. 10, Tangier, Morocco.

CAIRO DEMOGRAPHIC CENTRE LIBRARY
United Nations, Cairo Demographic Centre, 109 Qasr Al Aini Street, Cairo, Egypt.

POPULATION INFORMATION AND DOCUMENTATION SYSTEM FOR AFRICA
United Nations, Regional Institute for Population Studies, University of Ghana, P.O. Box 96, Legon, Ghana.

INTERNATIONAL INSTITUTE FOR POPULATION STUDIES LIBRARY
United Nations, International Institute for Population Studies, Govandi Station Road, Deonar-Bombay 4000-88, India.

UNITED NATIONS--ROMANIA DEMOGRAPHIC CENTRE LIBRARY
United Nations, Demographic Centre, P.O. Box 1-550, 39 Boulevard Ana Ipatescu, 70100 Bucharest, Romania.

GROUP OF EXPERTS ON URBAN AND REGIONAL RESEARCH
Economic Commission for Europe, Environment and Human Settlements Division, Palais des Nations, 1211 Geneva 10, Switzerland.

AGRICULTURAL INFORMATION DEVELOPMENT SCHEME
Economic and Social Commission for Asia and the Pacific, Agriculture Division, United Nations Building, Rajadamnern Avenue, Bangkok 2, Thailand.

ASIAN AND PACIFIC DEVELOPMENT INSTITUTE LIBRARY AND DOCUMENTATION CENTRE
Economic and Social Commission for Asia and the Pacific, Asian and Pacific Development Institute, P.O. Box 2.136, Sri Ayudhije Road, Bangkok, Thailand.

REGIONAL INFORMATION SYSTEM NETWORK FOR HUMAN SETTLEMENTS
Economic and Social Commission for Asia and the Pacific, ESCAP/UNIDO Division of Industry, Housing and Technology, United Nations Building, Rajadamnern Avenue, Bangkok 2, Thailand.

ESCAP LIBRARY
Economic and Social Commission for Asia and the Pacific, United Nations Building, Rajadamnern Avenue, Bangkok 2, Thailand.

ESCAP BIBLIOGRAPHIC INFORMATION MASTER FILE
Economic and Social Commission for Asia and the Pacific, Library, United Nations Building, Rajadamnern Avenue, Bangkok 2, Thailand.

ESCAP DOCUMENTATION INFORMATION SYSTEM
Economic and Social Commission for Asia and the Pacific, Library, United Nations Building, Rajadamnern Avenue, Bagkok 2, Thailand.

ESCAP LIBRARY SERIALS INFORMATION SYSTEM
Economic and Social Commission for Asia and the Pacific, Library, United Nations Building, Rajadamnern Avenue, Bangkok 2, Thailand.

ESCAP LIBRARY SERIALS DATA BASE
Economic and Social Commission for Asia and the Pacific, ESCAP Library, United Nations Building, Rajadamnern Avenue, Bangkok 2, Thailand.

POPULATION CLEARING-HOUSE AND INFORMATION SYSTEM
Economic and Social Commission for Asia and the Pacific, Clearing-house and Information Section, Population Division, United Nations Building, Rajadamnern Avenue, Bangkok 2, Thailand.

CURRENT RESEARCH IN FAMILY PLANNING
Economic and Social Commission for Asia and the Pacific, Clearing-house and Information Section, Population Division, United Nations Building, Rajadamnern Avenue, Bangkok 2, Thailand.

UNESCAP/STATISTICS INFORMATION SYSTEM
Economic and Social Commission for Asia and the Pacific, Statistics Division, United Nations Building, Rajadamnern Avenue, Bangkok 2, Thailand.

QUARTERLY BULLETIN OF STATISTICS FOR ASIA AND THE PACIFIC
Economic and Social Commission for Asia and the Pacific, Statistics Division, United Nations Building, Rajadamnern Avenue, Bangkok 2, Thailand.

STATISTICAL INDICATORS FOR ASIA AND THE PACIFIC
Economic and Social Commission for Asia and the Pacific, Statistics Division, United Nations Building, Rajadamnern Avenue, Bangkok 2, Thailand.

STATISTICAL YEARBOOK FOR ASIA AND THE PACIFIC
Economic and Social Commission for Asia and the Pacific, Statistics Division, United Nations Building, Rajadamnern Avenue, Bangkok 2, Thailand.

TRADE INFORMATION SERVICE
Economic and Social Commission for Asia and the Pacific, Trade Promotion Centre (TPC), International Trade Division, United Nations Building, Rajadamnern Avenue, Bangkok 2, Thailand.

HOUSEHOLD SURVEYS DATA BANK
Economic Commission for Latin America, Statistics Division, Casilla 179D, Edificio Naciones Unidas, Avenida Dag Hammarskjold, Santiago, Chile.

CARIBBEAN INFORMATION SYSTEM FOR ECONOMIC AND SOCIAL PLANNING
Economic Commission for Latin America, CEPAL Office for the Caribbean, Caribbean Documentation Centre, P.O. Box 1113, Room 300 Salvatori Building, Port of Spain, Trinidad and Tobago.

CARIBBEAN PLANNING DATA BASE
Economic Commission for Latin America, CEPAL Office for the Caribbean, Caribbean Documentation Centre, P.O. Box 1113, Room 300 Salvatori Building, Port of Spain, Trinidad and Tobago.

LATIN AMERICAN CENTRE FOR ECONOMIC AND SOCIAL DOCUMENTATION
Economic Commission for Latin America, Casilla 179-D, Edificio Naciones Unidas, Avenida Dag Hammarskjold, Santiago, Chile.

CLADBIB DATA BASE
Economic Commission for Latin America, Latin American Centre for Economic and Social Documentation (CLADES), Casilla 179-D, Edificio Naciones Unidas, Avenida Dag Hammarskjold, Santiago, Chile.

CLADIR DATA BASE
Economic Commission for Latin America, Latin American Centre for Economic and Social Documentation (CLADES), Casilla 179-D, Edificio Naciones Unidas, Avenida Dag Hammarskjold, Santiago, Chile.

CLAPLAN DATA BASE
Economic Commission for Latin America, Latin American Centre for Economic and Social Documentation (CLADES), Casilla 179-D, Edificio Naciones Unidas, Avenida Dag Hammarskjold, Santiago, Chile.

CENTRAL AMERICAN CENTRE FOR ECONOMIC AND SOCIAL DOCUMENTATION
Economic Commission for Latin America/Central American Higher University Council (CSUCA), Apartado 37, Universidad de Costa Rica, San Jose, Costa Rica.

CEPAL/CSUCA-CEDESC DATA BASE
Central American Centre for Economic and Social Documentation (CEDESC), Apartado 37, Universidad de Costa Rica, San Jose, Costa Rica.

LATIN AMERICAN POPULATION DOCUMENTATION SYSTEM
Economic Commission for Latin America, Centro Latinoamericano

de Demografia, Casilla 91, Edificio Naciones Unidas, Avenida Dag Hammarskjold, Santiago, Chile.

DOCPAL DATA BASE
Economic Commission for Latin America, Centro Latinoamericano de Demografia, Casilla 91, Edificio Naciones Unidas, Avenida Dag Hammarskjold, Santiago, Chile.

JOINT CEPAL/ILPES LIBRARY
Economic Commission for Latin America, Latin American Institute for Economic and Social Planning, Casilla 179-D, Edificio Naciones Unidas, Avenida Dag Hammarskjold, Santiago, Chile.

JOINT CEPAL/ILPES LIBRARY BIBLIOGRAPHICAL INFORMATION SYSTEM
Economic Commission for Latin America, Latin American Institute for Economic and Social Planning, Casilla 179-D, Edificio Naciones Unidas, Avenida Dag Hammarskjold, Santiago, Chile.

GROSS DOMESTIC PRODUCT BY KIND OF ECONOMIC ACTIVITY
Economic Commission for Latin America, Statistics Division, Casilla 179-D, Edificio Naciones Unidas, Avenida Dag Hammarskjold, Santiago, Chile.

DATA BANK
Economic Commission for Africa, Statistics Division, P.O. Box 3001, Africa Hall, Addis Ababa, Ethiopia.

ECA LIBRARY
Economic Commission for Africa, P.O. Box 3001, Africa Hall, Addis Ababa, Ethiopia.

ECWA LIBRARY
Economic Commission for Western Asia Administration, P.O. Box 4656, United Nations Building, Bir Hassan, Beirut, Lebanon.

INDUSTRIAL INFORMATION SYSTEM DATA BASE - INDUSTRIAL DEVELOPMENT ABSTRACTS
United Nations Industrial Development Organization, Industrial Information Section, P.O. Box 300, Vienna International Center, Wagramer Strasse 5, A-1400 Vienna, Austria.

INDUSTRIAL AND TECHNOLOGICAL INFORMATION BANK
United Nations Industrial Development Organization, Industrial Information Section, P.O. Box 300, Vienna International Center, Wagramer Strasse 5, A-1400 Vienna, Austria.

UNEP LIBRARY AND DOCUMENTATION CENTRE
United Nations Environment Programme, P.O. Box 30552, Nairobi, Kenya.

PROJECT INSTITUTIONAL MEMORY
United Nations Development Programme, Bureau for Programme Policy and Evaluation, One United Nations Plaza, New York, NY 10017.

PROJECT INSTITUTIONAL MEMEORY DATA BASE
United Nations Development Programme, Bureau for Programme Policy and Evaluation, One United Nations Plaza, New York, NY 10017.

UNITED NATIONS FUND FOR POPULATION ACTIVITIES LIBRARY
United Nations Fund for Population Activities, 485 Lexington Avenue, Room 2018, New York, NY 10017.

UNITAR LIBRARY
United Nations Institute for Training and Research, 801 United Nations Plaza, New York, NY 10017.

UNITED NATIONS UNIVERSITY LIBRARY
United Nations University, Academic Services, 29th Floor, Toho Seimei Building, 15-1 Shibuya 2-chome, Shibuya-ku, Tokyo 150, Japan.

REFERRAL PROGRAMME OF ACADEMIC SERVICES DIVISION
United Nations University, Academic Services, 29th Floor, Toho Seimei Building, 15-1 Shibuya 2-chome, Shibuya-ku, Tokyo 150, Japan.

CLINTERFOR DOCUMENTATION AND INFORMATION SERVICE
International Labour Office, Inter-American Centre for Research and Documentation on Vocational Training, Casilla de Correo 1761, San Jose 1092, Montevideo, Uruguay.

SOCIAL AND LABOUR BULLETIN DOCUMENTATION UNIT
International Labour Office, Working Conditions and Environment Department, Social and Labour Bulletin Section, 4 route des Morillons, 1211 Geneva 22, Switzerland.

LABOUR INFORMATION RECORD DATA BASE
International Labour Office, Working Conditions and Environment Department, Social and Labour Bulletin Section, 4 route des Morillons, 1211 Geneva 22, Switzerland.

CENTRAL LIBRARY AND DOCUMENTATION BRANCH OF THE ILO
International Labour Office, Bureau of Information Systems, Central Library and Documentation Branch, 4 route des Morillons, 1211 Geneva 22, Switzerland.

INTERNATIONAL LABOUR DOCUMENTATION
International Labour Office, Bureau of Information Systems, Central Library and Documentation Branch, 4 route des Morillons, 1211 Geneva 22, Switzerland.

TRAINING INFORMATION DATA BASE
International Labour Office, Training Department, Documentation, Information and Reports, 4 route des Morillons, 1211 Geneva 22, Switzerland.

AGLINET UNION LIST OF SERIALS
Food and Agricultural Organization of the United Nations,

Department of General Affairs and Information, Library and Documentation Systems Division, Via delle Terme di Caracalla, 00100 Rome, Italy.

AGRIS DATA BASE
Food and Agriculture Organization of the United Nations, Department of General Affairs and Information, Library and Documentation Systems Division, Via delle Terme di Caracalla, 00100 Rome, Italy.

AGRARIAN RESEARCH AND INTELLIGENCE SERVICE
Food and Agriculture Organization of the United Nations, Economic and Social Policy Department, Human Resources, Institutions and Agrarian Reform Division (ESH), Via delle Terme di Caracalla, 00100 Rome, Italy.

DEVELOPMENT EDUCATION EXCHANGE SERVICE
Food and Agriculture Organization of the United Nations, Development Department (DD), Via delle Terme di Caracalla, 00100 Rome, Italy.

FAO LIBRARY SERIALS INFORMATION SYSTEM
Food and Agriculture Organization of the United Nations, Department of General Affairs and Information, Library and Documentation Systems Division, Via delle Terme di Caracalla, 00100 Rome, Italy.

POPULATION DOCUMENTATION CENTRE
Food and Agriculture Organization of the United Nations, Economic and Social Policy Department, Human Resources, Institutions and Agrarian Reform Division (ESH), Via delle Terme di Caracalla, 00100 Rome, Italy.

TERMINOLOGY AND REFERENCE SECTION
Food and Agriculture Organization of the United Nations, Department of General Affairs and Information, Publications Division, Via delle Terme di Caracalla, 00100 Rome, Italy.

COMPUTERIZED DOCUMENTATION SYSTEM
United Nations, Educational, Scientific and Cultural Organization, Division of Library, Archives and Documentation Services, 7, place de Fontenoy, Paris 75700, France.

UNESCO DATA BASE
United Nations Educational, Scientific and Cultural Organization, Division of Library, Archives and Documentation Services, 7, place de Fontenoy, Paris 75700, France.

DARE DATA BASE
United Nations Educational, Scientific and Cultural Organization, Social Science Documentation Centre (SSDC), 7, place de Fontenoy, 75700 Paris, France.

UNESCO STATISTICAL DATA BANK SYSTEM
United Nations Educational, Scientific and Cultural Organization, Office of Statistics, 7, place de Fontenoy, 75700 Paris, France.

REGIONAL CLEARING-HOUSE FOR POPULATION EDUCATION
United Nations Educational, Scientific and Cultural Organization, Regional Office for Education in Asia and Oceania, P.O. Box 1425, Darakarn Building, 920 Sukumvit Road, Bangkok 11, Thailand.

IBE WORLDWIDE NETWORK FOR EDUCATIONAL INFORMATION
United Nations Educational, Scientific and Cultural Organization, International Bureau of Education, Documentation and Information Unit, Palais Wilson, 1211 Geneva 14, Switzerland.

LIBRARY AND DOCUMENTATION CENTRE OF THE UNESCO INTERNATIONAL INSTITUTE FOR EDUCATIONAL PLANNING
United Nations Educational, Scientific and Cultural Organization, International Institute for Educational Planning, 7-9 rue Eugene Delacroix, 75016 Paris, France.

INFORMATION SERVICES OF THE NETWORK OF EDUCATIONAL INNOVATION FOR DEVELOPMENT IN AFRICA
United Nations Educational, Scientific and Cultural Organization, Regional Office for Education in Africa (BREDA), B.P. 3311, 12, avenue Roume, Dakar, Senegal.

LIBRARY OF THE UNESCO REGIONAL OFFICE FOR SCIENCE AND TECHNOLOGY FOR AFRICA
United Nations Educational, Scientific and Cultural Organization, Regional Office for Science and Technology for Africa, P.O. Box 30592, Bruce House, Standard Street, Nairobi, Kenya.

LIBRARY OF THE UNESCO REGIONAL OFFICE FOR SCIENCE AND TECHNOLOGY
United Nations Educational, Scientific and Cultural Organization, Regional Office for Science and Technology for Latin America and the Caribbean, P.O. Box 3187, Bulevar Artigas 1320, Montevideo, Uruguay.

WORLD HEALTH STATISTICS DATA BASE
World Health Organization, Division of Health Statistics, 20 avenue Appia, 1211 Geneva 27, Switzerland.

WHO SOUTH-EAST ASIA REGION HEALTH LITERATURE, LIBRARY AND INFORMATION SERVICES NETWORK
World Health Organization, Regional Office for South East Asia (SEARO), SEARO Library, World Health House, Indraprastha Estate, Mahatma Gandhi Road, New Delhi 110002, India.

DOCUMENTATION AND HEALTH INFORMATION OFFICE
World Health Organization/Pan American Health Organization, 525 Twenty Third Street, N.W., Washington, D.C. 20037.

DOCUMENTATION REFERRAL SERVICE
World Bank, Records Management Division, Document Acquisition and Control, 1818 H Street, N.W., Washington, D.C. 20433.

SOCIAL INDICATORS
The World Bank, Economic Analysis and Projections Department,

Economic and Social Data Division, 1818 H Street, N.W., Washington, D.C. 20433.

WORLD TABLES
The World Bank, Economic Analysis and Projections Department, Economic and Social Data Division, 1818 H Street, N.W., Washington, D.C. 20433.

IMF DATA FUND SYSTEM
International Monetary Fund, Bureau of Statistics, 700 19th Street, N.W., Washington, D.C. 20431.

JOINT BANK-FUND LIBRARY
International Monetary Fund, 700 19th Street, N.W., Washington, D.C. 20431.

II. BIBLIOGRAPHY OF BIBLIOGRAPHIES

ANNOTATED BIBLIOGRAPHY OF COUNTRY SERIALS is a listing of periodicals, annuals and other serials containing information of economic, business or trade interest. The listing is organized on a regional and country basis. Copies are available from the Documentation Service, International Trade Centre UNCTAD/GATT, 1211 Geneva 10, Switzerland.

BASIC-NEEDS APPROACH: A SURVEY OF ITS LITERATURE, edited by M. Rutjes, contains a brief analysis of the concept of basic needs, its targets, its strategy and implications, followed by a concise bibliography related to the topic. Copies may be obtained from the Centre for the Study of Education in Developing Countries, Badhuisweg 251, The Hague, The Netherlands.

DEVELOPMENT PLANS AND PLANNING - BIBLIOGRAPHIC AND COMPUTER AIDS TO RESEARCH, by August Schumacher, is arranged in three parts. The first contains more than 100 selected bibliographies on development plans and planning, the second is concerned with a new source of empirical materials for the development planner - the automated documentation centre, and the third analyzes recent work on computer aids for the research library. The publication is available from Seminar Press Ltd., 24-28 Oval Road, London NW1, England.

BIBLIOGRAPHY ON DEVELOPMENT EDUCATION lists books, manuals, resource materials, magazines, and articles in the field of development education. The listing was prepared by the Dutch Central Bureau of Catholic Education. Copies are available from the Central Bureau of Catholic Education, G. Verstijnen, Secretary Foreign Department, Bezuidenhoutseweg 275, The Hague, Netherlands.

BIBLIOGRAPHY OF GERMAN RESEARCH ON DEVELOPING COUNTRIES, prepared by the German Foundation for International Development, is divided into two sections: Part A contains an index of research institutes, author index, subject-matter index, and a geographical index. Part B contains specific information on each of the studies listed. The text is in German with explanatory notes in German, English, French and Spanish. Copies may be obtained from the Deutsche Stiftung fur Internationale Entwicklung (DSE), Endenicher Strasse 41, 53 Bonn, Federal Republic of Germany.

BIBLIOGRAPHY OF SELECTED LATIN AMERICAN PUBLICATIONS ON DEVELOPMENT is a listing of over 200 titles in Latin American development literature, including subject and author indexes. The document was prepared by the Institute of Development Studies Library. Copies are available from the Librarian, Institute of Development Studies, University of Sussex, Brighton BN1 9RE, England.

CANADIAN DEVELOPMENT ASSISTANCE: A SELECTED BIBLIOGRAPHY 1950-70, compiled by Shirley B. Seward and Helen Janssen, covers Canada's foreign aid programs and policies from 1950 to 1970. Copies are available from the Distribution Unit, International Development Research Centre, P.O. Box 8500, Ottawa, Canada K1G 3H9.

DEVINDEX CANADA is a bibliography of literature on social and economic development in Third World countries, which originated in Canada in 1975. Copies may be obtained from the International Development Research Centre, Box 8500, Ottawa, Canada K1G 3H9.

The UNESCO Division of Scientific Research and Higher Education has compiled **A DIRECTORY AND BIBLIOGRAPHY ON THE THEME "RESEARCH AND HUMAN NEEDS"**, listing organizations, journals, newsletters, reports and papers, information services and data banks. The bibliographical section includes headings such as food and nutrition, health, housing and sanitation, environment, energy, technology. For copies contact "Research and Human Needs", Division of Scientific Research and Higher Education, UNESCO, Place de Fontenoy, 75007 Paris, France.

GUIDE TO CURRENT DEVELOPMENT LITERATURE ON ASIA AND THE PACIFIC is published every two months by the Library and Documentation Centre of the Asia Pacific Development Information Service. For more information write to the Centre, United Nations Asian and Pacific Development Institute, P.O. Box 2-136, Sri Aydudhya Road, Bangkok, Thailand.

Hald, Marjorie W.
A SELECTED BIBLIOGRAPHY ON ECONOMIC DEVELOPMENT AND FOREIGN AID, rev. ed., Santa Monica, CA: The Rand Corporation, 1958.

Hazelwood, Arthur
THE ECONOMICS OF "UNDERDEVELOPED" AREAS: AN ANNOTATED READING LIST OF BOOKS, ARTICLES, AND OFFICIAL PUBLICATIONS. London: Oxford University Press for the Institute of Colonial Studies, 1954. 623 titles.

THE ECONOMICS OF DEVELOPMENT: AN ANNOTATED LIST OF BOOKS AND ARTICLES PUBLISHED 1958-1962. London: Oxford University Press, for the Institute of Commonwealth Studies, 1964.

INTERNATIONAL BIBLIOGRAPHY, INFORMATION DOCUMENTATION (IBID) provides bibliographic details and annotations necessary to identify the full range of publications prepared by the United Nations and its related agencies, plus those of ten organizations outside the UN system. IBID is published quarterly by Unipub. Available from Unipub, Box 433, Murray Hill Station, New York, New York 10016, USA.

THE 1978/79 PUBLICATIONS LIST OF THIRD WORLD PUBLICATIONS contains over 300 titles of pamphlets, books and teaching materials about the Third World. The listing is available from Third World Publications, Ltd., 151 Stratford Road, Birmingham B11 1RD, England.

A list of 200 books on **NORTH-SOUTH WORLD RELATIONS** has been compiled by the Developing Country Courier. The listing is organized by subject and region. For copies write to the Courier, P.O. Box 239, McLean, Virginia 22101, USA.

United States Agency for International Development
A PRACTICAL BIBLIOGRAPHY FOR DEVELOPING AREAS. Washington, D.C., 1966. 2 vols. (Vol. 1 - A selective, annotated and graded list of United States publications in the social sciences. 202 pp.) (Vol. 2 - A selective, annotated and graded list of United States publications in the physical and applied sciences. 332 pp.)

PUBLIC ADMINISTRATION--A SELECT BIBLIOGRAPHY, prepared by the British Ministry of Overseas Development Library is the second supplement to the 1973 revised edition. Copies may be obtained from Eland House, Stag Place, London SW1E 5DH, England.

PUBLIC ADMINISTRATION--A SELECT BIBLIOGRAPHY, prepared by the Library of the British Ministry of Overseas Development, is a supplement to the revised edition which appeared in 1973. It includes material published in the period 1972-1975 with 1,600 references. Copies may be obtained from the Library, British Ministry of Overseas Development, Eland House, Stag Place, London SW1E 5DH, England.

The OECD Development Centre has gathered together in the catalog **PUBLICATION AND DOCUMENT, 1962-1979** all the books and documents it has published since its establishment in 1962 up to August 1979. Copies available from OECD Development Centre, 94 rue Chardon Lagache, 75016 Paris, France.

REGISTER OF RESEARCH PROJECTS IN PROGRESS IN DEVELOPMENT STUDIES IN SELECTED EUROPEAN COUNTRIES was prepared by the Centre for Development Studies of the University of Antwerp at the request of the European Association of Development Research and Training Institutes. Copies are available from the Centre, St. Ignatius

Faculties, University of Antwerp, 13 Prinsstraat, 2000 Antwerp, Belgium.

Re Qua, Eloise and Statham, Jane
THE DEVELOPING NATIONS: A GUIDE TO INFORMATION SOURCES CONCERNING THEIR ECONOMIC, POLITICAL, TECHNICAL AND SOCIAL PROBLEMS. Detroit: Gale Research Company, 1965.

The East African Academy has published two new bibliographies. **SCIENCE AND TECHNOLOGY IN EAST AFRICA** contains more than 5,000 titles about research in the agriculture, medical technological, and related fields in East Africa, with short summaries on the problems and progress of research in these areas. **TANZANIA EDUCATION SINCE UHURU: A BIBLIOGRAPHY--1961-1971** was compiled by Dr. George A. Auger of the University of Dar es Salaam. Both publications are available from the East African Academy, RIPS, P.O. Box 47288, Nairobi, Kenya.

SELECTIVE ANNOTATED BIBLIOGRAPHY ON BRAZILIAN DEVELOPMENT has been prepared by the SID Sao Paulo Chapter. This first issue contains only references that have appeared in 1975. Copies are available from the Society for International Development, Sao Paulo Chapter, Caixa Postal 20.270-Vila Clementino, 04023-Sao Paulo-S.P. Brazil.

A SELECTED ANNOTATED BIBLIOGRAPHY: INDIGENOUS TECHNICAL KNOWLEDGE IN DEVELOPMENT, compiled by Liz O'Keefe and Michael Howes, is contained in the January 1979 IDS BULLETIN. This issue of the BULLETIN is devoted to the importance of indigenous technical knowledge in rural areas. Single copies of the BULLETIN are from the Communications Office, Institute of Development Studies, University of Sussex, Brighton N1 9RE, United Kingdom.

SELECTED BIBLIOGRAPHY OF RECENT ECONOMIC DEVELOPMENT PUBLICATIONS covers a period of one year, from July 1977 to June 1978 and contains two main sections, one for general and theoretical works, the other for literature related to regions and countries. For copies write to the Graduate Program in Economic Development, Vanderbilt University, Nashville, Tennessee 37235, USA.

International Bank for Reconstruction and Development; Economic Development Institute
SELECTED READINGS AND SOURCE MATERIALS ON ECONOMIC DEVELOPMENT. A list of books, articles, and reports included in a small library assembled by the Economic Development Institute, Washington, D.C., 1961.

SOCIAL AND ECONOMIC DEVELOPMENT PLANS - MICROFICHE PROJECT is a cumulative catalogue listing the holdings of Inter Documentation Company AG on social and economic development plans around the world. About 1400 plans from over 180 countries are included. Copies of the catalogue and other catalogues of IDC's microfiche projects are free on request from Inter Documentation Company AG, Poststrasse 14, 6300 Zug-Switzerland.

Powelson, John
A SELECT BIBLIOGRAPHY ON ECONOMIC DEVELOPMENT. Boulder, Colorado: Westview Press, 1979.

THIRD WORLD BIBLIOGRAPHY AND RESOURCE GUIDE features a wide range of material on Third World issues. It is designed for students and general readers. Copies may be obtained from the Development Education Library Project, c/o OSFAM/Ontario, 175 Carlton Street, Toronto, Canada.

The United Nations Asian and Pacific Development Institute has prepared a **SPECIAL BIBLIOGRAPHY ON ALTERNATIVE STRATEGIES FOR DEVELOPMENT WITH FOCUS ON LOCAL LEVEL PLANNING AND DEVELOPMENT** in connection with a UNAPDI meeting, held in Bangkok, October 31 - November 4, 1978. Copies are available from the APDI Library and Documentation Centre. UNAPDI, P.O. Box 2-136, Sri Ayudhya Road, Bangkok, Thailand.

Vente, Role and Dieter Seul
MACRO-ECONOMIC PLANNING: A BIBLIOGRAPHY. Nomos Verlagsgesellshaft, Baden-Baden, 1970.

Volunteers in Technical Assistance (VITA) has published its 1979 **CATALOGUE OF BOOKS, BULLETINS AND MANUALS.** The listing contains VITA documents related to appropriate technology, as well as materials published by other development organizations around the world. Copies are available from VITA, 2706 Rhode Island Avenue, Mt. Ranier, Maryland 20822, USA.

DEVELOPMENT--A BIBLIOGRAPHY, was compiled by Vaptistis-Titos Patrikios (Rome: FAO, 1974) and updates the first edition, published in 1970, to cover the 1970/73 period. Contains eight sections relating to development: theories and problems; perspectives of the Third World countries; population and food production; aid, trade and international cooperation; agriculture; manpower and employment; education; and environment. A ninth section lists bibliographies.

III. DIRECTORY OF PERIODICALS

ACTUEL DEVELOPPEMENT, English Digest Edition, Paris.

AFRICA, London, Africa Journal, Ltd.

AFRICA INSTITUTE, Pretoria, Africa Institute.

AFRICA QUARTERLY, New Delhi, India Council for Africa.

AFRICA RESEARCH BULLETIN, Exeter, Eng. Africa Research, Ltd.

AFRICA, SOUTH OF THE SAHARA, London, Europa Publications.

AFRICA TODAY, New York, American Committee on Africa.

AFRICAN AFFAIRS, London, Journal of the Royal African Society.

AFRICAN DEVELOPMENT, London.

AFRICAN DEVELOPMENT BANK, Annual Report, Ibadan.

AFRICAN ENVIRONMENT, Dakar, United Nations Environmental Program.

AFRICAN STATISTICAL YEARBOOK, Addis Ababa, Economic Commission for Africa.

AFRICAN STUDIES REVIEW, Stanford, Boston, East Lansing, African Studies Association.

AFRICAN URBAN STUDIES, East Lansing, Mich., African Studies Center.

AGENDA, Washington, D.C., U.S. Agency for International Development.

Directory of Periodicals

APPROPRIATE TECHNOLOGY, London, Intermediate Technology Publications, Ltd.

APPROTECH, Ann Arbor, Mich., International Association for the Advancement of Appropriate Technology for Developing Countries.

ARTHA VIJNANA, Poona, Gokhale Institute of Politics and Economics.

ASIA AND THE WORLD MONOGRAPHS, Taipei, Asia and the World Forum.

ASIA YEARBOOK, Hong Kong, Far Eastern Economic Review.

ASIAN AFFAIRS, London, Royal Central Asian Society.

ASIAN DEVELOPMENT BANK, Annual Report, Manila.

ASIAN REGIONAL CONFERENCE OF THE INTERNATIONAL LABOR ORGANIZATION, Proceedings, Geneva, ILO.

ASIAN SURVEY, Berkeley, Institute of International Studies.

BANGLADESH DEVELOPMENT STUDIES, Dhaka, Bangladesh Institute of Development Studies.

BANGLADESH ECONOMIC REVIEW, Dhaka, Bangladesh Institute of Development Economics.

BULLETIN OF INDONESIAN ECONOMIC STUDIES, Canberra, Dept. of Economics, Australian National University.

CEPAL REVIEW, Santiago, Chile.

CANADIAN JOURNAL OF AFRICAN STUDIES, Montreal, Loyola College.

COMMUNITY DEVELOPMENT JOURNAL, Manchester, U.K., Oxford University Press.

DEVELOPING ECONOMIES, Tokyo, The Institute of Asian Economic Affairs.

DEVELOPMENT, Rome, Society for International Development.

DEVELOPMENT CENTER STUDIES, OECD, Paris.

DEVELOPMENT AND CHANGE, Beverly Hills, Calif.: Sage Publications.

DEVELOPMENT CO-OPERATION, Paris, OECD.

DEVELOPMENT DIGEST, Washington, D.C., U.S. Agency for International Development.

DEVELOPMENT DIALOGUE, Uppsala, Sweden, Dag Hammarskjold Foundation.

EASTERN AFRICA ECONOMIC REVIEW, Nairobi, Oxford University Press.

ECONOMIC DEVELOPMENT AND CULTURAL CHANGE, Chicago, University of Chicago Press.

ETHIOPIAN JOURNAL OF DEVELOPMENT RESEARCH, Addis Ababa, Institute of Development Research.

FAR EASTERN ECONOMIC REVIEW, Hong Kong.

FINANCE AND DEVELOPMENT, Washington, D.C.

IDS BULLETIN, Institute of Development Studies, University of Sussex, U.K.

IMPACT OF SCIENCE ON SOCIETY, Paris, UNESCO.

INDIAN JOURNAL OF INDUSTRIAL RELATIONS, New Delhi, India.

INDUSTRY AND DEVELOPMENT, Vienna, UNIDO.

INTERNATIONAL DEVELOPMENT REVIEW, Rome, Society for International Development.

INTERNATIONAL LABOR REVIEW, Geneva, ILO.

INTERNATIONAL STUDIES QUARTERLY, San Francisco.

JOURNAL OF AFRICAN STUDIES, Los Angeles, UCLA African Studies Center.

JOURNAL OF DEVELOPING AREAS, Macomb, IL, Western Illinois Univ.

JOURNAL OF DEVELOPMENT ECONOMICS, Amsterdam, North Holland Publishing Co.

JOURNAL OF DEVELOPMENT STUDIES, London, U.K.

JOURNAL OF ECONOMIC DEVELOPMENT, JOURNAL OF INTERNATIONAL AFFAIRS, New York, Columbia University.

JOURNAL OF MODERN AFRICAN STUDIES, New York, Cambridge University Press.

LATIN AMERICAN RESEARCH REVIEW, Chapel Hill, North Carolina.

MODERN ASIAN STUDIES, New York, Cambridge University Press.

MONOGRAPH, DEVELOPMENT STUDIES CENTER, AUSTRALIAN NATIONAL UNIVERSITY.

MONOGRAPH, OVERSEAS DEVELOPMENT COUNCIL, Washington, D.C.

ODI REVIEW, Overseas Development Institute, London, U.K.

OXFORD ECONOMIC PAPERS, Oxford, U.K.

PAKISTAN DEVELOPMENT REVIEW, Karachi, Pakistan.

PUBLIC ADMINISTRATION AND DEVELOPMENT, Sussex, U.K., Royal Institute of Public Administration.

THIRD WORLD QUARTERLY, London, Third World Foundation for Social and Economic Studies.

WORLD BANK STAFF WORKING PAPER, IBRD, Washington, D.C.

WORLD DEVELOPMENT, Pergamon Press, N.Y.

NOTE:

For more information on relevant periodicals please consult:

1. **DIRECTORY OF UNITED NATIONS INFORMATION SYSTEMS**

2. **REGISTER OF UNITED NATIONS SERIAL PUBLICATIONS**

Public by **Inter-Organization Board for Information Systems**, IOB Secretariat, Palais des Nations, CH-1211 Geneva 10, Switzerland.

IV. RESEARCH INSTITUTIONS

INTERNATIONAL (GENERAL)

AFRICAN INSTITUTE FOR ECONOMIC DEVELOPMENT AND PLANNING
United Nations Economic Commission for Africa, Dakar, Senegal.

AFRO-ASIAN ORGANIZATION FOR ECONOMIC CO-OPERATION
Chairo Chamber of Commerce Building, Midan el-Falsky, Cairo, Egypt.

ASIAN ASSOCIATION OF DEVELOPMENT RESEARCH AND TRAINING INSTITUTES
P.O. Box 2-136, Sri Ayudhya Road, Bangkok, Thailand.

ASIAN DEVELOPMENT CENTER
11th Floor, Philippines Banking Corporation Building, Anda Circle, Port Area, Manila, Philippines.

ASIAN INSTITUTE FOR ECONOMIC DEVELOPMENT AND PLANNING
P.O. Box 2-136, Sri Ayudhya Road, Bangkok, Thailand.

ATLANTIC INSTITUTE FOR INTERNATIONAL AFFAIRS
120, rue de Longchamp, 75016 Paris, France.

CARIBBEAN STUDIES ASSOCIATION
Inter-American University of Puerto Rico, P.O. Box 1293, Hato Rey, Puerto Rico 00919.

CENTRE FOR STUDIES AND RESEARCH IN INTERNATIONAL LAW AND INTERNATIONAL RELATIONS
The Hague Academy of International Law, The Hague, Netherlands.

CENTRE FOR THE CO-ORDINATION OF SOCIAL SCIENCE RESEARCH AND DOCUMENTATION IN AFRICA SOUTH OF THE SAHARA
B.P. 836, Kinshasa XI, Zaire.

CLUB OF ROME
Via Giorgione 163, 00147 Roma, Italy.

COMMITTEE ON SOCIETY, DEVELOPMENT AND PEACE
Oecumenical Centre, 150, route de Ferney, 1211 Geneve 20, Suisse.

COUNCIL FOR ASIAN MANPOWER STUDIES
P.O. Box 127, Quezon City, Philippines.

COUNCIL FOR THE DEVELOPMENT OF ECONOMIC AND SOCIAL RESEARCH IN AFRICA
B.P. 3186, Dakar, Senegal.

EAST AFRICAN ACADEMY RESEARCH INFORMATION CENTRE
Regional Building of East African Community, Ngong Road (rooms 359-60), Nairobi, Kenya.

EASTERN REGIONAL ORGANIZATION FOR PLANNING AND HOUSING
Central Office: 4a, Ring Road, Indraprastha Estate, New Delhi, India.

EASTERN REGIONAL ORGANIZATION FOR PUBLIC ADMINISTRATION
Rizal Hall, Padre Faura Street, Manila, Philippines.

ECONOMIC DEVELOPMENT INSTITUTE
1818 H Street, N.W., Washington, D.C. 20433, U.S.A.

EUROPEAN FOUNDATION FOR MANAGEMENT DEVELOPMENT
51, rue de la Concorde, Bruxelles, Belgique.

EUROPEAN INSTITUTE FOR TRANSNATIONAL STUDIES IN GROUP AND ORGANIZATIONAL DEVELOPMENT
Viktorgasse 9, 1040 Vienna, Austria.

EUROPEAN INSTITUTE OF BUSINESS ADMINISTRATION
Boulevard de Constance, 77 Fontainebleau, France.

EUROPEAN RESEARCH GROUP ON MANAGEMENT
Predikherenberg 55, 3200 Kessel-Lo, Belgique.

INSTITUTE OF INTERNATIONAL LAW
82, avenue de Castel, 1200 Bruxelles, Belgique.

INTERNATIONAL AFRICAN INSTITUTE
210, High Holborn, London WC1V 7BW, United Kingdom.

INTERNATIONAL ASSOCIATION FOR METROPOLITAN RESEARCH AND DEVELOPMENT
Suite 1200, 130 Bloor Street West, Toronto 5, Canada.

INTERNATIONAL CENTRE OF RESEARCH AND INFORMATION ON PUBLIC AND CO-OPERATIVE ECONOMY
45, quai de Rome, Liege, Belgique.

INTERNATIONAL CO-OPERATION FOR SOCIO-ECONOMIC DEVELOPMENT
59-61, rue Adolphe-Lacombie, Bruxelles 4, Belgique.

INTERNATIONAL INSTITUTE FOR LABOUR STUDIES
154, rue de Lausanne, Case Postale 6, 1211 Geneve, Suisse.

INTERNATIONAL INSTITUTE FOR STRATEGIC STUDIES
18, Adam Street, London WC2N 6AL, United Kingdom.

INTERNATIONAL INSTITUTE OF ADMINISTRATIVE SCIENCES
25, rue de la Charite, Bruxelles 4, Belgique.

INTERNATIONAL MANAGEMENT DEVELOPMENT INSTITUTE
4, Chemin de Conches, 1200 Geneve, Suisse.

INTERNATIONAL SCIENCE FOUNDATION
2, rue de Furstenberg, 75006 Paris, France.

INTERNATIONAL SOCIAL SCIENCE COUNCIL
1, rue Miollis, 75015 Paris, France.

INTERNATIONAL STATISTICAL INSTITUTE
Prinses Beatrixlaan 428, Voorburg, Netherlands.

INTERNATIONAL TRAINING AND RESEARCH CENTER FOR DEVELOPMENT
47, rue de la Glaciere, 75013 Paris, France.

LATIN AMERICAN CENTRE FOR ECONOMIC AND SOCIAL DOCUMENTATION
Casilla 179-D, Santiago, Chile.

ORGANIZATION FOR ECONOMIC CO-OPERATION AND DEVELOPMENT
Chateau de la Muette, 2, rue Andre Pascal, 75775 Paris Cedex 16, France.

REGIONAL ECONOMIC RESEARCH AND DOCUMENTATION CENTER
B.P. 7138, Lome, Togo.

RESEARCH CENTRE ON SOCIAL AND ECONOMIC DEVELOPMENT IN ASIA--INSTITUTE OF ECONOMIC GROWTH
University Enclave, Delhi 7, India.

SOCIETY FOR INTERNATIONAL DEVELOPMENT
1346 Connecticut Avenue, N.W., Washington, D.C. 20036, USA.

SOUTHEAST ASIAN SOCIAL SCIENCE ASSOCIATION
Chulalongkorn University, c/o Faculty of Political Science, Bangkok, Thailand.

UNITED NATIONS INSTITUTE FOR TRAINING AND RESEARCH
801 United Nations Plaza, New York, NY, USA.

UNITED NATIONS RESEARCH INSTITUTE FOR SOCIAL DEVELOPMENT
Palais des Nations, 1211 Geneve, Suisse.

AUSTRALIA

AUSTRALIAN INSTITUTE OF INTERNATIONAL AFFAIRS
P.O. Box E181, Canberra, ACT 2600.

INSTITUTE OF ADVANCED STUDIES
The Australian National University, P.O. Box 4, Canberra ACT 2600.

STRATEGIC AND DEFENSE STUDIES CENTER
Research School of Pacific Studies, Australian National University, P.O. Box 4, Canberra ACT 2600.

AUSTRIA

AUSTRIAN FOUNDATION FOR DEVELOPMENT RESEARCH (OFSE)
Turkenstrasse 3, 1090 Vienna, Austria.

VIENNA INSTITUTE FOR DEVELOPMENT
Karntner Strasse 25, 1010 Vienna, Austria.

BANGLADESH

BANGLADESH INSTITUTE OF DEVELOPMENT STUDIES
Adamjee Court, Motijheel Commercial Area, Dacca 2.

BELGIUM

CATHOLIC UNIVERSITY OF LOUVAIN
Center for Economic Studies, Van Evenstraat 2b, 3000 Louvain, Belgium.

FREE UNIVERSITY OF BRUSSELS
Department of Applied Economics, Avenue F-D Roosevelt 50, 1050 Brussels, Belgium.

UNIVERSITY OF ANTWERP
Centre for Development Studies, 13 Prinsstratt, 2000 Antwerp, Belgium.

BRAZIL

BRAZILIAN INSTITUTE OF ECONOMICS
Fundacao Getulio Vargas Caixa Postal 4081-ZC-05, Rio de Janeiro, Brazil.

PROGRAMME OF JOINT STUDIES ON LATIN AMERICAN ECONOMIC INTEGRATION
Caixa Postal 740, Rio de Janeiro, Brazil.

BULGARIA

SCIENTIFIC RESEARCH CENTRE FOR AFRICA AND ASIA
Academy of Social Science, ul. Gagarin 2, Sofia 13, Bulgaria.

INSTITUTE FOR INTERNATIONAL RELATIONS AND SOCIALIST INTEGRATION
Bulgarian Academy of Sciences, Boul. Pencho Slaveicov, 15, Sofia, Bulgaria.

CANADA

CANADIAN ASSOCIATION OF AFRICAN STUDIES
Geography Department, Carleton University, Ottawa, K1S 5B6.

CANADIAN COUNCIL FOR INTERNATIONAL CO-OPERATION
75 Sparks Street, Ottawa 4, Ontario.

CANADIAN INSTITUTE OF INTERNATIONAL AFFAIRS
Edgar Tarr House, 31 Wellesley Street East, Toronto 284, Ontario.

CENTRE FOR DEVELOPING-ASIA STUDIES
McGill University, Montreal.

INSTITUTE OF INTERNATIONAL RELATIONS
University of British Columbia, Vancouver 8.

INTERNATIONAL DEVELOPMENT RESEARCH CENTRE
60 Queen Street, P.O. Box 8500, Ottawa K1G 3H9.

REGIONAL DEVELOPMENT RESEARCH CENTER
University of Ottawa, Ottawa 2, Ontario.

CHILE

CATHOLIC UNIVERSITY OF CHILE
Institute of Economics, Avda. Libertador Bernardo O'Higgins, No. 340, Santiago, Chile.

CATHOLIC UNIVERSITY OF CHILE
Center for Planning Studies (CEPLAN), Avda. Libertador Bernardo O'Higgins, No. 340, Santiago, Chile.

UNIVERSITY OF CHILE
Planning Centre (CEPLA), Avda. Libertador Bernardo O'Higgins, No. 1058, Santiago, Chile.

COLOMBIA

UNIVERSITY OF ANTIOQUIA
Economic Research Centre, Apartado Aereo 1226, Medellin, Colombia.

CZECHOSLOVAKIA

INSTITUTE OF INTERNATIONAL RELATIONS
Praha 1 - Mala Strana, Nerudova 3, Czechoslovakia.

DENMARK

INSTITUTE FOR DEVELOPMENT RESEARCH
V. Volgade 104, DK-1552 Kobenhavn.

CENTRE FOR DEVELOPMENT RESEARCH
9, NY Kongensgade, 4K-1472 Copenhagen K, Denmark.

FRANCE

UNIVERSITY OF PARIS, INSTITUTE OF ECONOMIC AND SOCIAL DEVELOPMENT STUDIES
58 Boulevard Arago, 75013 Paris, France.

INSTITUTE FOR RESEARCH INTO THE ECONOMICS OF PRODUCTION
2 rue de Rouen, 92000 Nanterre, France.

INTERNATIONAL CENTRE OF ADVANCED MEDITERRANEAN AGRONOMIC STUDIES
Route de Mende, 34000 Montpellier, France.

INSTITUTE FOR ECONOMIC RESEARCH AND DEVELOPMENT PLANNING
B.P. 47, 38040 Grenoble Cedex, France.

GERMANY, FEDERAL REPUBLIC OF

INSTITUTE FOR DEVELOPMENT RESEARCH AND DEVELOPMENT POLICY
Ruhr-Universitat Bochum, 463 Bochum-Querenburg, Postifach 2148, Federal Republic of Germany.

INTERNATIONAL INSTITUTE OF MANAGEMENT
Wissenschaftszentrum Berlin, Criegstrasse 5-7, Berlin 33, D-1000.

GERMAN ASSOCIATION FOR EAST ASIAN STUDIES
Rothenbaumchaussee 32, 2 Hamburg 13.

GHANA

INSTITUTE OF AFRICAN STUDIES
University of Ghana, P.O. Box 73, Legon, Accra.

HUNGARY

INSTITUTE FOR WORLD ECONOMICS OF THE HUNGARIAN ACADEMY OF SCIENCES
P.O. Box 36, 1531 Budapest, Hungary.

INSTITUTE FOR ECONOMIC AND MARKET RESEARCH
P.O. Box 133, Budapest 62, Hungary.

INDIA

CENTRE FOR THE STUDY OF DEVELOPING SOCIETIES
29, Rajpur Road, Delhi 6, India.

INDIA INTERNATIONAL CENTRE
40 Lodi Estate, New Delhi 110003, India.

INDIAN COUNCIL FOR AFRICA
Nyaya Marg, Chankyapuri, New Delhi 21, India.

INDIAN COUNCIL OF WORLD AFFAIRS
Sapru House, Barakhamba Road, New Delhi 110001, India.

INDIAN INSTITUTE OF ASIAN STUDIES
23/354, Azad Nagar, Jaiprakash Road, Andheri, Bombay 38, India.

INDIAN SCHOOL OF INTERNATIONAL STUDIES
35, Ferozeshah Road, New Delhi 1, India.

INSTITUTE OF ECONOMIC GROWTH
University of Enclave, Delhi 7, India.

MADRAS INSTITUTE OF DEVELOPMENT STUDIES
74, Second Main Road, Gandhinagar Adyar, Madras 20, India.

INDONESIA

NATIONAL INSTITUTE OF ECONOMIC AND SOCIAL RESEARCH
Leknas, UC, P.O. Box 310, Djakarta, Indonesia.

ISRAEL

DAVID HOROWITZ INSTITUTE FOR THE RESEARCH OF DEVELOPING COUNTRIES
Tel-Aviv University, Ramat-Aviv, Tel-Aviv.

AFRO-ASIAN INSTITUTE FOR CO-OPERATIVE AND LABOUR STUDIES
P.O. Box 16201, Tel-Aviv.

ISRAELI INSTITUTE OF INTERNATIONAL AFFAIRS
P.O. Box 17027, Tel-Aviv 61170.

JAPAN

INSTITUTE OF DEVELOPING ECONOMIES
42 Ichigaya-Hommura-cho, Sinjuku-ku, Tokyo 162, Japan.

JAPAN CENTER FOR AREA DEVELOPMENT RESEARCH
Iino Building, 2-1-1 Uchisaiwai-cho, Chiyoda-ku, Tokyo, Japan.

KENYA

INSTITUTE FOR DEVELOPMENT STUDIES
University of Nairobi, P.O. Box 30197, Nairobi.

KOREA

INDUSTRIAL MANAGEMENT RESEARCH CENTRE
Yonsei University, Sodaemoon-ku-Seoul.

INSTITUTE OF OVERSEAS AFFAIRS
Hankuk University of Foreign Studies, 270 Rimoon-dong, Seoul.

INSTITUTE OF THE MIDDLE EAST AND AFRICA
Rom. 52, Dong-A Building, No. 55, 2nd-ka, Sinmoonro, Congro-ku, Seoul.

MEXICO

CENTRE FOR ECONOMIC RESEARCH AND TEACHING
Av. Country Club No. 208, Apdo. Postal 13628, Mexico 21, D. F.

NEPAL

CENTRE FOR ECONOMIC DEVELOPMENT AND ADMINISTRATION (CEDA)
Tribhuvan University, Kirtipur, P.O. Box 797, Kathmandu, Nepal.

NETHERLANDS

CENTRE FOR LATIN AMERICAN RESEARCH AND DOCUMENTATION
Nieuwe Doelenstraat 16, Amsterdam 1000, Netherlands.

INSTITUTE OF SOCIAL STUDIES
Badhuisweg 251, P.O. Box 90733, 2509 LS The Hague, Netherlands.

FREE UNIVERSITY, DEPARTMENT OF DEVELOPMENT ECONOMICS
De Boelelaan 1105, Amsterdam 1000, Netherlands.

CENTRE FOR DEVELOPMENT PLANNING
Erasmus University, Postbus 1738, Rotterdam, Netherlands.

DEVELOPMENT RESEARCH INSTITUTE
Hogeschoollaan 225, Tiburg 4400, Netherlands.

NEW ZEALAND

NEW ZEALAND INSTITUTE OF INTERNATIONAL AFFAIRS
P.O. Box 196, Wellington, New Zealand.

NEW ZEALAND INSTITUTE OF ECONOMIC RESEARCH
26, Kelburn Parade, P.O. Box 3749, Wellington, New Zealand.

NIGERIA

INSTITUTE OF AFRICAN STUDIES, UNIVERSITY OF NIGERIA
University of Nigeria, Nsukka, Nigeria.

NIGERIAN INSTITUTE OF INTERNATIONAL AFFAIRS
Kofo Abayomi Road, Victoria Island, G.P.O. Box 1727, Lagos, Nigeria.

NIGERIAN INSTITUTE OF SOCIAL AND ECONOMIC RESEARCH
Private Mail Bag No. 5, U.I. University of Ibadan, Ibadan, Nigeria.

NORWAY

INTERNATIONAL PEACE RESEARCH INSTITUTE
Radhusgt 4, Oslo 1, Norway.

NORWEGIAN AGENCY FOR INTERNATIONAL DEVELOPMENT (NORAD)
Planning Department, Boks 18142 Oslo Dep., Oslo 1, Norway.

THE CHR. MICHELSEN INSTITUTE (DERAP)
Fantoftvegen 38, 5036 Fantoft, Bergen, Norway.

PAKISTAN

DEPARTMENT OF INTERNATIONAL RELATIONS
University of Karachi, Karachi-32, Pakistan.

PHILIPPINES

ASIAN CENTER
University of the Philippines, Palma Hall, Diliman D-505, Quezon City, Philippines.

ASIAN INSTITUTE OF INTERNATIONAL STUDIES
Malcolm Hall, University of the Philippines, Diliman, Quezon City, Philippines.

INSTITUTE OF ECONOMIC DEVELOPMENT AND RESEARCH
School of Economics, University of the Philippines, Diliman, Quezon City, Philippines.

POLAND

RESEARCH INSTITUTE FOR DEVELOPING COUNTRIES
Rakowiecka 24, Warsaw, Poland.

CENTRE OF AFRICAN STUDIES
University of Warsaw, Al. Zwirki i Wigury 93, 02-089 Warsaw, Poland.

SINGAPORE

INSTITUTE OF ASIAN STUDIES
Nanyang University, Jurong Road, Singapore 22.

INSTITUTE OF SOUTH-EAST ASIAN STUDIES
Campus of University of Singapore, House No. 8, Cluny Road, Singapore 10.

SRI LANKA

MARGA INSTITUTE
P.O. Box 601, 61 Isipathana Mawatha, Colombo 5, Sri Lanka.

SUDAN

INSTITUTE OF AFRICAN AND ASIAN STUDIES
Faculty of Arts, University of Khartoum, P.O. Box 321, Khartoum, Sudan.

SWEDEN

INSTITUTE FOR INTERNATIONAL ECONOMIC STUDIES
Fack S-104 05, Stockholm 50, Sweden.

STOCKHOLM SCHOOL OF ECONOMICS, ECONOMIC RESEARCH INSTITUTE
Box 6501, 11383 Stockholm, Sweden.

UNITED KINGDOM

CENTRE FOR SOUTH-EAST ASIAN STUDIES
University of Hull, Hull HU6 7RX.

CENTRE OF AFRICAN STUDIES
University of Edinburgh, Adam Ferguson Building, George Square, Edinburgh 8.

CENTRE OF LATIN AMERICAN STUDIES (CAMBRIDGE)
University of Cambridge, History Faculty Building, West Road, Cambridge CB3 9ES, England.

CENTRE OF LATIN AMERICAN STUDIES (OXFORD)
Oxford University, St. Antony's College, Oxford OX2 6JF, England.

CENTRE OF WEST AFRICAN STUDIES
University of Birmingham, P.O. Box 363, Birmingham B15 2TT.

INSTITUTE FOR THE STUDY OF INTERNATIONAL ORGANISATION
University of Sussex, Stanmer House, Stanmer Park, Brighton BN1 9QA, England.

INSTITUTE OF DEVELOPMENT STUDIES
University of Sussex, Falmer, Brighton BN1 9QN, England.

INSTITUTE OF LATIN AMERICAN STUDIES
University of London, 31 Tavistock Square, London WC1, England.

INSTITUTE OF LATIN AMERICAN STUDIES (GLASGOW)
University of Glasgow, Glasgow.

ROYAL INSTITUTE OF INTERNATIONAL AFFAIRS
Chatham House, St. James' Square, London SW1Y 4LE, England.

UNITED STATES

AFRICAN STUDIES CENTER (BOSTON)
Boston University, 10 Lenos Street, Brookline MA 02146.

BROOKINGS INSTITUTION
1775 Massachusetts Avenue, N.W., Washington, D.C. 20036.

CENTER FOR ASIAN STUDIES
Arizona State University, Tempe, AZ 85281.

CENTER FOR COMPARATIVE STUDIES IN TECHNOLOGICAL DEVELOPMENT AND SOCIAL CHANGE
University of Minnesota, Minneapolis, Minnesota 55455.

CENTER FOR DEVELOPMENT ECONOMICS
Williams College, Williamston, MA 01267.

CENTER FOR INTERNATIONAL AFFAIRS
Harvard University, 6 Divinity Avenue, Cambridge, MA 02138.

CENTER FOR INTERNATIONAL STUDIES
Massachusetts Institute of Technology, Cambridge, MA 02139.

CENTER FOR LATIN AMERICAN STUDIES, ARIZONA STATE UNIVERSITY
Arizona State University, Tempe, AZ 85281.

CENTER FOR LATIN AMERICAN STUDIES, UNIVERSITY OF FLORIDA
University of Florida, Room 319 LAGH, Gainesville, FL 39611.

CENTER FOR RESEARCH IN ECONOMIC DEVELOPMENT
506 East Liberty Street, Ann Arbor, MI 48108.

CENTER FOR STRATEGIC AND INTERNATIONAL STUDIES
Georgetown University, 1800 K Street, N.W., Washington, D.C. 20006.

CENTER OF INTERNATIONAL STUDIES, PRINCETON UNIVERSITY
Princeton University, 118 Corwin Hall, Princeton, NJ 08540.

HARVARD INSTITUTE FOR INTERNATIONAL DEVELOPMENT
Harvard University, 1737 Cambridge Street, Cambridge MA 02138.

INSTITUTE FOR WORLD ORDER
1140 Avenue of the Americas, New York, New York 10036.

INSTITUTE OF LATIN AMERICAN STUDIES
University of Texas at Austin, Sid. W. Richardson Hall, Austin, TX 78705.

STANFORD INTERNATIONAL DEVELOPMENT EDUCATION CENTER
P.O. Box 2329, Stanford, CA 94305.

UNIVERSITY CENTER FOR INTERNATIONAL STUDIES
University of Pittsburgh, Social Sciences Building, Pittsburgh, PA 15213.

WORLD FUTURE SOCIETY
4916 St. Elmo Avenue, Bethesda Branch, Washington, D.C. 20014.

UNIVERSITY OF HAWAII
Centre for Development Studies, Department of Economics, Porteus Hall, 2424 Maile Way, Honolulu, Hawaii 96822.

URUGUAY

LATIN AMERICAN CENTRE FOR HUMAN ECONOMY
Cerrito 475, P.O. Box 998, Montevideo, Uruguay.

VENEZUELA

UNIVERSITY OF ZULIA
Department of Economic Research, Faculty of Economic and Social Sciences, Maracaibo, Venezuela.

YUGOSLAVIA

INSTITUTE FOR DEVELOPING COUNTRIES
41000 Zagreb, Ul. 8 Maja 82, Yugoslavia.

RESEARCH CENTRE FOR CO-OPERATION WITH DEVELOPING COUNTRIES
61 109 Ljubljana, Titova 104 P.O. Box 37, Yugoslavia.

INSTITUTE OF WORLD ECONOMICS AND INTERNATIONAL RELATIONS OF THE ACADEMY OF SCIENCES OF THE U.S.S.R.
Yaroslavskaya Ul. 13, Moskva I-243.

Appendix

COUNTRIES BY INCOME GROUP
(based on 1976 GNP per capita in 1976 US dollars)

INDUSTRIALIZED COUNTRIES

Australia
Austria
Belgium
Canada
Denmark
Finland
France
Germany, Fed. Rep. of
Iceland
Ireland
Italy
Japan
Luxembourg
Netherlands
New Zealand
Norway
South Africa
Sweden
Switzerland
United Kingdom
United States

DEVELOPING COUNTRIES BY INCOME GROUP
(Excluding Capital Surplus Oil Exporters)

High Income (over $2500)

American Samoa
Bahamas
Bermuda
Brunei
Canal Zone
Channel Islands
Faeroe Islands
French Polynesia
Gabon
Gibraltar
Greece
Greenland
Guam
Israel
Martinique
New Caledonia
Oman
Singapore
Spain
Venezuela
Virgin Islands (U.S.)

Upper Middle Income ($1136-2500)

Argentina
Bahrain
Barbados
Brazil
Cyprus
Djibouti
Fiji

French Guiana
Guadeloupe
Hong Kong
Iran
Iraq
Isle of Man
Lebanon
Malta
Netherlands Antilles
Panama
Portugal
Puerto Rico
Reunion
Romania
Surinam
Trinidad & Tobago
Uruguay
Yugoslavia

Intermediate Middle Income ($551-1135)

Algeria
Antigua
Belize
Chile
China, Rep. of
Colombia
Costa Rica
Dominica
Dominican Republic
Ecuador
Ghana
Gilbert Islands
Guatemala
Ivory Coast
Jamaica
Jordan
Korea, Rep. of
Macao
Malaysia
Mauritius
Mexico
Namibia
Nicaragua
Paraguay
Peru
Seychelles
St. Kitts-Nevis
St. Lucia
Syrian Arab Rep.
Trust Territory of the Pacific Islands
Tunisia
Turkey

Lower Middle Income ($281-550)

Angola
Bolivia
Botswana
Cameroon
Cape Verde
Congo, P.R.
El Salvador
Equatorial Guinea
Grenada
Guyana
Honduras
Liberia
Mauritania
Morocco
New Hebrides
Nigeria
Papua New Guinea
Philippines
Rhodesia
Sao Tome & Principe
Senegal
St. Vincent
Sudan
Swaziland
Thailand
Tonga
Western Samoa
Zambia

Low Income ($280 or less)

Afghanistan
Bangladesh
Benin
Bhutan
Burma
Burundi
Cambodia
Central African Empire
Chad
Comoros
Egypt
Ethiopia
Gambia, The
Guinea
Guinea-Bissau
Haiti
India
Indonesia
Kenya
Lesotho
Madagascar
Malawi

Maldives
Mali
Mozambique
Nepal
Niger
Pakistan
Rwanda
Sierra Leone
Solomon Islands
Somalia
Sri Lanka
Tanzania
Togo
Uganda
Upper Volta
Viet Nam
Yemen Arab Rep.
Yemen P.D.R.
Zaire

CAPITAL SURPLUS OIL EXPORTING DEVELOPING COUNTRIES

Kuwait
Libya
Qatar
Saudi Arabia
United Arab Emirates

CENTRALLY PLANNED COUNTRIES

Albania
Bulgaria
China, People's Rep. of
Cuba
Czechoslovakia
German Dem. Rep.
Hungary
Korea, Dem. Rep. of
Lao People's Dem. Rep.
Mongolia
Poland
U.S.S.R.

Index

Adelman, I, 194, 212, 213
Afghanistan, 153, 332
Africa, 22, 35, 38, 48, 56,
 72, 75, 76, 85, 91, 94, 110,
 113, 137, 140, 144, 156, 177,
 182, 260, 274, 290, 291, 292,
 294, 296, 335, 344, 345, 351,
 410
Agricultural Development, 267
Agriculture, 50, 108, 286
Algeria, 31, 291, 334
Allocation of Resources, 302
Anderson, G., 173
Argentina, 153, 200, 299, 317,
 228, 331
Arnold, W., 204, 214
Asia, 22, 32, 38, 71, 72, 85,
 91, 110, 137, 140, 144, 156,
 260, 261, 265, 268, 270
Atkinson, J., 215
Ayza, J., 407
Baer, W., 172, 173
Bangledesh, 22, 41, 43, 69,
 153, 156, 332, 335, 339
Barbados, 317, 321
Barton, C., 172, 173
Becker, G., 214
Bird, R., 313
Blaug, M., 297
Boeck, K., 195
Bolivia, 280, 321, 322, 328,
 338
Botswana, 153, 328, 331
Brazil, 17, 26, 145, 153, 173,
 228, 280, 283, 284, 286,
 287, 300, 332, 335, 345,
 351
Britain, 12
Burundi, 22
Buttler, A., 173
Cameroon, 177
Capital Accumulation, 267
Capital Formation, 134
Caribbean, 94, 101, 113, 150,
 260, 275, 283
Ceylone, 261, 263, 266, 267,
 269, 271, 298
Chad, 26, 48, 153, 353
Champernowne, D., 213
Chelliah, R., 313
Chenery, H., 213
Chile, 12, 153, 228, 241,
 276, 280, 283, 284, 286,
 287, 298, 300, 317, 321,
 345
Chiswick, B., 214
Cline, W., 193
Colombia, 153, 205, 276, 283,
 286, 287, 300, 345, 353
Consumption, 58
Corea, G., 216, 361
Costa Rica, 26, 153, 205, 317,
 321, 328, 331, 339
Cuba, 1, 12
Dandekar, V., 297
David, P., 173
Debt, 31, 216, 307
Della Valle, P., 173

Development, 7
Development Finance, 341
Development Process, 10
Development Trends, 79
Dominican Republic, 286, 317, 319
Dorrance, G., 172
Dualism, 189
Economic Growth, 38, 163, 204, 211, 267
Economic Policy, 154
Economic Trends, 17
Ecuador, 317, 321, 322, 332
Educational Planning, 263
Egypt, 291, 296, 345, 353
El Salvador, 321, 345
Employment, 178, 281
Employment Objectives, 292
Employment Policies, 284
Employment Strategies, 244
Erhardt, B., 203
Ethiopia, 23, 52, 61, 68, 153
Exports, 26
Family Planning, 289
Ferguson, J., 313
Fichet, G., 362, 407
Fiscal Policy, 302
Fohl, C., 213
Foreign Aid, 341
Frank, C., 241, 242
Frenkel, J., 203
Friedman, M., 173, 213
Galton, F., 213
Ghana, 153, 228, 235, 241, 293, 301
Gilbrat, R., 213
Glezakos, C., 163
Gonzalez, N., 362, 407
Gordon, R., 172
Greece, 22, 26
Guatemala, 153, 317, 321
Guyana, 345
Haiti, 150, 278
Hajela, P., 313
Harberger, A., 172
Heston, A., 28
Higgins, B., 173
Honduras, 23, 280
Human Capital, 207
IBRD, 192, 193
ILO, 193, 298
Imports, 26
Income Distribution, 176, 204, 278, 305, 349
India, 10, 35, 46, 48, 61, 68, 69, 156, 161, 228, 237, 241, 261, 262, 267, 298, 313, 317, 321, 322, 331, 332, 338, 339, 344, 345
Industrial Progress, 64
Industrialization, 117, 250, 269, 294
Industry, 364
Inflation, 163
Interdependence, 411
International Development strategy, 79
International Inflation, 159
International Liquidity, 195
International Policy, 11
Iran, 321, 345
Iraq, 343, 351
Israel, 26, 345
Ivory Coast, 177, 179, 193, 344
Jamaica, 344
Japan, 159, 174, 408
Jermidis, D., 176
Johnson, H., 172
Joski, H., 192
Kenessey, Z., 78
Kenya, 293, 294, 301, 317, 319, 328, 332, 335, 339,
Kerstenetzky, I., 172
Khalid, R., 313
Kmenta, J., 174
Korea, 17, 22, 26, 153, 265 344, 345, 351
Krauis, I., 78, 212
Kuznets, S., 212
Latin America, 94, 97, 110, 150, 172, 260, 275, 276, 277, 278, 281, 286, 288, 298, 362-407, 410
Layard, R. P. G., 297
Lebanon, 26
Lecaillon, J., 176
Lydall, H., 214
Malaysia, 153, 261, 262, 265, 274, 295, 317, 319, 321, 331, 335, 339, 344
Mandelbrot, B., 213
Manpower Planning, 258, 273, 289
Manpower Training, 296
Manufacturing Output, 68, 286

Maton, J., 193
Mauritius, 335, 345
McClelland, D., 215
McKinnon, R., 173
Measurement, 9
Mexico, 17, 145, 280, 299, 344, 345, 351
Mikesall, R., 172
Mincer, J., 214, 215
Mobilization of Resources, 314
Morocco, 291, 321, 331, 332, 335, 344
Morris, C., 191
Morrisson, C., 194
Mozambique, 23
Mouly, J., 194
Nepal, 332
Niedereichholz, H., 214
Niger, 71
Nigeria, 161, 298, 319, 321, 325, 338, 345
Nisbet, C., 172
OECD, 17, 37, 241, 242
Oldman, O., 513
Oshima, H., 212
Output, 18
Pakistan, 41, 52, 58, 68, 69, 71, 75, 153, 261, 262, 263, 264, 266, 273, 297, 344, 345
Panama, 317, 321, 328, 335, 339
Papanek, G., 297
Paraguay, 280
Per Capita Income, 155
Paukert, F., 212
Pearson, L., 175
Peru, 299
Philippines, 32, 261, 264, 267, 270, 273, 274, 298, 319, 321, 328, 331, 329
Population, 91
Population Policy, 259, 274, 296
Poverty, 39, 244
Prebisch, R., 193, 407
Price Instability, 165
Production, 38, 50, 58, 362
Rath, N., 297
Reder, M., 173, 214
Regional Cooperation, 384
Rhodes, E., 213
Rosser, C., 192
Roy, 213

Rural Development, 296
Rural-Urban Migration, 177
Rutherford, R., 213
Rwanda, 23
Sargent, T., 174
Savings, 186, 314, 335
Seers, D., 7, 172
Senegal, 117
Shoup, C., 313
Sierra Leonne, 317
Singapore, 26
Skolka, J., 193
Somalia, 335, 353
Sommers, R., 78
Sri Lanka, 23, 46, 58, 61, 68, 161, 205
Sudan, 34
Taiwan, 17, 22, 26, 205
Tanzania, 41, 43, 46, 55, 68, 71, 153, 205, 295
Tawney, R., 215
Taxation, 302, 306
Thirlwall, A., 172, 173
Tinbergen, J., 214
Tixier, G., 192
Tobago, 276, 283, 286, 287, 299
Togo, 345
Toyoda, T., 174
Trade, 23, 58, 131, 158, 364, 377
Trends in Foreign Aid, 346
Trinidad, 276, 283, 286, 287, 299
Tunisia, 344
Turkey, 228
Uganda, 52, 71, 345
Upper Volta, 26, 43, 48
Unemployment, 156, 245
Urbanization, 91
Uruguay, 22, 280, 322, 332
Van de Ven, P., 313
Venezuela, 317, 319, 321, 335, 351
Voekov, M., 408
Wai, U. T., 154
Watanabe, S., 193
Weber, M., 215
Williamson, J., 202, 203
Wolfson, D., 302, 313
Woodhall, M., 297
World Bank, 242, 243
Yemen, 344
Zaire, 344, 353
Zambia, 344, 345

Maton, J., 193
Mauritius, 335, 345
McClelland, D., 215
McKinnon, R., 173
Measurement, 9
Mexico, 17, 145, 280, 299, 344, 345, 351
Mikesall, R., 172
Mincer, J., 214, 215
Mobilization of Resources, 314
Morocco, 291, 321, 331, 332, 335, 344
Morris, C., 191
Morrisson, C., 194
Mozambique, 23
Mouly, J., 194
Nepal, 332
Niedereichholz, H., 214
Niger, 71
Nigeria, 161, 298, 319, 321, 325, 338, 345
Nisbet, C., 172
OECD, 17, 37, 241, 242
Oldman, O., 513
Oshima, H., 212
Output, 18
Pakistan, 41, 52, 58, 68, 69, 71, 75, 153, 261, 262, 263, 264, 266, 273, 297, 344, 345
Panama, 317, 321, 328, 335, 339
Papanek, G., 297
Paraguay, 280
Per Capita Income, 155
Paukert, F., 212
Pearson, L., 175
Peru, 299
Philippines, 32, 261, 264, 267, 270, 273, 274, 298, 319, 321, 328, 331, 329
Population, 91
Population Policy, 259, 274, 296
Poverty, 39, 244
Prebisch, R., 193, 407
Price Instability, 165
Production, 38, 50, 58, 362
Rath, N., 297
Reder, M., 173, 214
Regional Cooperation, 384
Rhodes, E., 213
Rosser, C., 192
Roy, 213

Rural Development, 296
Rural-Urban Migration, 177
Rutherford, R., 213
Rwanda, 23
Sargent, T., 174
Savings, 186, 314, 335
Seers, D., 7, 172
Senegal, 117
Shoup, C., 313
Sierra Leonne, 317
Singapore, 26
Skolka, J., 193
Somalia, 335, 353
Sommers, R., 78
Sri Lanka, 23, 46, 58, 61, 68, 161, 205
Sudan, 34
Taiwan, 17, 22, 26, 205
Tanzania, 41, 43, 46, 55, 68, 71, 153, 205, 295
Tawney, R., 215
Taxation, 302, 306
Thirlwall, A., 172, 173
Tinbergen, J., 214
Tixier, G., 192
Tobago, 276, 283, 286, 287, 299
Togo, 345
Toyoda, T., 174
Trade, 23, 58, 131, 158, 364, 377
Trends in Foreign Aid, 346
Trinidad, 276, 283, 286, 287, 299
Tunisia, 344
Turkey, 228
Uganda, 52, 71, 345
Upper Volta, 26, 43, 48
Unemployment, 156, 245
Urbanization, 91
Uruguay, 22, 280, 322, 332
Van de Ven, P., 313
Venezuela, 317, 319, 321, 335, 351
Voekov, M., 408
Wai, U. T., 154
Watanabe, S., 193
Weber, M., 215
Williamson, J., 202, 203
Wolfson, D., 302, 313
Woodhall, M., 297
World Bank, 242, 243
Yemen, 344
Zaire, 344, 353
Zambia, 344, 345

About the Editor

Pradip K. Ghosh is President of the World Academy of Development and Cooperation, Washington, D.C. and Adjunct Associate Professor and Visiting Fellow at the Center for International Development at the University of Maryland, College Park. He is the author of *Thinking Sociology* and *Land Use Planning,* and editor of the International Development Resource Books series for Greenwood Press.

LIBRARY OF DAVIDSON COLLEGE

LIBRARY OF DAVIDSON COLLEGE